VITRUVIUS

Ten Books on Architecture

The only full treatise on architecture and its related arts to survive from classical antiquity, the *De Architectura libri decem* (*Ten Books on Architecture*) is the single most important work of architectural history in the Western world, having shaped humanist architecture and the image of the architect from the Renaissance to the present. Extremely influential in the formation of the medieval and modern concept of a broad liberal arts education as the basis for responsible professionals, this work is remarkable also because over half of its content deals with aspects of Hellenistic art, science, and technology, music theory, law, artillery, siege machinery, proportion and philosophy, among other topics.

This new, critical edition of Vitruvius's *Ten Books on Architecture* is the first to be published for an English-language audience in more than half a century. Expressing the range of Vitruvius's style, the translation, along with the critical commentary and illustrations, aims to shape a new image of the Vitruvius who emerges as an inventive and creative thinker, rather than the normative summarizer, as he was characterized in the Middle Ages and Renaissance.

Ingrid Rowland is Associate Professor of Art History at the University of Chicago. She is the author of *The Culture of the High Renaissance* and has contributed to *The Art Bulletin, Sixteenth Century Journal,* and *Viator.* She contributes regularly to the *New York Review of Books*.

Thomas Noble Howe is Professor of Architectural History at Southwestern University.

VITRUVIUS

❖

Ten Books on Architecture

Translation by Ingrid D. Rowland

Commentary and Illustrations by Thomas Noble Howe

with additional Commentary by Ingrid D. Rowland and Michael J. Dewar

CAMBRIDGE
UNIVERSITY PRESS

PUBLISHED BY THE PRESS SYNDICATE OF THE UNIVERSITY OF CAMBRIDGE
The Pitt Building, Trumpington Street, Cambridge, United Kingdom

CAMBRIDGE UNIVERSITY PRESS
The Edinburgh Building, Cambridge CB2 1RU, UK   http: //www.cup.cam.ac.uk
40 West 20th Street, New York, NY 10011-4211, USA   http: //www.cup.org
10 Stamford Road, Oakleigh, Melbourne 3166, Australia

First published 1999

Printed in the United States of America

Typeset in Weiss in QuarkXpress [G&H]

Library of Congress Cataloging-in-Publication Data
Vitruvius Pollio.
    [De architectura.   English]
    Vitruvius : ten books on architecture / translated by Ingrid D.
Rowland ; commentary and illustrations by Thomas Noble Howe ; with
additional commentary by Ingrid D. Rowland and Michael J. Dewar –
New ed.
      p.   cm.
    Includes index.
    ISBN   0-521-55364-4   (hardback)
    1. Architecture – Early works to 1800.   I. Rowland, Ingrid D.
(Ingrid Drake)   II. Howe, Thomas Noble, 1949–   .   III. Dewar,
Michael (Michael J.)   IV. Title.
NA2515.V6135   1999
720 – dc21   98-11716
                                     CIP

A catalog record for this book is available from
the British Library.

ISBN 0-521-55364-4 hardback

PARENTIBUS AC PRAECEPTORIBUS
"Parentium cura et praeceptorum doctrinis . . . copias disciplinarum animo paravi" (6.pref. 4)

MATRI
MEMORIAE PATRIS

T. N. HOWE
"Itaque ego maximas infinitasque parentibus ago atque habeo gratias" (6.praef. 3)

and the memories of
HARRY J. CARROLL, JR.
COLIN EDMONSON
KYLE M. PHILLIPS, JR.

I. D. ROWLAND

CONTENTS

Acknowledgments   *page* ix

List of Illustrations   xi

Translator's Preface   xiii

Illustrator's Preface   xv

INTRODUCTION   1

LIST OF MANUSCRIPTS SEEN   19

THE TRANSLATION

    Book 1: First Principles and the Layout of Cities   21

    Book 2: Building Materials   33

    Book 3: Temples   46

    Book 4: Corinthian, Doric, and Tuscan Temples   54

    Book 5: Public Buildings   63

    Book 6: Private Buildings   75

    Book 7: Finishing   85

    Book 8: Water   96

    Book 9: Sundials and Clocks   107

    Book 10: Machines   119

COMMENTARY   135

Index   319

ACKNOWLEDGMENTS

Architecture, that most collective of the arts, engenders gratitude on a collective scale. To all you who passed through the cortile of the American Academy in Rome, through Notre Dame, New York, Austin, Texas, or Chicago with kind words and advice – and you are too many to single out here – thank you for providing so broad, and so genial, a community in which to live and work. Caroline Bruzelius, former Director of the American Academy in Rome, and Malcolm Bell III, former Mellon Professor of Archaeology at the same institution, sponsored an exhibition of preliminary drawings and draft translation in June 1994. To the Academy itself, with its resources physical, intellectual, and above all human, our debt can never be measured in its totality, but it can at least be gratefully acknowledged.

The translation would not have been possible without Michael Dewar, whose devotion to scholarship bravely overrode his unrivaled sensivity to Latin style when Vitruvius put both to the test.

Thomas Gordon Smith's energy and ambition to see a modern illustrated vernacular Vitruvius brought together the authors, as well as several other contributors to the present edition, among them Michael Dewar and Lou Harrison, to whom we extend special thanks for the information on ancient Greek music provided in Book 5. Jean Davison shared her expertise on *echea* in Greek theaters for Book 5 with like generosity.

The Chicago Humanities Institute at the University of Chicago, now the Franke Institute for the Humanities, furnished steady support, beginning with its sponsorship of a symposium in 1991 and culminating with the award of its first Scholarly Partnerships grant in 1996–97. Particular thanks to former Directors Norma Field and Arjun Appadurai, to Associate Director Margot Browning, and to Philip Gossett, Dean of the Division of Humanities at the University of Chicago.

William Jones, Interim Provost, and Carole A. Lee, Dean of Fine Arts, Southwestern University, kindly arranged a special split sabbatical for Thomas Howe in 1996–97, which allowed him to finish a final draft of text and drawings.

Evelyn Simha, Executive Director of the Dibner Institute at the Massachusetts Institute of Technology, made available to Thomas Howe the resources of the Berndy Library of the History of Science and Technology.

Ingrid Rowland would like to thank the Bayerische Staatsbibliothek, Munich; the British Library; the Bodleian Library, Oxford; the University Library, Cambridge; the Biblioteca Hertziana, Rome; the Biblioteca Casanatense, Rome; the Avery Library at Columbia University; the Biblioteca Apostolica Vaticana; the Regenstein Library at the University of Chicago; and the Newberry Library, Chicago, for their help with manuscripts and early printed editions.

For sage counsel, we would especially like to thank William Macdonald, J. J. Coulton, Joseph Rykwert, Lothar Haselberger, Christof Thoenes, Johan Mårtelius, and Richard Brilliant.

To the generosity and friendship of Joe Connors, Peter Hicks, Margie Miles, Ingrid Edlund-Berry, Lucy Shoe Meritt, Piero Meogrossi, Mark Wilson Jones, and Giangiacomo Martines we owe particular long-standing thanks.

For bold risks, fervid speculation, and magnanimous spirit, Ingrid Rowland would like to thank David Mayernik, Thomas Rajkovic, Richard Cameron, Donald Rattner, and John Onians.

A providentially timed Quantrell Award for Excellence in Undergraduate Teaching from the University of Chicago allowed the translator to purchase a copy of the 1522 Giunta edition of Fra Giocondo's Vitruvius one giddy morning in Venice.

Beatrice Rehl, editor extraordinary, made the book possible at all. Françoise Bartlett guided it through production with sharp eyes and imagination. Anne Lesser copyedited the manuscript with care and intelligence. Kathie Kounouklos produced the handsome page layouts. Mario Pereira lent his rare *ingenium* to the preparation of manuscript, proofs, and index. Carroll Joynes offered much-needed support. Thanks to all of them; the flaws that remain would have been far more numerous without their help.

Two long-deceased colleagues seem worthy of special mention, although nearly half a millennium separates us from them. Fra Giovanni Giocondo's contribution to the understanding of Vitruvius through his printed edition of 1511 is well known, but not for that reason any less remarkable. The influence of his protégé Angelo Colocci is still a well-kept secret, yet it is Colocci's carefully annotated version of Giocondo, Vatican Library R.I.III.298, that afforded many crucial insights into the magnum opus of that opinionated old Roman who has nurtured alert readers and conscientious builders for over two thousand years.

LIST OF ILLUSTRATIONS

Figure 1. Rome in the Time of Augustus (partly reconstructed).

Figure 2. Caryatids/*Korai* (Maidens) 1.1.5–6.

Figure 3. "Climates:" Mapmaking (1.1.10).

Figure 4. "Climates:" Measuring the Earth (1.1.10).

Figure 5. "Climates" and Latitudes (1.1.10).

Figure 6. ". . . discuss certain things in common" (1.1.16).

Figure 7. The Elements of Architecture: *Ordo, Ordinatio, Dispositio* (1.2.1–9).

Figure 8. The Elements of Architecture: The *Ordinatio* Grid (1.2.1–9).

Figure 9. The Elements of Architecture: *Eurythmia, Symmetria* (1.2.1–9).

Figure 10. Symmetry in Nature and Design (1.2.4).

Figure 11. The Siting of Cities (Health, 1.4.1–12; Defense and Surrounding Territory, 1.5.1; Allocation of Plots, Ports, Temples, and so on, 1.7.1–2).

Figure 12. Surveying and Augury ("Old Principles") (1.4.9).

Figure 13. Surveying and Augury: Etruscan Roots?

Figure 14. The Siting of Cities: "The rampart should encircle precipitous heights" (1.5.2).

Figure 15. Fortifications: Summary of Vitruvian Features; Typical Hellenistic Fortification (1.5.1–8).

Figure 16. Fortifications: Towers as Artillery Emplacements; Round and Polygonal Towers (1.5.1–8).

Figure 17. Fortifications: A Variety of City Gate Designs; Left-Hand Approaches (1.5.1–8).

Figure 18. Fortifications: Foundations Carried to the Solid; Hellenistic Compartment Walls; Walls with Tie Beams (1.5.1–8).

Figure 19. Fortifications: Vitruvius's Walls Type 1, Type 2A, Type 2B (1.5.1–8).

Figure 20. Physical Nature of the Winds (1.6.1–3).

Figure 21. Orientation of the Winds by Celestial Points and Regions (1.6.4–13).

Figure 22. Orientation of the Wind by Quadrants/Octants of the Compass (1.6.4–13).

Figure 23. Orientation of a City by Means of a Windrose (1.6.6–7; 1.6.13).

Figure 24. Eratosthenes' Measurement of the Circumference of the Globe (1.6.9).

Figure 25. Surveying and *Limitatio* (Centuriation): Methods

Figure 26. Surveying and *Limitatio* (Centuriation): Examples

Figure 27. Surveying and *Limitatio* (Centuriation): Examples

Figure 28. Dinocrates and Alexander (2.praef.1–4).

Figure 29. The Invention of Building (2.1.1–7).

Figure 30. Celestial and Terrestrial Chemistry (2.2.1–2).

Figure 31. [Mud-] Brick (*Lateres*) (2.3.1–4).

Figure 32. Facing (2.8.1–4).

Figure 33. "The Masonry of the Greeks" (2.8.5–7).

Figure 34. Halicarnassus (2.8.10–15).

Figure 35. "The Expedient of Tall Buildings" (2.8.16).

Figure 36. Felling Timber (2.9.1).

Figure 37. Common Units of Measure (3.1.1–9).

Figure 38. *Homo Bene Figuratus* (3.1.1–4).

Figure 39. Types (*Genera*) of Temples (3.2.1–8).

Figure 40. Hellenistic Ionic Temples in the Tradition of Hermogenes.

Figure 41. Species ("Aspects") of Temples (3.3.1–13).

Figure 42. "The Larger the Spaces Between the Columns, the Greater the Diameters of the Shafts . . ." (3.3.11).

Figure 43. Dependence of Hypotrachelium Contraction on Column Heights (3.3.12).

Figure 44. *Entasis* (*Intentio/Contentio* = Tensioning).

Figure 45. Foundations/Podia (3.4.1–2, 3.4.4).

Figure 46. *Scamilli impares*-Stylobate Curvature (3.4.5).

Figure 47. "Attic" Base (= Attic-Ionic) (3.5.2).

Figure 48. Column Inclination (3.5.4).

Figure 49. "Pulvinated" Capital (= Ionic) (3.5.5–8).

Figure 50. The Problem with Swinging the Arcs of the Volute (3.5.6, 3.5.8).

Figure 51. Ionic Epistyles (3.5.8–11).

Figure 52. Epistyle Height (Proportion) Dependent on Column Heights (3.5.8).

Figure 53. Flutes of the Columns (3.5.14).

Figure 54. Simas and Lionhead Waterspouts (3.5.15).

Figure 55. "The Corinthian Column Appears More Slender Than the Ionic" (4.1.1).

Figure 56. From *Genus* to *Symmetria* (4.1.3–8).

Figure 57. Corinthian Origins (4.1.8–11).

Figure 58. Symmetries of the Corinthian Capital (4.1.11–12).

Figure 59. Corinthian Capitals of the Late Republic and Augustan Age.

Figure 60. Structural Origins of the *Genera* and Their *Ornamenta* (4.2.1–6).

Figure 61. Doric Origins (4.2.2–4).

Figure 62. The Doric Angle Contraction Problem (4.3.1–2).

Figure 63. Doric Symmetries (4.2.4–6).

Figure 64. The Doric Triglyph (4.3.5–6).

Figure 65. Examples of Late Republican and Augustan Doric

Figure 66. Symmetries for Diastyle (Two-Triglyph) Doric; Symmetries for Systyle (Single-Triglyph) Doric (4.3.3).

Figure 67. Temple Interiors (4.4.1–4).

Figure 68. Optical Adjustments (4.4.2–3).

Figure 69. Orientation/Visibility of Cult Image (4.5.1–2; 4.9.1).

Figure 70. The Doric Door (4.6.1–2); The Attic Door (4.6.6).

Figure 71. The Ionic Door (4.6.3–4).

Figure 72. Door Panels (4.6.4–5).

Figure 73. Tuscan Design (*Tuscanicae Dispositiones*) (4.7.1–5).

Figure 74. Round Temples (4.8.1–3).

Figure 75. Hybrid Temples and New Types (4.8.4).

Figure 76. Hybrid Temples and New Types (4.8.4).

Figure 77. The Forum (5.1.1–3).

Figure 78. The Basilica (5.1.4–5).

Figure 79. The Basilica at Colonia Julia Fanestris (Fano) (1.6.1–10).

Figure 80. The Basilica at Colonia Julia Fanestris (Fano) (1.6.1–10).

Figure 81. Harmonic Principles: The Scales (5.4.1–9).

Figure 82. *Echea* (Sounding Vessels in Theaters) (5.5.1–8).

Figure 83. Theater Design: The Roman Theater (5.6.1–8).

Figure 84. Theater Design: The Greek Theater (5.7.1–2).

Figure 85. Porticoes (5.9.1–9).

Figure 86. Baths (*Balneae*) (5.10.1–5).

Figure 87. Baths (*Balneae*) (5.10.1–5).

Figure 88. Palaestras (5.11.1–4).

Figure 89. Ports/Moles (5.12.1–7).

Figure 90. Latitudes, Peoples, and Musical Intervals (6.1.1–12).

Figure 91. Types (*Genera*) of Interiors (*Cavaedia*) (6.3.1–2).

Figure 92. Proportions of *Atria* (6.3.3–6).

Figure 93. Peristyle Courtyards and Dependent Chambers (6.3.7–11).

Figure 94. Orientation of Rooms (6.4.1–2).

Figure 95. Rural Buildings (*Rusticorum Aedificiorum Expeditiones*) (6.6.1–6).

Figure 96. Natural Lighting (6.6.6–7).

Figure 97. Greek Houses (*Aedificia Graecorum*) (6.7.1–7).

Figure 98. More on Foundations (Summary: 6.8.1; 1.5.1; 3.1.1–2; 5.3.3; 6.8.1; 6.8.2–4; 6.8.4).

Figure 99. Retaining Walls and Buttresses (*Anterides sive Erismae*) (6.8.6–7).

Figure 100. Flooring (7.1.1–7).

Figure 101. Preparation of Lime (7.2.1–2).

Figure 102. Ceilings and Wall Plaster (7.3.1–11).

Figure 103. Plasterwork in Damp Locations (7.4.1–3).

Figure 104. Styles of Wall Painting: Pompeiian First and Second Style (7.5.1–3).

Figure 105. Styles of Wall Painting: Pompeiian Third Style (7.5.1–3).

Figure 106. Sources of Water (Map of the Mediterranean World) (8.3.1–28).

Figure 107. Levelling and the *Chorobates* (8.6.1–3).

Figure 108. Distribution of Water (8.6.1–2).

Figure 109. Aqueducts (8.6.3–11).

Figure 110. Useful Innovations of Mathematics (9.praef.1–4).

Figure 111. Planetary Motion (9.1.1–6).

Figure 112. Retrograde Motion for the Planets ("Stars") "Above" the Sun (9.1.11–15).

Figure 113. The Constellations (9.3.5).

Figure 114. The Analemma (9.7.1–7).

Figure 115. The Analemma (9.7.1–7).

Figure 116. Water Clocks (9.8.4–7).

Figure 117. Water Clocks: Winter Clocks (9.8.8).

Figure 118. First Principles of Machines (10.1.1–3).

Figure 119. Cranes: *Trispastos/Pentaspastos* (10.2.1–4).

Figure 120. Cranes for Heavier Loads (10.2.5–7).

Figure 121. Other Cranes (10.2.8–10).

Figure 122. Special Methods of Hauling Large Blocks (10.2.11–15).

Figure 123. All Machines Use Two Types of Motion (10.3.1–8).

Figure 124. Water Raising Machines (1.4.1–4).

Figure 125. Bucket Chains (10.4.4).

Figure 126. Waterwheels (10.5.1–2).

Figure 127. The Water Screw ("Water Snail," *Coclea*) (10.6.1–4).

Figure 128. Ctesibius's Water Pump (10.7.1–3).

Figure 129. Water Organs (10.8.1–6).

Figure 130. The Hodometer (10.9.1–7).

Figure 131. Artillery: The *Scorpio* (10.10.1–6).

Figure 132. Artillery: The *Ballista* (10.11.1–9).

Figure 133. The Tensioning of War Machines (10.12.1–2).

Figure 134. The Siege Engines of Diades (10.13.1–7).

Figure 135. The Siege Engines of Diades (10.13.6–7).

Figure 136. The Tortoise for Filling Moats (10.14.1–3).

Figure 137. The Tortoise of Hegetor (10.15.2–6).

Figure 138. Defensive Stratagems (10.16.3–6).

Figure 139. Defensive Stratagems: The Siege of Massilia (10.16.11–12).

TRANSLATOR'S PREFACE

Vitruvius is an important writer, quite possibly a highly innovative writer, and certainly among the most influential writers the world has produced, but he is not, perhaps, a very *good* writer. It is difficult to translate him without at the same time trying to improve his sometimes clumsy phrasing, his endless sentences, his abrupt digressions, and his congenital failure to use one word when he can use two, especially when they sound alike ("evade and avoid" is a typical example). Yet in the middle of the fourteenth century, a reader as sensitive as Petrarch found Vitruvian style perfectly acceptable (although another sensitive reader, Leone Battista Alberti, could lament around 1450 that the *Ten Books* were such a pastiche of corrupted Latin and Greek that it would have been better if Vitruvius had never written at all).

Vitruvius's chief problems as a writer stemmed from the fact that he was addressing a whole series of different subjects for the first time in Latin. There were no fellow writers to offer him suggestions; often, there were not even words in his own language to describe what he wanted to discuss. Sometimes, as in his treatment of column types in Books 3 and 4 or of war machines in Book 10, he is clearly translating as best he can from Greek authors who have written treatises on a particular subject, but on other occasions, as in his discussion of the Tuscan temple in Book 4, he is just as clearly working entirely on his own. Sometimes these new forays succeed admirably (the description of Tuscan architecture is quite concise); sometimes, however, the fledgling writer abandons a floundering description and simply refers his reader to an illustration at the end of the book, where he promises to draw what he cannot effectively explain.

Vitruvius wrote in an age when writing had already been sharply defined into genres, each with its own appropriate form of expression. In addition, however, the persuasive writer was expected to maintain readers' interest by constant variation in emotional tone and intricacy of language. In his prefaces, therefore, Vitruvius aims for the dense, complex rhetorical style that his contemporary Cicero had been perfecting for years on the Rostra, in the law courts, and in the Senate House; this was called the "high style," and its preferred quality was *gravitas*: weight or seriousness. These moments of high style are the occasions when two words are always better, "heavier," than one, and they are the moments when the twentieth-century writer's impulse to avoid "turgidity" obeys an aesthetic code that is utterly alien to the ancient Latin sense of what is appropriate.

In the rest of his *Ten Books*, with mixed results, Vitruvius tries above all to write clearly, using a narrative "middle style" for his anecdotes and a tersely descriptive "low style" for the technicalities of constructions, sundials, clocks, and machines.

By keeping closely to the Latin text (by making the English text account, one on one, for every single Latin word), the present translation tries to follow Vitruvius's shifts in style, from high rhetoric to halting description, and to resist, as much as possible, "improving" his roundabout attempts to find words where no words have been found before. Similarly, the translation opts for a vocabulary that is consistent with Vitruvius's own usage, most evident in its abandonment of the word "orders" to describe the types of Classical column. Vitruvius classifies his world by using the term "genus," here translated as "type," whether he is referring to columns, music, war machines, or levels of rhetoric, and it surely reveals more about his thought to take him at his word than to fit him into modern ideas of architectural terminology.

No translator can approach Vitruvius without making hard choices about individual words in a text that has come down from antiquity with significant alterations. All of the surviving medieval manuscripts have many confusing or nonsensical passages and impossible – or missing – numbers for the dimensions of buildings, aqueducts, and machines. From 1511 onward, however, readers of Vitruvius could avail themselves of a printed text in which many of these errors had been corrected by a brilliant process of guesswork. The editor of this printed Vitruvius was an Italian monk, Fra Giovanni Giocondo da Verona, who had worked both as a classical scholar and a practicing architect in Italy and France; he was one of the few people in the Renaissance, and one of the few people ever afterward, who have had the range of expertise to understand every aspect of Vitruvius's text and therefore to anticipate what might have been misread as generations of scribes copied down the *Ten Books* with all too human fallibility. Frequently Giocondo went too far in his conjectural corrections, for once he had begun to tinker with the Latin of the manuscripts, nothing and no one could warn him when to stop. Still, the notes to the present translation show how often the Veronese monk seemed to be the first reader in fifteen centuries to understand what Vitruvius must really have said.

In addition to Giocondo's pioneering edition, consulted in the 1511 Venetian original and in the 1522 Florentine revised edition, the present translation has relied closely on the work of more recent scholars, making extensive use of the well-documented Latin edition of Valentin Rose and Hermann Müller-Strübing (Leipzig: Teubner, 1867), as well as those of Friedrich Krohn (Leipzig: Teubner, 1912); Frank Granger (London: Heinemann, 1931–1934); Kurt Fensterbusch (Darmstadt-Wissenschaftliche Buchgesellschaft, 1964); and the multivolume edition with commentary still being published from Paris by Editions des Belles-Lettres. Furthermore, Michael Dewar in particular has consulted the two preceding twentieth-century English translations of Morris Hicky Morgan and Frank Granger; Morgan's stately English, especially, will always stand as an achievement, whatever the subsequent changes wrought on our understanding of Vitruvius by new archaeological findings and the continued study of ancient Latin.

Vitruvius set out clarity and comprehensiveness as the chief goals to which he strove as an author; a translator, by contrast, strives only for fidelity. Michael Dewar's careful comments on several drafts of the translation manuscript have made that goal more attainable than it would otherwise have been.

ILLUSTRATOR'S PREFACE

The illustrations of this project are designed with two principal purposes in mind: first, to investigate the possibility of a consistent design approach in Vitruvius; and second, to illustrate the relation of this approach to the broad principles of liberal knowledge that constitute approximately half of the material in the *Ten Books*.

The latter intent is more difficult to achieve within the scope of this project because a full commentary and illustration of the background knowledge of Vitruvius would almost constitute a complete panorama of Hellenistic liberal and technical knowledge. But any successful attempt to interpret Vitruvius must deal with the most salient feature of the *Ten Books*: that over half the material does not deal with architecture per se, but with other, supposedly supportive, fields of knowledge, like astronomy, geography, and natural philosophy. As Frank Brown has asserted, the mission of Vitruvius is to present architecture as a liberal art, based on a Hellenistic belief of the unity of knowledge.[1] The *Ten Books* must be read therefore with at least a general knowledge of the numerous fields that Vitruvius touches upon, and also attitudes toward religion and cultural tradition.

The references to scientific knowledge in particular can appear digressive, fragmentary, and even bizarre to the modern reader (e.g., fish, being "dry," can live in water, whereas humans, being "wet," can live in air; 1.4.7). In fact, virtually every illustrative digression is a fragmentary reference to a large and coherent body of knowledge, of which Vitruvius is more or less a firm master. Our example refers to the Empedoclean chemical theory which asserts that bodies are stable when they are a tempered balance of the four elements (earth-air-fire-water) and unstable when there is excess or lack of one.

They are stable when complemented by their environment and are corrupted when there is an excess or lack of an element in the conjunction of body and environment. Hence fish must be "dry" because, living in water, their lack is complemented by their environment, and they are corrupted in air because they then have an excess of air and a lack of water. This may sound strange to us, but in antiquity it was science.

Vitruvius's knowledge of science appears to be extensive and highly consistent, but some of his analyses suggest that it is still at a somewhat personal and popular level. His anthropological analysis of the difference between northern and southern cultures based on the image of the earth being similar to a harp (6.1.3–7, people of the north have the heaviest voices because they are farthest from the sun, just like the longest string) and his explanation of retrograde motion (9.1.11, based on the attractive power of heat rather than on geometrical epicycles and deferents) are apparently outside the "proper" science of the time. They are logical, but they may be personal attempts to demonstrate his own ability to extend commonly known scientific principles to explain other phenomena. A little knowledge can be a dangerous thing.

What we are attempting to do here is to show at least part of this background. Therefore, there is a limited selection of architectural comparanda, and there are graphic written attempts to summarize some of the scientific fields that Vitruvius brings into his discussions.

It is hoped that the comparanda will show certain tensions and selectivity in the relation between Vitruvius and his material. There are indeed similarities between some of Vitruvius's prescriptions and our archaeological picture of contemporary or earlier architecture (e.g., the temple at Tivoli is often taken as the closest parallel to his method of designing the Corinthian type of capital), but the comparanda also show that Vitruvius exhibits a strong but judicious preference for more innovative approaches. Features of his recommendations for city walls (polygonal towers and left-turn approaches) are

---

1 Strictly speaking, there may be no such thing as a Hellenistic belief in the unity of knowledge. This may be simply the common phenomenon of reading another culture from the outside, and hence seeing it as a simplified unity. In Vitruvius, as in most well-educated ancient writing, there is considerable awareness of the dynamic nature of advanced knowledge.

attested, but they are not the most typical form of Hellenistic, much less Roman fortification.

Our drawings of the Vitruvian prescriptions do not take the prescriptions all the way to full reconstructions of paradigmatic designs. In fact, the point is that none of Vitruvius's prescriptions constitute what could be called a full design.[2] Gaps and ambiguities in the drawings are left because that is probably the way he intended them to be understood.[3] The prescriptions seem to carry the act of design only up to a certain point, after which it seems that the final business of design is left until the time of execution, possibly to other artisans.[4]

This accords with Vitruvius's constant admonitions that the "symmetries" of any type of form must always be adapted to exigencies: to site, to the local materials, to optics and scale, to function. The prescriptions for the house and the basilica contain adjustable, rather than fixed, proportional parameters (the length of the basilica can be between two and three times its width). Hence the construction lines are left on our drawings of Vitruvian prescriptions because they, not the finished form, are the essence of the drawing. It is they that show the method and the potential for altering the design while still maintaining control.

Many of the prescriptions for building types, such as the Roman country house, the Greek-style house, and the palaestra, are presentations of a group of optimal orientations and features for rooms, and not an attempt at fixed relationships. In fact, in some cases Vitruvius seems to be shaping his prescriptions almost in the manner of a modern practicing architect when he writes an initial program, in that he includes a number of desirable, but sometimes mutually conflicting, features, which rarely can all be equally well satisfied in the actual design. The fact that these recommendations have produced such a wide variety of "reconstructions" from Palladio to the present is testimony to the fact that there are inherent ambiguities and contradictions in them and that using them to arrive at (or "reconstruct") a full design automatically produces different solutions. There is no such thing as "the Roman house" or "the Greek house" in Vitruvius. Vitruvian prescriptions seem to admonish that a designer work from principles, not paradigmatic forms.

As for dimensions (or rather proportions), the modern habit is usually to reduce them to a common denominator.[5] However, in antiquity the habit was to use "unitary fractions," that is, those with a numerator of 1. (Two-thirds is thus represented as one-half plus one-sixth.) This may seem like a small point, but it represents a profound difference in the way arithmetic is used. Modern Hindu-Arabic numerals in decimals allow much more rapid comparison of quantities; which is larger? $1/4 + 1/60$ ($4/15$) or $1/5 + 1/15 + 1/90$ ($5/18$; i.e., 0.2666 or 0.2777)? The ancient system of unitary fractions aimed less at systematic unity in presenting measurable reality.[6]

Therefore the drawings, and to some extent the translation, retain the unitary fractions and the sequential instructions for proportions rather than reducing them to the more "convenient" decimals or other common denominator, with the intent that this too may reveal more of a relatively open system of design.

---

2 The most nearly complete are probably the catapults in Book 10, but even these lack important dimensions. These descriptions are almost identical to the tradition of technical engineering description represented by Philo of Byzantiumw, and it is quite possible that Vitruvius modeled his most meticulous descriptions of architectural features (e.g., the column types) on this type of description, rather than on the form of earlier architectural treatises or contracts.

3 For example, what he calls a "cymatium" in Books 3 and 4 is drawn as a generic half round because the term seems to cover a variety of molding types. The projection of the intermediate moldings of the Ionic bases are shown with a small section of the various possibilities because several possibilities are permitted within the range of his prescriptions.

4 This suggestion was made in conversation by Dr. Lucy Shoe Meritt.

5 For instance, the Ionic epistyle relative to the frieze is proportioned 4 parts to 3, but the 4 is then divided into 7 to give the subdivisions of the epistyle (fascias, crown molding); thus one can relate the subdivisions of the frieze directly by a common denominator of 28.

6 Or at least this consistency was more difficult for the average practitioner to achieve. The cumbersome arithmetic also does much to account for ancient architects' preference for thinking geometrically rather than arithmetically. Graphic/geometric calculation allowed one to handle such irrational numbers as square root of two (diagonal of a square) or complex curves such as an ellipse (created by stretching the diameter of a circle) or conic sections. Similarly, the bases of trigonometry were known from the time of Hipparchus's tables of chords in the second century B.C., but the exercises of the *agrimensores* (surveyors) several centuries later still do not make use of them.

VITRUVIUS
Ten Books on Architecture

INTRODUCTION

Marcus Vitruvius Pollio wrote his ten books[1] on architecture in the first decade of the Pax Augusta, c. 30–20 B.C. This was a decade of renewed peace and prosperity that followed some two or three generations of brutal turmoil and civil war, starting with the conflict between Marius and Sulla in the 90s B.C. (or the "reforms" of the Gracchi in the 130s) and culminating in the civil war of the second triumvirate and the defeat of Marc Antony and Cleopatra at Actium in 31. It was a time of renewed building, both architectural and cultural, a time endowed with a confidence that the world was being remade anew. It was also a time when an educated person seeking to visualize this new world order could draw on a rich international Hellenistic and Italic culture of science, technology, literature, arts, and architecture.

Literary Genre

The *Libri Decem* are a hybrid type of literature that was common in the last century of the Republic: a technical handbook with literary ambitions.[2] As a loosely defined type, these books tend to be rather idiosyncratic and original because the approach tends to force the authors to combine topics in unusual ways.

Duality of style is necessarily inherent in these specialized books. Rhetorical language was focused on the prefaces, or excursus, and technical sections relied on more prosaic language.[3]

The readership of these books was intended to be fairly wide and almost certainly did extend well beyond the "experts" or "professionals" in the particular field.[4] Augustus was fond of books of precepts and would copy books he thought to be useful and send them to members of his household or to officers and to provincial officials.[5] He would commonly read such books to assemblies and on one occasion read sections of Rutilius's *De Modo Aedificiorum* to the Senate.[6] It is debatable whether Vitruvius's work was ever the "handbook" of Augustan architecture,[7] but he certainly must have hoped it would become so.

By Vitruvius's time, book copying appears to have become a substantial business, and books could be "published" and disseminated fairly widely in a sense not too different from modern use. Rightly or wrongly, Cicero's friend T. Pomponius Atticus is credited with putting publishing on a commercial basis in the middle of the first century B.C., establishing a large scriptorium with slaves.[8] The cost of a book was approximately the cost of wages for hand copying; a book of seven hundred lines of Martial cost five denarii, about two days' skilled wages. By this reckoning, a copy of the *Ten Books* might run about 100 denarii.

The book trade must have been considerable because private libraries of the wealthy could often run to several thousand volumes (cf. that of L. Calpurnius Piso, Caesar's father-in-law and consul in 58 B.C., found intact in Herculaneum, which supposedly has about three thousand vol-

---

1 Physically, a book was a scroll of papyrus (although from the second century B.C. it could also be parchment) and had to be held in two hands to be unrolled and read, which made checking references slow and difficult. Books did not normally have titles. Hence *De Architectura Libri Decem* is not a title but a description: ten books, or scrolls, on architecture (i.e., ten scrolls, "libri"). The work is so recorded in the oldest surviving manuscripts.

2 The following is derived largely from E. Nilsson Nylander, "Prefaces and Problems in Vitruvius's *De Architectura*" (Diss. Göteborg, 1992).

3 This idea is further developed by Michael Dewar at a seminar at the University of Chicago: "Stylistic Level and *poikilia* in Vitruvius'

Decem Libri de Architectura." Also see L. Callebat, "Rhétorique et architecture dans le 'de architectura' de Vitruve," *CollEFR* 192 (1972), 31–46.

4 ". . . non modo aedificantibus, sed etiam omnibus sapientibus . . ." (1.1.18).

5 Nylander (1992), 32.

6 Suet. Aug. 89.2. P. Rutilius Rufus was a senator, and this was more of a formal oration, not a technical or theoretical manual.

7 D. Favro, *The Urban Image of Augustan Rome* (Cambridge University Press, 1996), 145–146.

8 R. Ogilvie, *Roman Literature and Society* (London, 1980), 14–15; H. Blanck, *Das Buch in der Antike* (Munich, 1992), 120–132.

umes).[9] Private libraries were normally available to clients and would probably have been the primary means of access to books by those who were not wealthy until the first "public" libraries opened in Rome about the time Vitruvius was writing: that established by Asinius Pollio in the Atrium Libertatis in 39 B.C.; that honoring Marcellus placed in the Porticus Metelli/Octaviae by Octavia; or that established by Augustus near his house and the temple of Apollo on the Palatine.[10] Teachers would normally have to have their own small libraries of the classics, such as Ennius or Homer, for use in instruction.

Name and Date

Vitruvius is unknown to contemporary writers, and therefore virtually everything we know about his life must be extracted from the *Ten Books* themselves. The *Ten Books* were probably written and published between c. 30 and 20 B.C., and Vitruvius himself was probably born c. 80/70 B.C. and raised and educated in Campania or in Rome itself.

NAME: MARCUS VITRUVIUS POLLIO

The *nomen* Vitruvius is the only certain one repeatedly passed down by manuscripts.[11] The *cognomen* Pollio comes from a single reference from a building manual of the early third century, the *De Diversis Fabricis Architectonicae* of M. Cetius Faventinus.[12] Faventinus is largely a recension of those parts of Vitruvius that deal with domestic architecture. Its first line reads, *"De artis architectonicae peritia multa oratione Vitruvius Polio aliique auctores . . ."* which, it has been

pointed out, could mean, "Vitruvius, Pollio, and other authors . . ."[13] The praenomen is variously reported as Aulus, Lucius, and most frequently Marcus.[14]

The name of the *gens Vitruvia* is not well known in history. A Vitruvius Vaccus is cited for the year 329 as a *vir clarus* from Fundi.[15] The name is, however, well attested in gravestones, mainly from the coast of Latium and Campania between Gaeta and Naples, centering around Formia.[16] Campania and Rome are throughout the *Ten Books* clearly the central points of his reference. Vitruvius consistently refers to Rome simply as the "City," and the range of building materials he discusses is limited to this area; he refers to the Adriatic coast as the "other" side of Italy. It would be quite plausible, then, that he was born and raised in the area of Formia or the Bay of Naples. This area produced many of the innovations of Roman architecture in the last centuries of the Republic, such as the first amphitheater (that at Pompeii, c. 80 B.C.), the first stone theaters in Italy (second century B.C.), and even the invention of Roman "concrete" (as early as 300 B.C.); presumably it produced many of its professional architects as well.

The person of Vitruvius has also been associated with three other testimonia. One is the arch of the Gavii in Verona, dated variously from the end of the Republic to the end of the first century A.D. It bears the inscription "L(ucius) VITRUVIUS L(uci) L(ibertus) CERDO ARCHITECTUS."[17] Our Vitruvius, however, is certainly not a freedman (libertus), therefore this Vitruvius Cerdo was very possibly a freedman of the family of Vitruvius who, like a son, was also brought up and trained in architecture. The second is an inscription[18] from Thibilis (Annuna in Algeria), which refers to a Vitruvius building an arch from his own funds: M VITRUVIUS ARCUS S(ua) P(ecunia) F(ecit), hence probably not the architect. The third is the person of Mamurra, a native of Formia and the *praefectus fabrum* (chief engineer or supply officer) of Julius Caesar.[19] He was notorious for using his office to enrich himself enormously and supposedly was the first person to fill his house in Rome with marble;[20] not too surprisingly, he is

9 H. Blanck, *Das Buch in der Antike* (Munich, 1992), 152–160.

10 These public libraries were essentially private libraries writ large and made only slightly more available to the public than a "private" library would be available to friends and clients. Their purpose was to serve the personal political advertisement of the patrons in the environment of competitive patronage of the 30s and 20s B.C. A "public" library in effect asserted the right of Pollio – a partisan of Caesar but not necessarily a supporter of Octavian – or Octavian to the clientage of the entire public.

11 P. Ruffel, J. Soubiran, "Vitruve ou Mamurra?" *Pallas* 11.2 (1962), 174–176.

12 Dated to the later fourth century by H. Plommer, in *Vitruvius and Later Roman Building Manuals* (Cambridge, 1973), the first half of the third by most others: E. Pasoli, "Vitruvio nella storia della scienza a della tecnica," *Atti dell'Accademia delle Scienze dell'Istituto di Bologna, Classe di scienze morali, Memorie* 66 (1971–1972), 1–37, esp. 2.

13 P. Thielscher, *Realenzyclopädie der Klassischen Altertumswissenschaft* II series, vol. 9, A.1 (Stuttgart, 1961), cols. 419–489; P. Ruffel, J. Soubiran, op. cit., 141.

14 E. Pasoli, op. cit., 2–3.

15 Livy, 8.19.4.

16 E. Pasoli, op. cit., 2–3.

17 CIL 5.3464.

18 CIL 8, 18913.

19 Thielscher, loc. cit.

20 Pliny the Elder, *Natural History* 36.48.

never referred to in Caesar's own accounts. This type of man, however, simply does not accord with the personality and the details of the career we can get from the author of the *Ten Books*, who was living on a pension.[21]

DATE

The entire mood of the preface is one of the strongest reasons for dating the composition of the *Ten Books* to the decade or so after Actium (31 B.C.). The events of the period center around the struggle for supreme power between the partisans of Octavian and the partisans of Marc Antony (44–30 B.C.), and the establishment of the Pax Romana and one-man rule of Octavian-Augustus (in the 20s B.C.).

Octavian entered into the struggle for the inheritance of his adoptive father C. Julius Caesar immediately upon Caesar's assassination in 44. B.C. (Caesar was in actuality his great-uncle; Octavian's natural father, C. Octavius, died in 56 B.C.) Octavian was then eighteen years old, and from the first always referred to himself as Gaius Caesar, omitting his cognomen Octavius. (Marc Antony referred to him as "the youth who owed everything to his name."[22]) In 42 he obtained the admission of his "father" into a state cult and thereafter claimed for himself the title of "divi filius." In the same year he entered into the second triumvirate with Marc Antony and M. Aemilius Lepidus. The following ten years (42–32) were a period of tense competition between Octavian's partisans, who were centered in Rome, and Antony's, centered in the eastern empire, particularly Alexandria. There were other open conflicts, such as that with the sea power of Sextus Pompey, son of Gnaeus Pompeius Magnus, who was centered in Sicily, which was brought to an end by the victory of Octavian's admiral M. Agrippa at Naulochoi (36). Civil war broke out again among the triumvirate in 32, Antony and Cleopatra were defeated at Actium in 31, and Egypt finally fell in 30. In 29 Octavian celebrated a magnificent triple triumph (Illyricum, Egypt, and Actium) in Rome and dedicated the temple of Divus Iulius in the Forum, and in 27 he was given the honorific name of Augustus by the Senate in gratitude for the "restoration" of the Republic.[23]

The preface to the *Ten Books* makes it clear that the reason Vitruvius is writing at this particular time is that Octavian had previously been preoccupied with "taking possession of the world," which is clearly a delicate euphemism for the civil wars. Now a period of peace has brought about considerable building activity: "When, however, I perceived that you were solicitous not only for the establishment of community life and of the body politic, but also for the construction of suitable buildings . . ."

Vitruvius's delicacy in referring to events of the civil wars seems typical of the overall change in Augustan imagery in the 20s. Augustus himself, in his public propaganda, was careful not to make too much of these victories in the civil wars because they were, after all, victories over other Roman armies. In general, the public art of Augustus changed from triumphal imagery to abstract classicistic presentations of religious items, such as wreaths, tripods, and candelabra. Everyone, including the former partisans of Antony, could join in the general worship of the new age of peace through such generic, inoffensive images.[24] Vitruvius's own panegyric style seems to have more of the cautious classicistic abstraction of the 20s than the triumphal rhetoric of the 30s. This caution may also be the reason that Vitruvius rarely makes clear reference to his own travels in the *Ten Books* because it is possible that these too might have reminded readers of the places of the civil wars.

Another possibility is that the period of writing was a decade earlier, the time of the second triumvirate, 42–32. In this decade the rival factions of Octavian and Antony did in fact do a considerable amount of building in Rome. Octavian vowed the temple of Mars Ultor (after Pharsalus in 42) and was finishing the Forum of Caesar, the Temple of Divus Iulius, the Basilica Iulia, the Curia, his own mausoleum, and his temple of Apollo near his house on the Palatine (36–28), and his partisans C. Domitius Calvinus and L. Cornificius were rebuilding the Regia and the temple of Diana of the *plebs* on the Aventine (after 33). Antony's man C. Sosius set out to rival Octavian's temple of Apollo by rebuilding the temple of Apollo in the Campus Martius, and Munatius Plancus (consul 42) rebuilt the temple of Saturn in the

21 Pasoli, op. cit., 4–6.
22 Cicero, *Philippics* 13.11.24.
23 *Res Gestae* 34.

24 P. Zanker, *The Power of Images in the Age of Augustus*, trans. A. Shapiro (University of Michigan Press, 1988), ch. 3, esp. 82. Zanker argues that the imagery of Augustus changed radically after Actium from self-glorification to religious devotion. It did so because Augustus was in the delicate position of having to celebrate triumphs without referring to the enemies, as the defeated armies were also Roman, and to do so would have aroused bitter and divisive memories of the civil wars (hence the choice of abstract religious imagery of peace and prosperity).

Forum.[25] The preface makes it clear, however, that at the time of writing Octavian had achieved sole power, which was not the constitutional or de facto situation of the second triumvirate.

The fact that Vitruvius does not address Octavian as Augustus does not necessarily mean the *Ten Books* must predate 27 B.C. when the name was granted. The title was unusual and sacral in nature (meaning "stately," "dignified," or "holy," or possibly recalling "augur," the type of priest who reads omens),[26] and came into use gradually in the years after 27. As late as 14–13 Horace uses both Caesar and Augustus.[27] Vitruvius does refer to the Aedes Augusti in his basilica at Fano, which makes clear that the title and the imperial cult were well established at the time of writing.[28]

Various attempts have been made to date the composition by the buildings that are referred to in the *Ten Books*. Unfortunately, there is some contradiction. He mentions as existing buildings the temple of Equestrian Fortune (3.3.2), which had been destroyed by 22 B.C., the temple of Ceres on the Aventine (3.3.5), which was destroyed by fire in 31 B.C. (and not replaced until it was rebuilt by Tiberius in A.D. 17), and the Porticus Metelli (3.2.5), which existed under that name until 32/27, after which it was transformed into the Porticus Octaviae (dedicated 23). But he also refers to the *pronaos aedis Augusti* in his basilica at Fano (5.1.7), although Octavian was not given the title of Augustus until after 27. The temple of Divus Iulius in the Forum is the most recent building he mentions, dedicated 18 August 29 B.C., but possibly completed before (by 33 or 31). He refers only to one temple of Apollo, that in the Forum Holitorium, and ignores the temple of Apollo built by Octavian on the Palatine in 36–28 next to his own house. He refers to

the *theatrum lapideum* (3.2.2), thus implying there is only one stone theater in Rome (that of Pompey), and that the theaters of Marcellus (dedicated at the Ludi Saeculares in 17) and L. Cornelius Balbus (begun 19, dedicated 13) are not yet begun.

Others have suggested that the *Ten Books* were written separately and published at separate times; Lugli[29] suggests that Books 1–5 were written before 31 B.C., possibly 40–35, and Pellati that the first six books were written and published first (45–32), revised in 32–28 and republished in 27, and the last four published in 16–15.[30] The latter calculus is based partly on the expression *cubica ratione* (5.praef.4), which Vitruvius uses to describe how his work is ordered like a cube, that is, with six faces/six books. A work like this surely took a few years to compose, and it was indeed common practice to pass a manuscript in limited circulation around to friends for comment before publishing it, but the idea that it was originally conceived as complete in six books is contradicted by the clarity with which the content of the entire ten books is previewed in Book 1.

The latest chronological date proposed is after 14 B.C.[31] on the grounds that the prefaces are a derivation from literary devices of Horace,[32] but the devices (in particular the expression in 1.praef.1 that he did not "dare" to publish while Octavian was preoccupied with making peace) have a specific meaning in Vitruvius's writing in the 20s, whereas they were literary topoi for Horace in the 10s. Two other events may limit the completion date of the *Ten Books* to about 22.[33] In 10.praef.4 Vitruvius says that it is the joint responsibility of the praetors and aediles to sponsor the games, but this situation obtained only until 22 when sponsorship became the sole responsibility of the praetors.[34] In 2.1.4 he refers to straw huts of the sort that one can still see in Aquitania and Gallia, which means that Aquitania was no longer a part of Julius Caesar's three parts of Gaul (Belgica, Gallia/Celtica, and Aquitania), but a separate

---

25 For an analysis of the reflection of this political competition in the arts during the second triumvirate, see P. Zanker, *The Power of Images in the Age of Augustus*, trans. A. Shapiro, (University of Michigan Press, 1988), ch. 2, 33–77.

26 Zanker, op. cit., 98.

27 Caesar only in *Epistulae* 2.1.4; in the *Odes* once Caesar (4.15.4), once Augustus (4.14.3). Ovid uses Caesar twelve times, Augustus twice.

28 Wistrand argued that the section in 5.1.1–6 on the basilica at Fano with its Aedes Augusti was interpolated into the text at a later date, *Vitruvstudier*, Akademisk Avhandling (Diss. Göteborg, 1933) 6 f. We take the position that its inconsistency relative to the text that immediately precedes it is the result of one arithmetical error in the manuscript transmission, and that otherwise the differences between Fano and the prescriptions are meant to illustrate how innovations may be introduced into the prescriptions.

29 G. Lugli, *Tecnica edilizia romana* (Rome, 1957), 371, n. 1.

30 F. Pellati, "La Basilica di Fano e la formazione della trattato di Vitruvio," *RPAA* 33–34 (1947–1949), 153–174, esp. 155 ff.

31 P. Thielscher, loc. cit.

32 *Epistulae* 2.1.

33 F. Pellati, loc. cit.

34 Dio Cassius 54.2.3. M. H. Morgan, in *Harvard Classical Studies* 17 (1902), 19, envisaged a period of joint responsibility, based on this passage, but it is just as likely that the event in 22 simply transferred the responsibilities from the aediles to the praetors.

province, which occurred in 27; but in 22 Gallia Narbonensis and the other three parts of Gaul (Belgica, Lugdunensis, and Celtica) were elevated to senatorial provinces, erasing the simple distinction between Aquitania and Gallia.[35]

These indications and contradictions give the impression that the composition of the *Ten Books* reflects rapidly changing events of the 20s B.C. and that they were probably published before 22.

Probable Career

The evidence for Vitruvius's career is almost completely internal to the *Ten Books*. He was clearly a freeborn Roman citizen, although not likely of high (equestrian) class. It also is clear from the preface to Book 6 that he was given a broad "liberal arts" education by his parents as well as a professional education on which he depended to earn his living. This education was not necessarily the standard one for architects, but it may have been common to many. It is also clear that much of his erudition is the result of lifelong continuous study, the kind that would have been possible through access to libraries of the rich and powerful or, to a much lesser extent, through books of his own. The fact that his parents could afford such an education does not mean they were wealthy. Liberal education was probably not common in the early first century for families of modest means but became so later; Horace's father was a man of modest means (a small farmer) who financed his talented son's advanced education (including study in Athens) with the view that it was an important means of advancement.[36]

Vitruvius's principal frame of reference throughout the *Ten Books* is always the City (Rome), and less overtly, Campania, which is the principal location of inscriptional references to the Vitruvius *gens* (see earlier). It is likely that he grew up and was educated in one or both of these places; Campania was a principal source of architects and architectural innovation in the second and first centuries B.C. One intriguing question is how exactly he was trained as an architect; he refers six times to his *praeceptores* (teachers).[37] Presumably after his liberal education he was in effect apprenticed to an architect, or several, or to architectural teachers. At least some of these teachers may have been architects who were Greeks (not uncommon among teachers or any kind of profession, especially doctors) or who were trained by a Roman who was trained by a Greek. Gros has suggested that Vitruvius may have been trained by someone who was in turn trained by Hermodorus of Salamis, the (Cypriot) Greek architect hired by Q. Caecilius Metellus Macedonicus to build the Porticus Metelli in 146.[38] Vitruvius has often been taken to be a disciple of the conservative tradition of Ionian Hellenistic architecture deriving from Pytheos, the architect of Priene and the Mausoleum, in the fourth century, particularly as codified by Hermogenes in the later third or early second century. In any case, he clearly had some contact with Greek building and its theory of practice, whether at second or at first hand.[39] The extent to which the *Ten Books* (especially Books 3 and 4) accurately represent this tradition is affected by the extent to which he or his teachers were selective or revisionary.

If Vitruvius was born c. 85/80 B.C. his career would have started c. 50 B.C. when he was in his thirties, that is, at the time of the outbreak of the civil war between Caesar and Pompey (49 B.C.). It is logical that in the next two decades much of his career might have been primarily military; he mentions his responsibility for the catapults (a highly technical responsibility), but he also clearly built as designer the basilica at Fano, a Caesarian/Augustan foundation or refoundation. This is a mix of activities attested in the careers of other *architecti*. Trajan's architect, Apollodorus of Damascus, designed a campaign bridge over the Danube and wrote a treatise on siegecraft in addition to his spectacular public works in Rome itself. Magistrates and generals commonly retained architects among their professional technical staff, and it is thus likely that Vitruvius spent many years of his career as a Caesarian staff architect, either on campaign or in the foundation of colonies (at least of Fano). It has also been suggested, on the basis of the explicitness of much of the material on water in Book 8, that part of his professional activity included work on aqueducts.[40] This is very plausi-

---

35 E. Pasoli, op. cit., 9–10.

36 Horace, *Sermones* 1.4.105 ff.

37 4.3.3; 6.praef.4; 6.praef.5; 9.1.16; 10.11.2; 10.3.8.

38 P. Gros, "Hermodoros et Vitruve," *Mélanges de l'Ecole Française de Rome* 85 (1973), 137–161.

39 One should be cautious about arguing that this was his principal training in architecture merely because it is the approach that dominates his presentation of monumental architecture. Throughout the *Ten Books* Vitruvius is highly selective of his influences, and he tends to choose those approaches that illustrate strong theoretical fundamentals.

40 L. Callebat, ed., *Vitruve, de l'Architecture* viii (Paris, 1973), ix–x.

ble because it may have been an experience that would have especially qualified him to work as M. Agrippa's staff architect on the *cura aquarum* after writing the *Ten Books*.[41]

There are many tentative indications throughout the *Ten Books* of Vitruvius's probable association with Caesarian supporters. In addition to the very explicit statement that he maintained Caesar's artillery, and the other suggestions that he was on campaign with Caesar or branches of his army, his anecdotes mention people associated with Caesar,[42] and he cites other probable accomplishments of the Dictator.[43]

As to the question of whether Vitruvius traveled, readers are on their own to judge from the intimacy of knowledge revealed in various descriptions. The architect's strongest association is clearly with Rome and Campania. Clearly, too, he was sent on campaign or assignment in northern Italy (Gallia Cisalpina, Gaul "This-Side-of-the-Alps") and possibly Gaul itself. He obviously worked at Fano on the Adriatic coast, he is the only source for the siege at Larignum (2.9.15: somewhere in the foothills of the Alps; Caesar does not mention it in *Bellum Civile*), and he may have been present at the siege of Massilia (Marseilles) in 49. A hypothetical experience of North Africa is based mainly on the vividness of his descriptions in Book 8, but he could have gotten these descriptions from the recently published *Libyka* of Iuba of Numidia.[44] Possible travel to Greece is suggested particularly by the vividness of the description of Halicarnassus and his knowledge of Ionian buildings.[45]

Of Vitruvius's later career there are two indications: the first that through Octavian he received a *commoda*, which was continued through Octavia's[46] intervention (1.praef.2); the second is the testimony in Frontinus that he may have worked on the *cura aquarum*. The meaning of *commoda* is obscure,[47] but presumably it means "stipend," a regular annuity.[48] This may have given him leisure for study and writing, and he credits it explicitly with affording him the leisure to write, or at least finish, the *Ten Books* (Book 1.praef.). The *Ten Books* in turn may have secured him the post in the *cura aquarum*.

The extent to which Vitruvius was known or read in his lifetime, or influenced the development of early Imperial architecture, is a highly debatable subject.[49] There are probably no contemporary references or certain traces of influence,[50] but he was known later, at least to educated readers: he is mentioned five times in subsequent classical literature. The first is the encyclopedic *Natural History* of Pliny the Elder (died in A.D. 79),

41 *De Aquis Urbis Romae* 25.1. Sextus Iulius Frontinus was praetor, suffect consul, and military governor of Britannia (i.e., a man at the top of the *cursus honorum*), who became Trajan's *curator aquarum* in 97 and wrote an extensive technical report on the Roman aqueduct system. In it he reports that the plumbers of Rome standardized their pipe sizes according to instructions from the *architectus* Vitruvius; hence the conclusion that our author may very likely have been a staff architect of the *cura*. Regular administration of police protection, fire patrol, and water delivery did not exist in the city of Rome until early in the reign of Augustus, and its establishment was one of the *princeps'* major innovations. In 33 Octavian's right-hand man, M. Vipsanius Agrippa, took the office of aedile and became the perpetual *curator aquarum* until his death in 11, endowing the office with an attendant corps of slaves and professionals. Vitruvius would presumably have been Agrippa's staff architect, or one of them. See D. Favro, *The Urban Image of Augustan Rome* (Cambridge, 1996), 110–111.

42 Faberius Scriba (7.9.2), secretary to Caesar, Vestorius (7.11.1), banker of Puteoli, and Gaius Iulius, son of Masinissa (8.3.25), presumably related to the royal house of Numidia and who served with Caesar.

43 He mentions that Caesar, when a magistrate, may have started the habit of holding public trials in his own house (6.5.2). The draining of the marshes of Salpia (1.4.12; if the date is c. 40 B.C. See note loc. cit.) and the foundation or refoundation of Fano may have been Caesarian projects.

44 Published in 26/25, or 23. The *Ten Books*, 8.3.24 seems to be lifted directly from it. E. Nylander, *Prefaces and Problems in Vitruvius' 'De Architectura'* (Diss. Göteborg, 1992), 19; B. Baldwin, "The Date, Identity and Career of Vitruvius," *Latomus* 49 no. 2 (1990), 427; L. Callebat, ed., *Vitruve, de l'architecture* viii (Paris, 1973), 125–127.

45 Of course he could well have gotten his detailed knowledge of Hermogenean Ionic design from teachers or writings available in Rome.

46 On Octavia, see Commentary: 1.praef.2.

47 It can also imply a onetime dismissal payment or a fee for services. E. Nylander, *Prefaces and Problems in Vitruvius' 'De Architectura'* (Diss. Göteborg, 1992), 32–36.

48 Otherwise he would not have had to seek its continuance through appealing to Octavia.

49 See later: "Vitruvius's Position in the History of the Development of Roman Construction Methods and Forms."

50 It has been suggested that the panegyric of 1.praef may, including the use of *numen* and the topos of not wanting to publish these matters while the *princeps* was busy with weightier matters (i.e., the civil wars), have influenced Horace (*Epistulae* 2.1.1, and 2.1.16). B. Baldwin, "The Date, Identity and Career of Vitruvius," *Latomus* 49 no. 2 (1992), 426. The exact opposite has also been suggested, namely that this similarity shows Vitruvius must have been influenced by Horace and hence the *Ten Books* must date to after 14 B.C. Teufel-Schwabe, *A History of Roman Literature*, trans. G. C. W. Warr (London, 1900), vol. 1, 548. Also see F. Callebat, ed., *Vitruve, de l'architecture* viii (Paris, 1973), 125–127.

who refers to Vitruvius as a source of information on timber (N.H., Book 16), painting and pigments (N.H., Book 35), and stones (including *emplekton* walls, Book 36). The next is Frontinus, writing in A.D. 97. The next is M. Cetius Faventinus,[51] whose work is largely recension of parts of Vitruvius. Servius[52] refers to him; Sidonius Apollinaris regards him as the architect par excellence.[53] The references in Pliny the Elder and Sidonius Apollinarius imply that Vitruvius did indeed achieve what he had set out to do, namely, to write the only comprehensive account of ancient classical architecture, and his book probably remained authoritative in this regard throughout antiquity.[54]

Education and Encyclic Studies ("Liberal Arts")

The concept of *artes liberales* (liberal arts) as a basis for professional[55] training was based on a Greek Hellenistic type of education called *enkyklios paideia* or *enkyklia mathemata* (Vitruvius refers to it as *encyclos disciplina*). Vitruvius's own ideas on liberal arts as the basis of the education of the architect are not just an ideal, and they are not his own invention, because his education, designed by his parents, clearly embodies them (6.praef.4). Vitruvius's education, however, almost certainly does not represent the way all Roman architects were trained.

Enkyklios paideia may be traced to the appearance of the Sophists of the later fifth century B.C., whose instructional methods developed into a fairly standard group of disciplines in Hellenistic Greece. The curriculum's original intention was to serve as preparation (*propaideumata*) for leadership in society. In the common view of those who favored such a curriculum in Rome (e.g., Cicero), *enkyklios*

paideia was a type of education in general studies (or "other studies" as Aristotle termed them) whose intention was to "broaden judgment" before specializing in a certain field. In the Roman world liberal study became accepted as a standard prelude only to the study of law and rhetoric (which were not paid "professions" in Vitruvius's time, but rather the activities of "those who guide the affairs of the republic") and to the professions of medicine and teaching, as well as various of the literary arts.

The ideal of a liberal course of study began to permeate the upper levels of Roman society during the second century B.C. (e.g., in the Scipionic circle), and by the first century it had not only become firmly established but had also permeated further down the social scale. For the generation of Cicero and Caesar (born c. 100 B.C.), the idea of finishing off this education with a stay in Athens was relatively unusual; by the time of Horace, a little over half a century later, this kind of general education was seen as an important family investment even for a small farmer.

The encyclic subjects (Vitruvius calls them *encyclios disciplina*; Cicero, *artes liberales*) were seen as a tightly knit group of fields that were already standardized by the late Hellenistic period: the verbal arts of grammar, rhetoric, and dialectic (logic); and the mathematical subjects of arithmetic, geometry, music theory, and astronomy.[56] Vitruvius's list of *disciplinae* includes several of the presumably "standard" subjects, as well as additions that were, in his opinion, specially pertinent to architecture and probably not part of standard education (e.g., draftsmanship, knowledge of painting, sculpture, and law). Philosophy, which Vitruvius includes, was normally the goal of encyclic studies, but not part of them.

In the normal course of Roman education there would be some introduction to encyclic studies while a youth was studying literature with a grammarian (from age twelve to fifteen), but for most Romans "general education" would consist of a patchwork of tutors from different fields who taught youths from ages fifteen to eighteen before they went into specialized training or apprenticeship. It is to these tutors that Vitruvius refers when he says he learned geometry and astronomy from his "teachers" (9.1.16).

51 Probably early third century, but see H. Plommer, *Vitruvius and the Later Roman Building Manuals* (Cambridge, 1973). One should also probably include Palladius, whose work is dependent on Faventinus, and hence at secondhand, on Vitruvius.

52 Grammarian and commentator, late fourth century, *Ad Aeneidem* 6.43.

53 *Epistulae* 4.3.5. Mid-fifth century Christian writer.

54 For subsequent history of his influence, see H. Koch, *Vom Nachleben des Vitruv* (Baden-Baden, 1951). One might also include the question of whether Vitruvius plagiarized Athenaeus Mechanicus, or whether Athenaeus plagiarized Vitruvius, or whether they both share a common source in Agesistratus. See commentary, 7.praef.14, 10.13.1–2.

55 The development of the concept of "professional," or at least the use of that word in that sense, slightly postdates Vitruvius. See Commentary: 1.1.11.

56 The terms *trivium* and *quadrivium* are first found in Boethius, but the Greek term *hai tesseres methodoi* ("the four methods") is found from the first century A.D. (Gerasimus (c. A.D. 100, *Introductio Arithmeticae* 1.3.4). The fields were grouped this way by the late Hellenistic period.

There were three levels of education in late Republican and early Imperial Rome, and the first two levels had fairly standard curricula.[57] The first or primary level began at about age six or seven and went through age ten or twelve, depending on the child. In the early Republic, education was traditionally supposed to be the responsibility of the *paterfamilias* ("traditional" parents like Cicero would try to continue the tradition by carefully designing their sons' education), but by the later Republic the wealthiest families hired tutors into their homes. Most other parents would send their children out to the care of a *magister ludi*, who worked in a hired space in the city. Here they would learn letters, basic reading and writing, and basic arithmetic. The wealthier children were accompanied by a "pedagogue," a slave who saw to it that they did their lessons and who sometimes assisted in teaching.

The second level of Roman education was in effect a grammar school, designed for students from ages ten or twelve to about age fifteen or seventeen. The pupil was in the care of a *grammaticus* or *scholasticus*, and the curriculum focused on grammar and literature (learned mainly through memorization) and further arithmetic. It was at this stage, depending on the ambitions of the parents, that extra tutors would be hired for subjects such as geometry, music, or history. Those going on to study and practice oratory were sometimes even sent to a comic actor, to increase the range of emotional expression in delivery.

The third stage, as far as we know it,[58] was the highly specialized preparation for a "career" in oratory. It would begin at about the age of fifteen or seventeen, that is, the age at which a youth would assume the clothing of an adult male, the *toga virilis*, and he would be placed in the care of a speech instructor, a *rhetor*. It would be at this stage that he normally would have tutelage in fields such as philosophy and rhetoric, if ever. This third stage of education would also often coincide with a youth's first military service, or might precede it by a few years.

As mentioned earlier, study abroad served as a fourth stage of education for many, at least for the sons of the wealthiest Romans. Foreign study usually involved advanced training in rhetoric or philosophy and would take place with the best of Greek scholars in Rhodes, Athens, and Marseilles.

One can speculate that Vitruvius may have been apprenticed in the third phase of his education primarily to the care of an architect, or an architectural teacher, although he may have begun to pick up some skills, such as drawing, earlier.[59] He also probably continued some liberal education into this third stage, as his writing shows knowledge, if not easy mastery, of rhetoric.[60] Whether Vitruvius's travel comprised part of his education or of his career, or both, remains an open question. Clearly, however, he continued his self-education for the rest of his life (1.praef.3; 8.3.25).

In the first and second centuries A.D., liberal arts education fell somewhat out of favor as parents expressed more interest in their sons' rapid professional advancement; hence students were pressed more quickly to learn declamation, and rhetoric became more and more a matter of fluent showmanship without substance.[61]

Building in Augustan Rome (Figure 1)

During Vitruvius's lifetime the appearance of the city of Rome was radically transformed by considerable building activity in two areas: the open area of the Campus Martius and the densely built-up area of the old Forum. Most of this construction was sponsored by the principal political rivals of the last decades of the Republic and their partisans: Pompey, Caesar, Octavian, M. Agrippa, and to a lesser extent Marc Antony.[62]

Throughout the first century B.C. it became common

---

57 See S. F. Bonner, *Education in Ancient Rome* (Berkeley and Los Angeles, 1977), and R. A. Kaster, *Guardians of Language: The Grammarian and Society in Late Antiquity* (Berkeley and Los Angeles, 1988).

58 We know about the third level of education almost exclusively from descriptions of the preparation of a "career" in oratory: the anonymous *Rhetorica ad Herennium*, Cicero, Suetonius, and Quintilian.

59 There were, by the late Hellenistic period and into the first couple of centuries A.D., a few "schools" of medicine, complete with a curriculum (varying from as little as six months to as much as four to six years) and initiation rituals for the entering class of students. There is no evidence of any similar schools for architects, or even architects who offered orderly curricula to their apprentices.

60 E. Nylander, *Prefaces and Problems in Vitruvius' 'De Architectura'* (Diss. Göteborg, 1992), 22. Vitruvius also specifically states that he has read Cicero on the art of rhetoric and Varro on the Latin language, so that his knowledge of rhetoric could well be part of his lifelong self-education (9.praef.17).

61 Bonner, *Education in Ancient Rome* (Berkeley and Los Angeles, 1977), 332.

62 For a summary of Augustan architecture and its overall historical context, D. Favro, *Image of Augustan Rome* (Cambridge, 1996).

Figure 1. Rome in the time of Augustus (partly reconstructed).

for competing individuals or factions to restore or completely rebuild temples that had fallen into disrepair. Maintenance of temples was normally a senatorial prerogative, and individuals or military *triumphatores* were not permitted to build or restore temples in their own names; L. Opimius was the first to be allowed to do so when he rebuilt the temple of Concord in 121 B.C., setting a precedent that other ambitious Romans were eager to follow. Many of the temples Vitruvius refers to are restorations or rebuildings of this sort. Most of the rebuildings were in the form of up-to-date Hellenistic monumental architecture, although they existed side by side with the older form of Italic/Etruscan temple of mud brick, timber, and terracotta, quite a number of which survived into the first century A.D.

The buildings that set the style for the monumentalization of the Campus Martius were a series of Greek-influenced lavish temples and porticoes built mainly by victorious generals (*imperatores*) from the middle of the second century B.C.: the temples of Hercules Musarum, Juno Regina and Diana, built by the censors M. Fulvius Nobilior and M. Aemilius Lepidus in 179; the Porticus Octavia, built by Gn. Octavius, the victor in a minor sea battle, in 168; the Porticus Metelli, built by Q. Caecilius Metellus Macedonicus, the conqueror of Macedon, in 146–131; and the Porticus Minucia, by M. Minucius Rufus, the victor in a Thracian campaign in 107. The Porticus Octavia was either two story or two aisled (*porticus duplex*) and had Corinthian columns decorated in gilded bronze.

In contrast to the older part of Rome, these monuments struck contemporaries as a radiant new city. Strabo, c. 9–6 B.C., writes,

In fact, Pompey, the Deified Caesar, Augustus, his sons and friends, and wife and sister, have outdone all others in their zeal for building, and in the expense incurred. The Campus Martius contains most of these, and thus, in addition to its natural beauty, it has received still further adornment as the result of foresight. Indeed, the size of the Campus is remarkable, since it affords space at the same time and without interference, not only for the chariot races [in the Trigarium and Circus Flaminius] and every other equestrian exercise, but also for that multitude of people who exercise themselves by ball-playing, hoop-trundling, and wrestling; and the works of art situated around the Campus Martius and the ground, which is covered with grass throughout the year, and the crowns of those hills that are above the river and extend as far as its bed [i.e., the modern Pincio, ancient Collis Hortulorum, crowned with villa-gardens, like the Villa of Lucullus], which present to

the eye the appearance of a stage painting – all this, I say, affords a spectacle which one can scarcely draw away from. And near this campus is still another campus, with colonnades round about it in very great numbers [i.e., the southern end of the Campus Martius], and sacred precincts, and three theaters, and an amphitheater, and very costly temples, in close succession to one another, giving the impression that they are trying, as it were, to declare the rest of the city a mere accessory. For this reason, in the belief that this place was the holiest of all, the Romans have erected in it the tombs of their most illustrious men and women; the most noteworthy is what is called the Mausoleum [the Mausoleum of Augustus], a great mound near the river on a lofty foundation of white marble, thickly covered with evergreen trees to the very summit. Now on top is a bronze image of Augustus Caesar; beneath the mound are the tombs of himself, and his kinsmen and intimates; behind the mound is a large sacred precinct with wonderful promenades [i.e., public garden]; and in the middle of the Campus is the wall (this too of white marble) round his crematorium [*ustrinum*]; the wall is surrounded by a circular iron fence and the space within is planted with black poplars. And again, if, on passing to the old Forum, you saw one forum after another ranged along the old one, and basilicas, and temples, and say also the Capitolium and the works of art there and those of the Palatium and Livia's promenade [Porticus Liviae], you would easily become oblivious to everything else outside. Such is Rome.[63]

In addition, one other major feature of architectural activity in the reign of Augustus was the long overdue reorganization of the administration of building codes, water supply, police and fire brigades.[64] Agrippa himself, although he had been consul, took the lower office of aedile in 34/33 to take control of the aqueducts and organized a permanent staff. Vitruvius may later have served as a professional on that staff when he standardized the sizes of the water pipes in Rome.[65]

Throughout this entire period, however, the main part of the city of Rome was a warren of winding streets and precarious multistory tenements (6–8 stories high), of mud brick and half-timber with cantilevered wooden bal-

63 Strabo, *Geography* 5.3.8, trans. H. L. Jones (London, 1938).

64 See D. Strong, "The Administration of Public Buildings in Rome in the Late Republic and the Early Empire," *Institute of Classical Studies Bulletin* 15 (1968), 97–109; D. Favro, "Pater Urbis; Augustus as City Father of Rome," *Journal of the Society of Architectural Historians* 51.1 (1992), 61–84.

65 Frontinus, *De Aquis Urbis Romae* 1.25.

conies. Collapses, fires, and speculative rebuilding were constant. (Experiments in tilework, or fired brick, as Vitruvius himself reports in Book 2, were just beginning, and can be seen in buildings like the interior parts of the Theater of Marcellus.) By contrast, the residences (domus) of the wealthy, all built or rebuilt with the fashionable luxury of the last century, were one- to two-story enclaves of Hellenistic elegance; they were still clustered mainly in the upper Forum and the Palatine and a few other locations. They could be quite vast, even if built in the densest parts of the City; the Porticus Liviae occupies all of the site of the domus of Vedius Pollio. On the hills around the periphery of the city the "horti" (gardens) were the first ring of villas of the very wealthy, owned by such people as Lucullus, Caesar, and Pompey. The next "ring" was about four hours' ride away and could be reached by the senatorial nobility on weekends; they were located in places like Tivoli, Tusculum, Lavinium, and Laurentum. The third ring was more distant, most particularly the lavish seaside villas of the Bay of Naples. The walls of the City itself, although refortified as recently as 87 B.C. by Sulla, were probably in part falling into disrepair, and in any case did not contain the spreading population; the fourteen Augustan regions include considerable area outside the old walls.

Vitruvius's Position in the History of the Development of Roman Construction Methods and Forms

Vitruvius is often taken to represent a conservative point of view toward the construction of his time because he seems generally to be unaware of the potential for new forms that emerged in brick-faced concrete and vaulting in the subsequent century, and he was critical of the technology that led to them.[66] With the hindsight of modern archaeology, the argument is not difficult to appreciate. He makes very little reference to vaulting (the "vaulted" ceilings of Book 7 are suspended ceilings) and never treats vaulting as a potential covering for a major interior space. He is suspicious of the

durability of tufa-faced rubblework,[67] he makes almost no mention of "engaged" columns, and his imposition of "rules"[68] on numerous aspects of form is taken as a conservative attempt to impose Hellenistic-style regularity on the chaotic inventiveness of late Republican, especially Campanian, architecture.

It is also possible to formulate the opposite view, namely, that Vitruvius is creatively critical of just those aspects of Roman architecture which are in fact revolutionized in the succeeding two or three generations. Within his lifetime the process of replacing tufa-faced opus reticulatum with brick-faced concrete was begun. He seems to take masonry vaulting for granted, at least in utilitarian and interior applications, even if he does not include a special section that focuses on the technique of masonry vaulting; in 5.10.3 he says that ceilings in baths in this form (vaulted) will be "more efficient" if executed in masonry (as opposed to suspended ceilings). He does mention "engaged orders" in passing (the pseudo-peripteral temple, the Egyptian oecus, and perhaps the upper story of the Fano basilica).[69] Again, rather than to prescribe rules for them, he takes them for granted. The syntactical rules for engaged orders are, after all, the same as for freestanding, and therefore to Vitruvius they may not have been worthy of being distinguished as a separate genus (type) of object.

By Vitruvius's time, lime-mortared rubble with a facing (opus caementicium) had been common for at least two centuries, and he treats it as only one alternative along with mud brick, half-timbering, and, for monuments or fortifications, ashlar.[70] Opus caementicium was almost certainly in use by the end of the third century B.C. (it is well attested in dated buildings in the colony of Cosa,

---

66 For example, A. Boëthius, "Vitruvius and the Roman Architecture of his Age," in Dragma Martin Nilsson (Acta Instituti Sueciae Romae 1) (Lund, 1939), 114–143; H. Knell, Vitruvs Architekturtheorie (Darmstadt, 1991), 59.

67 For example, the eighty-year devaluation of concrete walls; reticulate allowing cracks to propagate along straight lines; the inability to judge how long opus testaceum walls will last. 2.8.8; 2.8.1; 2.8.19.

68 This is what is normally implied by the modern critical term "Vitruvian classicism."

69 4.8.6; 6.3.9; 5.1.6–7.

70 In actual fact, any of these techniques could be used interchangeably for either monumental or utilitarian architecture. The walls, as well as the podium, of the temples of the Arx at Cosa (later third century) and the walls of the temples at Tivoli (c. 100) are reticulate; Republican shops at the foot of the Capitol and the domus of M. Aemilius Scaurus (praetor 67) (of the later second and early first centuries, respectively) are tufa ashlar. For Vitruvius, most masonry (structura) is some type of small stone masonry, unless it is squared stone (saxa quadrata).

founded 273), and may have been first developed in Campania as early as the early third century.[71] The idea of facing a core may have developed from Hellenistic *emplekton*, but more likely it was simply the result of tidying up the facing stones of the rubble mass in Italic small stone masonry. It was a common technique in the second century.[72] The formulas that Vitruvius gives for mortars must have been worked out by generations of empirical experiment in the third and second centuries B.C. There was a considerable increase in quality from the late second century to Sullan times.[73]

Fired brick was very ancient in the Mediterranean but not yet common in Rome.[74] It appears in Pompeii in columns at the end of the second century B.C. (the Basilica) and is used somewhat in Pompeii, Ostia, and Rome as framing (coigns) in walls of *opus incertum* in the first century.[75] Its real period of development into the standard facing begins in the reign of Augustus, usually as cut tiles, and it is applied to large buildings under Tiberius (the Castra Praetoria) and becomes a common coigning material for reticulate. It almost completely replaces reticulate by the time of Caligula and Nero.

Voussoir vaulting was also moderately common in the Near East throughout the first millennium B.C. in some highly visible locations, mainly city gates and palaces. True vaulting may appear in a few locations in Greece and the West in the fifth and fourth century B.C. but its large-scale introduction probably is to be attributed to the engineers of Alexander's eastern campaigns, who introduced it into city gates, drains, and tombs. It is in these applications that it appears to be most common in Etruscan and Latin Italy from the later fourth century.[76] In Rome in the second century vaults seem to be begun to be constructed in *opus caementicium* as well as stone, and they are used for extensive spaces in utilitarian buildings such as the huge warehouse identified as the Porticus Aemilia (193/174 B.C.). Vaults became relatively common in certain rooms of bath complexes in the later second and early first centuries B.C. The arch entered the vocabulary of monumental architecture in the last decades of the second century B.C. in the form of the *fornix* (triumphal arch) and the arched aedicula (the archivolt framed by engaged columns, in the terraced sanctuary of Praeneste in the 130s and the basement of the Tabularium in the Forum c. 79).[77] It rarely appears as monumental interior space, although as true and false vaults (as Vitruvius implies) it is common in houses and baths.

From this survey we have the impression that in Vitruvius's lifetime faced concrete was a standard wall technique which was being evaluated in competition along with mud brick and half-timber, and that Vitruvius's critical comments seem to be part of this evaluation. There were some tentative experiments, as Vitruvius suggests, in how to make concrete more weatherproof by using other materials, including tiles, in sections of the facing (e.g., cornices), or how to strengthen it with stone piers embedded in the caementicium. Small span vaulting was taken for granted but was still largely a utilitarian device for substructures and for some types of chambers (e.g., baths).[78]

71 Lugli, *Tecnica edilizia romana* (Rome, 1957), 375. The reference to it is in an inscription from Puteoli, dated 105 B.C., where it is referred to as *opus structile*. CL 10.1781.1 r. 16–22, in Lugli, op. cit., 363. This strengthens the association of *opus caementicium* with Campania. Pozzolana seems to have been used in the mortar from the early first century B.C.

72 Cato, *De Agri Cultura*, 14 ff.

73 F. Coarelli, *Papers of the British School at Rome* 45 (1977), 1 ff.

74 It was moderately common in certain applications in architecture of the Near East in the first millennium B.C. in places where Greeks and Italians could have seen it (Vitruvius mentions the walls of Babylon as *testacea*, 8.3.8). It is used rarely and only for special circumstances in Greek architecture from the end of the fifth century. Perhaps the first known instance is for bases for wooden columns in houses in the Athenian colony of Olynthus. A. W. Lawrence, rev. Tomlinson, *Greek Architecture* (New Haven, 1996), 184. In Sicily and southern Italy there are local traditions of the use of brick for columns and some applications in walls, and extensively for paving (e.g., Solunto, Veleia), throughout the Hellenistic period. R. J. A. Wilson, "Brick and Tiles in Roman Sicily," in A. McWhirr, ed., *Roman Brick and Tile*, BRA Int. Ser. 68 (1979), 11–43.

75 The basic coigning material for incertum and reticulate of the first century B.C. is *vittatum* (i.e., small blocks), and "brick" becomes more common only in late Republican buildings. It is usually cut tile, not purpose-made brick. Lugli, *Tecnica edilizia romana* (Rome, 1957), 529–551; L. Richardson, *Pompeii, An Architectural History* (Baltimore and London, 1988), 374–376; 378–379.

76 T. Boyd, "The Arch and Vault in Greek Architecture," *American Journal of Archaeology* 82 (1978), 83. A. W. Lawrence, rev. Tomlinson, *Greek Architecture* (New Haven, 1996), 171.

77 This latter motif goes on, in Vitruvius's lifetime, to become one of the main ways of using the "orders" to articulate vaulted architecture, as in the Colosseum; it was used in the amphitheater of Statilius Taurus and the Theater of Marcellus, and possibly the Theater of Pompey.

78 Even most of its first monumental applications (in buildings such as Praeneste, the Tabularium, or the theaters) were technically still substructures.

Vitruvius has no special word for vaulting. His most common term, *concameratio*, can be used equally for masonry vaults and suspended plaster ceilings.[79] Its actual meaning is simply "chambered in" and can refer to the (arched) covering of a cart or a garden trellis, that is, an arched form. The word *fornix* or its derivatives can refer to masonry structures.[80] Aqueducts should be raised on arches (*confornicentur*). The word *arcus* is used to describe the frame for hides covering a battering ram (10.13.7). The entrance to the *vomitorium* of a theater is described as covered by *supercilia*, eyebrows; this may mean an archivolt, but elsewhere the word means flat lintels.

The development of the aesthetic of space-positive vaulted architecture in the first century A.D. at first glance seems particularly remote from the supposedly philhellene Vitruvius, but in fact many of Vitruvius's recommendations concern preserving the spaciousness of interiors: he recommends the pseudodipteral temple of Hermogenes in part because of the breadth of the portico (3.2.6); the pseudoperipteral temple allows one to "create a spacious interior for the cella by taking away the areas reserved for the colonnade" (4.8.6); and his design for the basilica at Fano (5.1.1–10) is spatially innovative, both for functional reasons (there is a lateral tribunal "so that those who are before the magistrates will not interfere with those who are doing business in the basilica") and aesthetic reasons ("Thus the double ridged design . . . and the top of the ceiling on the interior presents an elegant aspect.").

The early stages of creativity are always hard to discern, but we clearly recognize here part of the eventual

intent. The casting about for terms and distinctions is characteristic of experiment and innovation. The very word *architectura* was probably a neologism of about twenty years earlier,[81] and in the same manner Vitruvius's own terms and definitions are almost certainly a mix of inventions and conventions.

Interpreting Vitruvius

The *Ten Books* have two dominant themes: the first is that the field of "architecture" covers the entire built and mechanical environment and is an art of great complexity and one of the most essential of the arts of social humanity; the second is that its proper practice depends on the synthetic mastery of a vast range of theoretical and practical knowledge.

It is this second point – architecture as a "liberal art" – that is most peculiar to the "Vitruvian" ideal of architecture. It argues that an architect should have not only personal talent and specialized practical knowledge, but should also be broadly educated in *artes liberales* or *encyclios disciplina*.

Then as now, this was a controversial, and not a standard, view of what an architect and an architect's preparation should be. In twentieth-century America, most architects do not have a liberal arts education behind their professional training. In fact, most buildings are built without "architects" at all.[82] The status and role of an "architect" in antiquity also varied greatly. He could be a wealthy amateur, a patrician doing his own design;[83] a

79 Uses of *concameratio* that probably do mean masonry vault: (5.10) baths with roofs of masonry vs. timber; (6.11.1) ceilings of underground cellars; (2.4.2) concrete structures; 3.3.1 *concamerationes* in foundations; (5.11.2) *concamerata sudatio*, presumably a true vault in a sweat bath. Uses that are not structural vaults but only the shape: (2.4.3) pitsand can hold ceilings that are in this shape; (5.10.3) suspended ceilings; (7.3.1) the word refers to the wickerwork of the vaulted ceiling; Vitruvius clarifies this by saying that it should be laid out *ad formam circinationis*.

80 (5.5.2) chambers in the seating cavea of theaters for sounding vessels; (6.11.3) windows and relieving arches; (6.8.4) buildings built on piers, their *fornices* may be closed by wedges (*cuneorum*, presumably voussoirs). This latter is the most unambiguous description of an arch (on piers), but to assure his reader what he is talking about he has to give a very roundabout description: *idemque, qui pilatim aguntur aedificia et cuneorum et cuneorum divisionibus coagmentis ad centrum respondentibus fornices concluduntur*. This implies that he assumed the arch may not have been common knowledge to his readers.

81 Its first known appearance in Latin is Cicero's *De Officiis*, 1.151. Cicero was generally opposed to neologisms or direct translation from the Greek to supply technical and philosophical words that Latin lacked but was not above using them when necessity compelled him. Another possible inventor of the word may have been Varro in his lost *De Novem Disciplinae*.

82 Contemporary estimates are that architects are responsible for between a fifth and a quarter of all construction. A. Saint, *The Image of the Architect* (New Haven, 1983), 72.

83 In disparaging the ignorant and inexperienced who try to pass as architects, Vitruvius also says, "but I cannot refrain from praising the heads of households who, trusting in their own reading, build for themselves." (6.praef.6). James Anderson is sympathetic to the identification of [C.] Mucius, the architect of Marius's temple of Honos and Virtus with Q. Mucius Scaevola, curule aedile under Marius in 100 B.C. L. Richardson, Jr., "*Honos et Virtus* and the Sacra Via," *American Journal of Archaeology* 82 (1978), 240–246; discussion in J. C. Anderson, Jr., *Roman Architecture and Society* (Baltimore and London, 1997), 24–26.

trained slave, such as at least one of Cicero's architects; an outright charlatan, of the type Vitruvius disparages (6.praef.6); a sought after foreign artist, usually Greek, such as Hermodoros of Salamis; a salaried maintenance official or city architect;[84] a highly trained professional technician or engineer who is a member of the staff of *apparitores* (attendants) of a senatorial magistrate;[85] a multifarious contractor-entrepreneur with a family business, possibly quite wealthy, such as the families of the Cossutii or Haterii;[86] or the type of liberal arts–trained professional that Vitruvius describes. Varro includes architecture among his list of nine liberal arts, along with medicine, and Cicero describes architecture and medicine as "honestae."[87] In *De natura deorum* (1.8) Cicero describes the creation of the earth as similar to the labor of an architect. In contrast, in the early second century B.C. Plautus (in *Miles gloriosus*) generally depicts the architect as a deceiver and "machinator." In the first century A.D., Seneca, referring to high apartment buildings (*insulae*), says it was a happy day before the days of the first architects and the first builders.[88] And Martial (5.56) advises that if your son is dull-witted "educate him as a page or an architect." Opinion and fact obviously varied greatly.

The type of professional with a liberal arts background that Vitruvius describes did indeed exist because he himself clearly embodies it, and there were clearly other architects with his kind of erudition.[89] The range of duties and knowledge ascribed to an architect in the *Ten Books* therefore may have considerable basis in fact, but these circumstances apply only to certain practitioners whose families had placed their faith in a role for liberal arts in the education of a professional. The *Ten Books*

are thus not necessarily a guide to how Roman architects were trained and practiced, but more likely they were written as an argument for how architects *ought* to practice.

This probable polemical relationship to a dynamic historical context must be kept in mind by any reader when formulating an interpretation of Vitruvius's work. The *Ten Books*, in such a light, should be regarded as largely "prescriptive" rather than "descriptive" – that is, arguing a point of view rather than summarizing currently accepted standard practice – but present interpretations of our author still exhibit a wide variety of possibilities.

The most common thread through modern Vitruvius research is to consider him in some way conservative or even reactionary. As mentioned earlier, it has often been noted that Vitruvius seems to say nothing that points toward the great revolutions in brick-faced vaulted concrete, he has a slavish respect for the definitive achievements of ancestors, the core of his theory about monumental architecture is the somewhat jejune canonical Ionic classicism of Hermogenes, and he hardly seems aware of engaged orders at all. Axel Boëthius argued that the meticulous dictation of proportions that dominates Vitruvius's descriptions of the "orders" was an attempt to suppress the uncanonical inventiveness of late Republican decoration, particularly the tradition derived from Campania.[90] The core of Vitruvian aesthetics would then be based on the principles enunciated by the Hellenistic architect Hermogenes. This meticulous classicizing system, based on a modular grid, supposedly forms the basis of a total system of modular design that, in Vitruvius's view, covers everything from columns to catapults. Scholarly efforts to discover this system within Vitruvius are extensive but are usually frustrated by its inconsistencies.

This leads to the view of Vitruvius as well read but somewhat intellectually naive and inept, a person who is more a pretender than a master of his broad education. His theoretical terms, although clearly based on his Greek erudition, seem to fall short of consistency or clarity: in 1.1 he defines architecture as *firmitas, utilitas,* and *venustas;* in 1.2 he defines it as the six categories of *ordinatio, dispositio, eurythmia, symmetria, decor,* and *distributio.* Are the first four or five categories of the second list

84 As Diognetus and Epimachus, architects of the city of Rhodes. 10.6.3.
85 P. Gros, "Munus non ingratum; le traité Vitruvien et la notion de service," in *Le projet de Vitruve; objet, destinataire et réception du de Architectura* (Rome, 1994), 75–90.
86 E. Rawson, "Architecture and Sculpture: The Activities of the Cossutii," *Papers of the British School at Rome* 43 (1975), 36–47.
87 *De officiis* 1.42.151.
88 *Epistulae* 90.8.43.
89 Vettius Cyrus, an architect who worked for Cicero, justified the width of windows in a room called the Amaltheum by saying it was required to accommodate the progression of visual rays, a theory going back to Theophrastus. Cicero's correspondent (Atticus) was not impressed by the argument, but it shows that some architects relied on this kind of applied scientific (or pseudo-scientific) principle. *Ad Atticum* 2.3.2. Also A. Constans, *Révue Philologique* (1931), 231, and P. Gros, "Le statut social et rôle culturel des architectes (période héllenistique et augustéenne," *CollEFR* 66 (1983), 449.

90 For example, A. Boëthius, "Vitruvius and the Roman Architecture of His Age," in *Dragma Martin Nilsson* (Acta Instituti Sueciae Romae 1) (Lund, 1939), 114–143; H. Knell, *Vitruvs Architekturtheorie* (Darmstadt, 1991), 59.

subdivisions of *venustas* in the first, or just a parallel system of categorization?[91] The terms themselves (*ordinatio*, etc.) are notoriously elusive of clear definition. A further support to this view is the opinion that many scholars have of his command of Latin; Vitruvian prose clearly shows its ambitions in the high rhetorical style of his prefaces, but dangling modifiers, overstretched grammatical structure, and tortuous physical descriptions abound. Like most architectural writers of any epoch, he is more ambitious than able.

Two diametrically opposite interpretations assert that Vitruvius is purely a theorist or an intellectual dilettante with a shallow grasp of practical exigencies, a person who read a great deal but never built a building, or, contrariwise, that he is primarily a technician, the military catapult officer and hydraulic engineer, short on erudition and intellect and wedded to an engineer's fascination for tedious detail.

The most prevalent modern interpretation of Vitruvius continues a tradition of Vitruvius as the promulgator of canonical rules and paradigmatic form. "Vitruvian classicism" is its catch phrase. This view derives primarily from sixteenth- and seventeenth-century commentators and illustrators, starting, probably, with the circle of Bramante and Raphael and passing on to Serlio, Palladio, Vignola, and, in the next century, to, among others, Perrault. It involves the substitution of the term "orders"[92] for the columnar *genera* (types) of Vitruvius and the related concept that there are only five definitive forms of trabeation (despite Vitruvius's brief but explicit statements to the contrary). Illustrations of Vitruvius executed in this tradition present the Vitruvian "orders" as complete paradigmatic designs, restored down to their last detail, even though the text does not in fact provide sufficient information to do so. The attempt to create full reconstructions may seem to carry out a methodology obvious to modern readers, but it is actually representative of ideas that postdate profound social-intellectual consequences connected with the development of modern science in the sixteenth and seventeenth centuries, more specifically the idea that physical reality is a consistent single system and that, similarly, architectural forms must emanate from a single mutually consistent group of "orders" whose forms must be as definitive and

specific as the forms of nature. Ancient aesthetics, like ancient science, seems to have been more tolerant of parallel systems.

The view that Vitruvius aims at rigid paradigmatic prescription must be modified by the fact that throughout the *Ten Books* there are numerous admonitions that the actual process of design requires (unspecified) adjustments to the "symmetries" and other prescriptions.[93] "Now it is not possible to have the symmetries for every theater carried out according to every principle and to every effect. Instead it is up to the architect to note in which it will be necessary to pursue symmetry in which to make adjustments according to the nature of the site or the size of the project" (5.6.7). If a villa is to be "more refined," the residential part can be designed with the symmetries recommended for a town house, "so long as this does not interfere with its serviceability as a country house" (6.6.5). One can not use the same principles of fortification design in all places; one needs to adapt to the site and the character of the opponent. Anyone who wants to use these instructions must "select from their variety" (10.16.1–2).[94] In 6.2.1 Vitruvius could hardly be more clear: "Thus, once the principle of symmetries has been established and the dimensions [for a building] have been developed by reasoning, then it is the special skill of the gifted architect to provide for the nature of the site, or the building's appearance, or its function, and make adjustments by subtractions or additions. . . ."

91 H.-W. Kruft, *A History of Architectural Theory* (Princeton, 1994), 24–25.

92 I. D. Rowland, "Raphael, Angelo Colocci, and the Genesis of the Architectural Orders," *Art Bulletin* 76 (1994), 81–104.

93 Vitruvius was probably aware of erudite theoretical debates in the fields of rhetoric and music that argued the sufficiency or insufficiency of rule vs. adjustment. In first-century B.C. development of Latin language and rhetoric there was a debate between the "analogists," who asserted a belief in the possibility of establishing fixed rules for all things, and those who supported *consuetudo* (custom) and invention in the shaping of language, including the creation of new words. The former group derived from the theories of Alexandrian scholars and included Staberius Eros, possibly Julius Caesar, and Varro; the latter derived from Stoic influence in Rome and included Crates of Mallos, Cicero, and much later Quintilian. "Good speech demands constant departure from rule" (Cicero, *De Oratore*, Bonner, 206). "It is one thing to speak grammatically, another to speak Latin" (Quintilian, 1.6.27). See Bonner, *Education in Ancient Rome* (Berkeley and Los Angeles, 1977), 205, 206, passim, and Moses Hadas, *A History of Latin Literature* (New York and London, 1952), 106. In music, the best known theorist, Aristoxenus, argued that true harmony could not be achieved through geometrically pure intervals but required small adjustments of those intervals.

94 Other places include 3.3.13; 3.5.5; 6.2.2; 6.3.1; 10.10.6; 10.16.3.

One body of adjustments deals with optics.[95] Another sets down rules, but leaves the designer to complete them by deduction, interpolation, or invention.[96] For some building types (the bath, the palaestra, the country house),[97] the "prescriptions" seem more like a preliminary program with a list of optimum, almost conflicting, design criteria that can rarely all be solved equally well in any actual design.

Many of Vitruvius's prescriptions lie outside the system of symmetries entirely. They are instead rules of thumb given as sliding parameters: steps to temples should be no more than five-sixths of a foot high, and the tread at least three-fourths wide (3.4.4); sheep and goat pens should be between 4 1/2 and 6 feet wide (6.6.3). Symmetry sometimes is recommended simply for its practical clarity in laying out dimensions, as in the use of the Pythagorean 3-4-5 right triangle in proportioning stairs and determining the pitch of the Archimedean waterscrew (10.6.4; 9.praef.8).

Vitruvius's section on his own design at Fano may indicate how his prescriptions are meant to be understood. The excursus abruptly follows his general prescriptions for basilicas, and contrasts with the prescriptions so clearly in certain respects that some scholars have been led to suggest that the description of Fano must be a later interpolation, possibly by a different author, into the original manuscript: Vitruvius introduces a double ridge roof and a lateral apsed tribunal, and the interior has one "order" of columns that span two floors rather than, as prescribed, two superposed orders.[98] In our view, however, the descriptive section follows the general, prescriptive remarks in order to illustrate how the basic prescriptions can be "improved" in an actual design.[99]

His numerous asides, and the fact that in no case do prescriptions themselves allow a reconstruction of a full design, imply that Vitruvius's method of writing was meant to present an open, and not an inclusive or closed, system of design. It was also a system capable of accommodating steady progress and innovation.

Vitruvius says explicitly, for example, that there are other allowable types of capital whose vocabulary has been drawn from Corinthian, Ionic, and Doric (4.1.12). The pseudoperipteral temple and the type of porch that adapts a Tuscan plan to Corinthian or Ionic columns are presented as adaptive innovations (4.8.5; 4.8.6) of prescriptions that he has just presented. He advocates reading from the wisdom of earlier writers so "that we may adapt them to our own enterprise . . . so that trusting in such authors, we may dare to prepare new principles" (7.praef.10). His story of Paconius, the architect who dared to invent a "better" system of hauling blocks than Chersiphron or Metagenes but who ended in ruin (10.2.13–14), demonstrates that the boldness to innovate brings the concomitant risk of failure.

From his liberal arts education Vitruvius gains not only broad knowledge but a habit of critical selectivity. There were, for instance, several schools of medicine in contemporary Rome, but he seems to follow the most scientific, so-called rational medicine. (See Commentary: 1.1.10.) He is aware that there are at least two major contrary trends in optics (that the eye generates, and that the eye receives, rays: 6.2.3); that there are some who say there are more than eight winds (1.6.9); that there is mathematical debate as to whether 6 or 10 is the best "perfect" number (3.1.5–6); and that there are those who deny the accuracy of Eratosthenes' measurement of the globe (1.6.11). In general our author tends to favor innovation; he shows an awareness of intellectual multiplicity, and a respect for both the preciousness of tradition and the value of innovative progress.

Vitruvius is also highly independent in his use of intellectual influences. Lucretius's *De Rerum Natura* appears to be one of his strongest influences, and from it he probably derives his scientific atomism, his respect for the primacy of sensory experience in the evaluation of truth, and his habit of listing multiple explanations for a single phenomenon[100] (his use of the words *ratio* and *genus* seems very much shaped by Lucretius), but he does not

---

95 Most of these are in Books 3 and 4. 3.3.12: hypotrachelium contraction; 3.3.13: entasis; 3.3.4: stylobate curvature; 3.5.8–9: higher epistyles for higher columns; 4.4.2–3: in interiors increase the number of flutes; 3.5.13: all elements above the capitals: front surfaces should all incline outward by one-twelfth the height.

96 Interior columns should be thinner, but then one needs to figure out how to prorate the thickness of the walls on one's own (4.4.2–4). Features like hypotrachelium contraction and epistyle height are given for columns up to a certain height, but then readers have to continue the system if they wish to build larger columns (3.3.12; 3.5.8).

97 5.10; 5.11; 6.6.1–5.

98 F. Pellati, "La basilica di Fano e la formazione del trattato di Vitruvio," *RPAA* 33–34 (1947–1949), 153–174.

99 Fano, according to Vitruvius, is less expensive and more spacious than a canonically designed basilica, and prevents the law court in the tribunal from interfering with the businessmen in the nave.

100 In Lucretius this habit may be intended more to deny the validity of specific causality, which is not an idea that Vitruvius seems to be in sympathy with.

follow Lucretius all the way to the image of a godless universe created by the chance amalgamation and dissolution of atoms.

Vitruvius is aware of the importance of experimental method and direct observation in the cumulative growth of science.[101] He cites the use of aeolipiles as proof that wind is the result of the collision of fire and water (1.6.2; this was a common scientific tool for Alexandrian scientists), he narrates the famous incident of Archimedes and the bath (9.praef.9–11), and notes that Democritus sealed with his personal signet ring in his treatise "whatever he has tried himself" (9.praef.15). Vitruvius honestly asserts, relative to his knowledge of sources of water, that "I have seen some of these things myself, and I discovered the rest in Greek books . . ." (8.3.27). The preface to Book 7 serves to give careful scholarly acknowledgment to his numerous written sources.

This same selectivity characterizes his architectural tastes. Throughout the *Ten Books* Vitruvius normally shows a strong preference for ingenious or innovative approaches, and even for foreign ideas. His prescription for polygonal towers in fortifications and left-turn approaches in gates, his recommendation of the *chorobates* as the most accurate of surveying levels (the chorobate is otherwise unattested in ancient literature on surveying), the use of sounding vessels in theaters, his description of a peculiar (but not wholly unattested) form of retaining wall (the *anterides*), his version of the *castellum aquae*, a type of fortification construction laced with timber like the Gaulish *murus gallicus*, the discovery of fire-resistant larch wood (2.9.15), even features of his design for the basilica at Fano, all have characteristics that depart from standard contemporary practice. It is not possible to say whether any of these improvements are his personal inventions (except, obviously, for the design features at Fano), but they at least reflect his personal choice, a choice apparently made with the intent of continual refinement.

As mentioned, Vitruvius steadily turns a critical eye to building, and whether or not one sees his remarks as resistance to change, they are contemporary with the beginning of the shift to terracotta-faced rubble (i.e., *structura testacea*/brick-faced Roman "concrete") and "space-positive" vaulted design. This type of critical appraisal[102] may have been an essential part of the process of initiating that shift.[103]

If critical method is a part of the whole revolutionary-evolutionary process of creating Roman imperial architecture,[104] then Vitruvius himself may have been an influential writer even in his own day. After writing the *Ten Books* he was very likely a staff architect of the *curator aquarum* and was responsible for the standardization of water pipe sizes.[105] Even the core of what is assumed to be "Vitruvian classicism" – the detailed proportional rules of Books 3 and 4 – may have influenced first-century A.D. practice (and been influenced by specific early first-century B.C. traditions, like a "Hermogenes-Hermodorus" school), but as with water pipes, the prescriptions rarely correspond to actual practice.[106] However, a standardization of certain architectural design features did occur in the first century A.D. that had a conceptual and procedural similarity to Vitruvius.

The Vitruvius who professes faith in scientific progress and critical method also has a great reverence for religion and tradition. The Greek youth was supposedly trained to walk with his head proudly raised, but like Cato the

102 Critical method was an essential part of rhetorical training, in evaluating myths, in evaluating the plausibility of events in early Roman history, or composing exercise arguments. Students were trained to recognize the consistent/inconsistent, possible/impossible, clear/obscure, and so on. Bonner, *Education in Ancient Rome* (Berkeley and Los Angeles, 1977), 262–263; Quintilian, 2.4.28–29.

103 He further cautions that one needs to attach orthostates (i.e., revetment) to coursed, not rubble masonry (2.8.3–4), he warns of the weakness of traditional tufa and recommends Ferentine (2.5.6), and he even goes so far as to criticize "ancestors" (*maiores*) in that he advises not to build heavy stucco cornices as they did (7.3.3).

104 Mario Torelli, "Innovazioni nelle tecniche edilizie romane tra il I sec. a.c. e il I sec. d.C.," *Tecnologia, economia e società nel mondo romano. Atti del convegno di Como, 27.28/29 Settembre, 1979* (Como, 1980), 139–161; Filippo Coarelli, *Papers of the British School at Rome* (1977) 45, 1–17.

105 S. Julius Frontinus, *De aquis urbis Romae*, 25.1, 27–30. He says that the plumbers of Rome standardized their sizes based on instructions from the architect Vitruvius. The sizes given in Frontinus (27–30) do not completely correspond to those given in Vitruvius, but Vitruvius may nonetheless be responsible for the concept and the administration of the idea.

106 See Mark Wilson Jones, "Designing the Roman Corinthian Order," *Papers of the British School at Rome* 59 (1991), 89–150. The immediate conclusion that one might draw from this study is that Vitruvius had no influence on the Imperial practice described in it.

101 This is a commonplace among some of the more sophisticated technical manuals that Vitruvius read. Philo (*Belopoeica* 50.23) asserts that experiment is necessary to adjust pure theory in the design of sophisticated artillery pieces.

Elder, Vitruvius, as a well-brought-up Roman, is proud to walk with his head humbly bowed before his *maiores* (ancestors).[107] With regard to liver divination, "I assert emphatically my opinion that the old principles for selecting a site should be called back into service" (1.4.9). But like science, the cultural accomplishments of tradition and religion are also the result of cumulative progress (e.g., the story of the rise of the arts of humanity and the art of architecture, 2.1.1–7), and they too involve personal skill and critical evaluation (e.g., the admonition not to build heavy stucco cornices like our *maiores*).[108]

It is therefore a peculiarly Roman feature of Vitruvius that a virtually seamless relationship exists between the critical, rational methods of science and the maintenance of ancestral tradition, including religion.[109] The accomplishments of both tradition and science represent the cumulative result of a progressive but partial unveiling of that natural order; they are a precious fabric of wisdom which is to be guarded carefully, but also extended continuously by invention and good judgment.[110]

There is no real trace in Vitruvius's text of the notorious later conflict in architectural theory between absolute beauty and arbitrary beauty because all form, whether personal or inherited, is the result of cumulative critical ability and personal skill. The *Ten Books* may be read by some as a paean to order in architecture, by others as a paean to informed creative intelligence.

The fundamental lessons of Vitruvius may in fact be rather simple: architecture is a very complex art and needs the control of rich tradition, but also must advance through innovative personal talent and intelligent application. The view of architecture as a "liberal art" is simply the assertion that the cumulative wisdom of liberal culture is the best way of providing architecture with that kind of flexible, firm control and judicious richness of invention.

Vitruvius, like much of late Republican culture, exudes a confident synthesizing eclecticism, respectful of inherited tradition, selectively admiring of foreign accomplishments, and confident of personal ability creatively to synthesize these influences. Hence the *Ten Books* may, through the medium of an ambitious but imperfectly informed visionary, reveal, in a very unexpected way, not just a panorama of Hellenistic knowledge, or a personal, critical view of Augustan architecture, but much of the key to a great period of architectural creativity.

---

107 On his attitudes to education, Plutarch, *Cato Maior*, 20.

108 There is thus nothing sacrosanct about *maiores*; just as with the reverence of family ancestors and the honoring of *summi viri*, their worth is proven by their acts and their course through the *cursus honorum*.

109 This seamless relationship extended to many other aspects of Roman culture. A common kind of oral business contract, the *stipulatio*, had to be executed with ritual correctness in order to be legally valid. See J. C. Anderson, Jr., *Roman Architecture and Society* (Baltimore and London, 1997), 70. Vitruvius's attitude also meshed well with the Augustan political program, which responded to critical weaknesses (e.g., the lack of a regular water administrator or fire department) by making minimal changes that maintained the forms of the *mos maiorum*; to do so, of course, required critical evaluation of those weaknesses, in the manner of Vitruvius.

110 The highly practical, observational quality of Etruscan/Italic religion probably did much to ease the assimilation of Hellenistic science into Roman culture. (Liver divination makes a great deal of sense in evaluating a site because the liver is the most responsive organ to the environment.) The dependence of augury on the quartering of the horizon attaches religion to orthogonal measure.

LIST OF MANUSCRIPTS SEEN

FLORENCE, BIBLIOTECA NAZIONALE

Magliabechi XVII.5

LONDON, BRITISH LIBRARY

Additional 38818
Arundel 122
Cotton Cleop. D.1
Harleianus 2508
Harleianus 2760
Harleianus 2767
Harleianus 3859
Harleianus 4870
Sloane 296

OXFORD, BODLEIAN LIBRARY

Auct. F.5.7

ROME, BIBLIOTECA APOSTOLICA VATICANA

Barb. Lat. 12 extracts
Barb. Lat. 90
Chigi H.IV.113
Chigi H.VI.189
Archivio di San Pietro H.34
Ottob.lat.850
   I only
Ottob. Lat. 1233
Ottob. Lat. 1234
Ottob. Lat. 1522
Ottob. Lat. 1561
Ottob. Lat. 1930
Vat. Lat. 2229
Vat. Lat. 2230
Vat. Lat. 4059
   Angelo Colocci's "tabulation" of text
Vat. Lat. 6020

Vat. Lat. 8488 (formerly Cicognara 691)
   I–III only
Vat. Lat. 8489 (formerly Cicognara 692)
Pal. Lat. 867 extracts
Pal. Lat. 1562
Pal. Lat. 1563
Urb. Lat. 293
Urb. Lat. 1360
Reg. Lat. 786 extracts
Reg. Lat. 1007 extracts
Reg. Lat. 1328
Reg. Lat. 1504
Reg. Lat. 1965
Reg. Lat. 2079

VITRUVIUS MANUSCRIPTS

H: British Library, Harleianus 2767, 8–9C
G: Wolfenbüttel, Gudianus 69, 11C
L: Leiden, Vossianus 88, 11C
l: Leiden, Vossianus 107, 11C
c: British Library, Cotton Cleop. D.1, 11C

PRINTED EDITIONS

Ioc. Giocondo, Venice 1511*
Schn. Schneider, Leipzig 1807
Mar. Marini, Rome 1836
Rose, Leipzig 1867
Granger, Cambridge, Mass., and London, 1931

* Rose bases his text on the slightly different Florence, 1513, edition of Fra Giocondo; I have used the Vatican copy (R.I.III.298) of the 1511 edition owned and annotated by Angelo Colocci (1474–1549; *Colotius*) and the Giocondo edition of Florence, 1522.

A Note about Transliteration of Greek

Vitruvius often seems to have written his Latin treatise with Greek texts close to hand. On occasion, he must have filled his own text with terms and, three times, whole poems in Greek; on other occasions, the manuscript record seems to suggest that he transliterated Greek by a combination of Roman letters and Greek spellings (as in the name Pytheos). Frequently, especially in the case of famous Greeks, he seems to have used an entirely Latinate spelling (Lysippus for Lysippos, Phidias for Pheidias, Philo for Philon). The translation's inconsistencies mirror those of the manuscript tradition, which may mirror those of Vitruvius himself, and reflect the eternal dilemma of any writer who works between two languages.

Note to the Reader

Words or phrases marked by an asterisk (*) are discussed in the illustrated Commentary that follows the translated text.

❖

FIRST PRINCIPLES AND THE LAYOUT
OF CITIES

PREFACE

1. So long as your divinely inspired intelligence and your godly presence, Imperator Caesar,* were engaged in taking possession of the world, your enemies leveled one and all by your invincible might, so long as citizens were glorying in your triumph and in your victory, with all the subject peoples awaiting your command, so long as the Roman People and Senate, freed from fear, were piloted by your far-ranging deliberations and plans, I dared not, in the midst of such concerns, publish my writings on architecture, even though these had been formulated according to extensive researches,* for fear that by intruding at an inappropriate moment I might incur the disdain of your keen spirit.

2. When, however, I perceived that you were solicitous not only for the establishment of community life and of the body politic, but also for the construction of suitable public buildings, so that by your agency not only had the state been rendered more august by the annexation of entire provinces, but indeed the majesty of the Empire had found conspicuous proof in its public works – then I thought that I should not miss the opportunity to publish on these matters for you as soon as possible, given that I was first recognized in this field by your Father [Julius Caesar]* and was a devoted admirer of his qualities. Thus when the council of the Olympians consecrated him among the abodes of immortality and passed his sovereignty into your own jurisdiction, this same devotion of mine, fixed upon his memory, naturally transferred allegiance to you. And so I was put in charge, along with Marcus Aurelius and Publius Minidius and Gnaeus Cornelius, of outfitting catapults as well as the repair of all the other sorts of war machines, and along with these men I received a stipend, first awarded by you, and continued at the recommendation of your sister.*

3. Therefore, because I had been put in your debt for the favor whereby I will never harbor the fear of want for the rest of my life, I began to record these matters for you. For I perceived that you had already built extensively (Figure 1),* were building now and would be doing so in the future: public as well as private constructions, all scaled to the amplitude of your own achievements so that these would be handed down to future generations. I have set down these instructions, complete with technical terms, so that by observing them you could teach yourself how to evaluate the works already brought into being and those yet to be. For in these pages I have laid out every set of principles for the discipline.

CHAPTER 1: THE EDUCATION
OF THE ARCHITECT

1. The architect's expertise is enhanced by many disciplines and various sorts of specialized knowledge; all the works executed using these other skills are evaluated by his seasoned judgment. This expertise is born both of **practice** and of **reasoning**.[1] **Practice** is the constant, repeated exercise of the hands by which the work is brought to completion in whatever medium is required for the proposed design. **Reasoning,** however, is what can demonstrate and explain the proportions of completed works skillfully and systematically.

2. Thus architects who strove to obtain practical manual skills but lacked an education have never been able to achieve an influence equal to the quality of their exertions; on the other hand, those who placed their trust entirely in theory and in writings seem to have chased after a shadow, not something real. But those who have fully mastered both skills, armed, if you will, in full panoply, those architects have reached their goal more quickly and influentially.

1 The boldface labels duplicate the rubrics (headings) found in most manuscripts of Vitruvius.

3. In all things, but especially in architecture, there are two inherent categories: the **signified** and the **signifier**.* The **signified** is the proposed subject of discussion; it is signified by a reasoned demonstration carried out according to established principles of knowledge. Thus we see that whoever puts himself forward as an architect should be practiced in both. And furthermore he ought to have a native talent, and be amenable to learning the disciplines [of the profession]. For neither native talent without learning nor learning without native talent create the master craftsman. To be educated, he must be an experienced draftsman, well versed in geometry, familiar with history, a diligent student of philosophy, know music, have some acquaintance with medicine, understand the rulings of legal experts, and have a clear grasp of astronomy and the ways of Heaven.

4. Here are the reasons why this should be so. An architect should understand **letters** so that he may strengthen his own memory by reading what has been written in the field. Next, he should have knowledge of **draftsmanship** so that he can more easily use illustrated examples at will to represent the appearance of the work that he proposes. **Geometry,** in turn, offers many aids to architecture, and first among them, it hands down the technique of compass and rule, which enables the on-site layout of the plan as well as the placement of set-squares, levels, and lines. Likewise, through knowledge of **optics** windows are properly designed so as to face particular regions of heaven. Through **arithmetic** the expenses of buildings are totaled up, and the principles of measurement are developed; the difficult issues of symmetry are resolved by geometric principles and methods.

5. He should know a great deal of **history** because architects often include ornaments in their work, and ought to be able to supply anyone who asks with an explanation why they have introduced certain motifs. Consider, for example, if anyone has decided, in place of columns, to insert statues of women clad in *stolae* – the so-called Caryatids (Figure 2)* – into his work, and above them to set cornices and mutules. For those who inquire he will give the following rationale: the Peloponnesian city of Caryae had sided with the enemy, Persia, against Greece. Subsequently, the Greeks, gloriously delivered from war by their victory, by common agreement declared war on the Caryates. And so, when they had captured the town, slaughtered the men, and laid a curse on the inhabitants, they led its noble matrons off into captivity. Nor would they allow these women to put away their *stolae* and matronly dress; this was done so that they should not simply be exhibited in a single triumphal procession, but should instead be weighted down forever by a burden of shame, forced to pay the price for such grave disloyalty on behalf of their whole city. To this end, the architects active at the time incorporated images of these women in public buildings as weight-bearing structures; thus, in addition, the notorious punishment of the Caryate women would be recalled to future generations.

6. The Spartans, too, led by Pausanias son of Agesilas [son of Polis], with only a handful of troops defeated an endless number of Persian infantry at the Battle of Plataea, and after they had won decisively, they set up the Portico of the Persians as a trophy of victory for posterity – after, of course, a triumphal celebration glorious for its spoils and booty. This portico was financed by the prizes of war in praise of the citizens' courage and as a monument of their victory for future generations. There they placed images of the Persian captives, decked out in their ornate barbarian dress, holding up the roof, their pride punished with well-deserved outrage. In addition, by this means enemies might shrink back, terror stricken at the results of Spartan courage. At the same time, the citizens, looking upon this example of battle courage, uplifted by pride, would be prepared to defend their own liberty. After this many architects employed statues of Persians to hold up epistyles and their ornaments, and by this means added notable variety to their works. There are other histories of the same type, with which the architect is obliged to have some acquaintance.

7. **Philosophy*** completes the architect's character by instilling loftiness of spirit, so that he will not be arrogant, but rather tolerant, fair, and trustworthy, and, most important of all, free from greed. For there is no work that can truly be done without honesty and disinterestedness; let him not be too grasping, nor fix his mind on receiving gifts or rewards, but let him pay serious attention to protecting his dignity by maintaining a good reputation – for these are the things that philosophy recommends.

Furthermore, philosophy serves to explain the science which in Greek is called **physiology.*** It is necessary to know this subject thoroughly, for it has many and varied natural applications, as, for example, in the matter of aqueducts. For natural water pressures differ, depending on whether one is dealing with swift downhill runs, curvatures, or ascents up onto a gradual slope, and no one can compensate for the impact of these pressures except someone who, thanks to philosophy, knows the basic facts of nature. In addition, anyone who reads the handbooks of Ctesibius* and Archimedes,* or any of the other writers in this field, will not be able to absorb their reading without a grounding in these matters with the help of the philosophers.

8. The architect should know **music*** in order to have a grasp of **canonical** and **mathematical** relations, and besides that, to calibrate *ballistae*, catapults, and [the small catapults called] *scorpiones*. In the headpieces of war machines there are "hemitone" spring holes, right and left, through which the twisted sinew cords are pulled tight by windlass and handspikes; these cords should not be wedged in place or fastened down unless they give off a particular and identical sound to the ears of the catapult maker. For when the arms of the catapult have been cocked to these tensions, upon release they should deliver an identical and equivalent thrust; if they are not tuned identically, they will keep the catapult from launching a straight shot.

9. In theaters, likewise, the bronze vessels – the ones the Greeks call **echea*** – which are enclosed underneath the seats, are placed according to mathematical principle based on their pitch. The vessels are grouped in sections around the circle of the theater to create intervals of a fourth, a fifth, and so on, up to a double octave.* As a result, the voice, as it occurs onstage, should be so located in the theater's overall design that when it strikes the **echea** it will be amplified on impact, reaching the ears of the spectators as a clearer and more pleasant sound. As another example, no one could possibly create water organs and other such hydraulic devices without recourse to musical principles.

10. He should know the science of **medicine,*** as this depends on those inclinations of the heavens which the Greeks call **climates,*** and know about airs, and about which places are healthful and which disease ridden, and about the different applications of water, for without these studies no dwelling can possibly be healthful (Figures 3–5).

And he should know the **law,*** especially the law governing those things necessary to buildings that include party walls, that is, the courses of rain gutters and drains, and lighting, and also water supply. In addition, other subjects of this type should be known to architects, so that even before they begin their buildings they have taken care not to bequeath the patron a legacy of lawsuits along with their completed work. Indeed, they should exercise a legislator's care in their dealings both with contractor and with client. For if a law is expertly written, it will be such that each party may be released from the contract without undue dispute.

As for **astronomy**, he should know east, west, south, and north, and the principles of the heavens, the equinox, the solstice, and the course of the stars. Anyone who lacks this knowledge cannot understand the principle of a sundial.

11. Therefore, because so great a profession* must be adorned by and abundant in so many and such various types of expertise, I do not believe that architects can simply announce themselves as such, none but those who have climbed step by step, nurtured from an early age by education – in letters above all, and in the arts – to reach the loftiest sanctuary of Architecture.

12. But perhaps it will seem incredible to those unfamiliar with the profession that human nature could learn so great a number of disciplines thoroughly and still retain the memory of them. Yet if they notice how all these studies have interconnected subjects in which they participate in common, then they may easily believe it possible for such things to occur. For a well-rounded education,* just like a single body, is composed of quite different parts. And thus those who are educated from an early age in the various types of study recognize the same salient points in all types of writing, and the relationship of all the branches of knowledge, and because of this they come to know all manner of subjects with greater ease.

One of the architects of the past, Pytheos,* who gave the temple of Minerva at Priene its illustrious design, claims in his treatises that the architect ought to be more competent in every skill and discipline than those who have simply brought individual arts to a pinnacle of excellence through study and practice. But this is not what happens in fact.

13. For an architect should not and cannot be a philologist of Aristarchus's* quality, but neither should he be unlettered; if not a musician as gifted as Aristoxenus,* still he should know music; if not a painter equal to Apelles,* still not unskilled in draftsmanship; if not a sculptor on the order of Myron or Polycleitus,* still he should not be ignorant of sculptural technique. Again, although he may be no Hippocrates,* he should have working knowledge of medicine, nor may he be learned to an outstanding degree in the other individual disciplines – still, in all of them he should have some expertise. No one, after all, can possibly master the fine points of each individual subject, because it can scarcely be in his power to master and grasp their reasoning.

14. Neither is it the case that architects alone cannot achieve full mastery of all things, for even people who have separately mastered the individual details of par-

ticular arts do not all manage to reach the pinnacle of praise. Therefore, if for any individual skill, individual artisans – not all, but only a few – barely achieve distinction for all time, how can the architect, who ought to be skilled in so many arts, not simply to do some very great and wonderful thing, whatever it might be – how can he, without being deficient in any one of these arts, still do so well that he outshines all those artisans who have assiduously devoted themselves to individual skills?

15. Therefore Pytheos seems to be mistaken in this matter, because he fails to note that each individual art consists of two elements: the **work** itself and the **reasoning** behind it; one of these is the particular property of those who are trained in an individual skill, namely the execution of the work itself. The other [element, reasoning,] is shared in common with every learned person, just as doctors and musicians share knowledge of the rhythm of our veins' pulse* and the motion of our feet. However, if there is need to heal a wound or snatch a sick person from danger, the musician will not come forward, for this is the proper work of the doctor. Likewise, the musician, not the doctor, will play an instrument so that his ears will delight in song.

16. Similarly, astronomers and musicians discuss certain things in common: the harmony of the stars,* the intervals of squares and triangles, that is, the [musical] intervals of fourths and fifths, and with geometers they speak about vision, which in Greek is called *logos optikos,* the science of optics, and in the other disciplines many – or all – things are common property, so far as discussion is concerned (Figure 6). But as for embarking on the creation of works that are brought to elegant conclusion, whether through manual dexterity or skillful application, this is properly left to those who have been trained to practice a single skill. Whoever has a moderate grasp of the theory and the practical details of those individual disciplines necessary to architecture seems to have done enough, and more than enough; he will not fail, if need should arise, to judge and test decisions and evaluate these various areas and techniques.

17. But those to whom nature has granted such wits, acuity, and good memory that they are fully skilled in geometry, astronomy, music and related disciplines, pass beyond the business of architects and are turned into mathematicians. As a result they can easily hold their own in such fields of study, because they have a well-stocked scholarly arsenal with missiles from several disciplines. Nonetheless, such people are seldom to be found, such as once were Aristarchus of Samos, Philo-laos and Archytas of Tarentum, Apollonius of Perge, Eratosthenes of Cyrene, Archimedes, and Scopinas of Syracuse,* who made all manner of discoveries on measurement through mathematics and natural philosophy, and left treatises on these subjects for subsequent generations.

18. Because by Nature's wisdom it has not been granted that all nations everywhere have such talents, but a few men only, and yet at the same time an architect's task must be carried out by means of many skills, and reason permits that, because of the immensity of the enterprise, he have not a supreme, but only a moderate knowledge of these disciplines, I request, Caesar, both of you and of those who will read these volumes, that they forgive anything that has not been composed according to the rules of literary style. For I have striven to write them not as a great philosopher or an eloquent orator, nor as a grammarian* trained in the finer points of his art, but as an architect who has dipped into literature. But on the power of my own art and the systems of reasoning included in it, I promise that, as I expect, in these pages I will without a doubt prove myself possessed of the greatest authority – not only for those who intend to build, but also for all learned men.

CHAPTER 2: THE TERMS OF ARCHITECTURE*

1. Architecture consists of **ordering**, which is called *taxis* in Greek, and of **design** – the Greeks call this *diathesis* – and **shapeliness** and **symmetry** and **correctness** and **allocation**, which is called *oikonomia* in Greek.

2. **Ordering*** is the proportion to scale of the work's individual components taken separately, as well as their correspondence to an overall proportional scheme of symmetry (Figure 7). It is achieved through **quantity,** which in Greek is called *posotês.* **Quantity,** in turn, is the establishment of modules taken from the elements of the work itself and the agreeable execution of the work as a whole on the basis of the elements' individual parts (Figure 8).

Next, **design*** is the apt placement of things, and the elegant effect obtained by their arrangement according to the nature of the work. The species of design, which are called *ideai* in Greek, are these: **ichnography** (plan), **orthography** (elevation), and **scenography. Ichnography** is the skillful use, to scale, of compass and rule, by means of which the on-site layout of the design is achieved. Next, **orthography** is a frontal image, one drawn to scale, rendered according to the layout for the future work. As for **scenography,** it is the shaded rendering of the front and the receding sides as the latter converge on a point.

These species are produced by **analysis** and **invention. Analysis** is devoted concern and vigilant attention to the pleasing execution of a design. Next, **invention** is the unraveling of obscure problems, arriving, through energetic flexibility, at a new set of principles. These are the terms for design.

3. **Shapeliness (eurythmia)*** is an attractive appearance and a coherent aspect in the composition of the elements (Figure 9). It is achieved when the elements of the project are proportionate in height to width, length to breadth, and every element corresponds in its dimensions to the total measure of the whole.

4. **Symmetry*** is the proportioned correspondence of the elements of the work itself, a response, in any given part, of the separate parts to the appearance of the entire figure as a whole.

Just as in the human body there is a harmonious quality of shapeliness expressed in terms of the cubit, foot, palm, digit, and other small units, so it is in completing works of architecture (Figure 10). For instance, in temples, this symmetry derives from the diameter of the columns, or from the triglyph, or from the lower radius of the column; in a ballista, it derives from the hole that the Greeks call *peritrêton*, in boats from the [spacing of the] oarlock, which the Greeks call the *diapegma;** likewise for all the other types of work, the reckoning of symmetries is to be found among their component parts.

5. Next, **correctness (decor)*** is the refined appearance of a project that has been composed of proven elements and with authority. It is achieved with respect to **function,** which is called *thematismos* in Greek, or **tradition,** or **nature.** Correctness of function occurs when temples dedicated to Jupiter the Thunderer and Heaven or the Sun and Moon are made open-air shrines, beneath their patron deity, because we see the appearance and effect of these divinities in the light of the outdoor world. Temples of Minerva, Mars, and Hercules will be Doric, because temples for these gods, on account of their courage in battle, should be set up without a trace of embellishment. Temples done in the Corinthian style for Venus, Proserpina, or the Fountain Spirits (nymphs) are those that will seem to possess the most fitting qualities, because, given the delicacy of these goddesses, the works executed in their honor seem best to augment a

suitable quality of correctness when they are made more slender, ornamental, and are decorated with leaves and volutes. If temples are constructed in the Ionic style for Juno, Diana, Father Liber, and other gods of this type, the principle of the "mean" will apply, because their particular disposition will strike a balance between the stern lines of the Doric and the delicacy of the Corinthian.

6. Correctness of tradition will be expressed if, when buildings have magnificent interiors, their vestibules have been made equally harmonious and elegant, for if interiors were outfitted elegantly, but had entrances deficient in dignity and respectability they would lack correctness. Likewise, if Doric entablatures are sculpted with dentils in the cornices, or triglyphs show up atop cushion capitals and Ionic entablatures, so that characteristics from one set of principles have been carried over into another type of work, the appearance of the result will be jarring, because the work was established according to a different sequence of conventions.

7. Natural correctness occurs as follows: if, from the outset, temple sites are chosen in the most healthful regions, well supplied with suitable sources of water, but especially for the building of shrines to Asclepius, Health, and those gods by whose medicines the sick seem to be healed in the greatest numbers. When patients have been transferred from a pestilent to a healthful place and are afforded the use of waters from healthful springs, they will recover more quickly, and so it will be arranged that from the very nature of the place the divinity in question will receive a greater and greater reputation along with the dignity of divine rank. Likewise, natural correctness will obtain if the light source for bedrooms and libraries comes from the east, whereas the source for baths and winter quarters comes from the west in winter, while in the case of picture galleries and whatever areas need a constant level of illumination it should come from the north, because that region of the sky is neither made bright nor dark by the course of the sun, but remains dependable and unchanging throughout the day.

8. **Allocation*** is the efficient management of resources and site and the frugal, principled supervision of working expenses. This will be observed if from the outset the architect forbears to require things that cannot be found at all or only procured at great expense. After all, not every place has an abundant supply of pit sand or rubble or fir, or deal planks, or marble. Different resources occur in different places, and their transport elsewhere is difficult and expensive. Where there is no pit sand, river sand or washed seashore sand should be used instead; if there is a shortage of fir or of deal planks, use cypress, poplar, elm,

or pitch pine. Other problems should be resolved in a similar fashion.

9. The other level of **allocation** obtains when buildings are designed differently according to the habits of the heads of families, or the amount of money available, or to suit their prestige as public speakers. Urban dwellings ought to be set up in one way, and rustic holdings, where harvests must be gathered, in another; the homes of moneylenders, certainly otherwise, and still otherwise the homes of those who are fortunate and sophisticated. For those powerful men by whose counsel the republic is governed, dwellings should be designed to accommodate their activities, and in every case the allocation of buildings should be appropriate to every different type of person.

CHAPTER 3: THE DIVISIONS OF ARCHITECTURE

1. The divisions of architecture itself are three: **construction**, **gnomonics** (the making of sundials), and **mechanics**.* Construction in turn is divided into two parts, one of which is the placement of city walls and **public works** in public places; the other is the erection of **private buildings**. The allocations of **public works** are three, of which the first is **defense**, the second **religion**, and the third **service**. The architecture of **defense** is the set of principles devised so that walls, towers, and gates will be permanently effective in warding off enemy attacks. That of **religion** is the establishment of sanctuaries for the immortal gods and of temples; that of **service** is the design of public places for common use, such as ports, fora, porticoes, baths, theaters, promenades, and the other installations which are appointed in public places for the same purposes.

2. All these works should be executed so that they exhibit the principles of **soundness**, **utility**, and **attractiveness**. The principle of **soundness** will be observed if the foundations have been laid firmly, and if, whatever the building materials may be, they have been chosen with care but not with excessive frugality. The principle of **utility** will be observed if the design allows faultless, unimpeded use through the disposition of the spaces and the allocation of each type of space is properly oriented, appropriate, and comfortable. That of **attractiveness** will be upheld when the appearance of the work is pleasing and elegant, and the proportions of its elements have properly developed principles of symmetry.

CHAPTER 4: THE CHOICE OF A HEALTHFUL SITE

1. These should be the primary elements for constructing the walls themselves: first of all, the choice of a very healthful site (Figure 11).* It should be elevated, not cloudy, not liable to frost, facing those regions of the sky which are neither hot nor cold but temperate. In addition, if at all possible, proximity to swamps is to be avoided. For when the morning breezes enter the town with the rising sun, whatever mists have formed overnight are joined with them. Their gusts spew the poisonous exhalations of the swamp animals, which have been mixed in with the mist, at the bodies of the inhabitants, and these will make the place pestilent. Likewise, if the walls are built next to the sea, so as to face southward or westward, they will not be good for health, because in summer the southern sky warms at sunrise and by midday is burning hot; by the same principle whatever faces westward grows warm with the rising sun, heats up at noon, and boils by evening.

2. Therefore, from the shifts of heat and cold, the matter that occurs in such places is weakened. This can even be observed in inanimate objects. Among covered wine cellars, not one admits light from the south or west, but only from the north, because that region of the heavens never alters with the season, but stays forever firm and changeless. For the same reason granaries which face the sun quickly ruin their stores, and dried fish or fruits that are not stored out of the sun's way are never preserved for long.

3. Invariably, whenever heat cooks down the strength of air, and its roiling vapors suck out and snatch away matter's natural properties, its fervor dissolves and softens matter to the point of limpness. We see the same thing with iron, which, however hard it is by nature, softens so completely when it is heated by the vapors of fire in furnaces that it is easily fashioned into every kind of shape; and by the same token, when, soft and glowing, it is chilled by dousing in cold, it hardens again and is restored to its former character.

4. We may also draw the conclusion that this is so from the fact that in the summer, everything, not just in pestilential places but even in healthful ones, grows flaccid in the heat, while all through the winter even the most plague-ridden regions are made healthful on account of the fact that they are solidified by the cold. Nor is there any doubt about this: that when objects are moved from cold areas to hot ones, they cannot endure but dissolve, while those that are taken from hot loca-

tions to the cold northern regions are not only none the worse for the change of place, but actually grow stronger.

5. For this reason, in laying out walls, it seems best to avoid regions that can taint human bodies with hot vapors.

According to the principles which the Greeks call *stoicheia*, just as all bodies are composed of elements, that is of heat and moisture, earth and air, so, too, a mixture of these elements in a given proportion produces all the particular qualities of each sort of living being to be found in the world.

6. Therefore in those bodies where heat dominates, it destroys and dissolves all the rest with its fervor. The air itself creates this defect in certain regions, when it settles into open veins more than the body allows at its natural temperament and mixture. Likewise, if moisture lodges in the veins of the body and puts it out of equilibrium, the other elements, as if corrupted by liquefaction, are diluted, and the natural virtues of the composition are dissolved out. These flaws can also be introduced into the body from the chilling effects of the moisture contained in the winds and breezes. On the same principle, the natural composition of air and earth in the body, by increasing or diminishing, weakens the other elements: the earth by an excess of food, the air by the heaviness of the atmosphere.

7. But whoever would like to study these facts more closely, take heed and note the nature of birds, fishes, and land animals, and in this light consider the differences in their makeup. The birds have one mixture, fishes another, and animals still another, far different from that of the first two. Birds have less earth, less moisture, a moderate amount of heat, and a great deal of air: therefore, composed as they are of lighter elements, they are more easily supported on moving air. The aquatic natures of fishes, on the other hand, because they are tempered by a bit of heat and largely made up of air and earth, but very little moisture, endure all the more easily in water to the extent that they lack the element of moisture in their bodies. And thus, when they are brought out on land they leave their lives behind with the water. Likewise, the land animals, because they have only a moderate complement of air and heat, less earth and a great deal of moisture – for the moist parts are abundant – cannot maintain life for long in water.

8. If these things truly seem to be as I have shown them, and with our own faculties we perceive that the bodies of animals are composed of these elements, and we judge that they suffer and dissolve when there are excesses or failures of one element or another, I have no doubt that if a healthful environment is to be sought after in constructing city walls, we should seek with all diligence to select temperate regions of the heavens.

9. Thus I assert emphatically my opinion that the old principles for selecting a site should be called back into service (Figure 12).* Our ancestors used to sacrifice some sheep pastured in the area where they wanted to establish towns or military camps, and examine their livers (Figure 13). If these were discolored and defective, first they would sacrifice more sheep, wondering whether the original victims might have been ravaged by disease or spoiled feed. Once they had scrutinized several victims and decided that the local water and fodder had produced perfect, solid livers, there they would lay their fortifications; if, on the other hand, they discovered the livers to be defective, they would decide that the supply of food and water produced in such a locale would prove just as pernicious to human bodies. Thus they moved onward, changing regions in the search for an environment healthful in every respect.

10. The validity of this conclusion, namely that the health-giving properties of the earth can be seen in fodder and food, can be noted and taken to heart in the Cretan countryside, along the river Pothereus, which flows between the two Cretan communities of Cnossus and Gortyna. Flocks graze on both the right and left bank of this river, but those that pasture hard by Knossos have a conspicuous spleen, whereas those by Gortyna do not. Hence doctors, inquiring after this phenomenon, discovered a herb growing in these regions; by grazing on it the flocks diminished their spleens. By collecting this herb they cure splenetics with a medicine made from it – the Cretans call it "no-spleen," *asplênon.* Thus, on the basis of food and water, it is possible to ascertain whether the properties of a place are naturally healthful or pestilent.

11. If walls are constructed in swamplands that are near the sea, and they face northward or northeast, and the swamplands themselves are higher than the seashore, these walls will prove to have been constructed on sound principles. For putting in drainage ditches will create an outlet for water along the seashore, and when the seas are swollen by storms, the surrounding swamp water, agitated by the seas' motion and by mixture with sea water, does not support normal swamp life. Thus whatever creatures swim up from the depths to the seaside are killed by the waters' unusual salinity. Indeed, the swamps of Cisalpine Gaul can serve as an example of the phenomenon – those around Altinum, Ravenna, Aquileia, and other towns in locations of this sort, situated near marshes – because, for

the reasons stated earlier, these places are marvelously salubrious.

12. But swamps that are stagnant and have no flowing outlets, whether by river or through ditches, like the Pomptine Marshes,* grow rotten from stagnation and send out grim, pestilent vapors into the surrounding areas. As another example, in Apulia there is a town, Old Salpia,* which Diomedes founded on his return from Troy, or, as several authors have stated, Elpias the Rhodian. This was sited in just such a region as I have described, for which reason the inhabitants, suffering every year from various diseases, came at last to the consul Marcus Hostilius with a public petition. They requested that he seek out and select for them a suitable place where they might relocate their walls, and he granted their request. He made no delay, but after an immediate, penetrating inquiry purchased a promising property along the seashore and asked the Senate and People of Rome for permission to relocate the town. He established the city wall, divided the city into lots, and gave each townsman full legal possession of his lot for the token payment of a one-sesterce coin. Once these works were complete, he made an outlet from a local lake into the sea, transforming this lake into a port for the town. And so now the Salpini, by moving four miles away from their old town, dwell in a healthy environment.

CHAPTER 5: CONSTRUCTION OF CITY WALLS

1. Once the scheme for siting the city walls* has been drawn up according to the principles of good health just stated, and its regions are choice and fertile in produce to nourish the population, and the construction of roads or access to rivers or marine ports will supply easy transport up to the city walls, then the foundation trenches* for the walls should be made according to the principle that they should be dug, insofar as this is possible, down to the solid ground and in solid ground, as far as seems reasonable, going by the width of the planned work. The width of the foundation should be greater than the projected width of the aboveground portion of the walls, and their construction should be as sound as possible.

2. Likewise, the towers should project toward the exterior,* so that if the enemy force wants to rush the wall, it may be wounded from the towers on either side, where its flanks are exposed. Special care should be taken to ensure that there be no easy approach to the wall for

an attacker; rather the rampart should encircle precipitous heights* and be so planned that the approaches to the gates are not straight but on the left (Figures 14–17). For if the wall is made in this manner, then the right flank of those entering the gates, the side which will not be covered by a shield, will be closest to the wall. Furthermore, fortified towns should not be built in the form of a square, or with protruding corners, because the corner in this case protects the enemy more than it does the citizen within the walls.

3. I think that the thickness of the wall should be made in this manner: walking along its top, two armed men coming toward each other should be able to pass each other without difficulty; moreover, within its fabric, rods of scorched olive wood* should be installed at as frequent intervals as possible, so that each of the faces of the wall, linked together by these rods (which act as clamps), will maintain an everlasting fixity (Figure 18). For neither rot nor foul weather nor time can injure this material, and thus, when buried in dirt or sunk in water it remains undamaged, functional forever. These rods should be set not only in the curtain wall itself, but also in its substructure and in whatever partition walls are to be made to the thickness of the rampart; clamped by this principle they will not be weakened quickly.

4. The intervals between towers should be made so that the distance between them is never more than the length of a bow shot;* thus, if an attack is mounted at any particular point, the enemy will be thrown back by bolts from the catapults and the other missiles that have been launched from the towers on either side. And furthermore, the wall should be portioned off on the inner side of the towers at intervals as wide as the towers will be, so that there will be wooden catwalks set on the insides of the towers (Figure 19). Nor should these catwalks be nailed in place, for, if the enemy should occupy some part of the wall, the defenders may isolate that section, and, if they act quickly enough, they will not allow the enemy to penetrate to the other parts of the wall or the towers, unless they want to fall head over heels.

5. Towers should be made either round or polygonal,* as war machines break apart square towers more swiftly; the hammering of battering rams will smash apart the corners, but along curves a ram will simply act like a wedge; by pressing toward the center it will be unable to harm the structure (Figure 16). Likewise, the fortification of walls and towers is far more secure if these are joined to earthen ramparts, because neither rams, nor mining, nor any of the other war machines succeed in inflicting any damage on the latter (Figure 19).

6. But it is not reasonable to build ramparts everywhere, only in places where there is level access outside the fortifications from high ground to the walls under attack. In places of this sort first ditches should be made, as wide and as deep as possible, and then the foundations of the wall should be sunk within the hollow of the ditch, and these should be made so thick that they will easily sustain the earthworks.*

7. On the inward side of the substructure, there should be another foundation, this set far enough inside the exterior wall that whole cohorts of troops can be stationed for defense along the top of the completed earthwork, just as if they are in battle formation. Once foundations have been laid at this distance from one another, then cross walls, bonded into the exterior and interior foundations, should be laid out between them, comblike, as the teeth of a saw are arranged. With the weight of the earth partitioned and distributed into small units, never bringing its full burden to bear upon a single location, the sheer magnitude of the work will not be able to warp the wall's substructure for any reason.

8. As for the wall itself, and the materials of which it should be constructed and finished, there can be no hard and fast rules, because we cannot have exactly the resources we might desire in every locality. But where there is squared stone, or split stone, or rubble, or burnt brick, or mud brick, this is what should be used. Not every region can do as the Babylonians did, who with their wealth of liquid bitumen used this in place of lime and sand, and made their city walls of burnt brick. Every region may have peculiarities of the site or similar advantages of the same type, such that, using these materials, it, too, may have a faultless wall, perfect forever.

CHAPTER 6: ORIENTATION

1. Once the walls have been raised, the division into lots of the area contained within the walls should follow, and the orientation of streets and lanes according to the regions of the heavens.* This process will be properly accomplished if, with foresight, the lanes are kept from facing into the path of the prevailing winds.* For if the winds are cold, they injure; if hot, they corrupt; if moist, they are noxious. For which reason this defect should be avoided, nor should what happens in so many communities be allowed to occur, as, for instance, on the island of Lesbos, where the town of Mytilene is magnificently, elegantly constructed, but poorly sited. For in that com-

munity, when the south wind blows, people grow sick; when Corus blows, they cough; with the north wind, their health returns, but they cannot gather in the streets or side streets because it is so chilly.

2. Wind is a flowing wave of air with an excess of irregular movements (Figure 20). It is produced when heat collides with moisture and the shock of the crash expels its force in a gust of air. We can observe that this is true from bronze statues of Aeolus, and by means of such clever inventions we may wring divine truth from the hidden principles of heaven. Make hollow bronze Aeolus spheres; these have a pinhole opening. They are filled with water and placed over a fire, and before they heat up they have no breath at all, but as soon as they reach the boiling point they emit a powerful gust at the fire. Thus, on the basis of a small, very brief spectacle, it is possible to understand and evaluate the great and extensive principles underlying the nature of the heavens and the winds.

3. If they are kept out, not only will they create a healthful place for healthy bodies, but also, if by chance some epidemic should spring up from other infections, which might have antidotes or cures in different, more healthful climes, even in these cases, because the winds have been shut out, the epidemic will the more readily be cured by the mildness of the air. For there are distempers that are difficult to cure in such regions as have been described here. These are heaviness of the arteries, coughs, pleuritis, phthisis, consumption, and other maladies that are cured, not by purges, but by additive diets. These are healed with difficulty for the following reasons: first of all, because they are caught from chills, and furthermore because for those whose strength has been sapped by disease the air is agitated, thinned by the agitation of the winds, and together with them it drains out the sap from afflicted bodies and makes them still weaker. On the other hand, mild, dense air, which has neither drafts nor frequent circulation, on account of its motionless stability, by adding to the physique of those who are afflicted with these diseases, nourishes the patients and restores them to health.

4. It pleases some to say that there are four winds: from equinoctial east Solanus, from the south Auster, from the equinoctial west Favonius, and from the north Septentrio (Figures 21, 22). But those who have studied the matter more thoroughly insist that there are eight, above all Andronicus Cyrrestes, who even went so far as to demonstrate this by means of an octagonal marble tower in Athens. On each side of the octagon he designed sculpted images of the winds, each facing its

own blast, and atop this tower he put a conical column and above this he placed a bronze Triton holding a wand in its right hand, so contrived as to revolve with the wind, so that it will always face into the prevailing wind and hold its wand over the image of the wind that is blowing at the moment.

5. And so between Solanus and Auster in the southeast we find Eurus, in the southwest between Auster and Favonius we find Africus, between Favonius and Septentrio we find Caurus, which so many people call Corus, between Septentrio and Solanus, Aquilo. This seems to be a way to understand the number of winds, their names, and the direction from which the fixed blasts of the winds blow.

Now that the subject has been thus examined in depth, this is how to set up your reasoning in order to discover their regions and their places of origin (Figure 23):* 6. Let a marble benchmark be set in the middle of the space enclosed by the city walls, or let a surface be dressed with a rule and level so that a benchmark will not be necessary, and above the very center of this surface place a bronze gnomon, that type of sundial which is called "shadow-tracker" in Greek (*skiothêrês*). An hour before midday, and about the fifth hour of morning, the end of the shadow of the gnomon should be noted and marked by a point, and, opening compasses to the point that signals the length of the gnomon's shadow, a line of circumference should be drawn circling around from the center. Likewise, the lengthening afternoon shadow of this gnomon should be observed, and when it touches the line of the circle and the afternoon shadow comes to equal the length of the morning shadow, then this, too, should be marked with a point.

7. Around these points the compass should draw two arcs intersecting in an "X", and a line should then be drawn from the point of intersection, through the midpoint of the circle, to the circle's outer circumference, in order to obtain the southern and northern regions. Then the sixteenth part of the entire circumference should be obtained, and the point of the compass placed on the southern line where it intersects the circle, and a mark made to right and left along the circumference, both in the southern and the northern part. Then lines should be drawn forming an "X" between these four marks, from one side of the circle to the other. By this means Auster and Septentrio will have their designated eighth of the circle. The remaining three parts to right and left should be assigned around the circle so that the eight equal sections are designated to the winds, as in the drawing. Then it will be evident that the alignment of the streets

and side streets ought to follow the angles between the regions of two different winds.

8. By means of these principles and these divisions, the detrimental force of the winds will be shut out of dwellings and side streets, for when the broad streets are designed to face the winds head on, the force and the dense gusts coming from the open expanse of the heavens, trapped in the heads of alleyways, wanders about with more violent energy. For these reasons the orientation of streets should be rotated obliquely to the regions of the winds; then, when the gusts approach the corners of apartment blocks they break apart, and, repulsed, are dissipated.

9. Perhaps those who know many names of winds will marvel at the fact that we have given the number of the winds as eight. But if they will have noted that the circumference of the terrestrial globe was discovered by Eratosthenes of Cyrene (Figure 24),* using the course of the sun, the shadows cast by the gnomon at the equinox, and the heavens' inclination, on the basis of mathematical principles and geometric methods, to measure 252,000 stades, which made 31,500,000 paces, then the eighth part of that total, which is what a wind can be seen to occupy, measures 3,937,500 paces. Then they should hardly wonder that in so large an expanse a single wind's wandering, twisting, and receding should create varieties by shifting its breath.

10. Thus at the right and left of Auster, Leuconotus and Altanus are wont to blow; to either side of Africus, Libonotus and Subvesperus; around Favonius, Argestes and at certain times of year the Etesian breezes; at the sides of Caurus, Circias and Chorus; around Septentrio, Thracius and Gallicus, to the right and left of Aquilo, Supernas and Caecias; around Solanus, Carbas and at a certain time of the year the Ornithiae; and with Eurus occupying the middle range, Euricircias and Volturnus take up the extremes (Figure 21). There are many other names for other breaths of wind, derived from places, or rivers, or mountain tempests.

11. Then there are the morning breezes, when the sun, emerging on its rounds from the subterranean region, strikes the moisture of the air, and spilling forth in the onslaught of its rising, it thrusts out the breaths that precede the coming of the daylight. When these persist once the sun has risen, then they occupy the regions around Eurus, and for this reason, because it is created from morning breezes (*aurae*), it is evidently called *euros* by the Greeks. And "tomorrow" is said to be called *aurion* [in Greek] because of these same morning *aurae*.

There are some who deny that Eratosthenes could have derived the true measure of the terrestrial globe. Whether the measurement is true or false, however, our own treatise cannot have false definitions of the regions from which the currents of the winds arise.

12. With the nature of the winds such as it is, suffice it to say that the forces of individual winds do not have a fixed proportion relative to one another, but only greater or lesser degrees of force.

Because these things have already been set out by us briefly so that they be more easily understood, it seemed best to me that at the end of this book, I supply two figures or, as the Greeks say, *schêmata*, one so drawn that it displays the directions from which the various winds originate, and another showing how their harmful breaths may be avoided by the oblique orientation of streets and avenues.

13. On a plane surface there will be a center point at the letter A, and the morning shadow of the gnomon at the point B, and with the compass spread from the center A to the mark made by the shadow at B, make a circle. Setting the gnomon back in the place where it had been before, one must expect that after it has receded it will lengthen a second time to an extent equal to the length of the morning shadow and touch the afternoon line of the circle at C. Then, from the mark at B and the mark at C, mark an "X" with the compass where there will be a point D, and then through the "X" where there is the letter D and the center, a line should be drawn to the outer edge, and along this line there will be the letters E and F. This line will serve as the index to the northern and southern regions.

Then by means of the compass derive the sixteenth part of the whole circumference, putting the point of the compass on the southern line where it intersects the circle at letter E, and mark the intersections at left and right with G and H. Likewise in the northern section put the point of the compass at the intersection of the circumference and the northern line F, and mark I and K to the left and right. Then draw lines from G to K and H to I through the center point A. The space from G to H will be the space of Auster and the part belonging to due south. Likewise, the space from I to K will be that of Septentrio. The remaining sections should be equally divided: three on the right and three on the left, to the east where you see letters L and M and to the west where there are the letters N and O. From M to O and from L to N intersecting lines should be drawn. And in this way there will be eight equal spaces for the winds as you go around the circle. If they have been so drawn, and we begin going angle by angle from due south: in the angle between Eurus and Auster there will be the letter G; between Auster and Africus, H; between Africus and Favonius, N; between Favonius and Caurus, O; between Caurus and Septentrio, K; between Septentrio and Aquilo, I; between Aquilo and Solanus, L; between Solanus and Eurus, M. When these have been established, put the gnomon between the corners of the octagon, and this is how the division of side streets will be guided.

CHAPTER 7: ALLOCATION OF PUBLIC SPACES

1. Once the lanes have been laid out and the broad streets have been established,* it is time to explain the way in which sites should be selected for access, convenience, and the city's public use, for temples, the forum, and other public places (Figure 11). If there are city walls next to the sea, then the site for the forum should be chosen right next to the port; if, on the other hand, the city site is inland, the forum should be placed in the very center of town (Figures 25–27). But for temples whose gods are regarded as particularly involved in protecting the city: to Jupiter, Juno, and Minerva, for example, sites should be allocated in the very highest place, the vantage from which to see the greatest possible extent of the city walls. Temples to Mercury should be located in the forum, or, as with Isis and Serapis, in the marketplace. Temples to Apollo and Father Liber belong next to the theater, those to Hercules, in cities which lack gymnasia and amphitheaters, should be situated by the circus, those to Mars outside the city but near the drill grounds, and similarly, those to Venus should be situated by the harbor.

Furthermore, this same point is enshrined by the Etruscan seers in the priestly writings of their discipline, namely that shrines of Venus, Vulcan, and Mars should be located outside the city walls so that venereal lust will not become a commonplace for the city's adolescents and matriarchs. By summoning Volcanic energy out of the city by means of rites and sacrifices, the city's buildings are thought to have been delivered from the danger of fire. And if the divinity of Mars is honored outside the city walls, there will not be armed conflict among citizens; rather, he will ensure that the walls serve only to defend the city from its enemies and the danger of war.

2. Likewise the shrine of Ceres should be sited in a place outside the city where no one need go except to offer sacrifice; the place ought to be maintained religiously, chastely, and purely. The sites for other temples should be assigned to the other gods as befits the requirements of their sacrifices.

As for the construction of temples themselves and their proportional systems, I will account for their principles in the third and fourth volumes, because in the second volume I thought it better to begin with the supplies of material that should be assembled for buildings, the qualities they possess and the way they should be employed, and only then to move on to the dimensions of temples, their design sequences, and the individual types of proportional systems, and to explain them in subsequent volumes.

❖

BUILDING MATERIALS

PREFACE

1. Dinocrates the architect,* full of confidence in his ideas and his cleverness, set out from Macedonia for the army in the days of Alexander's rise to power, ambitious for royal favor. From home he carried letters of recommendation from neighbors and friends, addressed to the king's generals and highest court officials, in order to facilitate his access to them; when these generals received him, he asked them courteously to present him to Alexander as soon as possible. Despite their promises, they were slow to do so, waiting for some suitable occasion. And thus Dinocrates, supposing that they were playing games with him, sought help in his own resources. He was a very tall man, handsome, with a fine face and immense dignity. Trusting, then, in those gifts of Nature, he went back to his inn, undressed, and thoroughly oiled his body. Crowning his head with a poplar wreath, draping his left shoulder in a lion skin and brandishing a club in his right hand, he strode before the tribunal where the king was hearing petitions. 2. When the crowd began to take notice of this novelty, Alexander, too, looked Dinocrates's way. Impressed by the young man, the king ordered the crowd to make way for him to approach the tribunal, and asked who he was.

"Dinocrates," he answered, "an architect of Macedon, who brings you ideas and plans worthy of your renown. I have, for example, a project to carve all Mount Athos into the image of a man. In his left hand I have represented the walls of a spacious city; in his right, a libation bowl where the waters of all the rivers that run on that mountain will gather together and plunge into the sea" (Figure 28).

3. Alexander, delighted with the idea, inquired immediately about the nature of the plan – were there farmlands to furnish this city with a regular supply of grain? When the king learned that food would have to be imported by sea, he said, "Dinocrates, I appreciate the ingenuity of this plan, and I am charmed by it, but I also recognize that if someone were to found a colony there, his judgment would be found wanting. Just as a newborn

baby cannot be nourished and grow without its nursemaid's milk, so neither can a city grow without farmlands and the flow of their produce within its walls. Without abundant food, no city can maintain a large population nor, without resources, safeguard its people. As much, therefore, as I think that the design is to be commended, the choice of the site is to be condemned. Still, I want you with me, because I intend to make use of your talents."

4. From then on, Dinocrates never parted from the king, and followed him into Egypt. There, when Alexander had noticed a naturally secure port, a thriving marketplace, wheatfields all around Egypt, and the great usefulness of the immense river Nile, he ordered Dinocrates to lay out the city of Alexandria in his name.

So Dinocrates, because of the beauty of his face and the dignity of his physical presence, came with high recommendation to this privileged status. But to me, Imperator, Nature did not grant imposing stature, age has ruined my face, and bad health has carried off my strength. Therefore, because I am bereft of such defenses, it is through the help of my expertise and my writings that I shall – as I hope – attain your approval.

5. Now, because in the first volume I have written all about the duties of the architect and the [technical] terms of the art, and likewise about city walls and the division of the areas of the city within the walls, the order would follow that I should write about temples, public buildings, and private buildings, and the proportions and symmetries they should exhibit, described so as to make them plain. I thought that nothing else should take precedence – unless I were to show something about the supplies of material that are assembled to bring buildings to completion, both with regard to their construction and to the general principles of matter, and to have discussed as well what particular functional qualities they possessed, and to have explained of what natural elements they have been composed.

However, before I begin to explain the natural elements, I shall begin with the principles of construction:

where they had their beginning and how these discoveries have grown up, and I shall follow the initial steps of ancient science and of those who have made researches into the beginnings of humanity and its discoveries, setting these down in writing. I shall, then, explain as these writings have taught me.

CHAPTER 1: THE INVENTION OF THE ARTS AND OF BUILDING*

1. Humans, by their most ancient custom, were born like beasts in the woods, and caves, and groves, and eked out their lives by feeding on rough fodder. During that time, in a certain place, dense, close-growing trees, stirred by stormy winds and rubbing their branches against one another, took fire. Terrified by the flames, those who were in the vicinity fled. Later, however, approaching more closely, when they discovered that the heat of fire was a great advantage to the body, they threw logs into it and preserving it by this means they summoned others, showing what benefits they had from this thing by means of gestures. In this gathering of people, as they poured forth their breath in varying voices, they established words by happening upon them in their daily routines. Later, by signifying things with more frequent practice, they began by chance occurrence to speak sentences and thus produced conversations among themselves (Figure 29).

2. The beginning of association among human beings, their meeting and living together, thus came into being because of the discovery of fire. When many people came into a single place, having, beyond all the other animals, this gift of nature: that they walked, not prone, but upright, they therefore could look upon the magnificence of the universe and the stars. For the same reason they were able to manipulate whatever object they wished, using their hands and other limbs. Some in the group began to make coverings of leaves, others to dig caves under the mountains. Many imitated the nest building of swallows and created places of mud and twigs where they might take cover. Then, observing each other's homes and adding new ideas to their own, they created better types of houses as the days went by.
3. Because people are by nature imitative and easily taught, they daily showed one another the success of their constructions, taking pride in creation, so that by daily exercising their ingenuity in competition they achieved greater insight with the passage of time.

First they erected forked uprights, and weaving twigs in between they covered the whole with mud. Others, letting clods of mud go dry, began to construct walls of them, joining them together with wood, and to avoid rains and heat they covered them over with reeds and leafy branches. Later, when these coverings proved unable to endure through the storms of winter, they made eaves with molded clay, and set in rainspouts on inclined roofs.

EXCURSUS ON CONTEMPORARY HUT ARCHITECTURE

4. We can confirm that these things have been instituted for the reasons just described because even to this day in foreign places people make buildings of these materials, such as Gaul, Hispania, Lusitania, Aquitania – that is, of oaken twigs or straw. Among the Colchian nation in Pontus, on account of their abundance of forests, they lay two entire trees flat along the ground, one to the right and one to the left, and they leave a space in between, whatever the length of the trees will permit. Then they place two transverse trees above the ends of the first two, which close off the central space of the house. Above these go alternating beams joined at the four corners, and by creating walls of trees they have built towers, upright from bottom to top, and they stop up the spaces that are left in between the logs with potsherds and mud. They span the roofs in the same manner, by cutting back the crossbeams at each end and gradually reducing their size. By contracting on all four sides at the top of the walls they extend a conical roof over the center, and covering this with leafy branches and mud they create roofed towers – barbarian style.

5. The Phrygians, on the other hand, who inhabit plains, are at a shortage of wood because they have so few forests. They choose natural hillocks and carve a trench through their centers, and by digging out passages, they increase the available space as much as the nature of the site will permit. On top, they create cones by binding rods together, and covering these with straw and stripped branches they heap up immense mounds of earth above their dwellings. Thus they have devised a method of shelter that is exceedingly warm in winter and exceedingly cool in summer.

Some fit together hut dwellings out of swamp reeds. Among certain other peoples and in several places house construction is also carried out in the same way, for similar reasons. In Massilia, for example, we may notice houses without roof tiles, made of earth and straw. In

Athens, on the Areopagus, there is an ancient example to this day of a house daubed with mud. Likewise, on the Capitol, the house of Romulus shows us – and calls to mind – the ancient ways; so do the wattle houses in the Citadel precinct. 6. Reasoning from these indications about the way in which the ancients invented building we can conclude that this is exactly how it happened.

THE INVENTION OF BUILDING, CONTINUED

When by daily practice they had made their hands fully adept at building, and by exercising their talents in clever ingenuity they had arrived by habit upon the arts, then, too, the industry instilled in their spirits brought it about that those who were more dedicated to these pursuits declared themselves carpenters. Because these things had been so established in the beginning, and nature had not only equipped the people with senses like all the other animals, but had also armed their minds with ideas and plans and subjected all other creatures to their power, so from the making of buildings they progressed, step by step, to the other arts and disciplines, and thus they led themselves out of a rough and brutish life into gentle humanity. 7. Then, training their own spirits and reviewing the most important ideas conceived among the various arts and crafts, they began to complete, not houses any longer, but real residences, with foundations, built up with brick walls or stone, roofed with timbers and tiles. Furthermore, on the basis of observations made in their studies, they progressed from haphazard and uncertain opinions to the stable principles of symmetry.

After they had noted what a profusion of resources has been begotten by Nature, and what abundant supplies for construction have been prepared by her, they nourished these with cultivation and increased them by means of skill and enhanced the elegance of their life with aesthetic delights. Therefore, I shall tell as best I can about those things which are suitable for use in construction, what their qualities are and what properties they possess.

8. Now if there are those who wish to question the order of this book in the belief that all this information should have been put first, this is how I will render my account so that they will not think that I have wandered from the point. When I set out to write about the whole body of architecture, I thought that in the first volume I would explain with what knowledge and skill that art is equipped, define its aspects in technical terms, and tell of what matters it has come into being. Thus, in the appropriate place, I explained what is desirable in an architect. Accordingly, in the first book I discussed the duties of the profession, and in this one I will treat the natural materials that are of use. This book will not declare where architecture originated, but only where the origins of construction had their beginning, and by what principles they were nurtured and how they progressed step by step to this state of refinement. 9. And so, this is what the plan of the present volume will be, in its proper place and order.

Now I will return to the subject at hand, and account for the supplies suitable for completing buildings, how they seem to be produced by nature and by what mixture of elements their composition is tempered, so that these will be easily seen by the reader rather than obscure.* None of the types of matter, nor bodies, nor objects can come into being without the coming together first of elements, nor will natural phenomena submit to valid explanation according to the teachings of the natural philosophers unless the causes inherent to these things, how and why they are as they are, are demonstrated by subtle reasoning.

CHAPTER 2: FIRST PRINCIPLES
(FIGURE 30)*

1. Thales was first to think that water was the origin of all things. Heraclitus, the Ephesian, who was called "The Obscure" by the Greeks for the obscurity of his writings, [thought] that the first element was fire. Democritus and Epicurus, who followed him, proposed atoms, what our people call "inseparable bodies," and some call "indivisibles." The teachings of the Pythagoreans added earth and air to fire and water. Thus Democritus, to the extent that he did not name separate things as such, but rather created the hypothesis of indivisible bodies, seems to have meant that when separated from one another, they are undamaged and incapable of destruction – nor can they be cut into sections, but instead retain in themselves an infinite solidity for all time.

2. Therefore, because all things seem to come together and to be born from the conjunction of these bodies, and are distributed into infinite types of natural objects, I thought that I should expound on their varieties and the criteria for their use, as well as what qualities they have in building, so that when this information is known, those who are planning to build will avoid mistakes and assemble supplies suitable for buildings.

CHAPTER 3: MUD-BRICK MASONRY
(FIGURE 31)*

1. First, therefore, I shall discuss mud bricks, and from what type of earth they should be created. For they should not be made from sandy or pebbly clay, nor from loose sand, because if they are made from these types of earth they will be heavy at first, and then, as rain spatters against the walls, they break down and dissolve, and the straw mixed in them will not hold together because of their unevenness. They should be made from whitish clay or red earth or even coarse sand. For these types of earth, on account of their lightness, have durability without weighing the building down, and they are easily piled together.

2. The bricks should be made in springtime or autumn, so that they dry at a uniform rate.* For those prepared in midsummer are defective because when the sun has baked the outermost skin harshly and prematurely, it makes it so that the brick looks dry when the interior has not yet dried. Then, when it later contracts in drying, it will shatter what has already dried. Thus these bricks are rendered cracked and weak. They will also be most serviceable if they were made two years earlier, as they cannot dry thoroughly before that time. If they are laid while new and not entirely dry, then, when the plaster has been laid and remains there solidified, the mud bricks themselves, as they subside [in drying], cannot maintain the same level as the plaster, and as they contract they no longer bond with it, but instead pull apart at the join. Therefore the plaster, split away from the masonry of the building, can no longer stand by itself because of its flimsiness, but shatters, and the walls, having settled haphazardly, are themselves flawed. For this reason the people of Utica would use a mud brick in the construction of walls only if it were fully dry and made five years earlier, and approved as such by the judgment of a magistrate.

3. Now there are three types of mud bricks. One, which is called "Lydian" in Greek, is the one which we use, one and one-half feet long and one foot wide. The Greeks construct their buildings with the other two types. Of these one is called *pentadôron*, the other *tetradôron*. For the Greeks call a palm a *dôron*, because in Greek the giving of gifts is called *dôron*, and that is always done by the palm of the hand. Thus whatever is five palms long in every direction is a *pentadôron*, and what is four palms long is a *tetradôron*, and public works are constructed with *pentadôra*, private works with *tetradôra*.

4. Along with these bricks half-bricks are made, which are laid like this: rows of bricks should be laid on one side, and rows of half-bricks laid on the other. Therefore when they are laid on the level on each side, the walls will be tied together with alternating surfaces and the half-bricks, placed over the joins, lend a durability and an appearance on each side that is not unattractive.

There is a city called Maxilua in Further Spain, another called Callet, and in Asia one called Pitane, where bricks, once they have been made and dried, float when they are cast into water. Now these seem to be able to float because the earth from which they are made contains pumice. And because it is so light, once solidified by air it will not admit or absorb moisture. Thus, because they are of a light and porous nature, yet do not allow the power of moisture to penetrate into their body, whatever their weight, inevitably they are borne up in water just as pumice will be. And thus they are extremely useful, as they are neither heavy when used in construction nor, once made, will they dissolve in storms.

CHAPTER 4: SAND FOR CONCRETE
MASONRY*

1. In concrete structures one must first inquire into the sand, so that it will be suitable for mixing the mortar and not have any earth mixed in with it. These are the types of excavated sand: black, white, light red, and dark red. Of these the type that crackles when a few grains are rubbed together in the hand will be the best, for earthy sand will not be rough enough. Likewise, if it is thrown onto a white cloth and then shaken off, if it neither dirties the cloth nor leaves behind a residue of earth, it will be suitable.

2. If there are no sand beds where it may be dug out, then it will have to be sifted from riverbeds or gravel deposits, or, of course, extracted from the seashore. But this type of sand has these faults in construction: it dries with difficulty, nor will the wall support uninterrupted loading unless it is relieved at intervals, nor will it take ceilings. This is even more so of sea sand because the walls, when plaster is applied to them, give off salt and dissolve the surface.

3. Excavated sands, on the other hand, dry quickly in construction, and the plastering stays in place; they will also bear ceilings, but only those sands that are from newly discovered sand deposits. When sand beds lie

exposed for any stretch of time after they have been worked, subjected to sun and moon and frost, they break down and become earthy. And thus when such sands are mixed into the mortar, they cannot hold the rubble together. Instead, the rubble comes loose, and the weight of the masonry, which the walls can no longer sustain, collapses.

But even though newly excavated sands have so many virtues in construction, they are not useful for plaster precisely because in mixing with lime, because of its own density, and with straw, it cannot dry without cracks; it is too intense. Although its fine grain makes it useless for construction, as in *opus signinum*, river sand, when flattened down by the action of a plaster float, acquires firmness for plasterwork.

and water burned away and carried off, it is left with a residue of latent heat. When the stone is then plunged in water, before the water absorbs the power of its heat, whatever liquid penetrates into the pores of the stone boils up, and thus by the time it has cooled it rejects the heat given off by lime. 3. Therefore, whatever the weight of stones when they are cast into the furnace, they cannot have retained it by the time they are removed; when they are weighed, although their size remains the same, they will be found to have lost a third part of their weight because of the moisture that has been cooked out of them. And thus, because their pores and spaces lie so wide open, they absorb the mixture of sand into themselves and hold together; as they dry, they join together with the rubble and produce the solidity of the masonry.

CHAPTER 5: LIME FOR CONCRETE MASONRY*

1. Now that everything has been clarified about supplies of sand, then we must be careful about our lime, and whether it has been cooked down from limestone or *silex* (hard limestone). And that which is made from denser and harder stone will be useful in construction, and that made from porous stone, for plaster. When it has been slaked, then the materials should be mixed so that if we are using excavated sand, three parts of sand and one of lime should be poured together. If, on the other hand, it is river or sea sand, two parts of sand should be thrown in with one of lime. In this way the rate of mixture will be properly calibrated. Furthermore, if one is using river or sea sand, then potsherds, pounded and sifted, and added to the mixture as a third part, will make the composition of the mortar better to use.

2. When lime absorbs water and sand it reinforces the masonry. Evidently this is the reason: because stones, too, are composed of the four elements. Those which have more air are soft, those with more water are dense with moisture, those with more earth are hard, those with more fire are more friable. Because of this, if we take this stone before it has been cooked, pound it fine and mix it with sand in masonry, it will neither solidify nor bond. If, on the other hand, we throw it into the kiln, then, caught up in the flame's intensity, it will shed its original property of hardness, and with its strength burned away and sucked dry, it will be left with wide-open pores and voids. Therefore, with its air

CHAPTER 6: POZZOLANA FOR CONCRETE MASONRY*

1. There is also a type of powder that brings about marvelous things naturally. It occurs in the region of Baiae and in the countryside that belongs to the towns around Mount Vesuvius. Mixed with lime and rubble, it lends strength to all the other sorts of construction, but in addition, when moles [employing this powder] are built into the sea, they solidify underwater. Evidently this is why it happens: under these mountains are boiling earths and plentiful springs. These would not exist unless deep beneath there were huge fires, blazing with sulphur or alum or pitch. Therefore these interior fires and the vapor of their flames seep through veins in the ground and make this earth light, and the tufa created there has risen up without any component of moisture. Hence, when these three ingredients [lime, fired rubble, and pozzolana], forged in similar fashion by fire's intensity, meet in a single mixture, when this mixture is put into contact with water the ingredients cling together as one and, stiffened by water, quickly solidify. Neither waves nor the force of water can dissolve them.

2. This, too, may serve to indicate that there are deep fires in these localities: there are places in the hills of Cumae and Baiae which have been dug out as sweating chambers. In these, boiling vapor, created deep below, pierces the ground by the intensity of its fire. It rises up in these places where it has seeped through to the surface, creating outstandingly serviceable sweating

chambers. Antiquity records that fires cropped up in great abundance under Mount Vesuvius and that flames vomited forth from thence into the surrounding countryside. Thus that sponge or pumice called "Pompeian" seems to have been reduced to its present type of consistency by the firing of some other type of stone.

3. The type of pumice extracted from this place does not occur everywhere; only around Aetna and in those hills of Mysia which the Greeks call "scorched" (*katakekaumenê*) and anywhere else where the locality has these particular properties. If in such places there are boiling springs and hot vapors exuding wherever one digs, and these very places are recorded by the ancients as having had flames coursing through the countryside, it seems certain that the intensity of fire will have deprived the tufa and the ground in that place of its moisture, just as moisture is driven from lime in a kiln.

4. As a result, [in building with pozzolana underwater], unlike and unequal entities that have been forcibly separated are brought together all at once. Then the moisture-starved heat latent in these types of ingredients, when satiated by water, boils together and makes them combine. Quickly, they take on the qualities of a single solid mass.

Now this will leave open the question why, if hot-water springs occur just as frequently in Etruria, there is not some similar powder occurring there, through the use of which underwater masonry might consolidate in the same manner. I thought I had better anticipate the reader's question and explain how this happens. 5. The same types of earth do not occur in every place or every region, nor the same types of stone. Some terrains are mostly soil, others are sandy, and some consist of gravel. In other places the ground will be made of coarse-grained sand, and it is absolutely the case that earth has different qualities of unlike and unequal type that vary with each region. Especially, one can see that where the Apennine range encloses the regions of Italy and Etruria there is no lack of sand deposits in almost every locality. Across the Apennines, however, in that part which faces the Adriatic Sea, not one can be found, nor can I name a single one across the sea in all Achaea or Asia. Therefore the same opportunities cannot possibly combine in every place where there are plentiful hot springs. All things occur as Nature has decided, not determined for human pleasure[1] but scattered as if at random.

6. Therefore, in those places where the mountains are not earthy but are made instead of soft matter, the force of fire exiting through the veins of that matter parches it, for fire burns off whatever is soft and tender, leaving behind whatever is harsh. And thus, just as in Campania scorched earth becomes ash, so in Etruria the cooked matter becomes burnt ochre. Both of these are outstanding for construction, but one works in buildings on land while the other works as well for sea moles. This matter has a softer quality than that of tufa, yet more solid than earth, because it has been seared from within by the intensity of the vapor from deep below. That type of sand called "red earth" is produced in several places.

CHAPTER 7: STONE FOR CONCRETE MASONRY*

1. For lime and sand I have stated what their varieties are and what particular qualities they have. Now order demands that I explain about quarries, from which both squared blocks and the supplies of rubble for building are obtained and readied. These, in turn, will be found to have unequal and dissimilar qualities. Some are soft: around the City itself,[2] the stones of Saxa Rubra, Palla, Fidenae, and Alba are like this. Some are neither soft nor hard, like those of Tibur, Amiternae, and Soracte, and other stones of this type. Some are hard, like *silex* (hard limestone). There are many other types as well, like the red and black tufa in Campania, and white tufa in Umbria and Picenum and Venetia; this can be cut with a toothed saw as if it were wood.

2. But all these soft stones share this virtue, that the blocks made from them are easily handled at work. And so long as they are used in covered areas, they will sustain stress, but if they are put in open, uncovered places, then, once they have been saturated with ice and frost they crumble apart and dissolve. Likewise along the seashore they will wear away, eaten by the salt, nor do they endure summer heat. Travertine, on the other hand, and all stones of the same type, endure every strain, whether it be stress or the injuries inflicted by harsh weather, but they cannot be safeguarded against fire. As soon as they make contact with it, they crack apart and

---

1 Reading MSS *voluptas* rather than Giocondo's *voluntas*.

2 Vitruvius acknowledges only one Urbs. Other cities are *civitates* or *oppida*.

fall to pieces, because they have a natural composition with little water, and not much earth, but a great deal of air and fire. Therefore, because the moist and earthy components are scarce in them to begin with, and on top of this the forceful touch of fire will have driven out the component of air, then, pursuing deep within the stone and occupying every empty vein, it flares up, creating a compound as blazing as its own elemental bodies.

3. There are several quarries in the territory of Tarquinii called Anician, about the same as the Alban stone in color, whose workshops are mostly around the Lacus Volsiniensis and the prefecture of Statonia. Now these have endless virtues. For neither freezing storms nor the touch of fire can hurt them; they are firm and last to a great old age because they have little air and fire in their natural composition, a moderate amount of water, and a very great deal of earth. Thus consolidated by dense texture, they are harmed[3] neither by harsh weather nor the power of fire. 4. This can be concluded especially from the monuments around the town of Ferentum, which are made of stone from these quarries. There are large statues outstandingly crafted, and smaller statues, and flowers and acanthus plants elegantly carved, which, though they are old, look newly finished. Similarly the bronze workers who have prepared their models in the currents of air coming off these quarries find that they are of the greatest utility for casting bronze.

If these quarries were nearer the City, it would be fitting that all work be completed in these very workshops. 5. But because necessity compels the use of supplies from the quarries of Saxa Rubra and Palla because of their proximity, and whatever other quarries are nearby, whoever wants to bring his work to flawless completion should make preparations as follows.

When it is time to begin building, let the stone be extracted two years earlier, not in winter, but in summer, and lie about in an open place. Whatever stones have been touched and damaged by bad weather in the two years should be thrown into the foundation courses. All the rest that have not been damaged, once they have passed the test of Nature, will be capable of enduring in construction above ground. These provisions should be observed not only for squared stone but also in rubble structures.

3 The MSS all read *nocetur* for *nocentur*, hence the mistake of singular for plural entered the textual tradition early. There is no way of knowing whether it goes back to the author himself.

CHAPTER 8: STYLES OF CONCRETE MASONRY; STONE MASONRY*

1. These are the types of masonry: *reticulatum* ("network"), which is used by everyone now, and the old style which is called *incertum* ("random work"). Of these the more attractive is reticulatum, but it is inclined to split apart because it has discrete seams and junctures in every direction. Rubble in opus incertum, with stone sitting upon stone and sloping every which way, affords a masonry that is not pretty but is more durable than reticulate construction (Figure 32).

2. Either type of masonry should be built up of the most fine-grained ingredients, so that the wall surfaces, thickly saturated by a mortar of lime and sand, will hold together longer. For soft and porous in nature as they are, they dry out by sucking the sap from the mortar. When the supply of lime and sand superabounds, the wall surface, having more moisture, will not become feeble quickly, for it is held in bond by these two substances. As soon as the moist power has been sucked out from the mortar because of the porous structure of the rubble, the lime pulls away from the sand and dissolves; the stones, in turn, cohere with neither lime nor sand, and in the long run it makes for ruined walls.

3. This can be observed, indeed, in some monuments that have been erected around the City of marble or squared stone. Inside they have been filled with rubble work, and with the mortar weakened by age and sucked dry by the porous nature of the tufa, they go to ruin. With their bond pulled apart by the ruin of the joints they fall to pieces. 4. For which reason, if one wants to avoid falling into this error, reserve a hollow zone in the middle of the wall along the orthostates. On the inside, two-foot walls should be constructed of squared Anio tufa or terra cotta or split stone, and along with these the front surfaces should be linked by iron clamps and lead. For in this way the work is not heaped but coursed, forever flawless, because the beddings and joins, settling one with another and bound together at the seams, will not bulge the masonry outward, nor do they allow the orthostates (which are clamped together) to slip out of place.

5. Therefore the masonry of the Greeks is not to be condemned (Figure 33). They do not use a surfaced masonry of soft rubble, but whenever they depart from building with ashlar blocks, they lay courses of split stone or hard flagstone, and bind the joints together in alternate layers just as if they were building in brick, and thus they achieve powers of durability for the walls such that they will last an eternity.

They construct these walls in two types. Of these, one is **isodomic**; the other is called **pseudoisodomic**. 6. Masonry is called **isodomic** when all the layers are constructed of an equal thickness, **pseudoisodomic** when the rows are alternating and unequal layers are preferred. Both of them are durable for these reasons: first, because the flagstones themselves are of a dense and solid nature and will not, therefore, suck the moisture out of mortar; instead, they preserve its moisture intact even to the greatest age. And similarly, because the bedding for this masonry has been planed and leveled, it does not permit the mortar to settle, for it is bonded all along to the thickness of the walls, held in place to the greatest age.

7. There is another type of masonry which they call "interwoven" (*emplékton*); our Italian peasants use it as well. Its front surfaces are dressed; the rest is set in mortar untrimmed, with alternating joins. But our people, with their passion for quick results, put up only upright facings, and fill in the middle separately with broken rubble with mortar. Thus three layers are maintained in such masonry: two for the outer surfaces and one for the filling.

The Greeks, on the other hand, do not do it this way, but rather by laying the stones flat, heading every other one crosswise into the wall. Thus they do not fill the middle but rather give their walls a single unbroken thickness made from the two facings. Furthermore, all along they include single stones that reach right through and are dressed on either surface; they call these "stretchers" (*diatonoi*), and these especially reinforce the solidity of the walls by binding them together.

8. And so, anyone who wishes to consider and select a type of masonry from these commentaries has available the principles of what makes for permanence. Those structures made of soft rubble, for all their subtle attractiveness, are not the ones that will resist ruin as time passes. And thus when assessors are appointed to evaluate party walls, they never assess soft rubble walls according to their initial cost, but rather, when they look at the price recorded in the original contracts, they deduct one-eightieth of that sum for each subsequent year, and the remaining amount is fixed as the current value of the walls. They have rendered the judgment, in effect, that such walls cannot last more than eighty years.

9. For mud-brick walls, on the other hand, so long as they are standing upright nothing is deducted from their assessment, but whatever it cost to make them, they will always be assessed at this value. And so in some cities, public works and private homes alike, even royal palaces, are to be seen made of mud brick; to begin with, the wall in Athens that looks toward Mount Hymettus and Mount Pentele. Likewise, in the temple of Jupiter and Hercules at Patrae there are mud-brick cellas, although they are surrounded in that building by stone epistyles and columns. In Arretium in Italy there is an old wall outstandingly made. In Tralles there is the residence made for the Attalid kings that is always given as quarters to the person who holds the city priesthood. As for Sparta, pictures of inlaid brick were cut from certain walls, placed in wooden frames and brought over to decorate the Comitium and so adorn the aedileship of Varro and Murena. 10. The residence of Croesus is made of mud brick, the one which the people of Sardis have dedicated as a meeting house for the College of Elders, so that their citizens may spend their old age in restful leisure.

EXCURSUS: A TOUR OF HALICARNASSUS
(FIGURE 34)*

In Halicarnassus, the house of that mighty king Mausolus, although it had every part decorated in Proconnesian marble, also had walls constructed in mud brick; these exhibit remarkable durability to this day, so much so that the plasterwork has been polished to the point where it seems to have the transparency of glass. Nor did this king do as he did for lack of funds – he was glutted with endless tribute money because he ruled over the whole of Caria.

11. His sharp wit and expertise at building may be discerned from the following story: although he was born in Mylasa, when he perceived that Halicarnassus had a naturally fortified site, a suitable marketplace, and a handy port, he established his residence there. Now this site is similar to the curvature of a theater. In the lowermost part, next to the port, the forum has been set up. At a height halfway up the slope, at the landing between the tiers of seats, so to speak, there is a street of spacious breadth, in the center of which the Mausoleum has been made with such outstanding care that it is listed among the Seven Wonders of the World. In the center of the upper citadel, the shrine of Mars has a colossal acrolithic statue made by the noble hand of Leochares. (Some people say that Leochares made this statue; others think it the work of Timotheos.)

On the summit of the right-hand peak there is a shrine to Venus and Mercury, right by the fountain of Salmacis. 12. This is falsely believed to infect those who drink from it with venereal disease. However, I am not reluctant to show why this opinion has been spread around the globe by misleading rumors. It cannot have happened because – as they say – people are really made soft and shameless by that water, for the fountain's spring is utterly clear and its taste outstanding. However, when Melas and Arevanias led a colony in common from Argos and Troezen to be sited here, they had to eject the barbarian Carians and Leleges. These, in turn, driven away to the mountains, gathered together and made incursions down into the area, and set upon the colonists cruelly in their raids. Afterward one of the colonists outfitted a tavern next to the spring with every amenity, taking advantage of the excellence of the water to make some money for himself, and in running this business he attracted these barbarians as well. Coming down from the mountains one by one and taking part in city society they were gradually changed from their harsh and wild ways to Greek habits and were subdued into gentility by their own volition. Therefore this water did not gain its reputation from the vice of shameless disease but rather from the gentling of barbarian spirits by the allurements of humanity.

13. It remains, now that I have arrived at the description of the walls, for me to outline what the city is like as a whole. Just as the shrine of Venus and the spring mentioned above stand on the right-hand side, so on the left peak there is the royal residence which King Mausolus placed according to his own plan. For from its vantage, one looks out on the right toward the forum, the port, and the full extent of the city walls; hidden to the left under the walls is a secret port such that no one can see or know what happens there, yet the king himself could spot from his house what was needed for his soldiers and sailors without anyone else knowing.

14. And thus after the death of Mausolus, when his wife Artemisia reigned, the Rhodians, outraged that all the cities of Caria should be ruled by a woman, set out with an armed fleet to occupy the kingdom. When this was reported to Artemisia, she commanded that a fleet be concealed in that port, with hidden rowers and marines at the ready, while the remaining citizens were to man the walls. When the Rhodians, with their well-armed fleet, had disembarked in the main harbor, she ordered that her subjects raise a cheer and promise to betray the city. Just then, when the Rhodians had entered the city and left their ships behind empty, Artemisia led her fleet out of the small port along a canal made into the sea and thus she bore into the large harbor. Then, disembarking her soldiers [and boarding

them on the enemy ships], she led the Rhodian fleet out into the high seas. The Rhodians, in the meantime, having nowhere to retreat, were closed off on all sides and cut down right in the Forum. 15. Artemisia set out for Rhodes with her own soldiers and rowers boarded on Rhodian ships. Now when the Rhodians saw their own fleet coming into view covered with laurel, in the belief that they were welcoming back victorious fellow citizens, they received their enemies instead. When Artemisia had captured Rhodes and killed its leaders, she set up a trophy of her victory within the city of Rhodes itself and commissioned two bronze statues: one of the city of Rhodes and one an image of herself, this latter figure portraying her branding the city of Rhodes as her slave. Later, because the Rhodians were prevented by their religious beliefs from taking any other measures – for it is sacrilege for a trophy, once dedicated, to be removed – they built a structure around this site, and once that had been erected they covered it over with a Greek guardhouse, so that no one could see it, and ordered that it be declared a sacred precinct, off limits.

BRICK MASONRY

16. If, therefore, kings of such immense power did not disdain structures with mud-brick walls, kings for whom it was possible, thanks to tribute money and the booty of war, to have buildings in rubble work or squared stone masonry or even marble, I do not think it necessary myself to look down on buildings made of brick masonry, so long as they are roofed correctly. I shall, however, describe that type of structure which it is not right for the Roman people to have made in the City, and I shall not neglect to mention what the causes and reasoning are for such a phenomenon.

17. The law does not permit greater thicknesses than one and one-half feet to be reached in a party wall. All the other walls as well, except on the narrowest of sites, have been laid to the same thickness. However, brick walls at a thickness of one and one-half feet, unless they are going to consist of two or three layers of brick, cannot carry more than one story, whereas in a city of this grandeur and such endless density of population it is necessary to put up houses beyond number. Consequently, because a flat area cannot accommodate housing such a multitude in the City, the problem itself imposed arriving at the expedient of tall buildings (Figure 35).* By the use of stone piers, tile masonry and rubble-work walls, heights could be built up and lay-

ered with multiple stories, with the upper rooms partitioned off[4] for greatest efficiency. With various types of walls and roofing multiplied into vertical space, the Roman people have excellent dwellings without legal obstacle. 18. Now the reason has been made clear why there cannot be mud-brick walls in the City – because of the restrictions imposed by limited space.

If the plan is to use them outside the City, this is how to make them flawless even into great age. On the tops of the walls tile masonry should be put under the roof tiles to a height of about a foot and a half, and let it project like a cornice. In this way one can avoid the usual defects that occur in this type of wall, for when roof tiles are broken on the roof, or blown down by the wind, in those places where water can pour down from the tiles, the terracotta armor will not allow the brick to be harmed. 19. Instead, the projection of the cornice will cast the dripping water beyond the plane of the walls, thus preserving whole the brick masonry. Of the tile itself no one can judge immediately whether it will be excellent or defective for purposes of construction – once it has been placed on the roof, in storms and over time, if it is solid, it will prove itself. Tile that is not made from good clay or has been insufficiently baked will show that it is defective once it is set in place and exposed to ice and frost. It follows that the tile which cannot bear the work of roofing cannot hold firm in bearing the load of masonry.

20. This is why walls constructed with terracotta from old roof tiles will have a reliable durability.

HALF-TIMBERING AND LATTICEWORK

As for half-timbered walls, I for one wish they had never been invented. However advantageous they are in terms of speed and for covering broad expanses, they are a still greater source of disaster, and on a large scale, because they are as good as torches when it comes to catching fire. It ought to be clear, therefore, that the expense of paying for tile is better than putting oneself in danger for the convenience of half-timbering. Even the half-timbers used in plasterwork create fissures because of the placement of their uprights and cross-pieces. When they are first plastered over, they swell when they absorb the moisture, and then as they dry they contract; shrunk down like this, they break up the firmness of the plaster. Nonetheless, because haste, or

4 Reading MSS *dispertiones.*

poverty, or overhangs force some people to resort to it, this is how the work should be done: give them footings so that they do not touch the subfloor or the pavement. Otherwise, if they are set in these, they will become rotten with age. As they subside, they will lean and disrupt the appearance of the plaster.

To the extent that I could, I have explained about walls and their preparation according to their type, about the mortar used for them, and what virtues and defects they each possess. Now I will discuss floors, ceilings, and the materials from which they are prepared, so that even in old age they will not weaken, according to what science demonstrates.

CHAPTER 9: TIMBER

1. Timber should be cut from the very beginning of autumn to that time just before Favonius begins to blow (Figure 36).* The truth is that in the spring all the trees become pregnant, and all through the autumn and winter they transfer the strength in their possession to their branches and their annual fruits. Thus when they are empty and swollen as the season compels them, they become ineffectual and weak because of their lightness, just as women's bodies, once they have conceived, are not considered whole again until the birth of the child. Nor when slave women are put up for sale are the pregnant ones advertised as healthy, because the fetus growing in the body diverts all the nutrition afforded by the powers of food to itself, and the stronger it is as the time of birth approaches, so much less is it possible that what creates it be solid. After the child has been born, freed from having to create her offspring, she absorbs the nourishment that had hitherto been shunted off to foster another type of growth in empty, wide-open veins, and lapping up this sap grows solid and returns to the original strength of her nature.

2. By the same principle, when in autumn the leaves wither as the fruit ripens, the roots of the trees, receiving sap from the earth, recover, restored to their former solidity. In fact, the force of the winter wind compresses and consolidates trees throughout that season which has just been described. This is why wood, if cut during the time described, will be cut in season. 3. However, it ought to be cut so that the thickness of the tree is hewed to the central core and left to dry out by exuding sap. By this means the superfluous liquid in its veins, flowing out through the cambium, will neither keep

away bad humors nor let the quality of the wood be corrupted. When the tree is dry and no longer drips, it can be chopped down and will be at its best when put into use.

4. The truth of this can be seen in the case of pollarded trees.* When these are perforated at the bottom and pruned, through the openings they pour out whatever superfluous and corrupt liquid they may contain in themselves, and as they dry they take on durability. The moistures in trees that do not have an outlet coagulate and grow rotten within them, making these trees hollow and defective. If, therefore, trees do not grow old when they have dried out while standing and alive, when they are chopped down for timber and cared for according to these instructions, without a doubt they will prove of immense utility in buildings into great old age.

5. Trees have properties that are dissimilar and differ among themselves, such as oak, elm, poplar, cypress, fir, and the other trees especially suited for buildings. An oak cannot do what a fir does, nor a cypress what an elm does, nor do the others have exactly the same properties among themselves by nature. Instead, the individual types are composed with the properties of their first elements, and each type has its own particular utility at work. 6. Fir, first of all, which mostly has a great deal of air and fire and very little water and earth, is composed with the lighter powers of nature and is not a heavy wood. Kept in line by its natural rigidity, it is not easily bent under stress, and so remains very straight in joists. Because, however, it contains relatively more heat, it generates and fosters rot and is damaged by it. Furthermore, it ignites easily, for the reason that its body has the sparseness of air and with this open structure it accepts fire and indeed gives off an intense flame.

7. That part of it which is nearest the ground, before it is felled, because it receives water from the roots, is liquid and free from knots by virtue of this proximity. The higher part, on the other hand, because of the intensity of the heat in the branches that are extended into the air through the knots, when cut at about twenty feet up and worked with the axe, is called "club wood" because of the hardness of its knots. When the lowermost part of the same tree is cut and quartered, with the cambium removed, it is used for cabinetry and called fir.

8. Oak, by contrast, abounding to saturation with earthy first elements and possessing little water, air, or fire, lasts into eternity when it is buried in earthworks. For this reason, when exposed to water, and lacking the voids afforded by a looser structure on account of its

density, it cannot receive the moisture into its body. Instead, shrinking back from the moisture, it resists, grows twisted, and makes fissures in any work where it has been put to use.

9. Winter oak, on the other hand, which has an even composition of all the elements, proves immensely useful in construction. Still, when put into contact with water, by receiving moisture right through its pores and casting out air and fire, it is damaged by the powers of wetness. Turkey oak and beech, with an equal mixture of water, fire, and earth, and a very high proportion of air, decay quickly by absorbing moisture deep into their hollows. White and black poplar, also willow, linden, and agnus castus, have a full complement of fire and air, a moderate amount of water and little earth, and composed of this lighter mixture, they seem to have outstanding rigidity when put into use. Because they are not hard with the admixture of earth, they are bright white because of their loose structure and present a convenient malleability for carving.

10. Alder, which grows next to the banks of rivers and would hardly seem to be a useful wood, actually has outstanding properties. It is composed of a great deal of air and fire, not much earth, and little water. Therefore, when densely fixed as pilings under the foundations of buildings in swampy sites, by absorbing the liquid it lacks by nature it remains undecayed for eternity, bearing immense loads of masonry and preserving them flawless. In this way a wood that cannot last for even a short time out of the earth will last forever when submerged in water. 11. This is easiest to see in Ravenna, because all buildings there, public and private, have pilings of this type underneath their foundations. Elm and ash, on the other hand, have the greatest possible amount of moisture and a minimum of air and fire, and are composed with a moderate mixture of earth. In use, when they are worked they are flexible; because of their preponderance of water they have no rigidity and bend at once. At the same time, if they have been made dry with age, or because they have grown in an exposed place, they lose the liquid that was in them, become harder, and can be linked firmly in joins because of their elasticity.

12. Likewise, hornbeam, which has a minimal mixture of fire and earth, but has the greatest possible complement of air and water, is not fragile, and indeed has a most useful manageability. And thus, the Greeks, who make the yokes for their oxen from this wood, call it *zygia* – "yoke-wood." (They call yokes *zyga*.) No less remarkable are cypress and pine; these, with an abundance of water and an equal mixture of the remaining

elements, tend to bend in use because of their excess liquid, but they last into old age because the moisture held deep in their bodies has a bitter quality, and the sharpness of this will not permit rot to penetrate, nor pests. This is why projects carried out in these types of wood last forever, into eternity.

13. Cedar and juniper, too, have these same properties and uses, but in place of the resin in cypress and pine, cedars produce the oil called cedar oil. When other objects are rubbed with this oil, papyrus scrolls, for example, they will not be damaged by worms or rot. The leaves of this tree are similar to those of cypress, but the wood has a straight grain. The statue of Diana in the temple at Ephesus is made of this wood; so are the ceiling coffers, both there and in other noble shrines, thanks to its endless durability. These trees grow primarily in Crete, Africa, and several areas of Syria.

14. Larch, on the other hand, which is unknown except to the inhabitants of towns along the banks of the river Po and Adriatic coast, is not only undamaged by rot and worms because of the intense bitterness of its sap, but it also will not absorb flame from fire. Nor can it burn of itself unless it is thrown, like stone, into a lime kiln together with other types of wood. Even then, it will neither catch fire nor produce coals; instead, it is slowly consumed over a long period. Because its composition has the least possible complement of fire and air among the elements, and at the same time is densely packed with water and earth, there are no pores through which fire could penetrate. Instead, it throws back the force of fire, nor will it allow itself to be damaged by it quickly. Because of its weight it will not float in water, so that when it is transported it must be placed either in large ships or in barges made of fir.

THE DISCOVERY OF LARCH WOOD

15. It is worth knowing how this timber was discovered. The deified Caesar, when he commanded an army near the Alps, had ordered the surrounding communities to furnish supplies for him. There was in the area a fortified citadel called Larignum,* and those within it, trusting in their natural defenses, refused to obey the order. The Imperator, therefore, commanded his troops to draw up around it. Now there was a tower before the citadel gate, made of alternating cross beams of this wood, piled up to a great height as on a pyre, so that from its summit they could drive off attackers with sharpened stakes and stones. When it was noted that the garrison had no weapons other than lances, which

because of their weight could not be hurled far from the walls, the order went out to approach and to fling bundles of twigs and torches around the construction and set them afire. And these are what the soldiers quickly gathered together. 16. Once the flame, flickering toward heaven, had enveloped the twigs surrounding this wooden tower, it made the soldiers believe that they had already seen the whole structure collapse. But when the flames went out of their own accord, died down, and the tower appeared intact, an amazed Caesar ordered that a ditch be dug around the citadel, beyond the range of their lances. When the townspeople, terror stricken, surrendered, Caesar inquired where wood like this came from, that could not be harmed by fire. Then the townspeople showed him the trees, of which there is a great abundance in those very parts, and because this citadel was called Larignum, the wood is called larch.

This wood is transported down the Po to Ravenna, where it is then available to the citizens of Fano, Pesaro, Ancona, and the other towns in the region. If there were the possibility of transporting this wood to the City, it would be of the greatest usefulness in construction – if not everywhere, certainly at least if panels of this wood were placed around the eaves of apartment buildings, they would free the buildings from the danger of spreading fire, because they are impervious to flame or burning coals, nor can they create them themselves. 17. These trees have leaves similar to those of pines, and their timber is tall, adaptable to cabinetry no less than deal; it has a liquid resin, the color of Attic honey, which cures asthmatics.

I have explained about the individual types of timber, and with what properties nature seems to have composed them, and in what manners they are propagated. Let me follow with an account of why what are called "high-grown" pines in the City give an inferior timber; whereas those called "low-grown" afford outstanding utility in making buildings long lasting. Also, about related things: the way in which trees acquire virtues or defects from the properties of the locality itself, so that these matters may be more open to view for those who examine them.

CHAPTER 10: THE IMPORTANCE OF LOCATION IN TIMBER GROWTH

1. The first roots of the Apennine range arise from the Tyrrhenian Sea between the Alps and the outermost regions of Etruria. But the ridge of this mountain draws

itself around in a curve, and with the center of the curve almost touching the shores of the Adriatic Sea, it circles back to touch the sea on the other side. The nearer part of its curvature, which faces toward the regions of Etruria and Campania, has sunny properties, for it is always facing the course of the sun. The further side, which slopes down the Upper (Adriatic) Sea and is exposed to the north, is hemmed in by unbroken expanses of shadows and darkness. The trees in this part grow to immense heights, nourished not only on the power of water, for their veins, swollen and filled with an abundance of moisture, are also saturated with the superfluity of distending liquid. Furthermore, when they are felled and chopped into timbers and lose their vital powers, the rigidity of their veins persists as they dry; consequently their porosity makes these timbers spongy and weak, so that they will have no durability in construction.

2. Those that grow in areas facing the course of the sun, because they lack these open veins, are drained dry, and become solid, for the lapping of the sun not only draws moisture out of the earth but also out of trees. Thus the trees that grow in sunny regions, consolidated by the proximity of their dense veins to one another, do not have the loose texture created by water. When they are cut into timbers, they display great utility into old age. Low-growing woods, therefore, which are brought in from sunny localities, are better than those from dark highlands.

3. To the extent that I could assess them in my mind, I have set out what supplies are necessary in the preparation of buildings and what composition and temperament among nature's elements they seem to possess, as well as what virtues and defects occur in each individual type, so that none of this will be unknown to builders. Whoever is able to follow the recommendations of these precepts will be more prudent in his choice of what type of material to use in his projects. Now that matters of preparation have been explained, the remaining volumes will discuss the buildings themselves; first of all, in the next book I shall describe, as order requires it, the temples of the immortal gods, their symmetries and their proportions.

❖

TEMPLES

PREFACE: JUDGMENT OF ARTISTIC SKILL

1. Apollo of Delphi proclaimed in an oracle of the Pythian priestess that Socrates was the wisest man of all. Socrates, in turn, is recorded as having said, sensibly and knowledgeably, that human hearts should have been transparent and open, so that their feelings are not hidden, but rather open for inspection. Indeed, if only Nature had followed his advice, and had made them clear and open to view! In that case, not only would the praiseworthy qualities and the shortcomings of human souls be observable at close range, but, in addition, knowledge of the various disciplines, set out before our own eyes, would no longer be put to the test by uncertain judgments; instead, the truly learned and truly wise would acquire a preeminent, unshakable authority.

Yet because things have not been set up this way, but rather according to the will of Nature, it is not possible for men to judge the state of the knowledge of the arts that lies hidden within, because talent is concealed in darkness in men's breasts. Although artists themselves might profess their good judgment, if they are not wealthy, or well known because their shop is of long standing, and are unequipped with influence in the Forum and skill in public speaking, they cannot muster such authority with regard to their skill that what they profess to know will be believed.

2. We can observe this above all in the case of the ancient sculptors and painters, because those among them who had conspicuous position and the benefit of patronage are the ones who have been eternally commemorated to posterity, those like Myron, Polycleitus, Phidias, Lysippus, and the rest who achieved fame through their art.* As they executed their works for great cities, or kings, or prominent citizens, so, too, they acquired their great reputations. But those who were no less dedicated, talented, or skilled than the famous artists, and executed their commissions no less outstandingly, but for citizens of humble rank, those

artists have gained no fame whatsoever, because they were abandoned – not by dedication, nor by skill in their art – but by good fortune, men such as Hegias of Athens, Chion of Corinth, Boedas of Byzantium, and many others besides.* And the same is no less true for painters like Aristomenes of Thasos, Polycles and Androcydes of Cyzicus, Andron of Ephesus, Theo of Magnesia, and the others, whose dedication, training, and skill never failed them, but for whom personal poverty, or the shifts of fortune, or the victory of a rival in competing for bids blocked their advancement. 3. Not that it should be surprising when achievement in the arts is obscured by a lack of public awareness; still, it is particularly outrageous when, as so often happens, baseless approval is enticed away from truthful appraisal by the influence of social connections.

Therefore, if, as Socrates would have had it, our perceptions and opinions, and our knowledge of the various disciplines, were plain to see and thoroughly comprehensible, then influence and the currying of favor would be worth nothing. Instead, all commissions would be assigned automatically to the artists who obtained the greatest knowledge in a field by true, reliable work. But because these things are not as clear and as self-evident as we think they ought to be, and I observe that the ignorant outdo the learned in influence, I have decided not to contend with them in making the rounds canvassing favor, but rather, by publishing these remarks, to display the excellence of our profession.

4. And so, Imperator, in my first volume I showed you the art, what particular qualities it has, and in what disciplines the architect should be trained. I also added the reasons why one should acquire such skills. Then I classified the main branches of architecture and defined their contents. Then, as a necessary first step, I explained, on theoretical principles, about walls and how healthful sites are chosen, I named the winds and showed, with illustrations, the regions from which each of them blows, I gave instructions about how to place avenues and side streets

within the walls, and thus concluded the first volume. In the second I continued in the same vein, speaking of building materials: what uses they have in projects, and their respective properties according to Nature. Now in the third volume I will speak about the sacred dwellings of the immortal gods and shall explain how they should be designed.

CHAPTER 1: FIRST PRINCIPLES OF SYMMETRY

1. The **composition** of a temple is based on **symmetry,** whose principles architects should take the greatest care to master. **Symmetry** derives from **proportion,** which is called *analogia* in Greek. **Proportion** is the mutual calibration of each element of the work and of the whole, from which the proportional system is achieved. No temple can have any compositional system without symmetry and proportion, unless, as it were, it has an exact system of correspondence to the likeness of a well-formed human being (Figure 37).

2. For Nature composed the human body in such a way that the face, from the chin to the top of the forehead and the lowermost roots of the hairline should be one-tenth [of the total height of the body]; the palm of the hand from the wrist to the tip of the middle finger should measure likewise; the head from the chin to the crown, one-eighth; from the top of the chest to the hairline including the base of the neck, one-sixth; from the center of the chest to the crown of the head, one-fourth. Of the height of the face itself, one-third goes from the base of the chin to the lowermost part of the nostrils, another third from the base of the nostrils to a point between the eyebrows, and from that point to the hairline, the forehead also measures one-third. The foot should be one-sixth the height, the cubit, one-fourth, the chest also one-fourth. The other limbs, as well, have their own commensurate proportions, which the famous ancient painters and sculptors employed to attain great and unending praise (Figure 37).*

3. Similarly, indeed, the elements of holy temples should have dimensions for each individual part that agree with the full magnitude of the work. So, too, for example, the center and midpoint of the human body is, naturally, the navel* (Figure 38). For if a person is imagined lying back with outstretched arms and feet within a circle whose center is at the navel, the fingers and toes will trace the circumference of this circle as

they move about. But to whatever extent a circular scheme may be present in the body, a square design may also be discerned there. For if we measure from the soles of the feet to the crown of the head, and this measurement is compared with that of the outstretched hands, one discovers that this breadth equals the height, just as in areas which have been squared off by use of the set square.

4. And so, if Nature has composed the human body so that in its proportions the separate individual elements answer to the total form, then the ancients seem to have had reason to decide that bringing their creations to full completion likewise required a correspondence between the measure of individual elements and the appearance of the work as a whole. Therefore, when they were handing down proportional sequences for every type of work, they did so especially for the sacred dwellings of the gods, as the successes and failures of those works tend to remain forever.

PERFECT NUMBERS*

5. In the same way, they gathered the principles of measure, which seem to be necessary in any sort of project, from the components of the human body: the digit, palm, and cubit, for example, and grouped these units of measure into the perfect number which the Greeks call *teleion.* The ancients decided that the number called ten was perfect, because it was discovered from the number of digits on both hands. And if the number of digits on both hands is perfect by nature, it pleased Plato to state that the number was also perfect for this reason, that the decad (10) is achieved by adding together those [four] individual elements which the Greeks call *monades.* As soon as they reach eleven or twelve, because they will have passed beyond ten [and beyond the four of the tetrad] they cannot be perfect until they reach the next decad. In a manner of speaking, the first four integers are the component parts of the perfect number.

6. However, mathematicians who take the opposing side in this argument have said that the number which is called six is perfect, because that number has six components, all of which agree in their ratios with the number six. One-sixth of six (sextans = n/6) equals one. One-third of six (triens = n/3) equals two. Half of six (semissis = n/2) equals three. Two-thirds of six (bessis = 2n/3) equal four. Five-sixths of six (pentemoiros = 5n/6) equal five, and the complete number, the perfect number, is six. Now, if one increases the numbers in the direction of double six, by adding another unit, that is another sixth

of six (n + n/6), one obtains seven, called *ephekton*, when eight is reached, by the addition of another third of six to six (n + n/3), the sesquitertium (4:3) is obtained, which is called *epitritos*; adding one-half of six to six (n + n/2), which makes nine units, yields sesquialterum (3:2), which is called *hemiolios*. Adding two more units to make the decad (n + 2n/3) yields bes alterum, which they call *epidimoiros*; in the number eleven, because five units have been added (n + 5n/6), a fifth is made which is called *epipemptos*, but twelve, which is made by two whole numbers (i.e., 2 × 6; also 6 + 6) is called "the double," *diplasios*.

7. They also hold that number perfect because, just as the foot occupies the sixth part of human height, so, too, the number that brings the dimension of the feet to completion, when multiplied by six, delimits the height of the body. Furthermore, the ancients observed that the cubit is composed of six palms and twenty-four digits. On the basis of these observations, it seems that the Greek cities have made it a rule that just as a cubit consists of six palms, so in the drachma, which they would use as a coin, there should be six equal stamped bronze coins, like our pounds, which they called obols, and to have decided on quarter-obols, which some cities call *dicalcha* and several call *tricalcha*, with twenty-four in the drachma, in due ratio to the fingers as these correspond to the palm. 8. It was our ancestors who first fixed on the ancient number and invented the denarius of ten pounds, and this is why the name of our coinage to this day is *denarius*.* And the quarter-denarius, which is composed of two and one-half pounds, they called a *sestertius*. Later, when they had observed that both numbers, six and ten, were perfect, they combined them to obtain the most perfect number of all (i.e., sixteen). The source of this discovery was the foot. For if two palms are subtracted from a cubit, a foot measuring four palms is left, and the palm, of course, is formed of four digits. Thus it came about that the foot measures sixteen digits, and the bronze denarius, likewise, is composed of sixteen pounds.

9. Therefore, if it is agreed that from the limbs of the human body number was discovered, and also the fact that a correspondence of dimension exists among individual elements and the appearance of the entire body in each of its parts, then it is left for us to recognize that the ancients, who also established the houses of the immortal gods, ordered the elements of those works so that, in both their shape and their symmetries, fitting dimensions of separate elements and of the work as a whole might be created.

CHAPTER 2: TEMPLE TYPES
(FIGURE 39)

1. With temples, the first principles are those that determine the appearance of the plans. First there is the temple **in antis**, which is called *naos en parastasin* in Greek; then there are **prostyle**, **amphiprostyle**, **peripteral**, **pseudodipteral**, **dipteral**, and **hypaethral** temples.* Their forms are developed according to the following principles.

2. A temple is called **in antis** when its facade includes the ends of the walls which enclose its cella, and in between these two wall ends (antae) are two columns, on top of which a gable should be set in place according to the symmetries that shall be laid out in the present book. An example of this type of temple may be found at the sanctuary of the Three Fortunae; of the three temples, it is the one closest to the Porta Collina.

3. **Prostyle** temples have all the features of a temple in antis, but they also have two corner columns in front of the antae, and over them epistyles like those of the temple in antis, and two single columns on the sides to the right and left. An example is the temple of Jupiter and Faunus on the Tiber Island.

4. The **amphiprostyle** temple has all the features of the prostyle temple, but in addition it has the same sort of columns and gable in the back.

5. The **peripteral** temple will have six columns in the front and six in the rear, and, with the corner columns, eleven down each side. These columns should be placed so that there is a space, equal to the width of an intercolumniation, extending all around the walls to the outer edge of the rank of columns, so that there will be a walkway around the cella of the temple just as there is in the temple of Jupiter Stator in the Porticus Metelli, by Hermodorus, and in the temple of Honos and Battlecourage, made by Mucius next to the Mariana, which has no rear porch.*

6. A **pseudodipteros**, in turn, is so designed that there are eight columns each in front and rear, while on each side, counting the corner columns, there are fifteen. The walls of the cella should be opposite the four central columns of the front and rear. Thus the space between the cella walls and the outer edges of the rows of columns will be equal to two intercolumniations plus the thickness of a single column. There is no example of such a temple in Rome, but the temple of Diana in Magnesia, by Hermogenes,* and the temple of Apollo

at Alabanda executed by Menesthenes are of this type (Figure 40).*

7. The **dipteros** has eight columns front and back, but around the building it has two rows of columns, like the Doric temple of Quirinus, and the Ionic temple of Diana at Ephesus, set up by Chersiphron.

8. The **hypaethral** temple has ten columns across front and rear. All its other features are like those of the dipteros, but on the interior there are two rows of columns on the upper level, standing free from the walls all the way around to form a walkway as in the porticoes of peristyle courtyards. The central part, open to the heavens, is roofless. Folding doorways give access on either side of both the front and the back porch of these temples. There is no example of this type in Rome either, but in Athens there is an octastyle example in the temple of the Olympian [Jupiter].

CHAPTER 3: THE SPECIES OF TEMPLES

1. The species of temples are five, for which these are the terms: **pycnostyle**, that is, with close-set columns, **systyle**, with a slightly more ample intercolumnar space, **diastyle**, even more widely spaced, **araeostyle**, when the columns stand further apart than is desirable, and **eustyle**, when their placement is right (Figure 41).*

2. Thus **pycnostyle** is when one and one-half the thickness of a column can be put into the intercolumniation, as occurs in the temple of Deified Julius and the temple of Venus in the Forum of Caesar, and any others that are similarly designed.

Systyle, likewise, is a temple in which the thickness of two columns can be placed in the intercolumniation, while the plinths of the bases are equal in measure to the space between two plinths, as occurs in the temple of Equestrian Virtue (Fortune) by the stone theater and in any other temple that is composed according to this principle.

Each of these types is defective in its function. When matrons climb the steps of the pycnostyle temple to make their prayers, they cannot walk arm in arm through the intercolumniations; they must go in single file. Furthermore, the view of the doorways is blocked by the close placement of the columns, and the cult statues themselves are half hidden; also, because of the restricted space, movement round the temple portico is hindered.

4. The **diastyle** temple is composed so that we may put the breadth of three columns in the intercolumnar space, just as occurs in the temple of Apollo and Diana. This design has the following difficulty: because of the wide intercolumnar space the epistyle has a tendency to break.

5. It is not possible to make an **araeostyle** temple with epistyles in stone or marble; instead, above the columns wooden beams must be placed all round. The appearance of these temples is splayed, top heavy, low, and sprawling, while their roofs are decorated with terracotta ornaments or gilded bronze in Etruscan style, as in the temple of Ceres near the Circus Maximus, the temple of Hercules built by Pompey, and also the Capitoline Temple.

6. Now it is time to describe the system of the **eustyle** temple, which is the most laudable, and has principles developed with an eye to usefulness, attractiveness, and soundness. In the intercolumniations a space should be left which is equal to two-and-one-quarter times the thickness of a column, with the middle intercolumniation, both in front and back, equal to three times the thickness of a single column. Thus the building's design will have an attractive appearance, its unimpeded entrance, utility, and the walkway around the cella, authority.

7. This is how the system for such a building is developed: the front of the site to be occupied by the temple, if it is to be tetrastyle, should be divided into eleven and one-half parts, not counting the steps and the projection of the bases; if there are to be six columns across, divide into eighteen parts. If it is to be octastyle, divide it into twenty-four and one-half. Whether the temple is to be tetrastyle, or hexastyle, or octastyle, one of these units should be adopted, and it will be the **module**. This module is equal to the thickness of a column. The individual intercolumniations, except for the central one, measure two and one-quarter modules. The central intercolumniation, both front and rear, is three modules in breadth. The height of the individual columns is nine and one-half modules. From this calculation the intercolumniations and the heights of the columns will have the proper proportion. 8. There are no examples of such proportions in Rome, but in Asia, in Teos, they occur in the hexastyle temple of Father Liber.

Hermogenes established these symmetries; he was also the first to invent the eight-columned or pseudodipteral temple. From the proportional system [symmetry] of the dipteral temple he removed the inner row of thirty-four columns, and in that way he saved expense and labor. With great effect, he made room for a walkway around the cella, and did so without detracting in the slightest from the building's outward appearance; indeed, he preserved the dignity of the work as a whole with regard to its allocation of parts, and did so without our feeling the loss of what would have been superfluous.

9. Thus principles for the portico and the placement of the columns around the temple have been invented such that their severity lends authority to the building, and furthermore if the force of a downpour should surprise a large group of people and compel them to shelter under the portico, the added space will give them ample room to circulate in the temple and around the cella. These observations will explain the design of pseudo-dipteral temples. Thus one can see that Hermogenes had achieved great effects in his works, with acute and abundant skill, and that he has left behind him springs of knowledge from which subsequent generations may drink deeply of the principles of our profession.

10. The columns in an araeostyle temple should be made in such a way that their diameter is equal to one-eighth their height. In the diastyle temple the height of the column should be divided into eight and one-half parts, with the diameter of the column equal to one part. In the systyle temple the height should be divided by nine and one-half and one of these parts should be equal in measure to the diameter of the column. Likewise, in the pycnostyle, the height of the columns should be divided into ten parts with the diameter of the column equal to one of these parts. The height of the column of the eustyle temple, as with the systyle, should be divided into nine-and-one-half parts, and one of these units should be equal to the diameter of the bottom of the shaft. Thus the ratios of the intercolumniations will obtain for every part [of the temple].

11. The larger the space between the columns, the greater the diameters of the shafts must be (Figure 42). For if an araeostyle temple had columns whose diameters were equal to one-ninth or one-tenth the height of the column, the building would seem flimsy and inconsequential, because all along the intercolumnal spaces the air itself seems to diminish the apparent thickness of the shafts. In pycnostyle temples, by contrast, if the diameters of the columns were one-eighth of their height, what with the closeness and narrowness of the intercolumniations, the appearance of the building would be swollen and unattractive.

Thus the proportional system for each type of work should be fully observed. The corner columns, moreover, must be made thicker than the others by one-fiftieth of their diameter, because they are cut into by air on all sides and therefore seem more slender to the viewer. Thus where the eye deceives us, reasoning must compensate.

12. The neck contraction of the uppermost surface of the columns, it seems, must be made so that if the column measures up to fifteen feet, the diameter at the bottom should be divided into six parts and the diameter at the top should measure five of these parts (Figure 43). Again, if a column ranges from fifteen to twenty feet, the bottom of the shaft should be divided into six-and-one-half parts and the uppermost diameter of the column should measure five-and-one-half of these units. And again, for columns that measure between twenty and thirty feet, the bottom of the shaft should be divided into seven parts and the uppermost diameter should be contracted to measure six of these parts. A column that is between thirty and forty feet high should be divided at its base into seven-and-one-half parts, and the uppermost diameter should be contracted to six-and-one-half of these parts. Those columns that are between forty and fifty feet high should likewise be divided into eight parts, and the top of the shaft just below the capital should be contracted into seven of these parts. And if columns are higher than this, their contraction should be established to scale according to the same principle.

13. These adjustments to the diameter are added because of the extent of the distance for the ascending glance of our eyes.[1] For our vision always pursues beauty, and if we do not humor its pleasure by the proportioning of such additions to the modules in order to compensate for what the eye has missed, then a building presents the viewer with an ungainly, graceless appearance. At the end of the present book I shall record the illustration and method for the addition made to the middles of columns, which is called *entasis* (bowing) by the Greeks, and how to execute this refinement in a subtle and pleasing way (Figure 44).*

CHAPTER 4: TEMPLE CONSTRUCTION

1. The foundations of these works should be sunk down to solid ground and in solid ground, if it can be found, as much as seems reasonable for the size of the

---

1 Taking *species*, with Lucretius, as "gaze" or "glance," and reading a problematic passage, with Rose, as *scandente oculi specie*.

work, and the whole site should be built up with rubble work as solidly as possible.* Above ground level, walls should be constructed underneath the columns, half again as thick as the columns are to be, so that the lower parts of the building will be more stable than the upper parts. For this reason these walls are also called "ground-walkers," stereobates, because they bear the weight of the building. The bases of the columns should not project beyond the solid part of the substructure. Above this level, the thickness of the wall should be kept constant, and the spaces in between should either be vaulted over or rammed with fill in order to stabilize them.

2. But if it is not possible to find solid ground, and instead the site is on fill all the way to bedrock, or swampy, then the area should be dug out as much as possible, cleared, and reinforced with pilings of elder, olive, or oak that have been hardened by fire, and the palisade of pilings should be driven into place by machinery to be as densely packed as possible. The spaces between the pilings should be filled with charcoal, and thereafter the foundations should be filled with the most solid rubble work possible.

Once the foundations have been built up to the level, the stylobates should be placed. 3. The columns should be set on the stylobate according to the descriptions given earlier: if pycnostyle, then according to pycnostyle proportions, if diastyle, systyle, or eustyle, then they should be designed and placed just as we have already established and recorded. In araeostyle temples there is as much liberty as one likes in establishing the proportions. But the columns in a peripteral temple should be placed so that however many intercolumniations there are across the front, there should be exactly twice this number of intercolumniations along the sides. And thus the length of the temple will be twice its breadth. (Those who made double numbers of columns seem to have been in error, because there seems to be one more intercolumniation then there ought to be, that is, one ends up with one too many intercolumniations along the sides.)

4. The steps in the front should be constructed so that they are always an odd number (Figure 45).* In this way, if one begins to mount the temple steps with the right foot, it is again the right foot that will step into the temple proper. I think that the height of the steps should be made so that they are no greater than five-sixths of a foot and no less than three-fourths; in this way, the ascent will not be difficult. The treads of the steps should be no less than one-and-one-half feet wide and no more than two feet. If there are to be steps all around the temple, they should be made in exactly the same way.

But if there will be a podium on three sides of the temple it should be constructed so that the plinth, base molding, dado, cornice, and lysis fit the stylobate beneath the column bases.* The stylobate should be leveled so that in the middle it has an increment provided by the *scamilli impares* (Figure 46).* For if it is constructed exactly on the level, it will appear somewhat hollowed to the eye. At the end of the present book, the way in which the scamilli can be made to achieve this effect will be set out, both by means of a figure and by a demonstration of how to design them.

CHAPTER 5: IONIC COLUMN BASES, CAPITALS, AND ENTABLATURES

1. Once all these operations have been carried out, the bases can be placed in their proper locations, and this is how they should be finished to fit the symmetry: the height including the plinth should equal half the diameter of the column, and that projection which the Greeks call *ekphorá* should protrude enough so that the base will be as long and as wide as one and one-half times the diameter of a column (Figure 47).

2. If the base is going to be in the Attic style, then it should be divided off so that the upper part will measure one-third the diameter of a column, and the rest will be taken up by the plinth. Discounting the plinth, the rest of the base should be divided into four parts, of which the upper torus should measure one part, and the remaining three parts should be divided equally between the lower torus and the scotia with its fillets, which the Greeks call *trochilos*.* 3. If, on the other hand, the bases are to be made in the Ionic style, then their symmetries should be set up so that the width of the base on every side will measure one and three-eighths the diameter of the column. Its height should be calculated as if it were an Attic base, just like that of the plinth.[2] The rest of the base, not including the plinth, which should equal one-third the diameter of a column, should be divided into seven parts. Then the three uppermost parts ought to be reserved for the upper torus. The remaining four parts should be divided equally so that one part with its astragal and fillet becomes the upper trochilus, and the

2 Reading MSS *ita ut* rather than Giocondo's *ita et*.

remaining part should be left to the lower trochilus, but the lower part will seem larger inasmuch as it will project as far as the very margin of the plinth. The astragals should be made so that they are the eighth part of the trochilus. The projection (ekphorá) of the base should measure three-sixteenths of the thickness of the column.

4. Once the bases have been completed and set in place, the middle columns of the front and back porches should be set with their center axes vertical. Next set the corner columns and those that are to lead from them down the side of the temple to left and right, so that the surfaces facing the cella walls will be vertical, and the exterior surfaces will be contracted as has been stated before (Figure 48). For in this way the pattern of contraction in the composition of temples will be carried out according to proper procedure.

5. Once the shafts of the columns have been set up, this is the principle for their capitals (Figure 49).* If they are going to be Ionic, they will conform to the following symmetries: whatever the lower diameter of the shaft is to be, plus one-eighteenth part of that diameter, this is the length and width that the abacus will have. The height of the capital, including its volutes, will be half that measure. The fronts of the volutes must be set back from the outermost edge of the abacus toward the interior part by three-thirty-sixths of a column diameter. Next, the height is to be divided into nine and one-half parts. 6. At the outermost margin of the abacus, following along its edge, perpendicular lines are to be dropped in each sector of the volutes; these are called cathetoe. Then, of the nine and one-half parts, one and one-half are left as the thickness of the abacus, and the remaining eight are assigned to the volutes.

Next, after the line that has been dropped along the outermost edge of the abacus, another vertical should be dropped which is set inward from it by one part and a half [of the nine and one-half]. These lines should then be divided in such a way that four and one-half parts [of the remaining eight] are left under the abacus. The center of the oculus should be set at the division between the four and one-half parts and the remaining three and one-half. From this center a circle should be drawn, as large in diameter as one of the eight parts. This will be the size of the oculus; let its diameter be drawn to correspond to the cathetus. Then, beginning from the top of the axis beneath the abacus and circling around, reduce each successive axis by half the diameter of the oculus, until one finishes at the axis beneath the abacus.*

7. The height of the capital is to be made so that of nine and one-half parts, three overlap beneath the astra-

gal at the top of the shaft, and the remaining part should be reserved for the molding, minus the abacus and canalis. The molding should have a projection beyond the square of the abacus that equals the size of the oculus. The straps on the side of the capital should project this far beyond the abacus: if one point of the compass is placed at the midpoint of the capital and one is taken out to the edge of the molding, when the compass is brought around, it will touch the extreme parts of the straps. Let the axes of the volutes be no thicker than the size of the oculus, and the volutes themselves should be hollowed out to one-twelfth part of their height. These will be the symmetries of the capitals, and they will serve for any column from the smallest up to twenty-five feet. Columns above this size will have symmetries of the same sort for the rest of their proportions, but the abacus will be as long and as wide as the bottom of the column with one-eighth added on, because to the extent that there is less contraction for a taller column, there should be correspondingly more projection included in the proportioning of the capital, with the increment to this element coming, properly, at the summit.

8. As for drawing the volutes so that they are properly coiled with the use of a compass, and the way they are drawn, the form and the principle for these will be set down at the end of the book (Figure 50).

Once the capitals of the columns have been completed, then they should be set, not on the level, but according to a uniform unit such that whatever addition was made to the stylobate repeats in the upper elements. The principle for designing the epistyles should be as follows: if the columns are at least twelve and up to fifteen feet, the height of the epistyle should be half the diameter of the bottom of the column.* If the column is between fifteen and twenty feet, the height of the column should be measured out into thirteen parts, and the height of the epistyle will equal one of these parts. If the column is between twenty and twenty-five feet, the height should be divided into twelve and one-half parts, and one of these parts should be made into the measure of the height of the epistyle; if the column is between twenty-five and thirty feet, it should be divided into twelve parts, and let the epistyle be one of these parts in height. If the columns are higher than this, the height of the epistyle for each part should be derived from the height of the column in the same way. 9. For when the eye's glance* is directed higher and higher, it penetrates the density of the air with greater difficulty; therefore it falls away, drained by the extent and force of the altitude, and reports back an uncertain assessment of dimension to the senses. For which reason an increment must always be added on to the elements of the proportional system, so that when works are carried out in lofty sites or are themselves colossal, they have a method behind their dimensions.

10. The breadth of the epistyle at its lowermost edge, which will lie directly over the capital, should be made so that it is as thick as the diameter of the top of the columns directly underneath the capital; its thickness at the uppermost edge should be equal to the diameter of the bottom of the shaft (Figure 51).* The molding of the epistyle should be made to equal the seventh part of its total height, and should project to the same degree.* The rest of the epistyle, not counting the molding, should be divided into twelve parts. The lowermost fascia should be made of three of these parts, the second fascia of four, and the upper fascia of five. Likewise, the frieze over the epistyle should be smaller by one-fourth than the epistyle itself, unless one intends to decorate it with little figures, and then it should be taller by one-fourth than the epistyle, so that the sculptures will be imposing. Its molding should be one-seventh the height of the frieze, and its projection should equal its height.
11. Over the frieze the dentils should be made as high as the middle fascia of the epistyle, and their projection should equal their height.

The intersection which is called *metopê* in Greek should be so divided that the height of the dentils should occupy one-half of its height along the front, and the hollow of this intersection on the front should occupy two parts out of three; its molding will occupy one-sixth of its height. The fascia of the cornice, with its molding but without its sima, will be equal in measure to the middle fascia of the epistyle, and the projection of the cornice with the dentils should be made to equal the height from the frieze to the top of the molding of the cornice, and, in any event, the projections are always more attractive when they equal the height.
12. The height of the tympanum in the gable should be made such that the entire front of the cornice, from the outermost molding, is divided into nine parts, and one of these parts should be established as the midline to the peak of the tympanum; to this the epistyles and the necks of the columns should stand perpendicular. The raking cornices above should be placed in the same way

as the lower, except for the simas. Above the cornices, the simas, which the Greeks call *epaietides*, should be made higher by one-eighth than the height of the cornices. The corner acroteria should be as high as the midline of the tympanum, and the central acroteria taller by one-eighth than those at the corners.

13. All the elements to be placed above the capitals of the columns, that is, the epistyles, friezes, cornices, tympana, raking cornices, and acroteria, should have a front surface that inclines outward to one-twelfth its own height. This is why: when we stand opposite any facade, and two lines might be extended from our eye so that one would touch the lower margin of any part of the building, and the other touch the very top, that line which reaches the upper margin will be the longer of the two. Inasmuch as a longer line of sight extends to the upper part of the building, it will make it seem to tilt backward. But if, as we have stated earlier, the elements of the facade are made to incline, they will seem perfectly vertical to the viewer.

14. The flutes of the columns should be twenty-four, and hollowed out in such a way that when a set square is put into the hollow of the flute and rotated, the point of the set square will touch the right and left margins of the flute as it pivots (Figure 53).* The width of the flutes should be equal to the entasis, which has been added to the center of the column and derived on the basis of the drawing we have supplied.

15. On the simas that are placed above the cornices along the sides of the building, lion heads should be sculpted, placed so that a lion head appears over every column; the rest should be evenly spaced so that an individual lion head corresponds to the center of an individual pan tile of the roof (Figure 54).* Those lion heads that align with the columns should be pierced to form a channel, which will receive rainwater from the roof. Those in between should be solid, so that the force of the rainwater falling along the tiles and into the channels will not be cast out between the intercolumniations and drench the people entering the temple; rather, it will seem that those lions' heads which are in line with the columns are spewing forth spurts of water from their mouths.

In this volume, I have recorded as clearly as I could the design of Ionic temples, and in the following book I shall describe the Doric and Corinthian proportional systems.

❖

CORINTHIAN, DORIC, AND TUSCAN TEMPLES

PREFACE

1. When I had become aware, Imperator, that many writers had left behind them precepts and volumes of commentaries on architecture that were not set in proper order but taken up instead as if they were stray particles, I thought it would be a worthy and most useful contribution, first to set out the whole of such an excellent discipline in its full order and then in each volume to explain the particular qualities of each type of subject. And so, Caesar, in the first volume I told you about the duties of an architect and the subjects in which an architect ought to be well educated. In the second I discussed the supply of materials from which buildings are constructed. In the third volume, then, I offered instruction about the design of temples, and about the variety of their types, which species they have and how many, and what the distribution of the various components ought to be according to type. Of those three types whose proportions exhibit the most intricate modular systems, I taught the conventions of the Ionic. Now, in the present volume, I will speak about what have been set up as the Doric and Corinthian principles, and explain their distinctness and their special characteristics.

CHAPTER 1: THE DISCOVERY OF SYMMETRIES*

1. Except for the capitals, Corinthian columns have proportional systems like those of Ionic columns. The height of the Corinthian capital, however, makes these columns appear proportionately taller and more slender, because the height of the Ionic capital is one-third the diameter of the column, whereas that of the Corinthian measures the entire diameter of the shaft. Therefore, because the Corinthian capital is taller by two-thirds of a column diameter, its appearance, with this added height,

is more slender (Figure 55). 2. The rest of the elements that are placed over the columns may be designed either according to Doric symmetries or Ionic conventions, because the Corinthian type itself has not had its own set rule for the cornices or for the rest of its ornamentation, so that the building may either be designed with the arrangement of triglyphs and mutules for the cornice and guttae along the epistyle, in the Doric fashion, or it may be designed according to Ionic rules* with a sculpted frieze, dentils, and moldings. 3. Thus by the introduction of a third capital a third type has developed out of the two types used for building projects. The names of the three types are based on the formation of the columns: Doric, Ionic, and Corinthian, of which the Doric was the first to occur and did so in ancient times.

Dorus, the son of Hellen and the nymph Phthia, ruled Achaea and all of the Peloponnese, and in the ancient city of Argos he built a temple to Juno, a shrine whose shape chanced to be of this type. Thereafter, in other cities of Achaea he built other temples of the same type, although the principle of its symmetries had not yet come into being.

4. The Athenians, spurred by an oracle from Delphi, founded thirteen colonies in Asia at one time with the approval of all the rest of Greece.* They chose leaders for each of the colonies, and gave supreme authority to Ion, the son of Xuthus and Creusa. Apollo of Delphi had proclaimed Ion as his own son in oracular responses. Now Ion took these colonies into Asia and occupied the territory of Caria as well, and there he founded the great cities of Ephesus, Myus (which was long ago swallowed up by water, and whose holy places and voting rights the Ionians turned over to the Milesians), Priene, Samos, Teos, Colophon, Chios, Erythrae, Phocaea, Clazomenae, Lebedos, and Melite. This Melite, because of the arrogance of her citizens, was destroyed in a war declared by these cities in joint deliberation, and afterward, in its place, the city of Smyrna was received into the Ionian League, thanks to the good offices of King Attalus and Queen Arsinoë. 5. These cities, once they

had expelled the Carians and Leleges, called this region of the earth Ionia after Ion their leader, and establishing sacred precincts there, they began to build shrines. First of all, they decided to build a temple for Panionian Apollo like the ones they had seen in Achaea, and they called this temple "Doric" because they had first seen a temple of this type in the cities of the Dorians.* 6. When they had decided to set up columns in this temple, lacking symmetries for them, and seeking principles by which they might make these columns suitable for bearing loads yet properly attractive to behold, they measured a man's footprint and compared it with his height. When they discovered that for a man, the foot is one-sixth of his height, they applied this ratio to the column, and whatever diameter they selected for the base of the column shaft, they carried its shaft, including the capital, to a height six times that amount. Thus the Doric column came to exhibit the proportion, soundness, and attractiveness of the male body.

7. After this, the Ionians also built a temple to Diana; seeking a new type of appearance, they applied the same ratio based on footprints to a woman's slenderness, and began making the diameter of the columns measure one-eighth their height, so that their appearance would be more lofty. Instead of a shoe, they put a spira underneath as a base, and for the capital, as if for hair, they draped volutes on either side like curled locks. The front they adorned with moldings and festoons arranged in the place of tresses, and they let flutes down the whole trunk of the column to mimic, in matronly manner, the folds of a stola. Thus they derived the invention of columns from two sets of criteria: one manly, without ornament, and plain in appearance, the other of womanly slenderness, ornament, and proportion (Figure 56).

8. Later generations, more advanced in the elegance and subtlety of their aesthetic judgment, who delighted in more attenuated proportions, established that the height of the Doric column should be seven times the measure of its diameter, and the Ionic column should be nine times the width.* For that type of column is called Ionic, because it was first made by the Ionians.

DISCOVERY OF CORINTHIAN SYMMETRIES

Now the third type, which is called Corinthian, imitates the slenderness of a young girl, because young girls, on account of the tenderness of their age, can be seen to have even more slender limbs and obtain even more charming effects when they adorn themselves (Figure 57). 9. It is said that the invention of this type

of capital occurred in the following manner.* A young Corinthian girl of citizen rank, already of marriageable age, was struck down by disease and passed away. After her burial, her nurse collected the few little things[1] in which the girl had delighted during her life, and gathering them all in a basket, placed this basket on top of the grave. So that the offering might last there a little longer, she covered the basket with a roof tile.

This basket, supposedly, happened to have been put down on top on an acanthus root. By springtime, therefore, the acanthus root, which had been pressed down in the middle all the while by the weight of the basket, began to send out leaves and tendrils, and its tendrils, as they grew up along the sides of the basket, turned outward; when they met the obstacle of the corners of the roof tile, first they began to curl over at the ends and finally they were induced to create coils at the edges. 10. Callimachus, who was called "Katatexitechnos" by the Athenians for the elegance and refinement of his work in marble,[2] passed by this monument and noticed the basket and the fresh delicacy of the leaves enveloping it. Delighted by the nature and form of this novelty, he began to fashion columns for the Corinthians on this model, and he set up symmetries, and thus he drew up the principles for completing works of the Corinthian type.

CORINTHIAN SYMMETRIES

11. This is how to achieve the symmetry for this capital: whatever the diameter of the base of the column, the same unit should be the height of the capital with its abacus (Figures 58–59). The width of the abacus should observe this principle: whatever the height of the capital will be, there should be two diagonals of that length from one corner [of the abacus] to the other. In this way each face of the capital will have a properly proportioned appearance. Each of these faces should curve inward from the corner of the abacus by one-ninth the breadth of its face. The bottom of the capital will have the same diameter as the top of the column, not including its apophysis and astragal. The height of the abacus is one-seventh the height of the capital.

12. If the height of the abacus is set aside, the rest of the capital should be divided into three parts, of which

1 Reading MSS *poculis* as a version of *pauculis* along the lines of *plostrum* for *plaustrum*.

2 This reading from Pliny, *NH* 34.92; MSS have *Catatechnos* = "thoroughly skilled."

one should be assigned to the lowermost leaf. The second leaf should take up the middle space. The stalks (cauliculi) should have the same height; from these stalks sprout projecting leaves which take up the line of the tendrils that sprout from the stalks and extend to the very corners of the abacus. Smaller tendrils should be carved between them, in the middle of the capital underneath the flower on the abacus. The flowers on all four sides should be made as large as the height of the abacus. With these symmetries, Corinthian capitals will attain their standard.

There are, however, types of capitals that are put on the same columns yet called by different names. I am not able to give the special qualities of their symmetries, nor for that matter to name the types of columns, but it seems to me that their vocabulary has been drawn and modified from Corinthian, Ionic, and Doric, whose symmetries have been adapted to the refinement of new types of carving.

CHAPTER 2: ARCHITECTURAL ORNAMENT

1. Now, because the origins and invention of the three types of columns have been described earlier, I think it not out of place to talk about the ornaments of these types of architecture according to these same principles: that is, how they came about and by what first principles and origins they were discovered (Figure 60).*

In every building woodwork is put above the columns; this is called by a variety of names. Just as it has different names, so this woodwork has different purposes in the building. Beams are put over columns, pilasters, and antae, and joists and decking are put in floor structures. Under the roof, if there is a very large space, there are also tie beams and braces; if the space is comfortable, then the ridgepole and principal rafters should project to the edge of the eaves. Above the principal rafters, the purlins, and above these, underneath the roof tiles, the common rafters should overhang enough that the walls are protected by their projection.

2. And thus each element preserves its proper place, type, and order. Drawing from these elements and from the art of carpentry and applying them to the construction of sacred dwellings in stone and marble, craftsmen imitated these arrangements in their sculptures and agreed that these inventions ought to be adopted. The craftsmen of old, building in some place or another,

placed joists that protruded from the interior walls to the outer edges [of the buildings]. They built in between the joists and above them decorated the cornices and eaves with fine carpentry for a more attractive appearance. Subsequently they decided that these projecting joists should be cut off where they protruded beyond the plane of the walls, and because the result looked unattractive to them, they fitted plaques in front of the cuttings, which were shaped as triglyphs are made today, and they painted these with blue wax so that the cut ends of the joists would not offend the viewer (Figure 61).

And thus the covered sections of the joists in Doric works began to take on the arrangement of the triglyphs and, between the joists, the metopes. 3. Afterward various architects in various other buildings extended the projecting beams perpendicular to the triglyphs and leveled off the projections. From this, just as triglyphs derived from the arrangement of beams, so from the projection of the rafters the principle of mutules beneath the cornice was discovered. This is generally what happens in stone and marble works, in which the mutules are reshaped by slanted cutting, because they are an imitation of the rafters. Furthermore, they are placed of necessity at an angle because of rainfall. Thus, for Doric works the principle underlying the triglyphs and mutules was derived from these imitations.

4. Indeed, it is impossible that it happened the way some previous authors have said, mistakenly — that triglyphs are imitations of windows. Triglyphs are placed at the corners of a building and atop the centers of the columns, places where it is inadmissible to put windows. Indeed, if the open space for windows were left at the corners of a building, the joins at the corners would be destroyed. Moreover, if it were thought that the places where triglyphs occur now were supposed to have been window spaces, then by the same principle, the dentils in Ionic friezes ought to have taken the place of windows as well, because the intervals between both dentils and triglyphs are called metopes.

Now the Greeks call the beds of the joists and of the common rafters *opai*, just as we call these hollows "dovecotes" (*columbaria*). Accordingly, the space between two ceiling beams, which is, in other words, the space between two *opai*, is called *metope* in their language. 5. Just as the principle of triglyphs and mutules was discovered for Doric buildings, likewise in Ionic buildings the placement of dentils has its own underlying principle, and just as the mutules preserve the image of the projecting principal rafters, so in Ionic buildings the dentils imitate the projection of the common rafters. And thus in Greek construction no one ever puts dentils under a mutule, because there simply cannot be common rafters beneath major rafters (Figure 60).* Therefore, what in reality ought to be put above the rafters and purlins, if – even in imitation – it were to be put underneath, it would falsify the whole structural principle of the building. And so the ancient builders never approved, nor even so much as executed mutules or dentils on eaves, but only plain cornices, because neither chief rafters nor minor rafters are placed along a raking facade. Neither can they simply project outward; they must be placed on a slant to face the rain gutters.

And therefore they felt that there was no rationale for making an image of what would never obtain in fact. 6. For in the proper completion of their works, they expressed everything as it certainly was, drawn from the true customs of Nature, and they approved those things of which the explanations, when examined, can be shown to possess the ground of truth. And thus from these origins the ancient builders bequeathed us the established symmetries and proportions for each individual type of architecture, and following their precedent I have discussed the Ionic and Corinthian conventions. Now I shall briefly lay out the Doric proportional system and summarize its appearance.

CHAPTER 3: DORIC SYMMETRIES

1. Some ancient architects have claimed that temples should not be made in the Doric type because the proportional system was inevitably faulty and inharmonious. Arcesius was one of these, likewise Pytheos, and Hermogenes as well.* In fact, Hermogenes, once he had already acquired a supply of marble to complete a Doric temple, changed his mind and made this temple an Ionic shrine to Father Liber. He did not do this because the species and the type of Doric are unattractive, or because it lacks dignity of form, but because it is restrictive and inconvenient in working out the distribution of triglyphs and the spaces between them (Figure 62).*

2. Triglyphs must of necessity be placed in line with the center axes of the columns, and the metopes that are to be set in between the triglyphs ought to be as long as they are high. For the corner columns, however, the triglyphs are placed at the outer margins of the columns and not over their centers. As a result, the metopes that occur next to the corner triglyphs will not

come out square; instead, they are longer than they are high by half the width of a triglyph. But anyone who wants to make all the metopes equal to one another will have to reduce the last intercolumniations by half the breadth of a triglyph. Whatever is done, whether by adjusting the length of the metopes or by contracting the corner intercolumniation, is unsatisfactory. For which reason, the ancient builders appear to have avoided proceeding on the basis of the system of Doric proportions for their temples (Figures 63–65).

3. Now we shall describe these, as order requires it, and as we have understood from our teachers, in such a way that anyone who should want to enter upon such an enterprise and pays attention to the following principles shall have laid out for him the proportions by which he can execute temples in the Doric style that will be without blemish and irreproachable.

The facade of a Doric temple should be divided along the stylobate into twenty-seven parts if the building is going to be tetrastyle; if hexastyle, into forty-two (Figure 66). One of these parts will be the module, which is called *embatêr** in Greek. Once this module has been decided, all the calculations for the proportions of the whole project may be carried out.

4. The diameter of the columns will equal two modules, the height of the columns with their capitals, fourteen. The height of the capital will measure one module, the width two and one-sixth modules. The height of the capital should be divided into three parts, of which one will become the abacus with its molding,* another the echinus with its annulets, the third the neck (hypotrachelion). The columns should be contracted exactly as has been laid down for Ionic columns in the third volume. The height of the epistyle should measure one module including the taenia and guttae, the taenia should measure one-seventh of a module, and the length of the guttae underneath the taenia, in line with the triglyphs, including the regula, should hang downward one-sixth of a module. Likewise, the breadth of the epistyle on its underside should correspond to the top of the column at the neck. Above the epistyle the triglyphs should be set with their metopes, one and one-half modules in height and one module wide across the front; these are divided so that for both the corner columns and the middle columns the triglyphs align with the central axis of the column itself. Two more triglyphs should be placed in each remaining intercolumniation, except for the middle intercolumniation of the front and back porticoes, where the triglyphs should be three. With the center intercolumniation expanded in this

fashion, those who enter the building will have unimpeded access to the cult images of the gods.

5. The breadth of the triglyphs should be divided into six parts; draw five parts in the center of the triglyph with the rule, and two half-parts on either side. Form one "thigh" in the center (what the Greeks call *mêros*), and alongside this sink two little channels using the tip of the set square as a guide. Continuing this sequence, two other "thighs" are set up to the left and right, and then two half channels turn inward (Figure 64).

Once the triglyphs have been set up in this way, the metopes between the triglyphs should be as long as they are high, and at the extreme corners half metopes, half the width of a module,* should be pressed into the frieze. As a result, all the flaws of the metopes, of the intercolumniations, and of the ceiling coffers will be remedied, because they will have been made of equal units (Figure 63).

6. The capitals of the triglyphs should be made to measure one-sixth of a module, and above the capitals of the triglyphs the cornice should be placed so that it projects two-thirds of a module; it has a Doric molding at the bottom and one at the top. Thus the height of the cornice with its moldings will measure half a module.

Next, the course of the viae in the middle of the metopes and the distribution of the guttae should be laid out on the underside of the cornice, perpendicular to the triglyphs so that six guttae are visible along the length and three along the breadth [of the mutules].* The remaining spaces, because the metopes are to be broader than the triglyphs, should be left undecorated or should be sculpted with lightning bolts, and along the very chin of the cornice carve the line called *scotia*. All the rest of the building, the tympana, rain gutters, and cornices, should be completed as has been recorded earlier for Ionic temples.

7. This proportional system will be used for diastyle works. Now if one wants to do a systyle, single-triglyph work (Figure 66),* the facade of the building should be divided into nineteen and one-half parts if it is to be tetrastyle; if hexastyle, divide it into twenty-nine and one-half parts. 8. One of these parts will be the module; everything will be divisible by this unit as recorded earlier. Consequently, both two triglyphs and two metopes should be placed over each epistyle block. At the corners this dimension is broader by half, and this means the space equivalent to a half triglyph. The center intercolumniation, under the pediment, should extend to three triglyphs and three metopes; the temple will have this much more room for those who enter it, as well as allowing a dignified view of the cult statues.

9. The columns should be fluted with twenty flutes. If these are to be flat, they should have twenty angles marked. If, on the other hand, they are to be hollowed out, their form should be made as follows: whatever the span of the flute, a square should be drawn for the fluting whose sides are equal and of this same dimension. Then, in the center of the square set the point of a compass and draw a circle that touches the angles of the square. The difference between the square and the curvature is the amount that should be hollowed out from the flutes. This is the way in which the fluting of a Doric column is carried out appropriately to its type. 10. As for the entasis which is to be added to the center of the column, it should be carried out as prescribed in Book 3 with reference to Ionic columns.

CHAPTER 4: TEMPLE INTERIORS

Now that the external appearance of the Corinthian, Doric, and Ionic proportional systems has been set down, it is necessary also to explain the interiors of cellas and the design of the front portico (Figure 67).

1. The length of the temple is arranged so that its width will equal half its length, and the cella itself will be longer by one-fourth than its width, including the wall in which the doors are to be located. The remaining three parts of the front portico should extend to the antae of the walls, and the antae should have the same thickness as the columns. If the building will be wider than twenty feet across, two columns should be set in between the two antae; this will signal a separation between the space of the front portico and the colonnade. The three intercolumniations between the antae and the columns should be blocked off by parapets of marble or cabinetry, but in such a way that they have doors to provide access to the front portico.

2. If the width of the building is to exceed forty feet, additional columns should be placed on the interior, in line with those between the antae. These columns should have the same height as those on the facade, but their diameters should be diminished by the following principle: if the thickness of the front columns is one-eighth their height, these interior columns should be made so that their thickness is one-tenth their height, but if the front columns are one-ninth or one-tenth their height in diameter, the other principal dimensions should be suitably reduced. If the columns are somewhat elongated, it will not be noticeable in an enclosed

space. If they seem a little too slim, then, if the exterior columns have twenty or twenty-four flutes, give these twenty-eight or thirty-two. Whatever has been subtracted in reality from the body of the column shaft is apparently increased by the additional number of flutes, for the reason that the column's real diameter is less visible. Thus, for quite different reasons, the diameters of exterior and interior columns are brought into balance.

3. This happens because the eye is compelled to make a longer journey where it encounters more numerous and more frequent stimuli (Figure 68).* For if two columns of equal diameter are encircled by lines, and of these columns one is fluted and the other is not, one line makes contact with matter all along the hollows of the channels as well as the edges of the flutes. Thus, even if the columns are equal in diameter, the lines drawn around their perimeters will not be equal, because making the circuit of the edges and channels increases the length of the line that touches them. If this is how things seem to occur, it is not out of place in architectural works to employ narrower proportions for columns in narrow or enclosed spaces, since we have the adjustment of the fluting to come to our assistance.

4. The thickness of the walls of the cella itself should be made in accordance with the other principal dimensions, so long as the antae equal the diameters of the [exterior] columns. If these are to be built of rubble work, let the rubble be as fine as possible. If they are to be made of squared stone or marble, then they should be made of stones dressed most accurately and uniformly, because joins placed in line with the centers of the blocks below make the completion of any work more durable. Dressing the blocks so that they protrude around the beds and joints creates a chiaroscuro that is delightful to look upon.*

CHAPTER 5: ORIENTATION

1. Now the regions that the sacred dwellings of immortal gods should face should be established so that, if there is no impediment and there is unrestricted power to choose, both the temple and the cult statue which is to be housed in the cella should face the western regions of the heavens, so that those who approach with offerings and sacrifices will look toward the image within the temple beneath the eastern part of the heavens; and thus when they are raising their prayers, they will view both the temple and the rising heaven, while the images themselves will seem to be rising as well, to view the supplicants and sacrificers because it seems necessary that all altars of the gods face east (Figure 69).* 2. But if the nature of the site prevents this arrangement, then the layout of the site should be adjusted so that as much as possible of the city walls can be observed from the temples of the gods. If temples are to be erected alongside a river, as happens in Egypt in the region of the Nile, then the temples ought to seem to look toward the riverbanks. Similarly if there are to be temples near public roads, they should be placed so that passersby can take note of them and make their salutations within sight of the divine images.

CHAPTER 6: TEMPLE DOORS AND DOORWAYS

1. Next, these are the principles for designing temple doors and their frames, according to whatever type they are to be; the types of doorways are these: Doric, Ionic, and Attic.

The symmetries of the Doric are observed according to these principles (Figure 70): the uppermost cornice, which is placed above the vertical doorjambs, should be made on a level with the upper edge of the capitals of the columns in the front portico. The opening of the doorway should be designed so that whatever the height of the temple shall be from pavement to ceiling, this dimension should be divided into three and one-half parts. Of these parts, two and one-half should be assigned to the height of the opening. This in turn should be divided into twelve parts; of these, five and one-half should equal the width of the opening at the bottom. At the top of the doorway this space should be contracted so that if from the bottom, the width of the opening measures up to sixteen feet, the contraction equals one-third the measure of the jamb. If the opening measures from sixteen to twenty-five feet, the contraction should equal one-fourth of the jamb, if the space ranges from twenty-five to thirty feet, the upper edge of the opening should contract by one-eighth the measure of the jamb. 2. Those that are to be higher should be designed on the perpendicular.

The vertical jambs themselves should be contracted at the top by one-fourteenth of their thickness. The height of the lintel should equal the thickness of the vertical jambs at their upper margin. The molding should be made to measure one-sixth the thickness of the jamb, and its projection will equal its thickness. This molding, with an astragal, should be sculpted in the Lesbian manner. Above the molding of the lintel, a frieze equal to the height of the lintel should be placed, and on this should be carved a Doric molding and a Lesbian astragal. The uppermost[3] cornice should be carved flat with a molding, and its projection should equal its height. The lintel to be placed over the jambs should project to right and left in such a way that its lower margins are continuous and make a beveled join with the molding itself.

3. If, on the other hand, the doorways are to be made of the Ionic type (Figure 71), it seems that the height of the opening should be determined as for Doric doorways. The breadth should be calculated so that the height is divided into two and one-half parts, and the breadth of the lowermost edge of the opening should measure one part. The contractions are made as for Doric doorways. The thickness of the vertical jambs should equal one-fourteenth the height of the front door opening, and the molding be made to measure one-sixth of the thickness of the jamb. The rest of the jamb, excepting the molding, should be divided into twelve parts. Of these twelve parts, three parts make up the first fascia with its astragal, the second fascia is made to measure four parts, and the third, five. These fasciae, framing the door opening, should also have astragals. 4. The frieze should be composed exactly as for Doric doorways in all the principal dimensions. [Consoles], called "elbows" or "ear-lobes," carved on right and left, should extend down level with the lowest line of the lintel, not including the leaf. On their face, these should have a thickness equal to two-thirds the thickness of the vertical jambs, and at the lowermost part they should be more slender by one-fourth than at the uppermost part.

The doors should be assembled so that the hinge stiles are equal to one-twelfth the breadth of the door opening (Figure 72). In between the two stiles, the panels should each measure three parts out of twelve. 5. The placement of the rails should be such that once their heights have been divided into five parts, two parts should be relegated to the upper rails and three to the lower. The middle rails should be placed over the center of the door; the rest should be placed with some above, and some below. The height of the rails should

be one-third that of the panels, the molding of the rails one-sixth of their height. The breadth of the stiles should measure half that of the rails; the cover joint of the hinges two-thirds the measure of the rails. The stiles next to the vertical jambs should be made half the width of the rails. But if the doors are to have two folding panels, then they will maintain the same height, but to their breadth should be added the breadth of one door opening. If the opening is to have four panels, then the breadth should be increased by the height of the door space.

6. The Attic doorway is brought to completion by the same principles as the Doric (Figure 70). In addition, fasciae should be brought around the jambs below their moldings. These fasciae should be distributed so that if the width of the jambs without their molding is divided into seven parts, each [fascia] occupies two parts out of seven. Attic doorways have neither lattice-work nor double doors, but folding panels, and these should open outward.

To the extent that I was able to achieve my purpose, I have explained, in accordance with custom, by what principles of temple design Doric, Ionic, and Corinthian works should be made. Now I shall tell how a Tuscan design ought to be set up.

CHAPTER 7: THE TUSCAN TEMPLE (FIGURE 73)*

1. Take the site where the temple is to be established; whatever its length, divide this into six parts. Take away one part; assign what remains to the width. Divide the length in two. The inner part will be assigned to the spaces of the cellas. The part next to the facade will be left for the arrangement of the columns. 2. Also divide the width into ten parts. Of these, give over the three parts on the right and left of each one to the minor cellas, or to the wings if there will be wings instead; assign the four remaining parts to the center of the temple. The space that will be in front of the cellas in the front portico should be drawn up with columns in the following way: the corner columns should be placed opposite the antae of the outermost walls. The two center columns should be distributed so that they are opposite the walls between the center of the temple and the antae. Place a second set of columns exactly in the middle between the antae and the first range of columns.

---

3 *sima* MSS, *summa* Pontedera; reading *summa scalpatur* with Rose.

These columns should have a diameter at the bottom that is one-seventh their height; the height should be one-third the breadth of the temple,* and the upper diameter of the column should be contracted by one-fourth of the lower diameter.

3. Make the bases of these columns half as high as the columns are wide. The bases should have a circular plinth, half its breadth in height; above this, the torus with its apophysis should be exactly as high as the plinth. The height of the capital is half its breadth. The width of the abacus is equal to the lowermost diameter of the column. Divide the height of the capital into three parts, of which one is assigned to the plinth that is [contained] in the abacus, one to the echinus, and one to the neck with its apophysis.

4. Above the columns, compound beams should be placed; the module for their height should be appropriate to the size of the work. These compound beams should be set so they have a thickness equal to the upper diameter of the column at the neck, and they should be joined by spacers and clamps in such a way that there is a free space of two digits at the joins. Otherwise, if the beams touch each other and they cannot absorb the sighs and gusts of the winds, they heat up and quickly rot.

5. Above the beams and the walls, the projection of the mutules should extend to one-fourth the height of the columns. On their surfaces revetments should be fixed in place. Above this, the tympanum of the eaves, either of masonry or of wood, should be set in place. Above the eaves, the ridgepole, rafters, and purlins should be placed so that the slope of the roof responds to one-third of its entire run.

CHAPTER 8: ROUND TEMPLES (FIGURE 74)

1. Round temples are also made. Some of these are **monopteroe**, set up with columns but without a cella; others are called **peripteroe**. Those that are made without a cella have a platform* and staircase that measure one-third of the diameter. Above the stylobates columns are placed that are as high as the diameter of the sty-lobates from the outer edge of one wall to the other. The diameter of these columns is one-tenth their height counting the capitals and bases. The epistyle is half a column diameter in height. As for the frieze and the other elements that are placed above it; they are just

as described in Book 3, the book about proportional systems.

2. If, on the other hand, this temple is to be designed as a peripteros, then two steps and a stylobate should be designed from the bottom upward. Then the wall of the cella is placed, and its recession from the edge of the stylobate is about one-fifth of its total diameter. In the fabric of the wall, leave a place for the entrance and the doors. The cella itself, not counting the wall and its surroundings, should have a diameter equal to the height of the column, above the stylobate. The columns should be arranged around the cella with the same symmetries.

3. In the center, this is the principle for the roof: whatever the diameter of the entire work is to be, the height of the tholos should be made to equal half this, not counting the flower. The flower, in turn, should have the same height as a column capital, not counting its pyramid. The rest, it seems, ought to be made with the same symmetries and proportions as described earlier.

HYBRID TEMPLES AND NEW TYPES (FIGURES 75–76)*

4. Likewise, temples are made in other types, their scaling drawn from these same proportional systems, with their design in another type. The temple of Castor in the Circus of Flaminius is like this, and so is the temple of Veiovis-between-two-Groves; even more clearly this is the case for the temple of Diana Nemorensis, where columns have been added to the right and left along the sides of the front portico. It was first made in the same type as the temple of Castor in the Circus, the temple on the Acropolis in Athens, and in Attica, at Sunium, the temple of Pallas Minerva. The proportions of all these are not different from one another, but all the same. The cellas are of a length equal to double their width, as in other temples, and then everything that is usually on the front has been transferred to the sides.

5. Some designers take the column placements from Tuscan types and apply these to the ordering of Corinthian or Ionic works, and in the places where the antae of the front portico project forward, they place pairs of columns opposite the walls of the cella. By so doing, they effect a common reasoning for Tuscan and Greek work.

6. Others, removing the walls of the temple and applying them to the intercolumniations, are able to create a spacious interior for the cella by taking away

the areas reserved for the colonnade. However, in retaining all the other proportions and symmetries they seem to have created a new type of temple – the pseudoperipteros.

These types of temples are adapted for the purposes of sacrificial ritual. Temples should not be made according to the same principles for every god, because each has its own particular procedure for sacred rituals.

7. I have explained all the theories for temple design as they have been passed down to me. I have considered their design sequence and their symmetries item by item, showing, as best I could in my writings, in what respects their forms differ and by what criteria they differ among themselves. Now I shall tell about the altars of the immortal gods, so that they will have a suitable setup for the purposes of sacrifice.

CHAPTER 9: ALTARS

1. Altars should face east, and should always be placed lower than the cult images that will be in the temple, so that those who make supplication and sacrifices may look up at the deity; the heights of these differ and should be designed to fit the dignity of each particular god. Their heights should be set out so that those for Jove and all the other celestial divinities are set as high as possible, whereas they are placed low for Vesta, Earth, and Sea. According to these instructions, suitable designs for altars shall emerge from the planning process.

Now that the composition of temples has been explained in the present book, we shall account for the planning of public buildings in the next.

❖

PUBLIC BUILDINGS

PREFACE

1. Those, Imperator, who have set out their own thoughts and their researches in volumes more lofty than these in style, have contributed the greatest and most outstanding authority to their writings. So, too, with our own enterprise, the subject will obviously prove to be one whose authority would be enhanced by more elevated presentation, but this is not so easy to do as people think. Architectural writing is not like the writing of history or of poetry. Histories by their very nature maintain the interest of their readers; they present the ever-changing anticipation of learning something new. With poems,* on the other hand, it is the meters, the feet, and the elegant placement of words, as well as the varieties of expression adopted by various readers as they take their turns in reading aloud,* that carry our interest along to the end of the composition without a misstep. 2. This is not possible for architectural writing because the terms that have been devised to meet the needs of this art inflict the obscurity of their unfamiliar language on our senses. To begin with, then, these words are neither obvious in themselves nor are their names clear from common use. Furthermore, unless the wide-ranging writings of authorities on this subject have been condensed and expressed in a few, crystal-clear sentences, the density of the prose, not to mention the sheer length of it, confuses readers' minds.

Therefore, as I employ these esoteric names and the proportions derived from the components of architectural projects, I shall explain them briefly so that they may be memorized. In this way, readers' minds shall be able to absorb the information more quickly. 3. And no less emphatically, because I have observed that the city is thronged with people wholly engrossed in their business, public and private,* I have decided that it is better to write concisely, so that people reading in their restricted leisure time may understand these points quickly.

Pythagoras and those who followed his sect decided to write down their precepts using the principle of cubes; they thought that two hundred sixteen lines[1] constituted a cube and that there ought to be no more than three cubes in a single written composition.*

4. Now a cube is a body, squared all round, made up of six sides whose plane surfaces are as long as they are wide. When it is thrown, the part on which it lands (so long as it remains untouched) preserves an immovable stability; the dice that players throw onto the gaming board are like this. The Pythagoreans seem to have taken the image of the [literary] cube from dice, because this particular number of lines, landing like dice on any side whatsoever, will there produce immovable stability of memory. The Greek comic poets divided up the space of their plays by inserting a song by the chorus; defining the parts of the play by the principle of the cube they relieve the actors' speeches with these intervals.

5. Because these practices have been observed by our ancestors in so natural a fashion, and I note that I myself must write about many unusual and obscure matters, I have thought it best to write in short volumes in order best to reach the minds of my readers; in this way things will be readily understood. I have set up the organization of my subjects so that those seeking information will not have to gather it in separate sections — instead, they will have the explanations for each area of interest in one single body of text, and in individual volumes.

Thus, Caesar, in the third and fourth volumes I have demonstrated the principles of temples, and in the present book I shall explain the layout of public places. And first I shall tell where to set up a forum, because there matters both public and private are governed by the magistrates.

1 Emended by Giocondo; MSS read 250.

CHAPTER 1: THE FORUM; BASILICAS

1. The Greeks design fora on a square plan with exceedingly spacious double porticoes (Figure 77); they adorn these with closely set columns and stone or marble epistyles, and on the joists above they make walkways. In the cities of Italy, however, one should not proceed by the same method because from our ancestors we have inherited the custom of giving gladiatorial games in the forum.* 2. For this reason, distribute more spacious intercolumniations around the performance space. In the surrounding porticoes, place the moneychangers' shops and the balconies on the upper stories; then both will be correctly placed for the viewers' convenience and for bringing in revenue.

The dimensions of the forum should be based on the population; its area should neither be too cramped for efficiency nor so large that for lack of population it looks deserted. Make its breadth such that if the length is divided into three parts, two of these parts are assigned to it. Its configuration, then, will be oblong, and its design effective for mounting spectacles. 3. Make the upper columns smaller by one-fourth than the lower, because when it comes to bearing stress, the lower columns should be more substantial than the upper. Do this also because we should imitate the nature of growing things, as in the case of tapering trees, fir, cypress, or pine.[2] Each of these is thicker just above the roots, and then, as it grows upward, by a natural contraction narrows evenly, coming to a point. If the nature of growing things has so required it, then it has also been correctly decided that the upper components of a building be more reduced in their height and thickness than the lower.

4. The sites for basilicas should be chosen next to the forum in the warmest possible location, so that businessmen can meet there without being inconvenienced by bad weather. The widths of these sites should be no less than one-third but no more than one-half their lengths, unless the nature of the site prevents this and forces the builder to adopt another system of proportions. If the site is longer than this, then put Chalcidian porches on the ends, like the ones in the Basilica Julia and the Basilica Aquiliana.

5. The columns of basilicas ought to be made as tall as the porticoes are going to be wide (Figure 78). The

porticoes should be marked off at one-third the area of the central space, whatever that is to be. The upper columns should be made smaller than the lower as described earlier [3:4]. The parapet* between the upper and lower columns ought to be smaller by one-fourth than the upper range of columns, so that those who are walking around on the balconies of the basilica cannot be seen by the businessmen. The epistyles, friezes, and cornices should be laid out in proportion to the columns as we have explained in our third book.

6. Indeed, the planning of basilicas can attain the highest degree of dignified elegance; I myself have designed this type of building in Fano (the Colonia Julia Fanestris), and supervised its construction (Figures 79, 80),* in which the proportions and symmetries have been constituted as follows: the central hall, between the individual columns, is one hundred twenty feet long, and sixty feet wide. Its portico, which surrounds the central hall, is twenty feet wide between columns and walls. The columns are of a uniform height: fifty feet including their capitals, and five feet in diameter. Behind them, they have pilasters twenty feet high, two and one-half feet wide, and one and one-half feet thick. These hold up the beams onto which the upper floor structure of the porticoes is carried. Above these are a second set of pilasters of eighteen feet, two feet wide, one foot thick, and these, too, receive the supporting beams for the rafters and the ceilings of the porticoes[3] that are set underneath the main roof. 7. The areas remaining between the beams spanning columns and pilasters, that is, the areas along the intercolumniations, are left for the windows. The columns along the breadth of the central hall, including the left and right corner columns, number four; along the length nearest the forum, still including the corner columns, eight; on the opposite side, including corner columns, six, because the two central columns along that side have not been set in place; they would block the view from the front portico of the shrine of Augustus, which has been placed at the center of the wall surface of the basilica facing the forum and the temple of Jupiter. 8. The tribunal of this temple is formed on the segment of a hemicycle. The chord of this segment along its face measures forty-six feet, and it curves inward fifteen feet, so that those who are before the magistrates will not interfere with those doing business in the basilica.

---

2 "Tapering trees" for *arboris teretibus* is perhaps Frank Granger's best phrase from the Loeb edition.

3 Reading, with Giocondo, *porticuum* for MSS *porticum*.

Above the columns beams are set all the way around, made of three two-foot timbers fixed together, and these beams turn inward from the third column in on each side toward the antae that project from the pronaos of the shrine; these antae touch the hemicycle on right and left. 9. Above the beams, in line with the capitals of the columns, piers three feet high have been placed as supports; these measure four feet on every side. Above these, outward-sloping beams made of two two-foot timbers have been set in place; above these, in turn, the tie beams with their king posts, placed in line with the bodies of the columns and the antae and the walls of the front portico, come to one ridge over the interior of the basilica, and to a second ridge above the center of the pronaos of the shrine.

10. Thus the double-ridged[4] design of the roof on the exterior and the top of the ceiling on the interior presents an attractive appearance. In addition, the removal of the ornamentation of the epistyles and the apportionment of parapets and upper columns relieves us of labor and annoyance, and greatly reduces the sum total of the expenses. Indeed, the uninterrupted extension of the columns themselves to just under the beams of the roof seems to increase both the magnificence of the expenditure and the authority of the work.

CHAPTER 2: OTHER FEATURES OF THE FORUM

1. The treasury, the jail, and the senate house should be adjoined to the forum, but in such a way that the scale of their symmetries corresponds to that of the forum itself. And certainly, the senate house in particular should be built above all so as to enhance the dignity of the town or city. And if this senate house is going to be square, then whatever its length, its height should be half again as much. If, on the other hand, it is to be oblong, then the length and width should be added together, and half this measure should be given over to the height of the senate house up to the level of the ceiling coffers. 2. The centers of the walls, moreover, should be encircled by cornices of fine woodwork or white stucco, exactly halfway up. Without these cor-

nices, the voices of those debating in the senate house, carried upward, cannot be understood by their listeners. But when the walls are encircled by cornices, the voice, as it rises from below, will be delayed before it carries upward on the air and dissipates; it will be intelligible to the ears.

CHAPTER 3: THEATERS

1. Once the forum has been laid out, then a site should be selected for a theater for watching the entertainments on the feast days of the immortal gods. This site should be as healthful as possible, according to what I have written in my first book about the healthfulness of sites for laying out city walls. For the spectators at plays, sitting from beginning to end with their spouses and children, are held captive by their enjoyment; because of their pleasure their motionless bodies have wide-open pores, in which the breath of the wind can easily take hold.* And if these winds should come from swampy areas or other unhealthful places, they will pour their harmful vapors into the spectators' bodies. And therefore, if the site for a theater is chosen with slightly more care, defects will be avoided. 2. Also make certain that it does not have a direct southern exposure, for when the sun fills up the round hollow of the theater, the air, enclosed by the theater's curvature without the possibility of escape, heats up in its eddying. As it grows to white heat, it begins to burn up, and boils off and thus reduces the moisture in the bodies of the spectators. For these reasons, therefore, defective sites are especially to be avoided and healthy ones to be chosen.

3. The system of foundations will be easier to manage if the site is hilly, but if necessity compels laying foundations in a flat or swampy site, then do the work of consolidation and the substructures as described for the foundations of temples in the third book (Figure 98).

Above the foundations, stepped seats should be built up from the substructure, from supplies of stone or marble. 4. It seems that the transverse aisles of theaters should correspond in their dimensions to the total height of theaters, and in no case should the heights of the backs of the aisles exceed their breadth. If they are made higher, they will repel the voice, casting it out of the upper part of the theater; in the upper seats, those above the aisles, such theaters will not allow the endings of words to reach the ears of the listeners dis-

---

4 Reading *testudinatum;* Festus, p. 212, says that a *testudo* is a roof with four hip slopes, and a *pectinatum* roof has two gable slopes.

tinctly. In short, determine the height like this: if a line is extended from the lowest step to the highest, it should touch the edge of every step, that is, every angle. In this way the voice will not be obstructed.

5. Passageways should be designed to be plentiful and spacious. Do not mix access to the upper parts of the theater with that to the lower;* make the passageways direct and continuous from every place in the theater, without doubling back, so that when the audience takes its leave of the performance it will not be crowded. Instead, it will have a separate exit from every location.

It is also important to note carefully that the site itself not deaden sound; it should be the type in which the voice may travel with the utmost clarity. This can be accomplished if a site is selected where resonances are not impeded. 6. The voice is a flowing breath of air, and perceptible to the hearing by its touch.[5] It moves by the endless formation of circles, just as endlessly expanding circles of waves are made in standing water if a stone is thrown into it.* These travel outward from the center as far as they can, until some local constriction stands in the way, or some other obstacle that prevents the waves from completing their patterns. As soon as these obstacles interfere, the first waves bounce back and upset the patterns. 7. In the same way the voice makes circular motions; however, on the surface of water the circles move horizontally, while the voice at once advances horizontally and mounts upward, step by step. For the voice, therefore, just as for the pattern of waves in water, so long as no obstacle interferes with the first wave, it will not upset the second wave or any of those that follow; all of them will reach the ears of the spectators without echoing, those in the lowermost seats as well as those in the highest. 8. Therefore the architects of old, following in Nature's footsteps, perfected the stepped seating of theaters after their researches into the rising of the voice. They asked how, using the canonical theory of mathematicians and the principles of music, any voice onstage might reach the ears of the spectators more clearly and sweetly. For just as musical instruments achieve the clarity of their sounds by means of bronze panels or horn sounding boxes added to the sound of the strings, so, too, the calculations for theaters were established by the ancients on harmonic principles to amplify the voice.

CHAPTER 4: HARMONIC PRINCIPLES (FIGURE 81)*

1. Harmonics,[6] the literature of music, is an obscure and difficult subject, especially, of course, for those who cannot read Greek. However, if we are to explain this discipline, we must use Greek words because some of the concepts of harmonics do not have Latin names. I will therefore interpret, as clearly as I can, the writings of Aristoxenus, and I will include his diagram and his definitions of the notes, so that anyone who pays attention will be able to understand more easily.

2. When the voice is modulated by changes, some of these make it sharp, some heavy.* It moves in two manners: of these, one has a continuous effect, the other intervallic. The continuous voice has no boundaries and exists in no particular place; it produces no obvious terminations. Still, the intervals between sounds are clear, as when in conversation we say "slow," "looks," "flows," "stokes."* It is not entirely clear where the pitch begins or ends, but[7] the fact that it has turned from high to low and from low to high is apparent to the ears. When the voice moves by intervals the situation is completely reversed. In this case, the voice, when it is modulated, alters by placing itself firmly on one pitch, and then within the limits of another, and by doing this over and over, up and down, it appears changeable[8] to the senses, as when in singing we create a variety of modulations by flexing our voice. When the voice moves up and down by intervals in this fashion, and the places where it begins and where it leaves off appear within definite limits of sound, what lies in between is obscured by the intervals.

3. There are three types of modulation, first what the Greeks call **enharmonic**; second, **chromatic**; third, **diatonic**. The **enharmonic** modulation was systematically conceived; this is why its singing has a particularly solemn and dignified authority. The **chromatic**, with its subtle refinement and the closeness of its modulations, produces a more refined pleasure. The modulation of the **diatonic**, on the other hand, because it occurs in nature, has a distance between intervals that is more easily understood by the listener. Within these three types, the placement of the tetrachords differs, because the enharmonic tetrachord has two tones and two **dieses**. (The

5 *tactu* Rose *etactu* G *&actu* H; reading *e tactu*.

6 Reading *harmonice* with Rose; *harmonia* MSS.

7 *sed quid* G, *sed quod* H; reading *sed quod*.

8 *inconstans* Giocondo, *constans* G H; reading *inconstans*.

diesis is a quarter tone; thus the half tone contains two dieses.) In the chromatic type two half tones are placed in sequence, and the third interval spans three half tones. In the diatonic type two tones adjoin each other, and thirdly a half tone takes up the rest of the tetrachord. Thus for the three types of modulation [scales] the tetrachords are all calibrated from two tones and a half tone, but when the tetrachords are considered individually within the bounds of their own type, they have a different pattern of intervals. 4. Nature, therefore, distinguished the intervals of tones and half tones and tetrachords in the voice, defined their terms by quantitative measures, and established their qualities through certain distinct modes. Using what has been established by nature, the craftsmen who make musical instruments plan their finished construction with an eye to their effectiveness at producing harmony.

5. The notes, which in Greek are called phthongi, are ten and eight for each type.* Of these, eight are fixed in common among the three types, and the other ten, when they are tuned among themselves, are movable.

The fixed notes are those that are placed between the movable notes; they contain the unit of the tetrachord, and according to the differences between each type the sounds within the tetrachord will remain constant. These notes are called (i) proslambanomenos (added on at the bottom of the scale), (ii) hypatê hypaton (uppermost note on the uppermost string), (iii) hypatê meson (middle note on the uppermost string), (iv) mesê (middle string), (v) netê synêmmenon (joined note on low string), (vi) paramesê (next to middle string), (vii) netê diezeugmenon (low string, disjoined note), (viii) netê hyperbolaion (low string, highest note).

The movable notes are those that are placed in tetrachords in among the fixed notes, and depending on the type they change from place to place. Their names are (i) parhypatê hypaton, (ii) lichanos hypaton, (iii) parhypatê meson, (iv) lichanos meson, (v) tritê synêmmenon, (vi) paranetê synêmmenon, (vii) tritê diezeugmenon, (viii) paranetê diezeugmenon, (ix) tritê hyperbolaion, (x) paranetê hyperbolaion. 6. These receive differing values because they move; their intervals and distances between one another increase.

Thus parhypatê, which is a quarter tone distant from hypatê in the enharmonic type, has been moved in the chromatic type to a half tone away from hypatê. What is called lichanos in the enharmonic type stands a half tone away from hypatê, but when transposed into the chromatic scale this interval increases to two half tones, and in the diatonic type lichanos stands apart from hypatê by

three half tones. Thus these ten notes, on account of their transposition in the various types, create three varieties of modulation.

7. There are five tetrachords. The first is heaviest of all, the one the Greeks call hypaton, the second is in the middle range, the one called meson, the third is conjoined, the one called synêmmenon, the fourth disjoined, the one named diezeugmenon, and the fifth, which is sharpest of all, is called hyperbolaion in Greek.

The harmonies that human nature can measure out are called symphoniae in Greek, and number six: diatesseron (fourth), diapente (fifth), diapason (octave), and disdiatesseron (octave + fourth), disdiapente (octave + fifth) and disdiapason (double octave). 8. They took these numerical names because when the voice has held itself within the boundaries of a single note, as it turns away and arrives at the fourth interval off, this is called "through four" = diatesseron. When it arrives five intervals away this is called "through five" = diapente, at six intervals, "through all" = diapason, at eight and one-half intervals "through all and through four" = diapason et diatesseron, at nine and one-half intervals "through all and through five" = diapason et diapente, across twelve intervals "double through all" = disdiapason.

9. For if sound is made by plucked strings or by vocal singing, it cannot make harmonies between two intervals, nor with the third or sixth or seventh, but, as has been described, the harmonies of diatesseron and diapente and so on, up to disdiapason have boundaries that coincide with the nature of the voice, and these create harmonies from the conjunction of the notes, which in Greek are called "voices" = phthongi.

CHAPTER 5: THE ECHEA, SOUNDING VESSELS IN THEATERS (FIGURE 82)*

1. Thus, as a result of these investigations, let bronze vessels be made on mathematical principles in keeping with the size of the theater, and have these vessels so made that when they are touched, they can produce among themselves the diatesseron, diapente, and so on, up to disdiapason. Afterward place them in chambers set up for the purpose between the seats of the theater, and place them there according to the principles of music, so that they touch no walls and all around them they have an empty place and space above their heads. Set them upside down, and on the side facing the plat-

form put wedges underneath them, no less than half a foot high, and opposite these chambers leave openings along the footings for the lower tiers of seats that are two feet long and half a foot high.

2. Their pattern, and the places where they should be set, are laid out as follows. If the theater is not of an immense size, then mark off a horizontal area at the midpoint of the theater's height; in this area thirteen chambers should be vaulted over at twelve equal intervals. Those echea – the bronze vessels that have just been described – which have been tuned to nêtê hyperbolaion should be set in the chambers at the outermost points of the curve, and these should be placed first on both sides. The second from the ends should be tuned to sound a diatesseron to nêtê diezeugmenon, the third from the ends to sound diatesseron to paramesê, the fourth to sound diatesseron to nêtê synêmmenon, the fifth diatesseron to mesê, the sixth diatesseron to hypatê meson, and in the center one that sounds diatesseron to hypatê hypaton. 3. By this contrivance the voice onstage, poured forth from the stage – as it were, from the center of the theater – and circling outward, strikes the hollows of the individual vessels on contact, stirring up an increased clarity and a harmonic complement to its own tone.

If, however, the size of the theater is to be larger, then its height should be divided into four parts, to create three horizontal areas that are marked off for the chambers, one enharmonic, one chromatic, and the third diatonic. And from the bottom, which will be the first area to be completed, place the vessels tuned to the enharmonic type as described earlier for small theaters. 4. In the middle area, first place the vessels tuned to the note of hyperbolaion in the chromatic type on the outer ends, in the second chambers from the end place the vessels tuned at an interval of diatesseron, so that they sound diezeugmenon in chromatic. In the third chambers from the end they should sound synêmmenon in the chromatic tuning, in the fourth, at an interval of diatesseron, meson in chromatic, in the fifth, at another interval of diatesseron, hypaton in chromatic, in the sixth, paramesê, a note which in the chromatic type has these harmonies: diapente with chromatic hyperbolaion, and of diatesseron with the chromatic meson. 5. In the center chamber, place nothing at all, because there is no other quality [of note] among the sounds in the chromatic type that can create harmonies with the rest.

In the uppermost section, the uppermost area for these chambers, first, on each end, place vessels tuned to the note of hyperbolaion in the diatonic type, in the second,

at an interval of diatesseron in the diatonic type, vessels tuned to diezeugmenon, in the third, diatonic synêmmenon, in the fourth, at an interval of diatesseron, to diatonic meson, in the fifth, another diatesseron, to diatonic hypaton, in the sixth, another diatesseron to proslambanomenos, in the middle, tuned to mesê, because this note has the following harmonic relationships: diapason with proslambanomenos and diapente with diatonic hypaton. 6. And if anyone wants to bring these directions to completion with ease, please note the diagram at the end of the book, drawn according to the principles of music. Aristoxenus, with all his dedicated enthusiasm, devised this diagram with the tunings divided by type, and has left us this legacy. And anyone who truly pays attention to his reasoning will be more easily capable of using the principles of Nature to design theaters that enhance the voice for the pleasure of the audience.

7. Now perhaps someone will object that countless theaters have been built in Rome every year, and that none of the provisions we have described have been made in their construction, but he will be mistaken in this, because all the wooden public theaters have several floors that necessarily resonate.* Indeed, we can observe this from performers who sing to the lyre, who, when they want to sing in a higher key, turn toward the stage doors and thus avail themselves of the harmonic support that these can provide for their voices. When, however, theaters are constructed of more solid material, that is, of masonry, stone, or marble, which can not resonate, then they should be outfitted with echea for just that reason.* 8. If it is asked in what theater this has been done, we cannot provide any examples in Rome, but we can in the provinces of Italy and in a great many Greek cities. Indeed, we may point to Lucius Mummius* as an authority in this regard, for when he had razed the theater of Corinth he shipped its bronze echea off to Rome, and dedicated them as part of his war booty in the temple of the Moon. Many clever architects, moreover, who have designed theaters in towns of no great size, have achieved extremely serviceable results by taking clay jars tuned in the same fashion and assembling them according to the same set of principles.

CHAPTER 6: THEATER DESIGN

1. This is how to make the configuration of the theater itself (Figure 83). Whatever the size of the lower perimeter, locate a center point and draw a circle around

it, and in this circle draw four triangles with equal sides and at equal intervals. These should just touch the circumference of the circle. (By these same triangles, astrologers calculate the harmonies of the stars of the twelve heavenly signs in musical terms.) Of these triangles, take the one whose side will be closest to the performing platform. There, in that area that cuts the curvature of the circle, lay out the *scaenae frons*, and draw a parallel line from that place through the center of the circle; this will divide off the platform of the proscenium and the area of the orchestra. 2. Thus the platform will have been made deeper than that of the Greeks, because all the artists do their work on it.* In the orchestra, on the other hand, are the places reserved for the senators' seats. The platform itself should not be more than five feet high, so that those seated in the orchestra will be able to see all of the actors' gestures.

The wedges of seats in the theater should be divided like this. Have the angles of the triangles that run around the circumference of the circle determine the direction of the rise of the stairways in between wedges up to the first transverse aisle. Above this, the midlines of the upper wedges serve to direct the staircases in a staggered pattern. 3. The angles at the base of the theater, the ones that serve to orient the stairways, will be seven in number, and the remaining five mark off the design of the platform. The center angle should have the palace doors opposite it, and those to the left and right mark off the placement of the door to the guest quarters, while the two outermost angles will face the paths of the rotating panels.*

Make the steps up to the viewing areas (where the seats are to be laid out) no less than one palm high and no more than a foot and six digits. Their depth should be set at no more than two and one-half feet and no less than two. 4. The roof of the portico that will be put on the highest step should be completed on a level with the height of the scene building, for the reason that the voice will swell uniformly and so reach the top rows and the roof. If the theater is not level, then wherever it is lower, the voice will be interrupted at that point, because it has arrived there first.

5. As for the orchestra, whatever diameter it will have between its lowermost steps, take one-sixth of that measure. On each end of the theater, right by the entrances, make a perpendicular cut of this dimension along the lower rows of seats, and wherever the cut is, there place the lintels of the entrance passages.* In this way their vaults will have enough height.

6. The length of the platform ought to be twice the diameter of the orchestra. The height of the podium from the level of the platform, including its cornice and crowning molding, should be one-twelfth the diameter of the orchestra. Above the podium, the columns with their capitals and bases should have a height of one-fourth the same diameter, while the epistyles and the ornaments of these columns should be one-fifth their height. The attic (*pluteus*) above with its wave molding and its lower cornice should be half the size of the podium. Above this attic make the columns smaller by one-fourth than the lower set; the epistyles and ornaments for these columns should be one-fifth their height. It there is to be a third *episcaenos*, then have the upper attic be half the size of the middle attic, and the uppermost columns shorter by one-fourth than the middle columns. The epistyles and ornaments of these columns should likewise measure one-fifth the columns' height.

7. Now it is not possible to have the proportional systems for every theater carried out according to every principle and to every effect. Instead, it is up to the architect to note in which dimensions it will be necessary to pursue symmetry and in which to make adjustments according to the nature of the site or the size of the project. There are things that, because of their function, ought to be made of the same size both in a very small theater and in a large one: things like rows of seats, transverse aisles, podia, passageways, stairs, performing platforms, tribunals, and whatever else might occur where necessity compels departure from symmetry so as not to impede function. This is no less the case if some shortage of supplies is going to occur in the project, that is, of marble, wood, or one of the other materials that have been assembled. Then it will not be out of place to subtract or add a bit, so long as this is not done too imprudently, but rather with good sense. This will happen, of course, if the architect has experience, particularly if he is not wholly devoid of a quick mind and ingenuity.

8. Scene buildings have their own principles, developed as follows: the central doors have the ornaments of a royal hall, and the doors to the guest quarters (*hospitalia*) to the right and left are placed next to the area prepared for scenery. The Greeks call these areas *periaktoi* because there are machines in these places that have rotating triangles. Each of these has three different sets of decoration; when there is going to be a change of setting in a play, or the epiphany of a god in a clap of thunder, then these are rotated to change the appearance of the decoration on the exterior. Along-

side these places, their front panels should represent one entrance onstage from the forum, and one from abroad.

There are three types of sets:* one that is called tragic, one called comic, and the third satyric. Their ornamentation is unlike, and conceived on differing principles. Tragic sets are represented with columns and gables and statues and the other trappings of royalty. Comic sets look like private buildings with balconies, and the views from their windows are designed, in imitation, on the principles of private buildings. Satyric sets are ornamented with trees, caves, mountains, and all the other rustic features, fashioned to have the appearance of landscape.

CHAPTER 7: GREEK THEATERS
(FIGURE 84)

1. In Greek theaters, everything should not be made according to the same principles, because, first of all, whereas in a Latin theater there are four triangles inscribed in the lowermost circumference, in a Greek theater it is the angles of three squares that touch the circumference. Take the side of the square that is nearest the scene building. Where it cuts the curvature, this area is drawn as the limit of the proscenium. From that area to the outermost circumference of the circle draw a parallel line, along which the scaenae frons will be set up. Then draw a parallel line through the center of the orchestra from the area of the proscenium, and where[9] it intersects the line of the circumference on left and right, mark the points that signify the ends of each half circle. Place a compass on the right-hand point and draw a circle from the left interval to the left part of the proscenium. Likewise, with the point of the compass located on the left-hand point, describe a circle from the right interval up to the right part of the proscenium. 2. With three points laid out according to this design the Greeks have a broader orchestra, a more recessed scene building, and a shallower platform. This they call the *logeion* ("place of words") because on it the tragic and comic actors play their parts while the other artists participate in the production from

the orchestra. This is why the Greeks classify their artists separately as **scenic** or **thymelic**. The height of this *logeion* should be no less than ten feet and no more than twelve. The rise of the stairs between wedges of seats should be directed toward the corners of the three squares, up to the first transverse aisle. From the transverse aisle upward, the stairs should once again be laid out from the midline of the wedges, and, proceeding upward, whenever a transverse aisle occurs, increase the number of aisles by staggering them in the same way.

CHAPTER 8: THE SITING
OF THEATERS

1. Now when all these procedures have been carried out with the greatest care and expertise, then it is even more important to pay attention that a site be chosen in which the voice will apply itself gently; it should not be thrown back, echoing, so as to carry indistinct meanings to the ears. There are a number of places that naturally impede the motion of the voice, such as the dissonant places called *katêchountes* in Greek, the ones that disperse sound, which they call *perêchountes*, and the echoing ones called *antêchountes*. There are also the consonant ones which they call *sunêchountes*. **Dissonant** sites are those in which the voice first rises high, then meets resistance from solid surfaces higher up, and when it is deflected back it comes to rest low, preventing the rise of any other sounds. 2. **Dispersive** sites are those in which the voice, compacted by circling around, dissolves at a middle height, and by sounding without the ends of words it leaves their meanings unclear. **Resonant** sites are those where the voice, once struck by contact with a solid surface, echoes; by creating copies of sounds these places make the ends of words double for the listener. **Consonant** places, likewise, are those in which the voice, reinforced from below, rises with this increment and reaches the ears with precise clarity. Thus, if careful attention is paid to choosing sites, the effect of voices in the theater will be usefully improved as a result of this prudence. As for the illustrations, they can be identified by the following distinction: those drawn from squares follow Greek custom; Latin theaters are those drawn on the basis of equilateral triangles. Anyone who wants to make use of these instructions will bring flawless theaters to completion.

9 Reading *qua* with Philander for MSS *quae*.

CHAPTER 9: PORTICOES

1. Behind the scene building, set up porticoes,* so that when sudden rains interrupt the performances, the audience has a place to gather outside the theater, and the performers have a space in which to rehearse, like the porticoes of Pompey, and, in Athens, the portico of Eumenes next to the theater and the shrine of Father Liber. For those who exit on the left side there is the odeum that Themistocles set up with stone columns, and covered over with the masts and yardarms of ships from the Persian war booty. This same portico was restored by King Ariobarzanes after it had burned down in the Mithridatic War. There are also the Stratoniceum in Smyrna, and the porticoes in Tralles on either side of the scene building above the stadium, and in every city that has had conscientious architects there are porticoes and walkways around the theaters.

2. It seems that they ought to be placed so that they are double and have Doric exterior columns with epistyles and ornaments executed according to the principles of modulation [developed earlier]. Their width should be made such, it seems, that whatever the height of the exterior columns, the porticoes should be exactly that broad from the lower part of the outermost columns to the interior columns, and as broad again from the interior columns to the walls that enclose the walkways of the porticoes. The interior columns should be higher by one-fifth than the exterior ones, but they should be designed in the Ionic or Corinthian type. 3. The proportions and symmetries of the columns do not follow the same principles as I described for temples, for these dimensions should have one type of dignity in the sacred enclosures of the gods, and a different, lighter appearance in porticoes and other projects of the sort.

Thus, if the columns are to be of the Doric type, their heights, including the capitals, should be divided into fifteen parts, and of these parts one should be established as the module, on the basis of which the whole project's design shall be carried out. At the lowest edge of the column make the diameter two modules, the intercolumniation five and one-half modules, the height of the columns without the capital fourteen modules, the height of the capital one module, its breadth two and one-sixth modules. The dimensions of the rest of the work should be executed just as I have described for temples in Book 4.

4. If, on the other hand, the columns are to be made in the Ionic type, the column shaft except for its base and capital should be divided into eight and one-half parts, and one of these parts should be assigned to the diameter of the column. The base with its plinth should be set at half a diameter, and let the method for creating the capital be like that demonstrated in Book 3. If the portico will be Corinthian, design the shaft and base as for Ionic, and the capital as described in Book 4. The augmentation of the stylobate by means of the *scamilli impares* should be taken from the description recorded in Book 3. The entablatures, cornices, and all the other matters pertaining to columns are set out in the text of the preceding volumes.

5. The central spaces between the porticoes and open to the sky should be adorned with gardens because open-air walkways are of great benefit to health: for the eyes, first of all, because the subtle and light air from green plants flows in as the body exercises and clears the vision, carrying off the dense moisture from the eyes and leaving the sight fine and the image sharp. Furthermore, as the body heats up by moving around the walkways, the air, sucking away moisture from the limbs, reduces fullness and diminishes them by dissipating whatever the body has absorbed beyond what it can bear.

6. It is possible to observe that this is so because wherever sources of water are covered, or where there is a swampy flooding underground, no misty vapor arises from these places, whereas in open-air spaces, as soon as the rising sun touches the world with its vapor, it stirs up moisture from wet and flooded places, condenses it, and draws it upward. If it seems, therefore, that in open-air places the more noxious humors are sucked out of bodies, just as they seem to be drawn out of the earth on clouds, I think there can be no doubt that spacious and ornate walkways should be set up in cities outdoors and in the open air.

7. This is what to do to make them always dry and never muddy. Excavate the site as deeply as possible, and empty it out. To the right and left make masonry drains, and in the walls facing the walkways, insert tubes that slope on an incline into the drains. Once these have been completed, fill the site with charcoal, and above that spread the site with sand and then level it. Then, because of the natural permeability of charcoal and the arrangement of tubes and drains, any overflow of water will be carried off, and in this way the walkways will be dry, free from standing water.

8. Furthermore, such buildings were designated by custom as storehouses in times of need. In siege conditions, almost every provision is easier to come by than

timber: salt is easily brought in beforehand, grain is gathered quickly either by public or private agency, and if it runs out the deficiency may be made up by green vegetables or meat or dried beans. Water can be collected from the digging of wells or the runoff of rainwater from roof tiles. But supplying the wood that is supremely necessary for cooking our food can be difficult and bothersome because it is slow to transport and it is consumed in great quantities.* 9. During such emergencies, the walkways are opened up and rations are allocated to individuals according to their tribes. Thus open-air walkways offer two excellent advantages: a place of health in peacetime, and, secondly, a place of safety in time of war. For these reasons the layout of walkways, put in not only behind the scene building of the theater, but also in the precincts of all the gods, can offer great benefits to cities. Because these things now seem to us to have been set out in sufficient detail, the explanation of bath design shall follow.

CHAPTER 10: BATHS (FIGURE 86)*

1. First of all, choose as warm a site as possible; that is, one facing away from the north wind (Septentrio) and the northeast wind (Aquilo). Then the caldaria and the tepidaria will have light from the west in wintertime, or, if the nature of the site prevents this, at least from the south, as the most common time for bathing is generally from midday to evening. Care should also be taken that the men's and women's caldaria are connected and placed in the same area. In this way it will be possible for them both to share a common furnace for the tubs. Three bronze tanks should be assembled above the furnace, one a caldarium, one a tepidarium, one a frigidarium, and they should be so placed that however much hot water flows from the tepidarium into the caldarium, as much cold water is coming in from the frigidarium to the tepidarium in the same fashion. In addition, the ceilings of the tub rooms can be heated by this common furnace.

2. This is how to make the suspended floors of the caldaria (Figure 87). First, the floor is laid with one and one-half foot tiles that incline toward the furnace, so that if a ball is thrown in it cannot stay in place, but returns to the furnace of its own accord. In this way flame will circulate more easily under the suspended floor. On top of this piers of eight-inch tiles should be placed so that two-foot tiles can be placed over them. The piers should be two feet high and they should be mortared with clay mixed in with hair, and over them place the two-foot tiles, which will hold up the pavement.

3. If the vaults are going to be made of masonry they will be more efficient. However, if there are going to be ceilings made of wooden beams, then suspend a terracotta ceiling underneath – but this is how to do it. Have iron bars or arcs made; these should be hung from the beams on iron hooks set as closely as possible to one another. These bars or arcs should be set in rows so that flat tiles can sit between any two of them and can be laid in place. By this method all the ceiling can be completed so that it is supported on iron. The upper joins of these coffers should be spread with clay worked with hair; the lower surface, the one that faces the pavement, should be plastered first with terracotta mixed with lime, and then finished in stucco or plaster.* If these ceilings are made double in caldaria, they will be more efficient, for then the moisture from the vapor will not be able to rot the timber of the beams, but instead will wander aimlessly between the two ceiling chambers.

4. The dimensions of baths, it seems, are determined by the number of users (Figure 86). This is how they should be designed. Whatever the length is to be, take away a third part; that should be the breadth, except for the alcoves for the washbasin and the pool. The washbasin, in particular, should be built beneath the window, so that those standing around it will not obscure the light by casting shadows. The alcoves for the washbasins should be made spacious enough so that once the first comers have taken their places, the rest of the bathers can stand around comfortably and watch. The breadth of the pool, between the wall and the balustrade, should be no less than six feet, so that its lower step and the socle take up two feet.

5. The Spartan sauna and sweating chambers* should be joined onto the tepidarium, and however broad these are, they should have the same height up to the spring of the dome. Leave an oculus in the center of the dome, and from it suspend a bronze shield on chains, so that by adjusting its height the temperature of the sauna may be brought to perfection. These rooms ought to be constructed on a circular design, so that the force of flame and vapor can escape along the curvatures of the walls and out the center at an even rate.

CHAPTER 11: PALAESTRAS
(FIGURE 88)

1. Now I think it is time, even if they are not an Italian custom, to describe the traditions for building palaestras and to show how they are put up by the Greeks.* In palaestras square or oblong peristyles should be made so that their perimeter measures two stades, which the Greeks call *diaulos;* three of these porticoes will be laid out as single, and the fourth, which faces the south, will be double, so that when there are windy storms, the rain cannot spatter into the interior part. 2. In the three remaining porticoes spacious exedrae should be constructed, with seats, so that philosophers, orators, and everyone else who delights in study will be able to sit and hold discussions. In the double portico the following features must be installed. In the middle, an *ephebeum,* that is, a particularly large exedra with seats, which is one-third again longer than it is deep. On the right-hand side a leather punching bag, next to that a dust bath, and by the dust bath near the corner of the portico a cold-water sink, which the Greeks call *loutron.* On the left of the ephebeum an oiling room, next to the oiling room a frigidarium, and from this a passage to the *propnigeum* (steam room) at the corner of the portico. Next to this, inward from the area of the frigidarium, a vaulted sweating chamber should be placed, twice as long as it is wide, whose corners on one side should have a Spartan sauna, designed in the same way as recorded earlier. Across from the Spartan sauna there should be a hot-water washing room. This, as we have recorded, is how to arrange the peristyles of palaestras to perfection.

3. On the exterior, set out three porticoes: one for the people coming out of the peristyle, and two, to the left and right, measured out as running tracks. Of these, the one facing north should be made double and as broad as possible. The other two[10] should be single, so constructed that the parts nearer the walls and next to the columns will have borders to serve as paths no less than ten feet wide, and the central portion will be dug out so that there are stairs descending one and one-half feet to a level area which should measure no less than twelve feet. Thus those who are dressed may walk around the borders in their street clothes without

coming into contact with the athletes oiled for exercise. 4. This portico is called a *xystos* by the Greeks, because their athletes train in covered stadiums during the winter. Next to the *xystos* and the twin porticoes on either side, open-air walks should be designed. The Greeks call these *paradromides* (parallel tracks), but we call them xysta; here, throughout the winter, athletes can profitably exercise in good weather outside the [Greek-style] *xystos.* These [Latin] xysta should be made so that between the two porticoes there are woods or groves of plane trees, and in among these trees paths should be made with stopping places of opus signinum. Behind the xystus there should be a stadium, so designed that crowds of people can comfortably watch the competing athletes.

CHAPTER 12: PORTS (FIGURE 89)

1. I have furnished a full account of the things that are necessary to put within the walls of a city and how to set them out appropriately. The subject of the suitability of ports should no longer be deferred; now it is time to explain how ships may be safeguarded in port against bad weather. If harbors are well situated by nature so that they have headlands or projecting promontories, in which the inward curvatures and angles of the harbor have been formed by the nature of the site itself, they will work best. For all the way around, warehouses or ship sheds must be made, or passages from the warehouses to the marketplaces, and towers should be placed on either side, from which chains can be let out by machines.

2. However, if we are not going to have a natural site nor one that is suitable for safeguarding ships from stormy weather, it seems that this is what must be done: if no river prevents it at these sites, then there will be an anchorage on one side, and on the opposite side moles should be constructed in masonry or by earth embankments. This is how harbor enclosures should be designed. The masonry that will be underwater should be made by bringing in that powder found in the region from Cumae right down to the promontory of Minerva (pozzolana); this should be mixed two-to-one as if with a mortar and pestle. 3. Then, in the place that has been marked out for the purpose, caissons of oak planks, bound in chains, should be sunk into the water and set firmly in place. Then, within their

---

10 Reading the plural with Perrault rather than the singular of the MSS.

perimeter, from small crossbeams,[11] the lower part should be leveled underwater and dredged out, and the place should be heaped up with pounded rubble, and the mortar mixed as has been described, until the space between the caissons has been entirely filled. The places that have been described here have this gift of nature.

4. If, however, because of waves or the tossing of the open sea the supports cannot hold the caissons together, then from the land itself or from the edge of the shore a jetty should be constructed as solidly as possible, and this jetty should be built with a level area on less than half its surface; the rest, the part next to the shore, should have its surface incline upward. Then, along the water itself and around the sides of the jetty, one and one-half foot tiles should be laid to the same level as the plane surface mentioned earlier; this sloping area should be filled with sand to a height equal to that of the rim and the level area of the parapet. Above this leveled area a pier of equal dimensions should be constructed of masonry, and once it has been constructed, it should be left to dry for no less than two months. At that time, the brick rim that supports the sand should be demolished. Then the sand, carried off by the waves, will cause the pier to topple into the sea. By this means, moles can be constructed out into the water wherever they are needed.

5. In places where the powder (pozzolana) does not occur, build by this method. Double caissons made of planks bound together and encircled by chains should be set up in the place that is to be enclosed, and in between these supports clay in baskets made of swamp

reed should be dumped in. When the structure has been well compacted and is as dense as possible, then the place to be bounded by this enclosure should be dredged with water screws, wheels, and drums and allowed to dry. Within these enclosures the foundations should be excavated. If they are going to be in earth, they should be emptied out and dried to solidity at a greater thickness than that of the future wall, and then fill the place with a masonry of rubble, lime, and sand. 6. If the site is soft, it should be reinforced with pilings of burnt alder or olive and then filled with charcoal, as we have described for the foundations of theaters and city walls. Then, at last, a wall should be erected of squared stone blocks with the longest possible joins, so that the middle blocks in particular will be held together by the joins. Next, the space between the walls should be filled in with broken stone or masonry. And it will be so sound that even a tower can be built upon it.

7. Once these things have been completed, this is the method for setting up ship sheds. Above all, they should face north, for the southern regions, because of their heat, give rise to rot, worms, termites, and all the other types of pests, and then keep them alive by continuing to nourish them. These buildings are the last of all that should be built of wood, because of the danger of fire. There should be no set limit to their size; they should be made to the measure of the largest ship, so that when great ships are brought into them, they will be set in place there with room to spare.

In the present volume I have recorded those things that are necessary to facilitate the function of public places in cities, as they have occurred to me. Now, in the next volume, I shall discuss the functions of private buildings and their symmetries.

---

11 For an extremely problematic passage, reading *ex trastillis* (dim. of *transtrum*; Lewis and Short s.v.; cf. Granger ad loc.), for MSS *ex trastilis*.

❖

PRIVATE BUILDINGS

PREFACE

1. When Aristippus,* the Socratic philosopher, had been washed up on the shore of Rhodes after a shipwreck, and noticed that geometric diagrams had been drawn there, he is said to have exclaimed to his comrades: "Let us hope for the best; I see human footprints!" and forthwith he headed for the city of Rhodes. He came straight upon the gymnasium, and after discussing philosophy there was rewarded with gifts sufficient not only to outfit himself, but also to allow him to provide clothing and the other necessities of life to those who were with him. When later his companions wanted to return home, they asked him what messages he would like to have relayed back. This, then, is what he ordered them to report: that children should be furnished with the sort of possessions and travel money that can even survive a shipwreck in one piece.

2. For the real safeguards of life are those that neither the cruel storm of fortune nor political change nor the ravages of war can harm. Taking the same argument further, Theophrastus* put it this way, when he urged that people be well educated rather than relying on money: an educated person is the only one who is never a stranger in a foreign land, nor at a loss for friends even when bereft of household and intimates. Rather, he is a citizen in every country, and may look down without fear on the difficult turns of fortune. He, however, who thinks that he is fortified by the defenses of good fortune rather than learning will find himself a wanderer on shifting pathways, beleaguered by a life that is never stable, but always wavering.

3. Indeed, Epicurus says much the same thing: that fortune grants very little to wise men, but what she does grant are those gifts that are greatest and most necessary, namely to be governed by the contrivances of mind and imagination. Many other philosophers have said exactly the same things.

Likewise, the poets who wrote those old comedies in Greek declared these same opinions in verse onstage:

Eucrates, Chionides, and Aristophanes, for example, and with them, especially, Alexis,* who said that the Athenians should be complimented for this reason: the laws of all the Greeks compel parents to be cared for by their children, but the Athenians say that not all parents possess this right, but only those who have educated their children in an art. For all the gifts granted by fortune are just as easily taken away by her, whereas knowledge, coupled with intelligence, never fails; it stands steadfast to the very end of life.

4. And therefore I thank my parents immeasurably and bear them great and infinite gratitude because in accordance with the spirit of the Athenian law they had me trained in an art, an art, moreover, that cannot be mastered without education in letters and comprehensive learning in every field.* When, therefore, I had a stock of knowledge increased both by the solicitude of my parents and the erudition of my teachers, and enjoyed myself by reading both literary and technical writing,* I stored up all these assets in my mind, and this is the greatest reward of all: that there is no need to have more, for true wealth is to want nothing.

But perhaps some, thinking that these possessions are inconsequential, will think that wise people are those who are well supplied with money. And so, many people, striving to that end, apply bold methods and along with wealth, they have achieved celebrity too. 5. But I, Caesar, never devoted my efforts to making money by my art, but rather thought that I should pursue modest means and a good reputation – not wealth and infamy. Thus up to this point little fame has followed upon my work, yet I hope that once these volumes are published I will be known to future generations.

Nor is it any wonder that I am so unknown to most people. Other architects make the rounds* and ask openly to work as architects, but my teachers passed on the tradition that one was asked to take on a responsibility, rather than asking for it oneself. An honest person will blush from the shame of seeking something questionable, and it is those who grant a favor, not those who receive it, who are courted. For what are we to think about someone who is asked to make an expenditure from his patrimony for the gratification of a petitioner, other than that it is all to be done for the sake of the other man's profit and gain? 6. Our ancestors, therefore, would pass their projects to architects who, first of all, came from proven good family,* inquiring next whether they had been properly brought up, judging it best to entrust work to native modesty rather than aggressive audacity. As for the craftsmen themselves, they never trained anyone but their children and relatives, and educated them as good men on whom the financial responsibility of such massive undertakings might be conferred without misgiving.

But when I see that the importance of such a great profession is arrogated by the ignorant and inexperienced, and by those who not only lack knowledge of architecture, but even of construction technique, I cannot but praise the heads of households who, trusting in their own reading, build for themselves in the belief that, if they must entrust a commission to amateurs, they themselves are more worthy of the expenditure, which will be according to their own wishes rather than those of others. 7. No one tries to undertake any other craft at home, like shoemaking, fulling, or those that are easier – no craft but architecture, for the reason that those who profess it are called architects not on account of real skill, but falsely. This is why I thought that I should record the body of architecture and its governing principles as thoroughly as I can, thinking that this will be no unwelcome gift for all the nations.

Therefore, because in the fifth book I wrote about the proper construction of public buildings, in this volume I shall explain the calculations for private buildings,* and the dimensions of their symmetries.

CHAPTER 1: LATITUDES AND PEOPLES

1. These [symmetries] will be properly set out if first one takes into account in which regions and which latitudes* of the world they are established (Figure 90). It seems necessary to develop the types of building in one way in Egypt, another way in Hispania, still differently in Pontus, otherwise in Rome, and so on, according to the distinctive properties of other lands and regions. For in one part of the world the earth is overwhelmed by the course of the sun; in another it stands far distant from it, in still another part it is held at a middling dis-

tance. Therefore, just as the firmament has been established along the earth with the signbearing circle* and the course of the sun placed naturally at an incline and with dissimilar qualities,* so, too, the placement of buildings ought to be directed by the properties of the regions and the varied nature of the heavens.

2. Under the northern sky buildings should be entirely roofed over and be as enclosed as possible, oriented toward the warmer regions but not open to them. By contrast, under the onslaught of the sun in southern regions, because they are assailed by heat, buildings should be made more open and should face north and northeast. Thus, whatever Nature exaggerates will have to be restored by art. In the remaining regions the placement of buildings should be adjusted in the same way, according to the way the heavens are oriented because of the inclination of the cosmos.

3. These things should also be perceived and considered in Nature, and observed as well in the limbs and bodies of human populations. For the sun, in those places where it pours forth its heat in moderation, keeps bodies well balanced. Those that it inflames by coursing near them it robs of their complement of moisture by burning it away. In the cold regions, by contrast, because they are far distant from the south, the moisture is never drained away from their complexions[1] by heat. Instead, dewy air from the heavens, pouring more moisture into human bodies, gives them larger builds and a deeper sound to their voices. This is why the populations that have been nurtured in the north are formed with huge bodies, light color, straight red hair, blue eyes, and plentiful blood – because of the abundance of moisture and the chill of the heavens. 4. Those who are nearest the southern axis, subjected to the course of the sun, grow to maturity with shorter bodies, dark coloring, curly hair, black eyes, weak[2] legs, and meager blood because of the sun's assaults. Because of the meagerness of their blood they are more timid in resisting military attack, yet they fearlessly endure heats and fevers because their limbs have been nourished on heat. Bodies born in the north are made timid and helpless by fever, but because of their abundant blood they resist military attack without fear.

5. The sound of the voice, too, has unequal and various qualities among the different types of populations, because the endpoints of east and west, around the

---

1 Reading *coloribus* with H; so also Granger and Dewar.
2 Reading *invalidis* with Giocondo for the MSS *validis*.

equator of the earth, by which the upper and lower parts of the cosmos are divided, seem to have a circuit leveled in a natural manner; this the mathematicians call the *horizon*. Therefore, keeping this in mind as a certainty, if a line is cast from the margin in the northern region to the margin above the southern axis, and from it, a second, oblique line is cast upward to the top of the hinge beyond the stars to the north, we will note without hesitation that the firmament has the shape of a triangle, like that instrument which the Greeks call the *sambykê* (the angle harp) (Figure 90).* 6. And thus, what area there is next to the lowermost hinge, at the southern extremes along a line [drawn] from the axis, the nations that are underneath that place,[3] because of the short distance to the firmament, make a sound with their voice that is weak and extremely sharp [= high], just like the string nearest the angle of a harp. The rest of the nations along this line, all the way to central Greece, produce sounds that become progressively heavier [= lower] along the scale. In the same way, rising in sequence from the center to the far north, under the highest points of the firmament, the voices of the nations there are emitted with pitches that are still heavier by nature. Thus, it seems, the whole plan of the cosmos, because of its inclination, has been composed as symphonically as possible by modulating the sun to produce harmony.

7. Therefore, the nations that are situated in the middle between the hinge of the southern axis and the northern, have a middling pitch to their voice in conversation, just as if they were part of a musical diagram. Those nations that we find as we progress toward the north, because they have greater distances to the firmament, have moist tones of voice that resonate in the range of *hypatê meson*, *hypatê hypaton*, or *proslambanomenos*; they are compelled by Nature to produce a heavier [lower] sound. By the same principle, as we proceed from the center to the south, the populations there express the slender sound of their voices in the highest tones, the various notes of *nêtê* and *paranêtê*.

8. That this is true, namely, that low notes come from Nature's wet places and more piercing notes from those that are boiling hot, can be observed by the following experiment: take two cups, equally fired in the same kiln, of an equal weight and an identical tone when struck. One of these should be lowered into water, then removed, and then each is struck. When this is done, the sound will differ greatly between them and they cannot possibly be of the same weight. Likewise, human bodies formed to one type of shape and conceived at one conjunction of the cosmos* sometimes emit a piercing tone at the touch of air because of the heat of that region, whereas other bodies, because of an abundance of moisture, pour forth the deepest of tones.

9. Furthermore, because of the sparseness of their skies, the southern nations, having minds sharp with heat, move more quickly and efficiently to the invention of ideas. The northern populations, infused with the thickness of the air and chilled by moisture, have sluggish minds because of this air's resistance. That this is so can be observed in the case of snakes, which, once they have had the chill of moisture drunk dry by heat, move with great celerity, but when they are cooled by the change of the heavens in autumn and winter, they become immobilized in their stupor. Therefore it is no wonder that human minds are made more acute by hot air, whereas chill air makes them slower.

10. Still, although the southern nations may have acute minds and the infinite cleverness of invention, as soon as they are called on to make a show of strength they give way, because the vigor of their minds has been sucked away by the sun. Those, on the other hand, who are born in chilly regions are more prepared to meet the force of arms fearlessly, with great courage; but rushing in without thinking because of the sluggishness of their minds, and lacking cleverness, they thwart their own tactics.

Thus these things have been so positioned in the cosmos by Nature, and all nations have been made different from one another by their unequal composition. Within the area of the entire earthly globe and all the regions at the center of the cosmos, the Roman People has its territories. 11. The populations of Italy partake in equal measure* of the qualities of both north and south, both with regard to their physiques and to the vigor of their minds, to produce the greatest strength. Just as the planet Jupiter is tempered by running its course between seething Mars and chilly Saturn, so, for the same reason, Italy, in between north and south, partaking of each in her composition, has balanced and invincible qualities. With her prudent counsel she smites the barbarians' strength; her strong hand does the same to the southerners' scheming. Thus the divine intelligence established the state of the Roman People as an outstanding and balanced region – so that it could take command over the earthly orb.

3 An unusually convoluted sentence, meaning "the nations underneath the area next to the southernmost angle along a line from the axis . . ."

12. Now if it is the case that various regions have been created of various kinds according to the inclination of the heavens, and that the natures of the various peoples are created with unequal minds and frames and qualities of body, then neither should we hesitate to allot the principles of building among the nations and peoples according to their characteristics – for we have a clever and timely example in Nature herself.

To the extent that I could, I have presented for consideration the properties of places as they are set out by Nature according to the supreme principles, and I have also said that it is proper to determine the qualities of buildings according to the course of the sun and the inclination of the heavens to fit the physical characteristics of the population. Now I shall briefly explain the dimensions of the symmetries in buildings, according to their type, both in general terms and individually.

CHAPTER 2: THE IMPORTANCE OF PROPORTION AND OPTICS

1. Nothing should be of greater concern to the architect than that, in the proportions of each individual element, buildings have an exact correspondence among their sets of principles. Thus, once the principle of the symmetries has been established and the dimensions have been developed by reasoning, then it is the special skill of a gifted architect to provide for the nature of the site, or the building's appearance, or its function, and make adjustments by subtractions or additions, should something need to be subtracted from or added to the proportional system, so that it will seem to have been designed correctly with nothing wanting in its appearance.

2. It seems that there should be one kind of appearance for a building that is close by, another for one that is far off, yet another for an enclosed place, and another in the open; in these instances it is the business of sound judgment to decide what must be done. For it is clear that sight does not always produce true effects; indeed, the mind is quite frequently deceived by visual judgments. For example, in stage sets, one sees the projection of columns, the protrusion of mutules, and the fully rounded figures of statues, when these surfaces are beyond doubt flattened with a straightedge. Likewise, in ships, when the oars are straight underwater, they look broken to the eye: the parts that extend as far as the water's surface look straight (as indeed they are), but

once they are submerged underwater, they give off fluid images from their bodies; these, swimming through the shiny rarefaction of water's nature toward the upper surface of the water, and stirred up in that place, seem to create the appearance of broken oars to the eyes. 3. Thus either from the impact of images on our vision or by action of rays shed forth from our eyes, as the physicists would have it, for either reason it seems to be the case that the glance of our eyes may make false judgments.

4. Therefore, if things that are true appear false, and many things are taken to be other than they are by our eyes, I think there should be no doubt that it is proper to make additions and subtractions according to the natures and requirements of sites – but this should be done in such a way that nothing will be found wanting in the work. These adjustments must be made by sharp judgment on site, not only on the basis of standard method. 5. First of all, then, a system of symmetries must be established on the basis of which any change can be incorporated without hesitation. Then the lowermost extent of the length and width of the rooms of the future work will be laid out, and when its size has been constituted, then the implementation of proportion to obtain correctness will follow, so that its appearance will be shapely beyond question to those who behold it. I must, of course, declare by what methods this can be achieved, but first I shall tell about interiors and how they should be made.

CHAPTER 3: INTERIORS (CAVAEDIA) (FIGURE 91)

1. Interiors are distinguished into five types; these forms are called **Tuscan, Corinthian, tetrastyle, displuviate**, and **covered** (testudinate = "turtle-shelled"). **Tuscan** interiors are those in which the transverse beams of the atrium have hanging joists [between them] and gutters running inward from the corners of the walls to the intersections of the beams, with rafters sloping downward into a central compluvium to collect rainfall. In **Corinthian** [interiors] the beams and compluvia are placed in the same way, but the beams that project inward from the walls are arranged around a ring of columns. **Tetrastyle** interiors, with columns under their corner beams, offer both the greatest utility and the greatest soundness, as they are neither forced to sustain great stresses nor are they weighed down with joists. 2. **Displuviate** interiors are those in which outward-

sloping rafters, bearing the frame of the roof, throw off rainwater. These are most serviceable in winter quarters, because their upright compluvia do not interfere with lighting the dining rooms. But when it comes to upkeep, they are a great nuisance, because the walls contain pipes all round to collect rainwater, and these pipes are slow to take up the water as it flows down the gutters; thus they overflow and fill with standing water, which corrupts the plaster and the walls in these types of building. **Covered** interiors are made where there are no great stresses on the building; they provide ample living space on the floor above.

3. The lengths and widths of **atria** (Figure 92) are formed according to three types. The first type is designed as follows: when the length is divided into five parts, three are assigned to the width. For the second type, when the length is divided into three parts, two are assigned to the width. For the third type, make a square whose sides are equal to the width, draw a diagonal line, and whatever the distance of that diagonal, this is the length of the atrium. 4. To the underside of the beams, their height should be equal to the length minus one-fourth; within the remaining fourth the coffers and their frames above the beams should be apportioned.

The width of the **alae** (wings)* on right and left, if the length of the atrium is from thirty to forty feet, should be set at one-third this measure. From forty to fifty feet, the length should be divided into three and one-half parts, and of these one part should go to the wings. If, on the other hand, the length will be from fifty feet to sixty, a fourth part of the length should be assigned to the alae. From sixty to eighty feet the length should be divided into four and one-half parts, and of these one part will be the width of the wings. From eighty to one hundred feet the length divided into five parts will establish the proper width for the wings. Their lintel beams should be placed at a height equal to their width.

5. As for the **tablinum,** when the breadth of the atrium is twenty feet, take one-third of this sum away and the rest should go to the tablinum. If the atrium is from thirty to forty feet, half its width should be assigned to the tablinum. When it is from forty to sixty feet, its width should be divided into five, and of these, two go to the tablinum. For smaller atria cannot have the same principles of symmetry that larger ones do. If we use the proportions of larger atria in the design of smaller ones, the tablinum and the alae will be too small to be functional. If, on the other hand, we use the proportional systems of smaller atria to design the larger

ones, the dependent rooms will seem vacant and oversized. Therefore I thought that the principles for the dimensions of atria should be recorded precisely in the interests of function and appearance. 6. The height of the tablinum to the beam should equal the width with an eighth part added on. Its coffering should be elevated to one-third of the width added on to the height of the beam itself. The entryways for smaller atria should be determined by the width of the tablinum, minus one-third; those for larger atria should be one-half. Place the *imagines* (ancestral portraits), with their ornaments, at a height corresponding to the width of the wings.

As for the widths of the entryways in proportion to their height, complete them just as the proportional systems for doorways have been explained in the fourth book: if they shall be Doric, as for Doric doors; if Ionic, as described for Ionic. The opening of the compluvium should be left at no less than one-fourth and no more than one-third the width of the atrium; its length should be worked out in proportion with the length of the atrium.

7. **Peristyle courtyards** (Figure 93),* lying crosswise to the atrium, should be one-third longer than they are deep; the columns should be as tall as the porticoes of the peristyle are wide. The intercolumniations of peristyles should be no less than three, no more than four column diameters. But if the columns of the peristyle are to be made in the Doric manner, use the modules just as I have described them in the fourth book for Doric temples and place the columns according to those modules and the proportions of the triglyphs.

8. For **triclinia,** whatever the width is to be, the length should be twice that. The heights of all oblong enclosed rooms should have this kind of ratio: add together the length and width, and take one-half of this sum; this number is assigned to the height. If there are to be exedrae or square oeci, the heights should be extended to one and one-half times the width. **Picture galleries,** like exedrae, should be set up with generous proportions. **Corinthian oeci, tetrastyle oeci,** and those called **Egyptian,** should employ the same principles of length and width as recorded for triclinia, but because of the inclusion of columns they should be made more spacious.

9. This is the difference between Corinthian and Egyptian oeci. Corinthian oeci have single columns placed either on a podium or on the ground, and above they should have epistyles and cornices either of fine woodwork or of stucco. In addition, over the cornices

they have curved coffering bent along the arc of a circle. In Egyptian oeci there are epistyles above the columns, and from the epistyles to the surrounding walls joists should be installed, and flooring over the joists, so that there may be an open corridor all round. Then, above the epistyle, in line with the lower row of columns, a second row of columns should be placed, smaller by one-fourth than the first. The area above the epistyles and ornaments of this second row should be decorated with a coffered ceiling, and windows should be set in between the upper columns; the likeness will seem to be more that of a basilica than of a Corinthian dining room.

10. There are also those oeci which the Greeks call Cyzicene, although they are not an Italian custom. These are located to face the north and especially to face on gardens, and they have folding doors in the middle. These are so long and wide that two triclinia might be placed within them, facing each other, and still leave room to walk around them. To the left and right they have windows with folding shutters, so that from the dining couches there is a view from the windows onto the garden. Their heights are one and one-half times their width.

11. In these types of buildings all the features of their proportional systems should be carried out that can be completed without impediment by the site, and the windows, if they are not darkened by the height of the walls, will be easily laid out. If, on the other hand, they are blocked by crowding or other restrictions, this is when subtractions and additions are made to the proportional system with the help of inventiveness and judgment, in order that charms not unlike those of true symmetry will be achieved.

CHAPTER 4: ORIENTATION OF ROOMS

1. Now we shall explain where types of buildings with particular characteristics should face as befits their use and the regions of the sky. **Winter dining rooms** and **baths** should face the setting winter sun, both because they should make use of the evening light and also because the setting sun, shining full on and yielding up heat, makes this region warmer at evening time. **Cubicula*** and **libraries** should face east, for the morning light makes them serviceable, and furthermore, the books in libraries will not rot. For in libraries that face south and west, the books are spoiled by worms and

moisture, as the oncoming moist winds give rise to such things and nurture them, while as they pour forth their moist breath they corrupt the scrolls by discoloring them [with mold].

2. **Spring dining rooms** and **autumn dining rooms** should face east. Extended in this direction, with their windows facing the force of the sun, this, as it proceeds westward, moderates their temperature in the season when one is accustomed to use them. **Summer dining rooms** should face north because that region of the heavens does not, like the rest, become boiling hot in the heat of the solstice. Instead, because it is turned away from the course of the sun, it is always cool and when in use, a dining room so oriented affords good health and pleasure. The same orientation is appropriate for picture galleries and the workshops of brocaders, embroiderers, and painters, so that the colors in their work, thanks to the consistency of the light, will not change their quality.

CHAPTER 5: CORRECTNESS (DECOR)

1. Once these things have been set out with regard to the regions of the heavens, then it is time to note also by what principles the personal areas of private buildings should be constructed for the head of the family and how public areas should be constructed with outsiders in mind as well. **Personal areas** are those into which there is no possibility of entrance except by invitation, like cubicula, triclinia, baths, and the other rooms that have such functions. **Public areas** are those into which even uninvited members of the public may also come by right, that is, vestibules, cavaedia, peristyles, and any rooms that may perform this sort of function.

And so, for those of moderate income, magnificent vestibules, tablina, and atria are unnecessary, because they perform their duties by making the rounds visiting others, rather than having others make the rounds visiting them. 2. Those who deal in farm products have stables and sheds in their entrance courts, and in their homes should have installed crypts, granaries, storerooms and the other furnishings that have more to do with storing provisions than with maintaining an elegant correctness. Likewise, for moneylenders and tax collectors public rooms should be more commodious, better looking, and well secured, but for lawyers and orators they should be more elegant, and spacious enough to accommodate meetings. For the most prominent citizens, those who should carry out their duties to the citizenry by holding honorific titles and magistracies, vestibules should be constructed that are lofty and lordly, the atria and peristyles at their most spacious, lush gardens and broad walkways refined as properly befits their dignity. In addition to these, there should be libraries, picture galleries, and basilicas, outfitted in a manner not dissimilar to the magnificence of public works, for in the homes of these people, often enough, both public deliberations and private judgments and arbitrations are carried out.* 3. Therefore, if buildings are set out like this, by these principles and according to the individual types of persons, just as is written about correctness in Book 1, there will be nothing to reproach in them, for they will have comfortable and faultless execution in every respect. Furthermore, these principles will not only serve for buildings in the city, but also for those in the countryside, except for the fact that in the city the atria are customarily next to the entrance, whereas in the countryside and in pseudo-urban buildings the peristyle comes first, then afterward the atria, and these have paved porticoes around them looking into palaestras and walkways.

To the extent that I could record the principles for urban buildings I have set them down comprehensively. Now I shall state how the layout of rural buildings should be executed so that the buildings are convenient to use, and by what principles they should be designed.

CHAPTER 6: RURAL BUILDINGS (FIGURE 95)*

1. First of all, as regards a healthful site, just as was written in the first book about locating city walls, the area should be inspected and the villas located accordingly. Their size should be determined according to the amount of land available and the supply of crops. The courtyards and their size should be defined according to the number of cattle and however many yoke of oxen it will be necessary to keep in them. Within the courtyard, the kitchen should be laid out in the warmest possible place, the cattle stalls should adjoin them, with the mangers facing toward the hearth and the eastern region of the heavens, so that the cattle, by facing the light and fire, will not become shaggy. Likewise, farmers who are experienced[4] in the lay of land and sky do not think that cattle should face any region of the heavens except the rising sun. 2. Now the widths of the cattle stalls should not be less than ten feet and not more than fifteen, and their length such that each yoke will occupy no less than seven feet apiece. The baths should also adjoin the kitchen, for by this means the facilities for heavy-duty washing will not be far off. The olive press should also be next to the kitchen, for in this way access to the olives will be convenient. It should also have a wine cellar connected to it whose windows face north. If it has windows in any other part, which the sun might warm, the wine in this chamber, stirred up by the heat, will be weak. 3. The oil room should be placed so that there is light from the south and the warm regions, for the oil should not be chilled, but rather kept fluid by the warmth of heat. The size of these rooms should be made in accordance with the amount of harvest collected and the number of storage jars and if these measure one *culleus* (91 liters), they should occupy a space of four feet each in diameter. The olive press itself, if it is not turned by a screw, but rather compressed by handspikes and a pressing lever, should measure no less than forty feet; in this way there will be enough room for the man at the press. Its width should be no less than sixteen feet, for in this way there will be plenty of free movement and space available to the workers when work is fully underway. If the site calls for two presses, twenty-four feet should go to the width.

4. Sheep and goat pens should be large enough that individual sheep may have no less than four and one-half feet of space, and not more than six. Granaries should be elevated[5] and laid out so that they face either north or northeast, and in this way the grain cannot heat quickly; instead, chilled by the breeze it is preserved indefinitely. The other regions give rise to weevils and the other little creatures whose habit it is to ruin grain. The places in the villa that are especially warm should be designated for the horse stables, so long as they do not face the hearth. For when draft animals are stabled next to fire, they become shaggy. 5. Likewise, mangers that are located outside the kitchen in the open air facing east are certainly useful. For when cattle are brought into them in the morning, under a clear winter sky, they become more sleek because they

---

4 *inperiti* GH; *periti* Philander.

5 Granger has "with concrete floor," presumably following H *sublinata*; we follow G *sublimata*.

take their feed facing the sun. Storage barns for grain, haylofts, and spelt, as well as the bread oven, should be constructed outside the villa, so that it will be more protected from the dangers of fire. If the villa is going to be on the more refined side, it should be designed according to the symmetries that have been recorded earlier for urban buildings, so long as this does not interfere with its serviceability as a country house.

NATURAL LIGHTING (FIGURE 96)

6. One should take care that all buildings are well lighted, but clearly this is easier to achieve in villas, because no neighbor's wall will stand in the way; in the city, on the other hand, the height of party walls or the narrowness of a site may, by posing obstacles, create areas of darkness.

This is how you can make a test of the situation. Extend a line in the direction from which light is desired, beginning at the top of the wall that seems to stand in the way and toward the place where light is supposed to be admitted; if from this line, when one looks upward, an ample expanse of open sky is visible, then there will be light in that place without hindrance. 7. But if beams or lintels or joists stand in the way, then put an opening higher up and admit the light that way. In short, if there is a clear view of the sky from any part of the building, then space for windows should be reserved there; by this method, buildings will always be well lighted. To be sure, there is a great need for light in triclinia and other such chambers, but also in passageways, sloping corridors, and staircases, because people carrying various burdens often run into one another on stairs.

I have described the layout of the buildings of our countrymen as best I could, so that they would not be incomprehensible to builders. Now I will also give a cursory account of how buildings are laid out according to Greek customs, so that such buildings will not be unknown to the reader.

CHAPTER 7: GREEK HOUSES (FIGURE 97)

1. The Greeks do not use atria,* and so they do not build them; coming in from the front doors, they make narrow corridors. On one side of these there are horse stables and on the other the doorman's quarters, and

then immediately after this they install interior doors. The place between the two sets of doors is called *thyrôreion* in Greek. Next comes the entrance into the *peristylion*. This peristyle has porticoes on three sides; on the side facing south it has two piers standing a considerable distance apart, across which beams are carried. Whatever the distance between these piers, that expanse minus one-third goes to the depth of the portico. This place is named *prostas* by some, and *pastas* by others. 2. Inside these places large oeci are put up, in which the lady of the house sits with her woolworkers. To the right and left of the *prostas* cubicula are located, of which one is called the *thalamos* and the other the *amphithalamos*. Around this, under the porticoes, everyday dining rooms and cubicula are set out; also the servants' quarters. This part of the building is called the women's quarters, the *gynaeconitis*. 3. To these are connected larger residential quarters with more ornate peristyles, in which there are four porticoes of equal height; alternatively the portico facing south may be designed with more lofty columns. This peristyle with one taller portico is called Rhodian. These residential quarters have conspicuous vestibules and their own dignified doorways; the porticoes of the peristyles are decorated with stucco and fresco and inlaid coffers. In the porticoes that face north there are Cyzicene dining rooms and picture galleries, in those that face east there are libraries, exedrae in the porticoes facing west; those facing south have square oeci; these are of such ample dimension that four sets of couches could easily be spread within them and still reserve generous space for the providing of service and entertainment. 4. In these oeci the men's banquets take place. For it was never part of their custom for the ladies of their houses to join the men at dinner.[6]

Now these residential quarters with peristyles are called *andronitides*, for within them men move about without contact with women.

In addition, to the right and left small residential quarters are set up with their own entrances and convenient dining rooms* and bedrooms, so that upon arrival, guests are not shown into the peristyles but into these guest quarters. When the Greeks were more refined and more wealthy,* they outfitted dining rooms and bedrooms with well-stocked pantries for their arriving guests, and on the first day would invite them to dinner;

---

6 *Scripsi*, reading *maribus* for *moribus*. IDR.

subsequently they would send over chickens, eggs, vegetables, fruit, and other rustic produce. For this reason painters who in their pictures imitated the things that were sent to guests called such paintings "hospitalities," *xenia.* Thus heads of households, although guests, did not seem to be away from home, for they had in these guest quarters a generous amount of privacy.

5. Furthermore, between the two peristyles and the guest quarters there are corridors, called *mesauloe,* because they are placed "in the middle between two halls"; we call these corridors *androne.* But this is a very amazing thing, because it is not an appropriate term either in Greek or in Latin.* For the Greeks apply the word *androne* to the oeci where men's banquets usually take place because women do not enter there. Other terms, too, are similar in Greek and Latin, like *xystus, prothyrum, telamones,* and many other words of this kind. *Xystos* is a broad portico according to Greek terminology, where athletes train during the winter season. But we call outdoor walkways "xysta," whereas the Greeks call them *paradromides.* So, too, *prothyra* in Greek applies to the vestibules before entrance doors, and what we call "prothyra" the Greeks call *diathyra.* 6. Likewise, if statues of male figures hold up mutules or cornices, we call them *telamones* – the reasons for this or why they are so called are not to be found in the history books – and the Greeks call them *atlantes.* For Atlas is portrayed in history as holding up the cosmos, because he was first to see to it that, because of his vigorous intellect and his cleverness, the course of the sun and the moon and the principle of the revolution of all the stars would be passed on to humankind; because he bestowed this favor, he is depicted by painters and sculptors as holding up the firmament, and his daughters, the Atlantids, whom we call the Vergiliae and the Greeks in turn call the Pleiades, have been consecrated among the stars in the firmament. 7. Now I did not bring up these examples in order to suggest that the habits of naming and language be changed; however, I did think that they should be explained so that they are not unknown to lovers of learning.

I have explained the customs by which buildings are designed according to the Italian fashion and the traditions of the Greeks, and as for their proportional systems, I have recorded the proportions for individual types. Therefore, since I have written before about their beauty and correctness, now let us explain about sound construction, and how buildings can be designed to last until great age without flaws.

CHAPTER 8: CONSTRUCTION: RELIEVING ARCHES, SUBSTRUCTURES, RETAINING WALLS

1. Those buildings that have been laid out on ground level will be sound until old age without a doubt, so long as their foundations have been made as we described in previous books for city walls and theaters. But if, on the other hand, underground rooms or chambers* are going to be installed, then their foundations should be made thicker than the structures that will be in the upper parts of the building, and the walls, piers, and columns of the upper stories should be placed in line with those of the lower, centered so that they always correspond with solid masonry underneath. If the stresses of walls or columns were to be borne on unsupported spans, they could never attain lasting durability.

2. In addition, if posts are installed between the lintel blocks in line with the piers or antae, then they will not develop flaws. For if stone lintels[7] or wooden beams are loaded with masonry, they will sag in the middle and eventually break the deteriorated structure apart. If, on the other hand, posts are installed and wedged in place, they will not allow the lintels to sag or to injure the masonry.

3. Likewise, make certain that arches relieve the weight of the walls onto their voussoirs,* and that they are centered over the opening. For if arches spring from voussoirs that begin beyond the wooden beam or the head of a stone lintel, in the first place the wood will not bend because its load has been relieved, and secondly, if in time it begins to develop flaws, it can be replaced easily, and without piling up braces.

4. Similarly, if buildings are built up on piers, and their vaults are enclosed by voussoir arches with their joins pointing toward the center, then the outermost piers in these buildings should be made wider than the rest, so that they will have the strength to resist when the voussoir arches, compressed by the weight of the walls, push toward the center along their joins and force their imposts outward. Thus, if the corner piers are of a generous size, by containing the stresses of the voussoirs they will make the building itself sound.

5. Once it has been seen to that all these procedures have been carried out in construction, then it is no less imperative to ensure that all the masonry is absolutely

7 Reading *limina* with GH.

on the perpendicular, with no lean in any part of it. The greatest concern should be for the substructures, because in them the earth fill tends to bring about a host of problems. For the earth cannot always have the same weight as it does during the summer: in the winter season, it expands in weight and mass from the abundance of rainwater it absorbs, breaking apart sections of masonry or making them protrude. 6. In order to remedy this fault beforehand, do the following: first, the thickness of the masonry should be determined with respect to the amount of fill, and then on the facade buttresses or reinforcements should be built in bond with the masonry itself, and these should be as far distant from one another as the height of the projected foundation, and their thickness should be identical to its thickness (Figure 99). They should jut out at the bottom in relationship to the projected thickness of the substructure, and then they are contracted stepwise until at the top they have a projection equal to the thickness of the wall structure. Furthermore, buttresses should also be constructed on the inside facing the earth fill, in bond with the wall, in a sawtooth pattern so that each individual "tooth" projects as far from the wall as the projected height of the foundation; the teeth should have a thickness equal to that of the walls. 7. At the very corners, moreover, make a mark along each wall at a distance inward from the inner corner that is equal to the height of the foundation. Then construct an oblique wall connecting these two points, and from the center of the oblique wall connect another oblique wall to the corner of the exterior wall. The "teeth" and the oblique walls will prevent the fill from pressing on the wall with its full force by restraining and dissipating the stresses.

8. I have explained how a flawless project should be laid out and how those undertaking it may take precautions. (When it comes to replacing roof tiles or beams or rafters, there need not be the same degree of concern as with these former matters, because no matter how flawed these latter components may be, they are changed with ease.) As for elements that are not thought to be solid, I have shown by what methods they may be made durable and how they may be installed. 9. Now the exact type of material that should be used is not under the architect's control, because all types of building material do not occur in all places, as has been explained in the previous volume. Besides, it is the owner's prerogative to build in brick or concrete or squared stone as he wills. Therefore, the test of all architectural works should be made on the basis of three things: that is, the excellence of the craftsmanship, the magnificence of the expense, and the quality of the design.* When a magnificently completed work is looked upon, the lavishness is praised; this is the owner's domain. When it is completed with superior craftsmanship, the standards of the artisan are what is approved. But when the work has a masterful beauty because of its symmetries and their harmony, then the glory goes to the architect. 10. These distinctions are rightly made, because with their help the architect may accept advice both from the craftsmen engaged in the work and from the owner. For all people, not just architects, know how to recognize what is good, and the difference between the inexpert and themselves is this: the inexpert cannot recognize what the work will be until it is done, whereas the architect has both the finished and the unfinished project in mind, and before undertaking it has decided what it will be with regard to beauty and function and correctness.

I have recorded the things that I thought were useful for private buildings and how they should be executed. As for their final finishing, in the following volume I will show how they may be elegant and flawless into their old age.

❖

FINISHING

PREFACE

1. Our ancestors, not only wisely but also usefully, established the practice of transmitting their ideas to posterity through the reports of treatises, so that these ideas would not perish, but instead, as they grew with each passing age and were published in books, they would arrive, step by step, at the utmost refinement of learning. Thus it is not moderate, but infinite thanks that should be given those who did not jealously let their ideas pass in silence, but rather took care to hand on to memory their thoughts of every kind, preserved in their writings. 2. Indeed, had they not done so, we could not have known what deeds were done in Troy, nor what Thales, Democritus, Anaxagoras, Xenophanes, and the other physicists had thought about Nature,* nor what rules for living had been set down for humanity by Socrates, Plato, Aristotle, Zeno, Epicurus and the other philosophers,* nor what deeds Croesus, Alexander, and the other kings had done,* and for what reasons – not unless our ancestors, in compiling their precepts, had published them in treatises, commending them to the memory of all for posterity.

3. And just as thanks are due to these authors, those who, by contrast, steal the writings of these others and pass them off as their own should be censured, and those who do not rely on their own ideas in their writings, but rather, with envious character, do violence to other men's work and glory in it, these people are not only to be criticized, but, because they have lived impiously, should even be prosecuted as criminals. Nor indeed are these matters said to have been lightly punished by the ancients. It is not out of place to explain what outcomes such cases had before a court of law, when they have been handed down to us. 4. The Attalid kings, introduced to the manifold charms of literature, had established the great library of Pergamum* for the delight of all; then, likewise, Ptolemy, with boundless zeal and spurred by ambitious desire, had striven with no less passion to compete by establishing the library at Alexandria. Yet what he accomplished with the utmost devotion he thought insufficient unless he took care that, by sowing seeds, it be increased and extended. And so he dedicated games to the Muses and to Apollo and established prizes and honors for the victors among the public writers, just as usually happens with athletes.

5. Once they had been established, as the time came when the games were at hand, judges skilled in literature had to be chosen to evaluate the contests. When the king had chosen six men from the city, and could not come so quickly upon a seventh who was qualified, he referred his problem to the governors of the library, and asked them if they knew anyone who was available for the purpose. They told him then that there was a certain Aristophanes,* who with the utmost enthusiasm and the utmost diligence had been making daily readings through every one of the books, in sequence. And thus with the convening of the Games, when the judges' seats were apportioned, this aforementioned Aristophanes took his seat in his designated place. 6. The first array of poets had been brought in to compete and they recited their compositions; the whole audience signaled to the judges which work they should approve. And thus when the opinions of each were asked individually, six together said that they would award first prize to the poet who, they had noticed, had most pleased the crowd; second prize would go to the runner-up. But Aristophanes, when asked his opinion, ordered that the poet who had least pleased the crowd be proclaimed the winner. 7. Now when the king and everyone else took vehement exception to this, he stood up and was granted his request that he be allowed to speak. And so, once silence had fallen, he informed them that his choice alone was a true poet – the others had recited other people's verse, and in his opinion the judges should be concerning themselves with writing, not plagiarism.

The people were amazed, and the king still doubtful; then, relying on his memory he pulled volume after volume out of certain cabinets, and comparing their texts with those recited he forced the plagiarists to confess. With this, the king ordered the others to be prosecuted for theft and, when they had been convicted, ignominiously dismissed them, while he heaped Aristophanes with gifts and appointed him head librarian.

8. In later years Zoilus,* who took a nickname so that he would be called *Homeromastix* ("Homer's Scourge"), came from Macedonia to Alexandria and gave a reading before the king from the books he had composed *Against the Iliad* and *Against the Odyssey.* But when Ptolemy had learned that the father of poets and forerunner of all literature was being abused in absentia, and that he whose works were admired by all nations was being subjected to criticism by this man, he indignantly withheld any reaction to the reading. When Zoilus, meanwhile, had stayed on for a time in the kingdom, he was pressed for money; he finally applied to the king, asking whether something might be granted him. 9. The king is said to have replied that Homer, who had died a thousand years before, had nourished many thousands of people all through time, and likewise anyone who claimed to have a superior talent should be able to sustain not only themselves but many others besides. And, in short, various traditions report that he was condemned to death as a parricide, for some writers say that he was crucified by Philadelphus; others say that he was stoned in Chios, still others that he was burned alive on a pyre at Smyrna. Whichever of these fates he actually met, it was a well-deserved punishment. For no one seems to deserve otherwise if they bring charges against those who cannot explain in person what they meant when they were writing.*

10. But I, Caesar, have neither substituted my name on a text while altering the indications that it is another person's property, nor have I sought approval for myself by slandering another's work; instead I offer infinite thanks to all writers, because, with outstanding wisdom and talent, they have prepared abundant riches drawn from the ages, each of a different type, from which we, as if drinking in water from a spring, and adapting them to our own enterprise, will have more eloquent and ready proficiency in writing, and trusting in such authors we will dare to provide new precepts.

11. Therefore, because I observed that such were their initial steps readied for my enterprise, from that point, by absorbing them, I began to proceed further. In Athens, when Aeschylus was producing tragedies,[1] Agatharchus was first to work for the theater and wrote a treatise about it.* Learning from this, Democritus and Anaxagoras wrote on the same subject, namely how the extension of rays from a certain established center point ought to correspond in a natural ratio to the eyes' line of sight, so that they could represent the appearance of buildings in scene paintings, no longer by some uncertain method, but precisely, both the surfaces that were depicted frontally, and those that seemed either to be receding or projecting.

12. Later, Silenus published a volume on Doric symmetries, Theodorus on the Doric temple of Juno on Samos, Chersiphron and Metagenes on the Ionic temple of Diana at Ephesus, Pytheos on the Ionic sanctuary of Minerva, which is in Priene; likewise, Ictinus and Carpion on the Doric temple of Minerva, which is on the acropolis at Athens, Theodorus of Phocaea about the Tholus in Delphi, Philo on the symmetries of temples and on the arsenal, which was made in the port of Piraeus, Hermogenes on the Ionic pseudodipteral temple of Diana at Magnesia and the monopteros of Father Liber in Teos, likewise Arcesius on Corinthian symmetries, and the Ionic temple to Aesculapius at Tralles, which he is also said to have made with his own hands, Satyrus and Pytheos on the Mausoleum, designers to whom, indeed, happiness brought the greatest and highest reward.* 13. For their skills are judged to have the highest acclaim, ever flowering for perpetual ages, and indeed [those skills] had rendered their ideas outstanding service. For individual artists have taken on individual facades in competition with one another for the sake of the overall ornament and for individual acclaim: Leochares, Bryaxis, Scopas, Praxiteles, and – some think – Timotheus as well; their outstanding skill in their art propelled the fame of their work to a place among the seven wonders of the world.*

14. Aside from these, many others, less illustrious, recorded precepts on symmetries, like Nexaris, Theocydes, Demophilos, Pollis, Leonidas, Silanion, Melampus, Sarnacus, and Euphranor, not to mention those who have written about machines, like Diades, Archytas, Archimedes, Ctesibios, Nymphodorus, Philo of Byzantium, Diphilos, Democles, Charias, Polyidos, Pyrrhos, and Agesistratos.*

Of their treatises, I have noted what is useful, and brought it all together in a single body, and all the more because I realized how many Greek books have been published on the subject, but how very few have been written by our own people. For Fufius,[2] surprisingly, first of all,

---

1 Vitruvius's choice of the word "doceo" is a direct translation from the Greek *didaskô* = "to produce a drama." The MSS "ad scaenam fecit" may well be another direct translation from Greek (*ta kata skênên* or some similar phrase).

2 *Fuficius* GH; but see Q. Fufius Calenus, tribune of the plebs in 61 B.C., legate of Caesar in Gaul and Spain.

undertook to publish a volume; likewise Terentius Varro devoted one volume of his *On the Nine Disciplines* to architecture. Publius Septimius wrote two.* 15. So far, no one seems to have devoted himself to this kind of writing beyond one or two volumes, although our ancient citizens were great architects who could have composed writings no less elegantly [than they built]. For in Athens the architects Antistates and Callaeschros and Antimachides and Porinos³ laid the foundations for the temple to Olympian Jove, the one that Pisistratus was building, and then after his death they left off the work because the democracy intervened.* Some four hundred years later, when King Antiochus promised to take on the expense of this work, the great cellas, the setting out of a double colonnade, and the placing of the epistyles and other ornaments according to a proportional system, were designed, with great skill and the deepest learning, by Cossutius, a Roman citizen, acting with distinction as architect. This work is mentioned for its magnificence not only among the common people but also by the elite.

16. For in four places there are designs for temples outfitted [entirely] in marble work; they are known, to their conspicuous fame, by the names of their tutelary deities. Their excellence and the far-seeing magnificence of their inventions have their respect among the very thrones⁴ of the gods. The first of these, the temple of Ephesian Diana, was undertaken by Chersiphron of Cnossos and his son Metagenes, which afterward Demetrius, a temple slave of this very Diana, and Paeonius the Ephesian are said to have completed. This same Paeonius and Daphnis of Miletus undertook the temple of Milesian Apollo, also with Ionic symmetries.* Ictinus covered over the enormous cella of Ceres and Proserpina at Eleusis* in the Doric manner, without exterior columns, to increase the space available for the holy rituals. 17. Later, when Demetrius of Phaleron held power in Athens, Philo, by placing columns in front of the temple along the facade, made it prostyle. By this means he enlarged the space in the vestibule for the initiates and contributed the utmost authority to the building. In Athens itself, as we have said earlier, Cossutius is recorded as having taken charge of designing the Olympium, with a large-scale modular system, and Corinthian proportions and symmetries – but of his treatise on the project, nothing can be found. Nor are we lacking a treatise on these matters from Cossutius alone; we have none from G. Mucius either, who trusted

in his great learning to complete Marius's temple to Honor and Battle-courage,* establishing the symmetries of cella, columns, and epistyles according to the proper principles of art. Indeed, if this temple had been of marble, so that the authority it had for its magnificence and expense were equal to that earned by the refinement of its art, it would be named among the foremost works of architecture.

18. Therefore, because our ancients, too, can be found to be great architects no less than the Greeks, and there are many more such within living memory, and among them only a few have published treatises, I thought that I could not remain silent, but would instead describe individual matters of architecture in individual volumes in an orderly fashion. And thus, because I have recorded the principles of private buildings in my sixth volume, in the present, which is number seven, I will set forth the principles whereby the final finishing of buildings may achieve both beauty and durability.

CHAPTER 1: FLOORING (FIGURE 100)

1. First I shall begin with rubble subpavement, which is the first business of finishing, in order that it may have the highest principles of care and solidity. If ground level is to be paved, ensure that the soil is consistently solid, then level it and put in a rubble underlayer. If the site is entirely or partially on fill, then it should be carefully compacted by a leveller. In joist floors make careful note that any wall that does not extend to the very top of the building is not built up right underneath the pavement; instead, any such wall should have the decking hanging free above it. For if solid masonry comes right under the floor, then, as the floor beams dry out or begin to subside from sagging, the masonry, with its inflexible solidity, will necessarily create fissures in the pavement along its line to the right and left. 2. Equal care should be taken not to combine beams of winter oak with ordinary oak, because as soon as ordinary oaken beams absorb water they twist and make fissures in the pavement. But if there is no winter oak available and necessity demands that, because of the lack, they be made of ordinary oak, it seems that this is what to do: cut them into narrower sections. For the weaker they are, the more easily they are fixed in place with nails.* Then on the extreme ends of individual beams, fix two braces in place with nails, so that the

3 *Pormos* H; *Porinos* G.
4 Reading *sessimonio* with Giocondo.

beams cannot distort the corner joins with their twisting. Nothing made out of Turkey oak, beech, or ash can last for long.

When the decking is finished in an upper story, it should be strewn with fern, or otherwise, with straw, so that the woodwork will be protected from damage by lime. 3. Above this the underlayer is set down of stones no smaller than can fill the hand. Once the underlayers have been installed, if the rubble for the subpavement is new, then mix it three-to-one with lime; if it is reused, then the mixture should be five-to-two. Then the subpavement is laid in with wooden rods by ten-man work gangs, and compacted by steady pounding. By the time the pounding is done it should be no less than a *dodrans* (three-quarters foot) thick.* Above this, a core of crushed terracotta should be installed, mixed three-to-one with lime, and it should be no less than six digits thick. Above the core the pavements should be laid to the square and to the level, whether they are in stone inlay (*opus sectile*) or mosaic.

4. When the pavements have been laid and their inclines built up, then they should be polished like this: if they are going to be in stone inlay, none of the edges of the lozenges or triangles or squares or hexagons* should protrude; instead, their joints should be set level in every direction. If the pavements are to be of mosaic, take care that all the tesserae have been set in the same direction, for if their setting is not identically level, the polishing cannot be carried out as it should. Pavements in Tiburtine herringbone tile work should be carefully executed so that they have neither protuberances nor ridges, but are uniform and polished on the level.* Above this, once the floor has been ground with rough and fine polish, powdered marble is sprinkled over it, and coats of lime and sand are laid down over this.

5. It is most suitable to make pavements in open-air locations; floor joists, on the other hand, expanding with moisture or contracting as they dry, sagging and subsiding, create fissures in pavement as they shift, and besides, ice and frost do not permit them to last forever. Yet if necessity dictates, this is how to proceed in order to make pavements over floor joists as flawless as possible: once the decking has been installed, above them another layer of decking should be laid at right angles to the first and fixed in place with nails to provide a double framework for the joists. Then, together with [two parts of] fresh rubble, mix a third part of crushed terracotta; to this mixture lime should be introduced in the mortar in a ratio of two parts to five. 6. Once the underlayer [of fist-sized rocks] has been laid, then the subpavement is installed, and after it has been beaten it should be no less than one foot thick. After the core has been laid down as described, a pavement of tesserae trimmed to about two digits in size should be put in with a slope of two digits for every ten feet;* if this is well mixed and well polished, it will be safe from every flaw. In order to protect the mortar from the strains of frost, every year, before winter comes, saturate it with the residue from pressing olive oil; in this way it will not admit or absorb frost.

7. If it seems advisable to take even more care, two-foot tiles, joined together, should be placed over the subpavement with the mortar underneath, and these tiles should have small one-digit channels on each of their edges. When the tiles are joined together, these channels should be filled with lime that has been mixed with oil, and the joins are rubbed together once they have been compressed. In this way, the lime that has adhered in the channels solidifies in an interlocking pattern as it dries, and will not allow water, nor anything else, to penetrate the joints. Once this layer has been installed, then the core is laid over it and compacted by beating with rods. Over this put in a top layer either of large tesserae or of herringbone terracotta as described earlier;* if pavements are made in this fashion, they will not deteriorate quickly.

CHAPTER 2: PLASTERWORK

1. Now we shall take our leave of the care of pavements, and explain about plasterwork (Figure 101).* This will be done properly if clods of first-rate lime are softened long before there is need for them. If a clod is baked lightly in the kiln, then, as it is softened over many days the remaining liquid, forced to boil away, will bake the clod to an even degree. If it has not been softened all the way through, but is used when only recently fired, then, when applied, it will develop blisters, because it has raw grains hidden inside. If these grains are put into the work without having been softened to an even degree, they dissolve and break apart the finish of the plasterwork. 2. If the softening has been done reasonably, and the work is to be prepared with care, take an axe, and chop through the softened lime to its core as it lies in the pit, just as if it were wood being chopped. If the axe meets with granules,

then the lime is not yet ready. When the tool comes through dry and pure, it indicates that the lime is weakened and parched. When it is rich and properly softened, then, clinging all around that tool like glue, it shows that it has been tempered in every respect. Then get the machines ready and set in the ceilings of the rooms, unless they are going to be decorated with coffered ceilings.*

CHAPTER 3: CEILINGS (FIGURE 102)

1. Now that the method for ceilings is the matter at hand, this is what to do. Place straight battens at an interval of no more than every two feet, and these should preferably be of cypress, because silver fir will deteriorate quickly with rot and age. When these battens have been set in a circular pattern, they should be secured by a row of chains to the joists, or, under the roof (if this is the case) fixed with closely set iron nails, and these chains should be made of the kind of wood that neither rot nor age nor dampness can harm, that is, from boxwood, juniper, olive, oak (robur), cypress, and others like this, except for ordinary oak, because its twisting creates fissures in the projects that employ it.

2. Once the battens have been placed, then, with a rope made from Spanish broom, bind pounded Greek reeds to them as the design dictates. Then, on top of the ceiling, a mortar of lime and sand mixed together is laid on immediately, so that whatever seepage falls from the beams or the roof will be contained. But if there is no supply of Greek reeds, then narrow swamp reeds should be bundled together, and with a silken cord they should be adjusted to the proper length and thickness by attaching one to the next, provided that there will be an interval of no more than two feet between two knots of the attachments. These should be bound to the battens with a rope, as described earlier, and wooden pegs driven into them. Everything else should be prepared as described. 3. Once the ceilings have been laid out and interwoven, their lower surfaces should be plastered, then sanded, and then polished with chalk or marble.

When the ceilings have been polished, then crown moldings should be placed underneath them, which ought to be made as slender and fine as possible, for if they are large, they will be pulled down by their weight and unable to stay in place. For these, gypsum is the last thing one wants to mix in; instead, they should be composed of marble sifted to a uniform consistency, so that one part will not anticipate another in drying, but the whole will dry at a uniform rate. Equally one should avoid designs like those in our forebears' ceilings, because their surfaces, suspended over heavy cornices, are dangerous.

4. Some forms of crown molding are smooth, and others are decorated. In rooms where fire or several lamps are to be installed, they should be made smooth, so that they are more easily cleaned. In summer rooms and exedras, where there is hardly any smoke and soot can do little harm, then they should be decorated. For white work, in the pride of its whiteness, absorbs smoke not only from the building where it is located but also from those around it.

5. Once the crown moldings have been put in, the walls should be plastered as roughly as possible,* and afterward, when the plaster is nearly dry, the layers of sand mortar should be applied so that the planes of the walls are flat and on the level, their rise on the perpendicular, and their corners executed at right angles. This is how the appearance of the plaster in painted decoration will look faultless. As the plaster dries, a second and third layer should be applied. Thus the more solid the leveling produced by sanding, the sounder the solidity of the frescoes, and the more durable. 6. If no fewer than three layers of sand mortar have been applied, in addition to the rough plastering, then coats of large-grained powdered marble should be applied and leveled so long as the material is of this consistency: when it is being worked it never clings to the trowel, but instead allows the tool to come free when it is removed from the mortar. Once the layer of large-grained marble powder has been applied and is drying, then another layer of medium-grained powder should be laid on. When this has been worked and sanded down well, then a layer of fine-grained marble dust should be applied.

7. Thus, when the walls have been reinforced with three layers of sand mortar and as many of marble, they will not permit fissures or any other flaws. Instead, with a sound underpinning tamped down by plaster floats* and polished with marble of consistent whiteness, once the paints and the final polishing have been applied, they will exhibit brilliant color. For the paints do not dissipate when they are carefully applied to moist plaster,* but stay perpetually, because the lime, made weak and porous by having had its moisture baked out in the kiln, is forced by its emptiness to absorb anything with

which it happens to come into contact. When mixtures of various seeds or atoms with various qualities have been combined with it so that they solidify all at once, then as the lime dries among the components with which it has been worked, it is reduced so that it seems to take on their particular qualities. 8. Thus plaster that has been made correctly neither becomes rough with age, nor does it shed color when it is wiped, unless it has been applied carelessly and on dry plaster. And so when plaster is made on walls as described earlier, it has the capacity for soundness, brilliance, and durable quality. If, on the other hand, only one layer of sand mortar and one of fine marble have been applied, then the thinness of the plastering causes easy breakage, because it is less strong, nor can it take on a brilliant polish because of its insufficient thickness. 9. For just as a mirror with a surface of thin silver gives off an indistinct and weak reflection, so one made of a solid alloy, such that it absorbs the polish into itself with steadfast strength, gives off glittering images that are clear to the beholder. Even so, frescoes that are worked on a thin matrix not only develop cracks, but also fade quickly. Those, however, that are substantial in thickness, founded on the solidity of sand and marble, are not only shiny when they are worked with assiduous polishing, but actually reflect back images to their beholders from this kind of work. 10. The Greek plaster makers not only create long-lasting work according to these principles, but they also do this: when the mortar trough has been set in place, with the lime and sand poured together into it, they bring in ten-man work gangs who pound the mortar with wooden pestles, and they use it after it has been vigorously worked by these teams. Many people cut out the surfaces of old walls and use them as inlaid panels, and the frescoes themselves, with sections for inlaid panels and mirrors, have a particularly striking appearance.

11. But if the plaster is going to be made on half-timbering, in which it is unavoidable that cracks develop along the uprights and the cross pieces (because when the lattices are coated with mud they necessarily absorb moisture and then create fissures in the plaster as they shrink back in drying), this is the way for it not to happen: when the entire wall has been smeared with mud, then along the entire extent of the operation a layer of reeds must be fixed in place by pegs made of horsetails (*Equisetum*).* Then apply another layer of mud, and if the previous layer of reeds has been laid horizontally, then the second layer should be fixed vertically; then the sand and marble layers and all the plaster should be applied as

described here. In this way the double unbroken layer of reeds, fixed by perpendicular straws, will not allow flaking[5] or any other sort of fissures to develop.

CHAPTER 4: PLASTERWORK IN DAMP LOCATIONS (FIGURE 103)

1. I have told how plaster should be made in dry localities. Now I shall describe how the finishing of plaster can be completed in damp localities so that it can last without flaws. First of all, for rooms on ground level, instead of sand mortar, terracotta sherds should be rough plastered and applied up to a height of three feet above pavement level, so that these parts of the plaster will not be damaged by moisture. But if any wall is constantly damp, then just in back of that wall a second, narrow, wall should be constructed, as far apart from the first wall as the project permits. Between the two walls, a channel should be put in place at a level lower than the plane of the pavement of the room, with weep holes at an open spot. As construction continues upward, leave air holes in the wall, for if the dampness has no outlet through these holes, both above and below, then it will simply dissipate itself throughout the new masonry. Once these features have been completed, the walls should be rough plastered and leveled, and then plastered and polished.

2. If the site will not permit masonry, channels should be created whose openings give onto some open space. Then two-foot tiles (*bipedales*) should be placed on one side over the margin of the channel; on the other, piers of eight-inch bricks (*bessales*) should be constructed so that the corners of two tiles rest on each, and these piers[6] should stand away from the wall so that they are to extend for no more than a palm. Above these, footed tiles* should be fixed upright to the wall from bottom to top, their inward sides lined with pitch so that they are waterproof. Thus the walls will have ventilation at the bottom and at the top above the ceiling. 3. Then the walls should be whitewashed with lime dissolved in water, so that they will not reject the terracotta rough plastering, for because of the dryness induced in the tiles by baking them in the furnace, they cannot absorb the rough plastering nor hold it in place unless the addition

5 Reading *segmina* with Giocondo.
6 Reading *bae* (Llc) for GH *eae*.

of lime glues each component together and forces them to join. Once the rough plastering has been laid on, with broken terracotta in place of sand, then everything else should be completed as has already been described in the instructions for plastering.

CORRECTNESS IN PAINTING: WINTER DINING ROOMS

4. Now the walls themselves ought to have their own principles of correctness when it comes to finishing their decoration, so that they will have a dignity in keeping with their site and with the specific characteristics of the type of building. In winter dining rooms neither monumental painting nor subtle ornamentation of the ceilings with stucco and moldings will be of any value as decoration, because these will be marred by smoke from the fire and constant soot from the many lamps. Rather, for these rooms panels worked and finished in black should be arrayed above the podium, with inlaid wedges of ochre or cinnabar in between. Once the vaults have been completed and given a plain finish, this form of decoration for the pavements, used by the Greeks for their winter dining rooms, will give not unattractive, not to mention inexpensive and useful, results: (5.) underneath the level of the dining room one should excavate to a depth of about two feet, and when the soil has been packed down, either lay in a rubble underpavement or a terracotta pavement, sloped so that it has openings (nostrils) onto a channel. Then, onto coals that have been trampled to compactness, a mortar mixed of gravel and lime and ash should be laid to a thickness of half a foot. The topmost layer, planed to the rule and the level by polishing with a whetstone, presents the appearance of black pavement. Thus, during their banquets, any wine that is spilled from their cups or spat onto the ground will dry as quickly as possible, and those who do the pouring, even if they serve with bare feet, will not catch cold from this type of pavement.

CHAPTER 5: CORRECTNESS IN PAINTING: GENERAL REMARKS

1. In the remaining rooms, that is, the spring, autumn, and summer quarters, also in atria and peristyles, the ancients have established certain secure principles for painting, based on secure phenomena. For a painting is an image of that which exists or can exist, like those of people, buildings, ships, and other things with definite and certain bodies, of which examples may be found and depicted in imitation. On this principle, the ancients who established the beginnings of painting plaster first imitated the varieties and placement of marble veneers, then of cornices and the various designs of ochre inlay.*
2. Later they entered a stage in which they also imitated the shapes of buildings, and the projection into space of columns and pediments, while in open spaces like exedrae, because of the extensive wall space, they painted stage sets in the tragic, comic, or satyric style, and adorned their walkways, because of their extensive length, with varieties of landscape, creating images from the known characteristics of various places. For ports, promontories, seashores, rivers, springs, straits, shrines, sacred groves, mountains, herds, and shepherds are depicted; some places are portrayed in monumental painting with the likenesses of the gods or the skillfully arranged narrations of myths, such as the Trojan battles, or the wanderings of Ulysses through various landscapes, and other subjects that have been created according to nature on similar principles (Figure 104).

3. But these paintings, which had taken their models from real things, now fall foul of depraved taste. For monsters are now painted in frescoes rather than reliable images of definite things. Reeds are set up in place of columns, as pediments, little scrolls, striped with curly leaves and volutes; candelabra hold up the figures of aediculae, and above the pediments of these, several tender shoots, sprouting in coils from roots, have little statues nestled in them for no reason, or shoots split in half, some holding little statues with human heads, some with the heads of beasts (Figure 105).

4. Now these things do not exist nor can they exist nor have they ever existed, and thus this new fashion has brought things to such a pass that bad judges have condemned the right practice of the arts as lack of skill. How, pray tell, can a reed really sustain a roof, or a candelabrum the decorations of a pediment, or an acanthus shoot, so soft and slender, loft a tiny statue perched upon it, or can flowers be produced from roots and shoots on the one hand and figurines on the other? Yet when they see these deceptions, people never criticize them, but rather take delight in them, nor do they ever notice whether any of these things are possible or not. Minds beclouded by feeble standards of judgment are unable to recognize what exists in accordance with authority and the principles of correctness. Neither should pictures be approved that are not likenesses of

the truth, nor, if they are made elegant through art, is that any reason why favorable judgment should immediately be passed on them, not unless their subjects follow sound principles without interference.

5. As a matter of fact, in Tralles, when Apaturius of Alabanda had set his elegant hand to decorating the *scaenae frons* of the tiny theater, known as the *ekklêsiasterion* in those parts, on it he had made columns, statues, and centaurs holding up entablatures, the round roofs of tholoi, the projecting angles of pediments, and cornices decorated with lions' heads (all of these things that have their reason for being in channeling rainwater from roofs).* Above this *scaenae frons*, moreover, he put up nothing less than an *episcaenium*, with tholoi, temple porticoes, half pediments and pictures of every kind of building. Thus, when the appearance of this stage set captivated the sight of one and all because of its high relief, so that they were all ready to acclaim the work, then Licymnius, a mathematician, came forward and said. 6. "The people of Alabanda are considered intelligent enough when it comes to all matters political, but they have been regarded as foolish because of one trifling flaw: that of lacking a sense of propriety, for in their gymnasia all the statues are of lawyers pleading cases, whereas in the forum there are discus throwers, runners, and ballplayers. Thus the inappropriate placement of the statues with regard to their site has won the city the reputation for poor judgment. Now let us see to it that this scene building does not transform us, too, into Alabandeans or Abderites. Who among you could have houses above the tiles of your roofs or columns, or the outline of pediments? For these things are put above joists or beams, not above roof tiles. If, therefore, we are to approve things in pictures that cannot have any basis in truth, we will join the company of those cities that are considered foolish because of such flaws."

7. Apaturius did not dare make a reply, but rather removed the stage set, and once it had been altered according to the principles of truth, then Licymnius approved the later, corrected version. If only the immortal gods could have contrived for Licymnius to come back to life to correct this insanity, and the deviant practices of our fresco painters! But it will not be out of place to reveal why false reasoning wins out over truth: the ancients invested their labor and energy in competition to win approval for their skill, but now, [fresco painters] pursue approval through the deployment of colors and their elegant appearance, and whereas refinement of craftsmanship once increased the reputation of works, now sovereign extravagance makes it no longer desirable.

8. For who of the ancients can be caught using cinnabar except as sparingly as if it were medicine? And now it is lavished everywhere, on nearly every wall. Add to this malachite green, purple, Armenian blue – now these, even when applied without skill, present a glittering spectacle for the eyes, and because they are expensive, they are regulated by law, so that their use is determined by the patron rather than by the contractor.

What I could present so that deviant practice in fresco work might be avoided I have set out at sufficient length. Now I shall speak about the materials which will be necessary to undertake the work, and because lime was described in the beginning, now I shall record something about [powdered] marble.

CHAPTER 6: MARBLE POWDER

1. The same type of marble does not occur in every region; in some places there are clods with brilliant grains like those of salt, and these, when pounded and milled, are quite useful for stuccowork. In places where these resources are not available, smaller bits of marble, or chips, as they are called, the ones that marble workers discard on the job, are pounded and milled, and after sifting they can be used in projects. In other places, for instance, between the borders of Magnesia and Ephesus, there are places where marble powder can be dug up ready to use; there is no need either to mill it or sift it, for it is already as fine as any that has been pounded and sifted by hand.

CHAPTER 7: PIGMENTS

1. Some pigments are naturally found in certain locations and are mined there, whereas some are compounds, completed by treating or mixing various things in particular proportions so that they afford a consistent utility for stuccowork. First I shall discuss those that are excavated as is, like the ochre that the Greeks call *ôchra*. Now this can be found in many places, including Italy, but Attic ochre, the best of all, can no longer be found. This is because when the silver mines in Athens had their own slaves, then shafts were dug into the earth in order to strike silver. If they came across a vein of ore, they mined it for the ochre no less than for the silver, so the ancients used an immense amount of ochre in finishing their fres-

coes. 2. The red variety, too, is extracted in great abundance from many places, but the best comes only from a few of them, like Sinope in Pontus, Egypt, and the Balearic Islands of Hispania, also Lemnos; the Senate and People of Rome conceded the right to the proceeds from these ochre mines to the Athenians as part of their revenue. 3. White chalk is called Paraetonium after the very places where it is mined. For the same reason, white lead is called Melinum because its mines are said to be on the Cycladic island of Melos. 4. Green chalk is found in several places, but the best is from Smyrna. The Greeks call this *theodotion*, because the person on whose property this type of chalk was first discovered was one Theodotus by name. 5. Orpiment (arsenic sulfate), which is called *arsenikon* in Greek, is mined in Pontus. Red arsenic is likewise found in a number of places, but the best has its mines in Pontus next to the river Hypanis.

its own pressure. Thus there can be no denying that gravity is not a matter of weight but of the individual type of matter.

4. Now this quicksilver is useful for many things. For neither silver nor bronze can be properly gilded without it. When gold is woven into clothing, the garment, once it has been worn out with age, will no longer be fit for use; then the rags, placed in clay pots and put over the fire, are burned away. The ash is then cast into water, and to this quicksilver is added, which, in turn, snatches all the granules of gold to itself and forces them to merge with it. If the water has been poured into a cloth that is then wrung with the hands, then, as the water pours off, the quicksilver, too, because it is liquid, will slip through the intervals in the cloth, while inside pure gold will be found, compacted by compression.

CHAPTER 8: CINNABAR

1. Now I will proceed to explain the nature of cinnabar (mercury sulfide). This is first recorded as having been discovered in the Cilbian fields belonging to Ephesus, and both the pigment and its properties are marvelous enough. Its so-called clod, before it has been treated to become cinnabar, is mined in a vein like that of iron, but more reddish in color and surrounded by red powder. When it is extracted, under the blows of iron tools it sheds copious tears of quicksilver, which is immediately gathered by the miners. 2. When these clods of ore have been collected, because of their saturation with moisture they are cast into a kiln at the foundry in order to dry them out, and the smoke that is driven out of them by the heat of the fire, once it settles again along the floor of the kiln, will be found to consist of quicksilver. Once the clods have been removed, the droplets that have settled out cannot be gathered because they are so small, but they are swept into a tub of water and there they merge with one another and are finally poured together into a single mass. If there are four sextarii (= two liters)* of quicksilver, when they are poured out they will be found to equal a hundredweight. 3. If it is poured into any other tub, and a stone weighing a hundredweight is lowered onto it, the stone will float on top; it will not be able to compress the liquid with its weight, nor displace it, nor dissipate it. Take the hundredweight away and put in a scruple of gold, and it will not float, but rather sink to the bottom under

CHAPTER 9: THE PROCESSING OF CINNABAR

1. Now I shall return to the processing of cinnabar. Once the clods themselves have grown dry, they are pounded with iron pestles, and through repeated washings and bakings, the pigment begins to be brought out, leaving the impurities behind. Therefore, when the natural qualities present in the cinnabar have been lost through the removal of the quicksilver, its nature is made tender and feeble. 2. Thus, when it is applied to the plaster of covered rooms, it retains its color without deterioration, but in open rooms, in peristyles or exedrae or other places of the same kind, where the sun and moon can convey the splendor of their rays, then, when the place is touched by them, it deteriorates, and with the strength of the color gone it goes black. When Faberius the secretary [of Caesar and Antony], among many others, wanted to have his house on the Aventine elegantly frescoed, he applied cinnabar to the peristyles and all the walls, which after thirty days had taken on a mottled and unattractive color. And so he contracted as soon as he could for other pigments to be applied.

3. Now if anyone is more refined and wants cinnabar fresco to retain its color, then, once the wall has been frescoed and dried, Phoenician wax, liquefied in fire and tempered with a little oil, should be applied with a brush. Afterward, with coals assembled in an iron pot he should first make the wall sweat by heating it from close by, so that it can be evened out, and then work it with a candle and clean linens, just as unpainted marble

statues are maintained. 4. This is called "shining" (ganôsis) in Greek.* Thus the layer of Phoenician wax forms a barrier, and will not allow either the moon's splendor or the sun's rays to steal the color of the frescoes by lapping them up. The workshops that used to be in the Ephesian mines have now been transferred to Rome because this type of vein has since been discovered in regions of Hispania, and from those mines the clods of ore are brought to Rome and processed by contractors. These workshops are between the temples of Flora and Quirinus.*

5. Cinnabar is adulterated when it is mixed with lime. Thus, if anyone should want to test whether it is flawless, do this: take an iron strip, put cinnabar on it, and put it in the fire until the iron is red hot. When its color changes from glowing and it becomes dark, take the iron strip from the fire. Once it has cooled, if the strip is restored to its original color, the cinnabar has been proven to be faultless, but if the strip retains the black color, this means it has been spoiled.

6. I have discussed everything that came to my mind about cinnabar. Malachite green is imported from Macedonia, and it is mined in places that are near copper mines. Armenian blue and Indian indigo reveal where they are found by their very names.

CHAPTER 10: COMPOUND PIGMENTS

1. Now I shall pass on to those things that change and take on their properties of color by the working and mixing of different types of ingredients. First I shall discuss black – there is a great need for its use in fresco painting – so that it will be known how craftsmen prepare it in a reliable mixture. 2. A place is constructed, like a Spartan sauna, finely stuccoed with marble dust and polished. In front of it construct a little kiln which has outlets into the Spartan sauna, and its mouth is capped with special care so that the flame will not be dissipated outside. Resin is placed in the kiln. The power of fire, as it burns this resin, will force soot to be emitted through the outlets into the Spartan sauna, and this soot will cling all around the wall and the curvature of the vault. Then the resin is collected, and part is worked with gum for use as ink. Plaster workers will use the rest, mixed in with glue, for walls. 3. Now if these supplies are not ready to hand, then one will have to manage according to necessity, for work should not be halted in the waiting caused by some delay. Burn up brushwood and shavings of pitch pine and when they have turned to charcoal extinguish them.

Then grind them in a mortar with glue. This will make a black for fresco painters that is not without its charm. 4. Likewise if wine-lees are dried and baked in a kiln and these, ground with glue, are applied to the work, [the mixture] will produce a color that is even softer than standard black, but the better the wine from which it is prepared, the more closely it will approach the color, not of standard black, but of indigo.

CHAPTER 11: BLUE

1. The recipes for blue were first discovered in Alexandria, and subsequently Vestorius began to manufacture it in Puteoli as well.* Its story and how it was invented are quite marvelous. Sand is ground with flower of natron (first-class potassium nitrate) so finely that it almost becomes like flour. Copper, broken by coarse files until it is like sawdust, is sprinkled with this sand until it clings together. Then it is formed into balls by rolling it between the hands and bound together to dry. Once dry, the balls are put into a ceramic pitcher, and the pitchers are put into a kiln. In this way the copper and the sand, boiling with the energy of the fire, bond together, and exchanging their sweat between them they leave off their original properties; with their natures merged they produce a blue color.

2. Burnt ochre, which is quite useful for fresco painting, is obtained in the following way: clods of good ochre are baked until they glow in the fire. They are then quenched with vinegar and thus turn purple in color.

CHAPTER 12: WHITE LEAD
AND VERDIGRIS

1. It is not out of place here to tell how white lead and the verdigris we call "rust" are prepared. In Rhodes, they place branches in tubs with vinegar poured over them, and then put in lumps of lead; they cap these tubs with covers so that they do not emit any fumes. After a certain time they open the tubs and discover that white has been created from the masses of lead. By putting in strips of copper instead, they produce the verdigris called "rust" by the same method. When white lead is fired in the kiln, it changes its color because of the combustion of fire and becomes red arsenic. People learned this by observing what happened after chance fires, and

this kind is much more useful than the kind that is extracted as is from mines.

CHAPTER 13: PURPLE

1. I shall begin to tell about purple, which, of all the colors, has the most prized, and most outstanding, loveliness of appearance. This is extracted from a sea mollusk, from which purple dye is made, and whose marvels, when one considers them, are not inferior to those of any other natural phenomenon, for it does not have one type of color in every place where it is found, but is naturally tempered by the course of the sun. 2. Thus, what is collected in Pontus and Gaul[7] is black, because these regions are nearer the north. Proceeding to the northwest, we will find that it is bluish. That collected at the eastern and western equinox comes in a violet color. What is extracted in southern regions, however, comes out in the reddish range, and for this reason it is produced commercially on the island of Rhodes and in the other regions that are nearest the sun. 3. When these mollusks are gathered, they are cut all round with iron blades, and from these wounds a purple ooze, flowing out like tears, is shaken into mortars and prepared by grinding. Because it is extracted from the shells of marine mollusks, it is called oyster-purple, and because it is so salty it quickly becomes desiccated unless it has honey poured over it.

7 So the MSS; Rode emends to Galatia.

CHAPTER 14: SUBSTITUTE PIGMENTS

1. Purple pigments are made as well from chalk dyed with the root of madder, and from kermes (shrub oak, *Quercus coccifera*);* other pigments are also made from plants. Thus if fresco painters should want to imitate Attic ochre, they throw dried yellow violets into a vessel with water, boil it over a fire, and when it is ready they pour it into linen. Wringing the linen with their hands, they take up the water, which has been colored by the violets, in mortars, and when they pour chalk into these and pound it they create the color of Attic ochre. 2. Preparing blueberries by the same method and mixing in milk they create an elegant purple. Likewise, those who cannot use malachite green because of its high cost introduce blue pigment into weld (*Reseda luteola*),* and avail themselves of a deep green color. This they call "dyed" green. Likewise, because of the shortage of indigo, by dyeing Selinuntine chalk or jeweler's grout with woad (*Isatis tinctoria*), which the Greeks call *isatis*,* they create an imitation of indigo.

3. The principles and materials by which paintings ought to be made to achieve a design for sound construction, the principles by which correct painting should be executed, the powers possessed by pigments, all these I have recorded at length in this book as my memory presented them to me. And thus all the finished processes for buildings and the standards they should exhibit in the working out [of their designs] have been outlined in these seven books. In the following volume I will explain about water: how it can be found in places where it does not occur, by what methods it can be channeled, and by what means it can be verified as healthful and suitable.

❖

WATER

PREFACE

1. Thales of Miletus, one of the Seven Sages, declared that water was the first principle of all things. Heraclitus said that fire was; the priests of the Magi, water and fire; and Euripides, a follower of Anaxagoras, that philosopher whom the Athenians called "the actor," proposed air and earth, and said that the latter, inseminated by intercourse with heavenly rains, had conceived all peoples and all living things as her offspring in the world. He said as well that when her progeny dissolve, compelled by time's necessity, they return to her, while those things which have been begotten of air must return to the regions of heaven; they do not admit annihilation but rather revert, transformed by their dissolution, to their original characteristics. But Pythagoras, Empedocles, Epicharmos, and the other naturalists and philosophers proposed that the first principles of matter were four: air, fire, earth, and water, and that their adhesion to one another by natural formation creates the qualities particular to each type of substance.*

2. We observe, indeed, not only that all creatures have been begotten of these elements, but also that none can be nourished without them, nor grow, nor sustain themselves. Without the infusion of breath, bodies cannot have life, not unless inflowing air creates continuous respirations and contractions. And if there were not a proper supply of heat for bodies, they would not have vital spirit nor firm uprightness, and the energy of food would be unable to attain the temperature of digestion. If the parts of the body are not nourished by earthly food, they will fail, for they will be deprived of their proper component of the element earth. 3. If animals lacked the powers of water, they would dry out, bloodless, sucked dry of their liquid element. Therefore the divine intelligence decided that those things which were truly necessary to the nations would be neither difficult nor expensive to obtain, not like pearls, gold, silver, and the other things that neither the body nor nature requires. Those four elements without which the lives of mortals would not be secure she poured forth ready to hand throughout the world. Thus, for example, if by chance a body is short of breath, it is **air**, assigned to restore the lack, that supplies what is missing. So, too, the force of the sun's heat stands ready to help us, and the discovery of **fire** makes life more secure. Likewise, the fruits of the **earth**, offering attractions in supplies sufficient for the most bottomless desires, sustain and nourish animals by ceaselessly feeding them. **Water**, offering endless necessities as well as drink, offers services all the more gratifying because they are gratis.[1]

4. What Egyptian priests do by custom further demonstrates that all things are composed of the power of water. When water in a jar is brought with strict religious observance into the sacred precinct and the temple, then prostrating themselves on the ground and raising their hands to the heavens they give thanks to the divine beneficence for its discovery.

Therefore, because naturalists, philosophers, and priests alike judge that all things consist of the power of water, I thought that, because the principles of building have been laid out in the previous seven volumes, it was proper in this one to consider the finding of water, what qualities it has according to the characteristics of places where it is found, by what methods it can be transported, and how it may be tested. For water is indispensable for life and pleasure and daily use.

CHAPTER 1: FINDING WATER

1. Water will be easier to manage if there are open-air, flowing springs. But if they do not gush forth, their sources must be sought underground and merged together.

This is how to test for water: lie face down, before

---

1 The pun belongs to Vitruvius.

sunrise, in the places where the search is to be made, and with your chin set on the ground and propped, survey these regions. In this way the line of sight will not wander higher than it should, because the chin will be motionless; instead, the line of sight will take in a calculated height with definite limits in the direction of those regions.* In those places where moisture can be seen curling and rising into the air, dig on the spot, because this sign cannot occur in a dry location.

2. Now those searching for water should also take note of the localities and their type, for there are certain types in which water occurs. In clay the supply is thin and scanty, and not deep down; it will not be of the best flavor either. In gravelly sand it is also thin but found at a lower level, and this water will be muddy and unpleasant. In black earth seepages and droplets can be found that collect from winter storms and come to rest in dense and solid places; these will have a superb taste. In gravel, medium-sized, though unreliable,[2] veins of water can be found; these, too, will be of outstanding pleasantness. In coarse sand, sand, and sandstone, the supplies are more reliable and constant, and these, too, are of a good flavor. In red tufa the supplies are copious and good, if they do not dissipate through the pores and melt away. Under the roots of mountains and in hard limestone (silex) they are quite plentiful and flowing, and these waters are also cooler and more healthful. In the springs found in open fields the waters are salty, heavy, tepid, and unpleasant, unless they are those that flow underground down from the mountains and burst forth in the middle of level terrain, and in such places, covered by the shade of trees, they offer the delights of mountain springs.

3. These are the growing things to be found in the types of earth just described which are signs of water: slender rushes, wild willow, alder, agnus castus, reeds, ivy, and other things of this sort, which cannot occur on their own without moisture. These same plants tend to occur in the standing ponds that, all through the winter, collect rainwater more quickly than the surrounding countryside, and, because of their capacity retain it longer. Then, of course, they cannot be trusted as signs of underground water, but in those regions and soils – not ponds – where these signs occur naturally, not planted artificially, there water is to be sought.

4. In these places, once such [possible] discoveries of water have been indicated, this is how they should be tested. Dig a pit no less than three feet on each side and five feet deep.[3] In this, at sunset, place a bronze or leaden boat-shaped vessel or a basin. Whatever you choose, coat it inside with oil, place it upside down, and cover the pit with reeds or leaves, and cover that over with earth. Open it on the following day, and if there are droplets or seepage in the vessel, then the place will have water.

5. Likewise, if a vessel made of unfired clay is put in the pit and covered by the same method, if the place is going to have water, when the pit is opened up, the vessel will be damp, and already have begun to dissolve from the moisture. Or, if a fleece of wool is placed in the pit, and on the next day water can be wrung from it, this, too, means that the place will have a supply of water. Or, if a lamp has been prepared, filled with oil, lighted, and placed in the pit, and then covered over, if it has not gone out on the following day, but instead still has some of the oil and the wick remaining, and itself is discovered to be moist, it indicates that this place has water, because every sort of heat attracts moisture to itself. Also, if a fire is built in this pit, and the earth, once it is superheated and charred, exhales clouds of steam, this place will have water.

6. When tests have been made conscientiously in this way, and the signs just described have been found, then a well should be sunk in this place; if the water table is found, several wells should be dug near it, and through underground channels* all of them should be directed toward a single place. These are particularly to be sought in the mountains and the northern regions, because in these regions sweeter, more healthful, and more abundant water is to be found. For these regions are turned away from the sun, and in such places, first of all, the trees are plentiful and lush. Also, the mountains themselves have protective shade, so that the rays of the sun cannot arrive straight at the earth; hence they cannot burn off the moisture.

7. Valleys between the mountains receive the most rain, and because of the density of their forests they retain snow for more extended periods of time, thanks to the shade of the trees and the mountains. Later, the melted snows percolate through the veins of the earth and in this way they eventually reach the lowermost roots of the mountains, from which the flow of gushing springs breaks forth. Flat country, by contrast, cannot have copious supplies of water. Any that do exist cannot

---

2 *Non certae*, Giocondo; *non incertae*, MSS.

3 So Philander from the epitome of Vitruvius; *vacant codices.*

be healthful, because the intense force of the sun, unobstructed by shade, snatches the moisture away from the flat surface of the fields, drinking it up as it boils. If there are any visible waters, the air calls forth whatever is light, delicate, and of subtle healthfulness, dissipating it against the heavens' force, whereas those parts that are heaviest, harsh, and distasteful are left behind in flatland springs.

CHAPTER 2: RAINWATER; RIVER WATER (FIGURE 106)

1. Likewise, the water collected from rainfall has more healthful qualities because it is composed of the lightest and finest delicacies of all springs, which percolate through the movement of air in storms and then, liquefying, reach the earth. Furthermore, rain does not flow abundantly into plains, but in or near the mountains, because the fluids that have left the earth, stimulated at the rise of the morning sun, push away the air in that part of the heavens toward which they have been propelled; then, when they move, because of the vacuum left in their place, they bring in rushing waves of air after themselves.

2. Rushing air creates the gusts and growing billows of the wind by pushing moisture in every direction through the force of its blasts. The moisture condensed from springs, rivers, swamps, and the open sea is carried every which way by the winds; they are collected and drunk up with the heat[4] of the sun and thus clouds are raised aloft. Then, supported on the wave of air, upon reaching the mountains and on impact with them, they disperse, liquefying in stormy gusts because of their fullness and heaviness, and thus they are poured out toward the land.

3. This seems to be the reason that steam and clouds and moisture are born from the earth: because earth has in itself fervid heat, huge blasts and chills, and a great abundance of waters. For which reason, when the rising sun with its force touches the earth's sphere, chilled overnight, and gusts of wind spring up among the shadows, clouds emerge from damp places and rise aloft. Air, then, heated thoroughly by the sun, raises moisture from the earth by the same principles.

4. Take an example from baths. The ceilings of cal-

daria cannot have fountains above them, yet [they might as well, for] the atmosphere there, which has come from the mouths of the furnace and been heated through and through by the vapor of fire, snatches the water up from the pavements, rises with it into the curvature of the ceilings, and keeps it there, because hot vapor always pushes upward. First the air will not let the water come back down because there is so little of it, but as soon as it has gathered together more and more liquid, it can no longer hold it up because of its weight; then [just like a fountain,] it sprinkles water over the heads of the bathers. In the same way the air in the sky, when it has absorbed heat from the sun, drinks off moisture from every site, raises it up, and herds it together into clouds. Thus the earth, when it is touched by boiling heat, casts off its moisture, just as the human body gives off sweat in the presence of heat.

5. The winds are an indication of this fact, because those that come down after originating in the coldest regions, Septentrio (N) and Aquilo (NE), blow their gusts into the air when they have been stretched thin by dryness. Auster, on the other hand, and the rest that begin their onrush at the sun's course, are as moist as can be and always bring along rain, because they arrive thoroughly heated from the torrid regions, snatching the moisture from every land, lapping it up, and then they pour these fluids forth over the northern regions.

6. The sources of rivers can serve as proof that these things happen as we have described, for in the earthly globe (as depicted by the geographers and likewise in their written accounts) most of them, and the greatest, are found to emerge in the north.* First of all, in India the Ganges and Indus arise in the Caucasus; in Syria the Tigris and Euphrates; in Asia, in Pontus: the Borysthenes (Dnieper), Hypanis (Bug), and Tanais (Don), in Colchis: the Phasis; in Gaul, the Rhodanus (Rhone); in the land of the Celts, the Rhenus (Rhine); in Cisalpine Gaul, the Timavus (Timavo) and the Padus (Po); in Italy, the Tiber; in Maurusia, which we call Mauretania, from Mount Atlas, the Dyris, which after arising in the northern region proceeds west to Lake Eptabolos, where it changes its name and is called Agger. Then, from Lake Eptabolos it flows underneath the desert mountains through southern regions, and flows into what is called The Swamp, circles Meroë, which is the kingdom of the southern Ethiopians, and from these swamps it winds through the rivers Astansoba and Astoboa and many others, to pass through the mountains to the [sixth] cataract, and hurling itself over this it continues toward the north between Elephantis and Syene, and

---

4 *tempore* GH; *taepore* E; *tepore* c^ch and most editors.

the Theban countryside in Egypt – and there it is called the Nile.* 7. The fact that the head of the Nile flows forth from Mauretania can be understood above all from this: that on the other side of Mount Atlas there are other sources of rivers that also flow into the western Ocean, and there ichneumons occur, and crocodiles, and other beasts and fishes of similar nature, except for hippopotami.

8. Therefore, because all the rivers of any size in accounts of the earth seem to flow forth from the north, and the lands of Africa, which are in the southern region and exposed to the course of the sun, have their moisture lying hidden deep beneath them, but infrequent springs and rare rivers, one is left to conclude that the sources of springs that face Septentrio (N) or Aquilo (NE) will be found to be much better, unless they should occur in a place with sulphur, alum, or bitumen, for on those occasions they are transformed and whether they are hot or cold, the springs will flow forth with a bad odor and taste.

9. For hot water has no distinctive properties of its own, but when cool water, in its flow, happens upon a blazing place, it begins to boil and once it has been thoroughly heated it issues forth from the earth through pores. For this reason, it cannot stay hot for long, and cools down shortly. Now if it were hot by nature, its heat would never cool. Its taste and color are not restored, however, because it has been tainted and intermixed because of its own rarefied nature.

CHAPTER 3: SPRINGS

1. There are, however, some hot springs from which water of an excellent flavor flows forth, so delicious to drink that even the waters gushing from the fountain of the Camenae or the Aqua Marcia would not be missed.* These springs are created by nature in the following ways: when fire is stirred up deep within the earth through alum or bitumen or sulphur, its burning warms the earth above it to white heat, and so it sends off boiling vapor into higher regions. And thus if any sweet-water springs arise in the places above, when struck by this vapor they boil within the pores of the earth and so flow forth with uncorrupted taste.*

2. There are also cold springs with water of poor odor and flavor. These arise deep within the earth and pass through burning places, and from that point onward they flow through long tracts of earth to reach the surface with corrupted flavor, odor, and color, like the river Albula along the Via Tiburtina and the cold springs in the region of Ardea with the same odor, which are called "sulphurated," and in other similar places.* These, even though they are cold, look as if they are boiling, because when they encounter hot places deep within the earth, the converging water and fire, colliding with a violent clash, absorb powerful blasts, and then, inflated by the force of the condensed wind, they issue from the springs boiling abundantly. Springs of this kind that are without an outlet and, enclosed within rock, push the force of their gusts out through narrow pores near the tops of hillocks.*

3. And therefore, those who think that they can have[5] sources of springs at the same height as these hillocks will be sorely deceived once they begin to open pits far and wide. For just as a bronze vessel, filled with water not to the brim but to two-thirds capacity, and with a lid set in place, when touched by the intense fervor of fire, will force the water to become superheated, and the water in turn because of its natural rarefaction, as it absorbs the powerful inflation of the boiling, will not only fill the vessel, but raise the lid on its gusts as it grows and overflows, and then with the lid removed and its inflations emitted into the open air, recede back to its place again; so, too, in the same way, when the sources of springs are compressed by restricted space, the boilings of the water's gusts rush about at the surface, yet as soon as they are more widely exposed to the outside, they subside and are restored to balance, their breath escaped through the rarefaction of the liquid.

4. Certainly all hot water has medicinal properties, because in unhealthy conditions, when it is thoroughly heated it takes on another property in place of its own, to useful effect. Thus sulphurous waters refresh strain on the muscles by thoroughly heating and burning off the harmful humors from the body. Alum-saturated waters, when they receive the limbs of a body made feeble by paralysis or some other force of disease, restore them by entering their open pores and warming their chill with the opposing force of heat; by this means they are immediately restored to their original tone. Defects of the internal organs are usually cured with purges brought on by drinking bituminous waters. 5. There is a nitrous type of cold water, like that at Pinna Vestina, Cutiliae, and other similar places, which

---

5 Reading, with Giocondo, *posse habere* for the MSS *fosse habere*.

when drunk causes purging; when it passes through the digestive tract it also cures the swellings of scrofula.

However, although plentiful springs will be found where gold, silver, iron, copper, lead, and the other such things are mined, they are particularly harmful. Like hot springs, they, too, have sulphur, alum, and bitumen, and these substances, when they enter the body as drink and penetrate through the veins, attack the muscles and limbs, hardening them with swelling.[6] Therefore the muscles, swollen and inflated, contract in length, making people either gouty or arthritic, because the pores of their veins have been saturated with very hard, dense, and chilly substances. 6. This water has an appearance[7*] that is not particularly transparent, and on it, a kind of scum floats on its surface with the color of purple glass. This is particularly to be seen in Athens, for there fountains have been installed, both in the citadel and in the port of Piraeus, that draw from such places and such springs, and no one drinks from the fountains for that reason, although people use them for washing and other purposes. They drink water from wells and thereby avoid the defects of the fountain water. In Troizen the problem cannot be avoided, because no other type of water* is to be found anywhere except what the Cybdeli have, and thus in that city everyone, or at least the great majority, has foot problems. In Cilicia, on the other hand, in the city of Tarsus, there is a river called Cydnos, and if sufferers from gout soak their legs there they will be relieved of their pain.

7. There are many other types of water that have their own peculiarities. For example, in Sicily there is a river called Himeras; once it has emerged from its source, it divides in two. That part which flows in the direction of Etruria (North), because it runs through the sweet sap of the earth, is of an infinite sweetness; the other part, which courses through lands where salt is mined, has a salty taste. Likewise, in Paraetonium, on the way to the shrine of Jupiter Ammon, and in Casius, in neighboring Egypt, there are swampy lakes so salty that they have salt crystallized on their surfaces. In many other places there are springs and rivers and lakes that, because they run through salt deposits, have inevitably turned salty.

8. Other springs, flowing through rich veins of the earth, burst forth tinged with oil, as at Soli, which is a town in Cilicia, where there is a river by the name of Liparis; those who bathe or swim in it are oiled by the water itself. Similarly, there is a lake in Ethiopia that oils the people who swim in it, and in India there is one that produces great quantities of oil under clear skies. There is also a spring in Carthage in which oil floats on the surface of the water, with a scent like that of grated lemon rind; they also dip their sheep in this oil. On Zacynthus and around Dyrrachium and Apollonia there are springs that spew forth great quantities of pitch along with the water. In Babylon there is a lake of considerable size that is called *limnê asphaltitis*,[8] "the asphalt marsh," and has liquid bitumen floating on its surface; with this bitumen and earthen bricks Semiramis circled Babylon with a masonry wall. Also, in Joppa, in Syria, and in Numidian Arabia, there are lakes of immense size that give off huge masses of bitumen; the nearby inhabitants carry it away.

9. However, this phenomenon is not surprising: many quarries of hard bitumen are found there. When the force of water breaks through bituminous earth, it draws the bitumen along with itself; once it has emerged from the earth it separates and thus casts off the bitumen.

There is a broad lake in Cappadocia, on the road between Mazaca and Tyana, and if part of a reed or any type of object is partially sunk in its water and then removed the next day, the part which has been removed from the water will be found to have turned to stone, while the part which remained above water retains its own characteristics. 10. In the same fashion a great abundance of water boils up at Hierapolis in Phrygia, some of which is conducted in channels to the surrounding gardens and vineyards. Within a year this water creates a stony crust. Thus every year, after making earthen banks to the right and left, they bring in the water and make enclosed fields in the countryside by means of these crusts. It seems that this comes about naturally, because in these localities and in the earth where this water occurs, there is a pervasive sap similar to rennet. When the power of the water, mingled with this sap, emerges from the earth in springs, it is forced to congeal by the heat of the sun and the air, as can also be seen in salt flats. 11. Likewise the springs that emerge from the earth with bitter sap are themselves intensely bitter, like the river Hypanis (Bug) in Pontus. From its source it flows some forty miles with an

---

6 Reading *eademque* with H and Granger, and taking neuter plural *ea* as subject, assuming that the singular verb reflects translation from Greek or a grecism.

7 *Aquae* as dative. The passage is still corrupt.

8 *limnea spartacis* MSS *asphaltis* Sulpicius *asphaltitis* corr. Schott.

exceedingly sweet flavor, but then, when it reaches a place about one hundred sixty miles from its mouth, a little spring combines with it, the very tiniest little spring. The spring, when it flows in, makes even a river of that great size bitter, because that water has percolated through the type of earth and the veins where they mine red arsenic and has been turned completely bitter.

12. These waters then are made to have differing tastes because of the characteristics of the earth, as can also be seen in the case of fruits. For if the roots of trees or grapevines or the other plants did not produce fruit by absorbing sap with the characteristics of the earth, then the tastes of everything would be of one type in every place and region. But think of the island of Lesbos and the wine called *protropum*, and Catacaumenite wine of Maeonia, the Tmolite of Lydia, the Mamertinum of Sicily, the Falernian of Campania, the Caecubum from the area between Terracina and Fundi, and the endless multitudes of wines of different types and different characteristics that occur in all the other places.* These things could not happen unless, when the moisture of the earth, with its characteristic tastes, has entered into the roots of plants, it nourishes the wood, and then, proceeding through the wood to the very tip it pours forth the flavor particular to the place and to the type of fruit.

13. For if the earth were not unequal and manifold when it came to types of liquid, then it would not be only in Syria and Arabia that there were odors in the reeds and rushes and all the other plants, and incense-bearing trees, peppers giving forth their peppercorns and myrrh its clumps, nor silphium growing only among the reeds of Cyrene; instead, all things would occur, identical in kind, in every region of the earth. The inclination of the firmament* and the force of the sun, whether it is making its course close by or far removed, these are what make the varieties in quality of earth and water what they are according to region. They would not make the same thing happen, not only in these matters, but also in herds and flocks, unless the properties of individual lands were tempered according to their kind by the power of the sun. 14. For example, in Boeotia there are the rivers Cephisos and Melas, in Lucania the Crathis, in Troy the Xanthus, and springs in the countryside of Clazomenae, Erythrae, and Laodicaea. Along those rivers, when the flocks are readied for breeding in their season of the year, they are obliged to water there daily, and among them, no matter how white they may be, they bear ash-gray lambs in some places, brown in

some, and in others lambs as black as crows. Thus, when the property of the water has entered the body, it reproduces this dyed quality in its own kind. And hence, because in the Trojan countryside, red cattle and gray sheep are born next to the river, for that reason the people of Ilium are said to have called the river Xanthus ("reddish blond").

15. Deadly types of water can also be found; these, coursing through harmful sap in the earth, acquire a poisonous force in themselves. The fountain of Neptune, as it was called, in Terracina is said to have been like this, and those who unwittingly drank from it lost their lives. For this reason the ancients are said to have blocked it up. And there is a lake at Chrobs in Thrace, where not only those who drink its water die, but even those who bathe in it. There is also a gushing spring in Thessaly where no sheep will taste from that water nor will any type of animal go near it; near this spring is a tree that has flowers of a purple color.

16. Just so, in Macedonia, in the place where Euripides is buried, two streams flow together, coming from the right and left of the monument; travelers recline and picnic along one of these because of the excellence of its water, but no one approaches the bank that is on the other side of the monument, because it is said to have deadly water. In Arcadia there is a region of the earth called Nonacris, which has exceedingly cold waters that drip out of rock in the mountains there. This water is called *Stygos hudôr* "Styx water," and no vessels of silver or bronze or iron can hold this water without coming apart and dissolving. Nothing can contain and store it except a mule's hoof, in which this water is said to have been brought by Antipater, through the agency of his son Iollas, to the province where Alexander was, and that the king was killed by him with this water. 17. In the Alps, in the kingdom of Cottius, there is water that kills those who taste it on the spot. In the Faliscan countryside, along the Via Campana in the Campus Cornetus, there is a sacred grove in which a spring gushes forth, and there the bones of birds and lizards and other serpents are strewn about.

There are several springs with acid veins, like that of Lyncestus, and in Italy the Velinus, and in Campania at Teanum, and many other places, which have the ability, once they have been drunk, to break up the stones that occur in human bladders. 18. This seems to happen naturally, because a sharp and acid sap occurs in the soil there, and the veins of water exiting through this soil are tainted with its acidity; when these waters have then entered the body, they break up, as they encounter them, those sediments of water that have accumulated as concretions. We can observe the reasons why these things are broken apart by acids in the following way: if an egg is put in vinegar for a while, its shell will soften and dissolve. Likewise, if lead, which is highly flexible and extremely heavy, is placed in a vessel and vinegar poured around it, and this vessel is then covered and sealed, it will come about that the lead dissolves and creates white lead pigment.

19. For the same reasons, if copper, which is still more solid by nature, is similarly treated, it will dissipate and form verdigris. So will pearls. So will hard limestone (silex), which neither iron nor fire can dissolve on their own, but when these stones have been heated by fire, sprinkle vinegar on them and they break apart and dissolve. Since, therefore, we can see these things occur before our eyes, we can surmise on the same principles that so people with gallstones can be cured by nature in similar fashion by acids, on account of the sharpness of their sap.

20. There are also springs that, as it were, seem to be mixed with wine, like one in Paphlagonia, where those who drink from it become tipsy even without wine. Among the Aequicoli in Italy and in the Alps among the nation of the Medulli, there is a type of water that produces goiter.[9]

21. In Arcadia, on the other hand, there is a well-known city, Clitor, in whose countryside there is a cave running with water, and those who drink of it leave off drinking wine. There is an epigram inscribed in stone by this spring, with the following message in Greek verse: that this water is not suitable for bathing, and is an enemy to grapevines, for at this spring Melampus had purified the madness of the daughters of Proetus by means of sacrifices, and restored the minds of the girls to their original soundness. This is the [Greek] epigram inscribed there:

> Herdsman, if with your flocks you're heavy oppressed
>   at noonday,
> Thirsting, and coming upon Kleitor's outermost parts,
> Raise up a draft from the spring, [and drink it to your
>   refreshment,]
> Rest your entire herd here with the water nymphs.
> Do not attempt to bathe, or douse your skin in the
>   water,
> Lest the breeze bring you harm while you're in the
>   midst of a drunk.

9 Literally, "that swells the throats of those who drink it."

> Flee from the vine-hating spring, in which the hero
>   Melanthos
> Once loosed the daughters of Proetos from madness,
>   making them sane.
> In it he sank the secret means of purification
> When he had come from Argos to rough Arcadia's
>   peaks.

22. There is also a fountain on the island of Cea; those who unwittingly drink from it become stupid, and next to it is an inscribed epigram to the following effect: a drink from this fountain may be delightful, but those who drink from it will have the intelligence of a stone. These are the [Greek] verses:

> Sweet is the cooling drink of the waters that gush from
>   this fountain,
> Stone, however, is what that drinker's mind shall
>   become.

23. In Susa, the city in which the Persians have their capital, there is a little spring, and those who have drunk from it lose their teeth. On this, too, there is an inscribed epigram, which makes the following point: this is outstanding water for washing, but if it is drunk it knocks the teeth out at the roots. In Greek, these are the verses of the epigram:

> Spring water is what you see here, stranger, useful for
>   washing;
> Rinsing it off from their hands, its users remain
>   unscathed.
> But toss back this sparkling water into your hollow
>   gullet,
> Or just so much as touch it by reaching out with your
>   lip,
> On that same day, when you eat, all your teeth will be
>   uprooted,
> Tumbling out on the ground, and leaving you empty
>   jaws.

24. There are also springs in some locations that create outstanding singing voices in those who are born in the area, as in Tarsus, Magnesia, and other such regions, and also in Zama. Furthermore, Zama is an African city that King Juba* enclosed within a city wall of two layers, and there he established his royal palace. Twenty miles from there is the town of Ismuc, whose fields in the countryside are demarcated by an incredible sort of boundary. Although Africa is the mother and nursemaid of wild beasts* and especially of serpents, in the fields belonging to this town not a single beast is born, and if

any should be put out there, it dies immediately. Not only this, but the very soil from these places, if transported elsewhere, will be deadly in that place as well. This type of soil is also said to occur in the Balearics. But this soil has another still more marvelous property, of which I have heard the following account.

25. Gaius Julius, the son of Masinissa,* who owned all the fields of this town, served in the army with the elder Caesar. He was my house guest. In our daily contacts, it was only natural that we would turn to learned discussion. Once, when our conversation turned to the powers of water and its characteristics, he revealed to me that in his land there were springs such that those who were born in the area had outstanding singing voices, and for this reason, they would always buy handsome youths from across the sea, and mature girls, and mate them, so that the babies born to them would not only have excellent voices, but be good looking as well.

26. Thus we see that great variety has been distributed by nature among disparate phenomena. Now, given that a certain proportion of the human body is made of earth, and that in it, moreover, there are many types of liquid: blood, milk, sweat, urine, tears, then, if in these tiny particles of earth [which are our bodies] there can be such a discrepancy of flavor among the liquids, then it is hardly to be wondered at that in the great immensity of the earth itself there are indeed countless varieties of sap to be found, and that when water's power flows through the veins of these earths, it arrives at the heads of springs adulterated, and thus for this reason fountains are made diverse and various according to their types, because of the discrepancy of their localities and the dissimilar characteristics of their regions and soils.

27. I have seen some of these things myself, and I discovered the rest recorded in Greek books, and these are the authors of those texts: Theophrastos, Timaeus, Posidonios, Hegesias, Herodotus, Aristides, and Metrodorus,* who, with great powers of observation and boundless zeal declared in their writings that the properties of places, the characteristics of waters, and the qualities of the regions of the heavens have been distributed in this fashion because of the inclination of the cosmos. Following their lead, in this book I have recorded what I thought to be sufficient information about the varieties of water so that by using these remarks people may more easily choose sources of running water that they can bring into cities and towns for use there.

28. Of all things, none seems to be so necessary for use as water, because all nature's living creatures, were they deprived of the grain crop, could still maintain life

by using shrubs, or meat, or fish, or anything else as food, but without water neither the bodies of animals nor any other foodstuff can be created or conserved or prepared. For which reason springs should be sought and selected with great diligence and industry, in order to preserve the health of human life.

CHAPTER 4: TESTING WATER

1. This is how the testing and approval of springs should be carried out. If they are flowing and uncovered, before beginning to draw them, observe and note the build of the people who live around those springs, and if they have healthy bodies, glowing complexions, good legs, and clear eyes, then the waters will have passed the test outstandingly. Or, if a new fountain is to be dug, sprinkle this water into a Corinthian vase* or one of another type that is made of good bronze, and if it does not spot the vessel, then it is first rate. Likewise, if this water is boiled in a bronze kettle, and then allowed to cool and poured out, and in the bottom of the kettle no sand or mud is found, then this water has also passed the test. 2. If greens are thrown into a pot with this water, and cook rapidly when they are placed over the fire, they will indicate that the water is good and healthful. Equally, if the water in the future fountain is limpid and bright, and neither moss nor rushes grow where it emerges, nor is the place tainted by any source of pollution but instead preserves a pure appearance, on the basis of these signs it is given the nod as being light and of the highest healthfulness.

CHAPTER 5: LEVELING: THE CHOROBATE

1. Now I shall explain about conducting water into houses and city walls and how it ought to be done. Its first principle is that of leveling. Leveling can be done by diopters, or water levels, or a chorobate,* but it is more efficiently done with a chorobate, because diopters and water levels can be inaccurate (Figure 107).

A chorobate is a bar about twenty feet long. It has elbow joints at its extreme ends, finished identically, joined at a right angle into the ends of the bar, and transverse pieces between the bar and the elbows, fit together by hinges,* which have lines drawn straight on the perpendicular. The chorobate also has plumb bobs suspended from the bar on either side, one for each end. These, when the bar is set up and they touch the drawn lines to the same degree and simultaneously, indicate that the setup is level. 2. If the wind interferes and the lines cannot give a clear reading because of its motions, then on its upper surface give the straightedge a channel five feet long, one digit wide, and half a digit deep, and fill this with water, and if the water touches the upper edge of the channel equally all round, then it is known that the chorobate is level. When this chorobate has been so leveled, it is also known what the slope of the ground is.

3. Perhaps anyone who has read Archimedes' books will say that there cannot be a true leveling by means of water,* because he contends that water is not leveled, but instead has a spherical nature, and that it has the same center as the globe of the earth. But whether water is flat or spherical, it is still a fact that if the two extreme ends of the straightedge, right and left, are level with one another, then that straightedge is going to hold the water even, and if it inclines to either side, on the higher side the lip of the channel in the straightedge is not going to contain water. For it is a fact that no matter what it is poured into, water will have a bulging curvature in the center, but the extreme edges will be level with one another. An example of a chorobate will be drawn at the end of the volume.

If a slope is steep, the current of water will be easier to manage. If, however, the course is irregular, there will have to be recourse to masonry substructures.

CHAPTER 6: WATER SUPPLY

1. There are three types of watercourses (Figure 108): in open canals with masonry channels, or lead pipes, or terracotta tubing. These are the principles for each: for channels, the masonry should be as solid as possible, and the floor of the watercourse should have a slope calculated to be no less than half a foot[10] every hundred feet.* This masonry should be vaulted so that the sun touches the water as little as possible. When it reaches the walls of the city, make a reservoir (castellum aquae),* and adjoining the reservoir a three-part reservoir to receive the water. Within the reservoir itself, lay three

10 Reading *semipede* with GH.

systems of pipes, equally divided among three interconnected holding tanks, which are so joined that if there is overflow from the outer two, it will spill into the central tank.

2. The piping system for all the public pools and running fountains should be put in the middle tank, pipes for baths in one of the outside tanks, to provide tax revenue every year for the People of Rome, and in the third tank the piping system should be directed to private homes, so that there will never be a shortage of public water, for private citizens will not be inclined to divert public supplies if they have their own piping from the same source. These are the reasons that I have set up such divisions, because those who bring water into their own homes can, through taxes, provide for the transport of water by public contractors.*

3. If there are mountains between the city walls and the water source, this is what to do: tunnels are to be dug underground and the watercourse can be leveled to the fall just described (Figure 109). If the mountain is of tufa or stone, then the channel can be cut into the rock itself, but if it is of earthy or sandy soil, then masonry walls with vaults should be constructed in the tunnel and the water conducted by this means. Air shafts should be spaced so that there is one *actus* (120 feet) between every two of them.*

4. If waters are going to be conducted in systems of lead pipes, first a *castellum aquae* should be constructed at the source, and then the diameter of the pipes should be fixed on the basis of the water supply.* The piping system should be laid down to extend from this *castellum* to the *castellum* within the city walls. Pipes should be cast so that they are no less than ten feet long.

If they are going to be hundred-digit pipes, individually they should weigh 1,200 pounds; if they are eighty-digit pipes, 960 pounds; if fifty digits, 600 pounds; forty-digit pipes should each weigh 480 pounds; thirty-digit pipes, 360 pounds; twenty-digit pipes, 240 pounds; fifteen-digit pipes, 180 pounds; ten-digit pipes, 120 pounds; eight-digit pipes, 100 pounds; five-digit pipes, 60 pounds. The names of the sizes of lead pipes are taken from the sizes of their plate and however many digits they will be before they have been bent around into tubes. Thus the panels that are fifty digits wide, when made into pipe, will be called a fifty-digit pipe, and so on for the rest.

5. The conveyance of water through lead pipes is effected in this way. If the source has a downward incline toward the city walls, and there are no mountains in between that are so high as to interfere, but

only low valleys, then it will be necessary to construct underpinnings in masonry up to the level, just as with canals and channels. If bypassing is possible within a short distance, then the pipes should be carried around the low spot, but if there is a very broad valley, then their course should be directed down the slope. When the watercourse reaches valley bottom, it should not be elevated high on masonry substructures; the fall should be as long and as gradual as possible. This will be the "belly," which the Greeks call *coelia*, "gut." By the time the water will have arrived at the ascent opposite, its pressure has gradually increased because of the long extent of the "belly," and as a result it will be pushed up to the top of the ascent.

6. If a "belly" is not made in valleys, nor a substructure brought up to the level, but instead the pipe makes a "knee" bend, the water will break out and will dissolve the seams in the pipes. In a "belly," as well, dilations[11] should be made, through which water pressure may be alleviated.*

Thus those who conduct water through systems of lead piping according to these instructions will be able to make a beautifully calibrated slope all the way from the water source to the city walls, because the falls and bypasses and "bellies" and ascents can bring it about to this effect.

7. It is useful as well to place reservoirs at an interval of two hundred *actus** (= 24,000 feet) so that if one place along the line develops a flaw the entire work will not be ruined along its whole extent, and it will be easier to discover where the problem has arisen. However, these reservoirs should never be put on a downward fall, nor in the flat of a "belly," nor at an ascent, never by any means in valleys, but always on continuous flat ground.

8. If we want to limit expenses, this is what to do. Make terracotta piping with a wall whose thickness is no less than two digits, but make it in such a way that these pipes have tongues at one end, so that one can be fitted inside another and they can be joined together. Their joints should be lined with quicklime that has been worked with oil, and in the downward slopes of the "belly's" incline a stone of Anio tufa should be

placed at the "knee bend" itself and this should be perforated, so that the last pipe on the downward slope is fitted into the stone and the first pipe of the "belly," and in the same way at the ascent on the opposite side, the last pipe of the "belly" should be fixed in Anio tufa and the first pipe of the ascent should be fitted in the same fashion.

9. By this means the level plane of the pipes will not be displaced either along the fall or the ascent of the "belly." Strong pressure tends to develop in watercourses, strong enough even to break apart stone unless the water is let in lightly and sparingly initially at the source, and then, in knee bends or other turns the watercourse is restrained by bindings or loads of sand. All the rest of the system should be laid as for lead piping. Also, when water is first introduced at the source, put ash in beforehand, so that the joints, if they have not been sealed adequately, will be sealed by the ash.

10. Ceramic pipes have this advantage. First of all, if there is some flaw in the system, whatever it is, anyone may repair it. Furthermore, the water from clay pipes is much more healthful than that from lead, because it seems that lead is toxic;* white lead is derived from it, and that is said to be harmful to the human body. If that which is produced from lead is harmful, then there can be no doubt that lead itself is not healthful either. 11. We can take an example from the lead workers, whose coloring has been overcome by pallor. When lead exhales as it is poured, its vapor comes to rest in the limbs of their bodies; day by day it snatches away the strength of their blood by burning it away. It seems, then, that water should be conducted as little as possible through lead pipes if we want it to be healthful. That the flavor of water from terracotta pipes is better is clear from everyday cooking, because everyone, although they may have tables piled high with silver vessels, nonetheless uses terracotta for cooking, in order to preserve good flavor.

12. If there are no springs from which we can conduct water, it is necessary to dig wells. In digging wells a methodical approach is not to be undervalued: indeed, scientific principles should be taken into consideration with insight and great skill, because earth is of many and varied types. For it, like everything else, is composed of four elements. First of all, there is earth itself; then, from the moisture of water, it has springs. Likewise, it has heat, from which sulphur, alum, and bitumen are created, and it has huge breaths of air. When these, with their heavy breath, penetrate through pores in the earth to well shafts and there encounter the well diggers, they stop the breath of life within the workers' nostrils by the

---

11 Here, for the MSS *colliviaria, scripsi* "collaxaria," a *hapax* but one, at least, whose meaning works in the context. Other emendations (e.g. *colluviaria, collentaria, colliquiaria, columbaria*) do not make sense in the immediate context of the passage, with the possible exception of *collentaria*. Vitruvius is speaking of a way to reduce water pressure at the bottom of a "belly" by means of increasing the volume of the pipes (*laxamentum*).

natural force[12] of their vapor. If the workers do not escape quickly, they are killed on the spot.

13. By what methods can this be prevented? Do as follows: a lighted lamp should be sent down into the well shaft, and if it stays lit, then the descent can be made without danger. If the light is snatched away by the force of the vapor, than air shafts should be sunk alongside the well to the right and left, and in this manner the vapors will be dissipated out through the air shafts as if they were nostrils. When these procedures have been carried out and water has been reached, then the shaft should be lined with masonry, so that the veins of water will not be blocked.

14. Now if the ground is hard or the veins of water are too deep, then supplies of water have to be collected from roofs or other high places by hydraulic cement (*opus signinum*). This is how to make *opus signinum.** First of all, the purest and roughest sand should be readied, and then rubble of hard limestone should be broken up, no

---

12 Reading, with Rose, *vi* for MSS *ut.*

heavier than a pound, and mixed as vigorously as possible with lime in a mortar, so that five parts of sand correspond to two of lime.

15. The trench for the cistern should be dug down to the projected level and limed[13] using rods sheathed in iron. Once the walls have been limed, then the earth remaining in the center should be emptied to the level of the bottoms of the walls. Once these have been taken down to the level, the floor should be limed to the decided thickness. If these cisterns can be made double or triple, so that they can be used successively in filtering, they make the water supply much more healthful and flavorful, for if there is a place where the mud suspended in the water may settle, the water itself will become clearer and conserve its flavor without odor. Otherwise, it will be necessary to add salt and filter it.

In this volume, I have set down what I could about the properties and varieties of water, what uses it has, and the methods by which it can be conducted and tested. In the following book I shall write in full about matters concerning sundials and the principles of clocks.

❖

SUNDIALS AND CLOCKS

PREFACE

1. To the illustrious athletes who had won the Olympic, Pythian, Isthmian, and Nemean Games, the forebears of the Greeks awarded such great honor that not only are they given palms, garlands, and praises as they stand before the assembled public, but also, when they return home victorious to their cities, they are carried in triumph in four-horse chariots through their city walls to their homes, and at public expense they enjoy the rest of their lives on a pension. Now when I observe this, I am amazed that the same honors – or honors greater still – are not bestowed on writers, who provide every nation with endless utility for everlasting ages.* For this would have been a much more worthy institution to have set up, because athletes make their own bodies stronger by exercising, whereas writers strengthen not only their own wits, but indeed everyone's, by preparing books for learning and the sharpening of minds. 2. What good does it do humanity that Milo of Croton* was undefeated, or the others who were champions of this kind, other than that, so long as they were alive, they held distinction among their own fellow citizens? The valuable precepts of Pythagoras, on the other hand, of Democritus, Plato, Aristotle, and the other sages, cultivated by daily industry, not only produce ever fresh and flourishing fruit for their own fellow citizens, but indeed for all the nations. And those who from an early age enjoy an abundance of learning develop the best judgment, and in their cities they have established civilized customs, equal justice, and those laws without which no community can exist safely. 3. Since so many private and public gifts have been prepared for humanity by the wisdom of writers, I conclude that more than palms and garlands should be awarded them – indeed triumphs should be declared for them and to them it ought to be decided to dedicate thrones among the gods.

Now of their discoveries, which have been useful for people in improving their lives, I shall propose a few individual cases to serve as examples, from which it should be recognized that honors are due these writers. 4. First of all, I shall take one among many extremely useful findings of Plato as he explains it (Figure 110).* If there is a square plot or field with sides of equal length and it needs to be doubled in size, the need will arise for the type of number that cannot be found by means of calculation, but it can be found by drawing a succession of precise lines.* Here is a demonstration of the problem: A square plot that is ten feet long and ten feet wide gives an area of 100 square feet. If it is necessary to double this, and make one of 200 square feet, likewise with equal sides, then the question will arise as to how long the side of this square would be, so that from it two hundred feet should correspond to the doubling of the area. It is not possible to find such a number by counting. For if fourteen is established as the measure of each side, then when multiplied the sides will give 196 square feet, if fifteen, 225 square feet. 5. Therefore, it is not discovered by means of numbers.

However, if in that original square that was ten feet on a side, a line should be drawn diagonally from corner to corner, so as to divide off two triangles of equal size, each of fifty feet in area, then a square with equal sides should be drawn on the basis of this diagonal line. Thus, whatever the size of the two triangles defined by the diagonal line in the smaller square, each with an area of fifty feet, just so, four such triangles, of the same size and the same number of square feet, will be created in the larger square. Doubling by this method comes from Plato and is set out in the diagram at the bottom of the page.*

6. Likewise, Pythagoras discovered and demonstrated a set square without making one, and whereas artisans who create set squares with great effort scarcely ever succeed in making them accurate, an improvement can be set out as follows according to the principles and methods that he teaches.* If you take three rules, of which one should be three feet long, another four feet long, and the third five feet long, and these rules are arranged together so that the ends of each touch the ends of the two others

in the form of a triangle, they will create a flawless set square. And if individual squares with equal sides are drawn along the individual rules, that on the three-foot side will have an area of nine feet, the four-foot side, sixteen, the five-foot side, twenty-five. 7. Thus, the area in number of feet created by the sum of the two squares with sides three and four feet long is equally rendered by the square drawn with five feet to a side. When Pythagoras had discovered this, not doubting that the Muses had guided him to this discovery, he is said to have immolated sacrifices to them in thanksgiving.

And just as this ratio is useful in many things and many measurements, so, too, in the construction of stairways in buildings it serves to calibrate the incline. 8. If the height of a story from the topmost joist to the floor below is divided into three parts, then five of these parts will be the proper length for the run of the steps of the staircase. So, whatever these three parts of the distance between joist and pavement measure, move four such units horizontally, and there place the feet of the stringers. If this procedure is followed, then the placement of the steps themselves will be calibrated properly. The design of this matter will be illustrated as well.

9. As for Archimedes, although in his limitless wisdom he discovered many wonderful things, nonetheless, of all of them, one in particular, which I shall now describe, seems to convey his boundless ingenuity. It is no surprise that Hieron, after he had obtained immense kingly power in Syracuse, decided, because of the favorable turn of events, to dedicate a votive crown of gold to the immortal gods in a certain shrine.* He contracted for the craftsman's wages, and he [himself] weighed out the gold precisely for the contractor. This contractor completed the work with great skill and on schedule; it was approved by the king, and the contractor seemed to have used up the furnished supply of gold. 10. Later, charges were leveled that in the making of the crown a certain amount of gold had been removed and replaced by an equal amount of silver. Hieron, outraged that he should have been shown so little respect, and not knowing by what method he might expose the theft, requested that Archimedes take the matter under consideration on his behalf.

Now Archimedes, once he had charge of this matter, chanced to go to the baths, and there, as he stepped into the tub, he noticed that however much he immersed his body in it, that much water spilled over the sides of the tub. When the reason for this occurrence came clear to him, he did not hesitate, but in a

transport of joy he leapt out of the tub, and as he rushed home naked, he let one and all know that he had truly found what he had been looking for – because as he ran he shouted over and over in Greek : "I found it! I found it!" (*Eurêka! Eurêka!*)

11. On the basis of this discovery he is said to have made two masses whose weight was equal to that of the crown: one of gold and one of silver. When he had done this, he filled a large vessel to the brim with water, into which he sank the mass of silver. Whatever amount of silver was submerged, that much water spilled out. Then, once the mass had been taken out, he poured back the missing amount of water so that it would be level with the brim in the same way as before, using a one-sextarius pitcher [= 1/2 liter] as a measure. From this procedure he discovered that a certain weight of silver corresponded to a certain measure of water. 12. Once he had tried this, then in the same fashion he sank the gold mass into the full vessel, and when he had removed it, replacing the water by the same method, he discovered that not so much of the water had been lost, and less was required to replace it, as much less as a mass of gold will be smaller in body than a mass of silver which has the same weight. After this, once he had filled the vessel yet again, the crown itself was sunk into the water, and he discovered that more water was required to replace the crown than to replace the mass of gold of equal weight, and because there was more water in the crown's place than in the place of the mass of gold, he detected, by deduction, the mixture of silver in the crown and the contractor's flagrant theft.

13. Now let our attention be turned to the researches of Archytas of Tarentum and Eratosthenes of Cyrene.* For they made many welcome discoveries for humanity by means of mathematics. Therefore, just as they were appreciated for their other inventions, in this matter they are most greatly admired for their inspirations: each of them used a different method to carry out what Apollo had ordered in an oracle at Delos, namely that his altar, which had equal feet on all sides, be doubled, in order that the people of the island be freed from an ancient curse. 14. Archytas carried out the task by drawing a diagram of half cylinders,[1] and Eratosthenes achieved the same objective by using a machine, the mesolabe.

15. When these things are noted in all the exuberance of their erudition, we are naturally compelled by

---

1 So Philander; *cylindrorum* EGH.

these individual inventions to be deeply impressed as we consider their effects. In considering many such, I especially admire the volumes of Democritus on nature, and his treatise entitled "worked by hand" (*cheirokmêtôn*), in which he used a signet ring to mark in soft wax whatever he had tried himself.[2]*

16. Therefore the ideas of these men have not only been provided in order to improve our conduct, but also for the service of everyone in every age, whereas the achievements of athletes grow old in a short time together with their bodies; indeed, neither when they are at their peak nor later are they of any use for human existence, not in comparison with the thoughts of the sages. Although honors are awarded neither to the activities nor to the outstanding findings of writers, their minds themselves, looking up at the upper reaches of air, carried up to heaven on the staircase of human memory for all time, compel not only their thoughts but their very likenesses to be made known to later generations. And thus those who have minds imbued with the joys of literature cannot fail to have the image of Ennius the poet consecrated in their breasts as if he were one of the gods. Those who devotedly delight in the poems of Accius not only seem to have the power of his words but also his portrait present along with them.

17. Likewise many people born within our memory will seem to discuss science with Lucretius as if he were there in person, or the art of rhetoric with Cicero, and many subsequent generations exchange conversation with Varro about the Latin language,* and similarly most lovers of learning, who ponder many things along with the sages of the Greeks, will seem to be having private conversations with them, and to sum up, the ideas of wise writers, absent in body yet flourishing as they age, when they enter into our deliberations and discussions, they all have greater authority than those who are actually present. 18. Thus, Caesar, relying on these authors and applying their thoughts and advice, I have written these volumes: in the first seven about buildings, in the eighth about water, and in this one I shall explain about the principles of sundials, how, through the use of the shadows cast by the gnomon, these principles have been discovered by observing the behavior of the sun's rays in the firmament, and by what methods they can be expanded or contracted.

CHAPTER 1: THE COSMOS
(FIGURE 111)

1. These things have been prepared by the divine intelligence and contain great wonder for those who consider them, namely the fact that the shadow cast by a gnomon at the equinox is of one size in Athens, another in Alexandria, another in Rome, still different in Placentia and all the other places of the globe.* And so the designs of sundials must diverge just as drastically with a change in location. The shapes of the *analêmmata* are outlined by the sizes of the shadows at the equinoxes, on the basis of which the demarcation of the hours is made according to the place and to the shadows cast by the gnomon. The *analêmma* (Figure 114) is the principle derived from the observation of the sun's course and the growth of the shadow cast by the gnomon as that shadow increases up to the winter solstice; by using the principles of architecture and the compass its effects in the world itself will be discovered.

2. Now the cosmos is the all-encompassing system of everything in nature, and also the firmament, which is formed of the constellations and the courses of the stars. This revolves ceaselessly around the earth and sea at the extreme hinges of the axis. For thus the power of nature has acted as architect, and she has placed the hinges as central axes, one at the top of the firmament, far from land and sea, beyond the very stars of the North, and the other directly opposite, beneath the earth in the regions of the South. Right around these hinges she has fixed little wheels, rotating, as on a lathe, about these axes, which are called *poloi*[3] in Greek; through them the firmament is kept perpetually spinning. Thus the middle part of the earth, along with the sea, is naturally placed in the region where the center is.

3. Thus these things have been set out by nature so that in the northern half there is an axis higher above the earth, and in the southern half the axis is set low and obscured by the earth.* Furthermore, in the middle between them there is a broad circular belt[4] fashioned with twelve signs,* set transversely and inclined toward the south. The design of each sign shows an image taken from nature,* outlined in a pattern of stars among the twelve matched divisions of the belt. And thus these

---

2 Reading *ut signaret cera molli siqua esset expertus* (Soubiran) for a corrupt passage.

3 So Giocondo, surely correctly, as *polos* is the Greek equivalent of *cardo*. *pasde* EGH.

4 Reading *lata* rather than *delata*.

glittering objects, along with the firmament and the other constellations, perpetually spinning together in splendid array, complete their courses along the curvature of the firmament. 4. All these things have been created so that they are visible or invisible depending on the time of year. While six among the company of these signs wander above the earth* together with the firmament, the others, passing underneath the earth, are obscured by its shadow. Six of these signs, then, are always pressing forward, climbing above the earth. For however great a portion of the last sign, compelled by the downward progress of the firmament's rotation, passes under and is hidden beneath the earth, so an equivalent amount of its opposite sign, borne around by the same rotation, climbing upward by turning across the open reaches [of heaven], emerges from darkness into the light. For the power of a single force affects both east and west simultaneously.

5. These signs, therefore, are twelve in number and each individual sign occupies one-twelfth part of the firmament, and all of them are constantly rotated from east to west. Now through these signs, in a contrary course, the moon, the star of Mercury, the star of Venus, the sun itself, and likewise the stars of Mars and Jupiter and Saturn, journey from west to east across the firmament along a circuit of a different magnitude, traveling just as if they were at different points on a staircase. The moon, traversing its circuit in a little more, by about an hour, than once every twenty-eighth day, completes a lunar month by returning to the sign in which it had first set out. 6. In the turning of a month, the sun, in its journeys, traverses the space of a single sign, that is, one-twelfth part of the firmament. By traveling across the distance of twelve signs in twelve months, it completes the interval of the revolving year when it returns to the sign in which it began. In other words, that circuit which the moon runs thirteen times in twelve months, the sun measures out only once in the same number of months.

Just as the stars of Mercury and Venus are completing the circle of their journeys, describing orbits around the sun's rays as if about an axis, they regress backward, and slow their progress; they also delay at stopping places within the intervals of the signs (Figure 112).* 7. That this is so is best observed in the case of the star of Venus, which, as it follows the sun, appears in the sky after sunset, glittering brightly, and it is called Vesperugo, the evening star. At other times it courses ahead and rises before the sun; then it is called Lucifer, the morning star. And because of this, not infrequently

these stars spend several days in a single sign; whereas at other times they will quickly enter upon another. Therefore, because they do not spend an equal number of days in the individual signs, to whatever extent they have delayed, they compensate to complete their proper course by leaping across the signs at a more rapid pace. It happens, therefore, that although they may delay in several signs, when, of necessity, they tear themselves away from their lethargy, they quickly regain their proper circuit.

8. The path of the star of Mercury across the firmament circles in such a way that in running through the signs it returns every three hundred sixtieth day to the sign from which it had begun to make its course at the beginning of its revolution, and thus its path is balanced out so that in average it has some thirty days in each individual sign. 9. That of the star of Venus, when it has been freed from the impediment of the rays of the sun, traverses the space of a sign in thirty days. If it has spent fewer than forty days in individual signs, still, this is the number it will devote to a single sign when it comes to a standstill. Therefore, when it has measured out its entire circuit through the firmament, it reenters the sign from which it had first begun to make its rounds on the four hundred eighty-fifth day.

10. The path of the star of Mars, in traversing the space of the constellations on about the six hundred eighty-third day, arrives to the place from which it had initiated making its course, and although there are signs it has traversed quickly, when it makes its pause it fills out the measure of the number of days. The star of Jupiter, mounting with more placid steps against the rotation of the firmament, measures out some three hundred sixty days in individual signs, and pauses after eleven years and three hundred thirteen days, returning back to that sign in which it had been twelve years before. The star of Saturn, on the other hand, traversing the space of a sign in a few days more than twenty-nine months, is restored in the twenty-ninth year and about one hundred sixty days to the sign where it had been thirty years before; and from this fact, it can be seen that inasmuch as Saturn is less distant from the extreme end of the firmament, its progress across the firmament seems to be slower because it traverses a correspondingly greater circuit.

11. Those stars that travel their orbits beyond the path of the sun, particularly when they are about to be in the same triangle (trigon) as the approaching sun, do not proceed forward; they delay by regressing, and do so until the sun itself has passed out of that triangle and

into another sign. Some people think that this happens because, as they declare, the sun, when it stands at some distance off, envelops the stars, traveling through this distance on dim orbits, in toils of darkness. To us, however, this does not seem to be so. For the splendor of the sun is clearly to be seen and open to view without any sort of darkness throughout the cosmos, so that these stars are apparent to us even when they make their backtracking and delays. 12. Now if our own vision can observe this at such a great distance, why should we judge that darkness can obstruct the divine splendor of the stars?

This reasoning makes better sense to us: that just as boiling heat calls out all substances and draws them toward itself, just as we see fruits rising upward out of the ground because of heat, not to mention the vapors of water stirred up from springs toward the clouds along rainbows – for the same reason, the intense force of the sun, reaching forth its rays in the form of a triangle, pulls in the stars that follow it, and as if reining them in and restraining them, it prevents those that run before it from proceeding into another sign, and obliges them instead to return back in its direction.

13. Perhaps an explanation will be required about why, with its heat, the sun restrains the stars that are in the sign five places away from itself, rather than those stars in the second or third sign away, which are closer to it. I will show how this seems to happen. The sun's rays stretch out into the universe along lines that take the form of a triangle with equal sides.* This means that its ray extends directly to the fifth sign, no more and no less. Indeed, if the sun's rays poured out through the whole cosmos in expanding ripples, rather than having their reach held in line and extended only to conform to the shape of a triangle, they would set fire to all the closer signs. Euripides, the Greek poet, appears to have noticed this, for he says that those things which are further from the sun burn more intensely, whereas it keeps those nearer it temperate. This is what he writes in his play *Phaethon*:

He[lios] burns the more distant things, but keeps the nearer ones temperate.

14. If, therefore, the phenomenon, its principles, and the testimony of an ancient poet all point to the same conclusion, I do not think that one should decide except as we have written here about it.

The star of Jupiter, traversing its orbit between those of Mars and Saturn, flies along a course greater than that of Mars and less than that of Saturn. So, too, with the remaining stars, the farther distant they are from the limits of heaven and the nearer they keep their orbit to earth, the faster they seem to go, because each one of them, in traversing a smaller circle, more frequently passes underneath one which is higher up, and then overtakes it. 15. In the same way, if seven ants were to be placed on a potter's wheel, and as many channels were to be made around the center of the wheel, growing in size from the smallest to the outermost, and the ants were forced to make a circuit in these channels, then, as the wheel was spun in the opposite direction, it would be no less necessary for these ants to make their way against the rotation of the wheel, and the one whose channel was nearest the center would have to finish his circuit more quickly, but the one that traversed the outermost circuit of the wheel, even if it walked just as quickly, would complete its round much more slowly because of the circle's sheer size. In the same way, these stars, striving against the course of the cosmos, complete their orbit as they journey on, but because of the rotation of the firmament they are carried back in redoublings because of the daily twirling of time.

16. This appears to be the reason that some of these stars are temperate, some boiling hot, and still others frigid: every fire has a flame that rises to higher regions. Therefore, the sun, burning the ether above it with its rays, makes this ether white hot in exactly those places where the star of Mars sets its course. Thus it is made boiling hot by the sun's heat. The star of Saturn, because it is next to the ends of the cosmos and touches the frozen regions of the firmament, is intensely chilly. Hence the star of Jupiter, because it has its course between the circuits of these other two, can be seen to have the most harmonious and temperate of results from the meeting of their chill and heat in the middle.

As for the belt of the twelve signs, the contrary operation and course of the seven stars, and the principles and numbers according to which they travel from sign to sign in their orbits, I have laid out what I received from my teachers. Now I shall tell about the waxing and waning of the moon as it has been handed down to us from our forebears.

CHAPTER 2: THE MOON

1. Berosus, who proceeded from the city, or rather nation, of the Chaldaeans into Asia [Minor] and revealed the teachings of the Chaldaic discipline,* claimed as fol-

lows: the moon is a ball, half brilliant white and half of a sky-blue color, and when, making its way along its path, it passes underneath the orb of the sun, then it is caught up by the sun's rays and heat and turned, on account of its own property of light, toward the light of the sun. Summoned forth by the sun's orb, it faces upward, while its lower half, which is not a luminous white, appears dark because of its similarity to the color of air. When the moon is in line with the sun's rays, the entire luminous half is held facing upward, and it is called a "first moon."

2. When, in its progress, it moves toward the eastern parts of the firmament, it is released from the sun's power and the extreme edge of its bright half sends its splendor in the tiniest little line toward the earth, and then it is called a "second moon." The third and fourth moons are counted out, day after day, by a further daily withdrawal and rotation, and on the seventh day, when the sun is setting in the west, the moon occupies the middle regions of heaven between east and west; also, because it stands apart from the sun by half the extent of the firmament, it likewise has half its luminous part turned toward the earth. When, however, the whole space of the cosmos stands between the sun and moon, and the sun, setting in the west, stands opposite the moon rising in the east, then the moon, withdrawn to the greatest extent from the sun's rays, that is, on the fourteenth day, sends forth the splendor of its entire sphere as a full disk; for the remaining days, by a daily decrease until the completion of the lunar month, it submits in its rotation and its course to the renewed summons of the sun, creating the monthly pattern of the days in obedience to the solar disk and its rays.

3. Now I shall also describe how Aristarchus of Samos,* a mathematician of great ability, left behind the explanation for the moon's phases in his teachings. For it is no secret [in his theory] that the moon does not have its own particular glow, but rather it is like a mirror, and receives its splendor from the force of the sun. For the moon of all the seven stars traverses the smallest circuit in its journeys, the one nearest the earth. Thus every month, one day before the sun passes by, it is darkened underneath the solar disk and the sun's rays because it is hidden, and when it is with the sun, it is called the new moon. On the following day, which is the second in number, as it passes by it barely makes an appearance at the edge of its curvature. When it has receded three days' distance from the sun it waxes and is increasingly illuminated. And therefore, receding day by day, when it arrives at the seventh day, standing away from the sun

by about half the expanse of the firmament, half of it glows, and that part of it which faces the sun is illuminated. 4. On the fourteenth day, when it stands away from the sun by the diameter of the entire firmament, it becomes completely full and rises when the sun is setting in the west, because the whole expanse of the universe stands opposite it, and it receives the splendor of the entire disk of the sun onto itself. On the seventeenth day, when the sun rises, the moon is pressed toward the west. On the twenty-first day when the sun has risen, the moon occupies, roughly speaking, the regions at the middle of the firmament, and the part that faces the sun remains luminous; the rest is dark. Likewise, continuing its journey day by day, on about the twenty-eighth day it passes underneath the rays of the sun and thus rounds out the account of the months.

CHAPTER 3: THE SUN

1. Now I shall tell how the sun, in traversing the signs during individual months, increases and diminishes the space of the days and hours.* For when, after entering the sign of Aries, it traverses the eighth degree,* it completes the vernal equinox. When it advances to the tail of Taurus and the constellation of the Pleiades, from which the first half of Taurus projects, it courses through an expanse greater than half the cosmos, advancing toward the northern part. When it enters into Gemini from Taurus at the rising of the Pleiades, it ascends higher above the earth and increases the length of the days. Then, when it has entered from Gemini into Cancer, which occupies the shortest expanse of heaven, upon reaching the eighth degree of Cancer it brings to completion the time of the solstice, and continuing onward it reaches the head and breast of Leo, because those parts of Leo are still within the sign of Cancer. 2. From the breast of Leo and the boundaries of Cancer, the sun, coursing through the remaining parts of Leo on its way out, reduces the size of the day and of its circuit, returning to the same course as it had entering Gemini.* Then, crossing from Leo into Virgo and advancing to the fold of her dress it contracts the circle and matches the amount of its circuit to that of Taurus. Advancing out of Virgo by way of the fold of her dress, which occupies the first parts of Libra, in the eighth degree of Libra it completes the autumnal equinox. This circuit equals that occupied by Aries. 3. When the sun enters Scorpio at the setting of the Pleiades, in advancing southward it reduces the length of

the days. When, passing out of Scorpio, it has entered Sagittarius at the thighs, it flies through a narrower daily course. When it then begins from the thighs of Sagittarius, a part which is assigned to Capricorn, at the eighth degree of Capricorn it traverses the briefest expanse of the heavens. Because of the day's brevity these days are called *bruma*,[5] and *dies brumales*. Then, crossing from Capricorn into Aquarius it increases the length of the day to equal Sagittarius. When from Aquarius it has entered into Pisces, with Favonius blowing, it sets a course equivalent to that of Scorpio. Thus the sun, by making the circuit through these signs, increases or diminishes the extent of the days and hours at certain definite times.

CHAPTER 4: CONSTELLATIONS TO THE RIGHT OF THE RISING SUN (FIGURE 113)

1. Now I shall tell about the other constellations, arranged and portrayed with stars, to the left and right of the belt of signs – that is, in the southern and northern portions of the firmament. The North, which the Greeks call "The Bear" (*Arktos*) or "The Spiral" (*Helikê*), has The Warder (*Boötes*) posted behind it. Virgo has been formed not far from this, and above her left shoulder rests a brilliant star, which we call the "Forerunner of the Vintage" and the Greeks *Protrugetê*. Even more brilliantly white is the Ear of Grain* she carries. There is a colored star in the middle of the knees* of the Guardian of the Bear, who is called Arcturus, and he has been enshrined there.

2. In part of the very summit of the northern region, crosswise along the feet of Gemini, stands the Charioteer (*Auriga*), on the tip of the horn of Taurus; in fact he keeps the underside of his foot on the tip of the left horn of Taurus. The stars at the Charioteer's hands are called the Kids, and the She-Goat is at his left shoulder.[6] Above the signs of Taurus and Aries, Perseus has the Pleiades running beneath his stride to the right, and the head of Aries to the left; leaning with his right hand on the image of Cassiopeia, he brandishes the head of the Gorgon in his left above the sign of Taurus, laying it at the feet of Andromeda.

3. Andromeda is set above Pisces; her stomach and the belly of the Horse are above the dorsal fin of the northern Fish.[7] The brightest star in the belly of the Horse forms the division between itself and the head of Andromeda. The right hand of Andromeda has been set above the image of Cassiopeia, the left is alongside the northernmost fish of Pisces. Likewise the image of Aquarius is over the image of the Horse's head. The ears of the Horse just touch the cheeks of Aquarius.[8]

Cassiopeia is enshrined in the middle. Above the sign of Capricorn, high up, are the Eagle and the Dolphin. Following along them is the Arrow, and from there the Bird (Cygnus), whose right wing just touches the hand of Cepheus and his scepter; the left wing rests above Cassiopeia. 4. The hooves of the Horse are set under[9] the tail of the Bird. Then, above the images of Sagittarius, Scorpio, and Libra, the Serpent touches the Crown (Corona Borealis) with the tip of its snout. But near the middle of the Crown, the Serpent-handler (Ophiuchos) holds the Serpent in his hands, with his left foot stomping Scorpio full in the face. Not far from the region of the head of the Serpent-handler is placed the head of the Kneeler. It is relatively easy to distinguish the tops of their heads because they are not outlined by dim stars. 5. The foot of the Kneeler is propped on the temple of the head of that Serpent (Draco) in whose coils one of the Bears – which are also called the Northerners – is enfolded. The Dolphin curves slightly through these. Opposite the beak of the Bird the Lyre is held aloft. In between the shoulders of the Warder and the Kneeler, the Crown has been set in place.

In the northern circle there are placed the two Bears, with their backs facing one another and their breasts turned away. The smaller of these is called "Dog's Tail" (*Cynosura*) by the Greeks, and the larger is called "Spiral" (*Helikê*). Their heads are set to look away from one another. Their tails are portrayed so that each faces the head of the bear opposite; indeed, their tails extend beyond each other's heads and project upward.

6. Another Serpent (Draco) is said to be stretched

---

5 A contraction of *brevima*, which is in itself a contraction of *brevissima*.

6 Reading *appelluntur* for H *appellantur*, and *manui* for *manus*.

7 The preserved text of this paragraph has some serious problems. For the MSS "*Item pisces supra andromedam et eius ventris et equique sunt supra spinam equi cuius ventris lucidissima stella finit ventrem equi et caput andromedae,*" we read "*Item supra pisces andromeda, et eius ventris et equi sunt supra spinam aquilonalis piscis. Lucidissima stella finit ventrem equi et caput andromedae.*"

8 Reading, for the MSS *equi ungulae attingunt aquarii genua, equi auriculae attingunt aquarii genas.*

9 Reading *subiecti* with Philander for the MSS *subtecti*.

out between their tails; from this Serpent the star that is called the Pole Star* shines forth near the head of the larger Northerner (i.e., Great Bear). The Northerner nearest the Serpent (Draco) is wrapped in coils all around its head; indeed, together with all this, the head of Cynosura is inserted in the bend [of Draco], which is then extended all the way around to its feet. Here, bending inward and doubling on itself, rearing itself up, it is deflected away from the head of the Smaller Northerner back toward the Larger, at its muzzle and the right temple of its head. The feet of Cepheus are above the tail of the Small Northerner, and here there are stars making an isosceles triangle* with its very tip over the sign of Aries. Many of the stars of the Small Northerner and of the image of Cassiopeia are mixed in among one another.

I have told what constellations are set out to the right* of the rising sun between the belt of signs and the constellations of the North. Now I shall describe those that have been distributed by nature to the left of the rising sun and in the southern parts.

CHAPTER 5: CONSTELLATIONS
TO THE LEFT OF THE RISING SUN
(FIGURE 113)

1. First of all, set underneath Capricorn is the southern fish of Pisces, facing the tail of the Whale (Cetus). The region from here to Sagittarius is empty. The Incense-burner is under Scorpio's sting. The forward parts of the Centaur are next to Libra and Scorpio. In his hands the Centaur holds the image that those who are knowledgeable about the stars call the Beast. A Snake (Hydra), stretching along Virgo, Leo, and Cancer, twists back and binds together the line of stars, rearing its face up in the region of Cancer, holding up the Cup with the middle of its body hard by Leo, and setting down its tail, on which stands the Crow, at the hand of Virgo. The stars above its shoulders are of equal brightness.

2. Underneath, along the Snake's belly, just under its tail, is set the Centaur. Next to the Cup and Leo is the Ship, which is called Argo, whose prow is hidden – but the mast and the parts about the rudder can be seen emerging, and the poop of this little ship is connected through the tip of the Dog's tail. For the Little Dog follows the Twins of Gemini opposite the Snake's head. The Larger Dog follows the Little Dog. Orion is set

crosswise underneath, pressed by the hoof of Taurus,[10] holding a club in his right hand and raising his club with the other hand toward Gemini. 3. At his feet the Dog follows closely upon the Hare. The Whale (Cetus) is set under Aries and Pisces, and there is a light sprinkling of stars arranged in rows from his head to the space between the fish of Pisces, which in Greek are called the Harpoons. Some distance inward, a tight knot of snakes just touches the tip of the Whale's head. The river Eridanus flows forth – in a starry likeness – from a source making its beginning at the left foot of Orion, but the water that is supposed to be poured forth by Aquarius flows between the head of the southern fish and the tail of the Whale.

4. I have explained the images of the constellations that have been drawn and shaped in the firmament, designed by Nature and the divine intelligence, just as it has pleased Democritus, the natural philosopher, to describe them, but only those whose risings and settings we can observe and behold with our own eyes. For just as the Northerners, revolving around the hinge of their axis, neither set nor pass beneath the earth, so around the southern hinge, which because of the inclination of the cosmos remains set underneath the earth, there revolve hidden constellations; these do not have a way of rising up above the earth in the east. Therefore, because of the earth's interference, their configurations are unknown. Proof of this fact is the star of Canopus,* which is unknown in these regions, yet merchants who have been to the farthest reaches of Egypt and the boundaries near the last ends of the earth report its existence.

CHAPTER 6: THE HISTORY
OF ASTRONOMY

1. I have taught about the revolution of the cosmos around the earth and the arrangement of the twelve signs and of the constellations in the northern and southern parts so that they will be completely clear. For on the basis of this spinning of the firmament and the contrary course of the sun through the signs, as well as the shadows cast at the equinox by gnomons, we derive the design of *analêmmata*.

2. In the other concerns of astrology, for example,

10 *Centaurus* MSS.

the effect the twelve signs, the five stars, the sun and the moon exert upon the regulation of human life, we must yield to the learned reasoning of the Chaldaeans, because the system of casting horoscopes belongs to them, through which they make it possible for astrologers to explain past and future events by reasoning from the stars.* Those who went forth from the nation of the Chaldaeans itself and bequeathed us the discoveries of their people were of great wisdom and acumen in these matters, first among them Berosus, who settled in the island and city of Cos, and opened a school there. After him Antipater pursued the subject, and then again Achinapolus, who left us principles for casting horoscopes based not on time of birth but rather on time of conception. 3. After long thought, Thales of Miletus, Anaxagoras of Clazomenae, Pythagoras of Samos, Xenophanes of Colophon, and Democritus of Abdera bequeathed us the principles of natural science, by which natural phenomena are governed, along with how they come about, and what effects they have. Following upon their discoveries, Eudoxus, Euclemon, Callippus, Meton, Philippus, Hipparchus, Aratus,* and the rest discovered the risings and settings of the constellations and the meanings of the seasons on the basis of the teachings of astrology and the readings of the astronomical tables,* and bequeathed explanations of these to later generations.* The findings of these sages should be admired by people today, because they were made with such care that, as if guided by the divine intelligence, they still seem to predict the signs of times yet to come before the fact. For this reason deference must be shown to their diligence and study.

CHAPTER 7: MAKING THE ANALÊMMA (FIGURES 114, 115)

1. Among these subjects, we must now isolate and explain the principles of the shortening and lengthening of days from month to month. For the sun, in making the rounds in Aries and Libra at the time of the equinoxes, will cast a shadow of eight units if we have a gnomon nine parts in length and are at the incline of the heavens in which Rome is situated.* Likewise, in Athens, if a gnomon of whatever size is divided into four parts, the shadow will occupy three, in Rhodes the ratio will be seven to five, eleven to nine in Tarentum, five to three in Alexandria, and in every other place the shadows cast by a gnomon at the equinox will be found,

each in a different way, to be different from one another according to Nature.

2. Thus, wherever a sundial is to be laid out, the length of the shadow at the equinox particular to that place must be determined, and if, for example, the parts of the gnomon are nine, as in Rome, and the shadow occupies eight, a line should be inscribed on a plane surface, and in the middle of that surface an upright, the "right angle" (pros orthás), is erected with the help of the set square so that it stands on the perpendicular. This is called the gnomon. From the end of the plane line to the base of the gnomon, nine spaces are measured off with the compass, and at the place where the demarcation of the ninth part will be, a center is set where there will be a letter A. Once the compass has been spread from this center to the plane line, where there will be a letter B, circle the compass around; this is called the meridian. 3. Then, of the nine parts that extend from the plane line to the axis of the gnomon, take eight and mark them along the plane line, where there will be a letter C. This, then, will be the shadow of the gnomon at the equinox. From that demarcation and the letter C, draw a line through the center at the letter A; the ray of the sun at the equinox shall be here. Then, once the compass has been spread from the center to the plane line, mark two equal sides; at the extreme ends of the circle, on the left side there will be a letter E and on the right a letter I. Bring a line through the center, so that two equal hemicycles are divided off from one another. This line is called the *horizon* by the mathematicians. 4. Then take one-fifteenth part of the entire circle,* and set the point of the compass on the line of the circle where the equinoctial ray cuts this line, and put a letter F. To the left and right mark the letters G and H. From these and through the center, draw lines all the way to the plane line, and put the letters T and R. Thus one line will mark the sun's ray in the winter and another in summer. There will be a letter I opposite the letter E, where the line cast through the center cuts the circle at the letter A.* Opposite the letter G there will be the letters A and M, and opposite C and F and A there will be the letter N. [Opposite the letters R and H there will be the letter L.]¹¹ 5. Then draw two chords from G to L and from H to M. The lower chord will belong to the summer part, the upper chord to the winter. Divide these chords equally through the middle at the letters O and P, and mark centers there. Then draw a line

---

11 A sentence to this effect is needed but missing from the text.

through these marks and the center A to the extreme ends of the circle at letters Q and Z. This will be the upright line *pros orthás* that intersects the equinoctial ray on the perpendicular, and this line will be called the *axon* in mathematical terms. After the compass has been spread to the outermost diameters, from the same centers [O, P] draw hemicycles, one for summer and one for winter. 6. Where the parallel lines cut the horizon line there will be letter S to the right, and Y on the left, and from the letter S draw a line parallel to the axon toward the right hemicycle, and put the letter V. Likewise, from Y to the left hemicycle draw a parallel line to the center X. These parallel lines are called *loxotomus*. Then the point of the compass should be placed where the equinoctial ray cuts the line [GH], at the letter D, and a circle traced around to where the summer ray cuts the circle at letter H. From the equinoctial center, across the summer interval, the circuit of the monthly cycle is drawn, called *menaeus* ("monthly"). This is how to obtain the shape of the *analêmma*.

7. Once this construction has been drawn and executed as specified, for the winter lines and for the summer, for the equinoctial lines and the monthly lines, then, in addition, the system of the hours should be inscribed along the form of the *analêmma*. To these can be added many varieties and kinds of sundial, and they are all marked off by these inventive methods. However, the result of all these figures and their delineation is identical: namely, that the day at the equinox and at the winter solstice, and again at the summer solstice, is equally divided into twelve parts. Therefore, I have not chosen to omit these matters as if I were deterred by laziness, but so as not to cause annoyance by writing too much; nonetheless, I shall explain who discovered the various kinds and designs of sundials. At present, I cannot invent any new kinds myself, nor do I think it right to put forward someone else's invention as my own. Therefore I shall simply tell about the kinds that have been handed down to us,* and by whom they were invented.

CHAPTER 8: SUNDIALS AND WATER CLOCKS

1. Berosus the Chaldaean is said to have invented the semicircular one carved out of a squared block and undercut to follow the earth's tilt. The hemisphere, or

scaphê, is attributed to Aristarchus of Samos, and he also invented the disk on a plane. The Spider was invented by Eudoxus the astronomer; some say by Apollonius. The Plinth or Coffer, of which an example is set in the [region of the City known as the] Circus of Flaminius, was invented by Scopinas of Syracuse; Parmenion invented the "Sundial for Examination"; Theodosius and Andrias the sundial "For Every Climate," Patrocles the Axe, Dionysodorus the Cone, Apollonius the Quiver. The men named here invented other kinds, and many others have left us still other kinds, like the Spider-Cone, the Hollowed Plinth, and the Antiboreus ("Opposite the North"). Many, moreover, have left behind written directions for making portable and hanging versions of these kinds. Anyone who wants to may find additional information in their books, so long as they know how to set up an *analêmma.*

2. These same writers have also invented methods for assembling clocks that use water, Ctesibius of Alexandria first among them, who also discovered the power of natural breath and the principles of pneumatics. It is worthwhile for those who are interested to know how these things were discovered. Now Ctesibius was born in Alexandria to a father who was a barber. Greatly surpassing the rest in his ingenuity and his great industry, he is said to have delighted in clever inventions. When, for example, he wanted a mirror to hang in his father's shop in such a way that when it was lowered and then raised again, a hidden cord pulled a counterweight, this is how he set up the mechanism: 3. He fixed a wooden channel behind the lintel, and there he placed pulleys. Along the channel he laid a line toward the corner, and there he constructed little [vertical] tubes. In these he had a lead ball lowered along the cord. Thus the weight compressed the air as it ran down the narrowness of the tubes, and at the end of its furious descent it thrust the air, densely compacted by compression, through the mouth of the tube, where, meeting with an obstacle out in the open, it squeezed out a clear sound. 4. Therefore Ctesibius, when he had observed that the impact with the air and the emission of breath created sounds and voices, by building on these beginnings he was first to invent hydraulic machines.

And so he developed water jets and automata,* and many types of playthings, among them also the outfitting of water clocks (Figure 116). First he created an aperture, made of gold or a perforated gem, because these are not worn down by the impact of water, and not being susceptible to corrosion they will not plug up. 5. Now water, flowing evenly through this aperture, raises an inverted bowl, which is called *phellos* or *tympanum* (drum) by clockmakers. A bar is affixed to this float, with teeth on its other end that engage with similar teeth on a revolving drum. These little teeth, one propelling the next, create small rotations and movements. At the same time other bars and other drums, toothed in the same fashion, compelled by one motion, produce various effects with their rotations: statues move, goalposts are turned over, stones or eggs are thrown, trumpets blare out, and all the other amusements. 6. Among these, furthermore, the hours are marked out on a column or pilaster – a figurine, starting from the bottom, indicates them in turn with a wand all throughout the day.

The shortening and lengthening of the days must be corrected day by day and month by month through the addition or removal of wedges.* The stopcocks for the water should be made in the following way so that they can be regulated: make two cones: one solid, one hollow, finished on the lathe so that one of them can enter and fit inside the other, and their separation or telescoping on the same bar should make it so that there is either a forceful or a gentle flow of water into the tank. Thus, by these principles and this device, the outfitting of a clock for use in winter can be assembled using water.

7. But if, on the other hand, there is some question about compensating for the shortening or lengthening of days by adding or removing wedges, because the wedges frequently cause problems, this is how to outfit the water clock: the hours should be marked off transversely on a colonnette, just as they have been taken from the *analêmma*, and the monthly lines should also be marked on the little column. This column should be made to rotate so that the side facing the little statue with its wand (with which, when it comes out, the little statue points to the hours) will continually allow for the shortenings and lengthenings of each month as the column rotates.

8. Winter clocks of another kind are also made; these are called "pickup," and they are completed by the following method (Figure 117).* The hours are marked out by a bronze grille according to the outline of the *analêmma*, arranged from the center to the rim. Circles are drawn around these which delimit the spaces of the months. Behind this grille is a plate on which the cosmos and the signbearing circle are portrayed. The outline of the twelve signs should be made eccentrically, with one sign larger, one smaller. A rotating axle

is set into the back and fixed to the center of the plate. A pliable chain is wound around this bronze axle, and from one end hangs the float or *phellos*, which is raised by the water, while on the other end there is a counterweight filled with sand, of the same weight as the float. 9. Thus, however much the float is raised by the water, to the same degree the counterweight's burden, leading downward, will turn the axle, and the axle in turn will rotate the plate.

The rotation of this plate brings it about that sometimes the greater half of the signbearing circle marks out the boundaries of the hour, and at other times it will be the smaller half. For among the individual signs, each with its own month, the holes should be outfitted so that each month has its own number of days, in which a sphere indicates the space of the hours – in clocks this sphere tends to be decorated as an image of the sun.* 10. This sphere, carried from perforation to perforation, completes the round of the turning month. And so, just as the sun, traveling through the space of the constellations, lengthens or contracts the days and hours, in the same way the sphere in clocks, advancing point by point against the rotation of the center of the drum, as it is carried day by day across broader expanses in some seasons, narrower distances in others, creates the images of the hours and days through the divisions of the month.

As for regulating the water supply so that it will be systematically calibrated, do the following:* (11.) inside the clock, behind its face, place a reservoir, and water should plunge into this through a pipe and at the bottom there should be a hollow. At this point fix a drum with a hole, through which water flows into the hollow. Inside this enclose a smaller wheel, and this should have tenon-and-socket hinges fitting into one another so that this smaller drum, rather like a valve, will be turned tightly and gently as it shifts back and forth in the larger drum. The rim of the larger drum should have three hundred sixty-five dots marked at equal intervals around it, whereas the smaller wheel should have a little tongue fixed at its edge, whose tip points toward the dots, and in this little wheel a calibrated hole should be bored; water will flow from the larger into the smaller drum through this hole and this is how the water shall be regulated. 12. Because the rim of the larger drum will have images of the celestial signs, it must be motionless. At the top it should have the sign of Cancer, directly opposite at the bottom the sign of Capricorn, to the right of the observer that of Libra, to the left the sign of Aries, and the remaining expanse between them should be portrayed as the signs are seen in the heavens. 13. Therefore, when the sun is in Capricorn, the little pointer of the smaller wheel, daily touching individual dots of Capricorn in the parts of the larger drum, and having the forceful weight of the running water at a vertical angle, quickly thrusts it out through the hole in the small wheel and into the reservoir, which takes it up. When it is filled in a short time, it stops, and contracts the extent of the days and hours. When with daily rotation, the pointer on the smaller wheel advances into the dots of Aquarius, the outlet, deviating from the vertical[12] because of the forceful course of the water, is slower to send it jetting out. Thus, inasmuch as the reservoir takes up water from a less swiftly flowing source, it expands the space of the hours. 14. As it ascends, stepwise, the dots of Aquarius and Pisces, the hole in the small wheel, in touching the eighth degree of Aries, presents the hours appropriate to the equinox because of the moderately spurting water. From Aries through the area of Tau-

rus and Gemini to the topmost point of the eighth degree of Cancer, the hole, wandering through the months with the rotation of the drum and ascending back to the height, loses its strength, and thus, in flowing more slowly, it expands the spaces occupied during its hesitation, and reproduces the long hours of the summer solstice in the sign of Cancer. When it tilts away from Cancer and advances through Leo and Virgo to the dots at the eighth degree of Libra, turning back and gradually skimming them off, it contracts the spaces of the hours, and thus, arriving at the dots of Libra, again it mimics the hours of the equinox. 15. Then the aperture, pressing more and more directly downward toward the vertical through the spaces of Scorpio and Sagittarius, and returning in its circuit to the eighth degree of Capricorn, is restored by the swiftness of the spurting water to the shortness of the hours at the winter solstice.

As appropriately as I could, I have recorded the methods and practices needed for calibrating clocks so that they will be easier to use. Now it remains to discuss machines and their fundamentals. And so, in order to bring to completion a flawless and comprehensive account of architecture, I shall begin to write about these in the next volume.

---

12 Reading *discedens* with Rose instead of the MSS *descendens*.

❖

MACHINES

PREFACE

1. In the celebrated and spacious Greek city of Ephesus, there is said to be an ancient law established by the forefathers, harsh in its requirements but by no means partial in its justice. For an architect, when he has received the commission for some public work, promises in advance what the cost is to be. Once this estimate has been turned over to the magistrate, his goods are put in lien until the work is completed. Then, when it is finished, if the actual expenses correspond to the estimate, he is awarded special decrees and honors. Likewise, if it has exceeded the estimate by no more than one-quarter of the total, the difference is supplied by the public treasury and he is not obliged to pay any penalty. If, on the other hand, more than a quarter has been consumed by the project, then money is taken from his own assets to make up the difference.

2. If only the immortal gods had made it so that this law had also been adopted by the Roman People, not only for public buildings but also for private ones! Then the inexperienced would not run riot with impunity, and those who were well versed in the subtleties of the highest learning would practice architecture without hesitation. Neither would the heads of households be led on to an endless profusion of expenditures, so that they are even evicted from their own properties. The architects themselves, restrained by the fear of penalty, would be more careful and thorough in reckoning and declaring their estimates, so that heads of households would proceed with their buildings within the budget they had prepared, or adding only a little more. For people who can assemble four hundred thousand [sesterces] for a project will still be kept interested by the pleasure of anticipating its completion if they must contribute another hundred,* whereas those who are burdened with a subvention of half again and more are forced to give up entirely, hope renounced and money squandered, financially and spiritually bankrupt.

3. This is a problem not only for buildings, but also for the endowments made by magistrates for the festival games: the gladiators in the Forum and the players in the theaters. To these, no hesitation or delay is conceded; rather, necessity dictates completion within a limited time, that is, the seats for the shows, and the management of the awnings* and all the mechanical devices that are contrived according to the tradition of the stage for public viewing. In these matters there is a need for careful foresight and the inventions of a well-educated mind, because none of them can be created without a good grounding in mechanics as well as a varied and clever application to other studies.*

4. Therefore, because all these traditions have been handed down and established, it does not seem out of place that, before such projects are undertaken, these principles, too, be set down, carefully and with the closest attention. And because neither law nor custom can ensure that this be the case, and every year the praetors and aediles* must furnish mechanical devices for the festival games, I did not think it out of place, Imperator, because I have explained all about buildings in the preceding volumes, that in the present one, containing the very end of the work, I would set out the basic principles of machines, ordered by subject.

CHAPTER 1: FIRST PRINCIPLES
(FIGURE 118)

1. A machine is a continuous piece of joinery that has outstanding capacities for moving loads. It is moved systematically by the revolutions of circles, which the Greeks call *kuklikê kinêsis* – "circular motion."*

There is one type used for mounting (*scansorium*),* which the Greeks call *akrobatikon*, a second type that works by pressure (*spirabile*), which they call *pneumatikon*, and a third that drags loads (*tractor*), and this the Greeks call *baruoison*.[1]* It is a **mounting** machine when, for example, the machines are placed so that with the beams set to lead upward and the transverse pieces bound in place, it is possible to make an ascent without danger to view work in progress. It is a **pneumatic** machine when air is driven by pressure so that blows and voices are expressed instrumentally, *organikôs*. 2. It is a **tractor** when loads are dragged by machines and set in place after they have been raised aloft. In principle, the mounting machine revels not in skill but in daring and is held together by chains, transverse beams, interwoven bindings, and the propping of its braces. The type of machine that gets its impetus from an infusion of the power of air achieves elegant effects by the subtleties of art. But it is tractors that have the greatest and fullest opportunities for service and magnificence; they are also the machines that afford the greatest powers to those who employ them in acting prudently.

3. Of these machines, some move **mechanically**, *mechanikôs*, some **instrumentally**, *organikôs*.* The difference between **machines** and **instruments** seems to be that machines must be run by many workers, that is, with a great deal of force to have their effect, like ballistae, and presses, but instruments complete the task at hand with the knowledgeable touch of one skilled workman: the rotations of the scorpion or anisocycles are examples of this.* Therefore both instruments and the principles of machines are necessary in practice; without them, nothing could proceed without impediment.

4. Every mechanism has been created by nature and devised with the rotation of the cosmos as its teacher and governess. First let us take note and observe the continuous nature of the sun, the moon, and the five stars; if these had not been geared to rotate, we would not have had the alternations of light and darkness all this time, nor the maturation of crops. Therefore, when our forebears had observed that this is how things are, they took examples from nature and imitating them, spurred by these divine [exemplars], they achieved the development of life's conveniences. Thus they arranged some things to be more convenient by making machines and their rotations, and some instruments, and thus what they found useful in practice they took care to

improve, step by step, with the help of study, craftsmanship, and tradition.

5. Let us turn our attention first to what has been discovered by necessity, like clothing, and how the connection of warp to woof in fabrics by the application of an instrument not only protects the body by covering it but also contributes the attractiveness of adornment. Truly, too, we would never have had food in abundance unless yokes and plows, for oxen and all the other draft animals, had been discovered. If there had been no availability of windlasses, levers, and beams for presses, we would never have been able to have gleaming oil nor the fruit of the vine for our delight, nor would there have been a way to transport these, unless the rigs of carts or wagons on land, and boats at sea, had been invented. 6. The discovery of the means of testing by scales and balances redeems our life from iniquity through fair dealing. There are, indeed, virtually numberless principles for machinery, and these it seems unnecessary to discuss, as they are everyday matters, ready to hand, like mills, blacksmiths' bellows, passenger wagons, two-wheeled carts, lathes, and the other things that find general use in daily life. And so we shall begin by explaining those things which we only encounter on rare occasions, so that they will become familiar.

CHAPTER 2: CRANES AND HOISTS (FIGURE 119)

1. First, therefore, we will treat of things that must of necessity be provided for the completion of temples and public works. This is how they are made.

Two beams are prepared, in accordance with the size of the loads. They are fixed upright so that at the head they are joined together by a clasp and at the bottom they are spread apart, and they are kept erect by ropes fastened at their heads and arranged around. A pulley block is lashed to the top, which some call a *rechamus*. Two pulleys are set into the block, turning on little axles. A hoisting cable is sent through the upper pulley, and then let down and threaded through the pulley of a second, lower block. Then it is carried back up to the lower wheel of the upper block and fastened to its eye. The other part of the cable is carried down into the lower parts of the machine.

2. On the flat rear surfaces of the beams, where they spread apart, install socket pieces into which the heads of the windlasses are set, so that the axles will turn more

---

1 Reading *baruoison* for MSS *baruison*. The MSS reading was emended by Voss to *baroulkon* and is thus printed by all modern editions. The *baroulkos* appears later in a different context (as the anisocycle of X.1.3; see Note ad loc.), which suggests that the reading of Voss is not quite right and that, accordingly, the MSS reading might be taken seriously.

easily. These windlasses have twin holes near their heads, calibrated so that levers can fit into them. Then, at the lower block, iron forceps are lashed, with teeth designed to grip perforated stones. When the lower end of the cable is fastened to the windlass, which is rotated with the levers, the cable is wound around the windlass and pulled taut, and thus it raises loads up to a height, and to their place in a building project. 3. This type of machine,* because it turns on three pulleys, is called *trispastos.* If, on the other hand, there are two pulleys turning in the lowermost block and three in the upper, it is called *pentaspastos.*

Now if the machines are to be set up for greater loads, one will need to use greater lengths and thicknesses for the beams, and by the same principle for the clasp at the top and the rotation of the windlasses at the bottom (Figure 120). This accomplished, then install the supporting ropes, leaving them slack, and place control ropes far above the shoulders of the machine, and if there is no place to tie them down, then dig out places for inclined stakes and fill in around them with rammed earth so that the control ropes can be fastened to them.* 4. A pulley block should be bound to the top of the machine by a cord; from this block lead a rope down to a stake and to a pulley block that has been bound to the stake. Thread the rope around this pulley and lead it back to the block at the top of the machine, thread it around the pulley of that block, lead it downward and return it to the windlass at the bottom of the machine and there tie it in place. The windlass, propelled by the levers, will begin to rotate and will erect the machine by its action without risk. Then, by setting out stays and control ropes all around, attached to stakes, the machine can be secured more extensively. The pulleys and hoisting cables are outfitted as has already been described.

5. Now if, on the other hand, the loads involved in the work are colossal in their dimensions and weights, then there should be no reliance on windlasses; instead, just as the windlass is held in place by socket pieces, so an axle should be installed that has a large drum in the center; some call this a wheel, some Greeks an *amphiesis,* and others a *perithêkion.* 6. Now in these machines the pulley blocks are not made in the same way, but in another, for at both the top and bottom they have double ranks of pulleys. Thus the hoisting cable is threaded through the eye of the lower block so that its two ends are equal when the cable is stretched taut, and there along the lower block small cords, wrapped around and pulled tight, restrain each part of the hoisting cable so

that neither can slip, on the right or on the left. Then the ends of the cable are led to the upper block on the outside, threaded around its lower pulleys, and they return downward, connected to the pulleys of the lower block from the inside, and led, right and left, back to the head of the machine and around the upper pulleys. 7. Then, threaded from the outside, they are carried down to the right and left of the drum on its axle so that they will hold fast. Then another cable, wound around the drum, is led to a capstan, and this cable, by winding around the drum and the capstan, releases the hoisting cables equally, and thus they raise loads gently and without danger. If a larger drum is placed either in the center or off to one side without capstans, then people using it as a treadmill can complete the task still more quickly.

8. There is another type of machine that is clever enough, and useful for speeding the work, but no one but experts can use it (Figure 121). This is a beam that is set upright, then maneuvered by control ropes* extended in four different directions. Underneath the control ropes, two socket pieces are fixed, and a pulley block is fastened with ropes above the socket pieces; under the pulley block a bar some two feet long and six digits wide and four thick is set in place. Pulley blocks with three ranks of pulleys along their breadth are installed here. In this way three hoisting cables are fastened to the machine. These are then led back to the lower block and threaded from the inward side through its uppermost row of pulleys. Next they are led to the upper block and threaded from the exterior side to the interior through the lowermost pulleys. 9. When they are led downward, they are threaded from the interior side to the exterior through the second rank of pulleys, and led to the second rank of upper pulleys; threaded through, they return to the bottom; from the bottom they are led to the head of the machine; threaded through the uppermost pulleys they return to the bottom of the machine. At the very foot of the machine a third block is installed. The Greeks call it "leader," *epagonta,* and we call it *artemon.* This block, which is fastened to the foot of the machine, has three pulleys, through which the cables are passed and handed over for men to pull. By this means three ranks of men, pulling without a windlass, can raise a load quickly to the top. 10. This type of machine is called *polyspastos* because with its many rotations of pulleys it offers both the greatest ease and the greatest speed, and the erecting of a single upright has the advantage that by inclining it one can deposit the load anywhere, forward as much as one wishes, or to the right or left side.

All the types of machines that have been described are useful not only for the purposes outlined, but also for loading and unloading ships, with some machines set upright and some placed flat on revolving booms. Likewise, on the ground, without erecting beams, but using the same principles, ships can be hauled into shore by the adjustment of cables and pulleys.

11. It is not out of place to present the ingenious machine of Chersiphron as well (Figure 122). For when he wanted to transport the shafts of the columns from their quarries to the temple of Diana of Ephesus, given the immensity of their weight and the softness of the rural roads, and not trusting in carts, for fear that their wheels would be bogged down, he tried the following instead. He fitted together and secured four wooden planks with two crosspieces, of the same length as the column shafts, set in between them, and set iron pivots, like dowels, in lead at the ends of the planks, and installed wooden frames at the pivots to contain them. He also bound the ends of the frames with tin plates. The iron pivots, enclosed in their wooden bearings, had such free movement that when a hitch of oxen drew the shafts along, they were able to revolve ceaselessly by the turning of the pivots in their frames.

12. When they had transported all the column drums in this fashion and were embarking on the transport of the epistyle blocks, the son of Chersiphron, Metagenes, adapted the method for transporting the column shafts to bringing in the epistyles. And so he made wheels of about twelve feet in diameter, and enclosed the ends of the epistyles in the centers of the wheels, setting pins and bearings into their ends according to the same principle. Thus when the four-digit timbers were drawn by the oxen, the pins enclosed in the bearings turned the wheels, and the epistyle blocks, enclosed in the wheels as if they were axles, arrived at the building site without delay, just as the shafts had done. Another example of this would be the way in which rollers are used to level the walkways of palaestras. None of this could have occurred unless there had been short distances involved in the first place, for from the quarries to the temple it is not more than eight miles, and there is a level plain with no hills.

13. Within our own memory, when the base of the colossal statue of Apollo* had been broken apart by age, fearing that the statue might fall and shatter, they contracted for a base to be cut from the same quarries. A certain Paconius took the contract.* Now this base was twelve feet long, eight feet wide, and six feet high. Paconius, full of vainglory, did not convey it as Metagenes

had done, but decided instead to make a machine by the same principles, but of another type. 14. He made wheels some fifteen feet in diameter, and enclosed the ends of the stone in these wheels, and then, all around the stone, he fitted two-digit battens, extending from wheel to wheel all round, in such a way that the space between the battens was scarcely a foot. Then he wrapped a rope around the battens and once oxen had been hitched up, they began to pull the rope. Set up in this fashion, the rope turned the wheels, but it could not pull along the road in a straight line; instead, it continually veered to one side. Thus it was necessary to set the apparatus straight again, and in leading the oxen back and forth in this fashion, Paconius spent away his money until there was no longer enough to cover the expense.

15. I shall digress a little and tell how these quarries were discovered. Pixodarus was a shepherd who lived in these parts. When the citizens of Ephesus planned to execute the temple of Diana in marble and decided to seek marble from Paros, Proconnesus, Heraclea, or Thasos,* Pixodarus pastured his flock in that very place, driving his sheep before him. There, as two rams charged each other, they missed, swerving to either side. One, carried on by his momentum, struck rock with his horn, and a splinter of the most brilliant white was knocked down from the stone. Pixodarus is said to have left his sheep in the mountains and to have run into Ephesus bringing the splinter, because this was the time when the matter of the marble for the temple was most urgently under consideration. And so they decreed special honors for him on the spot and changed his name; rather than Pixodarus he would be called Evangelus – "Bringer of Good News." And today, once every month, a magistrate sets out for that place and makes Evangelus a sacrifice, and if he fails to do it, he will be fined.

CHAPTER 3: ALL MACHINES USE TWO TYPES OF MOTION (FIGURE 123)

1. As for the principles of tractors, I have briefly set out what I believe to be the essentials. As for their motions and effects, two different phenomena, unlike one another, combining like elements produce them in their final state, one of linear motion, which the Greeks call *eutheia*, and another of circular motion, which the Greeks name *kyklotê*, but the truth is that neither linear motion without circles nor revolution without linearity can raise loads.*

I shall explain so that this can be understood. 2. Little axles are installed as the axes of pulley wheels, and these pulleys in turn are placed in pulley blocks. A cable, threaded around the wheels and led straight downward, then fixed to the windlass, creates the upward lifting of loads by the rotation of handspikes. The pivots [literally, "hinges"] of these windlasses, extended like axles into the socket pieces, and the handspikes, enclosed within holes in the windlass, with their outer ends brought around in circles just as on a lathe, create the raising of loads by their rotations.

Also, just as when an iron bar is moved toward a load that a multitude of hands cannot move, when it is put underneath like a lever and extended across a linear fulcrum, what the Greeks call an "underbolt," *hypomochlion*, and with its tongue inserted under the load, its head end, depressed by the force of a single person, raises that load. 3. Because the shorter, forward, part of the lever reaches under the load from the fulcrum, which acts as an axis, and because the long end of the lever, which is more distant from the fulcrum, is pushed downward, through the fulcrum, in creating a circular motion it causes the weight of the heaviest burden to be counterbalanced by the pressure of a few hands.

Likewise, if the tongue end of an iron lever is inserted under a load and its head end, rather than being pushed downward, is lifted upward in the opposite direction, then the tongue, resting on the ground, will respond as if this is the load, and the corner of the load itself will now act as the fulcrum. Thus the weight of the load will be set into motion, not as easily as with downward pressure, but moved nonetheless. Therefore, if the tongue of the lever, placed over the fulcrum, were to go underneath the load and pressure were exerted on the head closer to the center, then the farther lever would not be able to raise burdens – not unless, as described earlier, a balance is obtained between the length of the lever and the pressure on its head.

4. It is also possible to observe this in the balances called *staterae*. If the handle [which acts as a fulcrum] is nearer the end from which the tray is suspended, and the counterweight in the other part of the shaft travels, point by point, farther and farther out to the very opposite end, then it produces considerable weighing power on its side by means of a small and unequal weight, and balance by leveling the shaft.[2] Moving away from the

axis, the feeble lightness of the counterweight, pulling down the more powerful weight by its own motion, gently, without sudden outbursts, causes its side of the balance to shift upward from beneath.

5. So, too, the pilot of the largest cargo ship, manning the tiller, which is called *oiax* by the Greeks, plying with pressure by the principles of his craft, pushing around an axis, as it were, turns the ship with the momentum of one hand, even when she is piled with abundant and bulky merchandise and a cargo of provisions.* And when the sails are unfurled to half the height of the mast, the ship cannot sail quickly, but if, on the other hand, the yards are drawn up to its summit, then it will move ahead more energetically, because the sails will take the wind into themselves not near the mast step, which is the place of the axis, but much nearer the top of the mast, where the distance is greater. 6. And so, just as when a lever is inserted under a load, if it is depressed in the middle, it is resistant and will not move, but if its very end is pushed downward, then it easily lifts up a burden, likewise sails, if they are adjusted to reach mid-mast, have less effect, but those that are fastened at the very topmost head of the mast, farther away from the axis, will, with the very same breezes, none sharper, cause the ship to advance more energetically by the pressure exerted on their uppermost reaches.

Oars too, fastened down by straps to the oarlocks, when pulled and returned by hand, the tips of their blades pushing off from their axis through the foamy waves, force the ship straight ahead in a burst of motion, its prow slicing the liquid's rarefaction.

7. Again, the weights of the greatest loads, when they are carried by gangs of four to six porters, are balanced at the exact centers of their carrying poles, so that the necks of individual laborers carry equal parts of the solid load's single mass according to a consistent principle of division. For the midpoints of the carrying poles, to which the bearing straps of the porters are attached and kept in line by pegs, will not shift to one side. If they are pushed off center they press down on the side nearer them, just like the weight in a balance, when it moves progressively outward on the arm of the balance in taking a measurement.

8. By the same principle, draft animals, when their yokes are held on center by the yoke straps, bear their burdens evenly. When, on the other hand, their strength is unequal and one, more powerful, forces the other, then one part of the yoke should be made longer by shifting the stay, because it will help the weaker animal. Thus with carrying poles and with yokes, if their bearing straps are

---

2 Reading *parte perficit* GH as *[sua] parte perficit*, and *examinationem* with Fleury.

not placed in the middle but off to one side, wherever the strap is moved off center, it will make one part shorter, and one longer. By this principle, if both ends of the carrying pole or yoke are rotated around the axis created by the placement of the bearing strap, the longer section will make a larger circle, and the shorter section a smaller one. 9. But just as smaller wheels have stiffer and more difficult movement, so carrying poles and yokes press down more heavily on the necks of the bearers or draft animals where the interval from the axis to the tip is less, while those that have a greater distance from the center relieve those who pull or carry their burdens.

Because these [machines] will have obtained their motions around the center by extensions and rotations, so, too, carts, wagons, wheels, screws, scorpions, ballistae, presses, and the other machines achieve their purpose by the same principles, [by moving] along a straight axis or by rotating in a circle.

CHAPTER 4: RAISING WATER

1. Now I shall explain about the instruments that have been invented to extract water, and how they are made according to their various types. First of all, I shall discuss the drum (Figure 124). This does not lift water very high, but it does extract a great quantity very quickly. An axle should be fashioned on the lathe or with a compass, with its ends sheathed in iron. Around its middle it should have a drum made of wooden panels joined together. This wheel is placed on uprights that have iron sheathing underneath the ends of the axle. Inside the hollow of this drum eight transverse panels should be laid so that they touch both the axle and the outermost circumference of the drum, dividing it off into equal compartments. 2. Around its rim, panels are fixed to leave openings of half a foot, for bringing in the water. Likewise, near the axle holes should be punched out on one side of each compartment. After this apparatus is coated with pitch, just as in ship making, it can be turned by people treading. Pulling in the water through the apertures along its rim, it then releases it through the holes near the axle; there is a wooden tub underneath which has a channel joined to it. Thus the machine furnishes an abundance of water for irrigating gardens or adjusting the level in salt works.

3. If there is a need to lift water higher, the same principle should be adapted as follows: a wheel should be built around an axle, large enough so that it suits the required height. Around the outermost edge of the wheel, square buckets should be attached, sealed with pitch and wax. When the wheel is turned by treaders, the full buckets, lofted to the top, will automatically pour out the water they have raised as they return downward; this they pour into a holding tank.

4. If still higher places must be supplied, then a double iron chain, wrapped around the axle of the same wheel and cast downward, should be placed at the lowermost surface of the water, with bronze buckets hanging from it that hold a *congius* (≈ 3½ liters) each (Figure 125).* The rotation of the wheel, by circling the chain toward the axis, will carry the buckets to the top, and when they pass over the axle they will be forced to overturn and pour out into a reservoir whatever water they have carried up.

CHAPTER 5: AN UNDERSHOT WATER WHEEL (FIGURE 126)

1. [Water]-wheels are also made in rivers according to the same methods as those described earlier. Around their edges paddles are fixed which, when they are struck by the surge of the river, force the wheel to turn as they proceed forward, and drawing the water and carrying it up in buckets, these wheels, turned by the force of the river itself rather than by workers' treading, furnish what is necessary for the job.

2. Water mills are turned by the same principle;* every feature is the same except that on one end of the axle a toothed wheel is installed. This, placed on the perpendicular, that is, on its edge, turns at the same rate as the wheel. Alongside it, a larger drum, also toothed, is placed on the horizontal so that the two engage. The teeth of the drum that is fixed to the axle, by driving the teeth of the horizontal drum, cause the circling of the millstones to occur. A hopper overhanging this machine provides the grain to the millstones and by means of the same rotation the flour is ground.

CHAPTER 6: THE WATER SCREW (FIGURE 127)

1. There is also a type of water screw that will drink up a great surge of water, but will not carry it as high as the wheel.* This is how to carry out the idea. Take a

beam, as many digits thick as it is feet long. This should be rounded out to an exact circle. At each end, the circumference will be divided by the help of a compass into eight segments, in such a way that the intersecting diameters of each circle, when the beam is laid flat, will correspond perfectly with one another on the level; then score circles around the beam along its entire length at intervals equal to one-eighth the circumference. Once the beam has been laid horizontal, lines should be drawn from one end to the other so that they are perfectly level. In this way equal intervals have been created along the curvature and the length of the beam. Where the lines have been drawn along the length, the transverse scorings create intersections, and these intersections determine specific points.

2. Once all these things have been drawn carefully, take a strip of slender willow or cut agnus castus which, once it has been dipped in liquid pitch, is fixed in place at the first point formed by the intersections. Then it is carried across obliquely to the next point of intersection between length and circumference, and proceeding row by row in this fashion, as the strip passes individual points, winding around, it is fastened at each intersection so that, by the time it reaches the eighth point away from the beginning and is fixed in place, it has arrived again at the same line in which it was fastened down in the first place. Thus, whatever distance it traverses obliquely along the eight points, it proceeds longitudinally as well, toward the eighth point. By the same principle, for the entire extent of the beam's length and circumference, strips should be fixed obliquely through each of the eight divisions of the diameter, to create spiral channels that wrap around, as well as an accurate, natural imitation of a seashell. 3. Along the same tracks other strips are attached upon others, coated with liquid pitch, and they are stacked to the point that their greatest thickness reaches one-eighth the length of the rotor.

Panels are placed around and over to cover this spiral, saturated with pitch and bound together with iron plates, so that they will not be broken apart by the force of the water. The ends of the rotor are iron. To the right and left of the water screw, beams are placed that have crossbeams attached to their ends on each side. Iron sockets are set into these, and into them pivots, and thus human treading will move the water screw. 4. It should be erected on a slope in such a way that it corresponds to a Pythagorean right triangle; that is, if the length is divided into five parts, the head of the water screw should be raised to three of these parts, and then the distance from the uprights to the lowermost

apertures will occupy four of these parts. Instructions for how to do this, and the form of the machine itself, are illustrated together at the end of the book.

CHAPTER 7: THE WATER PUMP OF CTESIBIUS

I have described, as clearly as I could, what instruments are made of wood for raising water, by what principles they are brought to completion, and from what phenomena they derive their motion to offer us endless convenience of their rotations, so that these will become more familiar.

1. Now it remains to demonstrate Ctesibius's machine, which conducts water to a height. It should be made of bronze. At its roots it has twin cylinders, standing slightly apart, with pipes that connect together in the figure of a fork, running together into a tank placed between them. In this tank disk valves should be closely fitted over the upper outlets of the pipes, so that when they are blocking these outlets they will prevent the escape of whatever water has been pushed into the tank by pressure.

2. Above this tank a hood rather like an inverted funnel is fitted and secured to the tank by a clasp with a wedge through it, so that the pressure of the incoming water will not raise it. Above this, a pipe called a "trumpet" should be set up, fitted in at the very top of the machine. The cylinders also have disk valves installed above the openings at the bottom of the pipes.

3. Hence, from above, pistons, turned and finished on the lathe and worked with oil, terminating in armatures and levers, compress whatever air is present there [in the cylinders] along with the water from above; with the valves obstructing the mouths of the pipes the pressure of the pistons pushes the water on through the outlets of the pipes and into the tank, where a little extra pressure is added, and finally forces it out upward through the "trumpet." By this means, from a reservoir in a lower place, water may be supplied for a fountain jet.

4. Nevertheless, this is not the only marvelous procedure said to have been discovered by Ctesibius; for indeed many others, and of various types, invented by him, are shown, when driven by liquid and by air pressure, to produce effects borrowed from nature, like the sounds of "blackbirds," caused by the motion of water, or the "bucket-climbers,"[3] or the little moving statues

---

3 Taking *angubatae* as Greek ἀγγοβάται with Callebat and Fleury.

that draw water and drink and the like, and all the other things that delight our senses for the eyes' enjoyment and the ears' engagement.* 5. Of these things, I have selected those inventions of his that I judged most useful and necessary. I thought that I should speak about clocks in the previous volume and in the present one about compressed water. Those who are taken with his cleverness can find the remaining machines, namely those inspired not by necessity but only by a wish to delight, in the treatise of Ctesibius himself.

CHAPTER 8: THE WATER ORGAN OF CTESIBIUS (FIGURE 129)

1. I shall not, however, omit water organs and the reasoning connected with them, and so, as briefly as I can, I will touch upon them next and commit them to writing.* Once a wooden base has been assembled, a box,[4] fashioned in bronze, is placed on it. Above the base, uprights are set to the right and left, fitted together in the form of a ladder in which bronze cylinders are encased, with moving pistons, which are precisely worked on the lathe and wrapped in sheepskin; these also have iron rods fixed in their centers, and are joined to levers with elbow joints. On the upper surface of the cylinders there are holes, each about three digits across. Bronze dolphins, set on pivots near these holes, have disks suspended by chains from their mouths, which are lowered into the holes of the cylinders. 2. Inside the bronze box, where the water is contained, the throttle is installed, like an inverted funnel, under it little cube-shaped blocks, about three digits high, are inserted, and these keep an even space at the bottom between the lips of the throttle and the bottom of the bronze box. Then, joined above the neck of the throttle, a small chamber holds up the headpiece of the machine; this headpiece the Greeks call the *canon musicus,* the "musical measure."[5] Along its length there are four channels if it is to be tetrachord; if hexachord, six; if octochord, eight. 3. Individual taps are enclosed in each of these individual channels, and set in place with iron handles. When these handles are turned, they open up the outlets from the small chamber into the channels. Leading from the channels, the *canon* has holes arranged in transverse rows that correspond to the openings on the top of the tablet; in Greek this tablet is called the *pinax.* Between the *canon* and the *pinax,* sliding tabs are installed that have holes bored in the same fashion; they have also been treated with oil so that they can be inserted and withdrawn easily, and thus they are able to block the holes. They are called *plinthides.* The back-and-forth movement of these sliding tabs covers some of the holes and opens others. 4. They also have iron hooks that are fixed to organ keys,[6] and it is touching the organ keys that continually creates the motion of the sliding tabs. Above the holes in the *canon,* where the pressure escapes through the channels, rings are glued down, the ones by which the tongues of all the organ pipes are fastened in place. From the cylinders, furthermore, there are continuous pipes joined to the neck of the throttle and extending to outlet holes that open into the small chamber. Here there are disk valves, fashioned on the lathe and then set in place; when the small chamber receives compressed air, the valves, by blocking the outlet holes, will not permit it to escape back. 5. Thus when the levers of the pistons are raised, they send the piston rods driving the pistons down to the bottom of the cylinders, and the dolphins that are set into the uprights lower their disks into the cylinders. This process fills the cylinders with air, and when the piston rods withdraw the pistons inside the cylinders with forceful, continuous strokes, with the disks still blocking the upper holes of the cylinders, their pressure pushes the compressed air that has been trapped there into the pipes. Through the pipes it rushes into the throttle and through the neck of the throttle into the small chamber. By a more forceful motion of the levers, then, the air is compressed still more closely, and flows into the openings of the taps and fills the channels with its breath.

6. Thus when the keys are touched by the hand, continuously driving the sliding tabs back and forth, blocking some holes and opening others, they produce sounds from the organ, pitched at all the different varieties of tuning according to the arts of music.

To the extent that I could apply myself to the task, I have striven to enunciate an obscure matter lucidly in writing, but this is not an easy subject, nor easy for everyone to understand, except those who have some

---

4 Reading *arcam* with Giocondo for MSS *aram,* although the sense of both readings ("box") is effectively the same.

5 So the manuscripts. The Latinized spelling of *canon* suggests that the term has become somewhat domesticated, like xystus, andron, and so on.

6 Reading *coracia* with Drachmann.

practical experience in this kind of work. But if anyone has failed to understand it fully from my writings, when he comes to know the thing itself, he will certainly discover that everything has been set out in order, carefully and precisely.

CHAPTER 9: THE HODOMETER
(FIGURE 130)

1. Now the attention of our treatise shall be shifted to a device that is not idle,* but has in fact been handed down to us by our ancestors with the greatest ingenuity, by means of which we can know how many miles we have traveled, whether on the road, sitting in a wagon, or navigating across the sea in ships. It will be like this.

Let the wheels of the wagon be four feet wide across their diameter, so that, when the wheel has a certain place marked on it and begins moving forward from that point, making its rotation along the roadbed, then to come to that point from which it had begun to turn it will have traversed a certain distance, namely twelve and one-half feet.* 2. When things have been set up in this fashion, then a drum should be made stationary on the inside of the hub of the wheel, and this drum should have a single tooth protruding from its edge. Above this, a frame should be firmly fixed next to the wagon box; this frame contains a revolving drum placed on edge and mounted on an axle, and on the edge of this drum teeth should be fashioned so that there are four hundred of them, evenly distributed, and engaged with the tooth of the lower drum. In addition, at the side of the upper drum one tooth should be fixed to protrude beyond the other teeth. 3. Then, above these, a horizontal drum should be installed, toothed in the same way, and set into another frame so that its teeth engage the tooth that has been fixed at the side of the second drum. Holes should be made in this last drum, as many as the number of miles that can be covered with the wagon in a day's journey. A few more or less will not interfere with the workings. Round pebbles should be placed in all these holes, and in the *theca* of this drum, that is, its frame, a single hole should be made that has a little channel, in which the pebbles that will have been placed in that drum may fall one by one when they come to that place, falling then into the wagon box and a bronze vessel that has been set underneath the channel.

4. Thus when the turning wheel propels the lower-most drum along with itself, and with every rotation, the tooth of this drum forces the drum above it to move forward by the propulsion of its teeth, it comes about that when the lowermost drum has rotated four hundred times, the drum above it will have rotated once, and the tooth affixed to its side will have driven the flat drum forward by one tooth. Now when, in four hundred rotations of the lowermost drum, the upper drum has turned once, the progress made will cover a distance of one thousand five feet – that is, a mile. On this principle, then, however many pebbles fall, by the noise they make they will announce each individual mile as it is covered, and the number of pebbles collected at the bottom will indicate the daily mileage by their total.

5. On seagoing vessels, these devices are made in the same way, with a few details changed, but following the same principle. An axle is carried through the hull from side to side, its ends protruding beyond the ship itself. On these ends wheels are mounted with a diameter that extends four and one-half feet; these wheels have paddles attached around the rim that touch the water. The center of the axle amidships has a drum with one tooth protruding from its edge. Here a frame is put up with another drum encased inside it; this drum has four hundred uniform teeth that engage with the tooth of the drum that is mounted on the axle, and in addition another single tooth is fixed to the side of the second drum, protruding beyond its curvature. 6. Above this, in another frame joined into the first, a horizontal drum is enclosed, toothed in the same manner, and the tooth that is fixed to the side of the second drum engages with the teeth of the horizontal drum, so that the tooth, by driving the teeth of the flat drum one by one, will turn the flat drum in a circle with every single rotation. Holes are let into the flat drum, and in these holes round pebbles are set in place. In the *theca* of this drum, that is, the frame, one hole should be hollowed out, which has a little channel down which a pebble, released from confinement, will fall into a bronze vessel with an audible noise.

7. Thus when a ship has been set into motion, either from the oars or from the wind's gusts, the paddles on the wheels, making contact with the water opposite them, are forced backward by the power of the impact and turn the wheels. The wheels, in turn, will drive the axle by their own rotation, and with the axle, the drum, whose tooth, brought around full circle by each single rotation, causes the gradual circling of the second drum by driving forward its individual teeth. When the wheels have been turned four hundred times by their

blades, the second drum, brought full circle once, will drive one tooth of the horizontal drum with the impetus of the single tooth on its side. Therefore every time the revolution of the horizontal drum brings the pebbles to the hole, it will let them fall through the little channel. In this way, both by sound and by number it will indicate the mileage of the sea journey.

CHAPTER 10: CATAPULTS (FIGURE 131)

I have thoroughly discussed how to make those things that can be set up for practical purposes and for amusement during settled times, times without fear. 1. Now, however, I shall demonstrate the things that have been invented for safety's sake as a protection against danger, that is, the principles for scorpions and ballistae,* and the proportional systems by which they should be prepared.

2. Every proportion of these instruments is derived from the proposed length of the arrow that the instrument is designed to shoot.* The spring holes in the capital, through which the twisted sinews are stretched to restrain the arms, measure one-ninth this amount. The [diameter of the] spring holes, in turn, should determine the height and breadth of the capital itself; the plates at the top and bottom of the capital, called "perforated," *peritrêta*, should have a thickness equal to the diameter of one hole, with a width of one and three-quarters diameters, and at the extreme ends one and one-half diameters thick. The right and left uprights, minus their tenons, are four diameters high and five-eighths of a diameter thick; the tenons measure half a diameter. From the upright to the spring hole is a distance of one quarter diameter, from the spring hole to the middle upright is also a distance of one quarter-diameter. The width of the middle upright is one diameter and three-quarters, its thickness one diameter. 3. The aperture in the middle upright, through which the bolt passes, is one quarter of a diameter. The four angles around the capital are reinforced on their sides and fronts with iron plates, or bronze pins and nails. The length of the trough, which the Greeks call *syrinx*, is nineteen diameters. The rails that are fixed to the sides of the trough, which some call *bucculae*, are nineteen diameters long, to make a height and thickness of one diameter. Two additional bars should be attached into which the windlass will be sunk; these have a length of three diameters and a breadth of half a diameter. The thickness of the cheekpiece (called

"little bench," or, as some would have it, "little box") is one diameter, its height one-half a diameter; it is fixed in place by dovetail joins. The length of the windlass is four diameters, the thickness five-twelfths of a diameter. The length of the claw is three-quarters of a diameter, its thickness one quarter-diameter, and its bracket is the same. The length of the trigger, or "handle" is three diameters, with a width and thickness of one quarter-diameter. 4. The length of the slide is sixteen diameters, its thickness one quarter-diameter, its height three quarter-diameters.

The base of the post at ground level is eight diameters, the breadth of the plinth on which the post stands is three quarters of a diameter, its thickness five-eighths. The length of the post up to its tenon is twelve diameters, its breadth three-quarters of a diameter, its thickness three-quarters. There are three struts, whose length is nine diameters, their width half a diameter, their thickness seven-sixteenths. The length of the tenon is one and one-half diameters, the length of the capital (= universal joint) atop the post is two diameters, the breadth of the antefix three-quarters of a diameter, with a thickness of one.

5. The rear minor post, which is called *antibasis* in Greek, is eight diameters [in length], its width three-quarters of a diameter, its thickness five-eighths. The lower prop is twelve diameters long, its width and breadth equal to that of the minor post. Above the minor post there is a hinge bracket, also called a "cushion," two and one-half diameters long, one and one-half high, three quarters of a diameter broad.

The handles of the windlasses are two and one-half diameters, their thickness half a diameter, their width one and one-half. The length of the handspikes including their hinges is ten diameters, the width one-half, and the thickness [is one-half] as well. The length of the arms is seven diameters, the thickness at the base nine-sixteenths of a diameter, at the top seven-sixteenths; the curvature measures eight diameters.

These [instruments] are prepared according to these given proportions, with additions or subtractions based on them. If the capitals are made taller than they are wide (these are called "tuned up," *anatona*), then the length of the arms must be reduced so that, inasmuch as the tension is softer because of the height of the capital, the shortness of the arm makes for a more powerful shot. If the capital is shorter than the one described here (this is called *catatonum*, "tuned down"), then, because of their power, the arms should be made a little longer, so that they can be drawn back more easily. For just as a five-foot lever might be able to lift a burden with the help of four people, one that is ten feet long will do the job with the help of two; so, in the same way, on a catapult longer arms are drawn back more easily whereas those that are shorter are more resistant.

CHAPTER 11: BALLISTAE (FIGURE 132)

1. I have given the principles for catapults, and the parts and pieces from which they are assembled. The principles for ballistae, however, vary, and they are assembled in various different ways to achieve the same results. Some are twisted by the principles of levers and windlasses, some by blocks and tackle, others by capstans, some, also, by geared drums. Nevertheless, no ballista is made except according to the weight of the stone shot that the instrument is designed to send. Therefore, their principles are not accessible to everyone, unless they have some preparation in the principles of geometry, number, and multiplication.

2. For holes should be made in the headpieces of ballistae, and through these spaces cables are stretched, preferably of women's hair or of sinew, of a size appropriate to the weight of the shot that this ballista is intended to launch. The proportions are adopted according to the principle of weight, just as in catapults they are based on the length of the bolts. And so, in order that even those who do not know geometry well may be equipped in such a way that they will not be detained by calculations amid the dangers of war, I shall set out what I know for certain by having done it myself and what I received already worked out from my teachers, and I shall give a full account of the units by which the Greek weights are proportioned to the modules.

3. Now if a ballista is intended to launch a two-pound stone, there will be a five-digit* spring hole in its capital; if 4 pounds, six digits; if 6 pounds, seven digits; 10 pounds, eight digits; 20 pounds, ten digits; 40 pounds, twelve and three-quarters digits; 60 pounds, thirteen and one-eighth digits; 80 pounds, fifteen digits; 120 pounds, one foot and half a digit; 160 pounds, one and one-quarter feet; 180 pounds, one foot and five digits; 200 pounds, one foot and six digits; 240 pounds, one foot and seven digits; 360 pounds, one and one-half feet.

4. Once the diameter of the spring hole has been decided, a lozenge is laid out, which is called "perforated" in Greek (peritrêtos), whose length is two and three-quarters diameters, and its width two and one-half. Let the middle be divided by a drawn line, and once it has been divided, the outermost parts of this figure are contracted, so that it has an oblique shape, one-sixth of whose length equals one-quarter of the width at the obtuse angles. On the sides where there is a curvature penetrated by the acute angles, the spring holes are turned, and contraction of the side returns inward by a distance of one-sixth. The spring hole will be elongated by an amount equal to the thickness of the tensioning rod (epizygis). Once the hole has been cut, its edge should be polished all round, so that it has a gentle curvature.

5. The thickness of this lozenge will be set at one unit. The washers will measure two diameters [in length], with a width of one and five-twelfths, the thickness aside from what will be set into the spring hole, three-quarters of a diameter, their outer width one-half diameter.

The length of the uprights is five and three-sixteenths diameters, the curvature of the holes half a diameter, their thickness eleven-eighteenths. Along the middle of the breadth the thickness should be increased around the spring hole as shown in the illustration. The connecting block[7] is one-fifth of a diameter broad and five diameters thick, one-quarter diameter high.

6. The length of the bar nearest the mounting table is eight diameters, its breadth and thickness half a diameter; the tenons are two diameters and half a diameter thick, curvature of the bar is three-quarters of a diameter. The front bar has an identical breadth and thickness; the length depends on its degree of curvature and the breadth of the uprights at their curvature. The upper bars are equal in their dimensions to the lower ones. The bars of the table are half a diameter.

7. The rails of the ladder are nineteen diameters, with a thickness of one quarter-diameter. The trough is one and one-quarter diameters wide, its height one and one-eighth diameters. The forward part of the ladder, that is, the part nearest the arms, which is joined to the table, should have the sum of its length divided into five parts. Of these five parts, two are assigned to [the trigger-cover which] the Greeks call the "turtle," chelônion; its breadth is three-sixteenths of a diameter, its thickness one quarter-diameter, and its length eleven diameters and one-half. The projection of the claw is half a diameter, the projection of the dovetail is one-fourth diameter. What is called the transverse front, at the windlass, measures three diameters.

8. The breadth of the interior rungs is five-sixteenths

---

7 *Regula est*: supplevit Schramm; there is a lacuna in the text.

of a diameter, the thickness three-sixteenths. The trigger cover is set into the rails of the ladder with a dovetail join, one quarter-diameter wide, one-twelfth thick. The thickness of the square along the ladder is seven-sixteenths of a diameter, one quarter-diameter at the ends. The diameter of the drum of the windlass will be on the same level as the claw, and by the pawls it will be seven-sixteenths of a diameter. 9. The length of the braces will be three and one-quarter diameters, the breadth at the bottom half a diameter, at the top the thickness will be three-sixteenths.

The length of the base, which is called the "hearth" or *eschara*, will be eight, the secondary base four diameters, and the thickness and width of both will be one diameter. The columns are joined together halfway up their height, their breadth and thickness half a diameter. Their length does not have a proportional relationship to the [diameter of the] spring hole, but will be whatever is necessary in practice. The length of the arm is six diameters, its thickness at the heel five-eighths of a diameter, and three-eighths at the end.

I have set out the proportional systems of ballistae and catapults in a way that I thought would make them of the greatest practical use. Now I shall not omit to tell how their tension is tempered by ropes twisted from sinew and hair, at least to the extent that I can treat this comprehensively in writing.*

CHAPTER 12: TUNING WAR MACHINES (FIGURE 133)

1. Take very long beams, and at the top of these brackets are fixed, into which windlasses are set. Along the space between the beams, forms should be cut and hollowed out, into which the capitals of catapults are inserted and then secured with wedges so that they do not move out of place during tensioning. Then bronze washers are set into the capitals and within them the little iron rods that the Greeks call *epizygides* are set in place. 2. Next, the ends of the ropes are threaded in through the spring holes of the capitals, and carried across to the other side, and then they are fastened around the windlasses and wound around them, so that when the ropes are stretched over them by the levers, when struck with the hand, each of them will give off a corresponding tone. Then they are secured with wedges at the spring holes so that they cannot uncoil. Thus, carried across to the other side of the capital, they are stretched with

handspikes on windlasses until they make an identical sound, and in this way catapults are adjusted to tone by propping with wedges according to the musical sense of hearing.

I have said what I could about these things. It remains for me to discuss siege engines, and how, by the help of machines, generals become victors and cities can be defended.

CHAPTER 13: DIADES AND HIS SIEGE ENGINES

1. First of all, the [battering] ram for attacking is said to have been invented in the following way:* the Carthaginians had set up camp near Gades (Cádiz)* in order to attack its fortifications. As they had already captured one fort, they attempted to demolish it, and because they had no iron tools for demolition, they took up a beam. Holding it in their hands, relentlessly pounding one end against the upper part of the city walls, they threw down the uppermost rows of stone masonry, and thus they gradually broke apart the entire fortification, course by course.

2. Afterward a Tyrian engineer, Pephrasmenos by name, inspired by the principle of this discovery, set up a ship's mast and suspended another from it sideways as if it were a balance, and by driving it back and forth with powerful blows he cast down the city wall of the Gaditani. Then Geras, another Carthaginian, having first made a base of timber with wheels set underneath, set up a frame of uprights and crossbeams, from which he suspended a battering ram. He covered this frame with oxhides, so that the men positioned on the apparatus to batter the wall should be better protected. Because the machine's movements were so slow, he began to call it the "tortoise for a ram."

3. With these first steps taken toward such a type of machine, later, when Philip, son of Amyntas, lay siege to Byzantium,* Polyidos the Thessalian developed it in several types, easier to use, and from him Diades and Charias, who fought with Alexander, learned their profession.

And so Diades, in turn, shows in his writings that he invented moving siege towers; these he took along unassembled as he accompanied the army. He also invented the drill and the climbing machine, by which a level passage could be made up to a city wall, and also the demolition grapnel ("crow"), which some call the crane.

4. He also used a wheeled ram [of his own invention], and left written principles for making it (Figure 134).

He says that the smallest tower should be no less than sixty cubits high and seventeen wide. The contraction of the uppermost part should be by one-fifth the dimension at the bottom, and the uprights for the towers should be three-quarters of a foot [per side] at the bottom, half a foot at the top. This tower ought to be made with ten levels, with windows on each level.

5. A larger tower is one hundred twenty cubits high, twenty-three and one-half cubits wide, its contraction similarly by one-fifth, its uprights one foot [per side] at the bottom, half a foot at the top. He made this tower with twenty levels, so that the individual levels had a gallery measuring three cubits [wide]. He covered it with rawhide so that these galleries should be protected from every blow.

6. The assembly of a "tortoise for a ram" was carried out according to the same method (Figure 135). It had a span of thirty cubits, a height, excluding the gable, of thirteen, and the height of the gable from the platform to the summit was sixteen cubits. The gable protruded upward above the middle of the canopy no less than two cubits, and above this a turret was erected of four cubits, and consisted of three levels. The catapults and ballistae were stationed on the top level; on the lower ones a great supply of water was gathered in order to extinguish the force of any fire that might be launched against it. Here, too, a ramming machine was set up, which in Greek is called the "ram-rack," *kriodochê*, on which a roller turned on an axle, and on this a suspended ram achieved the scheme's outstanding results through pulling and heaving on halyards. This, too, like the tower, was covered by rawhide.

7. He gave these instructions for borers in his writings: the machine itself was like a tortoise in appearance, but had a channel set between its uprights, just as in catapults or ballistae, fifty cubits in length, one cubit in height, into which is set a transverse windlass. At the head, on right and left, there are two pulleys; by means of these, the iron-headed beam contained in the channel was set into motion. Underneath, rollers encased close together in the channel itself made its movements quicker and more powerful. Above the beam that is set in the channel, densely set arches were placed close around the channel, in order to carry the rawhide in which the machine was wrapped.

9. He maintains that nothing need be written about the [demolition] grapnel, because he has observed that this machine has no practical use. As for the boarding

bridge, which in Greek is called *epibathra*, and seagoing machines, by which ships can be boarded, I have observed that he promised insistently that he would write about them, but that [in fact] he never explained their principles.

I have set out what Diades wrote about machines and how to make them. Now I shall explain what I have learned from my teachers and what I myself consider useful.

CHAPTER 14: SIEGE ENGINES OF VITRUVIUS AND HIS TEACHERS (FIGURE 136)

1. The tortoise that is prepared for filling moats (with its help, there can be access to the fortification wall) should be made as follows. A base is to be assembled, which is called the "hearth," *eschara*, in Greek, square, twenty-one feet to each side and with four crossbeams. These in turn should be held in place by two others, one and one-half feet thick, one-half foot wide. The crossbeams should stand about three and one-half feet apart. In their intervals casters should be inserted underneath, which in Greek are called "wagon-feet," *hamaxopodes*,[8] in which the axles of the wheels rotate, enclosed within iron plates. These casters are adjusted to have hinges and holes, in which levers can be inserted to facilitate their turning; thus, whether there is a need to move forward or backward, to the right or left side, or obliquely off at an angle, it is possible to move in that direction by turning the casters.

2. Above the base, two beams should be set in place, projecting six feet beyond each end, and around these projections two other beams are fixed into place, projecting seven feet from the faces, and as broad as has been recorded for the base. Above this framework connected posts are erected, of nine feet not counting the tenons, one and one-quarter feet thick on every side, with an interval between them of one and one-half feet. These are held in place at the top by tenoned beams. Above the beams, braces are joined to each other by hinges, raised up to a height of nine feet. Above the braces is a squared ridgepole to which the braces are connected.

3. These are held firmly in place all around by battens

---

8 Giocondo *hamaxapodes*; MSS *anaxopodes*.

and should be covered by planks, preferably made of palm;[9] if not, from some other wood that will be most practical, with the exception of pine and alder, for these are fragile and easily catch fire. Over all the planks, install wicker lattices, closely woven and as freshly cut as possible. Then the entire machine should be covered over by a double layer of the rawest hide, sewn together, stuffed with seaweed or straw that has been softened in vinegar. Thus the blows from ballistae and the attacks of fire will be repelled.

CHAPTER 15: MORE SIEGE ENGINES

1. There is also another type of tortoise that has all the other features as described earlier except for the braces; instead it has a parapet all round and merlon panels and above this inclined sills, and is enclosed above this by panels and hides firmly fixed in place. Above this, then, clay worked with hair is laid on so thickly that fire can in no circumstance harm the machine. If required, these machines can be outfitted with eight wheels, but it is necessary to determine this according to the terrain.

The tortoises that are outfitted for mining – they are called "diggers" in Greek (oryges), have all the features described earlier, but their faces are made like the angles of triangles, so that when missiles are launched at them from the walls, they will not receive frontal blows, but only glancing blows off the sides, and those who are inside are protected as they dig away without danger.

2. It seems not out of place for me to tell as well about the tortoise which Hegetor of Byzantium made, and the principles by which he made it (Figure 137).* The length of its base was sixty-three feet, its width forty-two. The uprights, of which four were set in place above the frame, were assembled of double beams, each thirty-six feet in height, one and one-quarter feet in thickness, and one and one-half feet in width. Its base had eight wheels, by which it was maneuvered. Their height was six and three-quarters feet, their thickness three feet. They were fashioned by three layers of wood, each joined to the next by dowels, and bound together by iron plates that had been worked cold, (3.) and these wheels made their rotations in casters, which are also called "wagon-feet" (hamaxopodes).

Above the surface of the level crossbeams, on the base, there were uprights eighteen feet high, three-quarters of a foot in width, five-eighths of a foot in thickness, standing one and three-quarters feet apart from one another. Above these, a frame of beams, enclosed all round, held the whole framework together; these were one foot wide and three-quarters of a foot thick. Above it, braces were raised to a height of twelve feet, and above the braces a ridgepole was set in place, uniting the joins of the braces. The braces had transverse battens, and above them decking to cover everything beneath.

4. It also had a center deck on smaller beams where the scorpions and catapults were set in place. Two compound uprights were erected of forty-five feet each, one and one-half feet in thickness, two feet in width, joined at their tops by a tenoned crossbeam and another tenoned beam halfway up between the two shafts, fixed in place with iron plates. On this, between the shafts and the crossbeam, another timber was set in place, pierced by bolts and firmly secured by clamps. In this timber two small rollers were made on the lathe, and lines attached to them restrained the ram.

5. Over the head of the axles that contained the battering ram, a parapet was set in place, equipped like a turret, so that two soldiers, standing, could look out without danger and report what manner of things the enemy were trying. The battering ram of this machine had a length of one hundred four feet, a width of one and one-quarter feet at its heel, while at its head, because of the contraction along the sides, it measured one foot, and three-quarters of a foot in thickness.

6. This ram had a beak of tempered iron, as warships do, and from this beak four iron plates of about fifteen feet each were attached onto the wood. From the head to the lowermost heel of the beam four ropes were stretched, eight digits in thickness, tied down just as a ship is stayed from poop to prow, and the ropes of this fastening were knotted transversely, having a space of one and one-quarter feet between them. The whole ram was enveloped above in rawhide. 7. The ropes from which it hung had quadruple chains made from iron at their ends, and these themselves were wrapped in rawhide.

The projecting part of this ram had a box, assembled of panels and secured in place, in which there was a [scaling] net, along whose sturdy ropes, when they had been spread, one could arrive at the walls with a firm foothold.

This machine could move in six directions: forward, backward, and to the right and left side, but it could

9 Reading Giocondo's *palmeis* with Callebat and Fleury.

also be raised upward and sent downward by inclining it. This machine was erected so that is was high enough to cast down walls of about one hundred feet in height; because of its mobility it covered a range of no less than one hundred feet to the right and left. One hundred men maneuvered it, and it had a weight of four thousand talents, which would be 480,000 pounds.

CHAPTER 16: DEFENSIVE STRATAGEMS

1. As for scorpions and catapults and ballistae, and also tortoises and towers, I have explained those that seemed to me most effective, by whom they were invented and how they ought to be assembled. Because the instructions for ladders and cranes and such things are simpler I saw no need to write about them. Soldiers usually make such things for themselves.

Nor can these things be useful in every place or according to the same methods, because fortifications differ from other fortifications, as do the strengths of various nations. Indeed, machines ought to be outfitted by one method for brave and daring people, in another way for careful ones, still otherwise for the timid. 2. And so if anyone should want to follow these instructions, and selecting from their variety, put them to work in preparing a single device, there will be no lack of helpful material here; he will be able without hesitation to lay out whatever may be necessary as situations or localities dictate.

Defensive methods, on the other hand, are not to be explained in writing, for attacking armies do not outfit their siege engines according to our descriptions; rather, their machines are most often rendered useless by the clever swiftness of an extemporaneous strategy, carried out without machines. Which, it is said, happened to the Rhodians.

3. Diognetus was an architect of Rhodes, and to him a certain honorary annual wage was assigned from the public budget because of his expertise. At that time, a certain architect from Arados, Callias by name, arrived in Rhodes, and upon arrival he gave a presentation in which he pulled out a model of a fortification wall. Atop this wall, he set a machine on a universal joint, by which he snatched up a siege tower that was advancing toward the wall and brought it inside the fortifications. When the Rhodians saw this, in their admiration they took away Diognetus's annual salary and transferred the distinction to Callias instead.*

4. Meanwhile, King Demetrius, who was called Poliorcetes, "Besieger of Cities," because of his obstinate temperament, prepared to make war on Rhodes, and brought Epimachus, a famous Athenian architect, along with him. Now Epimachus outfitted a siege tower at huge expense, and with the greatest exertion and labor, whose height was 120 feet and whose width was 60. This he reinforced with goatskins and rawhide, so that it could withstand the impact of a 360-pound shot launched from a ballista. This machine itself weighed 360,000 pounds.

When the Rhodians asked Callias to prepare a machine to defend the city against the siege tower and to carry it within the walls as he had promised, he said that he could not. 5. For not everything can be carried out according to the same principles. There are some things that achieve large-scale results like those achieved with small models. And then there are other things for which models cannot be made at all, and they must be built to scale in the first place. And some things that seem perfectly realistic in a model vanish when their scale begins to be enlarged, as we can observe in this case: a hole can be bored with a drill that is half a digit in diameter, or one digit, or one and one-half digits. But if we were to want to bore a hole a span across by the same method the job would never be done, for half-foot drills and larger do not even seem conceivable. 6. Thus in some models things that seem to happen on a tiny scale might seem to occur on a larger scale as well, and this is how the Rhodians, deceived along the same lines, inflicted insult and injury upon Diognetus. And so, once they saw the enemy stubbornly challenging them, the war machine readied to capture their city, the devastation in store for the community, they threw themselves at Diognetus's feet, begging him to help his homeland.

7. At first, he said that he would not. But after noble young maidens and the young men in military training (ephebes) came with priests to implore him, then he accepted, with these conditions: that if he succeeded in capturing the war machine, it would be his. With the agreement made, there where the war machine was to approach the city, there in that spot he pierced the wall and ordered everyone, by public proclamation and personal appeal, to take whatever stores they had of water, sewage, and mud, and dump them through that aperture, where they passed through sluices out before the walls. Because a huge quantity of water, mud, and sewage had been dumped in that place during the night, when on the next day the siege tower began its approach, before it could near the wall, it churned up a

sinkhole in the slime and stopped dead, unable either to advance or to retreat. And so Demetrius, when he had seen that he had been outwitted by the wisdom of Diognetus, retreated with his fleet.

8. Then the Rhodians, freed from war by the cleverness of Diognetus, thanked him publicly and bestowed upon him every honor and decoration. Diognetus, in turn, brought that siege engine into the city and set it up in a public place with the inscription: "Diognetus gave this gift to the citizen body from the spoils of war." Thus, in defense it is not so much machines that should be put at the ready, but, above all, strategies.

9. On Chios, likewise, when attackers had set up machines called storming bridges, *sambucae*, on boats, the Chiotes, during the night, heaped up earth, sand, and stone in the seawater before their fortification walls (Figure 138).* When the enemy had wanted to approach the walls the following morning, the ships grounded on the barriers under the water and were unable either to approach the fortification wall or to retreat backward. Instead, pinned to the spot by fire darts they were consumed by the flames.

In Apollonia, too, when it had been under siege and the attackers planned, by mining, to penetrate within the walls unsuspected, this fact was nonetheless reported to the Apolloniates by their lookouts.* Distressed by the news, at a loss for strategies because of their fear, they began to lose their spirit because they were certain neither of the time nor the place at which the enemy would emerge.

10. At that time, however, Trypho the Alexandrian was architect. He laid out several tunnels within the walls and mined outside the walls in several places until he was beyond the range of a bowshot, and in each of these tunnels he suspended bronze vessels. In one of these tunnels, which was up against the enemy mine, the suspended vessels began to clang at the impact of the picks and shovels, and by this means it was known where the adversaries planned to penetrate by digging their tunnel. Once the line of enemy approach was known, he prepared bronze vessels filled with boiling water and pitch, which would fall from above onto the heads of the enemy, and he filled others with human excrement and others with white-hot sand. Then, during the night, he bored many holes into the enemy mine, and by pouring out the contents of the vessels into these holes, he killed all the enemy engaged in the mining.

11. Likewise, when Massilia (Marseilles) was under siege, and more than thirty mines were underway, the Massilitani, suspecting something of the kind, lowered the level of the entire moat in front of their city wall by excavating it more deeply (Figure 139).* As a result, all the enemy mines had their outlets into the moat. In the places where it was not possible to make a moat, then within the wall itself they made a pit of the most extensive length and breadth, rather like a fishpond, opposite the place where the mines were underway, and filled it from the harbor and from wells. Thus when the mine suddenly opened out, a powerful surge of onrushing water uprooted all the shoring, and those caught inside were all overwhelmed by the sheer amount of water and the collapse of the mine.

12. Next, when a mound was being raised opposite them, right next to the wall, and trees had been cut down and set in place there so that the site of the operation would be elevated still farther, then, by launching white-hot iron rods from ballistae, they caused the entire palisade to catch fire. And when a "tortoise for a ram" approached the wall to batter it, they threw down a noose. Once the ram was entangled in that, by turning a drum mounted on a capstan, they pulled its head up into the air and prevented it from touching their wall. Finally they broke up the entire machine with fire darts and ballista shots.

And so these victories by besieged cities were not achieved by machines; instead, they were liberated by the cleverness of architects pitted against various types of machines.

In this volume, I have made a complete account of those principles of machines, both in times of peace and in times of war, that I could furnish myself and that I considered most useful. In the previous nine, on the other hand, I have assembled information about the individual types and parts of architecture, so that the entire body of that art might have all its components explained in the space of ten volumes.

[The tenth book of Vitruvius is successfully completed. Thank God.[10]]

FINIS

10 In MSS HLPfhEGbchpWV S: *Finis*.

COMMENTARY

BOOK 1

Imperator Caesar (1.praef.1)

Imperator means a victorious, charismatically acclaimed commander of troops. Under Augustus it has yet to mean "emperor," but it means more than commander. Immediately from the time of C. Julius Caesar's assassination in March 44 B.C., Octavian (then aged eighteen) referred to himself as C. Caesar (and often "*divi filius*," i.e., [adopted] son of the divine/deified Caesar), never Octavian, in order to emphasize that he was acceding to Julius Caesar's full political inheritance, including his clientage. He was awarded the title "Augustus" only in 27 B.C.

extensive researches (1.praef.1)

Presumably an indication that Vitruvius is relying not only on his youthful education but also on lifelong continuous reading.

your Father (1.praef.2)

C. Julius Caesar, by then deified Julius Caesar.

your sister (1.praef.2)

This is presumably Octavia, the full sister of Augustus, who had been married to M. Antonius as a political alliance (40–32) and who endowed the Porticus Octavia with its library dedicated to her son Marcellus. Octavia was not just a significant patron of the arts, but was also politically very active, and even crucial, in the relationships between Octavian and Antony (e.g., arranging the pact of Tarentum in 37, which renewed their alliance and avoided civil war). Coordinating matters for lesser clients, like the architect Vitruvius, would have been commonplace for her.

signified and the signifier (1.1.3)

These expressions appear to be adapted from Epicurean philosophy, particularly natural philosophy, and refer to the necessity of beginning all scientific investigations with a clear definition of terms.

"Epicurus held that the study of physics begins with the adoption of a method of inquiry," and the first rule of inquiry is to "have concepts which correspond to the words that are used,"[1] that is, define terms. Vitruvius knew and sympathized

with aspects of Epicurean philosophy (e.g., atomism), with which he was familiar through Lucretius's didactic poem *De Rerum Natura* (9.praef.17). Sextus Empiricus (late second century A.D.)[2] distinguished the methods of Stoics from Epicureans by pointing out that Stoics recognized three terms of discourse: "the significant" (*to semainon*), or the "voice" (*phonê*); the "signified" (*to semainomenon*,) also called "what is said" (*to lekton*); and the external point of reference (*to tygchanon*, "what happens"). Epicureans recognized only the "voice" and "what is said".[3]

In modern criticism, these phrases are normally taken to express such ideas as the opposition of *fabrica* (practice) and *ratiocinatio* (reasoning)[4] or the difference between the study of the "passive" work of architecture itself and what it "actively" expresses.[5] Vitruvius is more straightforward on this subject. That which is signified (*quod significatur*) is the actual object of discussion, such as building, and so on, and the "signifier" (*quod significat*) is the terminology that one needs to conduct the discussion.

Historiae: Korai/Caryatids and Persians (1.1.5–6) (Figure 2)

A *historia* is an *excursus* which serves as an explanation of subject matter, and it is an element typical of both rhetorical composition and secondary education. In rhetorical composition, an *excursus* or *egressio* was a description meant to relax the mind after the introduction of a point. It could precede or follow the *argumentatio*. In secondary education, which consisted extensively of memorization of literature (hence the popularity and usefulness of poetry in didactic and scientific works, like Lucretius's *De rerum natura*), a *grammaticus* would introduce a new piece of literature with a *praelectio* which included a first reading followed by explanatory information, mainly in the form of mythology.[6] Vitruvius does give a few other examples of this kind of historical aetiology: the origins of the types of columns (4.1.1–10); *telamones*/Atlantes (6.7.6).

---

1 E. Asmis, *Epicurus' Scientific Method* (Ithaca and London, 1984), 19–20.

2 *Adversus mathematicos* 8.11–12

3 E. Asmis, *Epicurus' Scientific Method* (Ithaca and London, 1984), 26.

4 P. Fleury, *Vitruve, De l'architecture*, i (Paris, 1990), 70.

5 F. Pellati, "Quod significatur et quod significat. Saggio d'interpretazione di un passo di Vitruvio." *Historia* 1 (1927), 53–59.

6 Quintilian, *Institutiones Oratoriae* 1.8.18–21. See M. L. Clarke, *Higher Education in the Ancient World* (London, 1971), 23–24.

The destruction of Caryae (a town in Arcadia near Sparta), presumably in 479 as a punishment for "Medizing," is obscure and otherwise unrecorded; the event may be confused with the destruction of Caryae in 368/67 by Sparta, when Caryae took the side of Thebes at Leuctra.[7] It has been suggested that this conflation occurred because Caryae's support for Thebes "raked up" memories of the medizing of the Persian Wars a century earlier.[8] Plataea (479 B.C.) was the decisive battle of Boeotia that ended the Persian Wars, but the father of the commanding general, Pausanias, was Cleombrotus, not Agesilas.[9] The stoa of the Persians at Sparta is recorded by another Pausanias (the second century A.D. traveller)[10] with figures representing recognizable Persians (e.g., the defeated general Mardonius), but they may have been attached to the columns or carved into their surface in the manner of the Archaic figure columns at Didyma or Ephesus.

Caryatids, known from the sixth century B.C. in Greek architecture, continue sporadically throughout the Hellenistic period and appear as furniture ornaments and bronze mirror supports. In Vitruvius's time Agrippa's Pantheon in the Campus Martius had caryatids[11] as did the attic of the porticus of the Forum Augustum.[12]

This is the first appearance of the word in Latin in the sense that it refers to a freestanding female figure used in the place of a column. It is common to refer to all female support figures in classical architecture as caryatids, but they probably did not all have that meaning in antiquity, that is, the recollection of citizens (matrons) punished for civic betrayal or cowardice.[13] Vitruvius's aetiology postdates the earliest caryatids by a century. The type of caryatids of the Erechtheion porch were apparently never called caryatids but simply *korai* ("maidens"). The "caryatids" in the Forum Augustum, which are copies of those of Erechtheion, probably have nothing to do with the iconography of punishment, but, according to B. Wesenberg, were mainly meant to carry the building into the realm of the fantastic and to serve as recognizably "Greek" works of art, demonstrating that the Forum had been built "ex

manubiis" (from the spoils of war).[14] Most caryatids, or least those of the much-copied Erechtheion type, should probably simply be called "korê/korai."

Therefore, Vitruvius's "historia" may be an anachronism, that is, the meaning may have been attached after the ornaments were invented. The extent to which these erudite meanings were broadly received and understood is debatable.[15]

philosophy and physiology (1.1.7)

By the Hellenistic period philosophy was commonly divided into two branches: moral and physical.

Greek philosophy became fashionable in certain circles in Rome in the later second century B.C. and in the first century there were three main schools of thought: Stoics; Epicureans; and the revived Academy (Platonism). Stoicism was brought to Rome by Panaetius (c. 180–110 B.C.), who was patronized by Scipio Aemilianus from 144 onward, and in the first century B.C. the leader of the school in Rome was Posidonius of Rhodes (135–50 B.C.), friend of Cicero and Pompey. Epicureans were briefly expelled from the City as early as 173 B.C. but the school became quite popular with Philodemus of Gadara (c. 110–35 B.C.), patronized by L. Calpurnius Piso, Caesar's father-in-law. The influence of the Academy was also pervasive; Cicero was taught in his youth by two of the leaders of the school, Philo and Antiochus.

It was a commonplace, particularly with the Stoics and Epicureans, that the practical purpose of philosophical education was the achievement of freedom from avarice and equanimity of soul in the face of misfortune. Cicero, in *De Officiis*, the definitive humanist handbook of civic duties written about ten years earlier than the *Ten Books*, uses very much the same language as Vitruvius to describe greatness of spirit, dignity, and freedom from greed, which are the benefits of study of philosophy.[16]

Physical or natural philosophy (physiology) is more or less what we distinguish as natural science. It and other specialist disciplines (such as medicine) generally became distinct from moral philosophy in the later fifth and fourth centuries (with such works as the Hippocratic corpus and Aristotle), although the distinction was never fully recognized. "Science" and even medicine continued to some extent to be considered a part of philosophy to the end of antiquity. Vitruvius clearly read the

7 Xenophon, *Hellenica* 6.5.25.

8 H. Plommer, "Vitruvius and the Origin of the Caryatids," *Journal of Hellenic Studies*, 99 (1979), 97–102; Xenophon, *Hellenica* 7.1.28.

9 H. Schaefer, in *Paulys Realencyclopädie der Klassischen Altertumswissenschaft* 8.4.2565–2578 s.v. Plataea.

10 Pausanias 3.10.7.

11 Pliny the Elder, *Natural History* 36.38: "Agrippae Pantheum decoravit Diogenes Atheniensis. In columis templi euius caryatides probantur inter pauca operum, sicut in fastigio posita signa, sed propter altitudinem loci minus celebrata."

12 Th. Homolle, "L'origine des Caryatides," *Revue Archéologique* 5.5 (1917), 1–67; M. Vickers, "Persepolis and the Erechtheum Caryatids: The Iconography of Medism and Servitude," *Revue Archéologique* (1985, 1), 3–28; H. Plommer, op. cit..

13 J. Rykwert suggests another possible conflation: that of the story of the destruction of Caryae with the stately dance of the maidens at the nearby sanctuary of Artemis Karneia. J. Rykwert, *The Dancing Column* (MIT Press, 1996), 135.

14 B. Wesenberg, "Augustusforum und Akropolis," *Jahrbuch des Deutschen Archäologischen Instituts in Rom* 99 (1984), 161–185.

15 Others, such as Vickers, "Persepolis and the Erechtheum Caryatids: the Iconography of Medism and Servitude," *Revue Archéologique* (1985), 3–28, would like to see that the story has some reference to the time described, that is, the Persian Wars, or, for Plommer, op. cit., column 368, when two types of "Caryatids" are added to the ornamental repertoire: one the punished women described by Vitruvius; the other dancing women taking part in the festival of Artemis Caryatidis at Sparta, probably the subject of a new figure group of Praxiteles (Pliny the Elder, *Natural History*, 36.23) from about that time.

16 *De Officiis* 1.61, 68, 69, 72.

Athens, Erechtheion

Syracuse, Hellenistic Altar

Forum of Augustus, dedicated 2. B.C.

Figure 2. Caryatids/*Korai* (Maidens) (1.1.5–6).

De rerum natura of T. Lucretius Carus (c. 94–55) and was persuaded by aspects of its atomistic natural philosophy. He uses many of the same analytical and descriptive terms in an identical way (e.g., *genus* and *ratio*). For Lucretius, "physiologia" is the fundamental science.[17]

Ctesibius (1.1.7)

Ctesibius of Alexandria (fl. c. 270) wrote on mechanical inventions and was a pioneer in pneumatics. He is one of Vitruvius's principal sources on several types of machine. (7.praef.14; 9.8.2.; 9.8.4; 10.7.4; 10.7.5).

Archimedes (1.1.7)

Archimedes of Syracuse (c. 287–212 B.C.) was one of the most famous geometers/mathematicians of antiquity and wrote definitive works on several subjects, including treatises on levers and equlibria (i.e., the basis of statics) (1.1.17; 7.praef.14; 8.5.3; 9.praef.9–10).

The architect should know music . . . to calibrate *ballistae*, catapults, and *scorpiones* (1.1.8)

The highly technical catapults of antiquity (described in 10.7) were twin armed torsion machines with independent springs. To ensure an even pull and a straight shot, both arms must have identical pull, and this was achieved by "tuning" the springs (i.e., identical tone would mean identical tension – in fact, the Greek word *tonos* means both "tone" and "tension").[18]

echea (1.1.9)

See Commentary, 5.4 and 5.8.

intervals of a fourth, a fifth . . . double octave (1.1.9)

The Greek terms are diatesseron (through-a-fourth), diapente (through-a-fifth), disdiapason. See Commentary 5.4.1.

inclination of the heavens . . . climates [and four element chemistry] (1.1.10) (Figures 3–5)

Throughout the *Ten Books* "climates" (*climata*) are equivalent to modern parallels of latitude. For their historical evolution in mapmaking, see figures. They were a powerful early tool for the scientific understanding of natural geography, because once the latitudes of various places were established, their natural characteristics could be compared to see to what extent natural features were dependent on latitude. Climates were therefore a major part of the framework of scientific evaluation of place, and the modern meaning of climate is a logical extension of that meaning (meteorologists refer to five major climatic zones: two polar, two temperate and one equatorial).

The inclination of the heavens (*inclinatio mundi*) refers to the inclination of the ecliptic, one of the most pervasive scientific catch phrases in Vitruvius. It refers to a great deal more than just celestial geometry. In Empedoclean chemistry there are only four elements (earth-air-fire-water) in the sublunary realm whose various combination accounts for the variety of all terrestrial phenomena. These elements have a natural inclination to their place (earth lowest and heaviest, then water, then air, then fire; hence the natural inclination of fire, or heated air, to rise, earth to sink through water). However, the rotation of the celestial spheres (i.e., the spheres that guide the movement of the planets and are made of the fifth element, ether) generates the disturbance and mixture of the sublunary/terrestrial elements. An important part of this destabilizing rotation is the movement of the sun along the ecliptic, which generates the seasons. (The relation of the movement of the moon to the tides was also obvious.) Hence the phrase "inclination of the heavens" is almost the short, but scientific, way of saying "the force that generates the diversity of the sublunary realm."

the science of medicine (1.1.10)

The introduction of rational medicine to Rome by professional Greek doctors occurred during the second and first centuries B.C. and medicine remained the one profession in the Roman Empire that was almost exclusively the province of Greek nationals. It was greeted with great suspicion in Rome (Cato regarded the profession as a plot by the conquered Greeks to assassinate their conquerors one by one),[19] in part because administering home remedies had always been the role of the *paterfamilias* (head of household);[20] as late as Pliny the Elder and Columella one finds discussions of medicine in this vein. By the later first century B.C. professional doctors were widely accepted, but continued to exist alongside priestly healers, midwives, herbalists, bone setters and other nonscientific providers of health care.

Ancient rational medicine held that health and illness were the result of balance or imbalance among the four elements (or "humors") of the body, and between the body and the environment. Therapy consisted of the adjustment of the four humors within the body, and of the adjustment between the body and the environment (including "climates," winds, waters, airs, etc.). Hence architecture, and even astronomy (which shaped the "climates"), was virtually an extension of medicine because architecture assisted the adjustment between body and environment.

Writings on rational medicine may have provided a particularly useful model for Vitruvius, because they included both scientific theory and (usually) a realistic appreciation of empirical observation and craft. In the second and first centuries B.C. there were several rival schools. That of the "rationalists" or

17 A. Merrill, "Notes on the Influence of Lucretius on Vitruvius," *Transactions of the American Philological Association* 35 (1904), 17.

18 Also see H. L. Ebeling, "The Value of a Musically Trained Ear in Modern and Ancient Warfare," *Classical Weekly* 25 (1935), 79, which describes an Austrian soldier during World War I who could localize gun emplacements by listening to the note made by a shell at the peak of its trajectory. Cited by Fleury, *Vitruve, De l'architecture*, i, 87.

19 *De Agri cultura* 2.7.

20 R. Jackson, *Doctors and Diseases in the Roman Empire* (London, 1988), 9–10.

"CLIMATES:" MAPMAKING

Rectangular world map of Ephorus (fl. c. 400 B.C.), as schematically represented in the <u>Christian Topography</u> of Cosmas Indicopleustes (sixth century A.D.)(Vat. Gr. 699 fol. 19r)

Reconstructed world map of Dicaearchus of Messana, c. 300 B.C., with "diaphragma" on the latitude of Rhodes. After Aujac, in <u>History of Cartography</u> (Chicago, 1987) fig. 9.2.

Reconstruction of Eratosthenes' <u>sphragides</u>, after Aujac, in <u>History of Cartography</u> 1 (Chicago, 1987) fig. 9.6

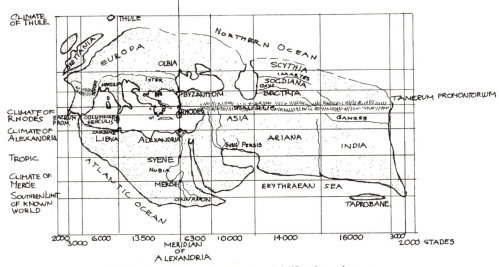

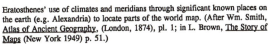

Eratosthenes' use of climates and meridians through significant known places on the earth (e.g. Alexandria) to locate parts of the world map. (After Wm. Smith, <u>Atlas of Ancient Geography</u>, (London, 1874), pl. 1; in L. Brown, <u>The Story of Maps</u> (New York 1949) p. 51.)

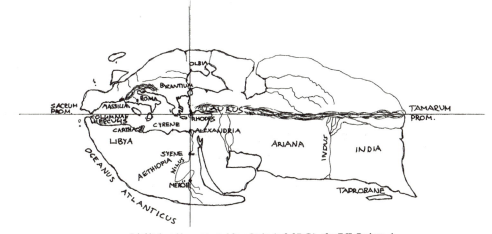

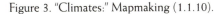

Inhabited world reconstructed from Strabo (c. 9-6 B.C.), after E.H. Bunbury, <u>A History of Ancient Geography</u>, 1-2 (1883; Dover reprint 1959) 2, map facing page 228.)

Figure 3. "Climates:" Mapmaking (1.1.10).

"CLIMATES:" MEASURING THE EARTH (1.1.10)

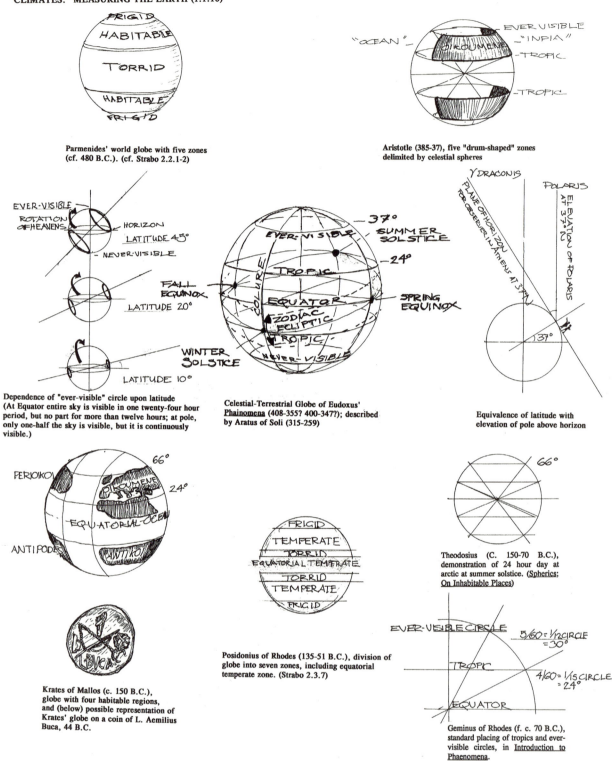

Figure 4. "Climates:" Measuring the Earth (1.1.10).

"CLIMATES" AND LATITUDES (1.1.10)

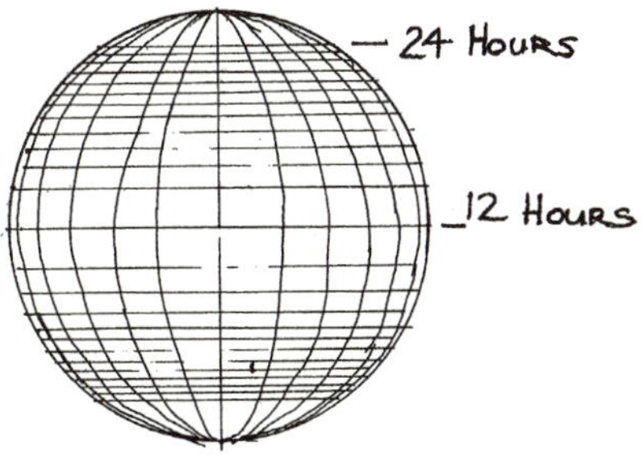
24 Hours
12 Hours

Hipparchus of Nicaea (fl. 161-126 B.C.), graticule for measuring the globe, with 24 meridians spaced one hour apart; the spacing of the "climata" is uncertain, possibly by solstitial hours.

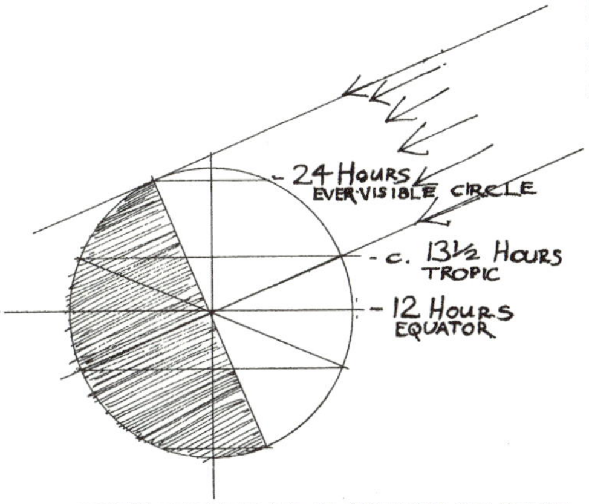
24 Hours
EVER-VISIBLE CIRCLE
c. 13½ Hours
TROPIC
12 Hours
EQUATOR

LENGTH OF THE DAY AT SUMMER SOLSTICE

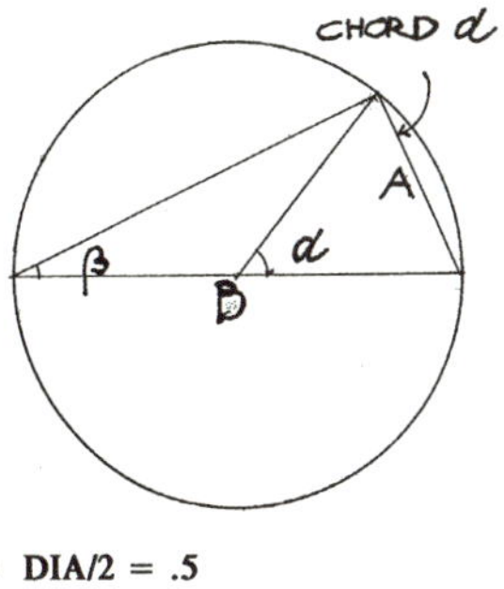
CHORD α
A
β
B
α

<u>Chords Expressed as Fractions of Diameter</u>

CHORD α = A/B

SIN β = A/B

$\alpha = 2\beta$

if α = 60°, CHORD α = DIA/2 = .5

β = 30°, SIN 30° = .5

RELATION OF HIPPARCHUS' CHORDS TO TRIGONOMETRY

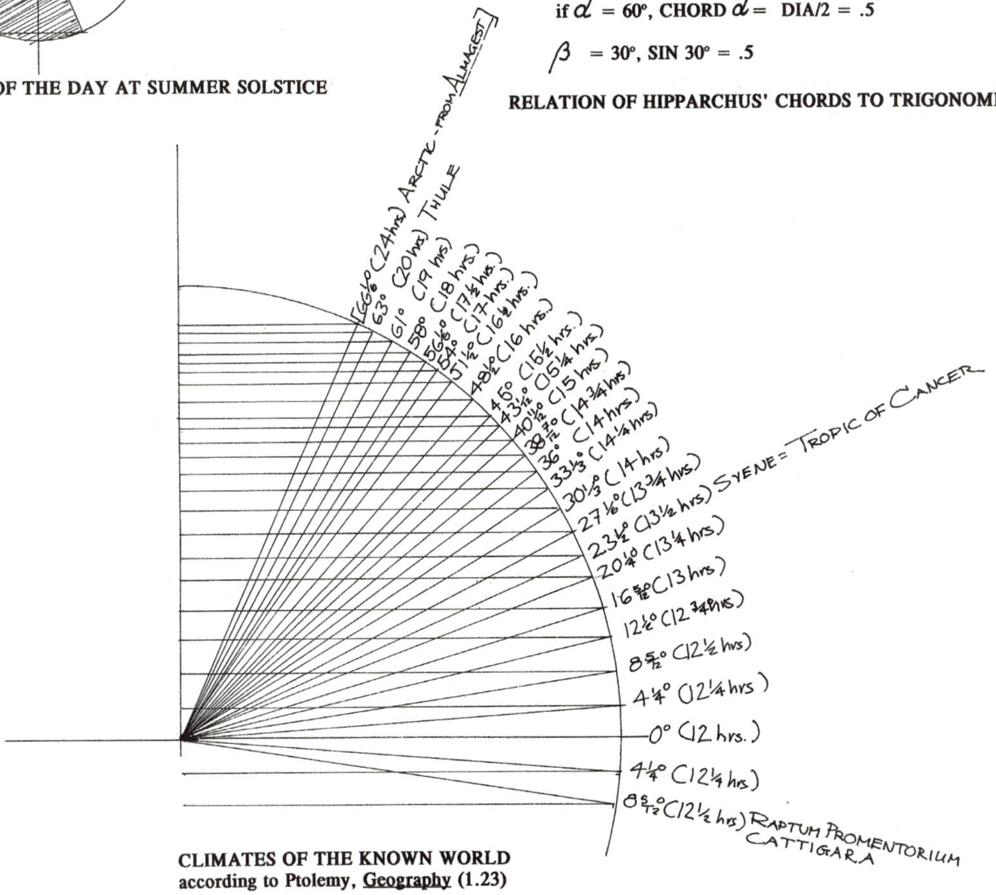
[66⅙° (24 hrs) ARCTIC - FROM ALMAGEST]
63° (20 hrs) THULE
61° (19 hrs)
58° (18 hrs.)
56⅙° (17½ hrs.)
54° (17 hrs.)
51½° (16½ hrs.)
48½° (16 hrs.)
45° (15½ hrs.)
43½° (15¼ hrs)
40½° (15 hrs)
38 7/12° (14¾ hrs)
36° (14 hrs)
33⅓° (14¼ hrs)
30⅓° (14 hrs)
27⅙° (13¾ hrs)
23½° (13½ hrs) SYENE = TROPIC OF CANCER
20¼° (13¼ hrs)
16 5/12° (13 hrs)
12½° (12 ¾ hrs)
8 5/12° (12½ hrs)
4¼° (12¼ hrs)
0° (12 hrs.)
4¼° (12¼ hrs)
8 5/12° (12½ hrs) RAPTUM PROMENTORIUM
CATTIGARA

CLIMATES OF THE KNOWN WORLD
according to Ptolemy, <u>Geography</u> (1.23)

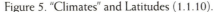

Figure 5. "Climates" and Latitudes (1.1.10).

"Dogmatists" descended from the advanced anatomical studies of Herophilus and Erasistratus in Alexandria in the third century. They were committed to theoretical and speculative medicine and the attempt to apply principles of natural philosophy to the discovery of the "hidden causes" of disease. The "Empiricists" rejected the search for hidden causes and instead concentrated on reading visible signs, avoiding serious interference with natural functions and limiting treatment to known successful cures. A third school, the "Methodists," was founded in Vitruvius's lifetime by Themison (first century B.C.), Thessalus (early first century A.D.), and popularized by Soranus of Ephesus (first century A.D.). They claimed the other schools had made medicine unnecessarily complicated and that all illness depended upon "tenseness" and laxness of the body; treatment followed "methodically" upon this assumption. This sect proved especially popular with Roman aristocrats, on the whole because of its pretension to simplicity. Other schools included the Stoic-based "pneumatists" and Asclepiades of Bithynia (fl. 90–75 B.C.), who rejected the four "humors" in favor of atomism.[21]

law (1.1.10)

Roman law relevant to buildings is divided into several different categories:[22]

- ❖ Building contracts.[23]
- ❖ Maintenance of public/common property. These laws determine responsibility for maintaining common property (party walls and terrace walls), controlling potentially damaging runoff from gutters, and the clearing of rubbish from the streets. This variety of law is particularly well recorded in the Astynomoi inscription of Pergamon, a group of statutes of the Hellenistic period reinscribed and still valid in the second century. In Greece, town officials called *astynomoi* checked compliance, in Rome the same task fell to the neighborhood bosses called *vicomagistri*, who served under the elected aediles.[24]
- ❖ Zoning/building regulations. Augustus introduced major regulations on building heights and materials in the *Lex Iulia de modo aedificiorum urbis*,[25] which was supposed to restrict speculative builders from building dangerous multistory tenements.
- ❖ As Vitruvius makes clear, architects also had to deal with "air rights," or rather light rights.

- ❖ A body of law is attested for a similar profession, the *agrimensores* (land surveyors) who had to deal with classification of types of land, boundaries and fraud and restitution.[26]

so great a profession (*disciplina*) (1.1.11)

Vitruvius slightly precedes the first use of the word *professio* as implying an ethical content to a paid skill or discipline. *Disciplina*, which normally meant a body of skills or knowledge, is his closest equivalent. One of the first references to *professio* that attributes ethical content to skill or workmanship occurs in a medical treatise, *On Remedies*, by Scribonianus Largus (early first century A.D.). Later references include Velleius Paterculus (1.16.2); Celsus, with regard to medicine (1.praef.11); Quintilian, with regard to the grammarian (*Institutiones Oratoriae*, 1.8.15); and Columella (1.praef.26). The earliest medical treatises of the Hippocratic corpus did not impose ethical rules or give love of humanity as a motive for service.[27]

a well-rounded education (*encyclios enim disciplina*) (1.1.12)

On *encyclios disciplina*, or *artes liberales*, see Introduction.

Pytheos (1.1.12)

Pytheos of Priene, mid-fourth century B.C. architect of the temple of Athena (i.e.,"Minerva") at Priene, c. 340 B.C., and the Mausoleum at Halicarnassus, c. 353–51 B.C. (1.1.15; 4.3.1; 7.praef.12).

Aristarchus (1.1.13)

Aristarchus of Samothrace, c. 215–143, head of the Library at Alexandria, and one of the founders of analytical grammar.

Aristoxenus (1.1.13)

Aristoxenus of Taras (Tarentum), c. 350?, pupil of Aristotle, the most influential writer on musical theory in antiquity (5.4.1).

Apelles (1.1.13)

Apelles of Colophon or Cos (fl. later fourth century B.C.), the most celebrated painter in antiquity.

Myron (1.1.13)

Myron of Athens (fl. c. 480–450 B.C.), celebrated early classical sculptor, author of the *Discobolus* (Discus Thrower).

Polycleitus of Argos (1.1.13)

Along with Phidias, probably the most influential high classical sculptor, author of the *canon*, a sculpture and a book explaining its proportions that was highly influential in the theory of proportions in antiquity, including 3.praef.2.

Hippocrates (1.1.13)

Hippocrates of Cos (c. 460–377), a real but somewhat shadowy figure around whom is associated the Hippocratic corpus, the foundation of Greek rational medicine.

21 David C. Lindberg, *The Beginnings of Western Science* (Chicago, 1992), 124; G. E. R. Lloyd, *Greek Science After Aristotle* (New York, 1973), 88–89.

22 M. Voigt, "Die Römische Baugesetze," *Sächsische Akademie der Wissenschaften, Philosophisch-Historische Klasse* 55 (1903), 175–198. D. F. Grose, *The Administration of the City of Rome Under the Republic* (Harvard University, Diss., 1975); J. C. Anderson, Jr., *Roman Architecture and Society* (Baltimore and London, 1997), 68–113 et passim.

23 J. C. Anderson, Jr., *Roman Architecture and Society* (Baltimore and London, 1997), 68–75.

24 R. Martin, *L'Urbanisme dans la Grèce antique* (Paris 1975–2), "Règlements d'urbanisme," 48–74, and to the Astynomoi inscription of Pergamon, one of the best preserved testimonia to property law, with translation in French, 58–59. Also H. Vetters, *Die Römerzeitlichen Bauvorschriften*, in *Forschung und Funde* (Festschrift B. Neutsch) (Innsbruck, 1980), 477–485.

25 Strabo, *Geography* 5.3.7.

26 O. A. W. Dilke, *The Roman Land Surveyors* (Newton Abbot, 1971), 63–65.

27 L. Edelstein, "The Ethics of Greek Medicine," in idem, *Ancient Medicine* (Baltimore and London, 1967, 1987), 319–348; 337–339.

doctors and musicians share knowledge of the rhythm of our veins' pulse (1.1.15)

In the absence of precise timepieces, musical theory was the most precise way of measuring, or characterizing, rhythm. The bases of diagnosing health by using the concepts of musical rhythm for analyzing the pulse were laid by Herophilus of Chalcedon, who was one of the founders of advanced medical study in Alexandria in the third century. As Galen reports, "as the musicians establish their rhythms according to certain definite arrangements of time periods, comparing the *arsis* with *thesis* [raising and placing of a step, i.e., upbeat and downbeat], so Herophilus supposes that the dilation of the artery corresponds to its *arsis* and its contraction to its *thesis*."[28] This gave the analysis of the pulse a mathematical basis, like the analysis of rhythm.

astronomers and musicians discuss certain things in common (1.1.16)

Many fields of Hellenistic knowledge shared common methods, including a reliance on diagrams based on Euclidean geometry. See figures.

the harmony of the stars (1.1.16) (Figures 6, 90)

What later became known as the "music of the spheres" was originally a concept of Pythagorean cosmology, which expressed the idea that the orbits of the planets are spaced according to musical intervals.[29] The tones were created by the rotation of the crystalline spheres, the pitch depended on the velocity of the sphere, and the velocity depended on distance from the center of the cosmos. The outer spheres were faster and produced higher notes.[30] The sound of the spheres produces a powerful harmony that we cannot hear because it is uniform and because we are used to it.

Aristarchus of Samos (1.1.17)

Astronomer (c. 310–230 B.C.), proponent of a radical heliocentric cosmos.

Philolaos of Tarentum (1.1.17)

A Pythagorean philosopher (died c. 390 B.C.?).

Archytas of Tarentum (1.1.17)

Geometer and mathematician (c. 450–360 B.C.), cited in 9.8.1 as the inventor of a type of sundial and in 9.praef.14 as the discoverer of a geometrical demonstration of doubling the cube.

Apollonius of Perge (1.1.17)

One of the most advanced mathematicians in antiquity (c. 262–190 B.C.); wrote on the sophisticated curvatures generated by conic sections; inventor of a type of sundial (9.8.1).

Eratosthenes of Cyrene (1.1.17)

Librarian of Alexandria (c. 284–192) and one of the greatest polymaths of antiquity (called "Beta" because he was the second most knowledgeable person in every field but the leader in none).

Archimedes of Syracuse (1.1.17)

See above, 1.1.7.

Scopinas of Syracuse (1.1.17)

Otherwise unattested; cited in 9.8.1 as the inventor of a type of sundial.

orator (*rhetor*), grammarian (1.1.18)

Grammarian and rhetor were two level of teacher: the *grammaticus* had younger students (ages 12–15); the *rhetor* taught specialized rhetoric and was paid higher fees. Cicero, *De Officiis* 2.19.79; 250 versus 200 denarii in the Diocletianic code of 301: *Ed. Pret.* 7.70.71.

The Terms of Architecture (1.2.1–9) (Figures 7–10)

The terms in this section are mainly adaptations from philosophical or theoretical literature (particularly discussions of rhetoric, but also music theory), but the basis of his concepts seems to be actual activities of the design process. The "five parts of rhetoric"[31] included *inventio*, *dispositio*, *elocutio* (variously translated eloquence, ornament or style), *memoria* (memory training), and *pronuntiatio* (the actual delivery, with gestures etc.). Vitruvius uses two of the same terms (*inventio* and *dispositio*) but otherwise the system seems to be his own invention, essentially an attempt to create analytical terms based on the activities of design. The terms *eurythmia* and *symmetria* are borrowed from Greek writings on aesthetics, eurythmia probably from music and visual arts.[32]

The strict linear sequence of design activities implied here is probably more of a literary convention than a reflection of standard practice. Throughout the *Ten Books* Vitruvius was very concerned also to lay out his work *in ordine*.[33] The concern for

---

28 C. G. Kuehn, *Claudii Galeni Opera Omnia*, (Leipzig, 1821–1833), vol. 9, 464; G. E. R. Lloyd, *Greek Science after Aristotle* (New York, 1973), 79–80.

29 It was a commonly known idea derived from the Chaldaean Babylonians in the later sixth century B.C. It continues to be known, although more as a philosophical or poetic idea than a scientific one, and Pliny the Elder reports the Pythagorean source in the first century A.D., *Natural History* 2.84.

30 Alexander of Aphrodisias, *Commentary on Aristotle's Metaphysics*, 542a, 5–18; translation in Coehna and Brabkin, *A Source Book in Greek Science* (Cambridge, Mass., 1948), 96. Aristotle, *De Caelo* 2.13.

31 The first mention of them is in Cicero's youthful textbook on rhetoric, *De Inventione*, c. 92–88 B.C., which suggests that they were already canonical at this time. G. Kennedy, *A New History of Classical Rhetoric* (Princeton, 1994), 120. Also Cicero, *De Oratore* 1.79. In 9.praef.17 Vitruvius specifically claims to have read Cicero on the art of rhetoric and Varro on the Latin language.

32 This appears to be the only ancient use of the term *eurythmia* in the field of architecture. P. Fleury, *Vitruve, De l'architecture* i, 112; R. Falus, *Sur la théorie de la module*, 255–256; L. Bek, "Venusta species. A Hellenistic Rhetorical Concept as the Aesthetic Principle in Roman Townscape," *ARID* 14 (1985), 142–143.

33 2.7.1; 2.10.3; 4.1.1; 10.praef.4.

"...DISCUSS CERTAIN THINGS IN COMMON" (1.1.16)

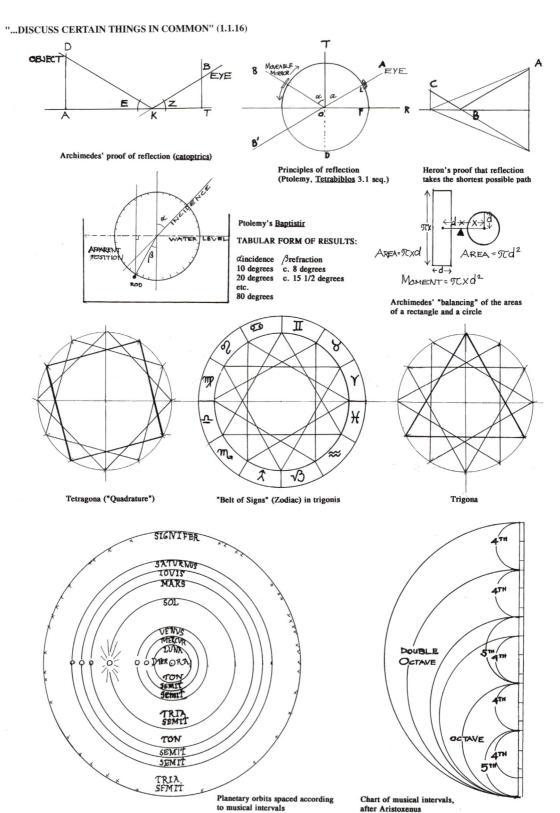

Archimedes' proof of reflection (catoptrics)

Principles of reflection
(Ptolemy, Tetrabiblos 3.1 seq.)

Heron's proof that reflection
takes the shortest possible path

Ptolemy's Baptistir

TABULAR FORM OF RESULTS:

αincidence   βrefraction
10 degrees   c. 8 degrees
20 degrees   c. 15 1/2 degrees
etc.
80 degrees

Archimedes' "balancing" of the areas
of a rectangle and a circle

Tetragona ("Quadrature")

"Belt of Signs" (Zodiac) in trigonis

Trigona

Planetary orbits spaced according
to musical intervals

Chart of musical intervals,
after Aristoxenus

Figure 6. "... discuss certain things in common" (1.1.16).

THE ELEMENTS OF ARCHITECTURE (1.2.1-9)

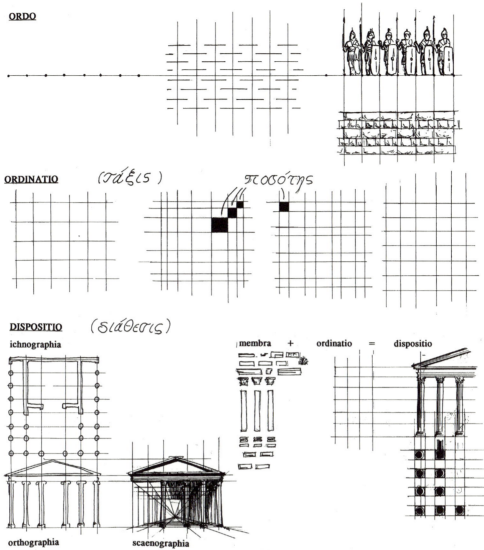

ORDO

ORDINATIO (τάξις) ποσότης

DISPOSITIO (διάθεσις)

ichnographia

membra + ordinatio = dispositio

orthographia scaenographia

Figure 7. The Elements of Architecture: *Ordo, Ordinatio, Dispositio* (1.2.1–9).

THE ELEMENTS OF ARCHITECTURE (1.2.1-9)

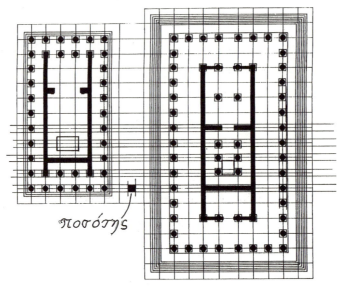

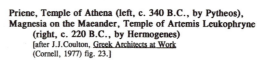

Priene, Temple of Athena (left, c. 340 B.C., by Pytheos),
Magnesia on the Maeander, Temple of Artemis Leukophryne
(right, c. 220 B.C., by Hermogenes)
[after J.J.Coulton, <u>Greek Architects at Work</u>
(Cornell, 1977) fig. 23.]

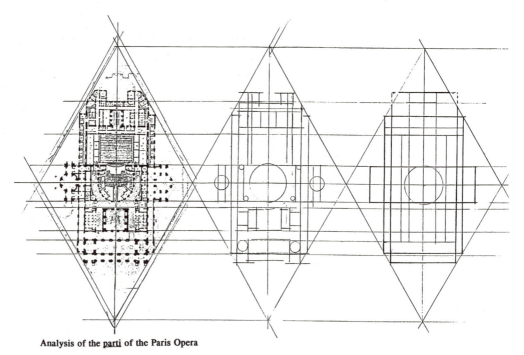

Analysis of the <u>parti</u> of the Paris Opera

Figure 8. The Elements of Architecture: The *Ordinatio* Grid (1.2.1–9).

THE ELEMENTS OF ARCHITECTURE (1.2.1-9)

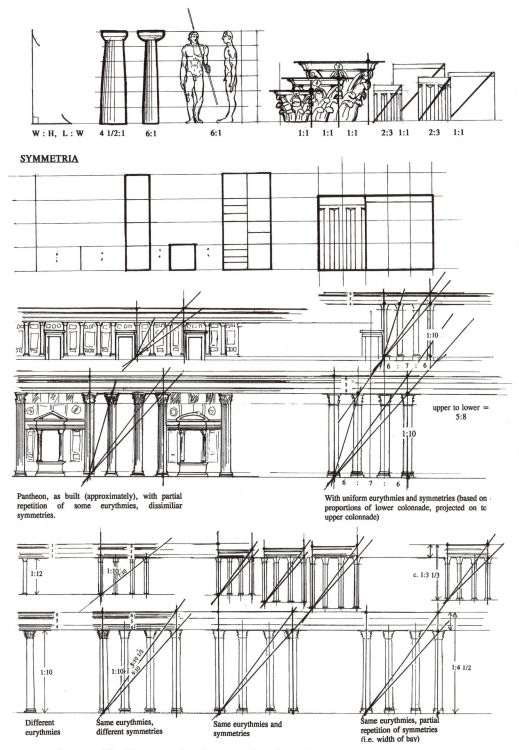

Figure 9. The Elements of Architecture: *Eurythmia, Symmetria* (1.2.1–9).

SYMMETRY IN NATURE AND DESIGN (1.2.4)

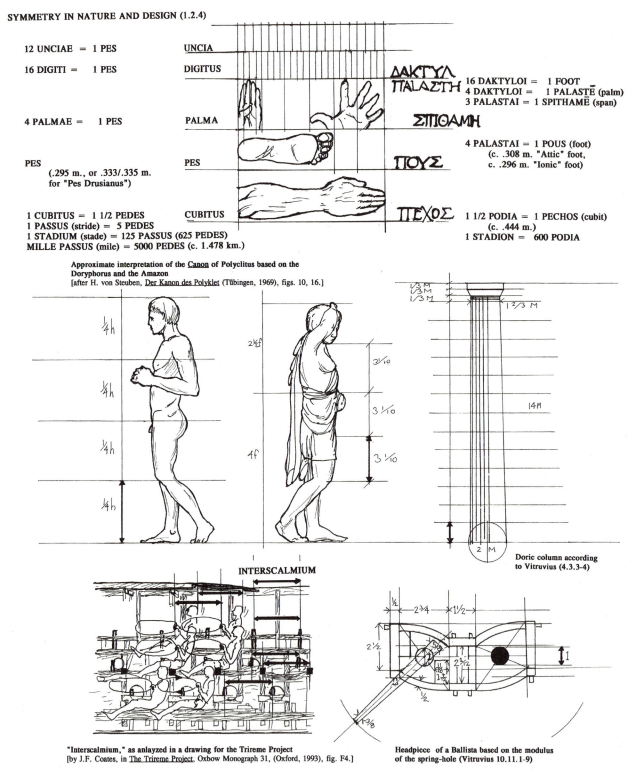

12 UNCIAE = 1 PES   UNCIA

16 DIGITI = 1 PES   DIGITUS   ΔΑΚΤΥΛ
     ΠΑΛΑΣΤΗ   16 DAKTYLOI = 1 FOOT
     4 DAKTYLOI = 1 PALASTĒ (palm)
     3 PALASTAI = 1 SPITHAMĒ (span)

4 PALMAE = 1 PES   PALMA   ΣΠΙΘΑΜΗ

     4 PALASTAI = 1 POUS (foot)
     (c. .308 m. "Attic" foot,
     c. .296 m. "Ionic" foot)

PES   PES   ΠΟΥΣ
     (.295 m., or .333/.335 m.
     for "Pes Drusianus")

1 CUBITUS = 1 1/2 PEDES   CUBITUS   ΠΕΧΟΣ   1 1/2 PODIA = 1 PECHOS (cubit)
1 PASSUS (stride) = 5 PEDES   (c. .444 m.)
1 STADIUM (stade) = 125 PASSUS (625 PEDES)   1 STADION = 600 PODIA
MILLE PASSUS (mile) = 5000 PEDES (c. 1.478 km.)

Approximate interpretation of the <u>Canon</u> of Polyclitus based on the
Doryphorus and the Amazon
[after H. von Steuben, <u>Der Kanon des Polyklet</u> (Tübingen, 1969), figs. 10, 16.]

Doric column according
to Vitruvius (4.3.3-4)

INTERSCALMIUM

"Interscalmium," as anlayzed in a drawing for the Trireme Project
[by J.F. Coates, in <u>The Trireme Project</u>, Oxbow Monograph 31, (Oxford, 1993), fig. F4.]

Headpiece of a Ballista based on the modulus
of the spring-hole (Vitruvius 10.11.1-9)

Figure 10. Symmetry in Nature and Design (1.2.4).

proper linear presentation, as well the analysis of various aspects into components, was a common feature of the analytical and informational literature of the first century B.C.[34]

Ordering (1.2.2) (Figure 7)

Ordering (*ordinatio*, gr. *taxis*), appears to be the initial commitment to a geometrical system that controls the subsequent design, usually a modular layout (not necessarily a grid), because it consists of deciding the quantity of the module, and unites the individual parts to the overall proportional system (*symmetriae*).[35]

design [*dispositio*] (1.2.2) (Figure 7)

Design (disposition, *dispositio*, Greek *diathesis*)[36] appears to describe the next stage of designing, which consists of placing (disposing) the major plan (and elevation) elements (walls, doors, columns) on divisions or subdivisions of the "ordinatio/taxis" grid. Vitruvius discusses disposition in terms of drawings. "Ichnography," "orthography" and "scenography" must refer to plans, elevations and rendered (shadow-cast) perspectives. Vitruvius discusses drawing as an appendage of *dispositio* because this activity of design involves, in effect, clothing the weightless and ordering abstraction of the *ordinatio-taxis* grid with the visible elements of architecture (*membra*).

Taken together *ordinatio* and *dispositio* sound remarkably like the concept of the *parti*, which has become familiar to twentieth century designers through their heritage from the late nineteenth century planning tradition of the Ecole des Beaux-Arts.[37] (Figure 8). The *parti* is now taken to be the fundamental geometrical diagram or pattern that is the basis of a given design; as the design develops, it continues to shape the decisions.

In Vitruvius the idea tends to be simpler, and apparently is thought of as a modular grid (although not necessarily rigidly confined to that). This grid sounds remarkably like the Hellenistic tradition of Ionic temple design codified by Hermogenes, which is the tradition in which Vitruvius probably was trained.[38]

Interpreting disposition as the point where the basic practical design decisions are made (i.e., walls, columns, doors are placed, or "disposed") is reinforced by Vitruvius's assertion that disposition is produced by **analysis** and **invention**, which implies analyzing the site and inventing arrangements or dispositions appropriate to the needs. Vitruvius uses the word again in 1.3.2 to state that utility depends on "the disposition of the spaces."

Shapeliness (1.2.3) (Figure 9)

"Shapeliness" (*eurythmia*) has long been a controversial term in ancient art criticism, but its most basic meaning is simply "good shape" and takes that meaning from its earliest appearances[39] in reference to such practical judgments as "well-fitting" armor, and later is extended to more aesthetic discussions, such as explanations of optical adjustments.[40] ("*Rhythmos*" means shape, and only by extension to dance becomes shape in movement, i.e., recognizable pattern in motion). Later and modern interpretations conclude that the basic meaning of eurythmy is "pleasing appearance" (*venusta species* in Vitruvius). This is often

---

34 Clarity of order was a major concern of the expository writers of the first century B.C. in many fields. They often felt that they had found the knowledge of their field in a disorderly heap and saw it being practiced with no sense of rules. Cicero, *De Oratore* 1.14, on the first enthusiasm for rhetoric: "At first, indeed, in their complete ignorance of method, since they thought there was no definite course of training or any rules of art, they used to attain what skill they could by means of their natural ability and of reflection." trans. E. W. Sutton, H. Rackham, Loeb Classical Library (London, 1988). The first handbooks of rhetoric, such as that of Marcus Antonius (late second century B.C.), did not as a whole develop a technical terminology. G. A. Kennedy, *A New History of Classical Rhetoric* (Princeton, 1994), 113.

35 The concept has roots in the original meaning of the Latin word *ordo*, which refers to the warp of the loom, the repetitive threads that hold the woven woof. In all cases it means orderly sequence or succession, and has strong implications of soundness, both moral and material. It is the type of linear repetition that holds together a military or social rank, a course of masonry, or a piece of fabric. Vitruvius uses the word in mundane ways that are in keeping with common Latin usage, to mean a line of objects placed next to one another. In the *Ten Books* Vitruvius uses *ordo* for a line of columns (3.2.6; 3.2.7); courses of masonry (2.8.4; 2.8.6); the order of nations from north to south (6.1.6); pulleys arranged vertically (10.2.5); and several times for the orderly sequence of his expositions in the *Ten Books* (2.7.1; 2.10.3; 4.1.1; 10.praef.4). It also had a common meaning of which he must have been aware, that of a line or rank of soldiers standing abreast. (The Greek word *taxis* has the same meaning.) He also uses the word more theoretically, as in "ordering" parts of a temple (3.1.9), transferring the dispositions of Tuscan temples to the "orderings" (i.e., types of plan) of Corinthian (4.8.5), and the ordering and symmetries of temples as taught by his ancestors. It never means the "orders" (i.e., types of trabeation.)

36 Literally, a putting down, placing.

37 Strictly speaking, what is diagrammed here on top of the plan of the Paris Opera is not, in the sense of the Ecole, the *parti*, but more an analysis of the compositional approach, the *composition pure*. By the late nineteenth century, *parti* seems to have meant the initial choice (*prendre parti* = to take a part, to take a stand) about the way the "network" of spaces (i.e., "circulations") should function. It was the generative idea of the subsequent development of the plan, but it might be seen as a pregeometrical idea. Plan development proceeded through "distribution," which was the relative apportionment of the amounts of spaces, "disposition," which was the development of their order, and "composition," which was the giving of a coherent overall shape. In architectural schools today, *parti* normally refers to the underlying, but often elusive, basic geometry which then is modified as the design develops. See David Van Zanten, "Architectural Composition at the Ecole des Beaux-Arts from Charles Percier to Charles Garnier," in *The Architecture of the Ecole des Beaux-Arts* (MIT Press, 1977), 112–324.

38 T. N. Howe, "An Early Imperial Pseudodipteral Temple from Sardis," *American Journal of Archaeology* 90 (1986), 45–68; idem, "The Stylobate Curvature of the Artemis Temple at Sardis and the End of the Hellenistic Tradition Temple Planning," in *Appearance and Essence: Refinements of Classical Architecture: Curvature* (University of Pennsylvania, 1997, in press).

39 Xenophon, *Memorabilia*, 3.10.10–12 (early fourth century B.C.).

40 Philo Mechanicus, *Syntaxis* 4.4.

taken to imply that symmetry is that aspect of appearance which is controlled by mathematical proportions, whereas eurythmy is the softening of that appearance by intuitive, non-mathematical modifications.[41]

In Vitruvius the term gains one very specific meaning; for him it seems to be the determination of the internal or immanent proportions of the individual members, that is, as he says, length to breadth, height to width, and so on. These internal proportions are, after all, what give the individual elements much of their particular character (i.e., their "shapes"). Hence the 1:6 relationship in a Doric column (lower diameter to height) provides eurythmy by giving it a character of "masculine" strength, which can then be made more "graceful" by changing the proportions to 1:7. In Vitruvius, therefore, eurythmy does have a geometric component, derived from the act of design, but unlike symmetry, eurythmy does not feature the repetition of modules. The proportion of length to breadth, and so on, can be chosen for irrational, aesthetic-intuitive reasons of "pleasing appearance" rather than mutual divisibility.

Symmetry (1.2.4) (Figure 9)

Symmetry (*symmetria*, commensurability) means that all of the elements in a building should not only have their own particular proportions (shapes or eurythmies), but those sets of particular proportions should also have common relationships, or common divisors, that bind them all into a whole. A triglyph, for instance, commonly has a particular proportion (eurythmy) of 2:3, and a metope of 1:1, but when they appear together in the same entablature symmetry demands that the 3 of the triglyph equals the 1 of the metope. Vitruvius gives the word *commensus* ("shared measure") as a Latin synonym in 1.3.2.

The ancient idea of symmetry, as the Greek word (and its Latin equivalent) specifically imply, demands that its relationships must be truly measurable. Irrational geometric relationships, like the diagonal of the square or the "golden section," are not strictly speaking "sym-metrical," measurable together, expressible as a ratio of fixed integers.

Analytic example (Figure 9): the Pantheon, for instance, has the notorious disjunction between the upper and lower trabeations ("orders") of the interior, which are of different scales and do not align vertically.[42] They are both similarly divided into four column units, but the entablature of the lower order is approximately one-fifth the height of the columns, and the entablature of the upper order is about one-third; the width of the four-column unit of the lower order is

about equal to the height of the columns, in the upper order it is about one and one-third the height of the columns. In other words, to correct Bernini,[43] if the columns and pilasters have the same proportions in both orders, then the two orders must be said to have the same eurythmy but different symmetries. If the upper order had the same proportions in all ways as the lower (height to column to height of entablature, height to intercolumniation), then they could be said to have had the same symmetries and eurythmies, but there would still be two distinct symmetry systems, at different scales. If there were some measurable relationship between the upper and lower symmetry systems, e.g., such that every dimension of the upper order were three-fifths of the lower, then both orders could be said to have a single symmetry.

In summary: eurythmy refers to the internal proportions that control the "shapeliness" of the individual parts; symmetry denotes the connecting measurable relationships between certain of the linear dimensions of all the individual shapes-eurythmies; the *ordinatio* grid is that which binds them all together to achieve the effect of symmetry, and design (*dispositio*) is the placing of the actual parts of the building on that grid.

human body . . . shapeliness . . . based on cubit, foot, palm; in a ballista; in boats from the oarlock (1.1.4) (Figure 10)

These are all examples of modular design, related by Vitruvius to the source of common units of measure in the parts of the human body. The exact term for the lower diameter of a Doric column is either *embatêr* or *embatês*, with little or no difference in meaning.[44]

Correctness (1.2.5)

Correctness (*decorum*, *decor*) generally means things as they are and as they have been handed down through the course of history, but for Vitruvius history is a critical process of discovery that accumulates across many generations. Things become accepted by "proven means" (*probatis rebus*) only by test, and by achieving a certain general acceptance.

---

41 For an excellent summary of sources and critical discussion, see J. J. Pollitt, *The Ancient View of Greek Art* (New Haven, 1974), 167–180.

42 T. Marder, "Bernini and Alexander VII: Criticism and Praise of the Pantheon in the Seventeenth Century," *Art Bulletin* 71 (1989) 628–645; W. Loerke, "A Rereading of the Interior Elevation of Hadrian's Rotunda," *Journal of the Society of Architectural Historians* 49 (1990), 22–43.

43 Marder ascribes Bernini's supposed opposition to removing the disjunctive upper order on the grounds that it had the same "euritmia" and "simmetria" as the lower, and therefore he was the first to recognize that the four-column unit of the upper followed the four-column unit of the lower. The proportions are not the same, however, which means that the interpretation ascribed to Bernini is not the same presented here. Marder, op. cit., 1989.

44 Both words are derived from the Greek *embainô*, "step into," and are attested in Greek sources. The basic sense of the word can be traced to the idea that the ground plan of a building was equivalent to its "footprint," an idea represented literally in the words *ichnographia* and *vestigium*. The manuscript tradition of the term, twice attested in Vitruvius, is entirely ambiguous; it reads *embatere* for 1.3.4 and *embates* for 4.3.3. Most modern editors follow Giocondo in choosing to read *embatêr*. Rose's emendation to *embate* was anticipated by Angelo Colocci in his annotations to his copy of Giocondo's edition: BAV, Stampati, R.I.III.298 (I).

For Cicero decorum represented a suitable harmony of thoughts, gestures, and words that were appropriate to a person's age, station, and activity.[45] It was a kind of self-control that had as its goal the approval of others, in other words, general acceptance, and this general acceptance is a constituent part of its authority. In Cicero this concern for others' opinions may represent the web of social obligations that acted as checks and balances on the family ambitions of the upper classes in Rome, but in Vitruvius this kind of mutual attention to the activities and accomplishments of others is a positive force in the growth of culture.[46]

Vitruvius subdivides *decor* into three aspects. **Function** (or prescription, *statio*, Greek *thematismos*) is laid down by tradition and is more or less formally described; **tradition** (or custom, *consuetudo*) is commonly, or tacitly, accepted through general use (*tradere* emphasizes the aspect of handing over; hence tradition and treason have a common root). Accordingly, the degree of elegance of "vestibules" and "interiors," or the fact that triglyphs do not appear over cushion (Ionic) capitals, are customary, not prescribed phenomena. By **nature** Vitruvius really does mean nature. Hence the three aspects of correctness are (1) formal cultural rules, (2) that which is tacitly accepted in a culture, and (3) that which is clearly prescribed by nature.

Allocation (1.2.9)

Allocation (*distributio*) is fairly straightforward and refers in general to practical management of costs and material. It might seem odd that the second aspect of allocation, the appropriateness of the expense of the house to the status of the owner, does not come under *decor*. In a sense it must, but in general allocation is the design consideration that involves overall estimate of cost, which is determined primarily by two things: the materials and the needs of the client.

The Divisions [or applications] of Architecture (1.3.1–2)

Vitruvius presents three parallel systems of analysis for the topic of "architecture." The habit of providing several parallel analyses for the same subject persists throughout the *Ten Books*. In Book 10 he provides three separate analyses of types of machines or their types of motion (10.1.1–3; 10.3.1–6). In these three contiguous sections he provides three subdivisions of architecture: 1.2.1–9; 1.3.1; 1.3.2.

the choice of a healthy site (1.4.1–1.5.1) (Figure 11)

There is considerable ancient literature on the siting of cities, much of it dominated by practical considerations of hygiene, agricultural land, defense, and commerce.[47] There is also substantial ritual attached to the foundation of new cities in Greek, Etruscan and Roman culture.

Almost all of the considerations which Vitruvius discusses in Chapters 4 through 7 about the process of setting up a new colony or town (winds, healthful sites, defense, roads and ports, etc.) would in fact have been the specific responsibility of a group of administrators delegated from the Senate and their staff of professional assistants. The fact that Vitruvius lists virtually all of the activities of planning in the *Ten Books* may indicate that, at least in his opinion, an architect, and not the *agrimensor* (land surveyor) or *mensor* (surveyor), was the chief professional whose duty it was to advise on the actual choice of site.

The foundation of colonies of Roman citizens in newly conquered territories became a common part of Roman policy from the fourth century B.C. and was still a continuous part of architectural activity in Vitruvius's time.[48] The administration of the new foundation was normally put in the hands of high-ranking commissioners (the *tresviri coloniae deducendae*), often of senatorial rank. (C. Asinius Pollio, for instance, a Caesarian and consul in 40 B.C., who in 39 founded the first "public" library in Rome in the rebuilt Atrium Libertatis, was a land commissioner who, in 42 B.C., was in charge of settling the veterans of Philippi on land near Mantua in northern Italy.)[49] It was their duty to choose the site, define the boundaries, subdivide the surrounding territory into allotments, enroll the new settlers, draw up and publish a foundation charter, and appoint the first officeholders. Normally each settler received a lot in the town and a farm plot in the surrounding territory. The commissioners received full discretionary powers, or *imperium*, to execute their task, and they were provided with a staff of trained *agrimensores* (surveyors), *finitores* (assistant land commissioners or "establishers of boundaries") and possibly architects. The records of land allotments were published, probably in the form of the publicly displayed stone plans of centuriated land of the town of Arausio (Orange) in southern France, and one copy of a bronze map was kept in the tabularium of the chief town of

45 Cicero, *De Officiis* 1.110 seq; 1.126–140. Written in the fall of 44 B.C. These sections are a catalog of types of behavior, dress, and so on, appropriate to various ages and stations, and end, as does this section in Vitruvius, with a description of what is appropriate in a nobleman's house.

46 As G. B. Conte points out, "The constant attention to what others may think and the concern not to hurt their feelings are a result of the dense web of social obligations in which the members of the upper classes at Rome find themselves enmeshed." G. B. Conte, *A History of Latin Literature*, trans. J. B. Solodow (Baltimore, 1994), 197–198. This is further expressed in Vitruvius by the history of the rise of the arts of humanity in 2.1.1–9.

47 Aristotle, *Politics* 7.10.1330a; Xenophon, *Memorabilia* 3.8.9; J. B. Ward-Perkins, *Cities of Ancient Greece and Italy: Planning in Classical Antiquity* (New York, 1974), 40; R. Martin, *Urbanisme dans la Grèce antique* (Paris, 1956), 38 ff.

48 For summary and critical discussions, see Ward-Perkins, op. cit., Appendices 1 and 2, 37–40; F. Castagnoli, *Orthogonal Town Planning in Antiquity* (Cambridge and London, 1972), 180–197; F. E. Brown, *Cosa 2* (Memoirs of the American Academy in Rome 26, 1960)9–19.

49 The founding of a colony of citizen landowners implied that the land was not previously owned or had been expropriated. It was this resettlement of Mantua that deprived Virgil of his hereditary estates. Virgil, *Eclogue* 9.27–29.

the district and another copy was supposedly deposited in the Tabularium in Rome.[50]

Thus I emphatically assert my opinion that the old principles for selecting a site . . . (1.4.9) (Figures 12, 13)

Vitruvius refers to the art of divination, or of reading the entrails of animals, especially the liver (haruspication), which was a widespread Italic practice; the *Etrusca Disciplina* was a particularly expert record of the practice.[51] The liver, which contains one-sixth of the body's blood, was regarded as the seat of life and therefore at any given time could serve as a mirror of the immediate world at the time of sacrifice. Over time priests developed a science of "correspondences" between the appearance of the liver and outward events, which became codified in traditions like the *Etrusca Disciplina*, with priests trained and licensed in the practices. The major preserved documents of this tradition are the Piacenza liver, a third-century B.C. bronze model liver presumably used for instruction, and the late Antique author Martianus Capella.[52]

The priestly discipline came about, therefore, by means of a tradition of critical observation and an assumption of a relationship between a body and its environment, features which it shared with later rational medicine. The taking of the auspices was no simple ritual matter; the results often were inconclusive and had to be carefully evaluated or repeated, or one type of divination (reading the liver or intestines) might cancel or reverse the reading of another, such as the reading of birds in the sky.[53] Cato the Elder also recommends that one examine the appearance of the inhabitants of a site before buying an agricultural villa there.[54]

There are also certain similarities between the practices of Roman surveyors and Etruscan-Latin augury.[55] Surveyors and augurs both "quartered" their view, usually as if facing west,

and they both referred to the division of territory by left-right, forward-back rather than north-south-east-west.

The first stage in the ritual (or science) of augury was the *conregio*, literally, the fixing of the regions, which amounts to defining the *templum*, or the place set aside for the taking of the auguries.[56] The augur would choose a position, presumably high ground with a clear view of the horizon,[57] and make a diagram on the ground in front of him with a *lituus*, a knotless staff, which divided his view into left and right (*sinistra et dextra*), and behind and forward (*postica et antica*). He would also note objects on the horizon to mark this division.[58] The pattern would have an outer boundary and the whole would constitute the *templum*, which is in effect an area "cut off" or set aside. Varro recommends that it should have a continuous fence with not more than one entrance.[59] The augur would stand some distance behind the *decussis* (intersection) of the two dividing lines, hooded, which would have focused his view.[60] The next stages of the ritual involved the observation of events (usually the flights of birds) in the four quadrants and the critical evaluation of them.[61]

In land surveying the placing of the *groma*, the surveying instrument, at the center point of the survey, was, like most serious acts in Roman society, preceded by the taking of auguries, and the area of the survey had the same kinds of conspicual designation as the *templum* of the augury: the area of the survey was orthogonally divided by a *cardo* and a *decumanus* and plots were identified by the terms "this side of

50 O. A. W. Dilke, *The Roman Land Surveyors* (Newton Abbot, 1971), 112–113, 63–65; Hyginus Gromaticus (ed. Blume) 1.196.

51 The *Etrusca Disciplina* was recorded in Etruscan on books of woven linen; it seems in particular to have concerned divination from thunder, lightning, livers, and bird omens, as well as the particulars of sacrifice. Ideas about Etruscan origins and practices are recorded in late Republican works by Cicero, the so-called prophecy of Vegoia, A. Caecina, and the Fasti (tables of religious festivals) set up at Praeneste by Verrius Flaccus.

52 Martianus Capella, *De nuptiis Mercurii et Philologiae*, in C. Thulin, *Die Götter von Martianus Capella und die Bronzeleber von Piacenza* (Giessen, 1906). See also Ambros Josef Pfiffig, *Religio Etrusca* (Graz, 1975).

53 See J. Rykwert, *The Idea of a Town. The Anthropology of Urban Form in Rome, Italy and the Ancient World* (Princeton, 1976), 44–49, 51–58.

54 *De Agri cultura* 1.

55 Ward-Perkins, *Cities of Ancient Greece and Italy*, 38–40; J. Rykwert, *The Idea of a Town* (London, 1976), 44–49, 51–58. Frontinus and Hyginus Gromaticus specifically say that the practice of establishing *limites* (land boundaries) derives from observing the course of the sun and from the practices of the augurs of the *Etrusca Disciplina*. Hyginus Gromaticus (ed. Thulin) 131; Frontinus (ed. Thulin) 10.

56 Varro, *De Lingua Latina* 7.8. The word *templum*, which derived from an Indo-European root meaning "to cut," originally referred to a consecrated place "cut off" from the profane world. This *templum* contained a section of earth, sky, and horizon, and might or might not include an altar (*ara*), shrine (*fanum*), or a building (*aedis sacra*, "sacred building"). Vitruvius always scrupulously uses the term *aedis sacra* to denote built temples, but in so doing he is probably distinctly old fashioned. His near contemporary Cicero, himself a stickler for precise language, uses *templum* as we use "temple" to refer to a religious building.

57 Although not always; auguries were sometimes taken from the rostra of the Comitium in the Forum. On the other hand, Cicero reports the destruction of an apartment building on the Caelian hill because it obstructed the view of the Capitoline *auguraculum*, even though it was 1.5 km away. *De Officiis* 3.66.

58 Varro, *De Lingua Latina* 7.8; Livy 1.18.

59 *De Lingua Latina* 7.13.

60 Frontinus and Hyginus, the surveyors, and Livy, the historian, say that he faced west because the sun and the moon travel that way; Varro says he faced south. Frontinus also says that this is why "some architects" have written that temples should face west. (Greek temples normally are supposed to face east.) Hyginus Gromaticus (ed. Thulin) 131; Frontinus (ed. Thulin) 10; Livy 1.18; Varro, *De Lingua Latina* 7.7.

61 The *conspicio*, which was the augur's observation, and the *contumio*, the assessment of the events. The entire ritual was called the *contemplatio*, referring to the process of making a *templum*. Romulus won his contest with Remus in the *inauguratio* of Rome because he saw more vultures from his perch on the Palatine than Remus did on the Aventine. Plutarch, *Romulus* 35; Dionysius of Halicarnassus 1.79.

THE SITING OF CITIES
(Health, 1.4.1-12; Defense and Surrounding Territory, 1.5.1; Allocation of Plots, Ports, Temples, etc., 1.7.1-2)

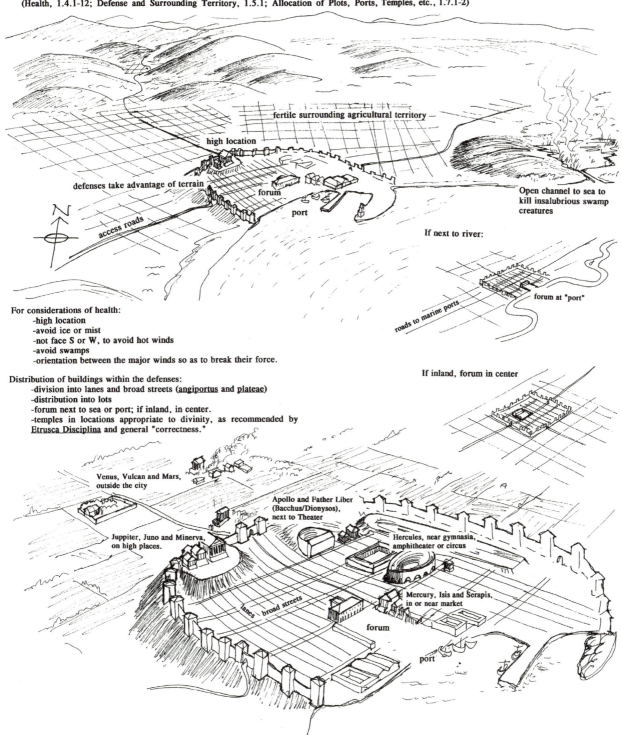

fertile surrounding agricultural territory —

high location

defenses take advantage of terrain

forum

port

access roads

N

Open channel to sea to
kill insalubrious swamp
creatures

If next to river:

forum at "port"

roads to marine ports

For considerations of health:
-high location
-avoid ice or mist
-not face S or W, to avoid hot winds
-avoid swamps
-orientation between the major winds so as to break their force.

Distribution of buildings within the defenses:
-division into lanes and broad streets (<u>angiportus</u> and <u>plateae</u>)
-distribution into lots
-forum next to sea or port; if inland, in center.
-temples in locations appropriate to divinity, as recommended by
<u>Etrusca Disciplina</u> and general "correctness."

If inland, forum in center

Venus, Vulcan and Mars,
outside the city

Apollo and Father Liber
(Bacchus/Dionysos),
next to Theater

Jupiter, Juno and Minerva,
on high places.

Hercules, near gymnasia,
amphitheater or circus

Mercury, Isis and Serapis,
in or near market

lanes broad streets

forum

port

Figure 11. The Siting of Cities (Health, 1.4.1–12; Defense and Surrounding Territory, 1.5.1;
Allocation of Plots, Ports, Temples, and so on, 1.7.1–2).

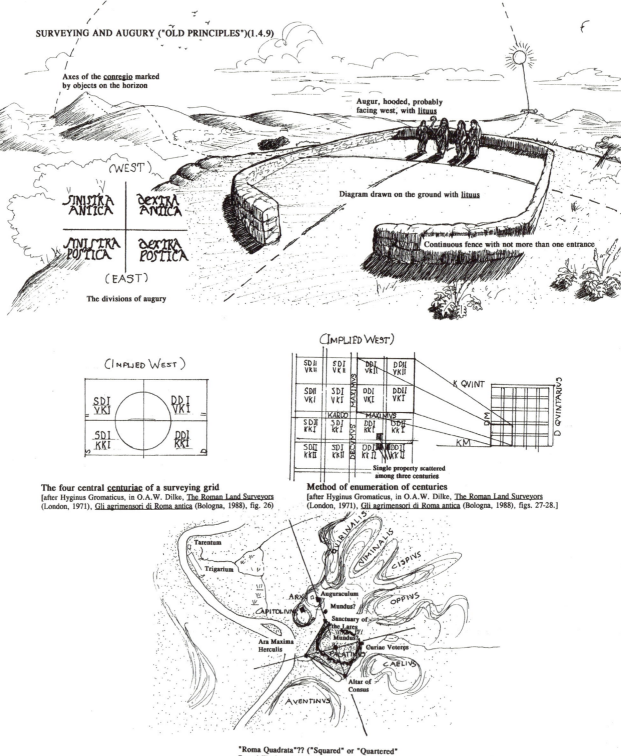

SURVEYING AND AUGURY ("OLD PRINCIPLES")(1.4.9)

Axes of the <u>conregio</u> marked by objects on the horizon

Augur, hooded, probably facing west, with <u>lituus</u>

Diagram drawn on the ground with <u>lituus</u>

Continuous fence with not more than one entrance

(WEST)

| SINISTRA ANTICA | DEXTRA ANTICA |
| SINISTRA POSTICA | DEXTRA POSTICA |

(EAST)

The divisions of augury

(IMPLIED WEST)

| SDI VKI | DDI VKI |
| SDI KKI | DDI KKI |

The four central <u>centuriae</u> of a surveying grid
[after Hyginus Gromaticus, in O.A.W. Dilke, <u>The Roman Land Surveyors</u> (London, 1971), <u>Gli agrimensori di Roma antica</u> (Bologna, 1988), fig. 26]

(IMPLIED WEST)

Single property scattered among three centuries

Method of enumeration of centuries
[after Hyginus Gromaticus, in O.A.W. Dilke, <u>The Roman Land Surveyors</u> (London, 1971), <u>Gli agrimensori di Roma antica</u> (Bologna, 1988), figs. 27-28.]

"Roma Quadrata"?? ("Squared" or "Quartered" Rome)(Tacitus <u>Ann</u> 12.24 et al.)

Figure 12. Surveying and Augury ("Old Principles") (1.4.9).

SURVEYING AND AUGURY: ETRUSCAN ROOTS?

BRONZE LIVER OF PIACENZA
(third cent. B.C.)
Used for instruction of <u>haruspices</u>
(practitioners of liver divination)?
[transcription by I.D. Rowland]

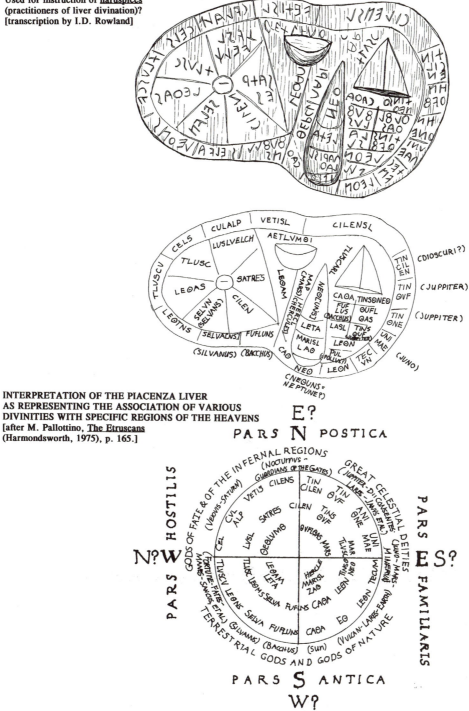

**INTERPRETATION OF THE PIACENZA LIVER
AS REPRESENTING THE ASSOCIATION OF VARIOUS
DIVINITIES WITH SPECIFIC REGIONS OF THE HEAVENS**
[after M. Pallottino, <u>The Etruscans</u>
(Harmondsworth, 1975), p. 165.]

Figure 13. Surveying and Augury: Etruscan Roots?

the cardo"/"beyond the cardo" (*kitra kardinem, ultra kardinem*),[62] "right of decumanus"/"left of decumanus" (*sinistra decumani, dextra decumani*).[63]

Pomptine Marshes (1.4.12)

Low malarial coastal plain south of Rome crossed by the Via Appia.

Salpia (1.4.12)

The foundation of Salpia may have occurred in the second century B.C., after the Social Wars in 89 B.C. or even c. 29, while Vitruvius was writing.[64]

City Walls (1.5.1–8) (Figures 14–19)

The first section of Chapter 5 amounts to a condensed version of book 5 of the *Mechanical Syntaxis* of the engineer Philo of Byzantium (second century B.C.), which has often been thought of as a virtually independent treatise on fortification.[65] Vitruvius's recommendations on defenses fit into the general practice of Hellenistic fortification, but with a distinct preference for the more inventive or experimental ideas rather than the most standard forms.

foundation trenches . . . down to solid ground (1.5.1) (Figure 18)

These were also recommended by Philo and were a consideration made more necessary by the need for firm foundations

to support the artillery that developed in the fourth century B.C.[66] It is quite common for the bottom two or three visible courses of a wall or tower to spread slightly, so that the foundation is wider than the upper wall, making sapping more difficult.

towers should project toward the exterior (1.5.2) (Figures 15–18)

The purpose of towers was hold to clear the curtains to either side with light artillery or bows as well as to clear the area in front of the wall with long-range artillery. The latter purpose required height; the former, projection from the face.

no easy approach . . . encircle precipitous heights (1.5.2) (Figures 14, 15)

The laying of fortifications along the ridges of high ground, so that the defenses correspond to the terrain and not the city area, is often thought of as a more peculiarly Greek approach, but Roman colonies of the Hellenistic period do the same (e.g., Cosa, founded 273 B.C.). Roman colonies, however, often had to be placed on flat land, apparently because greater consideration was given to access to the road network or ports (e.g., those in the Po valley of the later second and first centuries B.C., or Ostia, founded 338 B.C.).

the approaches to the gates are not straight but on the left (1.5.2) (Figures 15, 17)

This is unusual but is attested in several Greek sites and a few Roman (see figures).[67]

within its fabric rods (1.5.3) (Figure 18)

This sounds like a rather strange, or innovative combination of a Hellenistic curtain and the *murus gallicus* described by Caesar.[68] The idea may have been taken up later in wood and stone walls of forts on the northern frontier during the Empire (e.g., the Rhineland *limes*).[69] See figures.

The intervals between towers should be . . . a bow shot (1.5.4)

The range of a portable bow was about 30 to 40 m., and this is a common spacing for towers in Hellenistic circuits.[70] Philo recommends 100 cubits (150 feet, c. 46 m.).[71] At some places the spacing could be considerably more, such as at Rhodes, where the spacing was c. 330 feet.[72] (The effective range of a

62 *Citra* and *cardo* are among the few words in Latin that can be spelled with a "K" as well as with a "C." Agrimensorial records always use "K."

63 *Cardo* is the same word as the axis of the earth and therefore implies a N-S line, so that, like the augur, the surveyor is facing "west," along the *decumanus*. The existence of this kind of orthogonal organization is projected by historians back to the very founding of Rome in the controversial myth of Roma Quadrata supposedly laid out by Romulus around the Palatine, although the form of this area (round or square) is uncertain. Ennius, cited in Festus. s.v. Quadrata Roma; Plutarch, *Life of Romulus* 9; Dionysius of Halicarnassus 1.79; Tacitus, *Annals* 12.24; Varro, in Solinus 1.17–18. Tacitus gives the four corners at the Ara Maxima Herculis in the Foarum Boarium, the altar of Consus in the valley of the Circus Maximus, the Curiae Veteres at the NE corner of the Palatine and the altar of the Lares near the Lacus Iuturnae in the Forum. See E. Tübler, "Roma Quadrata und Mundus," *Römische Mitteilungen* 41 (1926), 212, 218; V. Basanoff, "Pomerium Palatinum," *Memorie dell' Accademia dei Lincei* 6.9 (1939), 3. for development of theories that certain aspects of *Roma Quadrata* may be preserved in the alignments of the later city, such as the line of the Via Flaminia, see. P. Meogrossi, "Topografia antica e restauro archeologico indicatori per il recupero della città," in *Mantenuzione e recupero nella città storica*, ed. M. M. Segarra Lagunes, convegno Roma, 27–28 Aprile, 1993, 81–89; and idem, "Allineamenti topografici tra Palatino e valle del Colosseo; ragioni e regole del disegno reale della *Forma Urbis*," in *La ciudad en el mundo romano*, XIV International Congress of Classical Archaeology, 2, Tarragona, 5–11 Sept, 1993 (Tarragona, 1994), 277–280.

64 M. Mingazzini, *Enciclopedia Italiana Treccani*, 30, 493, s.v. Salpia; E. Carraba, "La refondazione di Salpia," *Atheneum* 61 (1983), 514–516; A. Riontino, *Canne* (Trani, 1942), 200 ff.

65 Text, translation and commentary in Y. Garlan, *Recherches sur Poliorcétique grecque*, B.E.F.A.R. 223 (Paris, 1974), 279–404.

66 F. E. Winter, *Greek Fortifications* (Toronto, 1971), 327.

67 W. Andreae, *Hatra II*, Wissenchaftliche Veröffentlichungen der deutschen Orientgesellschaft 21 (Leipzig, 1912), fig. 26.

68 *De Bello Gallico* 7.23.

69 D. Baatz, "Keltische Einflüsse auf Römische Wehrbauten?", in *Bauten und Katapulte de Römischen Heers* (Stuttgart, 1994), 59–65.

70 The term "sagitta" in Vitruvius is ambiguous as to whether he is referring to a portable bow or a catapult.

71 Philo 5.89.

72 Y. Garlan, op. cit., 359, n. 45b.

THE SITING OF CITIES: "THE RAMPART SHOULD ENCIRCLE PRECIPITOUS HEIGHTS" (1.5.2)

Greek and Roman Cities Which Exploit Terrain

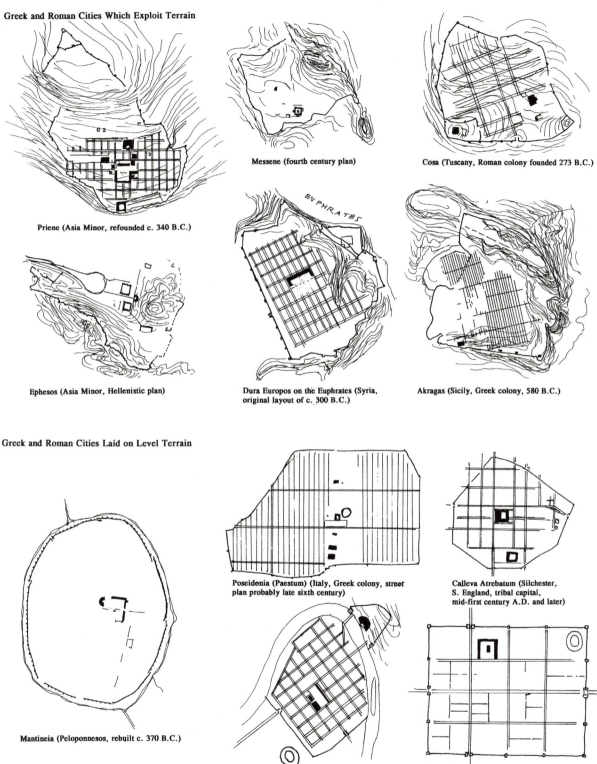

Priene (Asia Minor, refounded c. 340 B.C.)

Messene (fourth century plan)

Cosa (Tuscany, Roman colony founded 273 B.C.)

Ephesos (Asia Minor, Hellenistic plan)

Dura Europos on the Euphrates (Syria, original layout of c. 300 B.C.)

Akragas (Sicily, Greek colony, 580 B.C.)

Greek and Roman Cities Laid on Level Terrain

Mantineia (Peloponnesos, rebuilt c. 370 B.C.)

Poseidonia (Paestum) (Italy, Greek colony, street plan probably late sixth century)

Calleva Atrebatum (Silchester, S. England, tribal capital, mid-first century A.D. and later)

Verona (N. Italy, probably refounded by Augustus)

Aosta (Augusta Praetoria, veteran colony founded 25 B.C.)

Figure 14. The Siting of Cities: "The rampart should encircle precipitous heights" (1.5.2).

FORTIFICATIONS (1.5.1-8)
Summary of Vitruvius' Features for Fortification

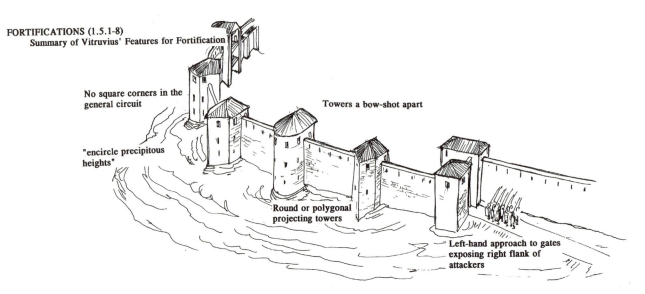

No square corners in the general circuit

Towers a bow-shot apart

"encircle precipitous heights"

Round or polygonal projecting towers

Left-hand approach to gates exposing right flank of attackers

Typical Hellenistic fortification:
Kydna, a small third century coastal fort in Lycia,
redrawn from drawings and reconstructions by J.P. Adam,
L'architecture militaire grecque (Paris, 1981), figs. 80, 84, 89.

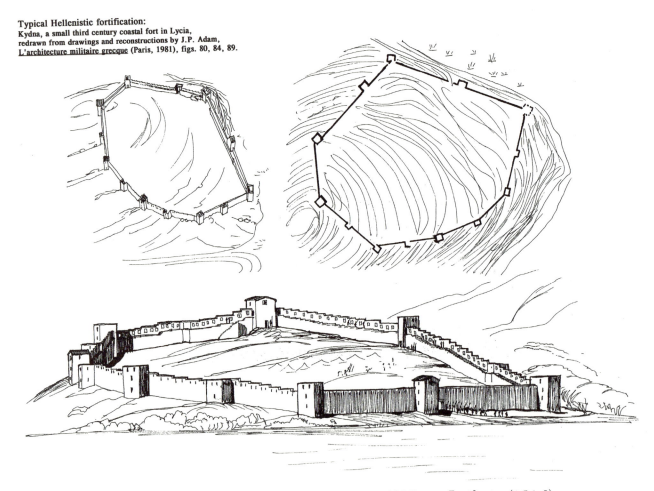

Figure 15. Fortifications: Summary of Vitruvian Features; Typical Hellenistic Fortification (1.5.1–8).

FORTIFICATIONS (1.5.1-8)

Towers as Artillery Emplacements
[after McNicoll, in <u>Fortification dans l'histoire du monde grec</u> (Paris, 1986),
fig. 158, and J.P.Adam, <u>L'Architecture militaire grecque</u> (Paris, 1981), fig. 74.]

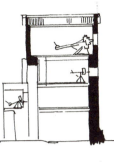

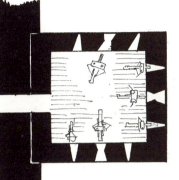

Side

Perge

Herakleia

Round and Polygonal Towers
[after J.P. Adam, <u>L'Architecture militaire grecque</u> (Paris, 1981),
figs. 29, 32, 43, 44, 65, and McNicoll, in <u>Fortification dans l'histoire
du monde grec</u> (Paris, 1986), fig. 159.]

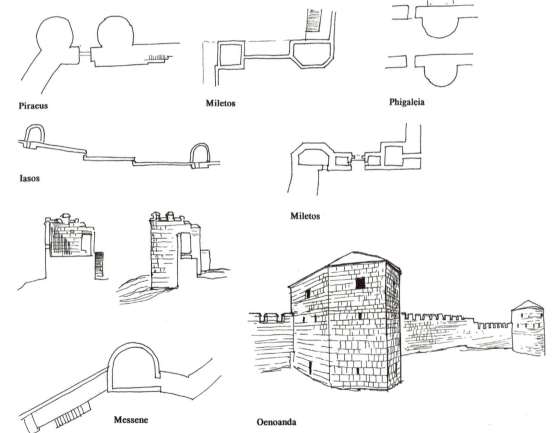

Piraeus　　　　**Miletos**　　　　**Phigaleia**

Iasos

Miletos

Messene　　　　**Oenoanda**

Figure 16. Fortifications: Towers as Artillery Emplacements; Round and Polygonal Towers (1.5.1–8).

FORTIFICATIONS (1.5.1-8)

A Variety of City Gate Designs

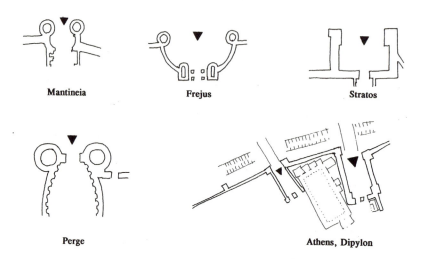

Mantineia   Frejus   Stratos

Perge   Athens, Dipylon

Gates with Left-Hand Approaches which Expose the Right Flank

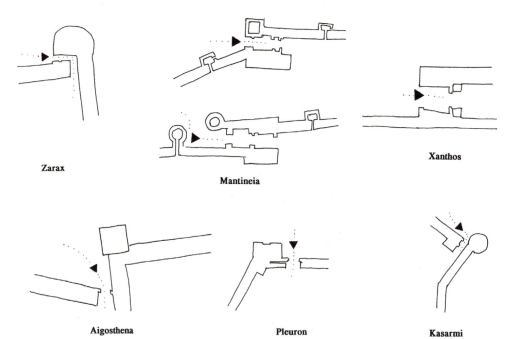

Zarax   Mantineia   Xanthos

Aigosthena   Pleuron   Kasarmi

Figure 17. Fortifications: A Variety of City Gate Designs; Left-Hand Approaches (1.5.1–8).

FORTIFICATIONS (1.5.1-8)

Foundations Carried "ad solidum"

..with the "width of the foundation...greater than the projected above ground portion"

"Steps" cut into the bedrock for ascending foundations

Herakleia ad Latmos

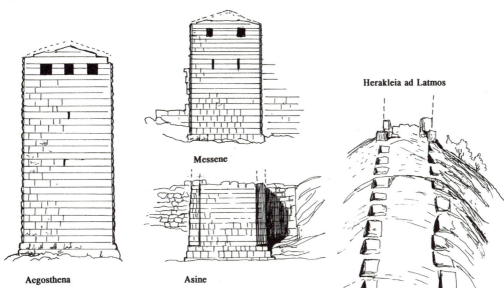

Aegosthena

Messene

Asine

Hellenistic compartment walls (supposed emplekton)

Sounion

Pleuron

Selinous, "masonry chain"

Walls with timber tie-beams

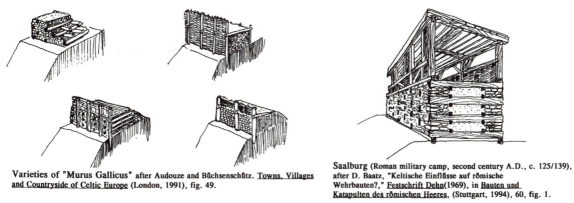

Varieties of "Murus Gallicus" after Audouze and Büchsenschütz. Towns, Villages and Countryside of Celtic Europe (London, 1991), fig. 49.

Saalburg (Roman military camp, second century A.D., c. 125/139), after D. Baatz, "Keltische Einflüsse auf römische Wehrbauten?," Festschrift Dehn(1969), in Bauten und Katapulten des römischen Heeres, (Stuttgart, 1994), 60, fig. 1.

Figure 18. Fortifications: Foundations Carried to the Solid; Hellenistic Compartment Walls; Walls with Tie Beams (1.5.1–8).

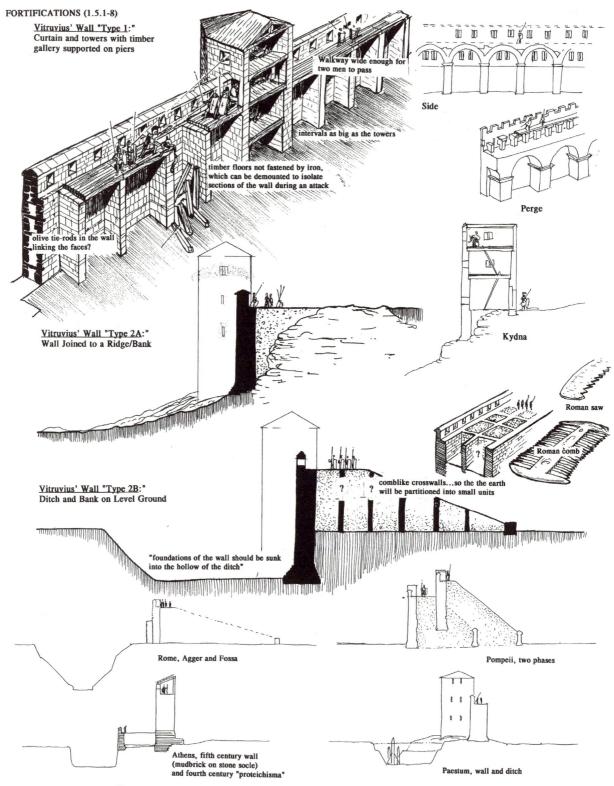

FORTIFICATIONS (1.5.1-8)

Vitruvius' Wall "Type 1:"
Curtain and towers with timber
gallery supported on piers

Walkway wide enough for
two men to pass

intervals as big as the towers

timber floors not fastened by iron,
which can be demounted to isolate
sections of the wall during an attack

olive tie-rods in the wall
linking the faces?

Side

Perge

Kydna

Vitruvius' Wall "Type 2A:"
Wall Joined to a Ridge/Bank

Roman saw

Roman comb

comblike crosswalls...so the the earth
will be partitioned into small units

Vitruvius' Wall "Type 2B:"
Ditch and Bank on Level Ground

"foundations of the wall should be sunk
into the hollow of the ditch"

Rome, Agger and Fossa

Pompeii, two phases

Athens, fifth century wall
(mudbrick on stone socle)
and fourth century "proteichisma"

Paestum, wall and ditch

Figure 19. Fortifications: Vitruvius's Walls Type 1, Type 2A, Type 2B (1.5.1–8).

catapult was about 300–400 m.) Caesar spaced towers at the siege of Alesia at 80 feet (24 m.).[73]

Towers should be made either round or polygonal (1.5.5) (Figure 16)

Towers in the Hellenistic period were commonly square, but various sorts of polygonal or round towers are common, as at Messene, Oenoanda, or Mantinea. Philo recommends both polygonal towers and the oblique approach.[74]

The fortification . . . is far more secure . . . if joined to earthen ramparts (1.5.5); but it is not reasonable to build ramparts everywhere . . . (1.5.6–7) (Figure 19)

The former sounds like a curtain wall revetting a natural ridge ("Type 2A"); the second, an earth-backed wall like the "Servian" wall in Rome (Type 2B).

the division into lots (1.6.1)

Normally the surrounding agricultural territory of a new colony was divided into regular plots by "centuriation," more commonly called *limitatio* in Latin, to facilitate the assigning of plots to colonists, or simply to keep records of land holdings. The practice of surveying the countryside by a regular grid goes back at least to the sixth century B.C. in Greek colonies of southern Italy (e.g., Metapontum). Each area to be "centuriated" begins from a central benchmark, which was oriented to the cardinal points, as Vitruvius describes, and the agrimensores recommend that whenever possible the grid itself be oriented to the cardinal points. Just as often it was not. Very often contiguous areas of centuriation have slightly different orientations, as in the areas of centuriation in the Po valley and around Arausio (Orange). The exercises of the *Corpus Agrimensorum* give many examples of how the surveyor needs to adapt the centuriaton grid to interruptions, such as water or a mountain. Obviously not all land in a territory was centuriated. In addition to centuriated land there was land that was measured but "excluded" from centuriation, and there was land which was unmeasured. Hyginus Gromaticus recommends that if the actual boundary of a centuriated territory does not correspond to the centuriation, it should be squared off. The agrimensorial exercises show that property boundaries are always approximated by simple rectangular and triangular shapes in order to make them measurable. The illustration, from a manuscript in the Vatican Library (Ms. Pal. Lat. 1564), shows centuriated area, a measured but "excluded" area, and the boundaries of two coloniae, a colonia Iulia and Mantua (probably not the actual city of Mantua).[75]

Winds and Orientation (1.6.1–13) (Figures 20–22)

In antiquity winds were held to be forced, focused streams that were impelled from specific quarters.[76] This idea obviously was derived from the ordinary observation that regions like the Mediterranean have certain characteristic winds, like the hot summer scirocco or the French mistral, which blow from certain directions, and often at certain seasons. It was also supported by physical theory; in earth-air-fire-water chemistry, wind was held to be the product of the collision of heat with moisture, as one could see in the producing of steam from boiling water in an aeolipile.[77] Hence it was not difficult to imagine that winds were impelled from certain quarters and were in fact generated at specific places or regions of the earth, where this type of collision took place.[78] The idea of winds being pushed from a specific place also accords with Aristotelian notions of dynamics which, in the absence of a concept of inertia, claimed that a thrown body continues to move after it has left the hand only because it receives a constant push from the rush of the displaced air behind.[79]

Winds were identified by dividing up the "horizon."[80] The more common way was by the solstitial risings; Vitruvius, and the Tower of the Winds in Athens, use regular divisions. Vitruvius conflates the two methods, referring in 1.6.5 to the "winter east," probably as a rhetorical equivalent of SE, and in then in 1.6.6–8 places these winds on the sides of an octagon, or true SE, and so on.

73 *De Bello Gallico* 7.72.4.
74 Philo 5.82; 5.89.
75 O. A. W. Dilke, *Greek and Roman Maps* (Ithaca, 1985), 94–95, fig. 15.

76 Pliny the Elder records more than twenty authors who wrote on winds. *Natural History* 2.117.
77 The aeolipile was attested from the third century B.C. as an experimental or didactic instrument, see Philo of Byzantium, *Pneumatica* 57, ed. Carra de Vaux. The best-known aeolipile is that of Hero of Alexandria (later first century A.D.), which was in effect a rotary jet-powered steam engine, and as close to the steam engine as antiquity ever got). Heron, *Pneumatica* 2.11; W. Schmidt, *Herons von Alexandria Druckwerke und Automatentheater* (Leipzig, 1899).
78 This idea persisted as late as the eighteenth century when the traveler ten Rhyne believed he had discovered in the cloud over Table Mountain at the Cape of Good Hope the "source" from which the mighty southwester was being "poured" into the atmosphere. Cited in B. Farrington, *Greek Science* (Nottingham, 1944, 1949), 263.
79 Aristotle, *Physics* 4.8, Discussions in O. Pedersen, M. Pihl, *Early Physics and Astronomy* (London and New York, 1974), 120–125. Aristotle held that there were three types of motion: natural motion, which was the innate property of earth to sink to the center of the universe and fire to rise to the edge of the celestial sphere; forced, which was that imparted by a hand to a stone; and voluntary, which comes from living things. Forced motion required a continuous force to be applied to a moving stone because the natural, innate motion of a stone would make it sink. Hence the hand imparted force to layers of air that kept the stone in motion as they rushed around behind it. This is known as the *antiperistasis* theory (i.e., to turn around the opposite side). Strato of Lampsacus criticized this theory, but no one in antiquity came close to the idea of inertia until John Philoponus's refutation of antiperistasis c. A.D. 500 (*Commentary on Aristotle's Physics* 641.13 ff.).
80 "Horos" is the Greek word for boundary, so that "horizon" in astronomical terminology means the limit or boundary of our view of the heavens.

PHYSICAL NATURE OF THE WINDS (1.6.1–3)

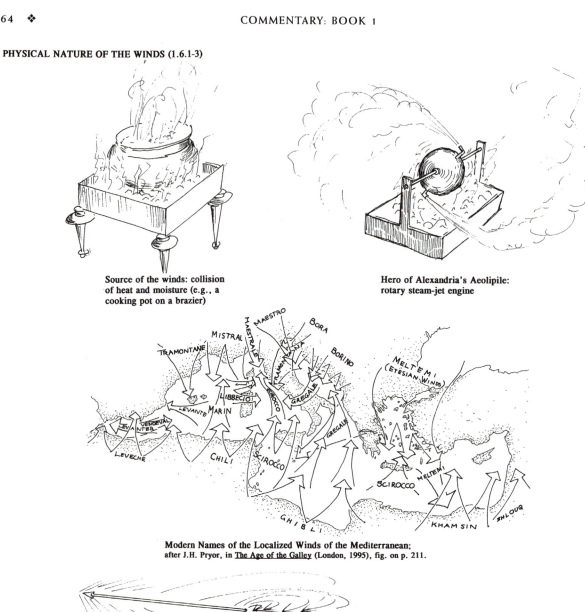

Source of the winds: collision of heat and moisture (e.g., a cooking pot on a brazier)

Hero of Alexandria's Aeolipile: rotary steam-jet engine

Modern Names of the Localized Winds of the Mediterranean; after J.H. Pryor, in The Age of the Galley (London, 1995), fig. on p. 211.

Antiperistasis: Motion impelled by continuous force from behind after release

Figure 20. Physical Nature of the Winds (1.6.1–3).

ORIENTATION OF THE WINDS BY CELESTIAL POINTS AND REGIONS (1.6.4-13)

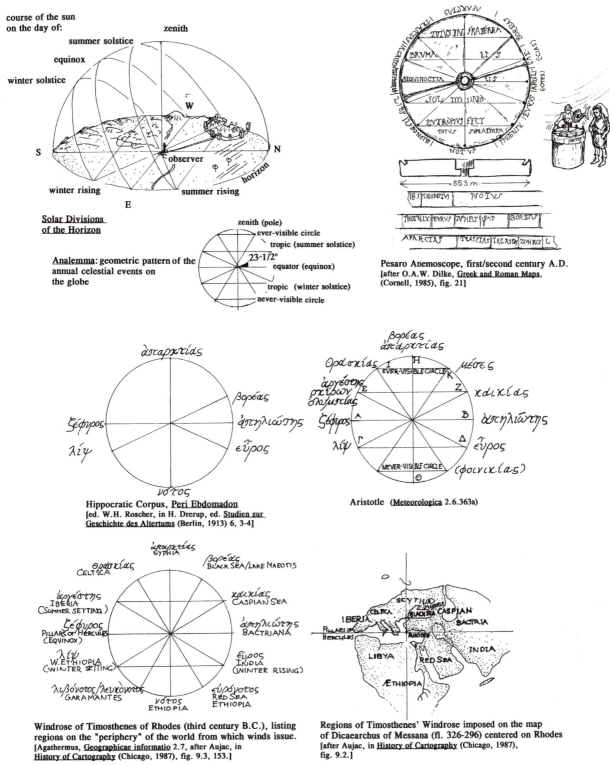

Figure 21. Orientation of the Winds by Celestial Points and Regions (1.6.4–13).

ORIENTATION OF THE WINDS BY QUADRANTS/OCTANTS, ETC. OF THE COMPASS   (1.6.4-13)

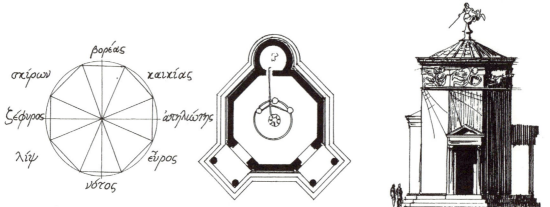

Winds according to Andronicus Cyrrhestes (left), and Tower of the Winds (center and right),
built by Andronicus in the Agora of Athens as a windrose, sundial and waterclock (later second,
early first century B.C.)
[after Stuart and Revett, <u>Antiquities of Athens</u> (London, 1759/65), pls. ii, iii.]

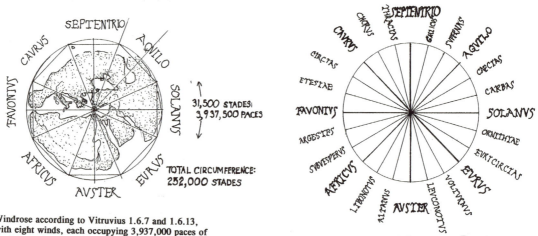

Windrose according to Vitruvius 1.6.7 and 1.6.13,
with eight winds, each occupying 3,937,000 paces of
the "circumference of the terrestrial globe" (according
to the circumference calculated by Eratosthenes).

Windrose according to Vitruvius 1.6.10,
with additional intermediate winds

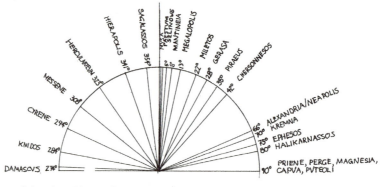

Orientation of "plateae" of classical and Hellenistic sites
[after H. von Gerkan, <u>Griechische Städteanlagen</u> (Berlin and Leipzig, 1924), fig 71.]

Figure 22. Orientation of the Wind by Quadrants/Octants of the Compass (1.6.4–13).

Vitruvius's recommendation on orientation differs from most other ancient writers on the subject. Aristotle, probably following the Hippocratic corpus, recommends that healthful cities should be opened to the winds.[81] Three centuries after Vitruvius, Oribasius, in a commentary on Galen, specifically says the streets should be oriented toward the cardinal points, because that is where the strongest winds come from, so the winds can sweep the streets unimpeded.[82] Vitruvius, on the other hand, believes that winds should break against the angles of city blocks and be stilled. The scientific reason for his conclusion, apparently, is that still air "adds" to the physique of ill individuals. This accords with his general physiology, which claims that moving air and heat tend to subtract "humors" from bodies. Aristotle and Xenophon recommend southern exposures; Vitruvius warns against southern exposures and hot winds.

Let a marble benchmark . . .
[Surveying and Centuriation] (1.6.6–13)
(Figure 23, 25–27)

Vitruvius's demonstration of finding true north on the *amusium* is drawn directly from actual surveying practice. The procedure is recorded in the compilation of treatises on professional surveying called the *Corpus Agrimensorum*;[83] the method which Vitruvius gives, based on two shadows, is given by the author Hyginus Gromaticus, who then follows his description by giving a more accurate method, using three shadows.[84] Pliny the Elder gives a more rough and ready rustic method, which is less accurate.[85]

The grid was extended from the central benchmark by means of the instrument called the groma.[86] Straight distances were sighted from plumb lines and measured by 10-foot wooden rods with metal tips (*decempeda*), and accuracy was checked by measuring diagonals.[87] Property boundaries were marked by boundary stones and the ditches or banks between fields. This type of simple orthogonal geometry naturally

favored square divisions, although not all centuriation was square. The unit of measure was the *actus* (120 feet, or the distance an ox was supposed to pull a plow before turning), two square *actus* made a *iugerum*, and two *iugera* a *heredium*, i.e., an inheritable farm; one hundred *heredia* made a century, the major land division, which was 20 *actus* on a side, or 400 square *actus*.[88]

Eratosthenes' Measurement
of the Globe (1.6.9) (Figure 24)

Eratosthenes effectively established the science of mathematical geography (the location of places by latitude and longitude), and one of his major accomplishments in this department was his measurement of the circumference of the earth.[89] It is based on four assumptions: that Syene (modern Aswan) is on the tropic of Cancer (it is close, about 35′ N; at the summer solstice sunlight would penetrate into a deep well, and hence the sun was directly overhead); that Syene and Alexandria were on the same meridian; that the distance between the two places was 5000 stades; and that the rays of the sun are parallel. When the sun was directly overhead at Syene, a gnomon at Alexandria cast a shadow which gave an angle of 7 1/5°, or just 1/50 the circumference of a circle. Hence the circumference of the earth was 50 × 2000 stades, or 250,000 stades, which Eratosthenes altered to 252,000 stades to make it divisible by 60. If the stade used by Eratosthenes was the Egyptian stade of 157.5 m, the value for the circumference was 39,690 km, which is within 1 percent of the modern value.[90] This gives a figure of 700 stades per degree.

The "meridian" of Alexandria-Syene was a commonly accepted approximation, and was often seen as extending south to Meroë and north to Rhodes, Byzantium and Olbia. It was not possible to measure longitude astronomically as it is dependent upon knowing absolute time, which could not be accurately measured until the development of the chronometer in the eighteenth century.[91] Hence in ancient mapmaking latitudes could be relatively accurate but longitude relied on dead-reckoning and overland distance measurements.

lanes . . . and broad streets (1.7.1) (Figures 14, 23)

The use of the terms "streets" and "lanes" (*plateae* and *angiportus*) implies a system not of square but oblong blocks, with major

81 *Politics* 7.10.11, 1330a. Hippocrates, *Aphorisms* 3.4–5; *Airs, Waters and Places* (ed. Littré), vol. 2, 20. R. Jolly, *Hippocrates* (Paris, 1964), 26 ff.

82 Oribasius (ed. Daremberg) 2.318 ff.

83 *Corpus agrimensorum romanorum*, ed. C. Thulin (Leipzig, 1913, reprint Stuttgart, 1971).

84 G. Martines, "La scienze dei Gromatici: un esercizio di geografia astronomica nel *Corpus Agrimensorum*, in *Misurare la terra: centuriazione e coloni nel mondo romano* (Rome, 1985), 23–27. The method by three shadows apparently is based on solid geometry.

85 *Natural History* 17.76–77.

86 The *groma* was the main surveying instrument in antiquity, and the word may derive from the Greek word *gnomon* probably transmitted through Etruscan (with the substitution of r for n; Dilke, 1971/88, 31). The accuracy of the grid depended on the accuracy of the right angle in the instrument itself and the accuracy of the setup. The accuracy of a right angle could always be checked by a 3-4-5 triangle, a technique known since Egyptian times. A reasonably accurate setup could be achieved by placing the pointed end of the *groma* into the ground a distance away from the *decussis* of the benchmark equal to the length of the support arm, then swinging the arm so that the center plummet was over the *decussis*, then straightening the *groma* so the shaft was parallel to the plumb line.

87 For the diagonal of an *actus*, surveyors used the near approximation of 170 feet (actual diagonal is 169.706).

88 On land surveying, see Dilke, op. cit. (1985), 88–101; Dilke (1971/1988), passim.; J. P. Adam, *La Construction romaine* (Paris, 1988), 22.

89 A. Thalamas, *La géographie d'Eratosthène* (Versailles, 1921), 128–164. The main ancient source is Cleomedes, *De motu circulari* (Greek: *Kuklikê theoria tôn meteôrôn*) 1.10.

90 The Greek *stadion* was normally 600 Greek feet, but there is great uncertainty on the actual length, even in terms of the number of feet; Vitruvius uses a stade of 625 feet or 125 paces (one pace/*passus* = two steps or five feet), so that 252,000 stades = 31,500 Roman miles (*mille passus*). At a Roman foot of .2957 m, the figure for the circumference of the earth would be 46,572 km. See Jakop Skop,"The Stade of the Greeks," *Surveying and Mapping* 10 (1950), 50–55; D. R. Dicks, *The Geographical Fragments of Hipparchus* (London, 1960), 42–46.

91 At the equator, an error of one second in time results in a locational error of c. 1/2 km.

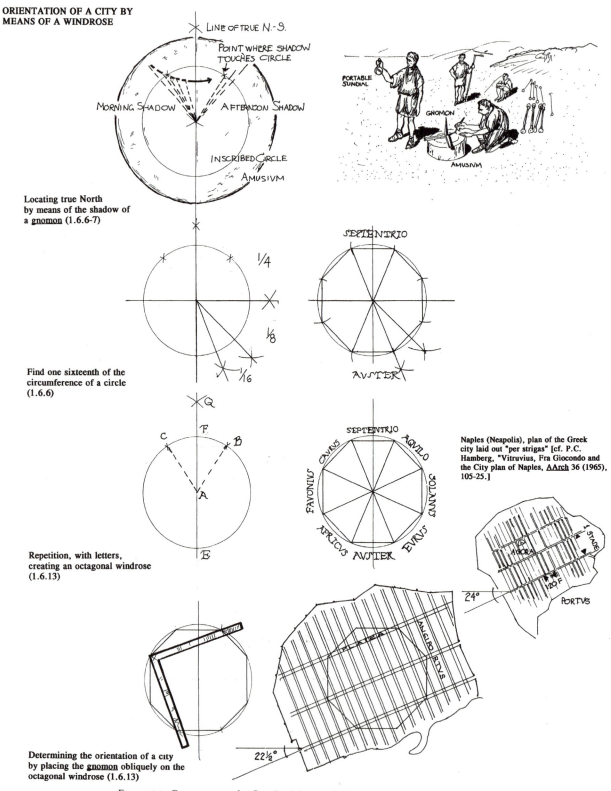

ORIENTATION OF A CITY BY MEANS OF A WINDROSE

LINE OF TRUE N.-S.

POINT WHERE SHADOW TOUCHES CIRCLE

MORNING SHADOW

AFTERNOON SHADOW

INSCRIBED CIRCLE

AMUSIVM

PORTABLE SUNDIAL

GNOMON

AMUSIVM

Locating true North by means of the shadow of a gnomon (1.6.6-7)

¼

⅛

¹/₁₆

Find one sixteenth of the circumference of a circle (1.6.6)

SEPTENTRIO

AVSTER

Q

F

C

B

A

E

Repetition, with letters, creating an octagonal windrose (1.6.13)

SEPTENTRIO

AQVILO

SOLANVS

EVRVS

AVSTER

AFRICVS

FAVONIVS

CAVRVS

Naples (Neapolis), plan of the Greek city laid out "per strigas" [cf. P.C. Hamberg, "Vitruvius, Fra Giocondo and the City plan of Naples, AArch 36 (1965), 105-25.]

AGORA

20 F

1 STADE

24°

PORTVS

ANGIPORTVS

PLATEA

22½°

Determining the orientation of a city by placing the gnomon obliquely on the octagonal windrose (1.6.13)

Figure 23. Orientation of a City by Means of a Windrose (1.6.6–7; 1.6.13).

ERATOSTHENES' MEASURE OF THE CIRCUMFERENCE OF THE GLOBE (1.6.9)

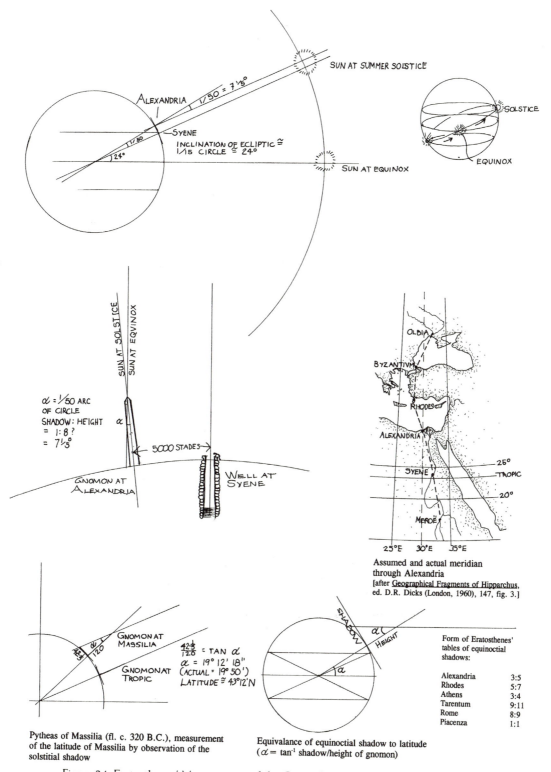

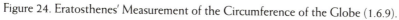

Figure 24. Eratosthenes' Measurement of the Circumference of the Globe (1.6.9).

SURVEYING AND LIMITATIO (CENTURIATION)

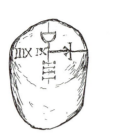

"Cippus" (Amusium?): Centuriation
boundary stone with decussis
(after J.P. Adam, 1989, fig. 6)

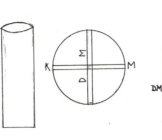

Cippus Gromaticus,
from Hyginus Gromaticus

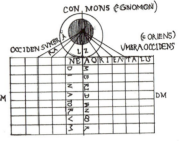

Hyginus Gromaticus: supposed diagram
for method of orienting grid by
shadow of gnomon

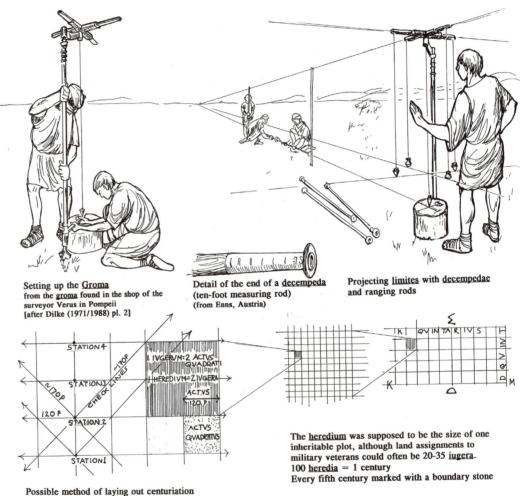

Setting up the Groma
from the groma found in the shop of the
surveyor Verus in Pompeii
[after Dilke (1971/1988) pl. 2]

Detail of the end of a decempeda
(ten-foot measuring rod)
(from Enns, Austria)

Projecting limites with decempedae
and ranging rods

Possible method of laying out centuriation
grid, including checking diagonals.

The heredium was supposed to be the size of one
inheritable plot, although land assignments to
military veterans could often be 20-35 iugera.
100 heredia = 1 century
Every fifth century marked with a boundary stone

Figure 25. Surveying and *Limitatio* (Centuriation): Methods

SURVEYING AND <u>LIMITATIO</u> (CENTURIATION)

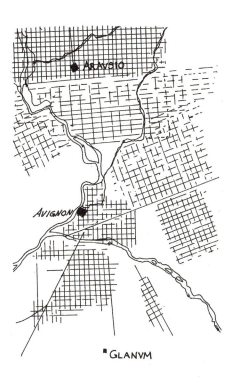

**Traces of eight different systems of
centuriation in the Orange-Avignon area**
[after O.A.W. Dilke, <u>The Roman
Land Surveyors</u> (London, 1971), <u>Gli agrimensori
di Roma antica</u> (Bologna, 1988), fig. 45.]

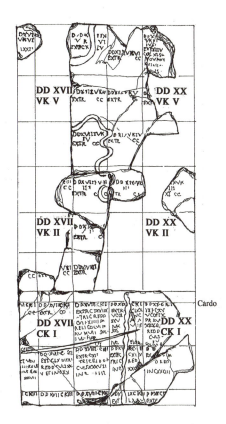

**Cadastral stone maps of Aurausio (Orange),
cadaster B, c. A.D. 77**
[after Dilke (1971/88), fig. 48]

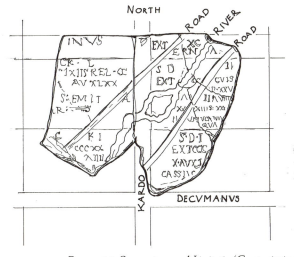

**Detail (left) of the Arausio cadasters
(cadaster A, fragment 7). This detail
shows a section adjacent to the principal
<u>decumanus-kardo</u> inersection, with a river
flanked by two roads.
Abbreviations:**

EXT(R) - <u>ex tributario</u>, i.e., removed from
tribute-paying status, applies only to Gauls.
REL COL - <u>reliqua coloniae</u>, lands remaining to
the colony, not given to veterans, rented.
RP - <u>rei publicae</u>, state lands.
SUBS - <u>subseciva</u>, land left over between
boundaries and centuriated sections, unoccupied.
[after Dilke,(1971/88), fig. 13, 16.)

Figure 26. Surveying and *Limitatio* (Centuriation): Examples

SURVEYING AND <u>LIMITATIO</u> (CENTURIATION)

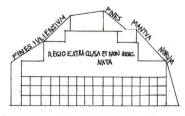

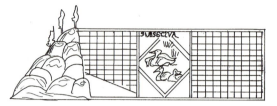

Centuriatio and "excluded" lands and boundaries, with two neighboring coloniae (Mantua and Colonia Julia).
Illustration of a surveying exercise by Hyginus Gromaticus, <u>corpus agrimensorum</u> [after O.A.W. Dilke, <u>The Roman Land Surveyors</u> (London, 1971), <u>Gli agrimensori di Roma antica</u> (Bologna, 1988), fig. 15.]

Centuriation interupted by a swamp and hills.
Illustration of a surveying exercise by Agennius Urbicus
Arcerianus A

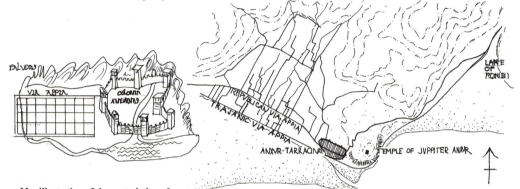

Ms. illustration of the centuriation of Terracina-Anxur, bounded by Via Appia, swamps, mountains and town.
from Hyginius Gromaticus, <u>corpus agrimensorum</u> (Pal Lat. 1564 89r.)

Modern Terracina showing traces of centuriation. The colony was founded in 329 B.C. Only cultivable land was centuriated.
[after Dilke (1971/88) fig. 34]

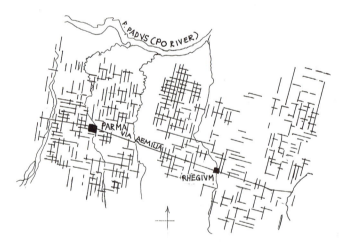

Traces of two different centuriations in the Po valley between Parma and Reggio. The section around Parma appears to use the section of the Via Aemilia west of the city as its decumanus.
[after Dilke (1971/88) fig. 41.)

Figure 27. Surveying and *Limitatio* (Centuriation): Examples

and minor streets, and this in turn sounds like a type of planning called *per strigas* ("by strips"), which is thought to be particularly characteristic of Greek planning and of Greek or Greek-influenced cities in southern Italy and Campania (e.g., Paestum). However, some Hellenistic Greek city plans had nearly square blocks (Priene and Miletus), and oblong blocks in the Hellenistic manner did continue to be used in early Roman colonies like Cosa (founded 273) to as late as Vitruvius's time (e.g., the refoundation of Carthage, c. 35–15 B.C.).[92]

The eventual dominance of uniform near-square city blocks in Roman planning is probably a result of the influence of the *agrimensores*. The centuriation grid is rarely an extension of the city grid, or vice versa, except in places like the Po valley where they both share a convenient common *decumanus* in the Via Aemilia. It should be noted that nowhere does Vitruvius say that the city is actually octagonal; the octagon is a surveying device to orient the city, not shape it. The city shape, according to what he says about putting defenses on on convenient high ground (1.5.2), will be determined by an evaluation of the site; it is not predetermined or fixed.

BOOK 2

Dinocrates and Alexander (2.praef.1–4) (Figure 28)

Dinocrates[1] is associated with the last phase of the Temple of Artemis at Ephesus as well as the city plan of Alexandria.[2] As Alexander seems to know, Mount Athos is an utterly barren rocky peninsula with high mountains (up to 2033 m), no arable land, and virtually no rivers (the only rivers are "streams of opportunity" that flow only during rainstorms and otherwise are dry torrent beds). The high mountains cause strong winds around the southern promontory, which made it notoriously dangerous to ancient seafarers because all navigation generally had to cling to visible coasts; it was thus worthwhile for Xerxes to cut a canal through the isthmus in 480 B.C. so his fleet could avoid the dangerous storms. Darius's fleet had been partly wrecked on the promontory ten years earlier. Alexandria was laid out in 332/331 as a new city on a coastal island at the Canopic mouth of the Nile and became the Hellenistic capital of Egypt and, by any measure, the most splendid and sophisticated city of the Hellenistic world.

The site is defensible and has an excellent sea port and access to the fertile regions of the interior by means of the Nile. It also had, and still has, a reputation as a remarkably breezy and salubrious site, despite its latitude.[3]

The Invention of the Arts and of Building (2.1.1–9) (Figure 29)

The *historia* of the rise of the arts of humankind is derived from a tradition of scientific-philosophical literature that amounted to the ancient equivalent of the science of anthropology, and it may go back to Democritus and the Hippocratic corpus of the fifth century B.C.[4] Vitruvius probably got most of his account from Lucretius, who wrote about twenty-five years before Vitruvius.[5] Diodorus Siculus, an exact contemporary of Vitruvius, also gives a rendition of the tale in the opening of his world history.[6]

by what mixture of elements their composition is tempered (1.praef.9)

This is stated in the terms of four-element chemistry, which analyzes the stability of objects in terms of a "tempered" mix of the four elements. See "Introduction: Interpreting Vitruvius," and Notes 1.1.10.

First Principles (2.2.1–2) (Figure 30)

The list of pre-Socratic philosophers chronicles the development of earth-air-fire-water chemistry, primarily through the speculations of the Ionian natural philosophers of the sixth and fifth centuries B.C. The proposition that all terrestrial things are various combinations of four elements, here attributed to the Pythagoreans and summarized by Empedocles and Aristotle in definitive form, in effect resolved a conflict

92 Ward-Perkins, *Cities of Ancient Greece and Italy*, 28, although the plan may be as early as 146 B.C. Castagnoli (1971), fig. 50, after P. Davin, *Révue Tunisienne* 1 (1930), 73ff.

1 Pliny the Elder, *Natural History* 34.42; B. M. Boyce, *Macmillan Encyclopedia of Architects* (London, 1982), i, s.v. Dinocrates, 533.

2 For Alexandria, see S. Shenouda, *Princeton Encyclopedia of Classical Sites* (Princeton, 1976), s.v. 36, and B. A. Pearson, *Oxford Encyclopedia of Archaeology in the Near East* (Oxford, 1997), s.v. Alexandria, 69, with refs. Alexandria was the first city in antiquity named after a living mortal rather than a divinity.

3 Strabo 17.1.7.

4 The attribution of the original theory to Democritus is made by K. Reinhardt [*Hermes* 47 (1912), 492 ff.] and is further argued by B. Farrington, *Greek Science* (Nottingham, 1944/49), 82–85. If the attribution to Democritus is correct, then the association of this story with atomistic thought may be consistent from the fifth century B.C. through Lucretius. The rise of the arts of humanity was a familiar *topos* in the fifth century. Aeschylus in *Prometheus Bound* records that humankind had "lived like an insect in sunless subterranean caves without knowledge of brick-making or carpentry," but now lived in well-built houses and could read the stars and the future (*Prometheus Bound* 436 ff.). Sophocles, in a famous passage of *Antigone* (332 ff.), sings that wonders are many but none so wonderful as humanity, who can harness the storm winds or the strength of a mule. Many of these concepts of the arts as a specific series of steps (a procedure) to attain a given end, that is, control over an object or an activity of nature, are probably due to Ionian philosophers of the sixth century B.C. See Farrington (1944/1949), 46–47, 136–137.

5 The passage in Lucretius's *De rerum natura* runs approximately from 5.925 to 5.1105. Lucretius 5.1091–1104, for fire coming from lightning of the friction of trees; 5.1028–1090 for origins of language. Vitruvius states in 9.praef.17 that he read Lucretius with admiration.

6 Didodorus Siculus, 1. 7–8.

DINOCRATES AND ALEXANDER (2.Praef.1-4)

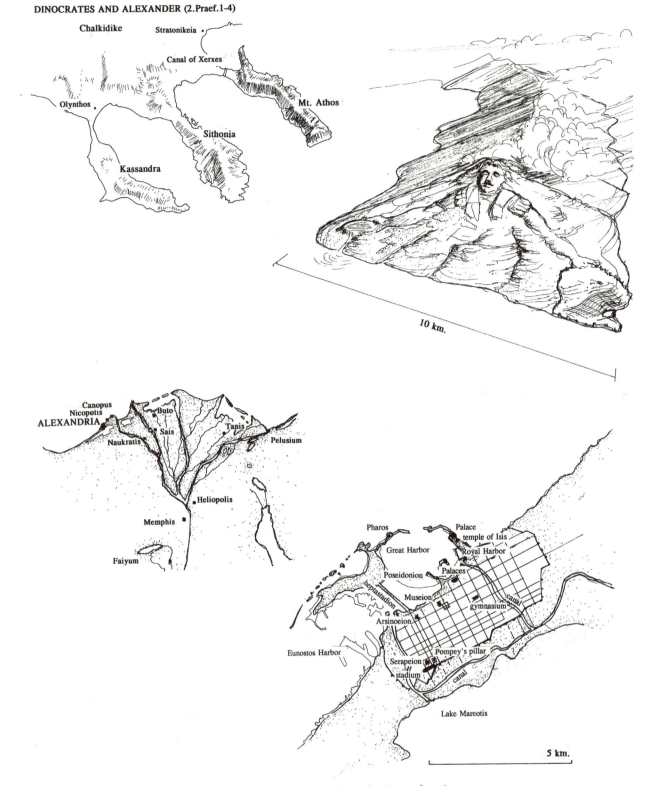

Figure 28. Dinocrates and Alexander (2.praef.1–4).

HISTORIA: THE INVENTION OF BUILDING (2.1.1-7)

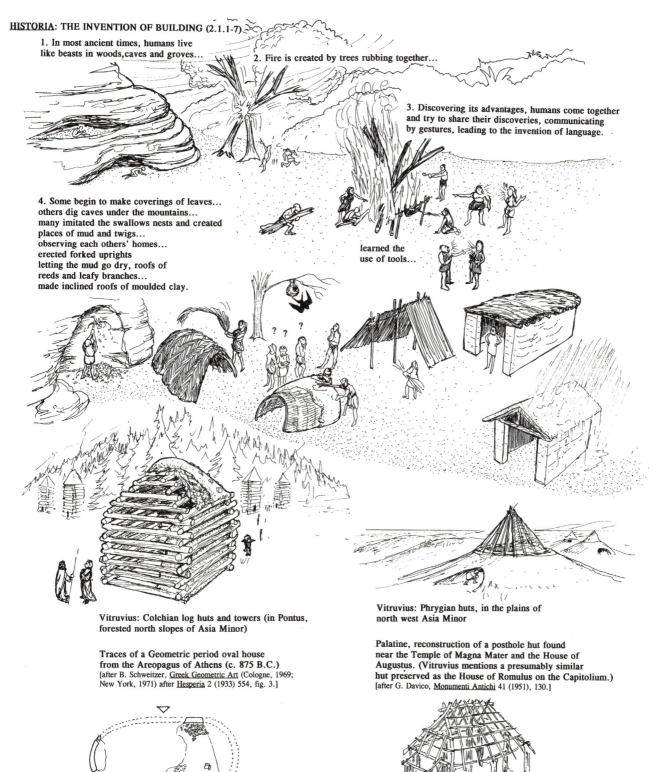

1. In most ancient times, humans live like beasts in woods, caves and groves...

2. Fire is created by trees rubbing together...

3. Discovering its advantages, humans come together and try to share their discoveries, communicating by gestures, leading to the invention of language.

4. Some begin to make coverings of leaves... others dig caves under the mountains... many imitated the swallows nests and created places of mud and twigs... observing each others' homes... erected forked uprights letting the mud go dry, roofs of reeds and leafy branches... made inclined roofs of moulded clay.

learned the use of tools...

Vitruvius: Colchian log huts and towers (in Pontus, forested north slopes of Asia Minor)

Vitruvius: Phrygian huts, in the plains of north west Asia Minor

Traces of a Geometric period oval house from the Areopagus of Athens (c. 875 B.C.) [after B. Schweitzer, Greek Geometric Art (Cologne, 1969; New York, 1971) after Hesperia 2 (1933) 554, fig. 3.]

Palatine, reconstruction of a posthole hut found near the Temple of Magna Mater and the House of Augustus. (Vitruvius mentions a presumably similar hut preserved as the House of Romulus on the Capitolium.) [after G. Davico, Monumenti Antichi 41 (1951), 130.]

Figure 29. The Invention of Building (2.1.1–7).

CELESTIAL AND TERRESTRIAL CHEMISTRY (2.2.1-2)

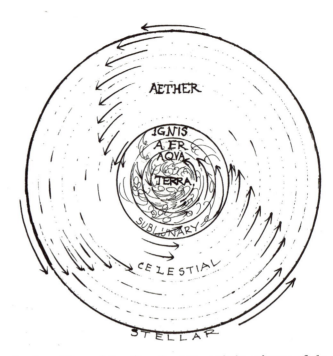

The natural positions of the five elements, and the mixture of the four sublunary elements impelled by motion of the stellar sphere

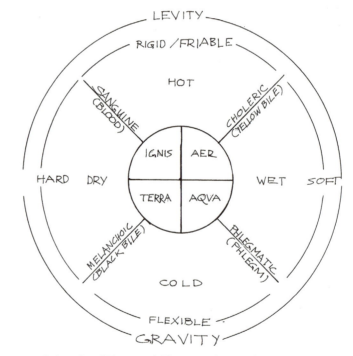

Figure 30. Celestial and Terrestrial Chemistry (2.2.1–2).

between a view of the world as perpetual change (Heraclitus) and changelessness (Protagoras). The development was not as cumulative as Vitruvius depicts here; the atomists, Democritus and Epicurus, actually stood somewhat outside this tradition and remained a minority approach in ancient science. Vitruvius, following Lucretius, combines aspects of both.

Throughout the *Ten Books* Vitruvius makes frequent use of the logic of scientific earth-air-fire-water terrestrial chemistry.[7] "Chemistry" was not really a separate field in antiquity, and in fact chemistry as a whole was not distinct from cosmology, astronomy, terrestrial physics, and even biology (medicine) and geology, and all were dependent on philosophy for their essential dialectic.[8] The system claimed to be remarkably all-encompassing because it could explain, in "chemical" earth-air-fire-water terms, the properties of both animate and inanimate objects – the phenomena of sickness and health in humans and durability or friability in building stones – and even phenomena of meteorology, dynamics, and cosmology.

Chemistry and Cosmology/Astronomy

The Aristotelian concept of the universe[9] was unitary and self-sufficient. (Vitruvius uses the term *mundus*, meaning both earth and universe.) It was a spherical plenum with no voids ("nature abhors a vacuum") but filled with continuous matter;[10] space was coterminous with matter, and therefore by definition the universe ended with the stellar sphere. There was nothing beyond that.

The universe was constructed of concentric nested spheres, the outer being the stellar sphere, the inner being the earth. In Aristotle there were fifty-five spheres, based on the spheres of Eudoxus and Callippus, and these accounted for the various separate movements of the stars, planets, sun, and moon. All of these touched each other and were driven by the outer sphere of the stars.

All of the spheres of the celestial realm (the spheres from the moon outward) were made of a fifth substance, "aether," which Aristotle thought of as a crystalline solid. It was pure and changeless, which accounted for the observable immutability of the heavens.

The sublunary realm, by contrast (i.e., terrestrial), consisted of four elements, or as Aristotle would have it, one continuous primal matter with four variously mixed sensible properties. (Most physicists, and those educated in the same tradition as Vitruvius, generally believed in four distinct elements. Vitruvius also followed atomism, which allowed the existence of voids, not the plenum concept.) In the absence of any external push, these would settle into a series of four concentric shells, with earth at the center, fire at the top, next to the celestial realm, and water and air filling the intermediate positions.

All these four elements had a natural propensity to move in one direction or another, depending on their properties of "gravity (heaviness)" and "levity (lightness)." These were seen as absolute forces tending to move elements to their "natural" sphere, observable in the motion of rocks through water to the center of the earth, and of fire through air toward the outer sublunary realm. Left alone, all four elements would return to their natural place.

However, the motion imparted to the universe by the stellar sphere caused all of the terrestrial elements constantly to be mixed so that they were never encountered in their pure state. The pulses of the stellar sphere passed through the mechanism of all of the touching crystalline spheres until they were passed to the earth by the lunar sphere, which, as the ancients easily observed, had a strong effect on tides. Hence the motion of the heavens was responsible for the variety of the sublunary realm.[11]

---

7 1.4.1–10 Explanation of strength and corruption in bodies.
   1.5.3 Scorched olive survives embedded in walls (explained with no chemistry).
   1.6.1–12 Physiology of winds on sites.
   2.2.1 Principles and history of early science.
   2.2.2 Mud-brick – no use of chemistry.
   2.5.2 Mortar.
   2.6.1–6 Pozzolana, geology and chemistry.
   2.7.2 Building stones.
   2.8.2 Strength and weakness of opus reticulatum.
   2.9.1–2.10.2 Types of timber.
   Books 3 and 4 (on temples) contain no chemistry.
   5.3.1 Motionless bodies in theaters, sitting with "pores open."
   5.9.5 Siting of porticoes, body heats with movement of exercise and is weakened by air sucking out moisture.
   6.1.1–11 Types of human physiology dependent on climate (i.e., latitude), which is basis for various forms of house design.
   6.2.2–3 Optics as basis for window placing.
   7.3.1; 7.8.3; 7.11.1; 7.13.1–2 Pigments.
   Book 8, Springs, numerous references, and assertion that variety of springs is due to "inclination of the heavens."
   9.1.12 Retrograde motion of planets explained as attractive power of heat.
   10. (Machines) no chemistry.
8 As Vitruvius says in (1.1.7).
9 The approach most widely accepted is best understood through Aristotle, mainly as it was expressed in *On the Heavens*. For summaries and discussions in histories of ancient science, see O. Pedersen, M. Pihl, *Early Physics and Astronomy* (London/New York, 1974), ch. 11, 141–152; T. Kuhn, *The Copernican Revolution* (Cambridge, Mass., 1957), 78–95; D. C. Lindberg, *The Beginnings of Western Science* (Chicago, 1992), 51–83.

10 The idea of continuous matter and "horror vacui" was not universally accepted. Democritean atomism insisted on the existence of void and matter, and Strato of Lampsacus, Aristotle's second successor at the Lyceum, demonstrated the existence of voids by experiments with the elasticity of air. Recorded in the opening of the *Pneumatics* of Heron of Alexandria. See B. Farrington, op. cit., 173–177.
11 When Vitruvius repeatedly uses the phrase "inclination of the Heavens" (*inclinatio mundi*) to explain the multifariousness of the earth, he is referring both to latitude ("climate") and to the inclination of the ecliptic, which accounts for the seasons and the never-repeating combinations of the orbits of the planets. (See further commentary on astronomy in Book 9.)

The System of Terrestrial Chemistry

All objects of the sublunary realm were regarded as various mixtures of the four primary elements and never thought to occur in their pure state. Aristotle claimed that the four elements were the result of combinations of the four sensible properties of material bodies:[12]

Dominant Quality	Secondary Quality	Elements
dryness	coldness	earth
coldness	moistness	water
moistness	heat	air
heat	dryness	fire

Each element was a combination of only two of the qualities, one primary, one secondary; an element could not contain two opposite qualities, such as fire and cold. Change, then, was explained by the intervention of some outside agent (an "adequate cause"), which altered the relation of primary to secondary properties and thus changed the element from one to another. Adding fire to water, therefore, drove out coldness, its primary quality, and replaced it with moisture, fire becoming the new secondary quality; that is, heat water and you get air.

In the system of the Stoic philosophers of the third century, each element had one property, and the elements were divided into active and passive:[13]

Quality	Element	
heat	fire	
		active
cold	air	
dryness	earth	
		passive
moistness	water	

Life involved the active elements of heat and air, which together constituted the divine *pneuma*, the life force that bound together the entire world and existed in eternal tension with passive or corruptive forces.

Vitruvius's Principles of Application of Chemistry

Chemistry is generally regarded by modern scholars as the weakest of the ancient sciences. It had a poor correlation with experiment,[14] a poor definition of observable properties, and poor predictive ability. The medical profession was the branch

of advanced knowledge most indebted to chemical knowledge, and limited by its limitations. Although the theory of the four elements was generally accepted by physicians, it also created skepticism in the profession from the time of the author of *On Ancient Medicine* (late fifth century B.C.?) to Galen (mid-second century A.D.); the former attacks all those who "attempt to practice medicine on the basis of a postulate,"[15] and Galen warns against the difficulty of dealing with the elements because they are so difficult to recognize in their pure state.[16] The difficulty of dealing with chemical concepts in a reliable and predictable way was one of the major causes of the creation of nondogmatic and empirical schools of medicine in the first centuries B.C. and A.D.

Vitruvius is one of our best sources outside medical writings for the attempt to use four-element chemistry as a predictive, or analytical, as well as a descriptive tool. He clearly believes objects can be combinations of all four elements in varying proportions, not just two. All bodies (*corpora*, and this refers equally to animate and inanimate bodies) are given their characteristics by the "tempering" (*temperatura*) of the four elements in them (i.e., mixture or adhesion). The goal of Vitruvius's scientific interest in a body is to maintain its solidity or health, or (like a doctor) to alter it by changing its character. The literal meaning of *temperatura* in Latin is regulation, or proportioning, that is, achievement of a consistency or stability of blend, or the adjustment between extremes that ensures the constitution of a body. By implication in this chemistry, it is indeed possible to change the *temperatura* of an object, but the result is a different object.

In general, from Vitruvius's descriptions, an object appears to be strengthened by being united with what it lacks and corrupted either by penetrating contact with what it already has in abundance, thus dis-tempering it, or by removal from an environment that supplies its natural lack.

❖ Hence fish, which, we are surprised to learn, have much fire and a fair amount of air and earth but little water, can live in water, because the ambience supplies the lack, but not on land, because they already have too little water;

❖ And land animals, which have moderate heat and air and less land but much moisture, can live on land, because they have little earth in them, but die in water, because they already have too much water in them.

❖ Alder (much air and fire, little earth and water) lasts forever as pilings in swamps because the earth and water are provided by the environment, but survives only a short time in the air, of which it has too much already.

❖ Or soft stones, like tufa, have much water and air in them, and hence dissolve in the rain from the excess of both; but travertine, which has much fire and air, little earth and water, resists weather, but not fire.

12 Pedersen/Pihl, op. cit., 144. The terminology mainly came from Hippocratic medicine in the later fifth century B.C.
13 Pedersen/Pihl, op. cit., 147–148.
14 Vitruvius does clearly indicate familiarity with experimental thought when he argues for the chemical change in limestone by pointing out that water is driven off when it is burned because it loses one-third its weight, and of course, does not combine with anything if simply ground up; 2.5.2.

15 Farrington, op. cit., 70.
16 *On Mixtures* 1.5.

The preceding examples are concerned to maintain the incorruptibility of bodies, but the same principles apply to altering *temperatura* to create new stable bodies. For Vitruvius matter seems to be particulate (atomic) and therefore capable of having voids. Thus some types of penetrating intervention, like heat, can "distemper" a body by removing one substance and leaving voids, and the presence of voids makes the altered body unstable and particularly vulnerable or eager to unite with some other matter.

❖ Hence, when one burns limestone to make lime (2.5.2), the process leaves voids and excess latent heat; when one plunges lime into water, it casts off its heat (water is cold as well as wet) and eagerly unites with sand or whatever other material it is mixed with.

❖ The best sand is that which is forged violently in volcanic regions. This sand has had its water and much earth driven off and has acquired excess heat; it is therefore eager to reunite with water or earth.

❖ In wall painting too (7.3.1) it is the "emptiness" of lime that makes it eager to reunite with pigment.

❖ Faced rubble work ("concrete") is unsound because tufa rubble continues a long slow process of sucking the "sap" (*sucus*) out of the mortar; the concrete can be made stronger by an abundance of mortar, but Vitruvius implies that the process of sap sucking goes on indefinitely and hence on chemical grounds is doomed to fail.

❖ Larch (2.9.14) has no pores and does not burn or sink.

In animate bodies, *venae* ("veins" or "pores") tend to be opened by heat, such as exercise or the attentive pleasure of being in a theater. Hence theaters and porticoes must be in healthful locations because the openness of the pores makes us vulnerable to foreign, "distempering" matter (5.3.1).

Changes in heat and cold weaken a body because the *temperatura* is adjusted for only one condition, and heat and cold are constantly either driving air or water out of pores in the fabric of matter or letting them in.[17] Heat in general is an attractive force, pulling things to it, like water in clouds, or steam in a bath. Vitruvius even observes the attractive power of heat in the celestial sphere, where a more sophisticated contemporary physicist would not, and uses heat's attraction to explain the retrograde motions of planets (9.1.12).

Certain other physical properties are associated with the presence or absence of the elements. Air is soft; water, obviously, moist; earth, hard; fire, rigid and friable. Hence fir is rigid (it has much air and fire, little water and earth), but burns and rots easily: burns because it already has much fire; rots, because if fire is driven out by cold (i.e., water) it is "rarefied" and made less solid by widely spaced voids.

The view of the physical world that Vitruvius acquired from his education and his reading seems, like that of Heraclitus, remarkably precarious. Even solid "stable" objects are compounds of warring opposites and complementaries coexisting in balanced tension. Any imbalance will cause corruption to another state. Stability is achieved by maintaining equilibrium between the body and its environment, or by "nourishing" or "sustaining" it.

The sections of the *Ten Books* that contain these "chemical" digressions are most similar in style to medical treatises, particularly those of the Dogmatic schools, and these are probably Vitruvius's main source and inspiration for adapting chemical theory to architecture.

Mud-Brick Masonry (2.3.1–4) (Figure 31)

For Vitruvius "brick" (*later*) automatically means mud brick, although on occasion he distinguishes *later coctus* from *later crudus*. Vitruvius's brick bond is basically the same as that for the fourth-century Servian wall.[18]

springtime or autumn (2.5.2)

Frontinus says that the building season was from April to November and stopped in the hottest times.[19]

Sand for Concrete Masonry (2.4.1–3)

SANDS, UNSUITABLE FOR MUD BRICK (MUD BRICK IS USUALLY MADE OF VERY FINE RIVER SILT):

[h]*arena*, *harenosus*: sand, sandy. (*harena fluviatica*, *fossicia*, *marina*: sand from rivers, excavation, sea.)
calculosa: pebbly.
glarea: pebbles, gravel, presumably larger than *calculosa*.
(*lutum*: clay); *lutum sabulosum*: again sandy, gritty clay.

SUITABLE FOR MUD BRICK:

creta: light clay, but sometimes chalk; chalky clay? Also the term for the material for fired tiles.
terra: a more imprecise term that can refer to anything from fine soil to clay to mud.
terra cretosa albida: whitish clay (-earth).
rubrica: red earth, presumably a red clay.
sabulo: usually sand, but Vitruvius includes it in materials suitable for mud brick, and hence it must be a type of clay/silt.
sabulo masculus: dense, serried silt?

The implication of this interpretation is that these terms may distinguish relative fineness from finest to coarsest: *creta* (*lutum*), *lutum* (clay), *rubrica* (red clay?), *sabulo* (silt), *terra* (earth, mud), *harena* (sand), *calculi*, pebbles, *glarea* gravel.

carbunculus: cinder.

Lime for Concrete Masonry (2.5.1–3)

calx: lime. The basic process of turning limestone into lime involves burning calcium carbonate (i.e., any stone rich enough in that compound to make processing worthwhile) to create calcium oxide:

---

17 6.1.4: in regions where the sun inflames, it robs bodies of moisture; where it is cold, vapors are never drained and bodies swell.

18 Lugli, *La tecnica edilizia Romana* (Rome, 1957), 530.
19 Frontinus. *De Aquis* 123.

$$CaCO_3 \rightarrow CO_2 + CaO$$

Adding water ("slaking" the "thirst" of the lime) reverses the process, in effect creating artificial limestone (calcium hydroxide):

$$CaO + H_2O \rightarrow CaOH$$

When combined with sand and other materials the calcium hydroxide in turn forms a variety of calcium silicate, aluminates, alumino-ferrates, and carbonates. Today, as in antiquity, the chemistry of concrete is very sensitive (and not completely understood), and very small variances in the mixture can destroy its strength. Hence Vitruvius emphasizes the importance of the proportions of the mixture as well as the definition of the materials:

sand:lime

If "excavated" sand, 3:1

if river or sea sand, 2:1; or add one further part pounded potsherds. (See *opus signinum* later.)

if pozzolana, 2:1 (he does not give the formula here but does later in 5.12.2, in describing the kind of mortar that will set under water).

in open air situations (7.1.5), 2 parts rubble,[20] 1 part terracotta (*testae*), 2 parts lime.

Pozzolana for Concrete Masonry (2.6.1–6)

See previous note.

Stone for Concrete Masonry (2.7.1–5)

saxum album: white stone, presumably limestone. Could refer to marble or travertine, although Vitruvius refers specifically to *marmor* (marble) some twenty-one times and distinguishes travertine.

Tiburtina (lapis tiburtinus): travertine (a porous sedimentary limestone), which he mentions as a medium hard stone, along with a presumed limestone from Amiternae and a presumed tufa from Soracte (2.7.1, 2.7.2).

tofus: tufa

saxa rubra: red tufa, probably from the Anio quarries.

Palla: unidentified quarries, possiby also the Anio quarries.

Alba: *lapis albanus*, "peperino," from near Castel Gandolfo, dark gray and fire resistant.

Fidenae, Amiternae, (Mt.) Soracte, all known places near Rome.

silex: this is one of the most mystifying of terms. In modern Italian it refers to volcanic *selce*, a basalt. It has been interpreted to mean flints,[21] but flints, although occurring as nodules in layers of chalk, are themselves a silicate of sandstone and cannot be burnt down to lime. (Flints will usually explode into sharp shards when put in a fire.)

Therefore it is likely that the term has been transferred to a totally different material since antiquity. Lugli interprets the term as meaning *"lapis duris,"* or hard stone, specifically that employed in polygonal masonry.[22] In Vitruvius *silex* can be: burnt for good lime; used as a material for fortification walls (1.5.8); a durable material for wall cores that is the equivalent of baked brick or squared tufa (2.8.4); a material for walls that can be used when one departs from squared stone, in alternation with "hard stone" (2.8.5); the type of *caementa* (rubble) to use in cisterns (*opus signinum*, 8.6.14). This implies that *silex* is a vague term which has no modern correspondent, but probably refers to a hard limestone, which can be squared (unlike flint or basalt) but, being very hard, is often used as split stone.

materia: also a very flexible term, which can mean either mortar or timber, as well as matter in general.

One of the major problems in trying to translate terms like these is that one culture will not recognize the distinctions in reality that another will. Ancient morphology was largely visual and tactile; hence, the pozzolana sand from around Puteoli, which is red, had exact equivalents elsewhere, which were ignored because they were yellow in color.[23] Thus certain types of flint or *selce* may have looked and felt a great deal like certain hard, blue limestones, and *"silex"* may have referred to a range of stones that we would distinguish from one another much more sharply.

Types of Concrete Masonry; Stone Masonry (2.8.1–10, 16–19) (Figures 32, 33)

Throughout the *Ten Books*, the term *structura*, generally translated here as rubble work, refers to various types of small stone masonry. This type of masonry, rather than large squared ashlar, seems to be Vitruvius's primary frame of reference.

caementa: rubble, the rough aggregate of "concrete," usually fist-sized blocks of tufa, but often *selce*, travertine, or any other material at hand.

opus caementicium: this refers to the mortared rubble core of the wall, not the whole wall; specifically, any "work" made of "rubble."[24]

opus incertum: literally "uncertain" work, an irregular pattern, hence slower to lay up but a masonry that, as he says, resists the propagation of cracks. *Opus incertum* provided the basic facing from the later third century, that is, the earliest "concrete," to mid-first century B.C.; in effect it was "invented" by building a wall of mortared rubble and tidying up the stones on the faces.

20 *rudus*, rubble, broken stone. There are several other formulas for mortars and plaster for special applications in Book 7. Oddly, these formulas leave out the sand.

21 L. Callebat, P. Fleury, *Dictionnaire des termes techniques du De Architectura de Vitruve* (Hildesheim, Zürich, New York, 1995), s.v. 36; F. Granger, *Vitruvius, on Architecture* (Cambridge and London, 1933), 97, translates "lava," and points out the quarrying of *silex* in four streams in Latium under the charge of the *procurator ad silices*.

22 G. Lugli, *La tecnica edilizia romana* (Rome, 1957), 46.

23 But by Vitruvius's time an identical sand from around Rome was replacing imports from Puteoli. J. B. Ward-Perkins, *Roman Architecture* (Harmondsworth, 1970), 247. Pliny the Elder, *Natural History* 16.202.

24 Lugli argues that terms like *opus caementicium*, *opus reticulatum*, and so on, are terms that should refer to the whole wall system. Hence a wall that is made in *"opus reticulatum"* implies that its facing is reticulate whereas its core is *caementicium*. It seems much more likely that Vitruvius applies terms to specific parts of the wall with precision. Hence any given wall is a combination of *opera*, based on the builder's discretion. G. Lugli, *Tecnica edilizia romana* (Rome, 1957), 47–49.

[MUD-] BRICK (<u>LATERES</u>) 2.3.1-4.

LYDION
(one by one and a half feet)

GREEK PENTADORON
(five palms)

GREEK TETRADORON
(four palms = one foot)

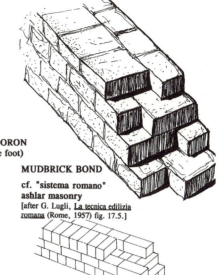

MUDBRICK BOND

cf. "sistema romano"
ashlar masonry
[after G. Lugli, <u>La tecnica edilizia</u>
<u>romana</u> (Rome, <u>1957</u>) fig. 17.5.]

IMPERIAL PERIOD FIRED BRICK SIZES (<u>testa</u>)
with standard patterns for cutting into facing tiles

<u>Bessales</u> (two-thirds foot)

<u>Sesquipedales</u> (one-and-a-half footers)

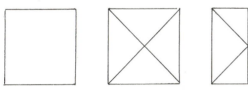

<u>Bipedales</u> (two-footers)

 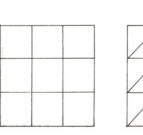

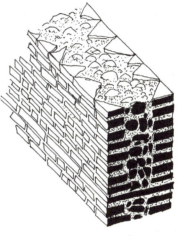

IMPERIAL PERIOD <u>OPUS TESTACEUM</u>

Bricks cut from Roof/floor tiles

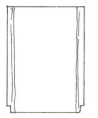 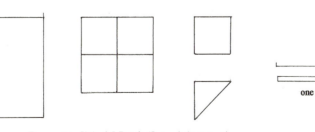

.5 m.

one foot (.295 m.)

Figure 31. [Mud-] Brick (*Lateres*) (2.3.1–4).

FACING (2.8.1-4)

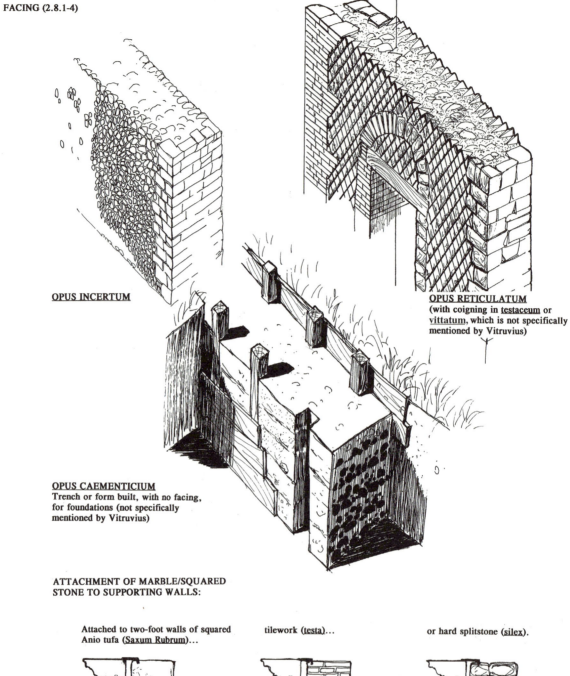

OPUS INCERTUM

<u>OPUS RETICULATUM</u>
(with coigning in <u>testaceum</u> or
<u>vittatum</u>, which is not specifically
mentioned by Vitruvius)

<u>OPUS CAEMENTICIUM</u>
Trench or form built, with no facing,
for foundations (not specifically
mentioned by Vitruvius)

ATTACHMENT OF MARBLE/SQUARED
STONE TO SUPPORTING WALLS:

Attached to two-foot walls of squared   tilework (<u>testa</u>)...   or hard splitstone (<u>silex</u>).
Anio tufa (<u>Saxum Rubrum</u>)...

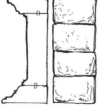
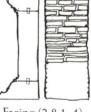
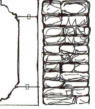

Figure 32. Facing (2.8.1–4).

"THE MASONRY OF THE GREEKS" (2.8.5-7)

ISODOMIC   **PSEUDOISODOMIC**   **EMPLEKTON**

Resistance of squared
stone walls to plastic
flow when mortar desiccates

Collapse of rubble
walls by plastic
flow

Hellenistic Walls on Delos
[after Delos viii (1932) pl. 37.]

TRADITIONAL INTERPRETATIONS

Isodomic   Pseudoisodomic

<u>Emplekton</u>

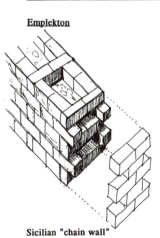

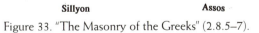

Sicilian "chain wall"   Sillyon   Assos

Figure 33. "The Masonry of the Greeks" (2.8.5–7).

opus reticulatum: standard-sized small pyramidal blocks (c. 4–10 cm) in a regular reticulate pattern, first attested in the Theater of Pompey, 60–55 B.C. Coigns and arches are usually built of small tufa blocks from c. 60 B.C., and begin to be built from tiles/bricks in the time of Augustus.[25]

structura testacea: terracotta,[26] or tile-work walls (2.8.17), or the weatherproof capping for mud-brick walls (2.8.18) or weatherproof flooring (7.1.4, 7.1.7, 7.4.3, 7.4.5); it becomes what we later know as the standard brick facing of Roman "concrete" in the Imperial age. Vitruvius's term makes it clear that brick-faced concrete was "invented" by replacing soft tufa reticulate by a more durable material: broken tiles. His critical discussion and suggestions make clear that the process of reevaluating and improving concrete facing was under way in the decade in which he was writing.[27] Brick-faced concrete became standard in the reign of Tiberius.

opus signinum:[28] in modern archaeology this term signifies mortar with a high addition of crushed terracotta in order to make it waterproof. Vitruvius is aware of this kind of mortar (2.5.1; 7.1.5), which became very common for all kinds of hydraulic application throughout the empire in the first century A.D., but he has no special term for it. For him *opus signinum* refers to mortar with "silex" in the aggregate; the fact that he recommends it for cisterns (8.6.14) implies that it too is appropriate for waterproof construction.

isodomum, pseudoisodomum, and *emplekton:* these are normally taken to be patterns of ashlar masonry, and the latter term is very controversial. The traditional interpretation of *emplekton* relates it to a number of common and well-attested techniques of Greek Hellenistic ashlar masonry, particularly in fortification walls, but also in the walls of large buildings like stoas. It is usually seen as a type of compartment wall, with two faces of ashlar around a mud and rubble core, and long headers penetrating the core at intervals.[29] However,

the crucial operating phrase in Vitruvius is "whenever they depart from building with squared blocks. . . ." they build walls like this (isodomic, etc.).[30] In fact the whole section (1.8) is about small stone masonry, walls built of everything from mud brick to rubble (French *petit appareil* fits the meaning), not about large ashlar.[31] Vitruvian use of the term *emplekton* therefore seems to mean that the two facings are laid to a level surface (i.e., not dressed),[32] that headers and stretchers of the two faces intertwine, with no real separate core, and that at intervals certain extra long stretchers (*diatonoi*) extend through the entire wall. The walls of most of the buildings in Delos, which was one of the most central and most visited seaports of the Mediterranean in the second and early first century B.C., and which from 197 was dominated by an Italian merchant community, are similar to this; they are basically flagstones bonded in mud mortar, the pattern being what might be called in modern terminology random ashlar.

Halicarnassus (2.8.10–15) (Figure 34)

Halicarnassus was an Ionian Greek city that from the sixth century was ruled by a Carian dynasty, who became the satraps under the Persian empire; the population remained mixed Ionian Greek and Carian (Vitruvius records that the Greeks drove away the Carians but they were drawn back by the quality of the springs). Halicarnassus rose to importance when Mausolus became satrap of Caria (377–353) and made it his capital instead of Mylasa (an inland town). He rebuilt the walls, transplanted the population of several towns to the site, and began his massive tomb, the "Mausoleum." He was succeeded by his sister-wife Artemisia II (died 350), who completed the tomb. She also repelled an attack from Rhodes, for which Vitruvius 2.8.14–15 is the only source.

Vitruvius's account is the principal ancient source for the topography of the city. Of the buildings mentioned, only the Mausoleum has been located. The first or inner harbor of Artemisia was clearly the inner harbor of today, but the outer harbor was probably only the open roadstead, connected to

25 Lugli, *Tecnica edilizia romana* (Rome, 1957), 505–508.

26 *Testaceus* normally refers to the material, *tegula* to the form, of tiles. Utilitarian earthenware pottery can be *testaceus.* Vitruvius does not use the term *opus testaceum.* He does refer to *opus figlinum* (5.10.3), meaning "potterywork" (referring to suspended tile ceilings), and *spicatum/tiburtinum,* meaning herringbone pavements.

27 It is worth noting that in Roman remains today the tufa reticulate of the facing has often eroded deeply while the hard mortar still projects.

28 Literally masonry in the Signian manner; Signia, a small town in the hills of Latium to the southwest of Rome.

29 A. W. Lawrence, *Greek Architecture* (Harmondsworth, 1957), 230. F. E. Winter, *Greek Fortifications* (Toronto, 1971), 135–137. Some writers think that this kind of compartment wall was one of the models for Roman-faced concrete because the mud mortar of these walls was usually carefully produced and sometimes had admixtures of lime; hence, by a gradual process of purification, Hellenistic stone facing with a rubble core became Roman-faced lime-mortared rubble (e.g., H.-O. Lamprecht, *Opus Caementitium* [Duesseldorf, 1987], 21; R. L. Vann, *A Study of Roman Construction in Asia Minor* [Diss., Cornell, 1976]; M. Waelkens, "The Adoption of Roman Building Techniques in Asia Minor," in *Roman Architecture in the Greek World* [London, 1987], 94–102.) R. A. Tomlinson suggested that the term *emplekton* referred only to the outer "woven" appearance of the wall (R. A. Tomlinson, "Emplekton Masonry and Greek Structura," *Journal of Hellenic Studies* 81 [1961],

133–140.) Lars Karlsson recently suggested that Vitruvius was referring to a type of Hellenistic masonry common primarily in Sicilian fortifications which has a virtual wall of headers penetrating the core every 10 feet or so, something he refers to as a "masonry chain" (L. Karlsson, *Fortification Techniques and Masonry Towers in the Hegemony of Syracuse, 402–211 B.C.* [Stockholm, 1992], 67–95.) Pliny the Elder (*Natural History* 36.171–172) gives a description that is clearly a scholarly recension of Vitruvius. He gets the description a little wrong, claiming that *diatonicon* means the core is packed with rubble, whereas in Vitruvius it means that stones penetrate from one face to the other, and there is no rubble core.

30 *sed cum discesserunt a quadrato* explicitly refers to ashlar.

31 The fact that the technique is also compared to rustic construction (*nostri rustici*) further confirms that Vitruvius refers to small stone walling, not massive dressed ashlar. Hence *isodumum* and *pseudoisodomum* as well as *emplekton* refer to small stone construction.

32 *plana conlocantes* does not imply that they are dressed, but merely laid with one edge creating a level surface.

HALICARNASSUS (2.8.10-15)

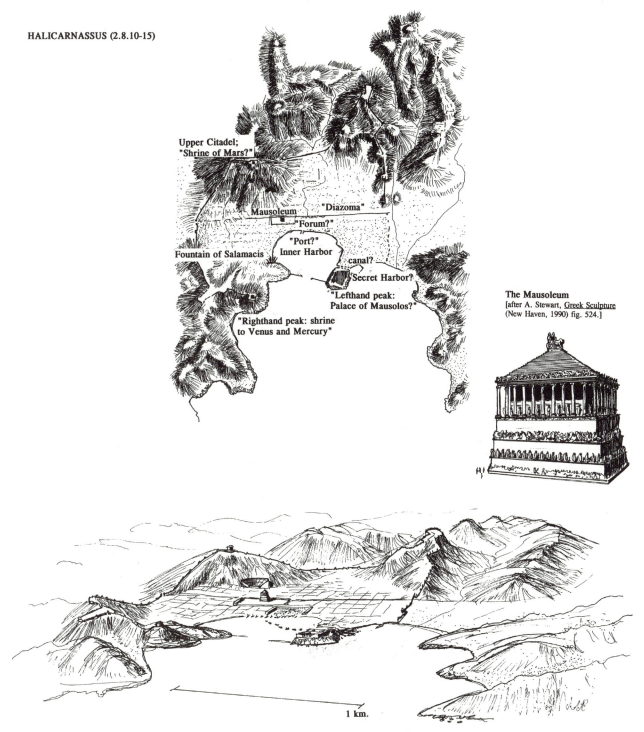

1 km.

Figure 34. Halicarnassus (2.8.10–15).

(2.8.16–20)

RECONSTRUCTION OF LATE REPUBLICAN <u>INSULAE</u> IN THE SUBURA

VITRUVIUS: MUDBRICK WALLS WITH <u>TESTACEUM</u> CORNICES (2.8.19)

↓1½ FEET

POMPEII: SMALLSTONE (<u>OPUS CAEMENTICIUM</u>) WALL STRENGTHENED BY PIERS (SO-CALLED <u>OPUS AFRICANUM</u>)
(after Overbeck-Mau, <u>Pompeii</u>, fig. 262)

<u>OPUS CRATICIUM</u>

Figure 35. "The Expedient of Tall Buildings" (2.8.16).

FELLING TIMBER

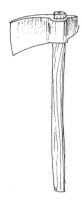

CHOPPING DOWN TREES TO BUILD AN ENCAMPMENT
(from Trajan's Column)

SLEDGING A LOG WITH CORDS
(from a relief in the Archaeological Museum in Bordeaux)

Figure 36. Felling Timber (2.9.1).

the first by a secret canal across the palace isthmus.[33] The form of the Mausoleum – a colonnade on top of a high podium – was developed in non-Greek lands of western Asia Minor in the later fifth century (e.g., the Nereid monument at Xanthos) and became one of the most influential forms of Hellenized architecture in the classical Mediterranean.

Parts of the city wall, the Mausoleum and the principal street – the one that Vitruvius likened to the diazoma of a theater – are locatable. Other parts of his description match the site if its first part is taken as looking from the acropolis: the spring of Salamacis and the shrine of Venus and Mercury (Aphrodite and Hermes) is probably near the west horn of the harbor (the right-hand peak looking south), where fresh water rises from the seafloor today; and the palace must have been on the central promontory, the left-hand peak. The secret harbor was probably just part of the more open east harbor,[34] connected with the other by a canal through the palace isthmus.

the expedient of tall buildings (2.8.17) (Figure 35)

Multistory *insulae* (apartment buildings with shops on the ground floor and rental apartments above) are attested in Rome from as early as 218 B.C., when Livy tells us that a runaway ox fell out of the third story of a house in the Forum Boarium.[35] Vitruvius's critical discussion is part of the background of Augustus's law of 27 B.C. limiting the heights of buildings and foreshadows Nero's requirement that buildings be faced in fired brick after the fire of A.D. 64.[36]

Favonius begins to blow (2.9.1) (Figure 36)

The Favonii blow at the beginning of spring. See Horace, *Carmina* 1.4.1. Pliny the Elder confidently asserts they begin to blow on 18 February (*NH* 2.122).

pollarded trees (2.9.4)

Arbusta can be trees as well as shrubs, especially the kind set between vines in a vineyard, usually elm.

Larignum (2.9.15)

This is the only source for the siege of Larignum, either in the Gallic wars or the Civil Wars; it is not mentioned by Caesar.

BOOK 3

Myron, Polycleitus, Phidias, Lysippus (3.praef.2)

This is a standard list of the most renowned classical artists in chronological order, as passed on from Xenocrates, lacking only Pythagoras of Rhegium and Praxiteles of Athens from the usual list.

Hegias of Athens, Chion of Corinth, Boedas of Byzantium . . . (3.praef.2)

This is, as Vitruvius implies, a list of less known artists. Those elsewhere attested include Hegias (or Hegesias or Hagias), master or pupil of Phidias,[1] Chion,[2] Myagrus,[3] Boedas,[4] Polycles,[5] and Theo of Magnesia.[6]

For Nature composed the human body . . . which the famous ancient painters and sculptors employed (3.1.2) (Figure 37)

This passage refers to the Canon (Greek *Kanôn*) of Polycleitus of Argos and other literature on proportions that it inspired. The *Canon* was the title of both a statue and a treatise created by Polycleitus, probably in the third quarter of the fifth century B.C., to demonstrate the application of *symmetria*, or a theoretical, ideal system of proportions, to the human figure.[7] The best summary of its content comes from Galen, the encyclopedic physician of the second century A.D. In paraphrasing the opinion of the Stoic philosopher Chrysippus that health is the result of the harmony of the constituent elements of the body, he says: "Beauty . . . resides not in the commensurability of the constituents [of the body], but in the commensurability of parts, such as the finger to finger, and of all the fingers to the metacarpus and the carpus (wrist), and of these to the forearm, and of the forearm to the arm, in fact of everything to everything, as it is written in the *Canon* of Polycleitus."[8] Philo Mechanicus adds a remark, which may be a direct quotation from the *Canon*, that "perfection [*to eu*, the good, excellent] arises *para mikrôn* [from the small] through many numbers."[9] The exact meaning of this statement is much debated (see figure) but it appears, from the phrase *para mikrôn*, and from the rhetorical sequence in Galen's description,[10] that there is a module based on the smallest part

33 G. E. Bean, s.v. in *Princeton Encyclopedia of Classical Sites* (Princeton, 1976), 375–376; E. Akurgal, *Ancient Civilizations and Ruins of Turkey* (Istanbul, 1978), 248–251.

34 Cf. the separately enclosed Royal Harbor at Alexandria.

35 Livy, 44.16.10.

36 Tacitus, *Annals* 15.43; Strabo, 5.3.7 (235).

1 Pliny the Elder, *Natural History* 34.49, 34.78.

2 Pausanias, 10.13.7.

3 Pliny the Elder, *Natural History* 34.91.

4 Pliny the Elder, *Natural History* 34.66, 34.73.

5 Possibly the son of Timarchides, a Greek painter active in Rome in the later second century B.C.

6 Pliny the Elder, *Natural History* 35.144.

7 *Kanôn* in Greek is a wooden measuring rod used by, among others, architects. The written version of Polycleitus's treatise was probably like a workshop manual that explained the system of proportions in great detail. It appears to have been the best known of all ancient treatises on aesthetics. See J. J. Pollitt, *The Ancient View of Greek Art* (New Haven, 1974), 14–22. The manuscript is lost, but there are several ancient references to its content: Pliny the Elder, *Natural History* 34.55; Lucian, *De morte peregrina* 9; and especially Galen, *De Temperamentis* 1.9.

8 Trans. Pollitt, op. cit., 15.

9 *Syntaxis* 4.1.49. trans. Pollitt, loc. cit. On attempts to derive the *canon* from known Roman copies of statues of Polycleitus, see R. Tobin, "The Canon of Polykleitos," *American Journal of Archaeology* 79 (1975), 307–320, or H. Von Steuben, *Der Kanon des Polyklet* (Tübingen, 1969); also F. W. Schlikker, *Hellenistische Vorstellungen von der Schönheit des Bauwerks nach Vitruv* (Berlin, 1940), 55, 60.

10 Galen was a well-trained writer and proud of his prose style.

or parts, or some sort of modular progression from the smallest to the largest determinate parts.

In the fourth century B.C. Lysippus modified the proportions of Polycleitus's canon in the direction of attenuation (e.g., foot to height equals 1:7 instead of 1:6); he was one of the last sculptors to place emphasis on *symmetria* in practice, as opposed to *eurythmia*, "grace, pleasing appearance" (i.e., an intuitive modification of proportion). Xenocrates, who more or less founded written art criticism in the fourth century B.C., was a sculptor trained in Lysippus's school, and it was through him that the concept of symmetry was passed on to literature in general as a fundamental critical tool.

Modern interpretation of the *canôn* remains unresolved,[11] but the general idea is that the smallest part must have served as the module, and this module generated all the other major dimensions by means of some sort of mathematical or geometrical exercise. R. Tobin, for instance, suggested an "areal" method, in which each linear measurement was squared, and the diagonal of that square formed the next linear measurement.[12]

the center and midpoint
of the human body . . . (3.1.3) (Figure 38)

The famous problem with this Vitruvian image is the fact that the arms and legs of a human body have separate pivots, and hence when rotated form four arcs with four centers, not a single circle with the center at the "umbilicus"-navel. (The inscribing of the extended arms within a square usually is true.) However, the actual rotation of limbs conforms rather closely with the image that Vitruvius suggests because the positions of the joints themselves move as well as the arms and legs. Vitruvius is aware that he is only speaking of the body's approximation to a geometric ideal, for he says "to whatever extent (*quemadmodum*) the circular scheme may be present in the body."

Perfect Numbers (3.1.5–6)

The concept of "perfect" numbers (*teleios*, which has the same meaning as Latin *perfectus*: finished, a completed process) is almost certainly part of Pythagorean number mysticism (late sixth century B.C.). There were two different attitudes as to what the perfect number ought to be. The number 10 is definitely associated with original Pythagorean doctrine (the "ancients," sixth century B.C.),[13] being the sum of the numbers 1, 2, 3, 4 that form the *tetraktys* (triangle of four units on each side). This

figure was the "most sacred oath" of the Pythagoreans and the "principle of health:"[14]

```
    1              1
   1 1            2 3
  1 1 1          4 5 6
 1 1 1 1        7 8 9 10
```

The numbers of the *tetraktys* also comprise the ratios of the principal musical intervals: the fifth (4:3), the fourth (3:2), and the octave (2:1). The triangle surrounds an inscribed hexagon (thus including the other perfect number), and its center is 5, the midpoint between 1 and 10.

The other tradition ("the mathematicians"), that six is the perfect number, may derive as well from Pythagorean tradition, but there is no mention of it in the fragments of Philolaos, Plato, or Aristotle (the earliest sources for Pythagorean doctrine). The earliest definition is from Euclid, c. 300 B.C. (7. Def. 22) and hence is likely to lie more purely in the realm of mathematical speculation. A perfect number is a number that is equal to the sum of its own parts, that is, all of its factors, including 1:

$$6 = 1 + 2 + 3$$
$$28 = 1 + 2 + 4 + 7 + 14$$
$$496 = 1 + 2 + 4 + 8 + 16 + 31 + 62 + 124 + 248$$

Nicomachus knew of only four perfect numbers: 6, 28, 496, 8,128. (There are others, the next being 33,550,336.) Vitruvius's explanation, by naming the constituent fractions of 1 to 12, is slightly awkward, and not the way a professional mathematician would have done it, but it is probably his way of explaining the factors of six.[15]

The notion that sixteen is a perfect number is probably Vitruvius's own rhetorical invention, based on observation of common events, and not necessarily part of the erudite mathematical traditions.[16]

denarius of ten pounds (3.1.8)

The Vitruvian term here translated as "pound" is *as* (pural *asses*). In Greek and Roman currency, coin values were essentially units of weight, and the units of the two systems were similar. Roman *unciae* (ounces, twelve to an *as*) could also be linear measurements (inches, twelve to a foot). Digital linear

---

11 H. Diels, *Antike Technik* (Leipzig, 1914), 14 ff.; S. Ferri, "Nuovi contributi esegetici al "Canone" della scultura greca," *Rivista dell' Istituto Archeologico di Atene* (1920), 133 ff.; J. E. Raven, "Polyclitus and Pythagoreanism"; D. Schulz, "Zum Kanon Polyklets," *Hermes* 23 (1950), 200–220; Th. Lorenz, *Polyklet* (Wiesbaden, 1972); H. von Steuben, *Polyklet* (Tübingen, 1969/1975).

12 R. Tobin, "The Canon of Polykleitos," *American Journal of Archaeology* 79 (1975) 307–321.

13 Aristotle, *Metaphysics* M 8, 1024 a 32–34.

14 Theo of Smyrna, p. 93, 17–94.9; Lucian, *De Lapsu in salutando*, 5; both in Heath, *A History of Greek Mathematics* (Oxford, 1921), I, 75. The triple interwoven triangle, or pentagram – that is, star-shaped pentagon – was the principal symbol of health and the main sign of recognition among Pythagoreans. Scholiast on Aristophanes, *Clouds*, 609; Lucian, *De Lapsu* . . . 5.1.447–8, ed. C. Jacobitz.

15 The passage has sometimes been considered a later addition.

16 The numbers 6 and 10 and their arithmetical derivatives were common in Roman building practices of the first centuries B.C. and A.D. (i.e., simple fractions or multiples: 3, 12, 24; 5, 20, etc.). M. Wilson Jones, "Designing the Roman Corinthian Order," *Journal of Roman Archaeology* 2 (1989), 62.

COMMON UNITS OF MEASURE (3.1.1-9)

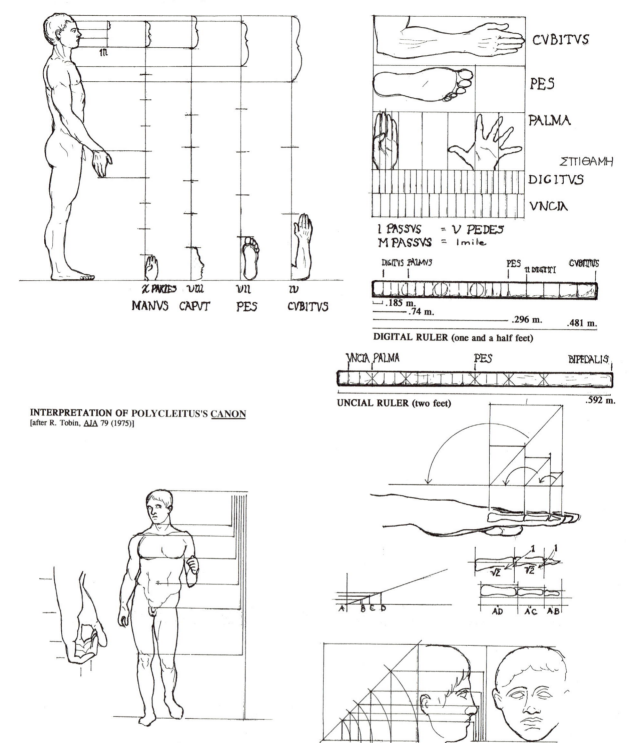

INTERPRETATION OF POLYCLEITUS'S <u>CANON</u>
[after R. Tobin, <u>AJA</u> 79 (1975)]

Figure 37. Common Units of Measure (3.1.1–9).

HOMO BENE FIGURATUS (3.1.1-4)

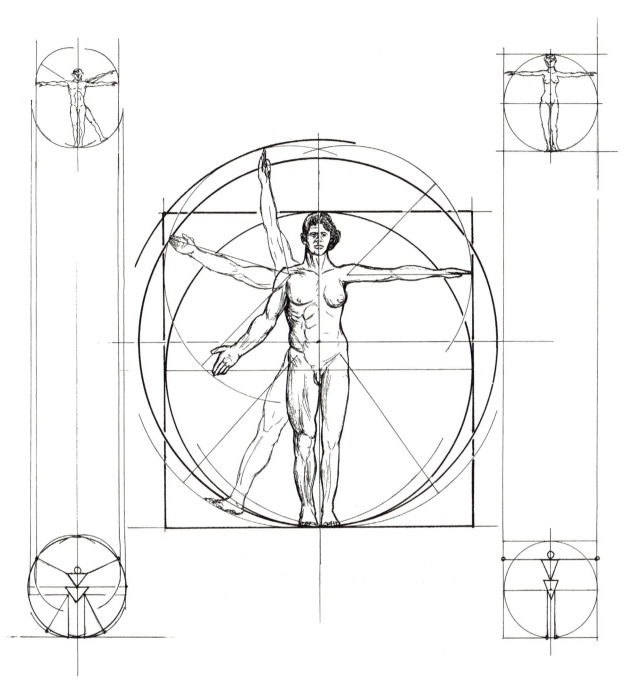

Figure 38. *Homo Bene Figuratus* (3.1.1–4).

measurement (16 *digiti* to a foot) was more common in building, and in Vitruvius.

Pliny records that during the crisis of Hannibal's invasion the denarius was revalued from ten to sixteen *asses*.[17] Vitruvius's argument here seems to be that this revaluation was a result of, or in line with, mathematical-philosophical speculation. His equation of the Greek *obolos* with the Roman bronze *as* is not very close, although the denarius and the drachma had roughly similar values.

Greek

4 tricalcha = 1 obolos
obolos = 1.04 gr., Aeginetan, 0.73 gr. Athenian
6 oboloi = 1 drachma
100 drachmai = 1 mna
60 mnai = 1 talent (6,000 drachmai)

Roman

1 uncia = .27–27,5 gr.
12 unciae = 1 as (originally = 1 libra/pound, 88 gr., gradually reduced to 55 gr. in mid-second century, to less than half that by late second century)
[4 quadrantes (fourths) = 1 as]
[3 trientes (thirds) = 1 as]
4 asses = 1 sestertius (originally 2 1/2 asses = 1 sestertius, contraction of "semis tertius," i.e., 2 1/2 asses)
4 sestertii = 1 denarius (16 asses, originally 10/*decem* asses)
[2 quinarii = 1 denarius]
25 denarii = 1 aureus
6,000 denarii or c. 25,000 sestertii = 1 talent

Temple Types (3.2.1–8) (Figures 39, 40)

Throughout the *Ten Books* Vitruvius uses the terms "pronaos" and "posticum" simply to refer to any space under a colonnade in the front and back. The modern use of the terms tends to restrict their meaning to the space between the antae, the columns in antis, and the short walls of the cella ("pronaos" and "opisthodomos"), particularly as determined by the plans of Greek temples, but in Vitruvius the terms are more flexible, or less specific, and refer to all the space at front and back, that bounded by the peripteral colonnade, if there is one, as well as that bounded by the antae and columns in antis.

Hermodorus . . . Mucius (3.2.5)

Hermodorus of Salamis (Cyprus), architect of this building, the first all-marble Greek-style temple in Rome (supposedly), architect of the temple of Mars, and restorer of the *navalia*

(ship sheds), active c. 146 to c. 110 B.C.[18] On the Roman architect [C.] Mucius, see Commentary: 7.praef.17.

Hermogenes (3.2.6; also 7.praef.12)

Architect of Artemis Leukophryne ("Diana") at Magnesia and Dionysos (= "Pater Liber") at Teos in western Asia Minor. See Commentary: 7.praef.12.[19]

Apollo at Alabanda . . . by Menesthenes (3.2.6)

A small pseudodipteros in western Asia Minor, second century B.C.; Menesthenes, unknown elsewhere, was presumably a student of Hermogenes.

The *Species* ["Aspects"] of Temples (3.3.1–13)

"Species" generally means visual appearances or aspects, the effect of visual appearance, and therefore it is here more or less the same as the elevation of a building.

There are two ways of looking at how the proportional system given by Vitruvius works: the first is that, given a consistent diameter, column height reduces with increase in intercolumniation, or span; the second is that, given constant height, column diameter increases with increase in span. Vitruvius phrases it the latter way, which gives priority to structural considerations (see figures).

A further necessary implication is that, taking the entire Vitruvian system presented by Books 3 and 4 together, as the thickness of the column increases, the capital and base are higher in proportion to the total height of the column, and the shaft less. The reason is that both base and capital are a fixed fraction of the lower diameter of the column, and that as thickness increases (i.e., lower diameter becomes a larger proportion of the total height), the base and capital obviously become a larger part of the total height as well.[20] The actual practice, as it became established in the first century A.D., seems to have been quite different, and more practical: namely, that the shaft was normally fixed at five-sixths of the full height of the column regardless of the thickness.[21] Variations could still occur in the height of the capital and base, but if the capital were higher, the base had to be lower, and vice versa.

Entablature height in the Vitruvian system, like the degree of neck (hypotrachelium) contraction, is dependent on absolute scale, not proportion.

---

17 Pliny the Elder, *Natural History* 33, 42–46. The revaluation of 213/ 212 is actually fairly complex and controversial, and may (or may not) have involved, as Pliny reports, the reduction of the *as* to an ounce (*uncia*); the change of the denarius from ten to sixteen *asses* may more likely have occurred in the later second century, about the time of the Gracchi. C. H. V. Sutherland, *Roman Coins* (New York, 1974), 45–47.

18 P. Gros, "Hermodorus et Vitruve," *Mélanges de l'Ecole Française de Rome. Antiquité* 85 (1973), 137–161.

19 For recent discussion and earlier bibliography, see W. Hoepfner, "Bauten und Bedeuten des Hermogenes," in *Hermogenes und die Hochhellenistische Baukunst* (Mainz, 1990), 1–34.

20 This is pointed out by Mark Wilson Jones, "Designing the Roman Corinthian Order," *Journal of Roman Archaeology* 2 (1989) 60–61. The figure here is adapted from his figure 12.

21 M. Wilson Jones, loc. cit.

entasis (3.3.13) (Figure 44)

There is no indication in the Vitruvian text of the method for creating *entasis* since Vitruvius relies wholly on a diagram that was originally at the end of each copy of the scroll for Book 3. No manuscript survives with a version of the diagram.

Entasis in Greek means tension or bowing, and therefore the basic meaning is clear: it refers to some sort of swelling curvature that was a common feature of Greek Doric columns from the early sixth century B.C. and of Ionic from the later fourth. The most likely method of creating that curvature is represented by full-scale third-century sketch drawings incised into the unfinished walls of the Temple of Apollo at Didyma (which would have been erased when the walls were given their final dressing).[22] The drawing shows one of the columns of the external colonnade, with the horizontal dimension in full scale and the vertical reduced to one-sixteenth (i.e., each vertical division of a dactyl/digit represents one foot). It also shows the upper torus of the base, the flare, the conical taper of the hypotrachelium contraction and, outside of that, the arc of a circle. The circle, which gives the curve of the entasis, is presumably swung from a center on the line that is perpendicular to the line of the contraction taper. The execution of the actual column simply required the translation of each vertical digit into a foot, which is a kind of multiplication that required only the use of the standard ruler, and no arithmetic. By this kind of multiplication the arc of the circle, and hence the actual curvature of the entasis, becomes stretched to an ellipse.

An alternative, and even simpler, way to obtain entasis seems to have been used for columns in Rome from the first century A.D.[23] The rough cut of the column shaft is guided by two lines: one from the lower diameter just above the flare to the projection of the astragal at the top of the shaft (more or less a vertical); and the second from the hypotrachelium (the upper diameter beneath the flare) to the projection of the lower astragal. The intersection of these two lines shapes the shaft as a truncated cone above a cylinder. The junction is then simply rounded off by eye.

The foundations (3.4.1–4) (Figure 45)

Earlier Greek and Etruscan foundations were continuous linear masses of bonded ashlar masonry running under the entire line of each colonnade as well as under all the walls, but the foundation described here is typical of what became standard practice in the later Republic and most of the Empire: isolated ashlar pier foundations to take the concentrated loads under columns, which are stabilized with a mass of concrete rubble infill or with vaulted chambers, all of this resting on a raft or footing of concrete ("structura"). The use of piles in soft ground under foundations is also fairly common. Pile drivers were relatively common and could even be floated on rafts to work over water. The use of charcoal (and fleeces) is attested in literature for the foundations of the archaic Artemision of Ephesus.[24]

The concern in monumental buildings was that the foundations should be, if not immobile, capable of settling as a unit, rather than differentially. In buildings of unmortared stone, any differential settling will open visible cracks in the joints of the blocks of the walls and epistyles, causing large blocks to be unevenly supported or loaded, eventually leading them to split. In Roman temples the substructure chambers could be used as storage vaults; the state treasury of Rome kept its reserve supply in the basements of the Temple of Saturn in the Forum; the mint hoarded its assets in the temple Juno Moneta on the Capitoline.

The steps in front . . . always an odd number (3.4.4) (Figure 45)

There are several testimonia in Roman literature that entry into a room with the right foot is a sign of fortune or respect for a sacred place, even if it is a house.[25]

plinth, base molding, dado, cornice, and lysis (3.4.5) (Figure 45)

In practice there were several variations on the forms of the podium listed in Vitruvius. See figures.

scamilli impares: Stylobate Curvature (3.4.5)

"*Scamilli impares*" (or *inpares*) literally means "unequal little benches," and the little benches are some sort of physical leveling tool for controlling the curvature.[26] In vertical surveying, the one certain starting point for all operations is a leveled line or plane, established with the use of a surveyor's level. If one face of a set of unequal little blocks are lined up, they are most likely lined up on the line of the horizontal; the gradation or "inequality" in the other ends can control a curvature.

The curvature can, of course, be anything one desires, but if one follows the procedure suggested in the Didyma drawings of column entasis – stretching a circle to form an ellipse – one can shape a convenient set of scamilli by fitting their heights under the arc of a compass-drawn circle.

22 L. Haselberger, "Werkzeichnungen am jüngern Didymaion," *Istanbuler Mitteilungen* 30 (1980), 192–215; idem, "Bericht über die Arbeit am jüngeren Apollontempel von Didyma," *Istanbuler Mitteilungen* 33 (1983), 123–140.

23 Proposed by Mark Wilson Jones in a paper given at the Williams symposium on stylobate curvature at the University of Pennsylvania, April 2–4, 1993. In press for *Appearance and Essence: Refinements of Classical Architecture: Curvature* (Philadelphia, 1997).

24 Pliny the Elder, *Natural History* 36.95; A. Bammer, *Die Architektur des jüngeren Artemisions von Ephesos* (Wiesbaden, 1972), 3.

25 Virgil, *Aeneid* 8.302; Petronius, 30.5; Horace, *Epistles* 2.2.37, Statius, *Silvae* 7.172.

26 First proposed by Bournof, reprised by W. H. Goodyear, *Greek Refinements* (New Haven, London, and Oxford, 1912), 114.

TYPES (<u>GENERA</u>) OF TEMPLES (3.2.1-8)

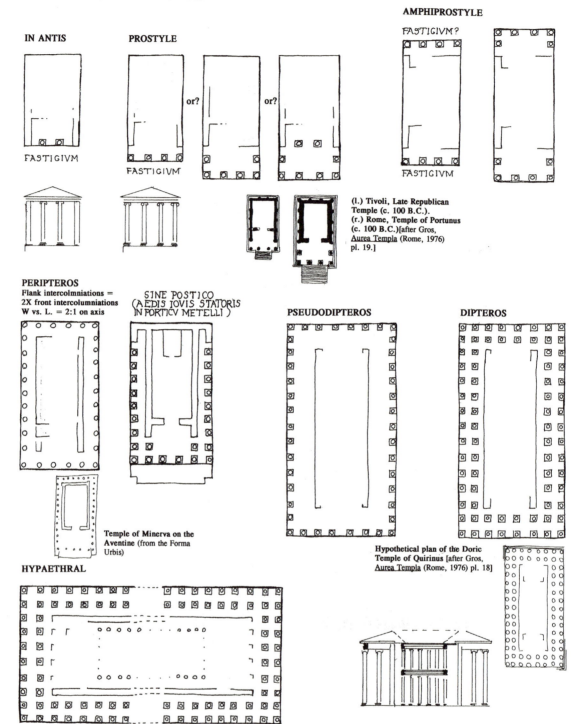

Figure 39. Types (*Genera*) of Temples (3.2.1–8).

HELLENISTIC IONIC TEMPLES IN THE TRADITION OF PYTHEOS AND HERMOGENES:

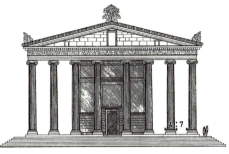

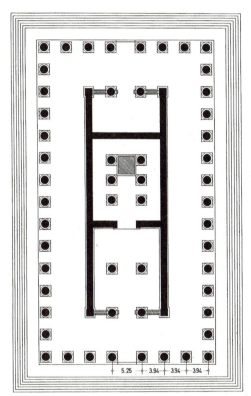

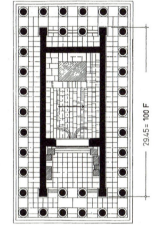

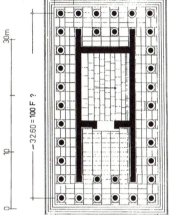

(above) **MAGNESIA-ON-THE-MAEANDER,** Artemis Leukophryne, attributed to Hermogenes, c. 220 B.C.

(above center) **PRIENE,** Temple of Athena Polias, attributed to Pytheos, c. 340 B.C.

(above right) **TEOS,** Temple of Dionysos, attributed to Hermogenes, c. 200 B.C.?

(right) **MAGNESIA-ON-THE-MAEANDER,** Agora, Temple of Zeus, c. 220/200?

(far right) **PRIENE,** Agora, Temple of Zeus, later fourth century?

[from W. Hoepfner, "Bauten und Bedeuten des Hermogenes," in <u>Hermogenes und die Hochhellenistischen Baukunst</u> (Mainz, 1990), 1-34, figs. 11, 17, 32.]

Figure 40. Hellenistic Ionic Temples in the Tradition of Hermogenes.

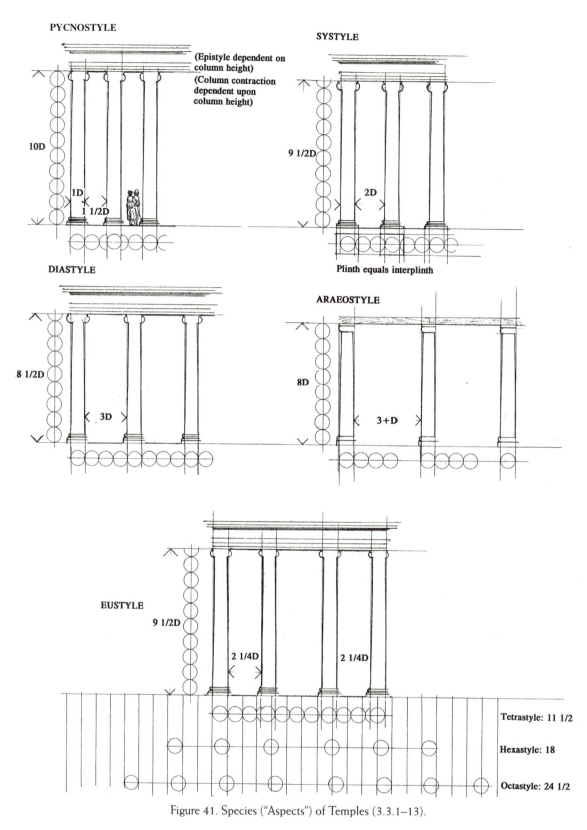

Figure 41. Species ("Aspects") of Temples (3.3.1–13).

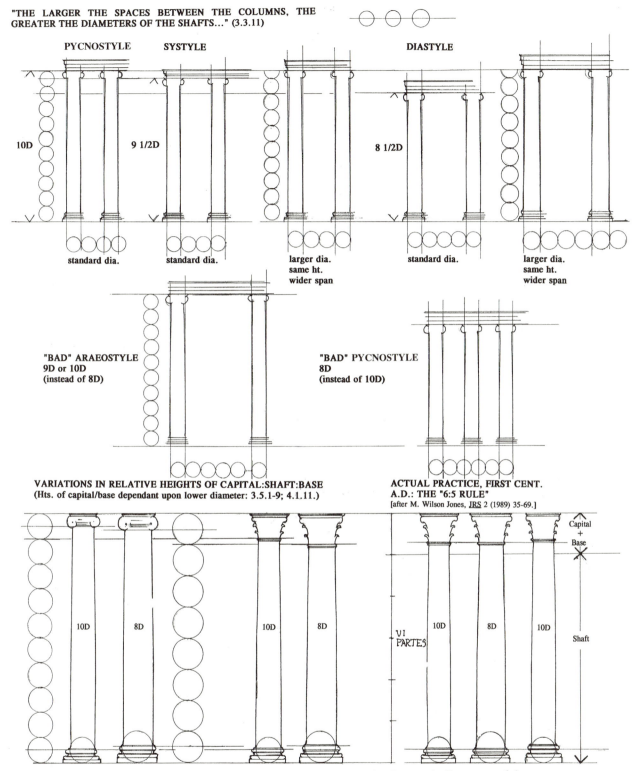

Figure 42. "The Larger the Spaces Between the Columns, the Greater the Diameters of the Shafts . . ." (3.3.11).

<u>**DEPENDENCE OF HYPOTRACHELIUM CONTRACTION ON COLUMN HEIGHTS**</u> (3.3.12)

DRAWN TO CONSTANT MODULE (LOWER DIA), VARIABLE SCALE

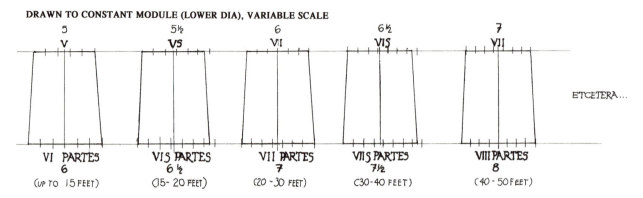

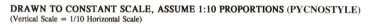

DRAWN TO CONSTANT SCALE, ASSUME 1:10 PROPORTIONS (PYCNOSTYLE)
(Vertical Scale = 1/10 Horizontal Scale)

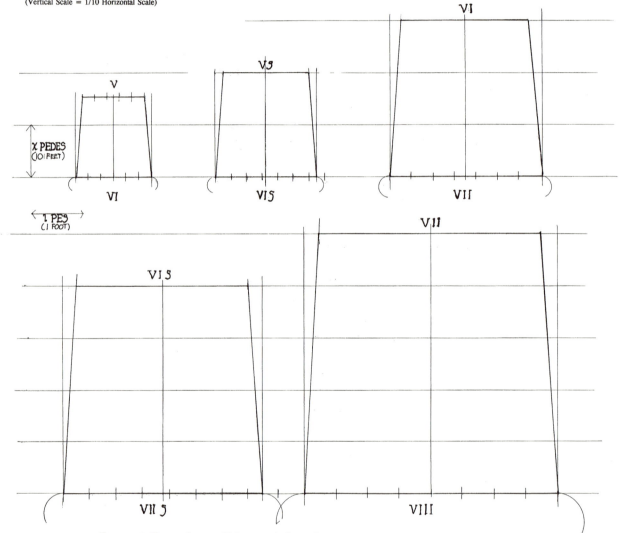

Figure 43. Dependence of Hypotrachelium Contraction on Column Heights (3.3.12).

ENTASIS ἔγτασις (**INTENTIO/CONTENTIO** = **TENSIONING**) (3.3.13)

ELLIPTICAL CURVATURE

ALTERNATE METHOD, FIRST CENT. A.D.
Smoothing Down Truncated Cone
(after M. Wilson Jones, 1993)

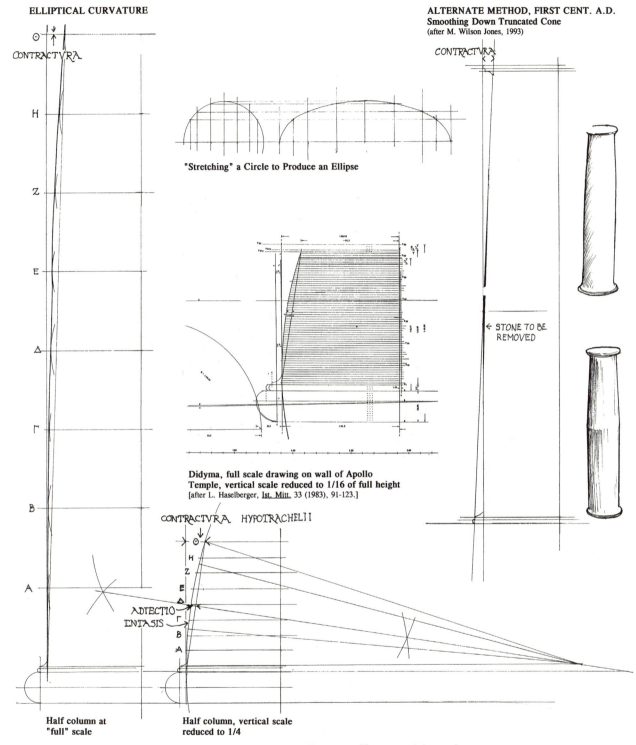

"Stretching" a Circle to Produce an Ellipse

Didyma, full scale drawing on wall of Apollo
Temple, vertical scale reduced to 1/16 of full height
[after L. Haselberger, Ist. Mitt. 33 (1983), 91-123.]

← STONE TO BE
REMOVED

Half column at
"full" scale

Half column, vertical scale
reduced to 1/4

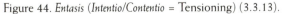

Figure 44. *Entasis* (*Intentio/Contentio* = Tensioning) (3.3.13).

FOUNDATIONS/PODIA (3.4.1-2, 3,4,4)

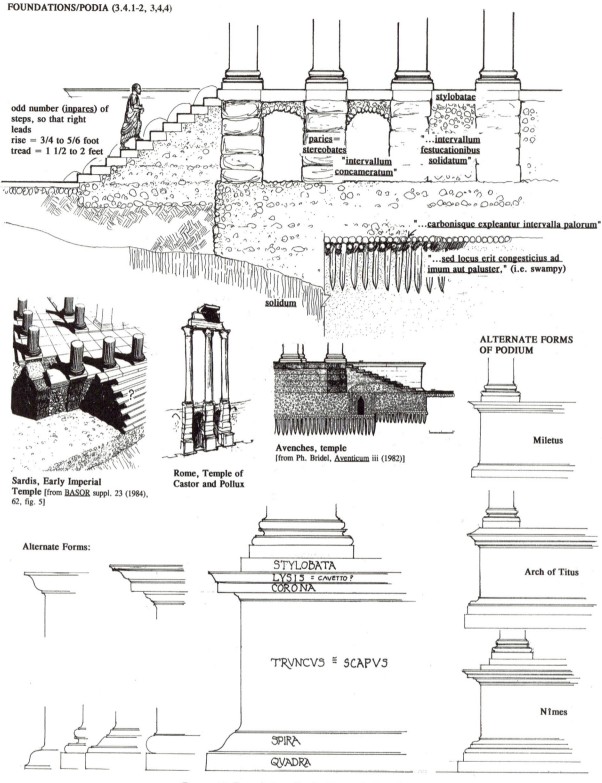

Figure 45. Foundations/Podia (3.4.1–2, 3.4.4).

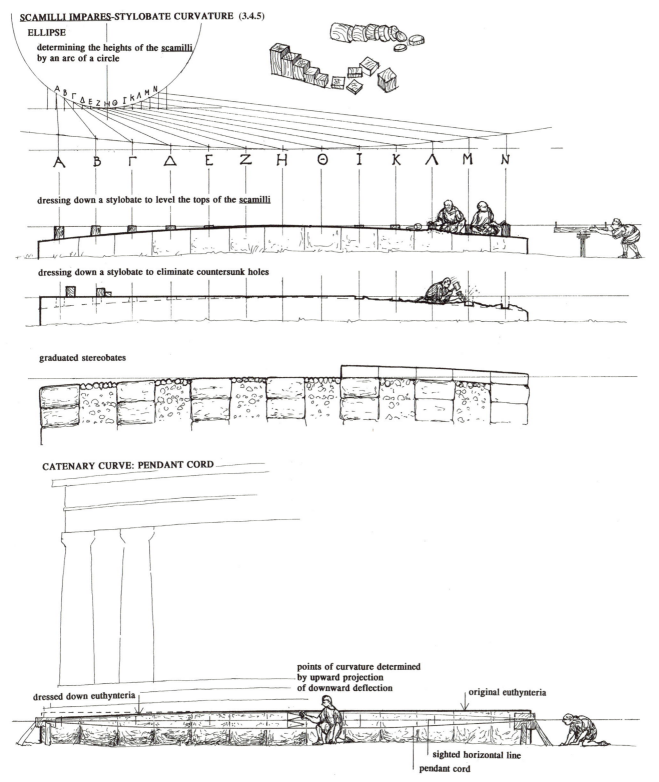

SCAMILLI IMPARES-STYLOBATE CURVATURE (3.4.5)

ELLIPSE

determining the heights of the scamilli by an arc of a circle

A B Γ Δ E Z H Θ I K Λ M N

dressing down a stylobate to level the tops of the scamilli

dressing down a stylobate to eliminate countersunk holes

graduated stereobates

CATENARY CURVE: PENDANT CORD

points of curvature determined by upward projection of downward deflection

dressed down euthynteria

original euthynteria

sighted horizontal line

pendant cord

Figure 46. *Scamilli impares*-Stylobate Curvature (3.4.5).

There are several different possible methods of executing the curvature (see figures): dressing down the stylobate until all the top surfaces of the blocks are level or countersinking the blocks from a level stylobate and dressing it down till the countersunk holes disappear.[27] The curvature can be averaged, or smoothed out, between points by the use of flexible wooden rods and red lead, which is the normal final stage in dressing stylobates.[28] Vitruvius's statement implies that the dressing down is done in the stylobate blocks, but the amount of labor could be reduced if the curvature was established in the foundations (i.e., the "stereobates").

A second method has been proposed for the fifth-century B.C. Greek temple at Segesta, Sicily, namely inverting a catenary curve given by a pendant cord (see figure).[29]

Vitruvius states that this procedure applies only to the stylobate course and everything above; in Greek temples the curvature was usually determined much lower down in the foundations, sometimes even in the foundation trench.

the base . . . lower torus and the scotia (3.5.2) (Figure 48)

In the bases, the projection of the flare is not specified, and this affects the projection of the other elements of the base, except the projection of the lower torus, which has to be tangent with the face of the plinth. In the "Ionic" base (Attic-Ionic, in modern common parlance) there are several alternative forms for the arrangement of the fillets and astragals on the trochili.

the capitals (3.5.5–8) (Figure 49)

In the capital, Vitruvius says nothing to imply that the canalis is straight between the volutes, although that was largely standard practice in the entire Hellenistic world by the late first century B.C., nor does he specify the relative height of the canalis to the "cymatium" (normally referred to as cushion or echinus in modern parlance). The only way of guessing the height of the echinus is to assume that, like other cymatia, its projection is supposed to equal its height. For the smallest column, the upper diameter is 15 units across, the projection of the cymatium/echinus equals the plinth plus one on each side (19 + 2 = 21); hence the projection and height ought to

be 2 1/2. This, of course, would have to vary with the overall height of the column because larger columns have less contraction, and hence the echinus projects less. Hence it is possible that Vitruvius did not mean for the height of echinus and canalis to be fixed.[30]

circling around (3.5.6)

"Tetrans" (quartering) means any figure – intersection of two lines – which divides an area into four (hence it is not quite the same thing as axes of a grid or quadrant). "Summa tetrans" implies starting the compass on the top axis (the cathetus), but that does not work because the two arcs do not meet at their tangents to the horizontals and verticals; see figure.[31]

One should note that Vitruvius design creates a rather short spiral of only two turns; it is common for Hellenistic capitals to have two and a half or even three full turns. It is also common for the spiral to reduce in width, and Vitruvius's maintains a constant width. In Vitruvius's system, one changes the design simply by changing the arithmetic of the vertical divisions of the capital. The eight-part division allows the radius to reduce four units (one-half unit per quadrant through eight quadrants equals two full turns); ten parts would allow two and a half turns; and so on.

the eye's glance (3.8.9)

See Commentary on 4.4.3.

the epistyle (3.8.10) (Figure 51)

In the entablatures Vitruvius leaves unspecified whether the cymatium of the dentils is included in the given height or added to it; the former seems more likely, as the latter produces a very high dentil course, and normally he includes the crown molding in the height of the course. He also leaves unspecified the position of the frieze and the middle fascia of the epistyle.

molding (3.8.10)

The word *cymatium* is here translated as "molding"; Vitruvius seems to make no distinction between Lesbian cymatium or ovolo because he refers to almost all of the moldings as "cymatia." "Cymatium" seems to be his generic term for any larger molding with a curved profile. When there is an astragal, he usually specifies it. Only in the description of the doorways (3.6.2) does he define the profile of the cymatium: for the jambs, Lesbian cymatium with astragal; for the cornice bed molding, Doric cymatium with Lesbian astragal.

27 The latter technique has recently been attested in the stylobate of a fourth-century B.C. building at Knidos. Hansgeorg Bankel, in a paper to be published in *Appearance and Essence: Refinements of Classical Architecture: Curvature* (Philadelphia, 1997). This technique, incidentally, is similar to the "pointing" technique for producing copies of statues: points are taken off the master and then stereometrically drilled into the unworked block of the copy until there are enough points for the intervening spaces to be worked by eye.

28 As indicated by the Lebadeia and Delian building inscriptions. J. Bundgaard, "The Building Contract from Lebadeia," *Classica et Mediaevalia* 8 (1946).

29 D. Mertens, "Herstellung der Kurvatur am Tempel von Segesta," *Rheinisches Museum* 81 (1974), 107–114; idem, *Der Tempel von Segesta und die dorische Tempelkunst des griechischen Westens in klassischer Zeit* (Mainz, 1984), 34–35, Beilage 21.

30 In late Hellenistic capitals in Asia Minor the canalis was higher than the echinus. In the early Imperial period, the relationship was reversed. O. Bingöl, *Das ionische Normalkapitelle in hellenistischer und römischer Zeit in Kleinasien, Istanbuler Mitteilungen Beiheft* 20 (1980), 149 ff.

31 This is essentially the position of the four points of the compass visible in a fragmentary Ionic capital from the Villa of Hadrian. P. Gros, ed., *Vitruve, de l'architecture* iv (Paris, 1992), 165, fig. 32; M. Ublacker, *Das Teatro Marittimo in der Villa Hadriana* (Mainz, 1985), fig. opposite p. 38.

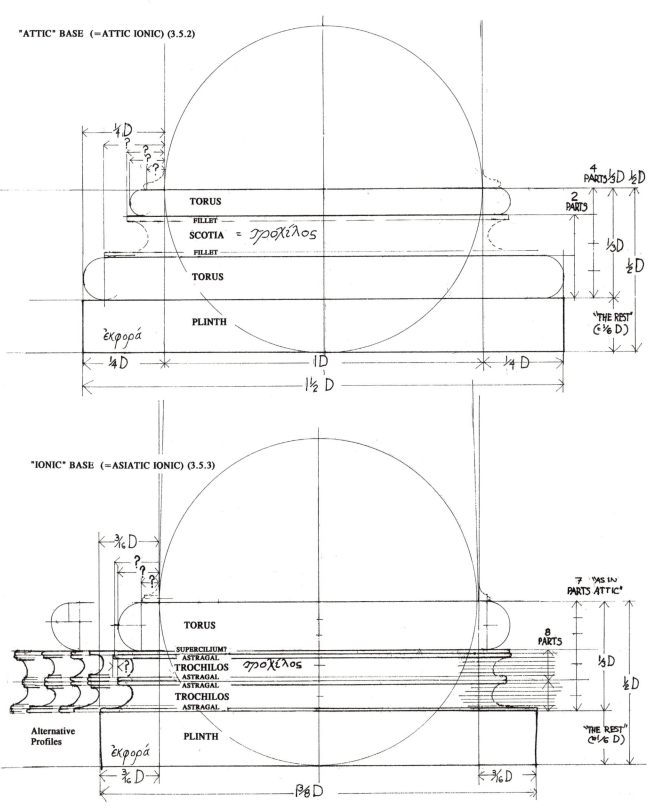

"ATTIC" BASE (=ATTIC IONIC) (3.5.2)

TORUS

FILLET

SCOTIA = τροχίλος

FILLET

TORUS

PLINTH

ἐκφορά

"IONIC" BASE (=ASIATIC IONIC) (3.5.3)

TORUS

SUPERCILIUM?
ASTRAGAL
TROCHILOS   τροχίλος
ASTRAGAL
ASTRAGAL
TROCHILOS
ASTRAGAL

Alternative
Profiles

PLINTH

ἐκφορά

Figure 47. "Attic" Base (= Attic-Ionic) (3.5.2).

COLUMN INCLINATION (3.5.4)

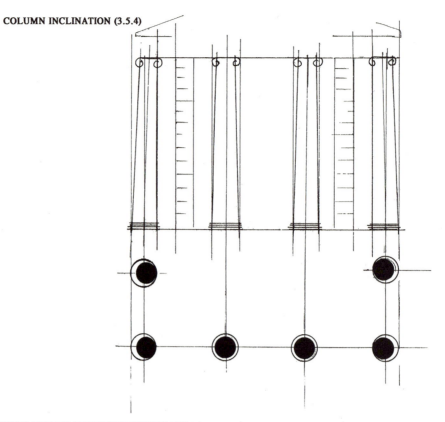

TOTAL EFFECT OF COLUMN INCLINATION AND STYLOBATE CURVATURE

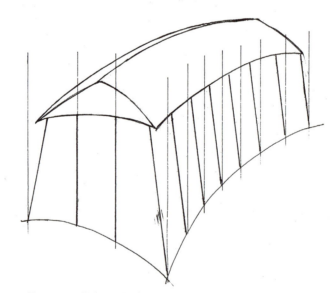

Figure 48. Column Inclination (3.5.4).

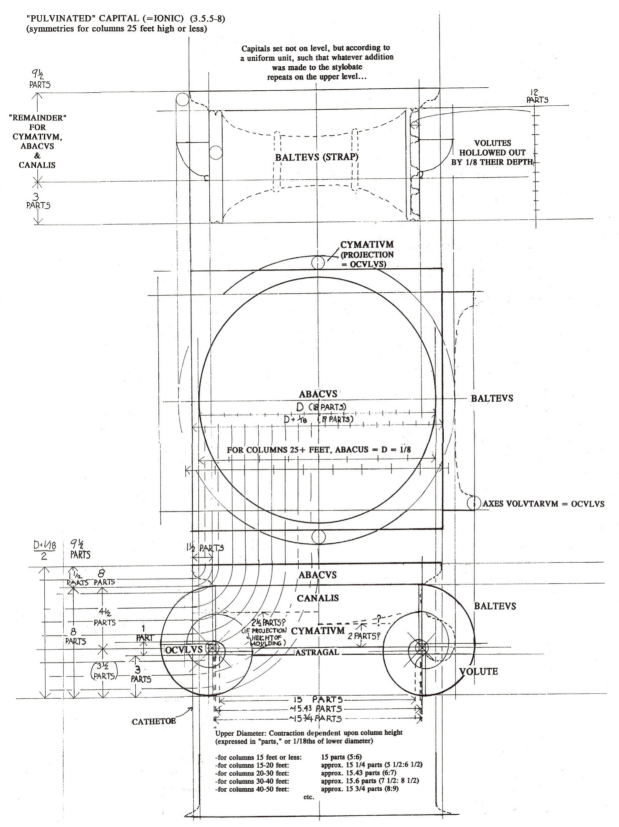

Figure 49. "Pulvinated" Capital (= Ionic) (3.5.5–8).

THE PROBLEM WITH SWINGING THE ARCS OF THE VOLUTE   (3.5.6, 3.5.8)

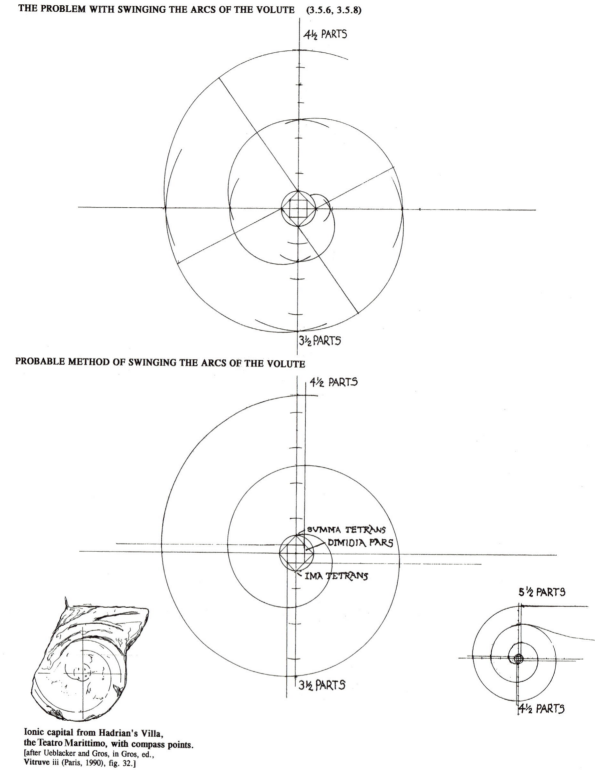

PROBABLE METHOD OF SWINGING THE ARCS OF THE VOLUTE

Ionic capital from Hadrian's Villa,
the Teatro Marittimo, with compass points.
[after Ueblacker and Gros, in Gros, ed.,
Vitruve iii (Paris, 1990), fig. 32.]

Figure 50. The Problem with Swinging the Arcs of the Volute (3.5.6, 3.5.8).

IONIC EPISTYLES (3.5.8-11)
symmetries for columns 12 to 15 feet.

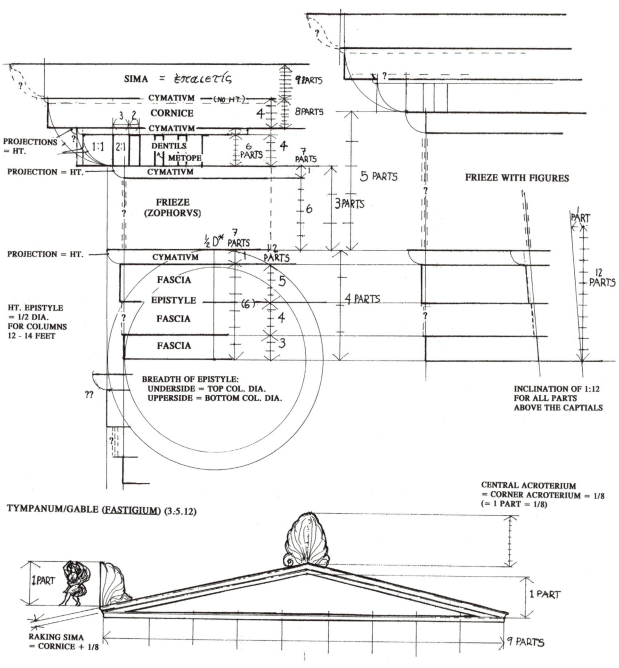

SIMA = ἐπαιετίς

CYMATIVM — (NO HT.)

CORNICE

CYMATIVM

9 PARTS

8 PARTS

4

3 2

PROJECTIONS = HT.

1:1 2:1

DENTILS

METOPE

CYMATIVM

6 PARTS

4

7 PARTS

PROJECTION = HT.

FRIEZE WITH FIGURES

5 PARTS

FRIEZE (ZOPHORVS)

6

3 PARTS

PROJECTION = HT.

½ D 7 PARTS

CYMATIVM

1 2 PARTS

FASCIA

EPISTYLE

5

4 PARTS

12 PARTS

HT. EPISTYLE = 1/2 DIA. FOR COLUMNS 12 - 14 FEET

(6)

FASCIA

4

FASCIA

3

BREADTH OF EPISTYLE:
UNDERSIDE = TOP COL. DIA.
UPPERSIDE = BOTTOM COL. DIA.

INCLINATION OF 1:12
FOR ALL PARTS
ABOVE THE CAPTIALS

CENTRAL ACROTERIUM
= CORNER ACROTERIUM = 1/8
(= 1 PART = 1/8)

TYMPANUM/GABLE (FASTIGIUM) (3.5.12)

1 PART

1 PART

9 PARTS

RAKING SIMA
= CORNICE + 1/8

Figure 51. Ionic Epistyles (3.5.8–11).

EPISTYLE HEIGHT (PROPORTION) DEPENDENT UPON COLUMN HEIGHT (3.5.8)
Drawn to variable scale, constant modulus (lower dia.)
For systle or eustyle symmetries (9 1/2 dia)

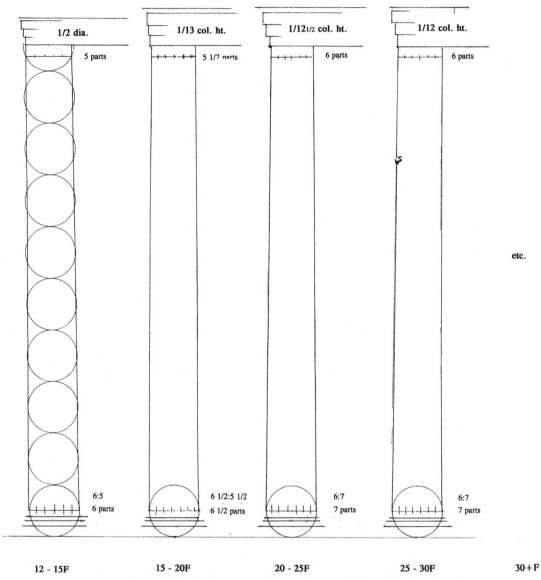

Figure 52. Epistyle Height (Proportion) Dependent on Column Heights (3.5.8).

FLUTES OF THE COLUMNS (3.5.14)

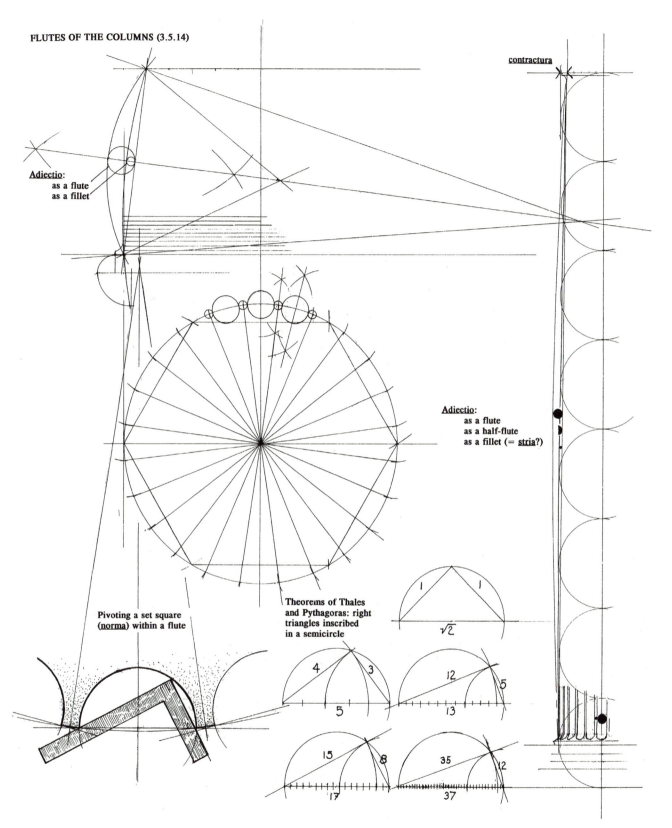

Adiectio:
as a flute
as a fillet

contractura

Adiectio:
as a flute
as a half-flute
as a fillet (= stria?)

Pivoting a set square
(norma) within a flute

Theorems of Thales
and Pythagoras: right
triangles inscribed
in a semicircle

√2

Figure 53. Flutes of the Columns (3.5.14).

SIMAS AND LIONHEAD WATERSPOUTS (3.5.15)

Vitruvius 3.5.15: Pierced lionhead spout over each column,
so that rainwater will not "drench the people entering the temple,;"
other spouts aligned with centers of tegulae (rooftiles).

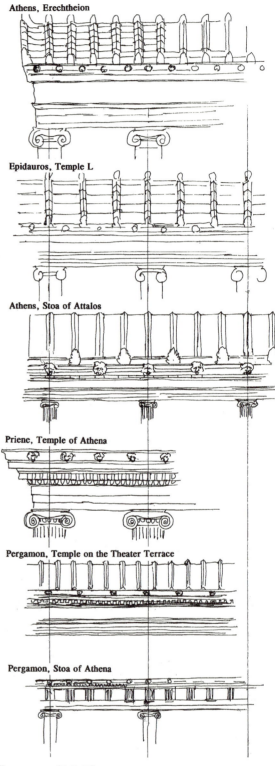

Athens, Erechtheion

Epidauros, Temple L

Athens, Stoa of Attalos

Priene, Temple of Athena

Pergamon, Temple on the Theater Terrace

Pergamon, Stoa of Athena

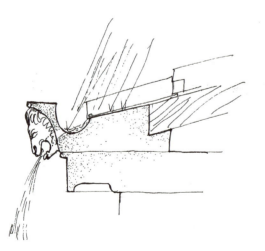

Figure 54. Simas and Lionhead Waterspouts (3.5.15).

the flutes of the columns (3.5.14) (Figure 53)

Vitruvius, as usual, does not give any indication of how one divides the arc of a circle into twenty-four parts; in many cases these numerous subdivisions of a given dimension may simply be achieved by progressive experiment and adjustment of the compass and divider, but here it can be achieved by starting from a hexagon and progressively halving its sides.[32]

It seems unlikely that Vitruvius really means that the flutes themselves are as wide as the *adiectio* added to the column for entasis. If the entasis were as wide as a flute, the curvature would bulge out beyond the vertical before tapering back inward, producing a curve like a cigar.[33] *Stria* is supposed to mean "flute" or "channel" but can also mean pleat or fold. It is related to *stringo*, which can mean banding, confining, stringing a bow. Hence the term does not necessarily mean the channel, or depth – what we call the flute – but the ridge, what we call the fillet. If the method of determining entasis is anything like the method suggested by the Didyma drawings, then it is more likely that the "*adiectio*" equals the size of the fillet between the flutes.[34]

Vitruvius (3.1.13) says nothing about the quantity of the *adiectio* of the entasis, but he implies here that the method is shown in the drawing at the end of Book 3. The *adiectio* is presumably an amount added to the line of the taper (the *contractura*) at "the middle" of the column. If *stria* means the fillet of the flute, it could be that the way the drawing indicates the quantity of the *adiectio* is an amount (like the small black circle in our drawing), which can be added to the taper of the column without making the curve bulge out beyond the vertical, that is, a small circle which at the midpoint of the column fits in between the vertical line and the tapered line of the *contractura*.

The controlling of the section of profile of the flute by rotating a set square inside it is simply a functional demonstration of one corollary of the theorem of Thales of Miletus (early sixth century B.C.): all triangles inscribed inside a circle with the diameter as the hypotenuse are right triangles.

on the simas . . . lion heads
should be sculpted (3.5.15) (Figure 54)

Vitruvius specifies that spouts align with the centers of *tegulae* (pantiles) and with the centers of columns. This requires that to some extent the roof tiles must correspond to the symmetrical system of the colonnade, but there are no stipulations as to how many tiles there are to a bay or whether every row of *tegulae* must have a spout. Some Hellenistic sima and spout patterns correspond to Vitruvius's preferences, but others have spouts aligning with *imbrices*, rather than *tegulae*, and most seem to have pierced spouts in the centers of the bays as well as over the columns.[35]

Terracotta roof tiles were normally about one foot across, but sizes varied, particularly in the late Republic, and for monumental buildings, tiles of terracotta or marble could be special ordered. Spouts could often be centered not on the tegula but on the imbrex (cover tile), but in smaller Hellenistic buildings (e.g., stoas) it was fairly common for there to be spouts centered on each tegula.

In the reconstruction of the Stoa of Attalos in Athens by the American School of Classical Studies in the 1950s, it was discovered that it was important for the tongues of the lions to protrude in order to cast the water away from the cornice; as executed, the tongueless spouts tend to drool and stain.

BOOK 4

The Discovery of Symmetries
[inventions of the ornaments] (4.1–2)

There are two aspects to Vitruvius's historical analysis of the origins of architectural form: the symmetries, or proportions of each type, and the formal vocabularies ("*ornamenta*" or "*membra*"). The symmetries (4.1.3–8) are abstracted from selective analysis and development of certain features of human proportions (Vitruvius focuses only on slenderness); the formal vocabularies derive from analyzing and abstracting the principles of timber roof structure (Doric and Ionic, 4.2) or vegetal representation (Corinthian, 4.1.8–10).

the Corinthian type itself has not had its own
set rule for the cornices . . . may . . . be designed
with . . . triglyphs . . . or . . . Ionic rules (4.1.2) (Figure 55)

"Mixed orders" appear almost as soon as the Doric and Ionic types themselves; placing dentils in Doric entablatures or Doric entablatures over Ionic columns appears as early as the fifth century B.C. (e.g., terracotta reliefs in Tarentum). In the Hellenistic period, both these features became fairly common

---

32 Working with a divider can in fact be extremely accurate once the user has acquired a high level of manual skill. Therefore many subdivisions that are not obtainable by geometric theory are achievable to considerable precision by skillful "fudging." Much of an architect's geometric work, after all, needs only to be functionally precise, not theoretically so.

33 This interpretation of *stria* = flute largely accounts for the extensive Renaissance through eighteenth-century tradition of columns that swell outward before tapering back inward.

34 Choisy and A. Claridge interpret *stria* as fillet; P. Gros insists [correctly. Translator's note.] that it must mean the channel of the flute. See L. Haselberger, "Bericht über die Arbeit am jüngeren Apollontempel von Didyma," *Istanbuler Mitteilungen* 33 (1983), 96; A. Claridge, *Tempio di Adriano* (Rome, 1982), 28; P. Gros, *Vitruve, de L'architecture*, iii (Paris, 1990), 199.

35 The archaeological reconstruction of the patterns of tile and sima spouts is often lacking or difficult on surviving monuments; they are often not worked out with certainty in scholarly publications.

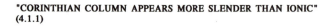

"CORINTHIAN COLUMN APPEARS MORE SLENDER THAN IONIC"
(4.1.1)

Ionic capital is one third the
height of the Corinthian...

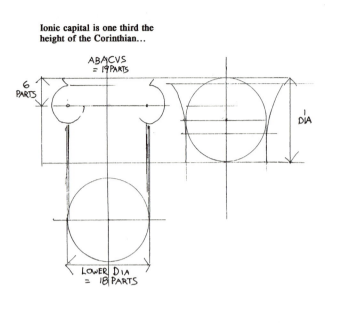

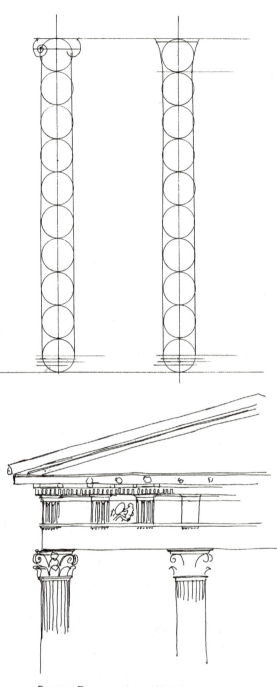

Elements placed over Corinthian capitals may be
either Doric symmetries or Ionic conventions...

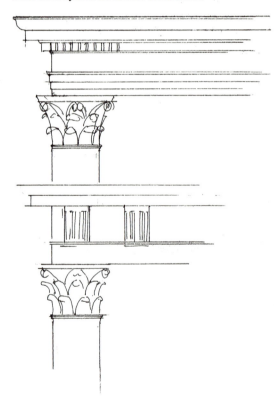

Paestum, Forum temple, c. 100 B.C.

Figure 55. "The Corinthian Column Appears More Slender Than the Ionic" (4.1.1).

options, especially in the upper stories of Pergamene stoas in Asia Minor. "Mixed orders" are not particularly common in Rome, but are in Campania, Vitruvius's likely homeland, even in monumental buildings (e.g., the second phase of the Forum Temple in Paestum c. 100 B.C.).[1]

The Athenians . . . founded thirteen colonies (4.1.4–5)

This account combines the semilegendary "Ionian" migration of c. 1000 B.C. with historical events under Lysimachus of Thrace, one of Alexander's successor generals.

Panionian Apollo (4.1.5)

The sanctuary of the Ionian League situated somewhere on the north side of Mt. Mycale between Ephesus and Miletus.[2]

Later generations, more advanced in the elegance and subtlety . . . (4.1.8) (Figure 56)

This account of the development of taste effectively corresponds with Greek architectural history: in the fifth century B.C. Doric columns are set at between 4 1/2 and 5 times their lower diameter; in the fourth century and Hellenistic period the proportions are raised to 6:1 or even 7:1.[3] This development also corresponds with changes in the figural arts in the fourth century B.C.[4]

the invention of this type of capital [Corinthian] (4.1.9–10) (Figure 57)

The earliest known Corinthian capital is that from the interior colonnade of the temple of Apollo Epikourios at Bassae (later fifth or early fourth century B.C.), where the column may have served as the aniconic cult image. The invention seems to have been brought about by the combination of the simple bell shape of the kalathos (basket) with a type of acanthus leaf and tendril which was becoming popular in Athenian grave stelai in the later fifth century B.C.[5] If Bassai, or at least its interior, was in fact by the Athenian architect Ictinus,[6] then Vitruvius's attribution of the invention of the capital to the Athenian sculptor Callimachus (late fifth century) may represent historical fact. ("*Katatêxitechnos*" means "refined"; some MSS read *catatechnos*, meaning "thoroughly skilled.")[7] The name *Corinthian* may refer not to the place, but to the possibility that the leaves were first attached in bronze.[8] The earliest form, at Bassai, was not particularly coherent as a tectonic unit. The evolution, or critical refinement and revision, which lead to the "definitive" form, occurs over the course of the fourth century and is more or less complete by the time of the interior capitals of the Tholos at Epidaurus (end of fourth century).[9]

---

1 Technically the Forum Temple is not Corinthian but features a Corinthianizing figural capital, mixed Doric entablature, and dentils. The bases are also extremely eccentric: a torus over a flare. F. Kraus, R. Herbig, *Der Korinthisch-dorische Tempel am Forum von Paestum* (Berlin, 1939). On mixed orders: H. Lauter, *Die Architektur des Hellenismus* (Darmstadt, 1986), 257–259 et passim; H. Knell, *Vitruvs Architekturtheorie* (Darmstadt, 1991), 50–51.

2 Herodotus, 1.143; Strabo, 14.1.20.

3 The only major correction one might make to the Vitruvian scheme is that the first generation of Doric buildings, c. 600–570 B.C., features not only the thickest columns in Greek history, but also the thinnest (i.e., the widest range of proportions).

4 That is, increasing height of figure from six to seven times the measure of the foot. This is interpreted as part of a general change in the symmetries of the *canôn* of Polycleitus carried out by Lysippus. Lysippus is seen at one and the same time as the ultimate representative of the use of symmetry to control the proportions of the human figure in sculpture and painting, and the change to a sensibility which favors the concept of "eurythmy," the sense of pleasing motion or grace, over clarity of measure. See F. W. Schlikker, *Hellenistische Vorstellungen von der Schönheit des Bauwerks nach Vitruv* (Berlin, 1940), 72–95.

5 On this idea of the origin: G. Roux, *L'Architecture de l'Argolide aux quatrième et troisième siècles avant J.C.* (Paris, 1961), ch. 12, 359–367. On the column as cult image, N. Yalouris, "Problems Relating to the Temple of Apollo Epikourios at Bassae," *Acts of the XI International Congress of Classical Archaeology* (London, 1978), 89–104. The kalathos would be a relatively simple invention because it is in effect a rotated cavetto, or rotated archaic sofa capital. Roux, op. cit., fig. 104. It is also the same shape as a common type of krater.

6 Pausanias, 8.41.9.

7 The nickname is securely transmitted in MSS of Pausanias, 1.26.7, less so in Pliny the Elder, *Natural History* 34.92.

8 Corinth was a center of Greek bronze work throughout antiquity, and the term *Corinthian* came to mean bronze work in general. The Porticus Octavi in Rome (built by Gn. Octavius, 174 B.C., probably next to the later Porticus Metelli/Octavia) was referred to as the Corinthian portico because it had capitals revetted with leaves of gilded bronze; Pliny the Elder, *Natural History* 34.7.1. Vitruvius would have known the building, as it was among the first of the splendid new porticus structures built in the Campus Martius. Vitruvius is the first direct source to use the term *Corinthian* to describe this type of capital. Others: Strabo, 4.4.6; Pliny, 34.7.2; Pausanias, 8.45.4; Athenaeus, 5.205.c, quoting Kallixenos (second century B.C.) describing the pleasure barge of Ptolemy IV. In this context, it is not totally out of the question that Vitruvius was the first to attempt to establish the term as standard, and succeeded, although the reference from Pliny might suggest that the term had long been in general use to describe the Porticus of Octavius (the Corinthian portico, meaning the bronze portico).

9 Strictly speaking, the Epidauros capital is not referred to in the scholarly literature as a "normal" capital because the central tendrils do not touch the abacus, but the fundamental proportions and effect are achieved: the leaves and tendrils, objects which in reality are highly fragile, are rearranged into a compact, three-tiered upward accelerating mass that gives the illusion of powerful support. Tegea and the Lysicrates Monument represent intermediate stages in the evolution. They show that, as in early Doric temples, the evolution was not gradual (literally step by step in a single direction), but cast about on all sides of the final solution before hitting upon it: too tall, too short, and so on. On the fourth-century evolution of the Corinthian capital: Roux, op. cit., ch. 12, 359–387; H. Bauer, *Korinthische Kapitelle des 4. und 3. Jahrhunderts vor Christus* (Berlin, 1973) DAI Beiheft 3; W. D. Heilmeyer, *Korinthische Normalkapitelle* (Heidelberg, 1970); H. von Hesberg, "Lo sviluppo dell'ordine corinzio in età tardo-repubblicana," in *L'art decoratif à Rome à la fin de la République et au début du Principat*, Rome, EFR (1981), 19–53.

FROM <u>GENUS</u> TO <u>SYMMETRIA</u> (4.1.3-8)

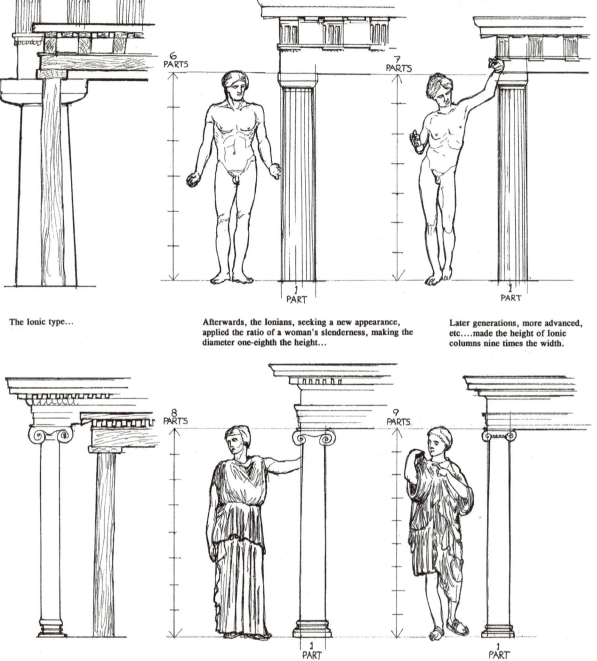

Dorus built a shrine to Juno [Hera] in Argos which "happened" to be of the this [Doric] type..

The first Ionians desired to build a shrine to Panionian Apollo of the same "Doric" type, and seeking principles for columns suitable for bearing loads, they measured the footprint of a man, and discovered that it is one-sixth of his height.

Later generations, more advanced in elegance and subtlety, and delighting in more attenuated proportions, established that the height of the Doric column should be seven times...

The Ionic type...

Afterwards, the Ionians, seeking a new appearance, applied the ratio of a woman's slenderness, making the diameter one-eighth the height...

Later generations, more advanced, etc....made the height of Ionic columns nine times the width.

Figure 56. From *Genus* to *Symmetria* (4.1.3–8).

CORINTHIAN ORIGINS (4.1.8-11)

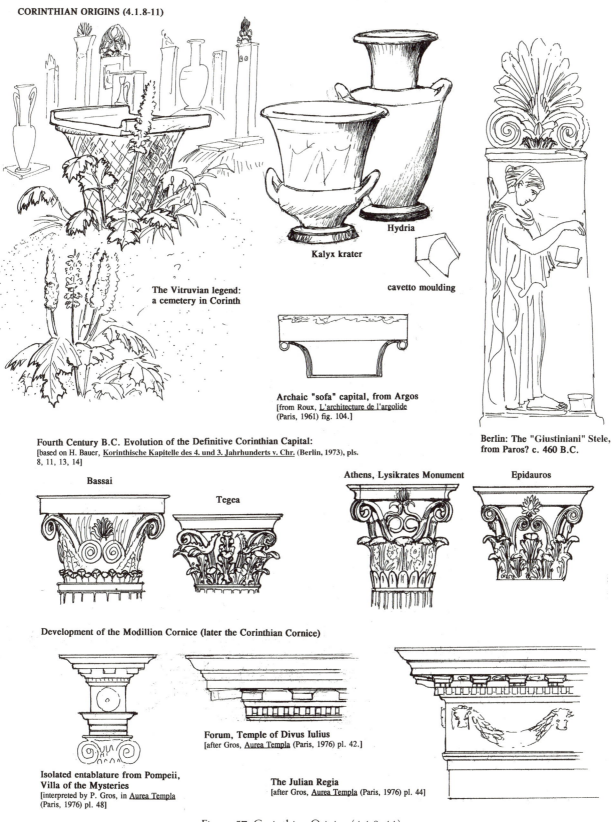

The Vitruvian legend:
a cemetery in Corinth

Kalyx krater

Hydria

cavetto moulding

Archaic "sofa" capital, from Argos
[from Roux, L'architecture de l'argolide
(Paris, 1961) fig. 104.]

Berlin: The "Giustiniani" Stele,
from Paros? c. 460 B.C.

Fourth Century B.C. Evolution of the Definitive Corinthian Capital:
[based on H. Bauer, Korinthische Kapitelle des 4. und 3. Jahrhunderts v. Chr. (Berlin, 1973), pls.
8, 11, 13, 14]

Bassai

Tegea

Athens, Lysikrates Monument

Epidauros

Development of the Modillion Cornice (later the Corinthian Cornice)

Isolated entablature from Pompeii,
Villa of the Mysteries
[interpreted by P. Gros, in Aurea Templa
(Paris, 1976) pl. 48]

Forum, Temple of Divus Iulius
[after Gros, Aurea Templa (Paris, 1976) pl. 42.]

The Julian Regia
[after Gros, Aurea Templa (Paris, 1976) pl. 44]

Figure 57. Corinthian Origins (4.1.8–11).

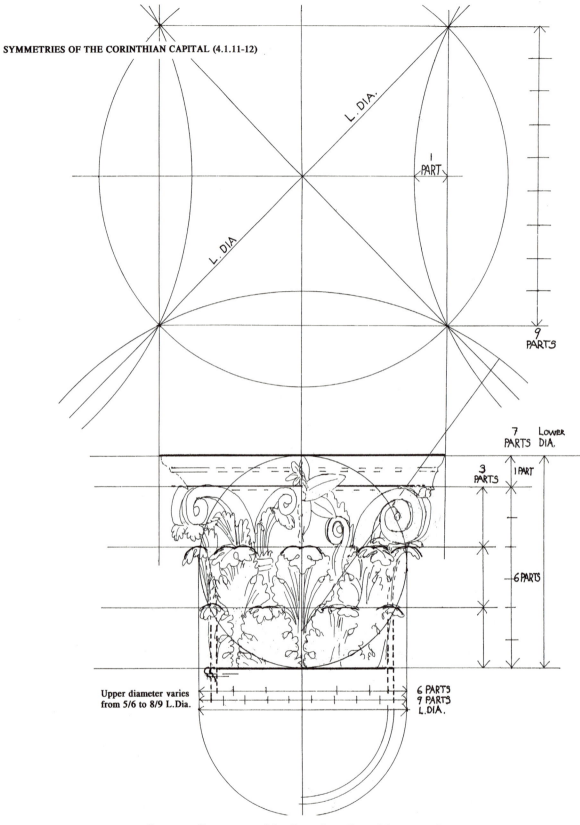

SYMMETRIES OF THE CORINTHIAN CAPITAL (4.1.11-12)

Figure 58. Symmetries of the Corinthian Capital (4.1.11–12).

CORINTHIAN CAPITALS OF THE LATE REPUBLIC & AUGUSTAN AGE
[from M. Wilson-Jones, "Designing the Roman Corinthian Capital,"
PBSR 59 (1991), fig. 2, reproduced here to different scales.]

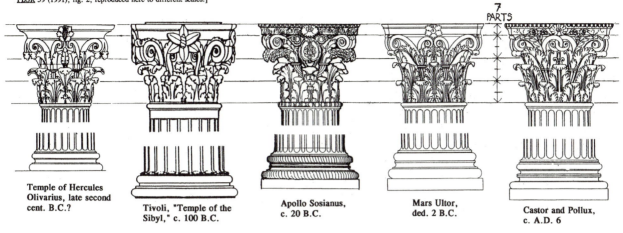

Temple of Hercules
Olivarius, late second
cent. B.C.?

Tivoli, "Temple of the
Sibyl," c. 100 B.C.

Apollo Sosianus,
c. 20 B.C.

Mars Ultor,
ded. 2 B.C.

Castor and Pollux,
c. A.D. 6

"There are, however, types of capitals which are put on the same columns yet
called by different names. I am not able to give their symmetries, nor for that
matter to name the types of columns, but it seems to me that their vocabulary
(vocabula) has been drawn from Corinthian, Ionic and Doric, whose
symmetries have been adapted to the refinement of new types of carving."
(4.2.8)

Pompeii, a selection of capitals
(from Mau)

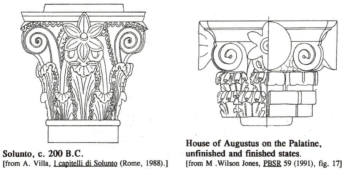

Solunto, c. 200 B.C.
[from A. Villa, I capitelli di Solunto (Rome, 1988).]

House of Augustus on the Palatine,
unfinished and finished states.
[from M .Wilson Jones, PBSR 59 (1991), fig. 17]

Figure 59. Corinthian Capitals of the Late Republic and Augustan Age.

the origins . . . the ornaments (4.2.1–6) (Figures 60, 61)

Vitruvius, of course, considerably postdates the actual time of origin of the Doric and Ionic column types, and there is no earlier clear reference to their "origins." Doric appears c. 600 B.C. in our archaeological evidence, Ionic about the same time or possibly a little later. According to Vitruvius's analysis, Doric and Ionic are simply two different interpretations of the same structural sequence: Doric exposes the beam ends of the *transtra* (or *trabes*), and projects the *cantherii*, shaving off the underside to form mutules; Ionic suppresses the *transtra* and *cantherii* and projects the *asseres*-common rafters – to form dentils.

The origin of the Doric type is one of the most debated issues in architectural history. In modern scholarship there are essentially three theoretical approaches.[10] The first, deriving from Vitruvius, is the wood origin theory. In modern archaeological theory this assumes that the vocabulary was worked out somehow in seventh-century buildings with stone foundations and timber colonnades, and hence there are no preserved traces until the first stone Doric temples appear in our evidence c. 600 B.C.[11]

The second is a loose collection of evolutionary theories. This assumes that Doric "ornamenta" may have developed gradually through steady, cumulative modifications of earlier motifs, such as the Mycenaean "split-rosette," or the Mycenaean cushion capital, possibly combining with some wood structural forms.

The third is that the Doric type was created suddenly, perhaps in a single ambitious building project c. 620/600 B.C. by the adaptive imitation of one type of Egyptian colonnade called proto-Doric, which has long been noted to have an uncanny similarity to Doric (see figures). This Egyptian type of colonnade was modified in two ways: by the insertion of a cushion below the abacus; and the dividing of the cavetto cornice into distinct vertical and horizontal surfaces, with the invention of a decorative, rhythmic pattern for those surfaces.

The Vitruvian question of origins has been a very important vehicle for modern theory.[12] The debate accepts, as does Vitruvius, that it is largely a question about the nature of "tectonic signification," that is, that the Doric in some manner is an expression, or suggestion, of structure. The first of the three theories, and to some extent the second, assume that logical expression of structure derives from actual structure. To a considerable extent, this is what Vitruvius seems to assume, although he also seems to emphasize the act of analytical abstraction as opposed to imitation. The third theory, the Egyptian-imitation theory, presents the more disturbing prospect that expression of structure may derive from forms that do not derive from the forms of structure.

The same debate also applies, if to a lesser extent, to Ionic architecture. Its first identifiable forms now appear to date only shortly after the appearance of Doric, to the early sixth century.[13] It seems also to have been created as an assemblage of motifs, in this case the stylized plant motifs gathered from the Near East and Asia Minor.

simply can not be common rafters beneath major rafters (4.2.5) (Figure 60)

Vitruvius was quite right in saying that in his time there was no form of entablature which was specific or unique to the Corinthian column (4.1.2). This remark appears to be a reference to the attempt to develop a type of cornice (the so-called modillion or console cornice) specific to the Corinthian type.[14] The modillion or console cornice, with double scroll brackets directly under the cornice and above the dentils, was, however, being developed in the 40s and 30s B.C. The rectangular bracket or modillion appeared c. 150 B.C. as a version of the Doric mutule, mainly in the upper Ionic stories of Pergamene stoas, and it appeared in Roman stucco (and second style wall painting) in the early first century. In the 30s and 20s, this kind of bracket, along with double volute scroll consoles (adapted from door frames) appear for the first time in monumental architecture in a number of buildings built or rebuilt in the second triumvirate and early principate, such as the temple of Divus Iulius in the Forum, Magna Mater on the Palatine, and the Temples of Castor, Saturn, and Concord in the Forum. The Composite capital may also have been invented at this time.[15] The internal cornice of the Tower of the Winds in Athens almost follows the Vitruvian recommendations.[16]

10 The following is a summary of T. N. Howe, *The Invention of the Doric Order* (Diss., Harvard, 1985, University Microfilms).

11 A. von Gerkan did the most thorough development of this hypothesis, finding a part for part carpentry origin for all features. "Die Herkunft des dorischen Gebälks," *Jahrbuch des Deutschen Archäologischen Instituts in Rom* 63–64 (1948–1949). The figure here summarizes his approach.

12 The Vitruvian wood-origin theory has been known to most architects since the later fifteenth century, but the issue of origins does not become a hot topic of debate until the middle decades of the eighteenth century, that is, just when modernity begins to question the authority of the classical orders.

13 G. Gruben, "Das älteste ionische marmorne Volutenkapitell," *Istanbuler Mitteilungen* 39 (1989), 161 ff.

14 D. E. Strong, "The Temple of Castor in the Forum Romanum," *Papers of the British School at Rome* 30 (1962), 1–30; idem, "Some Observations on Early Roman Corinthian," *Journal of Roman Studies* 53 (1963), 73–84; idem, "Some Early Examples of the Composite Capital," *Journal of Roman Studies* 50 (1960), 119–128; H. von Hesberg, *Konsolengeisa des Hellenismus und der frühen Kaiserzeit* (Mainz, 1980).

15 D. E. Strong, "Some Early Examples of the Composite Capital," *Journal of Roman Studies* 50 (1960), 119–128. Composite type capitals also appear on second style wall painting. If second style wall painting is dependent on Alexandria, some of this formal invention may have come from Alexandrian architecture.

16 This was built by a Near Eastern merchant, Andronicus Cyrrhestes (Andronikos of Kyrrhos, a town near the Euphrates), probably within twenty years of Vitruvius's writing (c. 50–37 B.C.). It almost follows the Vitruvian sequence, but with modillions under the cornice and dentils above the cornice and under the sima. Stuart and Revett, illustrated in A. W. Lawrence, *Greek Architecture* (Harmondsworth, 1973), plate 133A, and p. 137.

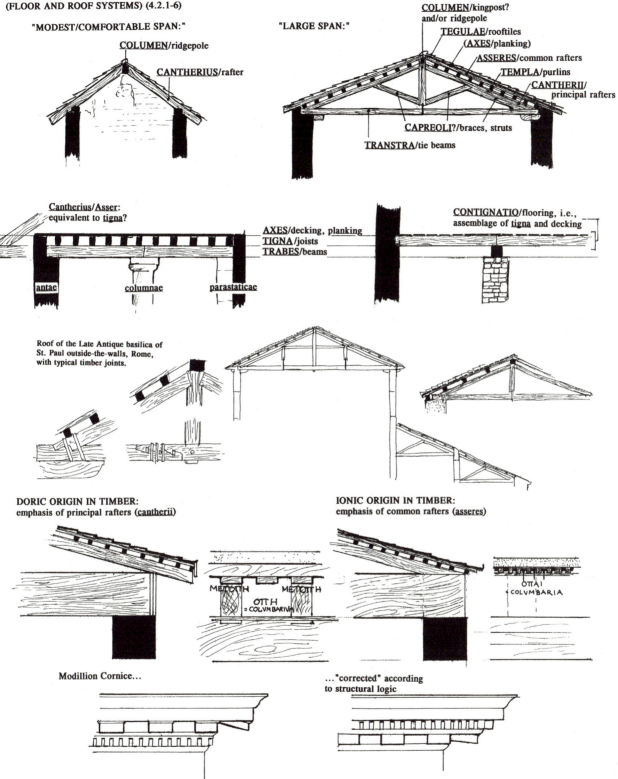

STRUCTURAL ORIGINS OF THE GENERA AND THEIR ORNAMANETA
(FLOOR AND ROOF SYSTEMS) (4.2.1-6)

"MODEST/COMFORTABLE SPAN:"

COLUMEN/ridgepole

CANTHERIUS/rafter

"LARGE SPAN:"

COLUMEN/kingpost?
and/or ridgepole

TEGULAE/rooftiles
(AXES/planking)

ASSERES/common rafters

TEMPLA/purlins

CANTHERII/
principal rafters

CAPREOLI?/braces, struts

TRANSTRA/tie beams

Cantherius/Asser:
equivalent to tigna?

AXES/decking, planking
TIGNA/joists
TRABES/beams

CONTIGNATIO/flooring, i.e.,
assemblage of tigna and decking

antae   columnae   parastaticae

Roof of the Late Antique basilica of
St. Paul outside-the-walls, Rome,
with typical timber joints.

DORIC ORIGIN IN TIMBER:
emphasis of principal rafters (cantherii)

IONIC ORIGIN IN TIMBER:
emphasis of common rafters (asseres)

Modillion Cornice...

..."corrected" according
to structural logic

Figure 60. Structural Origins of the *Genera* and Their *Ornamenta* (4.2.1–6).

DORIC ORIGINS (4.2.2-4)

Vitruvius' Wood-Origin Theory

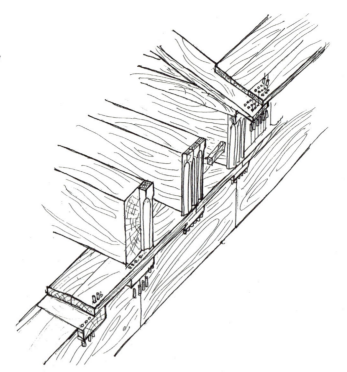

Adaptive Imitation of Egyptian Colonnade

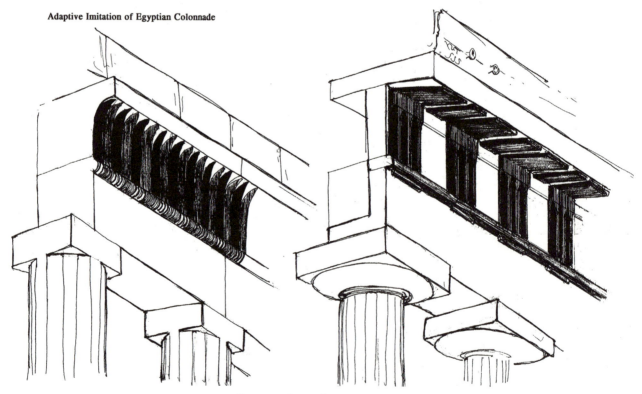

Figure 61. Doric Origins (4.2.2–4).

Arcesius, Pytheos . . . Hermogenes (4.3.1)

Arcesius is unknown outside Vitruvius, who also attributes to him a temple in Tralles and an essay on Corinthian symmetries (7.praef.12). Pytheos: 1.1.12; 1.1.15; 7.praef.12. Hermogenes: 3.2.6; 3.3.8; 3.3.9; 7.praef.12.

inconvenient in working out the distribution of triglyphs (4.3.1) (Figure 62)

This is the so-called angle conflict of Doric. The problem comes about because of innate conflict in the formal rules: metopes must be square; columns must be centered under triglyphs; at the corners, triglyphs must meet; epistyles must be centered over columns; epistyles are usually wider than triglyphs, so that at the corner the triglyph and epistyle cannot correspond. One must either stretch the metopes of the corner bay or contract the spacing of the columns of the corner bay.

There is no conflict only when the epistyle width equals the triglyph width. Vitruvius appears to give the wrong formula: to keep the frieze elements equal, the actual contraction equals half of the difference between the width of the triglyph and the width of the epistyle. This equals half the breadth of the triglyph only when the epistyle equals twice the triglyph.[17] Vitruvius's extraordinary suggestion that the problem should be solved with a split metope at the corner seems to have no known precedent in Greek architecture and no known progeny in large-scale Roman architecture. Similar examples exist only in stuccowork or painted representations.

embatêr (4.3.3)

See Commentary, 1.2.4.

[crowning] molding (4.3.4)

As in Book 3, Vitruvius uses the word cymatium for what must be several different types of molding, usually an ovolo or a cyma. Here it is translated simply as "molding."

width of a module (4.3.5) (Figure 63)

Vitruvius seems to be thinking of the width of the module without column contraction.

the viae (4.3.6) (Figures 64, 65)

The one major feature of the description of Doric that is unclear is whether there are mutules only over the triglyphs or over the metopes as well. A number of cornices in contemporary Doric buildings have mutules only over the triglyphs (the Theater of Marcellus, the Basilica Aemilia), with the broad spaces between (presumably the "viae") decorated usually with rosettes.

single-triglyph work (4.3.7–8) (Figure 66)

This means one triglyph in the center of each bay and one over each column (i.e., a two-metope span).

the eye is compelled to make a longer journey [optics] (4.4.3) (Figures 67, 68)

In Books 3 and 4 there are six references to the need to adjust forms for the sake of appearances:

> 3.3.12: Hypotrachelium contraction
>
> 3.3.13: Entasis . . . for both, the eye "pursues beauty," and we need to "humor it" (blandimur) by additions for what the eye has missed.
>
> 3.4.5: Stylobate curvature by means of scamilli impares. The purpose is to correct the hollowed (alveolatus) appearance given by uncorrected perception.
>
> 3.5.8–9: Higher epistyles for higher columns. Over higher columns, "the eye's glance . . . penetrates the air with greater difficulty. Therefore it falls away, drained by the extent and force of the altitude, and reports back an uncertain assessment to the senses."
>
> 4.4.2–3: In interiors, if column height is increased, increase the number of flutes. "Whatever is subtracted in reality . . . is apparently increased . . . because the eye is compelled to make a longer journey where it encounters more numerous stimuli."
>
> 3.5.13: In epistyles, friezes, cornices, tympana, raking cornices, and acroteria (i.e., all elements above the capitals): front surfaces should all incline outward by one-twelfth the height.

Virtually all of the adjustments that Vitruvius mentions are attested in one way or another in numerous Greek and Roman buildings;[18] the rationale he gives for the adjustments, however, derive from his general knowledge of the science of optics.

Early optics (i.e., the atomist Democritus of Abdera, c. 460–370) asserted that vision was due to a thin film of particles emitted by objects and received by the eye. For Plato, a fire in the eye blended with sunlight to create a medium, which received "motions" from objects and transmitted them

---

17 . . . unless the phrase "dimidia latitudine" can be taken to mean an approximation. His own symmetries (4.3.7) result in something less than half a triglyph width. The actual width of the split metope is a half triglyph (half module) less the hypotrachelium contraction. If one follows his detailed directions, it is perfectly clear what has to be done: the glyph is centered over the column "tetrans," and the metope gets whatever is left over, that is, a half module less a bit. He later (4.3.4) makes this principal criterion totally clear: "these [the metopes] are to be divided so that both for the corner columns and the middle columns they [the triglyphs] align with the central axis of the column itself." Hence the phrase "half triglyph" could be a conscious verbal efficiency, not just formal sloppiness.

18 Despite general familiarity with Vitruvius, the existence of refinements in Greek temples (e.g., stylobate curvature) was generally not believed by antiquarians until they were first noticed in the Parthenon and other classical Greek buildings by Allason and C. R. Cockerell (1814), Donaldson (1820), and Hoffer and Pennethorne (1836–37). F. C. Penrose, Principles of Athenian Architecture (London, 1888, 2nd ed.); J. Pennethorne, The Geometry and Optics of Ancient Architecture (London and Edinburgh, 1878); A. Thiersch, "Optische Täuschungen auf dem Gebiete der Architecktur," Zeitschrift des Bauwesens, 1878. The principal summary remains W. H. Goodyear, Greek Refinements: Studies in Temperamental Architecture (New Haven, 1912).

THE DORIC ANGLE CONTRACTION PROBLEM (4.3.1-2)

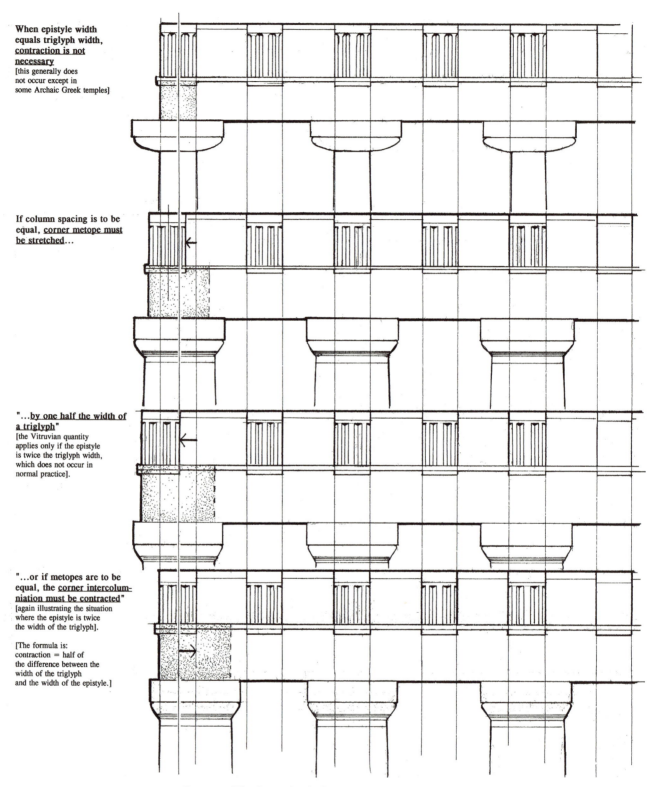

When epistyle width
equals triglyph width,
**contraction is not
necessary**
[this generally does
not occur except in
some Archaic Greek temples]

If column spacing is to be
equal, **corner metope must
be stretched**...

"**...by one half the width of
a triglyph**"
[the Vitruvian quantity
applies only if the epistyle
is twice the triglyph width,
which does not occur in
normal practice].

"**...or if metopes are to be
equal, the corner intercolumniation must be contracted**"
[again illustrating the situation
where the epistyle is twice
the width of the triglyph].

[The formula is:
contraction = half of
the difference between the
width of the triglyph
and the width of the epistyle.]

Figure 62. The Doric Angle Contraction Problem (4.3.1–2).

DORIC SYMMETRIES (4.2.4-6)

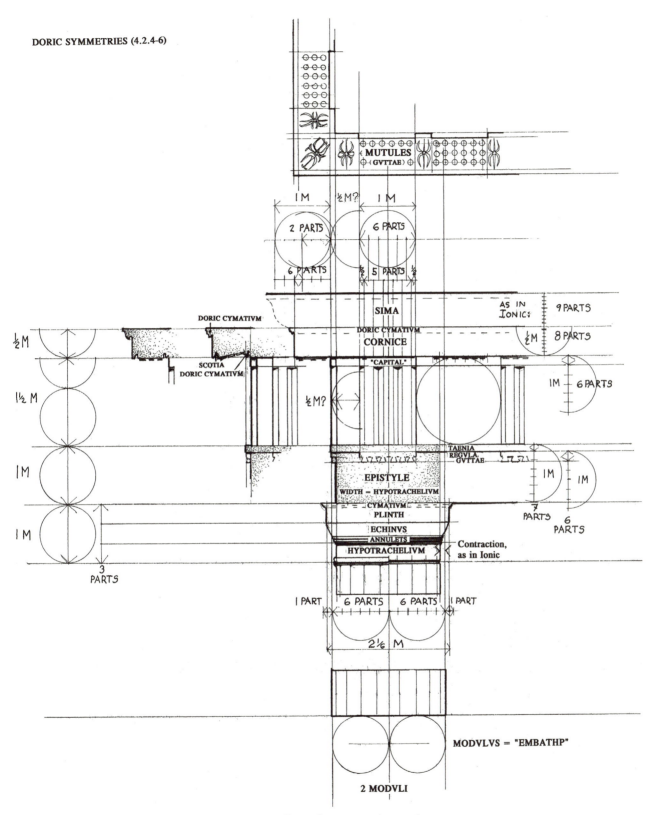

Figure 63. Doric Symmetries (4.2.4–6).

THE DORIC TRIGLYPH (4.3.5-6)

THE FLUTES OF A DORIC COLUMN (4.3.9)

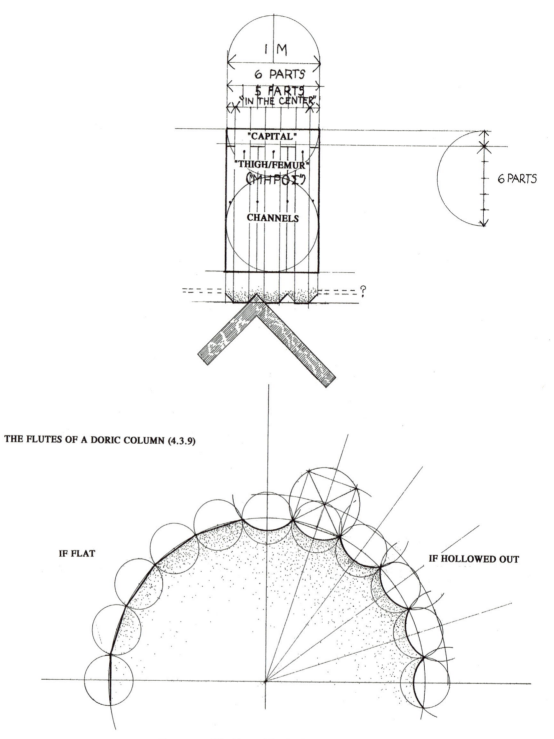

Figure 64. The Doric Triglyph (4.3.5–6).

EXAMPLES OF LATE REPUBLICAN AND AUGUSTAN DORIC

Six Late Republican Doric Entablatures
[after F. Töbelmann, Römische Gebälke, 1, (Heidelberg, 1923) figs. 20, 23-27.]

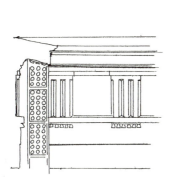

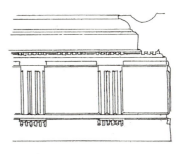

Pompeii

Theater of Marcellus, ded. 17 B.C.
(after a drawing by Giuliano da Sangallo)

Cori

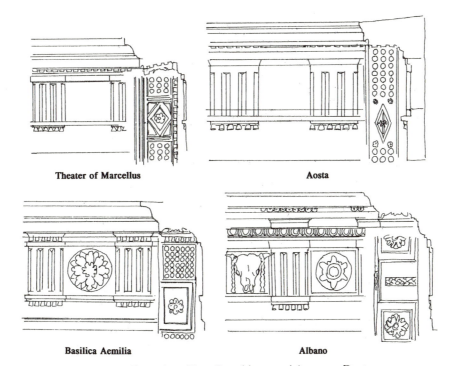

Theater of Marcellus

Aosta

Basilica Aemilia

Albano

Figure 65. Examples of Late Republican and Augustan Doric

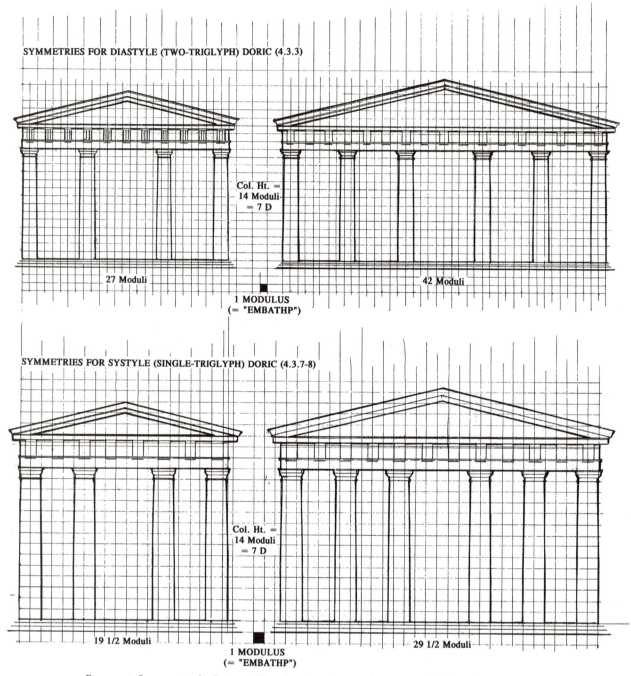

Figure 66. Symmetries for Diastyle (Two-Triglyph) Doric; Symmetries for Systyle (Single-Triglyph) Doric (4.3.3).

TEMPLE INTERIORS (4.4.1-4)

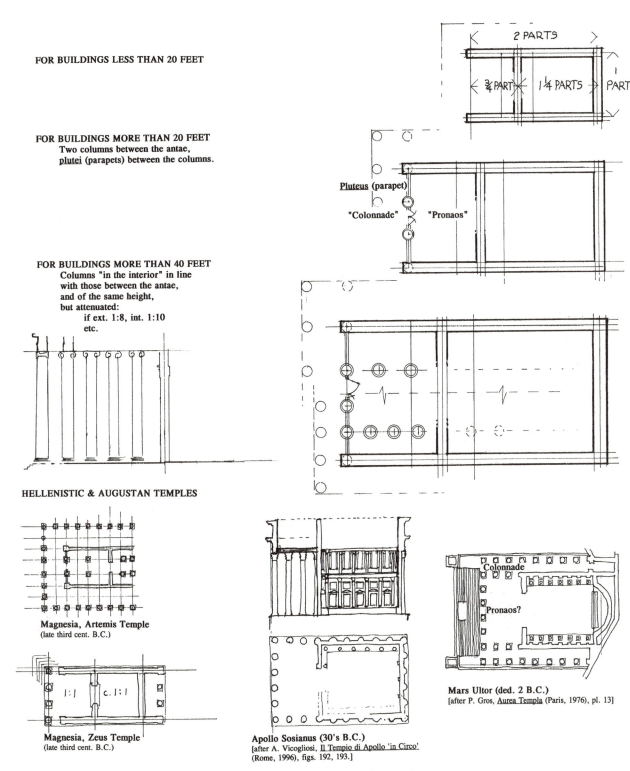

FOR BUILDINGS LESS THAN 20 FEET

FOR BUILDINGS MORE THAN 20 FEET
Two columns between the antae,
plutei (parapets) between the columns.

FOR BUILDINGS MORE THAN 40 FEET
Columns "in the interior" in line
with those between the antae,
and of the same height,
but attenuated:
  if ext. 1:8, int. 1:10
    etc.

HELLENISTIC & AUGUSTAN TEMPLES

Magnesia, Artemis Temple
(late third cent. B.C.)

Magnesia, Zeus Temple
(late third cent. B.C.)

Apollo Sosianus (30's B.C.)
[after A. Vicogliosi, Il Tempio di Apollo 'in Circo'
(Rome, 1996), figs. 192, 193.]

Mars Ultor (ded. 2 B.C.)
[after P. Gros, Aurea Templa (Paris, 1976), pl. 13]

Figure 67. Temple Interiors (4.4.1–4).

OPTICAL ADJUSTMENTS (4.4.2-3)

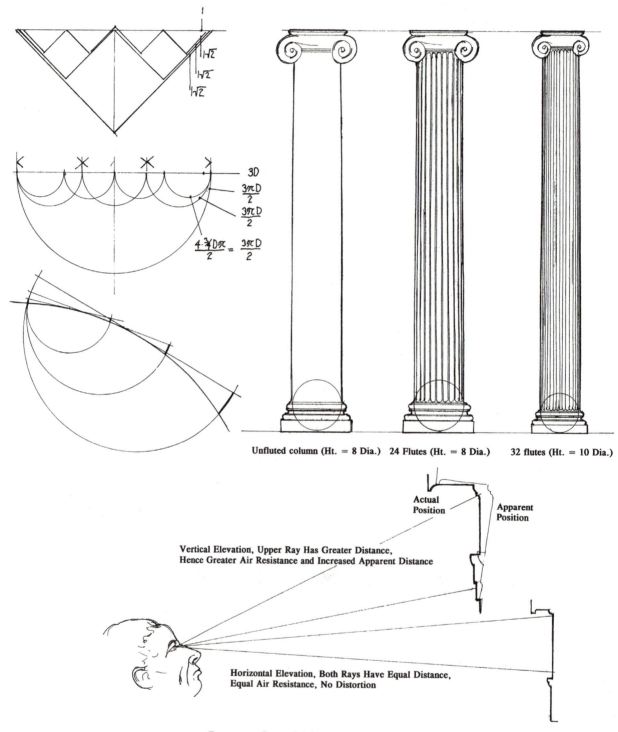

Unfluted column (Ht. = 8 Dia.)   24 Flutes (Ht. = 8 Dia.)   32 flutes (Ht. = 10 Dia.)

Actual
Position

Apparent
Position

Vertical Elevation, Upper Ray Has Greater Distance,
Hence Greater Air Resistance and Increased Apparent Distance

Horizontal Elevation, Both Rays Have Equal Distance,
Equal Air Resistance, No Distortion

Figure 68. Optical Adjustments (4.4.2–3).

to the eye. Aristotle contested the physical, particular basis of these theories and asserted that air or water are potentially transparent media (i.e., opaque when dark), that are brought to a state of actual transparency by contact with fire. Light, according to this theory, is not an emanation of particles, but a state of the medium. Color is a mixture of light and dark. Much light gives red, less gives green, and least violet. Hence in the rainbow, red is on the inside, the side closest to the sun, that with most light.[19]

Euclidean optics (c. 300 B.C.) became the dominant tradition and made optics effectively a branch of mathematics. It proceeded from the assumption that vision was the result of a rectangular ray emanating from the eye, creating a "cone of vision," with the eye at the apex. Euclidean tradition was relatively unconcerned with whether or not there really was a ray projected from the eye; the "cone of vision" was essentially a convenient geometric premise. Thus Euclidean optics abstracted experience, reducing it to questions of geometry.

Euclidean "optics" per se deal mainly with the geometry of perspective and such problems as the apparent size of an object versus its distance from the eye. One of its postulates stated that the apparent size of an object was a function of the angle at which it was observed; another postulate claimed that the location of an observed object depended on (or could be determined by) its location within the visual cone: that is, objects subtended by, or observed by, rays higher in the cone were farther from the viewer. Another division of Euclidean optics, catoptrics (the science of mirrors), dealt with the geometry of reflection and refraction.

In architecture, the use of refinements (the almost invisible curvatures) exists already in the first generation of stone Doric buildings.[20] In sculpture, the alteration of figures to correct for the impression gained from certain viewpoints can be seen as early as the early fifth century B.C. (e.g., the pedimental sculptures at Olympia). One finds an early literary awareness of this practice in Plato,[21] and the increasing interest in subjectivism made the nature of optical distortion – the distinction between actual and apparent – a common topic in the fourth century.[22]

Vitruvius seems to be aware of the whole tradition of scientific optics[23] – both physical and Euclidean/geometric. His fundamental principle is Euclidean: every proposition he makes considers the action of the line of vision from the eye. From optics he gets an awareness that the apparent position of an object depends on its contact with the line of vision. From catoptrics he develops an awareness of the constant possibility of "a false report" caused by interference with the line of vision.

Vitruvius's chief criterion in his optical analyses is the consideration of obstacles or impediments to the line of vision, either in terms of geometry or the nature of the medium: distance (the height of columns); darkness (the interior of temples); the number of stimuli (the number of flutes of columns).[24]

The intended purpose of the curvatures is highly controversial. There are two chief modern lines of interpretation. One approach asserts that the curvatures were deliberate departures from geometric regularity in order to add the imperceptible sense of life ("the eye is continually influenced by what it can not detect"[25]); the other maintains, with Vitruvius, that they are indeed optical "corrections."[26]

Dressing the blocks so that they protrude (4.4.4)

That is, drafted margins.

face toward the western regions (4.5.1–2) (Figure 69)

The "normal" Greek practice is literally to orient, that is, to face east. Frontinus (*Gromatica* 2.4.) and Hyginus (*Gromatica* 1692) say that Roman temples face west, but their common source seems to be Vitruvius. There is no other firm evidence for such a rule.

Tuscanicae Dispositiones (4.7.1–5) (Figure 73)

"Tuscanicae" implies more "Tuscanoid" than "Tuscan" or "Etruscan," and thus puts some distance between the Etruscans and the present, suggesting that what is given here is a Tuscan-ish contemporary adaptation of an ancient type.

breadth of the temple (4.7.2)

Templum here does mean "temple."

---

19 Summaries in O. Pedersen, M. Pihl, *Early Physics and Astronomy* (New York and London, 1974), ch. 10, 127–139; D. C. Lindberg, *The Beginnings of Western Science* (Chicago, 1992), 105–108; G. E. R. Lloyd, *Greek Science After Aristotle* (New York, 1973), 134–137.

20 Entasis at Hera I at Paestum, c. 600–580; stylobate curvature at the Apollo temple at Corinth, c. 570.

21 *Sophist*, 235–236. Plato divides figural art into *eikastikê*, the making of images that are other than what they represent (i.e., "stylized?"), and *phantastikê*, the making of things that appear to be like what they represent but in reality are very different. Plato notes the habit of sculptors of intentionally altering the true proportions – *alêthinê symmetria* – by shortening legs and lengthening torsos "in order to compensate for the low vantage point." J. J. Pollitt, *The Ancient View of Greek Art* (New Haven, 1974), 46–47.

22 Pollitt, op. cit., 162.

23 He is aware of the debate as to whether vision is the result of the impact of images emitted by the object, or of visual rays shed from the eyes: "Thus either from the impact of images on our vision, or by action of rays shed forth from our eyes, as the physicists would have it, for either reason it seems to be the case that the glance of our eyes may make false judgements" (6.2.3). Just as Vitruvius reflects it, the debate was never resolved in the scientific literature.

24 He uses a similar criterion in evaluating acoustics: echoes are caused by impediments to the circular wavelike spreading of sounds. 3.3.6–8.

25 Ruskin, *The Stones of Venice*, 2.5.

26 Some refinements must be intentionally optical, and for the reasons Vitruvius gives; corner columns should be increased by one-fiftieth their diameter "because they are cut into by the air on all sides and therefore seem more slender to the viewer" (3.3.11)

ORIENTATION/VISIBILITY OF CULT IMAGE (4.5.1-2; 4.9.1)

"...if there is no impediment...both the temple and the cult statue should face toward the Western regions of the heavens, so that [offerers/sacrificers] will see the image within the temple beneath the Eastern regions of the heavens...while the images themselves will seem to look from the East upon the supplicants."

"But if the nature of the site prevents this...then the layout of the site should be adjusted so that as much as possible of the city defenses can be observed from the temples..."

"If temples are to erected alongside a river, as happens in Egypt in the region of the Nile, then the temples ought to seem to look out on the river banks."

"...if near public roads, they should be placed so that passersby can look upon them...within sight of the divine images."

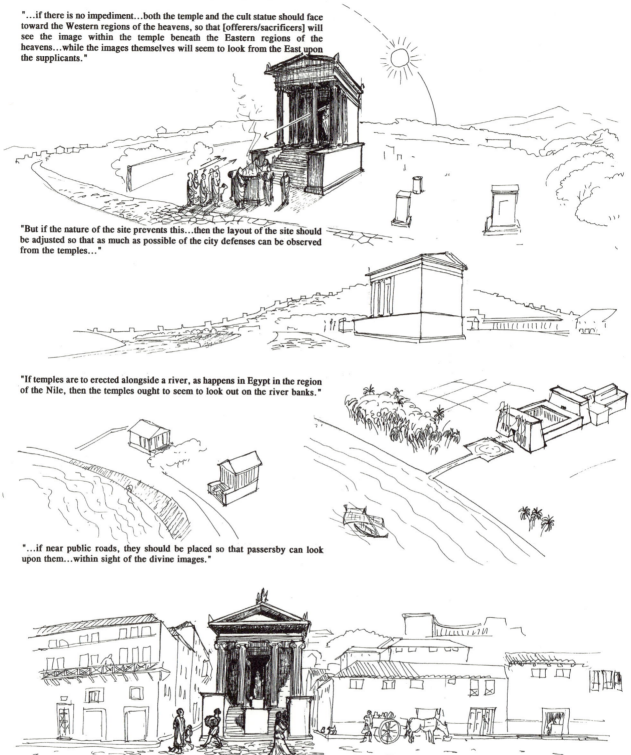

Figure 69. Orientation/Visibility of Cult Image (4.5.1–2; 4.9.1).

THE DORIC DOOR (4.6.1-2)
(THE ATTIC DOOR, 4.6.6)

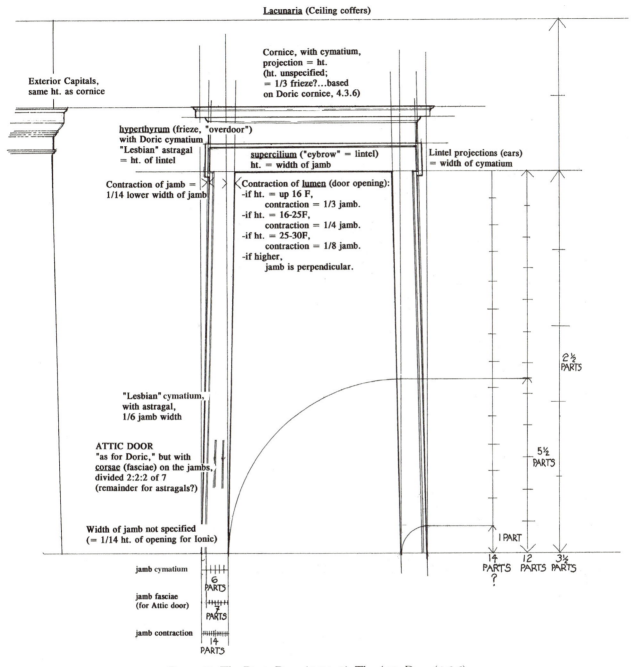

Lacunaria (Ceiling coffers)

Cornice, with cymatium,
projection = ht.
(ht. unspecified;
= 1/3 frieze?...based
on Doric cornice, 4.3.6)

Exterior Capitals,
same ht. as cornice

hyperthyrum (frieze, "overdoor")
with Doric cymatium
"Lesbian" astragal
= ht. of lintel

supercilium ("eybrow" = lintel)
ht. = width of jamb

Lintel projections (ears)
= width of cymatium

Contraction of jamb =
1/14 lower width of jamb

Contraction of lumen (door opening):
-if ht. = up 16 F,
    contraction = 1/3 jamb.
-if ht. = 16-25F,
    contraction = 1/4 jamb.
-if ht. = 25-30F,
    contraction = 1/8 jamb.
-if higher,
    jamb is perpendicular.

"Lesbian" cymatium,
with astragal,
1/6 jamb width

ATTIC DOOR
"as for Doric," but with
corsae (fasciae) on the jambs,
divided 2:2:2 of 7
(remainder for astragals?)

Width of jamb not specified
(= 1/14 ht. of opening for Ionic)

2½ PARTS

5½ PARTS

1 PART

14 PARTS ?   12 PARTS   3½ PARTS

jamb cymatium
6 PARTS

jamb fasciae
(for Attic door)
7 PARTS

jamb contraction
14 PARTS

Figure 70. The Doric Door (4.6.1–2); The Attic Door (4.6.6).

THE IONIC DOOR (4.6.3-4)

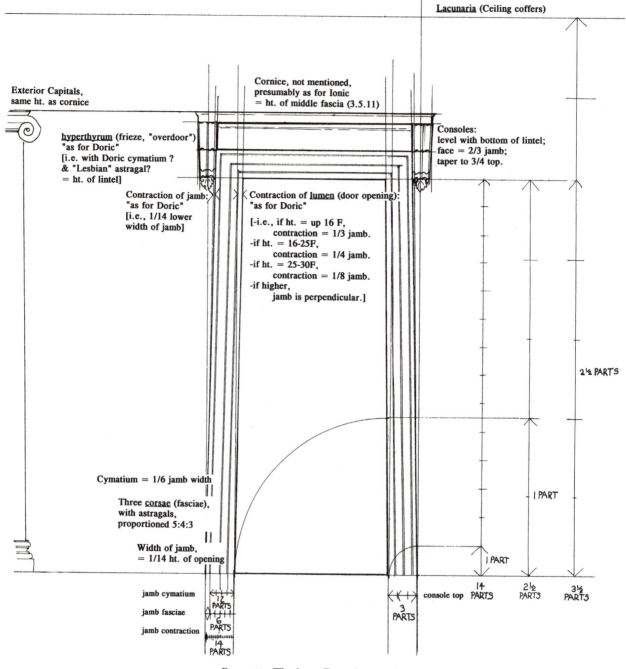

Lacunaria (Ceiling coffers)

Exterior Capitals,
same ht. as cornice

Cornice, not mentioned,
presumably as for Ionic
= ht. of middle fascia (3.5.11)

hyperthyrum (frieze, "overdoor")
"as for Doric"
[i.e. with Doric cymatium ?
& "Lesbian" astragal?
= ht. of lintel]

Consoles:
level with bottom of lintel;
face = 2/3 jamb;
taper to 3/4 top.

Contraction of jamb:
"as for Doric"
[i.e., 1/14 lower
width of jamb]

Contraction of lumen (door opening):
"as for Doric"

[-i.e., if ht. = up 16 F,
         contraction = 1/3 jamb.
-if ht. = 16-25F,
         contraction = 1/4 jamb.
-if ht. = 25-30F,
         contraction = 1/8 jamb.
-if higher,
         jamb is perpendicular.]

Cymatium = 1/6 jamb width

Three corsae (fasciae),
with astragals,
proportioned 5:4:3

Width of jamb,
= 1/14 ht. of opening

jamb cymatium

jamb fasciae

jamb contraction

12
PARTS

6
PARTS

14
PARTS

3
PARTS

console top

2½ PARTS

1 PART

1 PART

14
PARTS

2½
PARTS

3½
PARTS

Figure 71. The Ionic Door (4.6.3–4).

DOOR PANELS (4.6.4-5)

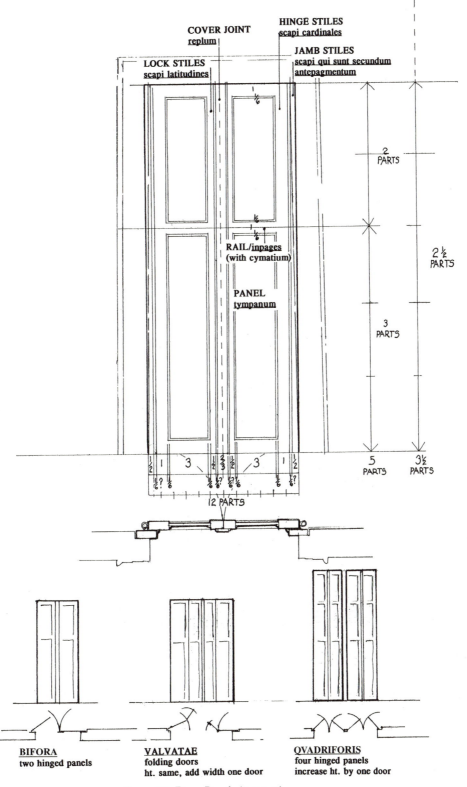

Figure 72. Door Panels (4.6.4–5).

TUSCAN DESIGN/TUSCANICAE DISPOSITIONES (4.7.1-5)

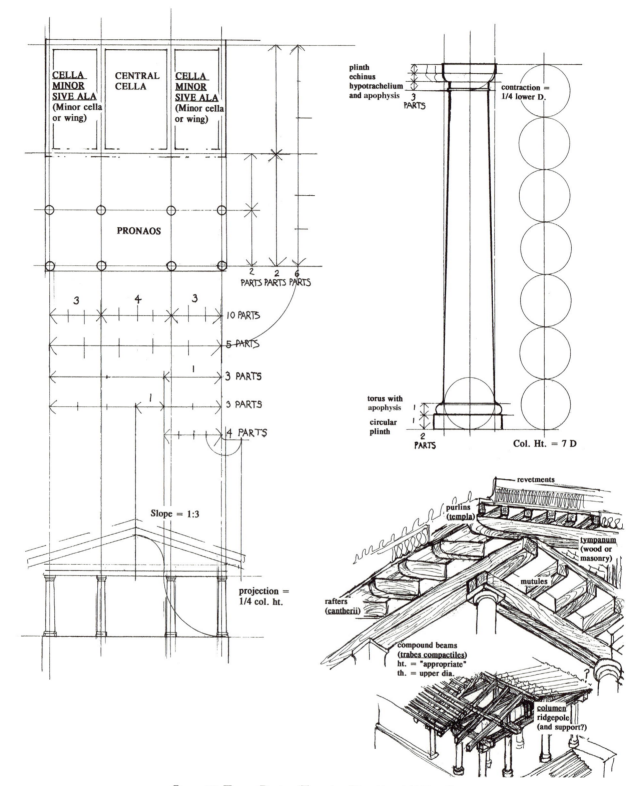

Figure 73. Tuscan Design (*Tuscanicae Dispositiones*) (4.7.1–5).

platform (4.8.1) (Figure 74)

A "tribunal" could be just the floor of the porch, but it implies a speaking platform, hence possibly a platform inserted into a staircase.

other types (4.8.4–7) (Figures 75, 76)

Five times in Book 4 Vitruvius mentions the possibility of creating new architectural forms by analyzing principles and combining elements:

4.1.2: Corinthian entablature can be either Doric or Ionic.

4.1.3: By the introduction of a third type of capital (Corinthian), a third type of column has developed out of the other two.

4.1.12: The existence of other types of capitals, whose names and symmetries he is not able to give, but which seem to have had their vocabulary drawn from Corinthian, Ionic, and Doric.

4.2.5: Criticism of placing representations of mutules over dentils, which is the reverse of logical structure (*asseres* over *cantherii*).

4.6.4–6: Creating a new type of plan by taking everything that normally is on the front and transferring it to the side (i.e., transverse cella), or transferring Tuscan principles of plan disposition to Corinthian or Ionic buildings.

BOOK 5

poems . . . reading aloud (5.praef.1)

Education and didactic literature relied a great deal on poetry as an aid to memorization (e.g., verse descriptions of astronomy or science, such as Manilius or Lucretius). Most reading, even in libraries, was aloud, or at least mumbled.

the City is thronged (5.praef.3)

This probably refers to the increase of business activity under the Pax Augusta.

Pythagoras . . . [principle of] cubes (5.praef.3)

MSS read 250, Fra Giocondo supplies 216, the cube of six.

custom of giving gladiatorial games in the forum (5.1.1)

This continued down into the end of the Republic. See Commentary 10.praef.3.

parapet (5.1.5)

Pluteus, generally a parapet or screen. Also means a movable screen or protective parapet, or the protective back to a couch.

I myself have designed this type of building . . .
and supervised its construction (5.1.6) (Figures 79, 80)

The phrase *conlocavi curavique* almost certainly means "I designed and supervised it," not just that he was the contractor or construction architect. The primary meanings of *conlocare* (*collocare*) are to put out, set out, lay out, arrange, determine (i.e., as in a design). Secondary meanings include to station (soldiers), give

in marriage, deposit or spend money, or to put out a contract. *Curare* means to tend, administer, have care of.

Colonia Julia Fanestris (5.1.6)

The former Fanum Fortunae, made a colony by Augustus, on the Adriatic coast.

The Basilica at Fano (5.1.6–10) (Figures 79, 80)

It has been suggested that the section of the *Ten Books* on the basilica at Fano was inserted into the manuscript later, perhaps after publication, because it seems to have features that blatantly contradict the prescriptions for basilicas which immediately precede it.[1] Vitruvius says first that the upper columns of basilicas should be three-quarters the height of the lower, then at Fano he makes them eighteen feet over twenty. However, with one emendation of the text (xv for xviii feet) the reconstruction can be made to correspond almost completely with the preceding prescriptions (with the obvious exception that the one large colonnade instead of two stories of columns is an innovation). Also, as suggested in our introduction, this may be Vitruvius's example of how innovations may be introduced into his prescriptions.

spectators . . . wide open pores (5.3.1)

Vena (fissure, vein, pore, cavity) appears in numerous other passages that use the language of chemical analysis (e.g., 8.3.2, referring to springs welling up from within mountains). The condition of veins serves for Vitruvius as one of the major determinants of what we term chemical bonding because how one material's bond with another may be determined by whether its "pores" are already densely filled with another substance or whether they are open.

Do not mix access to the upper parts
of the theater with that to the lower (5.3.5)

The theater of Marcellus, dedicated in 17 B.C., does as Vitruvius recommends, and this practice becomes standard in Imperial period theaters and amphitheaters. Spectators in cheaper seats were thereby segregated from wealthier theatergoers, and quick access made easy.

voice is a flowing breath of air . . .
endless formation of circles (5.3.6)

This analysis is related to the "antiperistasis" theory of impelled motion (cf. 1.6.2), and stands in contrast to the theory of radial projection of rays (9.1.13).

Harmonics (5.4.1–9) (Figure 81)

Vitruvius is obviously conversant with Greek musical theory, especially Aristoxenus, and he depends heavily on musical theory for terms such as *genus* (type), *dispositio* (disposition-design),

---

1 F. Pellati, "La basilica di Fano e la formazione del trattato di Vitruvio," *Rendiconti della Pontificia Accademia* 33–34 (1947–49), 153–174.

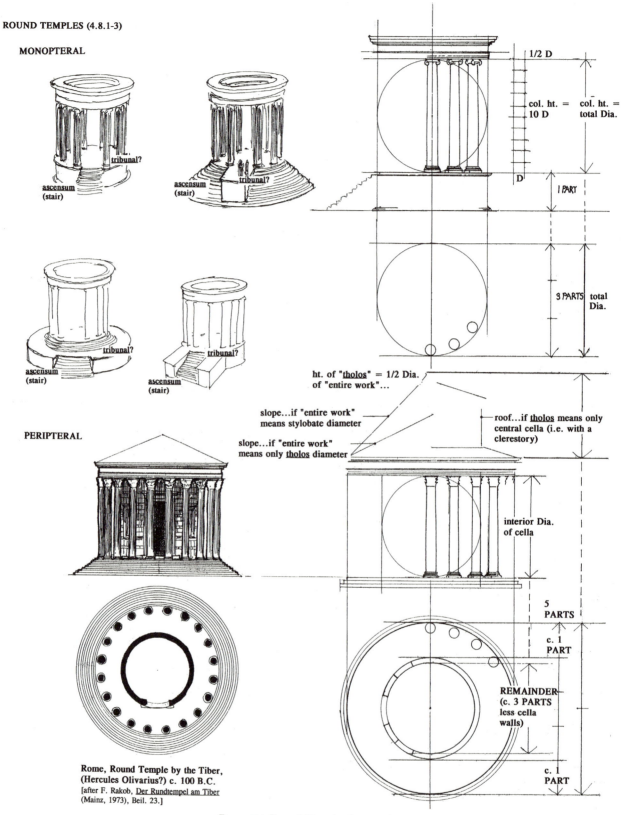

ROUND TEMPLES (4.8.1-3)

MONOPTERAL

ascensum (stair)   tribunal?

ascensum (stair)   tribunal?

ascensum (stair)   tribunal?

ascensum (stair)   tribunal?

1/2 D

col. ht. = 10 D   col. ht. = total Dia.

D

1 PART

3 PARTS total Dia.

ht. of "tholos" = 1/2 Dia. of "entire work"...

slope...if "entire work" means stylobate diameter

slope...if "entire work" means only tholos diameter

roof...if tholos means only central cella (i.e. with a clerestory)

PERIPTERAL

interior Dia. of cella

5 PARTS

c. 1 PART

REMAINDER (c. 3 PARTS less cella walls)

c. 1 PART

Rome, Round Temple by the Tiber, (Hercules Olivarius?) c. 100 B.C.
[after F. Rakob, Der Rundtempel am Tiber (Mainz, 1973), Beil. 23.]

Figure 74. Round Temples (4.8.1–3).

HYBRID TEMPLES AND NEW TYPES (4.8.4)

LATERAL TEMPLES:
"Proportions are all the same...a length equal to double their width...
...everything that is usually in the front has been transferred to the
sides."

Agrippa's Pantheon
(Hadrianic Pantheon in outline)
[after H. Kähler, Der römische Tempel
(Berlin, 1970), fig. 9.]

**Temple of Veiovis "Between
the Two Groves," (next
to the Tabularium)**
[after A.M. Colini, BollComm (1942), 5seq.)

**Temple of Castor in
the Circus Flaminius**
[after M. Conticello de'Spagnolis, Il tempio dei
Dioscuri nel Circo Flaminio (Rome, 1984), 43, 59.]

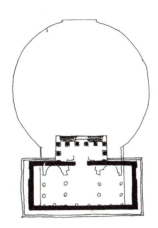

**Temple of Diana Nemorensis
(Diana at Nemi):**
hypothetical reconstruction,
"...where columns have been added to the
right and left along the sides of the
pronaos."

...from the remains at Nemi:

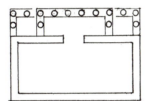

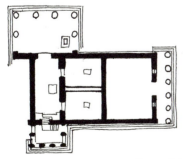

**The temple on the Acropolis at Athens
(i.e., the Erechtheion)**

Minerva (i.e. Athena) at Sounion
(after W.B. Dinsmoor Jr.)

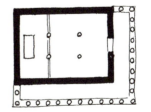

Figure 75. Hybrid Temples and New Types (4.8.4).

HYBRID TEMPLES AND NEW TYPES (4.8.4)

TUSCAN DESIGN APPLIED TO CORINTHIAN/IONIC ORDERING
"...in the places where the antae of the pronaos project forward, they place pairs of
columns opposite the walls of the cella..."

Tuscan Design   Plus   Corinthian/Ionic Ordering   equals...

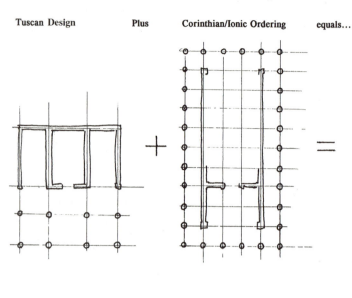
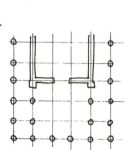

Temple of Castor and Pollux
in the Forum

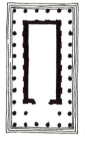
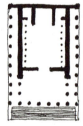

Forum Holitorium Temple   Tivoli, Hercules Victor
(after Palladio)

PSEUDOPERIPTEROS (False Peripteros):
        Removing the walls of the temple...to the intercolumniations...to create a spacious
interior...

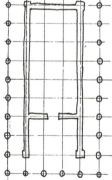
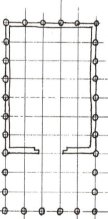
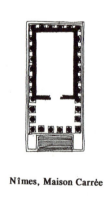

Nîmes, Maison Carrée

Temple of Apollo Palatinus

Figure 76. Hybrid Temples and New Types (4.8.4).

THE FORUM (5.1.1-3)

THE GREEK FORUM (i.e. Agora)
 -laid out on the square
 -"double" colonnades, with ambulatories above
 -narrow intercolumniations

THE ITALIAN FORUM
 -sized appropriate to the city
 -oblong, 2:3
 -accommodates Italian custom of gladiatorial shows
 -wider intercolumniations
 -shops (for moneychangers et al.) and balconies
 -upper columns 1/4 less than lower,
  (implied continuous taper?)

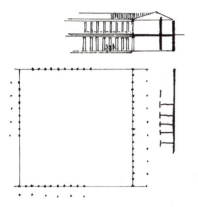

3 PARTS

4 PARTS

Athens, Agora, as in the mid-second cent. B.C.
[after J. Travlos, Pictorial Dictionary of Ancient Athens (New York, 1971) fig. 31.]

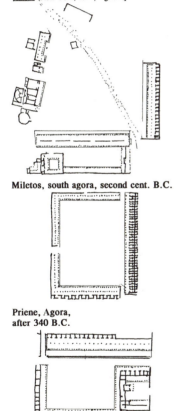

Miletos, south agora, second cent. B.C.

**Priene, Agora,
after 340 B.C.**

**Pompeii, Forum,
as in c. 89 B.C.**
[after P. Zanker, Pompeii (Trier, 1987) fig. 7.]

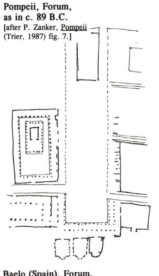

**Baelo (Spain), Forum,
mainly first cent. A.D.**
W. Trillmich, Th. Hauschild, Denkmäler der Römerzeit. Hispania Antiqua (1993) fig. 137.]

**Iuvanum, mainly
first cent. B.C.**
[after A. Pellegrino, ArchCl 36 (1984), 172, fig. 2.]

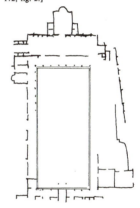

**Verona, refounded
late first cent. B.C.**
[after J.B. Ward Perkins, Cities of Ancient Greece and Italy: Planning in Classical Antiquity (New York, 1974) fig. 59]

Figure 77. The Forum (5.1.1–3).

THE BASILICA (5.1.4-5)

-site in the warmest location, in order
  to be able to conduct business in winter

-width of the site, unless nature of the site prevents it,
  should be between 1/3 and 1/2 length

-if longer, "Chalcidian"
porches (presumably open
porticos or courtyards)
are to be placed at ends

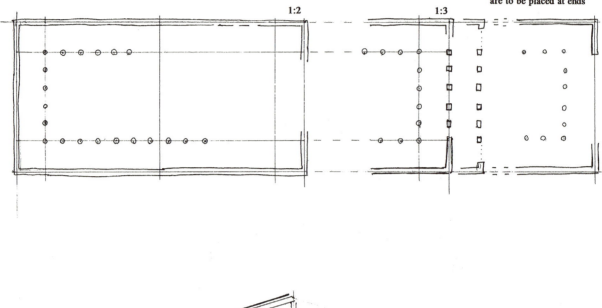

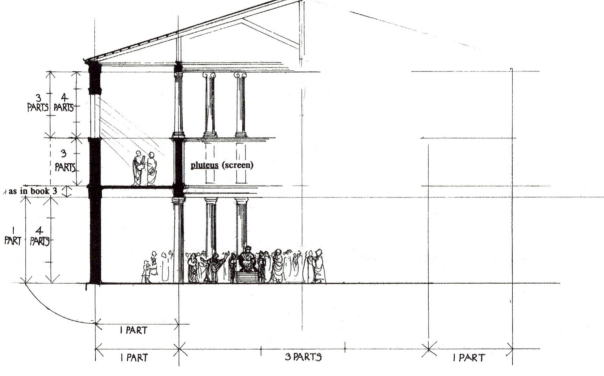

Figure 78. The Basilica (5.1.4–5).

THE BASILICA AT COLONIA JULIA FANESTRIS (FANO)(5.1.6–10)
Drawn with on-center dimensions

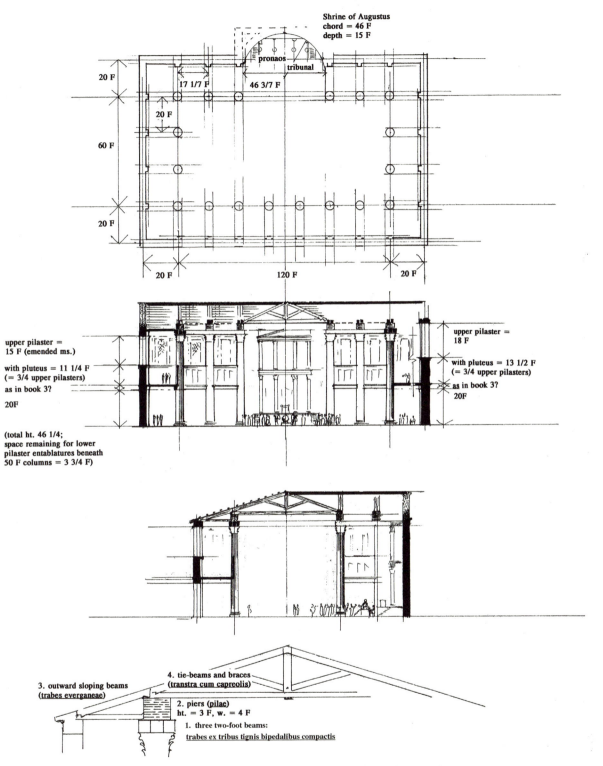

Shrine of Augustus
chord = 46 F
depth = 15 F

pronaos
tribunal

20 F

17 1/7 F   46 3/7 F

20 F

60 F

20 F

20 F   120 F   20 F

upper pilaster =
15 F (emended ms.)

with pluteus = 11 1/4 F
(= 3/4 upper pilasters)
as in book 3?

20F

(total ht. 46 1/4;
space remaining for lower
pilaster entablatures beneath
50 F columns = 3 3/4 F)

upper pilaster =
18 F

with pluteus = 13 1/2 F
(= 3/4 upper pilasters)
as in book 3?
20F

3. outward sloping beams
(trabes everganeae)

4. tie-beams and braces
(transtra cum capreolis)

2. piers (pilae)
ht. = 3 F, w. = 4 F

1. three two-foot beams:
trabes ex tribus tignis bipedalibus compactis

Figure 79. The Basilica at Colonia Julia Fanestris (Fano) (1.6.1–10).

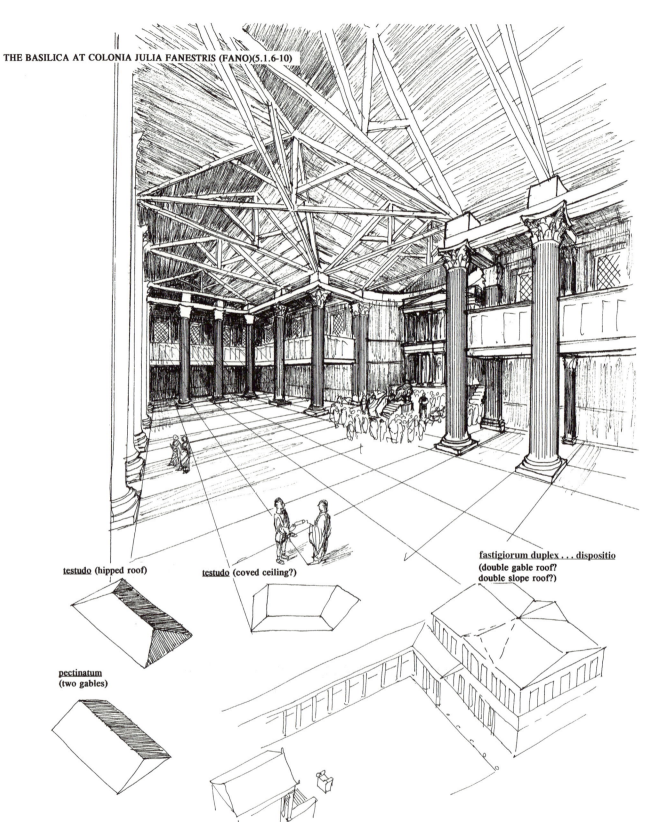

THE BASILICA AT COLONIA JULIA FANESTRIS (FANO)(5.1.6-10)

<u>testudo</u> (hipped roof)

<u>testudo</u> (coved ceiling?)

fastigiorum duplex . . . dispositio
(double gable roof?
double slope roof?)

pectinatum
(two gables)

Figure 80. The Basilica at Colonia Julia Fanestris (Fano) (5.6.1–10).

HARMONIC PRINCIPLES: THE SCALES (5.4.1-9)

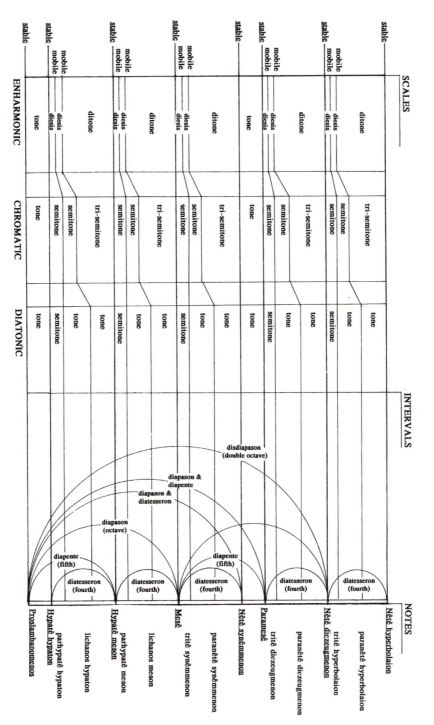

Figure 81. Harmonic Principles: The Scales (5.4.1–9).

pyknon (closely spaced, as in pycnostyle spacing of columns), and certain aspects of the term *eurythmia*. He is also probably dependent on musical theory for awareness of much more sophisticated concepts, such as the difference between empirical measurement and abstract principles (i.e., the phenomenal and the noetic);[2] this awareness informs his constant opinion throughout the *Ten Books* that design by *symmetria* and other rules must almost always be modified for practical, optical, or aesthetic considerations.

This section in effect introduces Vitruvius's readers to the intervals of the three principal *genera* of harmony: enharmonic, chromatic, and diatonic.

Greek musical theory makes a strong distinction between intervals that were *symphona* (concordant, those which blend together) and those that were *diaphona* (discordant).[3] The concordant intervals were the octave, fifth, and fourth, and all those compounded from them; all others were discordant. The concordant intervals were those that were treated as fixed in the musical scales.

Scales were built on tetrachords, that is, intervals of a fourth. Two tetrachords could either be "conjunct" when they shared a tone (i.e., the top note of one was the bottom note of the other) or "disjunct" (when they did not share a note and there was an interval of a tone between them). An octave consisted of two disjunct tetrachords (each usually divided into three smaller intervals by four notes), which amounted to the same thing as a fourth and a fifth (the latter divided into four intervals by five notes).

A tetrachord was an interval of two and a half tones. The two outer notes were, obviously, fixed; the two inner ones were movable. In the *enharmonic* mode the two middle tones were crowded down at the bottom of the tetrachord only a quarter tone (*diêsis*) apart, followed by an interval of two tones ("ditone"). (The term for this "crowding" is *pyknon*). In the *chromatic* the intervals were semitone, semitone, and a tone and a half, or trisemitone. In the *diatonic* (which is the basis of almost all modern Western music), the intervals of the tetrachord were tone-tone-semitone (although not necessarily in that order).

> *enharmonic*: quarter tone, quarter tone, ditone
> *chromatic*: semitone, semitone, trisemitone
> *diatonic*: tone, tone, semitone

Vitruvius gives here a list of the standard names of the intervals and notes covering two octaves and a fourth. He starts with the fixed intervals and then gives the movable intervals, whose various positions determine the type of scale. The terms for the types (or magnitudes) of fixed intervals are these:

i.	diatesseron	fourth
ii.	diapente	fifth
iii.	diapason	octave
iv.	disdiatesseron	octave + fourth
v.	disdiapente	octave + fifth
vi.	disdiapason	double octave

These two octaves and a fourth constituted the range of a lyre (a modern piano covers seven octaves), and the somewhat elaborate Greek names of the specific intervals and notes of this range were based on the names for the strings (*chordai*) of the lyre.[4] The strings used to name the fixed notes were as follows:

Hypatê [chordê] ("uppermost string"): uppermost position, lowest pitch
Mesê [chordê] ("middle string")
Nêtê [chordê] ("lowermost string"): lowermost position, highest pitch
Tritê ("third") occurs between mesê and nêtê; used for movable notes

Tetrachords

lower octave:
hypaton [systêma]	"lowest system"
meson [systêma]	"middle system"

upper octave:
synêmmenon [systêma]	"joined system"
diezeugmenon [systêma]	"disjoined system"

upper fourth:
hyperbolaion [systêma]	"uppermost," "additional system"

The names for the individual notes describe the string (*chordê*), and then end in -ê, or the tone (*tonos*), and then end in -os or the chordal system, and then end in -on.

Fixed Notes

i.	proslambanomenos	added on at the bottom of the scale
ii.	hypatê hypaton	uppermost note on uppermost string
iii.	hypatê meson	middle note on uppermost string
iv.	mesê	middle string
v.	nêtê synêmmenon	joined note on middle string
vi.	paramesê	next to middle string
vii.	nêtê diezeugmenon	low string, disjoined note
viii.	nêtê hyperbolaion	low string, highest note

Movable Notes

i.	parhypatê hypaton	next to uppermost string, uppermost note
ii.	lichanos hypaton	forefinger-struck uppermost note
iii.	parhypatê meson	next to uppermost string, middle note
iv.	lichanos meson	forefinger-struck middle note

---

2 Aristoxenus, a student of Aristotle, and hence presumably an empiricist, held that precise numerical harmonies could not account for experience on the simple grounds that they were developed from first principles; pleasing harmonies were dependent on slight variations on string length from mathematical prescriptions. This need is recognized in modern "well-tempered" tuning. See T. Levenson, *Measure for Measure: A Musical History of Science* (New York, 1994), 39–70.

3 The following material is derived largely from M. L. West, *Ancient Greek Music* (Oxford, 1992), 160–164, which is the best source for the basics of harmonics.

4 Our thanks for the following to the composer Lou Harrison.

v.	tritê synêmmenon	third string, joined note
vi.	paranêtê synêmmenon	next to lowest string, joined note
vii.	tritê diezeugmenon	third string, disjoined note
viii.	paranêtê diezeugmenon	next to lowest string, disjoined note
ix.	tritê hyperbolaion	third string, highest note
x.	paranêtê hyperbolaion	next to lowest string, highest note

In the fifth century B.C. most serious music (i.e., that associated with classical drama) was enharmonic; as Vitruvius says it has "a particularly solemn and dignified authority."[5] Its name means simply "in tune." Chromatic was a sort of deviation, a "coloring" of it (more for "refined pleasure," as Vitruvius says), the province of professional citharodes and with a tendency to "effeminacy." In the Hellenistic period chromatic and diatonic came to dominate because they were easier to appreciate, and by the Late Republic in Rome almost all music was diatonic.

The drawing at the end of Book 5 that Vitruvius refers to was probably very similar to our Figure 81. The custom of illustrating musical intervals by half circles of various diameter is standard for medieval and Renaissance manuscripts.

sharp . . . heavy (5.4.2)

Our "high" and "low" but also related to "sharp" and "flat."

"slow," "looks," flows," "stokes" (5.4.1)

The Latin words are sol, lux, flos, vox.

The notes . . . each type (5.4.5)

This is the same use of genus as in the "types" of Doric, Ionic, and Corinthian columns.

Echea (Sounding Vessels) (5.5.1–8) (Figure 82)

These vessels, of bronze or clay, may be another example of Vitruvius singling out a highly technical feature of Greek architecture that was uncommon, but between eight and sixteen potential sites with evidence of echea have been identified. It is debatable whether such vessels amplified or deadened sound.[6]

that countless theaters
have been built in Rome every year (5.5.7)

For the numerous temporary theaters built for annual festivals in Rome, see Commentary for 10.praef.3.

masonry, stone, or marble, which can not resonate (5.5.7)

In literature poetic fantasy allowed several resonant structures: for example, a musical tower in Megara described by Ovid (Metamorphoses 8.14–16).[7]

Lucius Mummius (5.5.8)

Conqueror of Corinth, 146 B.C.

all the artists do their work on it (5.6.2)

Artifices is a fairly common term for actors, especially in the Imperial period.

rotating panels [periaktoi] (5.6.3, 5.6.8)

These devices probably go back to the fifth century B.C., but there are almost no archaeological indications of how they functioned in the Hellenistic or Roman theater. From Vitruvius's description they appear to have been rotating prisms that may have been placed behind or in front of the outermost doors of the scene building to indicate locality. To indicate a change of locality within the same town, the convention was to turn only the right periaktos; to change the entire scene, both were turned. The right entrance normally indicated an entrance from the town, the left an entrance from the country. To change the scene more than three times, the paintings on the rearward two panels of each periaktos could be changed before the next scene change.[8]

lintels (5.6.5)

Supercilia, literally "eyebrows"; these could be archivolts, although in other cases they are flat lintels.

three types of sets (5.6.8)

Reflections of this much discussed passage have been seen in certain types of Pompeiian fresco scenes.[9] Some types of classical tragedy and comedy did continue to be performed, but the most popular types of theater performance were Atellan farce (a sort of commedia dell'arte with stock characters) and mime (a combination of dancers and actors).

The thymelê is the altar to Dionysus in the orchestra of a Greek theater (Figure 84). Scenic artists are the protagonist, deuteragonist, and tritagonist; thymelic artists would include the chorus and the aulos player (piper).

5 M. L. West, Ancient Greek Music (Oxford, 1992), 164.

6 On pithoi beneath the floor causing the house auditorium to resound, Aristotle Problemata 9.8; on empty pots deadening sound, Pliny the Elder, Natural History 11.12.270. On eight potential sites with evidence of echea, P. Thielscher, "Die Schallgefässe des antiken Theaters," Festschrift Frans Dornseiff, ed. H. Kusch (Leipzig, VEB Bibliographisches Institut, 1953), 334–371. Our thanks to Profs. Jean Davison and Robert Arns of the University of Vermont for information on their researches; article forthcoming in Technology and Culture.

7 Also Horace, Carmina 3.11.2, "movit Amphion lapides canendo," and Statius, Thebaid 1.9 seq.

8 See M. Bieber, The History of the Greek and Roman Theater (Princeton, 1961), 75.

9 H. G. Beyen, "The Wall Decoration of the Cubiculum of the Villa of Publius Fannius Synistor near Boscoreale in Relation to Ancient Stage Painting," Mnemosyne 4th ser. 10 (1957), 147–153; A. M. G. Little, Roman Perspective Painting and the Ancient Stage (Kennebunk, Maine, 1971); R. Ling, Roman Painting (Cambridge, 1990), 30–31, 77–78, 143.

ECHEA (SOUNDING VESSELS IN THEATERS) (5.5.1-8)

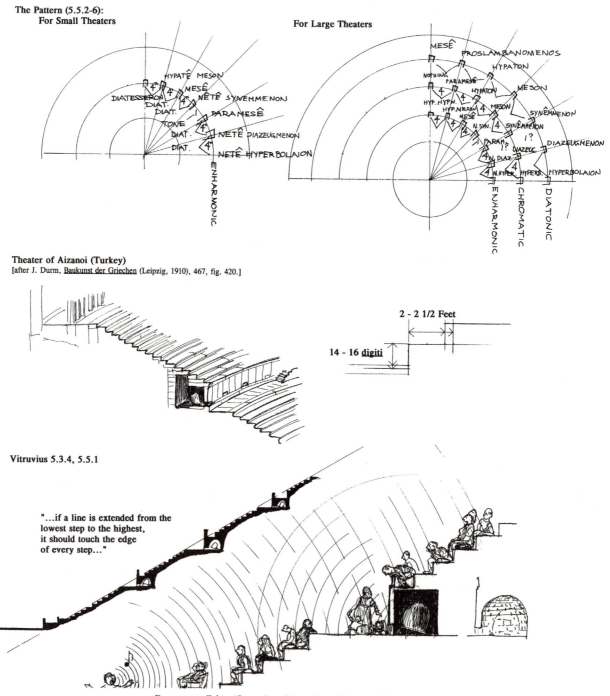

Figure 82. *Echea* (Sounding Vessels in Theaters) (5.5.1–8).

THEATER DESIGN: THE ROMAN THEATER (5.6.1-8)

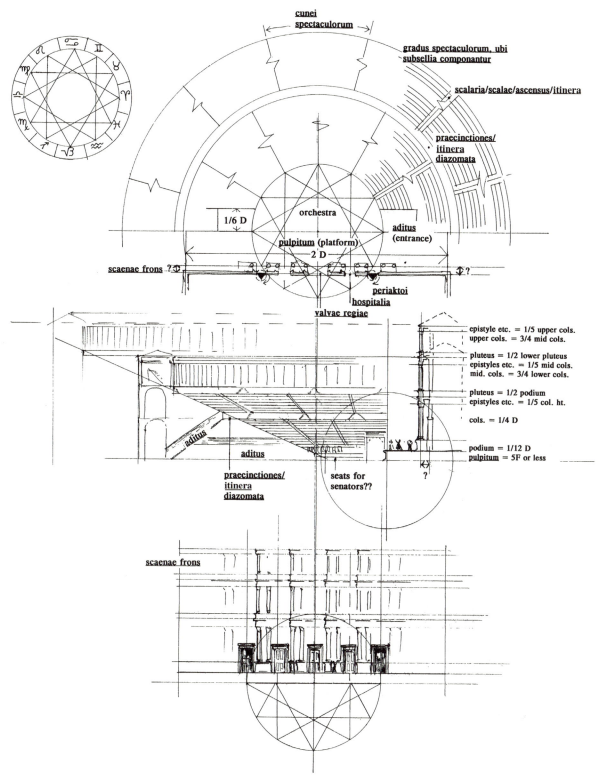

Figure 83. Theater Design: The Roman Theater (5.6.1–8).

THEATER DESIGN: THE GREEK THEATER (5.7.1-2)

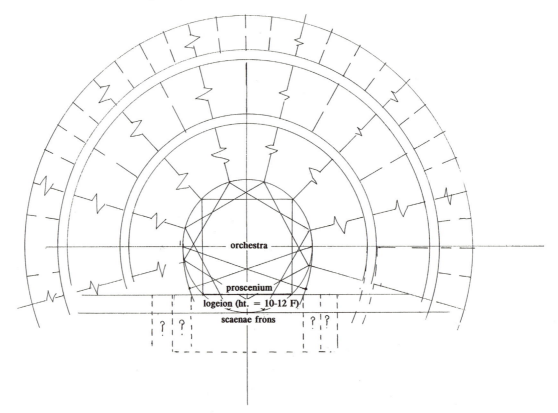

GREEK THEATERS
[after Bieber, The History of the Greek and
Roman Theater (Princeton, 1961), fig. 476.]

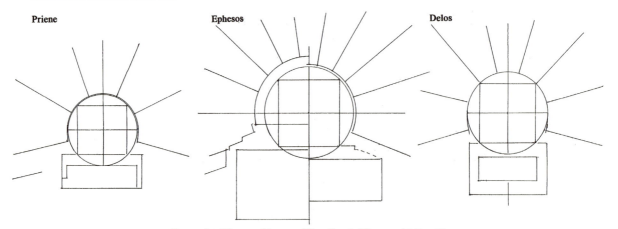

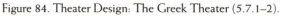

Figure 84. Theater Design: The Greek Theater (5.7.1–2).

Behind the scene building,
set up porticoes (5.9.1) (Figure 85)

Vitruvius refers in part to the great quadriporticus attached to buildings like the Theater of Pompey, but the custom of building porticoes of some sort in the region of theaters goes back to the late classical period (see figure). As Vitruvius implies, these could be remarkably multifunctional spaces. The Senate sometimes met in the porticus behind the Theater of Pompey (as it did on the Ides of March, 44), and the Saepta, the huge courtyard built by Caesar as a voting precinct, also housed gladiatorial games.

supplying the wood . . . in great quantities (5.9.8)

Roman cities did indeed consume a great quantity of wood, especially for baths and industry, and the huge consumption has been linked to deforestation and the silting of harbors in late antiquity.

the explanation of bath design . . . (5.10.1–5) (Figures 86, 87)

In the view of the old-fashioned moralists, baths were part of the disintegration of morals not only because they attracted purveyors of corruption and ease, but also because heat was considered enervating (cf. 1.4.6).[10]

stucco or plaster (5.10.3)

Albario (here translated "stucco") implies worked, molded plaster; tectorio implies plaster, including the fresco layer.

Spartan sauna and sweating chambers (5.10.5)

Laconicum, a dry heat chamber with, or near, a cold water plunge, that is, bathing in the Spartan manner; sudatio, wet heat, or steam room.

building palaestras (5.11.1) (Figure 88)

In Greek usage a palaestra was a wrestling school and a building, usually a courtyard building. A gymnasium was an athletic ground, with or without buildings, mainly equipped with running tracks, and almost always public. The palaestra could often be privately owned, but also often city owned, and was the main place of instruction for ephebes.[11]

BOOK 6

Aristippus (6.praef. 1)

Aristippus of Cyrene, a contemporary and associate of Socrates, and a man of luxurious habits, or his grandson, a founder of the Cyrenaic school of philosophy, which taught a sensationalist theory of knowledge and that immediate pleasure is the goal of action.

Theophrastus . . . a citizen in every country (6.praef.2)

Presumably Theophrastus, successor of Aristotle at the Lyceum.

The poets who wrote those old comedies . . . (6.praef.3)

Eucrates and Chionides and, of course, Aristophanes were the poets of Old Comedy (mid/late fifth century B.C.); Alexis was a poet of Middle Comedy (c. 375 B.C.).

And therefore I thank my parents immeasurably . . .
an art . . . that can not be mastered without
education in letters and comprehensive learning (6.praef.4)

The type of education that Vitruvius refers to (litteratura encyclioque doctrinarum omnium disciplina) would have been contracted out by his parents to several different specialist teachers while he was in his middle teens, which would have been a considerable expense to a family of modest means.

both literary and technical writing (6.praef.4)

The distinction between philologia and philotechnia is observed in Greek technical literature (e.g., Philo of Byzantium). These technical writers make very little use of literary devices in the manner of Vitruvius's treatise.

make the rounds (6.praef.5)

Presumably Vitruvius means that architects appeared among the crowds of clients who visited the atria of prominent Romans during the morning ritual known as the "greeting," salutatio. The reading chosen here, ambiunt, is directly related to the English word ambition. The oldest manuscript of Vitruvius contains another word, ambigunt, whose meaning is "they wander about."

good family (6.praef.6)

Ingenuo pudori implies strongly that Vitruvius and his parents are freeborn citizens.

private buildings (6.praef.7)

Vitruvius studiously avoids using the word domus, "house," except when referring to the public spaces of the most sumptuous houses.

latitudes (6.1.1) (Figure 90)

Climata. The idea that national or racial characteristics are created or shaped by climate goes back to the Ionian philosophers.[1]

signbearing circle (6.1.1)

Vitruvius always refers to the zodiac by this or other circuitous Latin phrases because "zodiac" is a specifically Greek term rather than a native one.

10 Seneca, Epistulae 51.6, Dialogi 7.7.3. See C. Edwards, The Politics of Immorality in Ancient Rome (Cambridge, 1993), 175–193.

11 E. N. Gardiner, Athletics of the Ancient World (Oxford, 1930; reprint Chicago, 1980).

1 See also Herodotus 9.122; Euripides Medea 826 seq.; Seneca Epistulae 51.10, Lucian 8.363–368. On the Augustan ideal of Italy as the land of the Golden Mean (as far as climate and temperament go), Virgil, Georgics 2.136–176. Caesar, on the other hand, praises the ingenuity of northern-dwelling, thick-air breathing Gauls (De Bello Gallico 7.22).

PORTICOES (5.9.1-9)

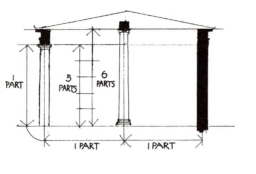

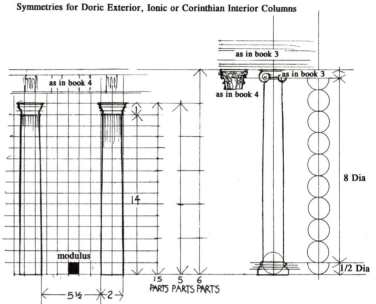

Symmetries for Doric Exterior, Ionic or Corinthian Interior Columns

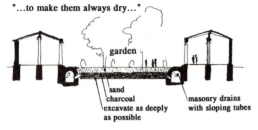

"...to make them always dry..."

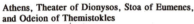

garden

sand
charcoal
excavate as deeply
as possible

masonry drains
with sloping tubes

Athens, Theater of Dionysos, Stoa of Eumenes, and Odeion of Themistokles

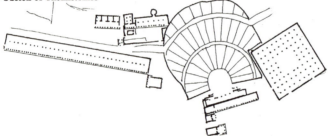

Pompeii, Large Theater and Quadriporticus

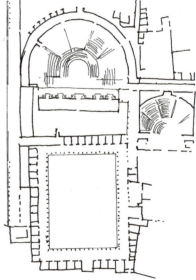

Rome, Theater and Porticus of Pompey
(partly reconstructed after the Forma Urbis)

Figure 85. Porticoes (5.9.1–9).

BATHS <u>BALNEAE</u> (5.10.1-5)

Orientation: avoid Septentrio (N.) or Aqvilo (NE.); face afternoon sun

SEPTENTRIO
AQVILO

General Layout:
-facing SW or W (afternoon sun)

-men's and women's <u>caldaria</u> in same area to share common furnace

-<u>sudatio</u>/<u>laconicum</u> attached to <u>tepidarium</u>

-<u>frigidarium</u> (location unspecified)

(-<u>apodyterium</u>, dressing room, not mentioned)

Frigidarium?/Apodyterium?

Tepidarium

Sudatio/Laconicum

Caldarium

furnace

Caldarium

Tepidarium

Sudatio/Laconicum

Frigidarium?/Apodyterium?

Pompeii, Stabian baths, as in c. 80 B.C.: plan, section through laconicum and tepidarium, and reconstruction. [Reconstruction after H. Eschebach, <u>Die Stabianerthermen in Pompeii</u> (Berlin, 1979).]

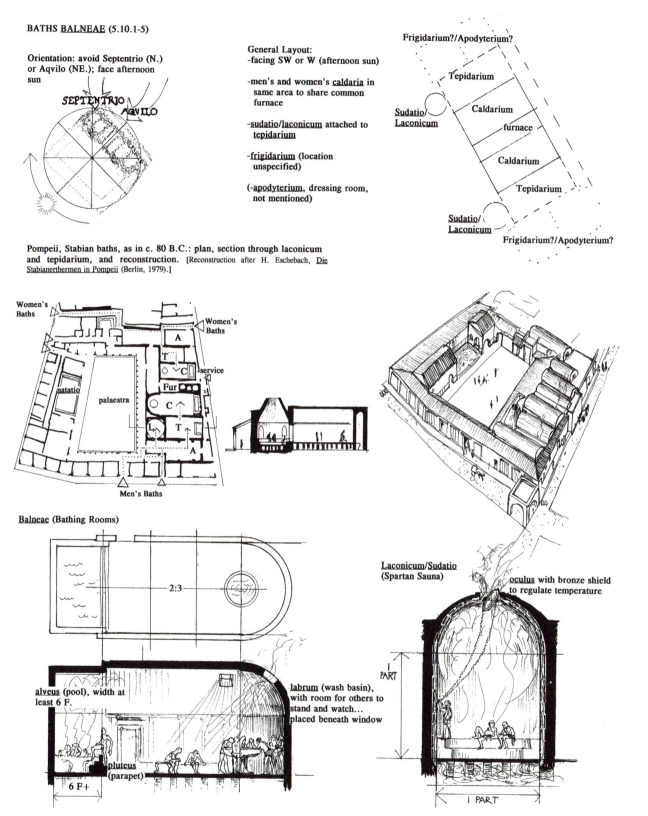

Women's Baths

Women's Baths

service

natatio

palaestra

Fur

Men's Baths

<u>Balneae</u> (Bathing Rooms)

2:3

<u>alveus</u> (pool), width at least 6 F.

<u>labrum</u> (wash basin), with room for others to stand and watch... placed beneath window

<u>pluteus</u> (parapet)

6 F+

Laconicum/Sudatio (Spartan Sauna)

<u>oculus</u> with bronze shield to regulate temperature

1 PART

1 PART

Figure 86. Baths (*Balneae*) (5.10.1–5).

BATHS <u>BALNEAE</u> (5.10.1-5)

WATER TANKS

reservoir

Bronze Tanks:
cold (<u>frigidarium</u>) tepid (<u>tepidarium</u>) hot (<u>caldarium</u>)

SUSPENDED FLOORS OF <u>caldaria</u>:

testudo

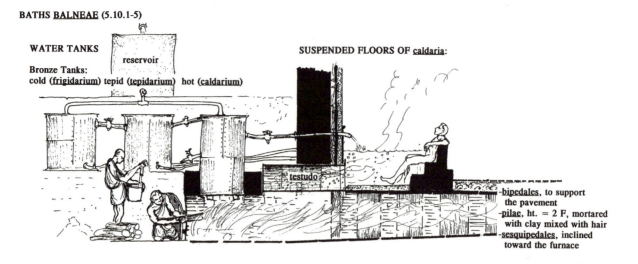

-<u>bipedales</u>, to support
  the pavement
-<u>pilae</u>, ht. = 2 F, mortared
  with clay mixed with hair
-<u>sesquipedales</u>, inclined
  toward the furnace

CEILINGS/VAULTS

<u>concamerationes</u> (chambering, ceiling)
"are more efficient if made of masonry."

Flat Ceilings (Suspended)   Arched Ceilings (Suspended)   Double Ceilings (for <u>caldaria</u>)

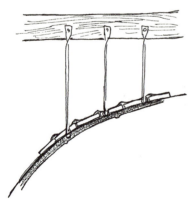

Ceilings made of timbers:

-iron hooks

-rods (for flat ceilings) or arcs
  (for vaulted ceilings), set in
  rows to support flat tiles.
-upper surface: joints spread
  with clay and hair.
-flat tiles.
-under surface: plastered with lime and
  terracotta; then <u>albarium</u> or <u>tectorium</u>

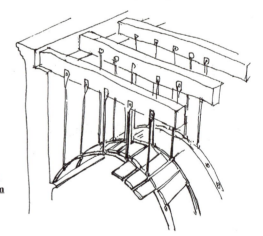

Figure 87. Baths (*Balneae*) (5.10.1–5).

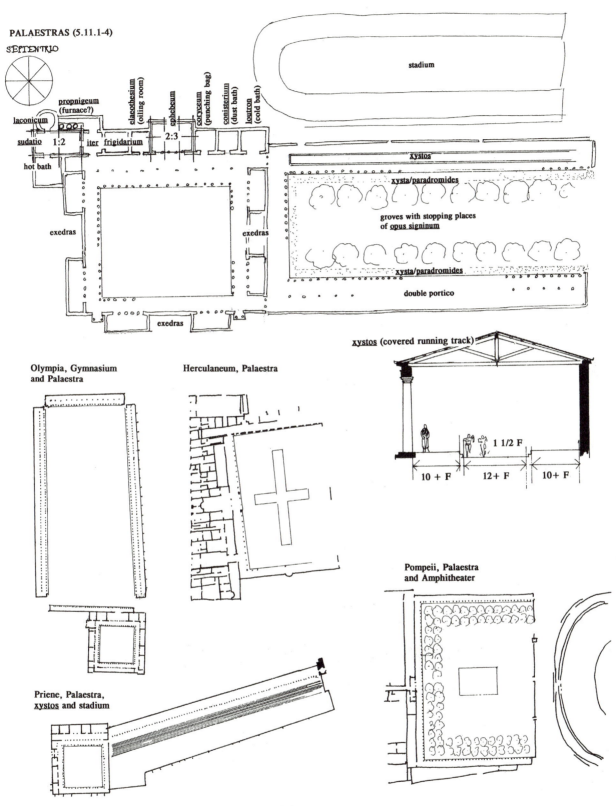

Figure 88. Palaestras (5.11.1–4).

PORTS/MOLES (5.12.1-7)

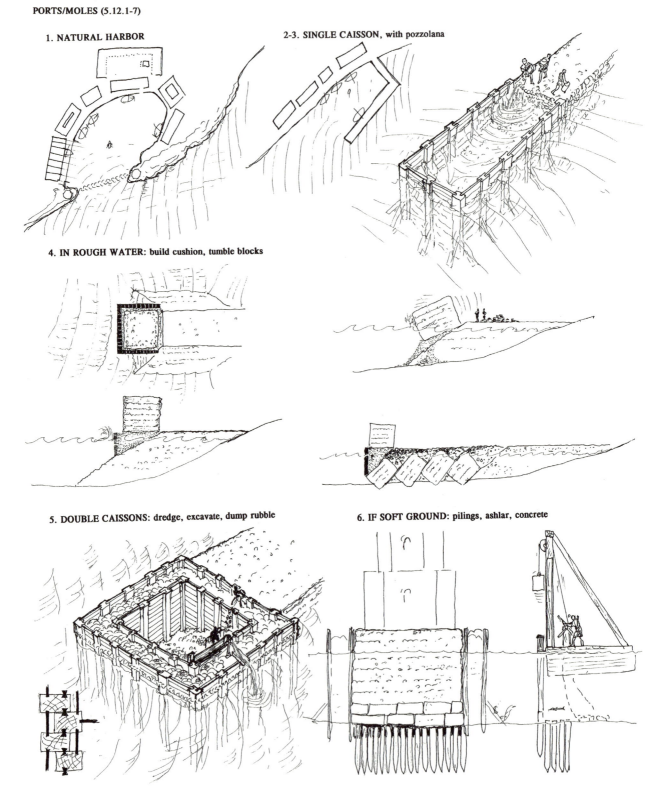

1. NATURAL HARBOR

2-3. SINGLE CAISSON, with *pozzolana*

4. IN ROUGH WATER: build cushion, tumble blocks

5. DOUBLE CAISSONS: dredge, excavate, dump rubble

6. IF SOFT GROUND: pilings, ashlar, concrete

Figure 89. Ports/Moles (5.12.1–7).

LATITUDES, PEOPLES AND MUSICAL INTERVALS (6.1.1-12)

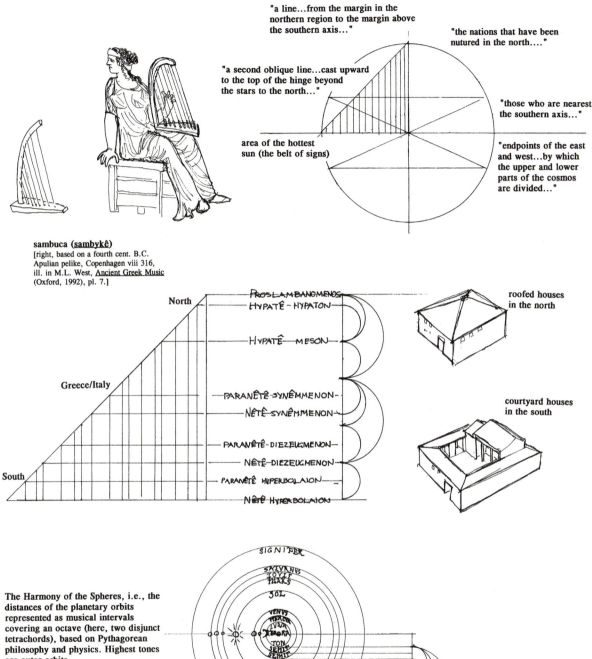

Figure 90. Latitudes, Peoples, and Musical Intervals (6.1.1–12).

the sun placed naturally
at an incline . . . with dissimilar qualities (6.1.1)

This is another reference to the idea that the dissimilarity of terrestrial phenomena is caused by the rotation of cosmic spheres and particularly the obliquity of the ecliptic.

that the firmament has the shape of a triangle . . . like . . .
the *sambykê* (6.1.5) (Figure 90)

The key to understanding this rather difficult image, which is probably Vitruvius's own invention, is that, although technically all places on the earth's surface are equidistant from the firmament (the sphere of stars), he is thinking of distance north being "up" from that part of the earth which is hottest and "closest to the firmament," that is, the equatorial regions.

conjunction of the cosmos (6.1.8)

Language borrowed from astrology.

partake in equal measure (6.1.11)

Temperatissimae, tempered, is language borrowed from chemistry. Tempering means the proper balance of elements appropriate to the object or being, which guarantees its integrity or vigor.

alae . . . *tablinum* . . . (6.3.4.5) (Figure 92)

The functions of the rooms in a house are hard to define, probably in part because they were highly multifunctional. The *tablinum* apparently began as the principal dining room of the *domus*, but its primary function came to be the usual place where the *dominus* of the house, seated, with secretaries and others, conducted the business of the morning *salutatio* with clients. The *alae* might have served as any other kind of "breakout" space, for example, for dining for an entourage or multiple groups at a banquet (a pattern maintained in Imperial dining areas). The tablinum became little more than a passage to a garden peristyle but may still have functioned as the normal seat of the *salutatio*.

peristyle courtyards . . . triclinia . . . picture
galleries . . . oecus . . . libraries . . . baths . . .
winter/summer dining rooms (6.3.7–11, 6.4.1–2) (Figure 93)

This list of elegant specialized rooms is a trait of the spectacular luxury villas and domus of the late Republic. The triclinium (a three-couch dining room) and oecus became the principal types of dining room. It is unclear what was meant by an oecus; it is probably simply a fashionable "Grecian" equivalent of an ornamental triclinium.

cubicula (6.4.1)

The cubiculum was the private bedchamber of those members of the family whose status merited it. But it also served as the place for those family members to do business with other family members or intimate friends that could not be dealt with in the more public space of the atrium.

the most prominent citizens . . . for in the
homes of these people . . . both public
deliberations and private judgments . . . (6.5.2)

The business carried on with guests and clients in the cavaedia of prominent citizens was very much an extension of the public affairs. It may have been a new custom of the period to hold trials in the private *domus* of the magistrates. Trials were normally held out of doors in the Forum or in basilica.[2]

rural buildings (6.5.3; 6.6.1–6) (Figure 95)

Vitruvius does not talk about the distinction between pars (sub-)urbana, pars rustica, the elegant residential versus agricultural/industrial parts of the villa. The implied combination comes only at the end of this section; the term *villa urbana* comes from Varro.[3]

The Greeks do not use atria . . . (6.7.1–5) (Figure 97)

The source of Vitruvius's ideas for the planning of a "Greek" house is highly debatable, but then there is probably no real "source." The image, or program, given here is likely an amalgam or analytic invention of Vitruvius based on typical Greek multicourt peristyle palaces (e.g., Pella, Pergamum, presumably Alexandria; other large Greek houses and palaces – for example, Vergina – were often just a single courtyard), common hearsay about the social segregation of Greek women, compounded with images of Pompeiian atrium-peristyle houses, which are palatial in scale. (The House of the Faun at Pompeii is larger than any known Hellenistic ruler's palace.) J. Raeder[4] has suggested that *gynaikonitis* probably meant the general living quarters, the *andronitis* the representational quarters, those dominated by men, sometimes excluding women. These terms probably were used to distinguish between types of apartments on Delos when there was a major presence of Italian businessmen there. In any case, Vitruvius's discussion of houses, Greek and Roman, deals with the very highest level of status.

larger residential quarters (6.7.3)

Here the word *domus* is used for the first time since Book 2.

convenient dining rooms (6.7.4)

A euphemism for small (*commoda*).

When the Greeks were more
refined and more wealthy (6.7.4)

This suggests that Vitruvius's description is taken from some past time, presumably before the decline of Greek independence, c. 198–145 B.C.

---

2 The trial for which Cicero delivered *For King Deioarches* was held in Caesar's house. G. Kennedy, *A New History of Ancient Rhetoric* (Princeton, 1994), 150.

3 *De Re Rustica* 1.13.6.

4 *Gymnasium* 95 (1988), 316–368.

TYPES (<u>GENERA</u>) OF INTERIORS (<u>CAVAEDIA</u>) (6.3.1-2)

Tuscan

Corinthian

tetrastyle

displuviate

covered (testudinate)

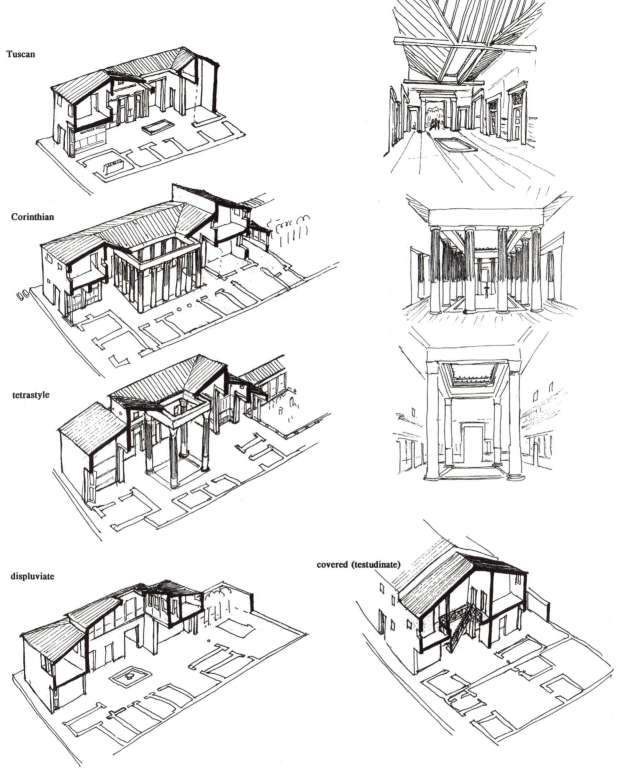

Figure 91. Types (*Genera*) of Interiors (*Cavaedia*) (6.3.1–2).

PROPORTIONS OF <u>ATRIA</u> (6.3.3-6)

Types of <u>atria</u>:

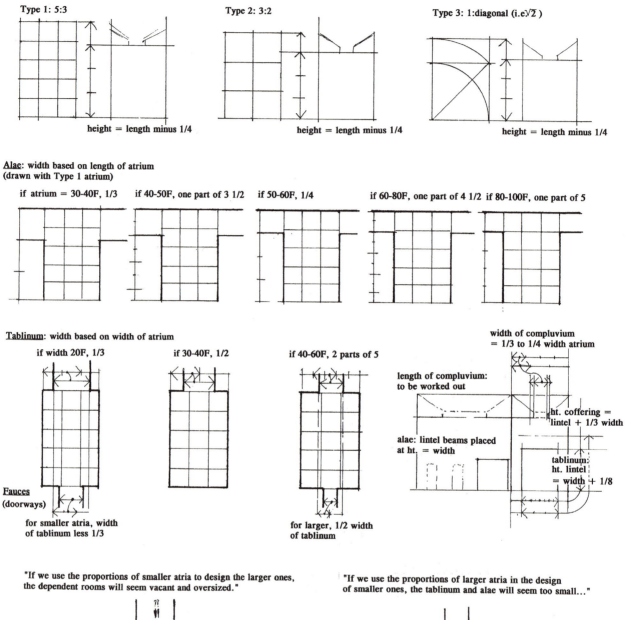

Type 1: 5:3   Type 2: 3:2   Type 3: 1:diagonal (i.e√2̄)

height = length minus 1/4   height = length minus 1/4   height = length minus 1/4

<u>Alae</u>: width based on length of atrium
(drawn with Type 1 atrium)

if atrium = 30-40F, 1/3   if 40-50F, one part of 3 1/2   if 50-60F, 1/4   if 60-80F, one part of 4 1/2   if 80-100F, one part of 5

<u>Tablinum</u>: width based on width of atrium

if width 20F, 1/3   if 30-40F, 1/2   if 40-60F, 2 parts of 5

width of compluvium
= 1/3 to 1/4 width atrium

length of compluvium:
to be worked out

ht. coffering =
lintel + 1/3 width

alae: lintel beams placed
at ht. = width

tablinum:
ht. lintel
= width + 1/8

<u>Fauces</u>
(doorways)

for smaller atria, width   for larger, 1/2 width
of tablinum less 1/3   of tablinum

"If we use the proportions of smaller atria to design the larger ones,
the dependent rooms will seem vacant and oversized."

"If we use the proportions of larger atria in the design
of smaller ones, the tablinum and alae will seem too small..."

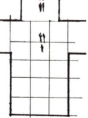

TRICLINIA

Figure 92. Proportions of *Atria* (6.3.3–6).

PERISTYLE COURTYARDS AND DEPENDENT CHAMBERS (6.3.7-11)

Peristyle Courtyards

length = width + 1/3

ht. cols. = width of porticoes

Intercol. = 3-4 L. Dia.
for Doric, see book 4

Pompeii, House of the Menander

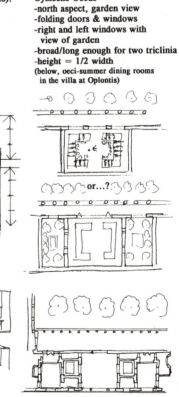

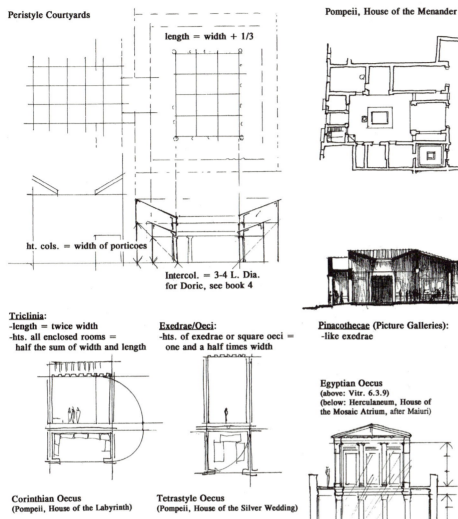

Triclinia:
-length = twice width
-hts. all enclosed rooms =
  half the sum of width and length

Exedrae/Oeci:
-hts. of exedrae or square oeci =
  one and a half times width

Pinacothecae (Picture Galleries):
-like exedrae

Egyptian Oecus
(above: Vitr. 6.3.9)
(below: Herculaneum, House of
the Mosaic Atrium, after Maiuri)

Cyzicene Oecus
-north aspect, garden view
-folding doors & windows
-right and left windows with
  view of garden
-broad/long enough for two triclinia
-height = 1/2 width
(below, oeci-summer dining rooms
  in the villa at Oplontis)

Corinthian Oecus
(Pompeii, House of the Labyrinth)

Tetrastyle Oecus
(Pompeii, House of the Silver Wedding)

Figure 93. Peristyle Courtyards and Dependent Chambers (6.3.7–11).

ORIENTATION OF ROOMS (6.4.1-2)

SEPTENTRIO

facing north:
-summer dining triclinia
  also...
-pinacothecae
-workshops of
  brocaders
  embroiderers
  painters

"...in the city atria customarily come next to the entrance, whereas in the country and the pseudo-urban buildings, the peristyle comes first..." (6.5.3)
(Pompeii, Villa of the Mysteries)

facing west:
-baths
-winter dining triclinia

facing east:
-libraries
-cubicula
-spring/autumn
  dining triclinia

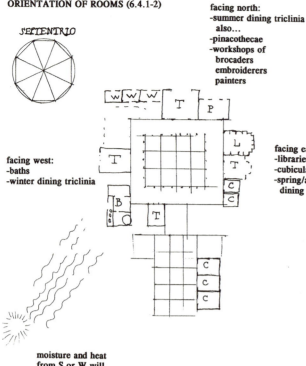

moisture and heat
from S or W will
discolor or corrupt
books in libraries

DIVISION OF PUBLIC vs. PRIVATE AREAS (6.5.1)

Private:
-cubicula
-triclinia
-baths
-etc. (service?)

Public...accessible even
  to the uninvited (??)
-vestibules
-cavaedia
-peristyles...
-etc. ("basilicas?")

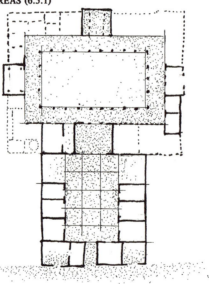

Figure 94. Orientation of Rooms (6.4.1–2).

RURAL BUILDINGS (6.6.1-6)

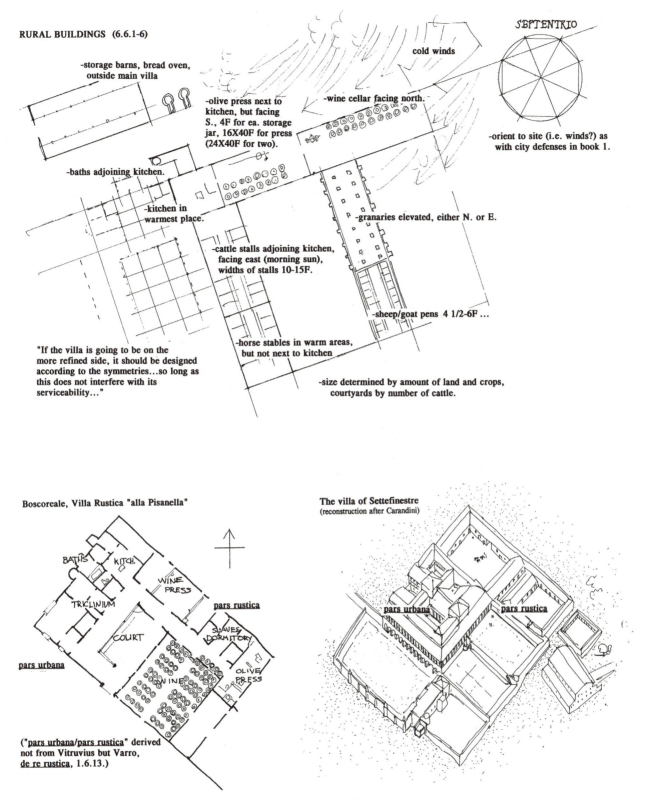

-storage barns, bread oven, outside main villa

SEPTENTRIO

cold winds

-olive press next to kitchen, but facing S., 4F for ea. storage jar, 16X40F for press (24X40F for two).

-wine cellar facing north.

-orient to site (i.e. winds?) as with city defenses in book 1.

-baths adjoining kitchen.

-kitchen in warmest place.

-granaries elevated, either N. or E.

-cattle stalls adjoining kitchen, facing east (morning sun), widths of stalls 10-15F.

-sheep/goat pens 4 1/2-6F ...

-horse stables in warm areas, but not next to kitchen

"If the villa is going to be on the more refined side, it should be designed according to the symmetries...so long as this does not interfere with its serviceability..."

-size determined by amount of land and crops, courtyards by number of cattle.

Boscoreale, Villa Rustica "alla Pisanella"

BATHS   KITCH.

WINE PRESS

pars rustica

TRICLINIUM

COURT

SLAVES DORMITORY

pars urbana

WINE

OLIVE PRESS

("pars urbana/pars rustica" derived not from Vitruvius but Varro, de re rustica, 1.6.13.)

The villa of Settefinestre
(reconstruction after Carandini)

pars urbana   pars rustica

Figure 95. Rural Buildings (*Rusticorum Aedificiorum Expeditiones*) (6.6.1–6).

NATURAL LIGHTING (6.6.6-7)

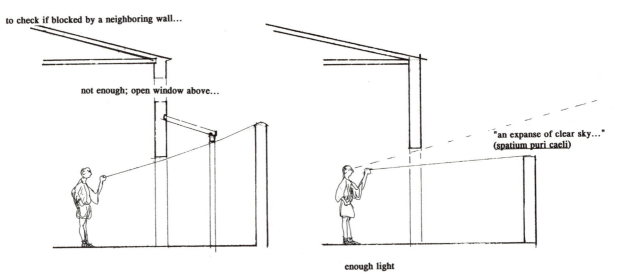

to check if blocked by a neighboring wall…

not enough; open window above…

"an expanse of clear sky…"
(spatium puri caeli)

enough light

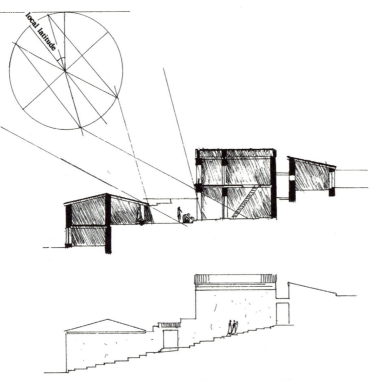

Seasonal sunlight in the courtyard of
a typical house in Priene
[after W. Hoepfner, W.D. Heilmeyer,
Haus und Stadt im klassischen Griechenland
(Munich, 1994²), fig. 303.)

local latitude

Figure 96. Natural Lighting (6.6.6–7).

GREEK HOUSES (AEDIFICIA GRAECORUM) (6.7.1-7)

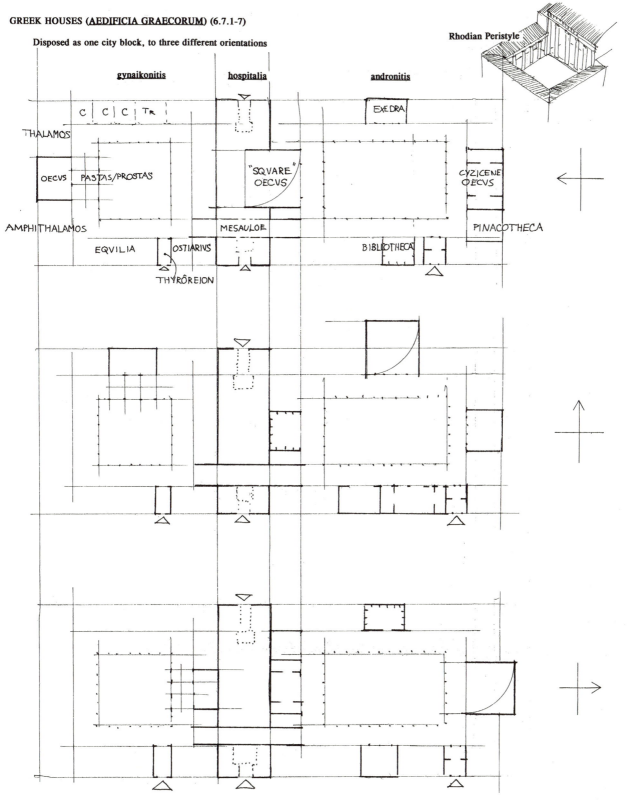

Figure 97. Greek Houses (*Aedificia Graecorum*) (6.7.1–7).

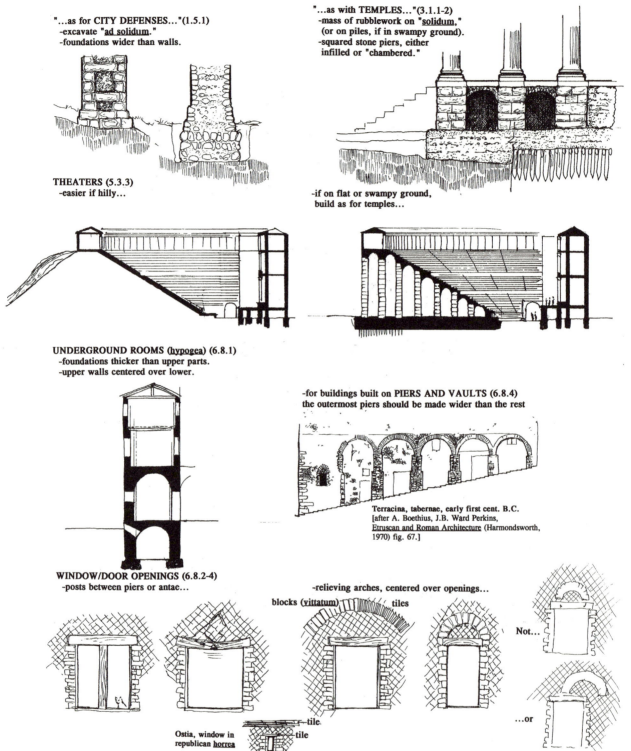

MORE ON FOUNDATIONS (summary...)(6.8.1)

"...as for CITY DEFENSES..."(1.5.1)
-excavate "ad solidum."
-foundations wider than walls.

"...as with TEMPLES..."(3.1.1-2)
-mass of rubblework on "solidum,"
  (or on piles, if in swampy ground).
-squared stone piers, either
  infilled or "chambered."

THEATERS (5.3.3)
-easier if hilly...

-if on flat or swampy ground,
  build as for temples...

UNDERGROUND ROOMS (hypogea) (6.8.1)
-foundations thicker than upper parts.
-upper walls centered over lower.

-for buildings built on PIERS AND VAULTS (6.8.4)
the outermost piers should be made wider than the rest

Terracina, tabernae, early first cent. B.C.
[after A. Boethius, J.B. Ward Perkins,
Etruscan and Roman Architecture (Harmondsworth,
1970) fig. 67.]

WINDOW/DOOR OPENINGS (6.8.2-4)
-posts between piers or antae...

-relieving arches, centered over openings...
blocks (vittatum)   tiles

Not...

Ostia, window in
republican horrea   -tile.
                           tile

...or

Figure 98. More on Foundations (Summary: 6.8.1; 1.5.1; 3.1.1–2; 5.3.3; 6.8.1; 6.8.2–4; 6.8.4).

RETAINING WALLS AND BUTTRESSES (<u>anterides</u>/<u>erismae</u>) (6.8.6–7)

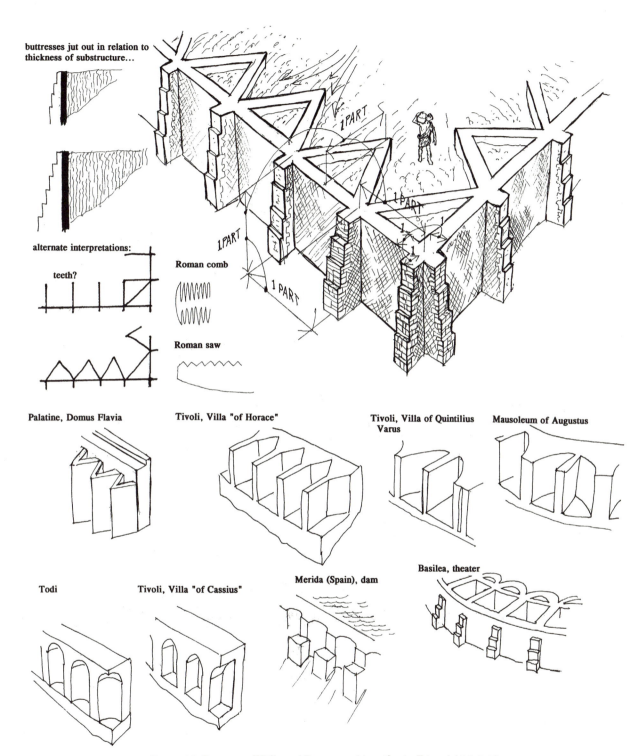

buttresses jut out in relation to thickness of substructure...

alternate interpretations:

teeth?

Roman comb

Roman saw

Palatine, Domus Flavia

Tivoli, Villa "of Horace"

Tivoli, Villa of Quintilius Varus

Mausoleum of Augustus

Todi

Tivoli, Villa "of Cassius"

Merida (Spain), dam

Basilea, theater

Figure 99. Retaining Walls and Buttresses (*Anterides sive Erismae*) (6.8.6–7).

an appropriate term either in Greek or in Latin (6.7.5)

This passage addresses the technical problems of many Latin writers of the first century B.C.: how to develop Latin equivalents for essential Greek terms.

underground rooms or chambers (6.8.1) (Figure 98)

hypogea concamerationesque. Concameratio, at least in this instance, presumably means vault, but the literal meaning is "chamber." Discussions of foundations are scattered in several places in the *Ten Books*: 1.1.5, fortifications sunk to solid; 3.4.1–2, on temple foundations, presumably the main section; 5.3.3 on theaters, built as recommended for temples; 5.12.1–7, harbor moles; 8.16.14, *opus signinum* in trenches.

voussoirs (6.8.3)

Vitruvius's use of the word *cuneus*, wedge, makes it clear that he means a real keystone arch with wedge-shaped voussoirs, both here and in 6.8.4.

and the quality of the design (6.8.9)

Dispositione (disposition).

BOOK 7

Thales, Democritus, Anaxagoras, Xenophanes (7.praef.2)

This is a partial, and not strictly chronological, list of "classic" natural philosophers: Thales of Miletus (fl. c. 580 B.C.), the first of the Ionian philosophers; Democritus of Abdera (c. 460–c. 365 B.C.), founder of atomism; Anaxagoras of Clazomenae (c. 500–428 B.C.), master of Euripides, an astronomer, formulator of theories of perspective; Xenophanes of Colophon (fl. c. 540 B.C.).

Socrates, Plato, Aristotle, Zeno, Epicurus (7.praef.2)

These two lists follow the distinction between physical and moral philosophy, the first being moral, the second being physical, although most members of this second group would also classify as natural philosophers.

Croesus, Alexander (7.praef.2)

Croesus of Lydia (560–546 B.C.), Alexander the Great (336–323 B.C.).

the great library of Pergamum (7.praef.4); Aristophanes (7.praef.5)

The library at Alexandria was traditionally founded in 307 by Ptolemy I Sotêr, supposedly with the help of Demetrius of Phalerum. The library at Pergamum was founded afterward by Eumenes II (197–159). Pliny the Elder reports that the political rivalry between the Ptolemies of Egypt and the Attalids of Pergamum had an impact on the libraries because Ptolemy V Epiphanes (205–182), jealous of Pergamum's success, placed an embargo on the export of papyrus, leading the Pergamenes to invent parchment for writing (the word for parchment in German is still *Pergament* and *pergamena* in Italian). Pliny the Elder, *Natural History* 13.17. The tale of Aristophanes of Byzantium (257–180 B.C.), who succeeded Eratosthenes as Librarian, dates from the second century as well.

Zoilus (7.praef.8)

Apparently Vitruvius is referring to Zoilus of Amphipolis (later fourth century B.C., not contemporary with the period of this story), Cynic philosopher, pupil of Anaximenes, noted for his bitter attacks on Isocrates, Plato, and especially Homer.

For no one (7.praef.9)

The translation, for reasons of clarity, departs more than usual from Vitruvius's own syntax.

Agatharchus [in Athens] (7.praef.11)

Agatharchus of Samos (c. 490–c. 415), collaborator with Aeschylus (c. 468–456), has been credited with the invention of something very like linear perspective. The nature of his invention is still debatable, but his generation was contemporary with developments in pictorial rendering of space, such as shadows and modeling, and a sort of deep landscape space rendered in vertical perspective that has been attributed primarily to Pythagoras of Samos. Agatharchus is presumably the same painter who was kidnapped by the wealthy, disdolute Athenian Alcibiades c. 420 to decorate his house.[1]

Silenus, Theodorus . . . et al. (7.praef.12)

The following is a highly significant list of architects, most of them well attested by other ancient authors. Silenus (writing on Doric symmetries) is otherwise unknown, as is his date. Theodorus is usually associated with Rhoecus, who was possibly his father, as one of the architects of the great Heraion of Samos (c. 560 B.C.).[2] Rhoecus is one of the great hero-inventors of early Greek history, credited with bronze casting (i.e., lost wax), the set square, lever, lathe, lock and key.[3] The reason that Vitruvius calls the temple Doric is that in its incomplete state, completed to the cushions of the capitals but without the volutes, it may have looked like a Doric type with an egg-and-dart echinus. The works of the following architects are well attested by remains: Pytheos and the temple of Athena at Priene (c. 340) and, with Satyrus, the Mausoleum at Halicarnassus; Ictinus and Carpion of the Parthenon ("Minerva") at Athens; Theodorus of Phocaea and the Tholos at Delphi (c. 380–370 B.C.), Philo, architect of the porch of the Telesterion at Eleusis (7.praef.17) and the Arsenal in Piraeus;[4]

---

1 Plutarch, *Alcibiades* 17.
2 Herodotus 60; Pausanias 8.14.8; Diodorus Siculus 1.98.5–9; Diogenes Laertius 2.103.
3 Pliny the Elder, *Natural History* 7.198.
4 The Arsenal is known through a meticulous inscribed building contract or description, *Inscriptiones Graecae* 2², as is also the porch of the Telesterion, *IG* 2² 1666, referred to in 7.praef.17. See J. J. Coulton, *Greek Architects at Work* (London and Ithaca, 1977), 55.

Hermogenes and the temples of Artemis (Diana) at Magnesia and Dionysos (Father Liber) at Teos.[5] Arcesius (possibly fourth century B.C. is known only through Vitruvius (also 4.1.1 as a detractor of Doric).

The nature of these publications on "symmetries" is debatable. Many must have been essentially technical descriptions, perhaps very similar to the Prostoon inscription of Eleusis and the Arsenal inscription,[6] although others must have expressed broader opinions (such as Pytheos's assertions that the architect should master all of his constituent disciplines).

Leochares, Bryaxis, Scopas, Praxiteles, Timotheus (7.praef.13)

Vitruvius lists acknowledged major sculptors of the mid- or later fourth century B.C. Leochares (fl. c. 372–320 B.C.); Bryaxis (second half of the fourth century); Scopas of Paros (mid-fourth century, also architect of the temple of Athena Alea at Tegea); Praxiteles (c. 400–330/325 B.C.); Timotheus, also sculptor of the temple of Asclepius at Epidaurus (c. 375 B.C). On the collaboration of these on the Mausoleum, see Pliny the Elder, *Natural History* 36.30.

Nexaris, Theocydes . . . (7.praef.14)

This is a list of artists who, like Polycleitus, wrote on symmetries. Surviving manuscripts of Vitruvius are inconsistent in spelling Greek names, sometimes using Greek -os, sometimes Latin -us. The translation follows the manuscript. Nexaris, Theocydes, and Sarnacus are otherwise unknown. Demophilus, possibly Demophilus of Himera (first half of the fifth century B.C.); Pollis, probably a sixth-century bronzeworker; Leonidas, painter (fourth century B.C.); Silanion, Athenian bronze sculptor (fourth century B.C.); Melampus, unknown, unless identified as Melanthios, painter of the school of Sicyon and author of a treatise;[7] Euphranor of Corinth (c. 395–330/325), painter, sculptor, and author of a treatise on symmetries.[8]

Diades, Archytas, Archimedes, Ctesibios, Nymphodorus, Philo of Byzantium, Diphilos, Democles, Charias, Polyidos, Pyrrhos, and Agesistratos (7.praef.14)

Again, Vitruvius spells Greek names inconsistently, sometimes with the Greek ending -os and sometimes with the Latin ending -us. The translation follows manuscript tradition in observing the inconsistency. Polyidos, engineer of Philip II, and his students, Diades and Charias, engineers of Alexander, laid the foundations of advanced siegecraft in the later fourth century B.C.; Diades's treatises were probably the core of the material

later developed by Philo of Byzantium and Vitruvius's contemporary Athenaeus. Agesistratos may be the joint source for both Vitruvius (10.13–15) and Athenaeus. Archytas of Tarentum (c. 460–365), Archimedes, and Ctesibios are among the best known mathematicians/engineers. Nymphodorus, Diphilos, and Democles are otherwise unknown. Pyrrhos, king of Epirus (319–273 B.C.), was one of the boldest military campaigners of Greek antiquity and an author of a treatise on siegecraft.

Fufi[ci]us, Terentius Varro, Publius Septimius (7.praef.14)

Fufius, or Fuficius, is otherwise unknown. M. Terentius Varro (116–27), was an encyclopedic polymath, author of *De lingua latina* and an encyclopedia of the liberal arts, *De novem disciplinae*, which included architecture and medicine. P. Septimius is otherwise unknown, but may be Vitruvius's source for the teachings of Hermodorus of Salamis and hence possibly also for the symmetries of Hermogenes, who is not included in this list.[9]

Antistates, Callaeschros, Antimachides, Pormos (Porinos), Cossutius (7.praef.15)

The first four personages on Vitruvius's list are otherwise unknown, but apparently the original architects of the colossal Olympieion of Athens, begun but left unfinished by Pisistratus, tyrant of Athens (566–528 B.C.), and continued as a Corinthian dipteros by Antiochus IV (175–164) with the Roman architect Cossutius. This Cossutius is very likely a member of a large family of architect-entrepreneurs from Campania.[10]

Ephesian Diana . . . Milesian Apollo (7.praef.16)

The Cretans Chersiphron and his son Metagenes were presumably the architects of the first Artemision of Ephesus, which, according to Pliny the Elder (*Natural History* 16.213; 36.95), took 120 years to complete (c. 560–440?). The "completion," by the temple slave Demetrius and by Paeonius of Ephesus, must be the reconstruction after the temple was burnt in 356 B.C. (supposedly on the night on which Alexander the Great was born, by an arsonist who wanted his name to be immortal). Alexander contributed funds to the rebuilding after his victory on the Granicus in 334. The colossal Ionic dipteral temple of Apollo at Didyma outside Miletus was, along with the great dipteroi of Samos and Ephesus, built in the first half of the sixth century B.C.; it was burnt in the Ionian revolt of 494, and rebuilt presumably after Granicus, with Paeonius and Daphnis of Miletus as architects, the latter of whom is otherwise unknown.

Demetrius of Phaleron (7.praef.17)

An intellectual, the Macedonian puppet ruler of Athens (317–307), he supposedly assisted in the foundation of the Library of Alexandria.

---

5 Pater Liber is an ancient Italic god of vegetation, and hence was assimilated to Dionysos/Bacchus. The temple is not a monopteros but a peripteros.

6 *IG* 2², 1666, 1668; J. Bundgaard, *Mnesicles, A Greek Architect at Work* (Copenhagen, 1957), 97–98, 117–132; K. Jeppesen, *Paradeigmata* (Aarhus, 1958), 69–101, 109–131; discussion in J. J. Coulton, *Greek Architects at Work* (Ithaca and New York, 1977), 54–55.

7 Pliny the Elder, *Natural History* 35.50; Diogenes Laertius 4.18.

8 Pliny the Elder, *Natural History* 35.129.

9 P. Gros, "Hermodoros et Vitruve," *Mélanges de l'Ecole Française de Rome. Antiquité* 85 (1973), 137–161.

10 E. Rawson, "Architecture and Sculpture: The Activities of the Cossutii," *Papers of the British School at Rome* 43 (1975), 36–37.

the enormous cella of Ceres and Proserpina at Eleusis (7.praef.16)

The Telesterion of Demeter and Korê (Proserpina) at Eleusis.

G. Mucius; Marius's Temple to Honor
and Battle-courage (7.praef.17; also 3.5.2)

G. Marius's temple of Honos et Virtus was built in 101 B.C. from the *manubiae* (spoils) of G. Marius's victories over the Cimbri and the Teutones; the site is unknown but possibly near the Capitol or the Velia. Vitruvius mentions it earlier (3.5.2) along with the temple of Jupiter Stator in the Porticus Metelli, designed by Hermodorus of Salamis, as an example of a temple *sine postico*. G. Mucius may have been a client/freedman of the "anti-Hellene" Q. Mucius Scaevola Augur (speculating from the name alone) and a student of Hermodorus; his significance may be that he tried to adapt Greek symmetries to traditional Italic plans.[11]

nails (7.1.2)

Hand-wrought iron nails were cheap and plentiful by the first century B.C.

dodrans (7.1.3)

Three-quarters foot = three palms = one span.

hexagons (7.1.4)

Literally, "honeycombs."

Tiburtine herringbone tile work (7.1.4)

Testacea spicata tiburtina, Tiburtine herringbone terracotta, called *opus spicatum* by modern archaeologists. The term derives from Latin *spica*, an ear of grain, whose interlocking seed husks also show a herringbone pattern.

slope of two digits for every ten feet (7.1.6)

1:80; cf. 8.7.1, for slope of aqueducts 1:250.

herringbone terracotta [blocks] (7.1.7)

Spica testacea.

plasterwork (7.2.1)

The translation follows the sequence: *trullissatio* = rough plastering; *tectorium* = plaster (suitable for painting); *albarium* = stucco, with the connotation that stucco can be molded.

the machines (7.2.2)

Presumably scaffolding (cf. 10.1.1).

plastered as roughly as possible (7.3.5)

This means leaving a rough surface to assist in the adhesion of the next layer.

plaster floats (7.3.7)

Reading with the MSS as *liaculorum*. Tertullian uses the word *lio*, to level.

moist plaster (7.3.7)

The fresco layer.

horsetails (7.3.11)

The bryophyte *equisetum*, which is strong enough to go into mud.

footed tiles (7.4.2) (Figure 103)

Reading the MSS either as *mammatae* (nippled) or *hamatae* (hooked).

beginnings of painting
[polished] plaster (7.5.1) (Figures 104, 105)

Vitruvius's description gave rise to modern scholars' distinction of four styles in Pompeiian wall painting.[12]

Tralles . . . Apaturius of Alabanda (7.5.5)

Tralles and Alabanda are both in western Asia Minor. Apaturius and Licymnius (or Lykinos) are otherwise unknown, but the story probably dates from the second century B.C. or later because it is probable that this is when this kind of fantasy architecture (i.e., the basis of the second and third Pompeiian styles) was developed in real and painted architecture in Alexandria.[13] An ekklesiasterion is a council house that supposedly can hold the entire citizen body of a town.

four sextarii (7.8.2)

One sextarius = c. 0.5461 l.; 6 sextarii = 1 congius; 16 sextarii = 1 modius.

shining (ganôsis) (7.9.3–4)

This is apparently a final polishing, not to be confused with encaustic, painting in hot wax.

the temples of Flora and Quirinus (7.9.4)

The temple of Quirinus (Doric dipteral, according to 3.2.7; restored by Augustus in 16 B.C.) was near or on the Alta Semita on the west edge of the Quirinal hill. The temple of Flora was also on the hill or in the valley below, outside the Servian walls. The cinnabar workshops may have been in an industrial quarter just outside the walls.

Vestorius (7.11.1)

A wealthy banker and innovative entrepreneur of Puteoli, known to Cicero and Atticus.[14] Puteoli was and remained the principal port for the Egyptian grain fleet in Italy until the

---

11 P. Gros, "Les premières générations d'architectes hellénistiques à Rome," *L'Italie préromaine et la Rome républicaine, Mélanges J. Heurgon* (Rome, 1976), 407.

12 Especially see A. Mau, *Geschichte der dekorativen Wandmalerei in Pompeii* (Berlin, 1882).

13 J. R. Clarke, *The Houses of Roman Italy* (Berkeley, 1991), 45; J. McKenzie, *The Architecture of Petra* (Oxford, 1990), 85–100.

14 Cicero, *Ad Atticum* 14.9.1; 14.12.3.

FLOORING (7.1.1-7)

FOR JOIST FLOORS (in contignationibus...)

"...make careful note that there is no wall that...
has been built up right underneath the pavement..."

-braces for beams of ordinary oak.

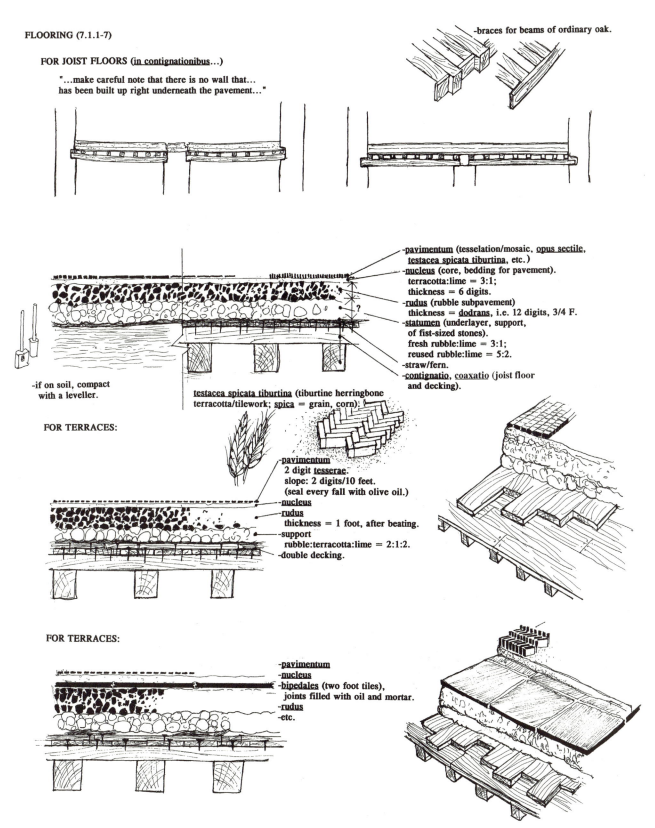

-pavimentum (tesselation/mosaic, opus sectile,
testacea spicata tiburtina, etc.)
-nucleus (core, bedding for pavement).
terracotta:lime = 3:1;
thickness = 6 digits.
-rudus (rubble subpavement)
thickness = dodrans, i.e. 12 digits, 3/4 F.
-statumen (underlayer, support,
of fist-sized stones).
fresh rubble:lime = 3:1;
reused rubble:lime = 5:2.
-straw/fern.
-contignatio, coaxatio (joist floor
and decking).

-if on soil, compact
with a leveller.

testacea spicata tiburtina (tiburtine herringbone
terracotta/tilework; spica = grain, corn)!

FOR TERRACES:

-pavimentum
2 digit tesserae.
slope: 2 digits/10 feet.
(seal every fall with olive oil.)
-nucleus
-rudus
thickness = 1 foot, after beating.
-support
rubble:terracotta:lime = 2:1:2.
-double decking.

FOR TERRACES:

-pavimentum
-nucleus
-bipedales (two foot tiles),
joints filled with oil and mortar.
-rudus
-etc.

Figure 100. Flooring (7.1.1–7).

PREPARATION OF LIME (7.2.1-2)

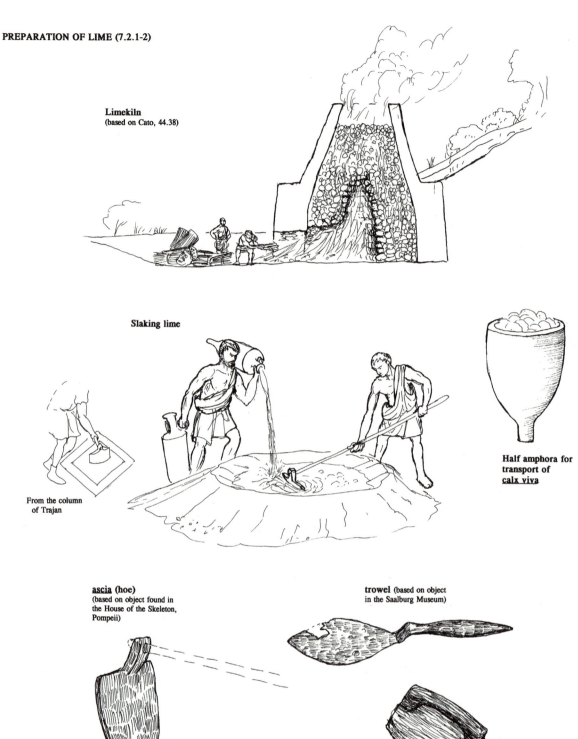

Limekiln
(based on Cato, 44.38)

Slaking lime

From the column
of Trajan

Half amphora for
transport of
calx viva

ascia (hoe)
(based on object found in
the House of the Skeleton,
Pompeii)

trowel (based on object
in the Saalburg Museum)

liaculum (plaster float)
(based on object in the
Saalburg Museum)

Figure 101. Preparation of Lime (7.2.1–2).

CEILINGS AND WALL PLASTER (7.3.1-11)

Suspended Ceilings

Plaster (tectorium) for Painted Decoration

Finishing Sequence

roughcast (trullissatio)

sand plaster (harenata)

polish coats/marble plaster (politiones)

2. upper surface of ceiling

3. lower surface of ceiling

4. stucco cornices

5. walls

1. floor

Plaster on opus craticium

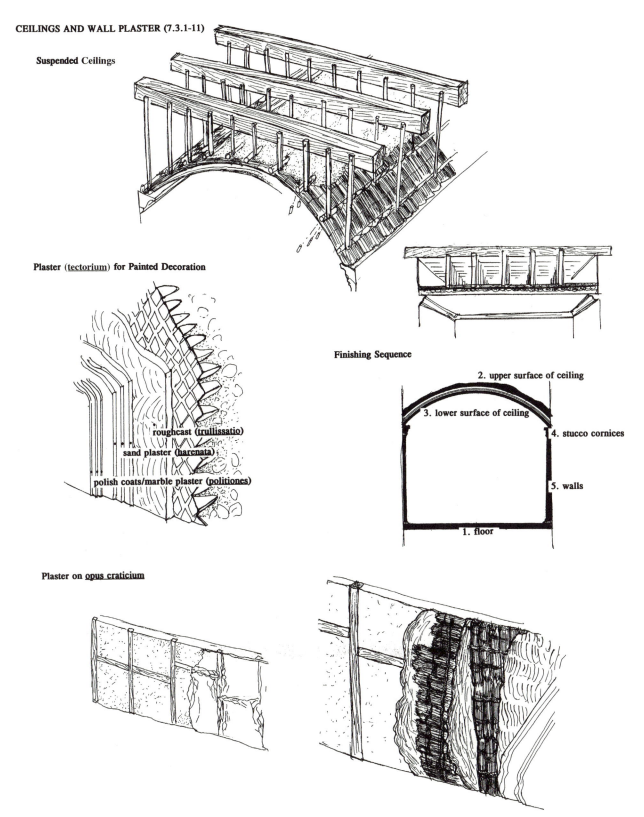

Figure 102. Ceilings and Wall Plaster (7.3.1–11).

PLASTERWORK IN DAMP LOCATIONS (7.4.1-3)

Double wall, damp barrier/drain

Praeneste, basilica

Single wall, <u>tegulae mammatae</u> with subfloor drain

WINTER DINING ROOMS (7.4.4)

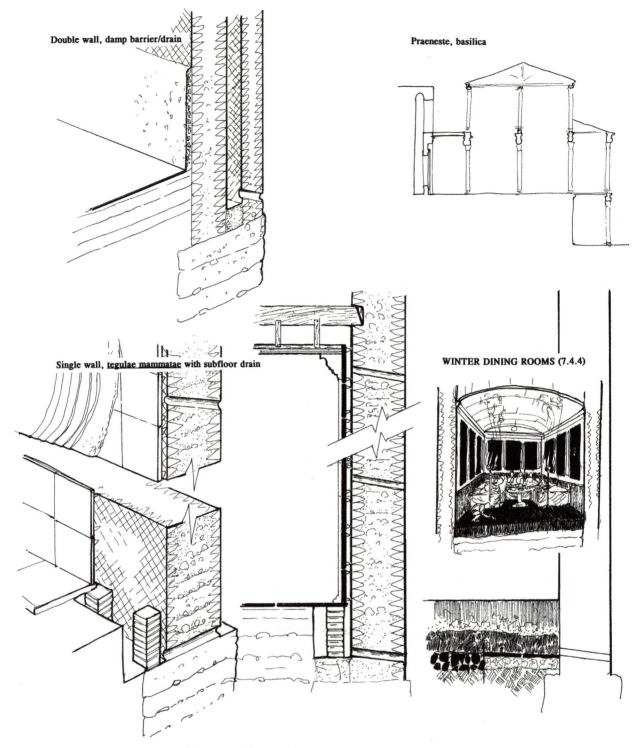

Figure 103. Plasterwork in Damp Locations (7.4.1–3).

STYLES OF WALL PAINTING (7.5.1-3)

Pompeiian First Style: "...imitated the varieties and placement of marble veneers..."

Pompeiian Second Style: "...later...also imitated the shapes of buildings and the projection into space of columns and pediments..." (c. 100 B.C.)

Pompeii, House of Sallust, c. 100 B.C.
[after Mau, <u>Geschichte der dekorativen Wandmalerei in Pompeii</u> (Berlin, 1882), pl. 2A.]

Pompeii, House of the Stag
(early Second Style)

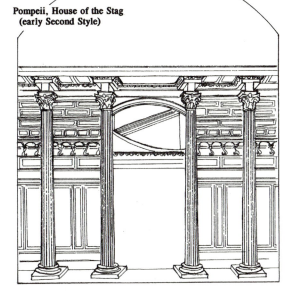

Pompeii, House of the Cryptoporticus
(later Second Style)

Figure 104. Styles of Wall Painting: Pompeiian First and Second Style (7.5.1–3).

STYLES OF WALL PAINTING (7.5.1-3)

Pompeiian Third Style: "...monsters are now painted in frescoes..."

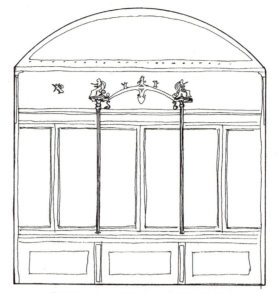

Pompeii, House I.11.12, early Third Style

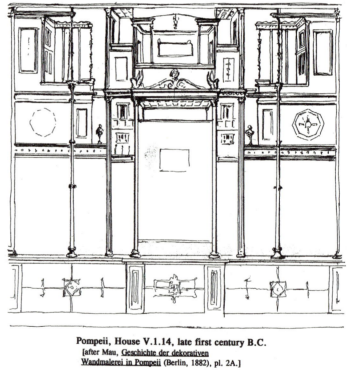

Pompeii, House V.1.14, late first century B.C.
[after Mau, Geschichte der dekorativen
Wandmalerei in Pompeii (Berlin, 1882), pl. 2A.]

Figure 105. Styles of Wall Painting: Pompeiian Third Style (7.5.1–3).

early second century A.D., when it was displaced by the Trajanic harbor at Ostia.

kermes (7.14.1)

Quercus coccifera, a shrub oak whose fruit produces a crimson dye.

weld (7.14.2)

Reseda luteola, a swamp plant used to make yellow dye, also known as dyer's rocket, yellowweed, or dyer's mignonette. Pliny the Elder, *Natural History* 33.87, 91.

woad (7.14.2)

Isatis tinctoria, also called dyer's weed (as are several other plants), a blue dye superseded by indigo.

BOOK 8

Heraclitus, Euripides, Anaxagoras . . . Pythagoras, Empedocles, Epicharmos (8.praef.1)

This is another list of the formulators of the fundamental theories of natural philosophy. Euripides is the playwright of the later fifth century, Empedocles (fl. c. 444 B.C.) is the figure normally credited with formulating the definitive form of earth-air-fire-water chemistry. Again Vitruvius is inconsistent in his spelling of Greek names.

definite limits in the direction of those regions (8.1.1)

The vocabulary here is much the same as that for laying out a *templum* in augury.

underground channels (8.1.6)

This method of collecting water from several weak wells sounds very much like a Persian qanat, although there are some systems in Rome that consist of mazes, *cuniculi*, which appear to function as seepage collectors.[1]

the earthly globe (8.2.6)

Vitruvius's discussion is contemporary with M. Vipsanius Agrippa's world map in the Porticus Vipsania and may be informed by it.

the Nile (8.2.6–7)

This idea that the Nile rises in the West (Mauretania) and flows underground, reemerging in the Sudd, goes back at least to Herodotus (2.28–34), who presents a slightly different theory about how it may flow from the West.

Camenae, Aqua Marcia (8.3.1)

The spring of the Camenae is located on the south side of the Caelian Hill. The Aqua Marcia was completed in 144 B.C. and thought to be the best of the aqueducts.

---

1 In the Horti Aciliani and the Forte Antenne (ancient Antemnae). I. Riera, in I. Riera ed., *Utilitas Necessaria: Sistemi idraulici nell'Italia romana* (Milan, 1994), 330.

sweet-water springs (8.3.1)

Taking *dulcis* to mean good-tasting water, although it may simply mean fresh water as opposed to salt or brackish.

the river Albula (8.3.2)

The source of the Albula outside Tivoli is at the travertine deposits, and the functioning baths there still emit a strong sulphurous smell.

push the force of their gusts; sources of springs at the same height as these hillocks (8.3.2–3)

This discussion of the force of springs depends on Empedoclean chemistry (wind as the result of a collision of heat and water) rather than a concept of a pressure head.

This water has an appearance (8.3.6)

Aquae here is not a genitive but a dative of possession; *species* in this case can not be a term of classification.

type of water (8.3.6)

Vitruvius here uses *genus aquae*, not *species*.

wine . . . of Lesbos, and so on (8.3.12)

This is a list of the best known ancient wines. Maeonia is in the upper Hermos valley in western Asia Minor, Lydia in north-central western Asia Minor. Falernian of Campania had the reputation as being among the best of ancient wines.

the inclination of the firmament (8.3.13)

This is another reference to the scientific theory that all terrestrial diversity is generated by the oblique rotation of the celestial spheres, particularly the sun.

Juba (8.3.24)

Presumably Juba II, son of Juba I, who as a child was led in Caesar's triumph of 46 B.C. Given Roman citizenship by Octavian, he was reinstated as a client king in Numidia and, in 25 B.C., in Mauretania. He was a man of considerable learning and wrote many books on geography, history, language, and natural philosophy.

Africa is the mother and nursemaid of wild beasts (8.3.24)

This phrase is similar to Horace *Odes* 1.22.15–16, published in 23 B.C., but it also may be lifted from the *Libyka* of Juba, published in 26/25 B.C.

Gaius Julius, the son of Masinissa (8.3.25)

The identification of this person is uncertain, but presumably he was a scion of the royal house and descendant of Masinissa, king of Numidia and client of Rome until his death in 148 B.C. The name and the information Vitruvius gives indicates he may have been awarded Roman citizenship as a reward for service with Caesar.

Theophrastos, Timaeus, Posidonios, Hegesias, Herodotus, Aristides, and Metrodorus (8.3.27)

Again, Vitruvius's spelling of Greek names is inconsistent. Theophrastus, pupil and successor of Aristotle at the Lyceum;

SOURCES OF WATER (8.3.1-28)

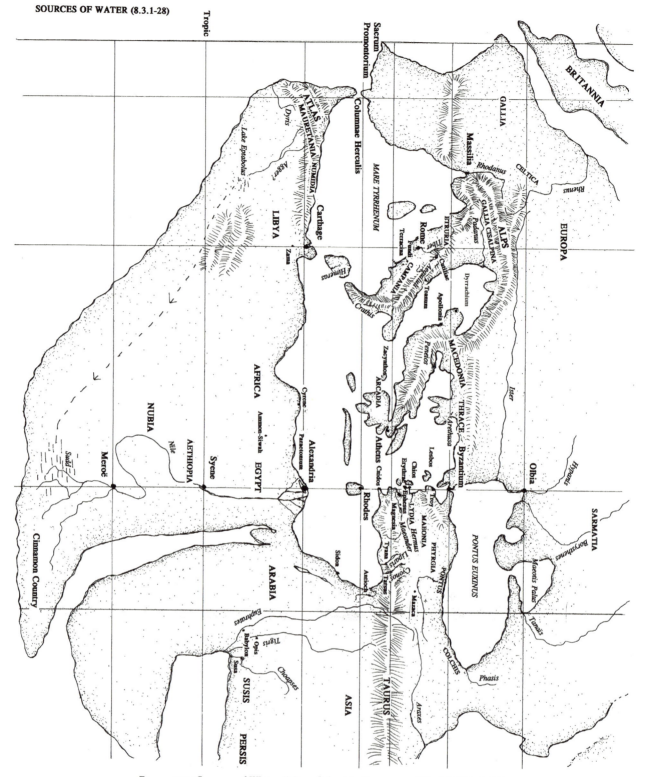

Figure 106. Sources of Water (Map of the Mediterranean World) (8.3.1–28).

Timaeus of Tauromenium (c. 346–250 B.C.), author of a history of Sicily; Posidonius of Apamea (c. 140/130–59/40 B.C.), philosopher, historian, geographer, and naturalist; Hegesias could be Hegesias of Maroneia or Hegesias of Magnesia; Herodotus (d. c. 425 B.C), the great historian of the mid-fifth century; Metrodorus of Skepsis and Aristides are uncertain.

Corinthian vase (8.4.1)

An alloy of bronze, gold, and silver (Pliny the Elder, *Natural History* 9.13.9; 34.6–9; 37.49).

diopters, or water levels, or a chorobate (8.5.1) (Figure 107)

The diopter was an instrument apparently like a modern transit or theodolite and must have had some capacity for measuring angles, probably both vertical and horizontal. As such, it also would have been serviceable as a level (although like a modern transit, it may have been less accurate as such than a dedicated level). The diopter was known to Archimedes, Hipparchus, and Ptolemy, and the most detailed description is in Hero of Alexandria.[2] (True triangulation surveying with trigonometric functions seems not to have been used in antiquity; it generally dates to the end of the sixteenth and early seventeenth centuries.) The water level is unattested in representations, but its general principle can be guessed fairly easily (see figure). The chorobate is known only through Vitruvius (it is not mentioned in the *Corpus agrimensorum*), and therefore it may have been an unusual instrument and a personal recommendation of Vitruvius.

fit together by hinges (8.5.1)

This implies that, like any surveying instrument, the chorobate could be dismantled and transported.

Archimedes' books will say that there cannot be a true leveling by means of water (8.5.3)

Although in a way Archimedes is right (the course of the water in a water channel follows the curvature of the earth), Vitruvius is also right to note that in functional circumstances the curvature is insignificant, and what counts is the relationship between the two ends of the water vessel, which when level are tangent to the earth's curvature.

slope . . . no less than half a foot every hundred feet (8.6.1)

There are two possible readings of the MSS here: *sicilicos* or a quarter of an inch per 100 F, or a slope of 1:4,800; or *semipede*, a half foot, or a slope of 1:200. The range of the slope in Roman aqueducts varies greatly, normally from 1:150 to 1:2,900 (with an extreme in the aqueduct of Nîmes at 1:14,000), and sometimes within a single aqueduct (the aqueduct of Gier varies from 1:151 to c. 1,000, that at Basse-Fontaine from 1:59 to 1:2,500).[3]

1:200 seems steep, but immediately above (8.5.3) Vitruvius says that "If a slope is great, the current of the water will be easier to manage," and in 7.1.6 Vitruvius recommends a slope of two digits (one-eighth foot) for every ten feet for open-air floors (slope of 1:80).

castellum aquae (8.6.1) (Figure 108)

A reservoir for water distribution is usually just inside the city gates at the highest point of the circuit of the walls.

those who bring water into their own homes (8.6.2)

An *actus* is 120 feet, the standard unit for measuring centuriated plots.

there is one *actus* (120 feet) between every two (8.6.3)

The illegal tapping of public mains for private homes was a major problem for Agrippa's and Frontinus's administrations.[4]

the diameter of the pipes (8.6.4)

Roman lead water pipes were made as lead sheets rolled around a form with either a folded or a soldered join. The ten standard calibers that Vitruvius recommends are measured in terms of the width of the sheet, which is in effect the circumference of the pipe plus the overlap for the join. Frontinus gives a somewhat more complicated system and attributes to Agrippa or Vitruvius the introduction of a different measure, the *quinaria*, which refers either to a five-digit sheet rolled into a pipe, or a pipe five *quadrantes* (quarter-digits) in section.[5] Vitruvius also gives the weight of each sheet, which implies that the standard wall thickness for a pipe is one-quarter inch (9.0627 m.), regardless of diameter.[6]

but if there is a very broad valley . . . the "belly" (8.6.5) (Figure 109)

Although Vitruvius mentions inverted siphons in conjunction with a closed pipe system, they can be combined with open-channel masonry aqueducts with the siphon running from one open castellum on one side of the valley to another on the other. The economic break-even point between building a lead-pipe siphon, which required high craftsmanship and maintenance, seems to have been c. 150 feet; in valleys of less depth, aqueducts were normally carried across on masonry arches, from c. 155/160 feet to c. 375 feet, normally lead pipes with an inverted siphon.[7] The upper limit for lead siphons is the amount of pressure head that the lead pipe can sustain. The siphon at Pergamum has a pressure head at one point of c. 500 feet (250 lb./sq. in. or 18.5 kg/cm²), although it was later replaced by an open-channel aqueduct.[8]

2 C. Germain de Montauzan, *Essai sur la science et l'art de l'ingénieur aux premiers siècles de l'empire romain* (Paris, 1908), 46 seq.; A. G. Drachmann, *The Mechanical Technology of Greek and Roman Antiquity* (Munksgaard, 1963), 197–198.

3 C. Germain de Montauzon, *Les Aqueducs de Lyon* (Paris, 1909), 170; L. Callebat, ed., *Vitruve, de l'architecture*, viii (Paris, 1973), 146–148.

4 Frontinus, *De Aquis*, 112–114.

5 The system is measured in *quinarii* up to the *fistula vicenaria* (five-digit pipe), then in *digiti quadrati*, which implies a more advanced system of adjusting to accurate cross section than Vitruvius's system. Frontinus *De Aquis* 25, 26–34.

6 J. G. Landels, *Engineering in the Ancient World* (Berkeley, 1978), 42–45.

7 A. F. Norman, "Attitudes to Roman Engineering and the Question of the Inverted Siphon," *History of Technology* 1 (1976), 45–71, esp. 61.

8 Landels, op. cit., 47–49.

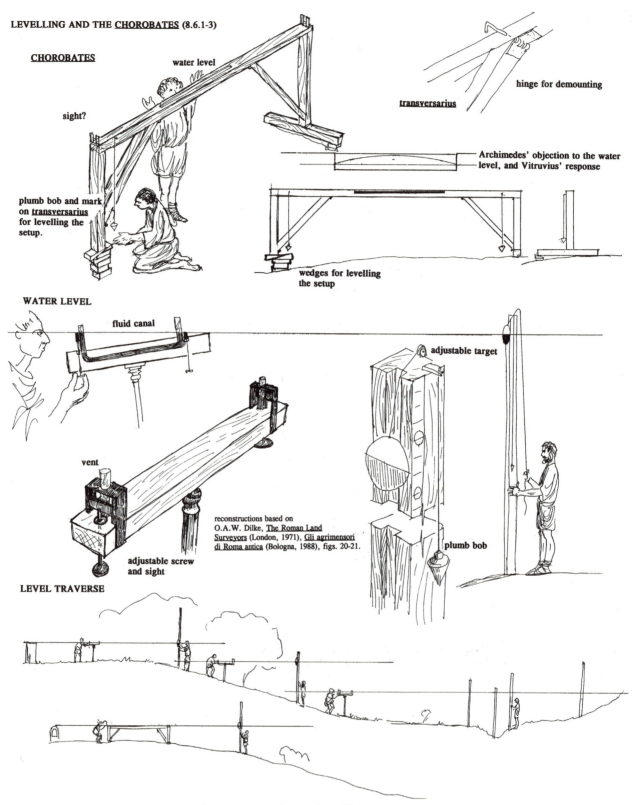

LEVELLING AND THE **CHOROBATES** (8.6.1-3)

CHOROBATES

water level

sight?

transversarius

hinge for demounting

Archimedes' objection to the water level, and Vitruvius' response

plumb bob and mark on transversarius for levelling the setup.

wedges for levelling the setup

WATER LEVEL

fluid canal

adjustable target

vent

reconstructions based on O.A.W. Dilke, The Roman Land Surveyors (London, 1971), Gli agrimensori di Roma antica (Bologna, 1988), figs. 20-21.

plumb bob

adjustable screw and sight

LEVEL TRAVERSE

Figure 107. Levelling and the *Chorobates* (8.6.1–3).

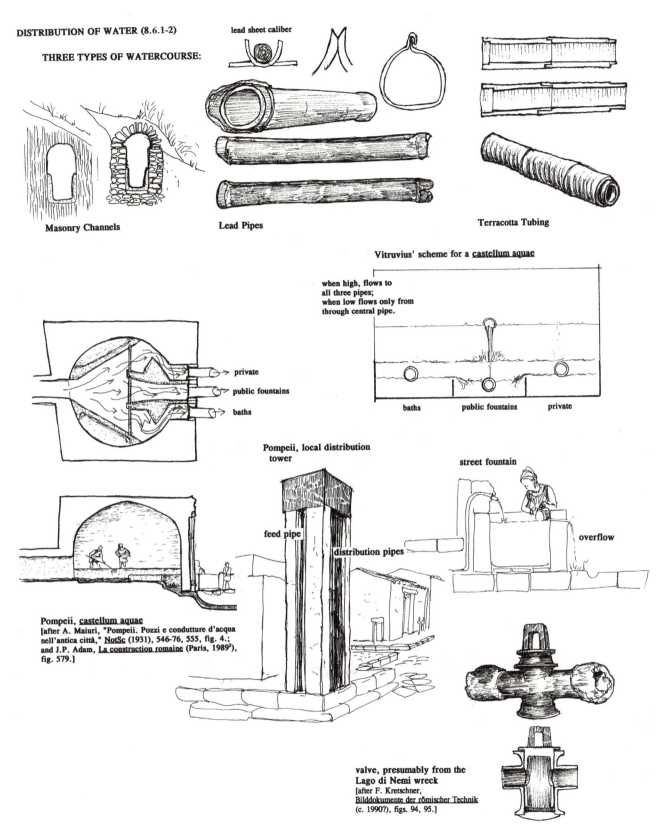

Figure 108. Distribution of Water (8.6.1–2).

AQUEDUCTS (8.6.3-11)

MASONRY CHANNELS, CONTINUOUS GRADIENT

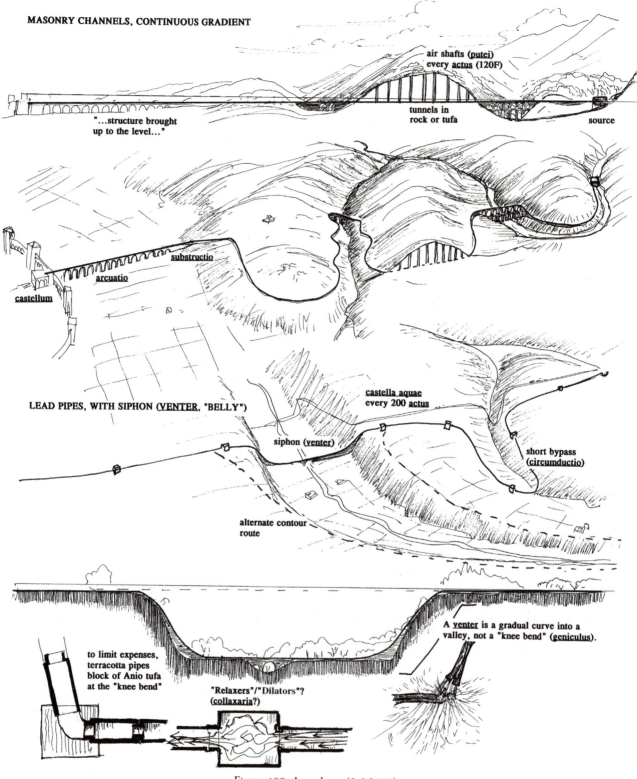

air shafts (putei)
every actus (120F)

"...structure brought
up to the level..."

tunnels in
rock or tufa

source

substructio

arcuatio

castellum

castella aquae
every 200 actus

LEAD PIPES, WITH SIPHON (VENTER, "BELLY")

siphon (venter)

short bypass
(circumductio)

alternate contour
route

to limit expenses,
terracotta pipes
block of Anio tufa
at the "knee bend"

"Relaxers"/"Dilators"?
(collaxaria?)

A venter is a gradual curve into a
valley, not a "knee bend" (geniculus).

Figure 109. Aqueducts (8.6.3–11).

dilations (8.6.6)

The MSS reading *colliviaria* is much disputed. The reading proposed here, *collaxaria*,[9] implies that at the rise of the pipe some sort of expanded pipe was inserted with the belief (right or wrong) that it relaxed the pressure on the bottom of the upslope. Technically, such a device should cause the speed of the current to decrease but not necessarily the pressure.

reservoirs [*castella aquae*]
at an interval of two hundred *actus* (8.6.7)

Equivalent to 24,000 feet. Note that one does not put *castella aquae* in masonry open-channel aqueducts because this type of aqueduct cannot be shut down except at the source, and then one has to wait for the entire system to drain before one can do repair work. Frontinus points out that one can build temporary bypasses around sections of open-channel aqueducts in order to do repair work (*De Aquis*, 2.124).

lead is toxic (8.6.10)

Vitruvius is the first writer to mention lead poisoning. White lead oxide forms in water pipes. Probably most lead water pipes did not pose a serious health problem because almost all Roman water mains worked by continuous flow, and therefore the water was not in the pipe long enough to absorb much lead. The problem would be greater in off-flow pipes with spigots, where the water was static between times when the tap was opened.

opus signinum (8.6.14)

This is supposedly waterproof cement, but it is not what is commonly called *opus signinum* by modern archaeologists; this now refers to any mortar with admixture of crushed terracotta, usually intended for waterproof situations.

limed (8.6.15)

Here and in the next sentence, context demands that *calcetur* derive from *calx* "lime," and not *calx* "heel" = "trample." This usage is again a *hapax*, but not a surprising one; liming cisterns does not occur in Latin literature. For the formation of the word, compare *statuminetur* at 7.1.3.

BOOK 9

illustrious athletes . . . same
honors . . . are not bestowed on writers (9.praef.1)

In several of the Greek games, prizes were awarded to authors as well as athletes. Augustus created the *Ludi Actiaci* after Greek fashion, and there were six *ludi* for which the aediles and praetors commissioned plays. Poets received prizes by the later first century A.D.

Milo of Croton (9.praef.2)

Recognized as one of the greatest athletes of antiquity, six-time victor at the Olympic Games (later sixth century B.C.).

useful findings of Plato (9.praef.4) (Figure 110)

Vitruvius recasts an anecdote in Plato, *Meno* 82b–85b, where Socrates coaxes an ignorant slave to deduce the principle of doubling the square. This kind of exercise is similar to land calculation exercises in the agrimensorial treatises (e.g., Columella, *De Agricultura* 2.8–9).

the type of number that cannot
be found by means of calculation (9.praef.4)

All "*numeri*" are rational in the Vitruvian lexicon, that is, a ratio of positive integers (1/2, 15/17, etc.). Functions like pi and the diagonal of a square ($\sqrt{2}$) are irrational, and hence not "numbers."

bottom of the page (9.praef.5)

Vitruvius refers here to one of the eleven drawings originally included in his text; manuscripts preserve none of them.

Pythagoras . . . demonstrated
a set square (9.praef.6) (Figure 110)

The Pythagorean theorem is represented by the discovery of the 3-4-5 right triangle.

Archimedes; Hieron (9.praef.9)

Cf. 7.8.3 on specific gravity. Hieron II was tyrant of Syracuse (270–215 B.C.).

one sextarius (9.praef.11)

Equivalent to c. 0.546 liter.

Archytas of Tarentum and Eratosthenes of Cyrene; what
Apollo had ordered . . . at Delos; the mesolabe
(9.praef.13–14)

Archytas (first half of fourth century), and Eratosthenes (284–204), librarian of Alexandria and correspondent of Archimedes, were both mentioned earlier (1.1.18; 7.praef.14; 1.6.9). For the calculation of the mesolabe based on the solution of two mean proportionals, see figures.

Democritus . . . in which he uses
a signet ring to mark (9.praef.15)

The text here may be corrupt, but Soubiran's interpretation at least corresponds to Vitruvius's respect, in the tradition of Lucretius, for crediting direct observation.

Accius (9.praef.16–17); Lucretius; Cicero; Varro (9.praef.17)

Reference to L. Accius (c. 140 B.C.–c. 90 B.C.). T. Lucretius Carus (c. 94–c. 55 B.C.), M. Tullius Cicero (106–42 B.C.), and M. Terentius Varro (166–27) are older contemporaries of Vitruvius and probably his strongest intellectual influences; directly or indirectly he cites the *De rerum natura* of Lucretius, *De oratore* of Cicero, and *De lingua latina* and the *Disciplinarum libri ix* of Varro.

---

9 *Collaxo* appears in Lucretius, 6.233.

USEFUL INNOVATIONS OF MATHEMATICS (9.Praef.1-14)

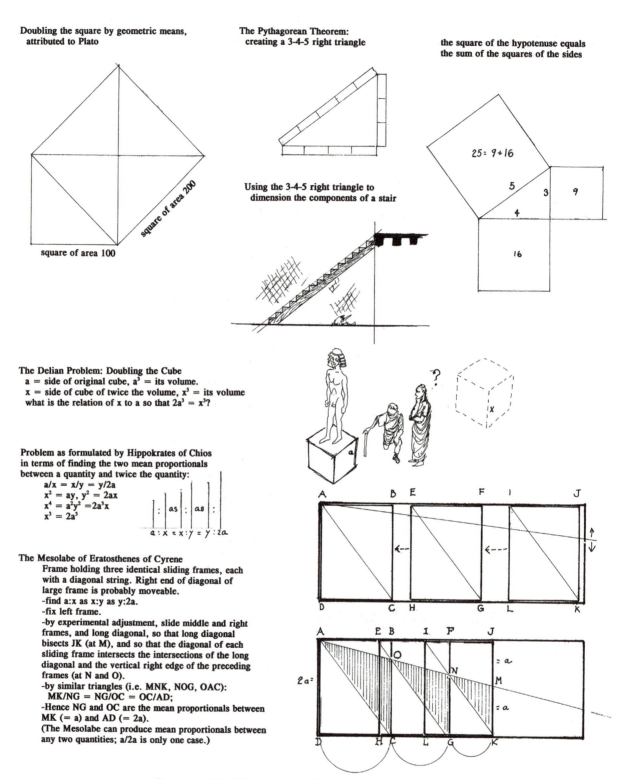

Doubling the square by geometric means, attributed to Plato

square of area 200

square of area 100

The Pythagorean Theorem: creating a 3-4-5 right triangle

the square of the hypotenuse equals the sum of the squares of the sides

$25 = 9 + 16$

5

3

9

4

16

Using the 3-4-5 right triangle to dimension the components of a stair

The Delian Problem: Doubling the Cube
a = side of original cube, a^3 = its volume.
x = side of cube of twice the volume, x^3 = its volume.
what is the relation of x to a so that $2a^3 = x^3$?

Problem as formulated by Hippokrates of Chios in terms of finding the two mean proportionals between a quantity and twice the quantity:
$a/x = x/y = y/2a$
$x^2 = ay, y^2 = 2ax$
$x^4 = a^2y^2 = 2a^3x$
$x^3 = 2a^3$

: as : as :

$a : x = x : y = y : 2a$

The Mesolabe of Eratosthenes of Cyrene
Frame holding three identical sliding frames, each with a diagonal string. Right end of diagonal of large frame is probably moveable.
-find a:x as x:y as y:2a.
-fix left frame.
-by experimental adjustment, slide middle and right frames, and long diagonal, so that long diagonal bisects JK (at M), and so that the diagonal of each sliding frame intersects the intersections of the long diagonal and the vertical right edge of the preceding frames (at N and O).
-by similar triangles (i.e. MNK, NOG, OAC):
  MK/NG = NG/OC = OC/AD;
-Hence NG and OC are the mean proportionals between MK (= a) and AD (= 2a).
(The Mesolabe can produce mean proportionals between any two quantities; a/2a is only one case.)

Figure 110. Useful Innovations of Mathematics (9.praef.1–4).

shadow cast by a gnomon at the equinox (9.1.1)

The normal method after Eratosthenes of measuring and recording latitude was the equinoctial shadow, not the solstitial; on that day the angle cast by the gnomon is equivalent to the latitude (angle = tan^{-1} shadow of gnomon/height of gnomon). Once one knows the size of the earth (or the length of a degree) one can use this kind of measure to calculate any N–S location where one has measured the equinoctial shadow. Eratosthenes also created a table of equinoctial shadows relative to latitude. Vitruvius may be quoting Eratosthenes' table in 9.1.1, or at least its format. This was in effect the first step toward the establishment of mathematical trigonometry because it recorded the ratio of length of shadow to height of gnomon (i.e., the tangent) for each latitude.[1] Placentia (Piacenza) is in this list because its latitude is a few minutes off 45° (45° 03'), and hence its ratio is expressed as 1:1.

in the southern half the axis is set low and obscured by the earth (9.1.3) (Figure 4)

This is a reference to the "never-visible circle" of celestial astronomy, the amount of the celestial sphere that is obscured by the earth and dependent on the viewer's latitude (i.e., at the poles one sees 90° of the firmament, at the equator, with the rotation of the earth, all of it, at 45° N one sees everything down to 45°S. See figures for Book 1).

broad circular belt . . . with twelve signs (9.1.3)

Reading *lata* rather than *delata*. Because Vitruvius never uses the term *zodiac*, it has been avoided here. Hyginus (second century A.D., not the *gromaticus* or Augustus's librarian) and Ptolemy (second century A.D.) use *zodiac*, a term of Greek derivation (*zoôn* = animal).

each sign shows an image taken from nature (9.1.3)

Vitruvius makes the constellations obey his precepts for good art (7.5.3–4). Manilius (*Astronomica* 1.456, slightly later than Vitruvius) tells his readers that the images of the constellations are not completely outlined with stars because the heavens could not withstand so intense a conflagration.

above the earth (9.1.4) (Figure 111)

That is, above the equator. Only in the night sky do the signs of the Zodiac appear to climb and fall with the seasons.

stars of Mars and Jupiter (9.1.5)

The phrase "star of" expresses the idea that the names of the planets refer to gods but are not identical with them.

Just as the stars of Mercury and Venus are completing . . . their journeys . . . they regress; [t]he sun's rays stretch out into the universe . . . form of a triangle (9.1.6–13) (Figure 112)

Vitruvius provides two explanations for retrograde motion. The first is conventional, that Mars and Venus orbit around the sun's rays, but the other is unusual because it relies on an application of Empedoclean chemistry (i.e., the attractive power of heat), and a very peculiar image: that the sun emanates rays not like sound or ripples, in circles,[2] but in rays, like a focused searchlight. Hence he is led to the odd (but in its way, scientifically logical) speculation that the sun's rays stretch out only to the fifth sign of the zodiac, because otherwise the planets would be incinerated if they orbited closer to the sun. See Figure 112.

in the same triangle (9.1.11)

Trigon is the normal astrological term but because it simply means *triangle* in Greek, the latter translation is used to relate the present passage to Vitruvius's description of theater design (6.5) and other triangles in 9.praef.5–6 and 9.4.6.

Berosus (9.2.1)

Priest of Bel (fl. c. 290 B.C.) and author of a history of Babylon. This book was one of the main vehicles for the later transmission of Babylonian astronomy to Hellenistic Greece.

Aristarchus of Samos (9.2.3)

Astronomer (first half of third century B.C.), best known as the author of a heliocentric theory of the universe.

the sun . . . diminishes the space of the days and hours (9.3.1)

One of the major problems in the design of timepieces was that in antiquity the day and the night were divided into twelve equal hours each, but because the day and the night were never equal (except at the equinoxes) the length of the hours of each changed throughout the seasons; daylight hours were long in summer, short in winter, and so on. Any clock had to account for that.

the eighth degree (9.3.1) (Figure 111)

The signs are begun differently in different traditions: Hipparchus, on the entry of the sun into a sign (the first degree); Meton on the eighth degree of the sign. Also note that the precession of the equinoxes (caused by the gradual wobble of the earth's axis, discovered by Hipparchus in the second century B.C.) has displaced the entire zodiacal calendar by about a month. Vitruvius works from the state of the stars c. 200 B.C., as do modern newspaper horoscopes.

---

1 Pliny the Elder, *Natural History* 2.182; 6.211–220. The next major step was taken by Hipparchus in the next century with his calculation of the tables of chords.

2 Cf. 5.3.6, on the acoustics of theaters: "The voice is a flowing breath of air. . . . It moves by the endless formation of circles."

PLANETARY MOTION (9.1.1-6)

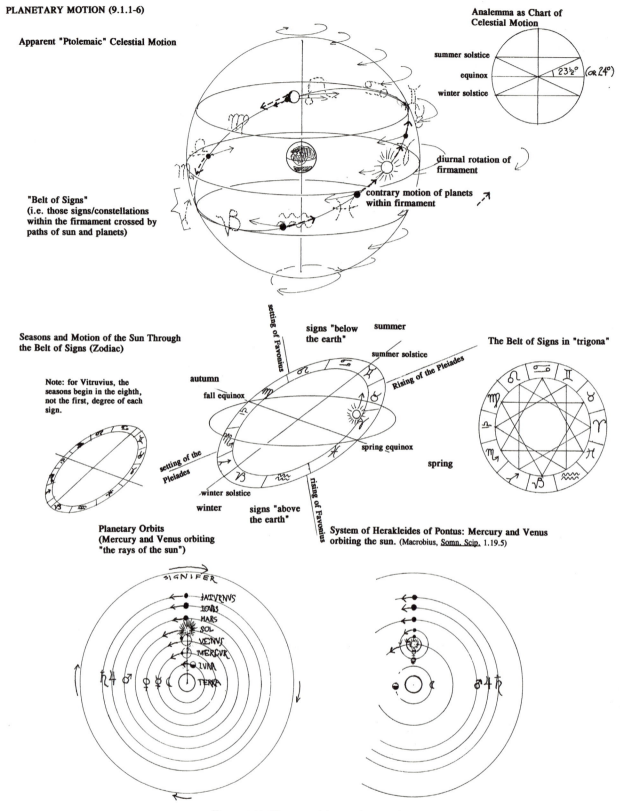

Figure 111. Planetary Motion (9.1.1–6).

RETROGRADE MOTION FOR PLANETS ("STARS") ABOVE THE SUN
(9.1.11-15)

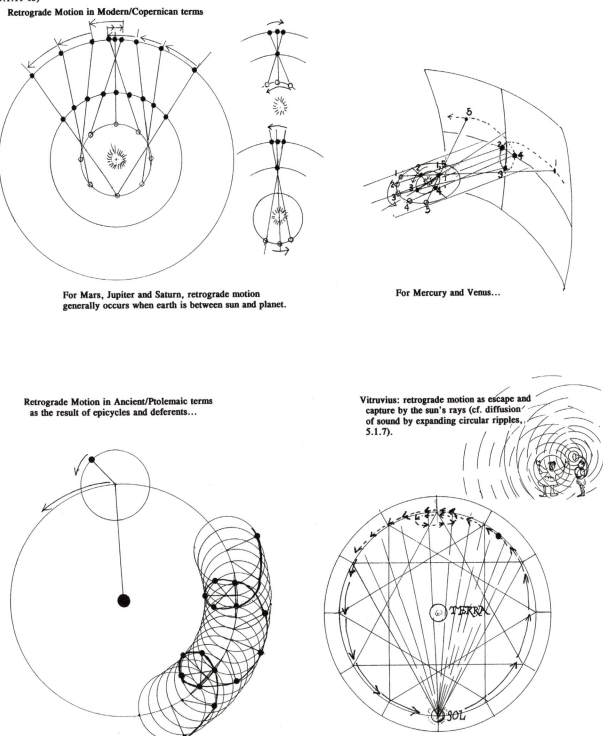

Retrograde Motion in Modern/Copernican terms

For Mars, Jupiter and Saturn, retrograde motion generally occurs when earth is between sun and planet.

For Mercury and Venus...

Retrograde Motion in Ancient/Ptolemaic terms as the result of epicycles and deferents...

Vitruvius: retrograde motion as escape and capture by the sun's rays (cf. diffusion of sound by expanding circular ripples, 5.1.7).

Figure 112. Retrograde Motion for the Planets ("Stars") "Above" the Sun (9.1.11–15).

same course as it had entering Gemini (9.3.2)

This is an attempt to emphasize the symmetry of the seasons.

the ear of Grain (9.4.1)

The star Spica, now Spiga.

colored star in the middle of the knees (9.4.1)

Arcturus. The word *genuorum* is very plebeian Latin.

Pole Star (9.4.6)

There was no real pole star at the time. The Pole was between the tail of the Little Bear and Draco. Vitruvius uses an approximate pole star in Draco, which he distinguishes from the real, unmarked pole.

isosceles triangle (9.4.6)

An isosceles triangle is also equilateral (two sides) in Vitruvius.

right (9.4.6)

Right and left are confused in Vitruvius or the MSS, or both. The ancient travel writer Pausanias has the same problem in distinguishing between the viewer's right and the object's right in his guidebook to Greece.

the star of Canopus (9.5.4)

This implies reports of the firmament as far south as 60° S, which, of course, would be visible from Syene at c. 23 1/2° N.

learned reasoning of the Chaldeans . . . future events by reasoning from the stars (9.6.2)

The border between scientific astronomy and astrology was recognized in antiquity, but it was rather difficult to place. There was a certain revival of traditional augural/astrological practices in the Augustan period, including technical works on astrology by Varro, Nigidius Figulus (praetor 58, died 5 B.C.), and Manilius.

Anaxagoras of Clazomenae,
Pythagoras of Samos, Xenophanes of Colophon,
Democritus of Abdera . . . Eudoxus, Euclemon,
Callippus, Meton, Philippus, Hipparchus, Aratus (9.6.3)

Many of these natural philosophers/astronomers have been mentioned already several times. Xenophanes of Colophon (later sixth century B.C.); Eudoxus of Cnidos (390–337 B.C.), student of Plato, who took up the latter's challenge to devise a rational explanation for the movement of the planets, and the originator of the mathematically sophisticated and influential theory of homocentric rotating invisible ethereal spheres to explain the motions of the planets (including retrograde motions) by means of combinations of "perfect" uniform circular motions; Euclemon (or Euctemon), a collaborator of Meton; Callippus of Cyzicus (c. 370–334), who modified the system of Eudoxus; Meton (fl. 432 B.C.), the orginator of the nineteen-year "Metonic cycle" to synchronize the cycle of the moon with the motions of the sun; Hip-

parchus of Nicaea (mid-second century B.C.), probably the greatest astronomer of antiquity and the basis of much of the work of Ptolemy; Aratus of Soli (315–240/39 B.C.), author of the very popular *Phaenomena*, a versification of the prose essays of Eudoxus undertaken at the behest of Antigonus Gonatas, king of Macedon, which led to several Latin translations, including one by Cicero.

astronomical tables [*parapegmata*] (9.6.3)

Written tables/calendars of star positions, such as survive in Ptolemy's *Almagest*.

Rome . . . 9:8 (9.7.1) (Figures 114, 115)

Rome is at 41° 54', 9:8 = 41° 38'. 9:8 is also the value given by Pliny for Rome (*Natural History* 2.182, 6.217).

one-fifteenth part of the entire circle (9.7.4)

This counts as Vitruvius's approximation of the inclination of the ecliptic, 360°/15 = 24°. It was actually about 23° 51' 19" at the time of Vitruvius.[3]

the letter A (9.7.4) (Figure 114)

The text for the next few sentences is corrupt; our text follows the logic of the illustration.

the kinds that have been handed down to us (9.7.7)

The most common type of sundial now, in which the gnomon is made more accurate by making it parallel to the earth's axis, seems to have been invented about fifty years after Vitruvius.[4] See sundial of Berosus, 9.8.1: "undercut to follow the earth's tilt."

water jets and automata (9.8.4)

This is a reference to the complex field of entertainment automata used mainly in the theater.[5]

removal of wedges (9.8.6) (Figure 116)

Wedges were a very basic method for controlling, tightening, and leveling all sorts of machines or structures in antiquity, including, presumably, leveling the chorobate.

winter clocks . . . "pickup" (9.8.8) (Figure 117)

For use when it is dark. "Anaphoric" = pickup.

sphere indicates (9.8.9) (Figure 117)

This is the pointer that indicates the current time in the outer grill.

As for regulating the water
supply (9.8.11–12) (Figure 117)

This is a different clock from the above, and it functions by differential water pressure.

3 J. Soubiran, ed., *Vitruve, de l'architecture*, ix (Paris, 1969), 223.
4 R. Newton Mayall, M. W. Mayall, *Sundials* (Boston, 1938), 15.
5 See R. S. Brumbaugh, *Ancient Greek Gadgets and Machines* (New York, 1966).

THE CONSTELLATIONS (9.3-5)

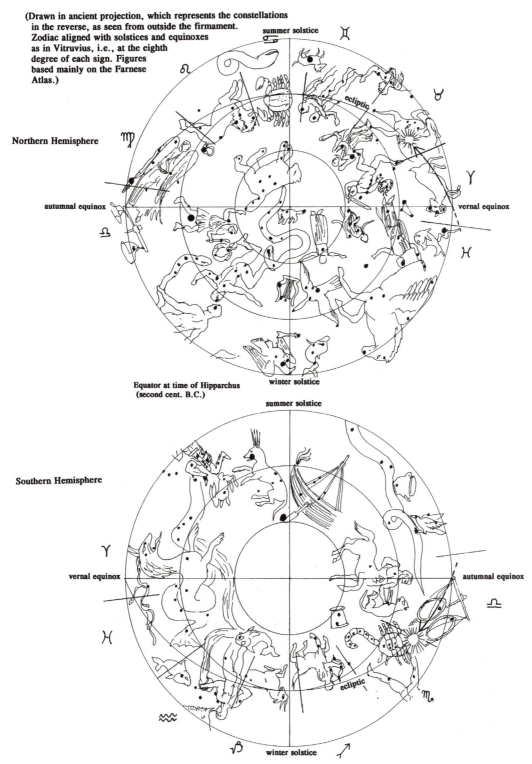

(Drawn in ancient projection, which represents the constellations in the reverse, as seen from outside the firmament. Zodiac aligned with solstices and equinoxes as in Vitruvius, i.e., at the eighth degree of each sign. Figures based mainly on the Farnese Atlas.)

summer solstice

ecliptic

Northern Hemisphere

autumnal equinox

vernal equinox

Equator at time of Hipparchus
(second cent. B.C.)

winter solstice

Southern Hemisphere

summer solstice

vernal equinox

autumnal equinox

ecliptic

winter solstice

Figure 113. The Constellations (9.3.5).

THE ANALEMMA (9.7.1-7)

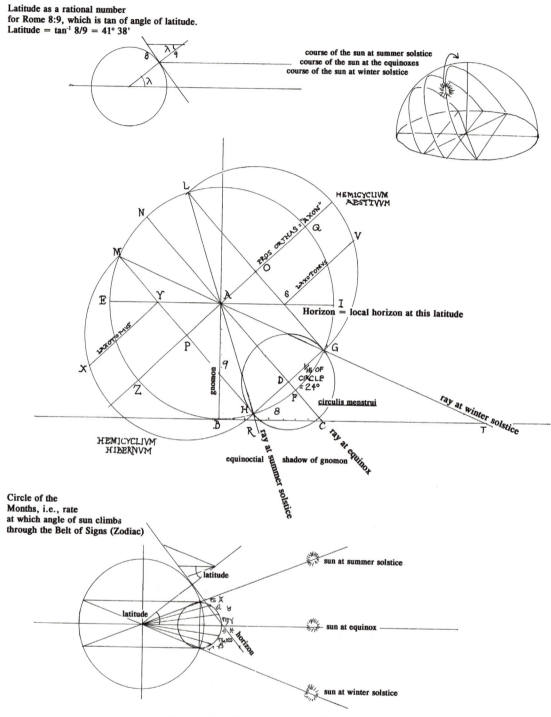

Latitude as a rational number
for Rome 8:9, which is tan of angle of latitude.
Latitude = tan⁻¹ 8/9 = 41° 38'

course of the sun at summer solstice
course of the sun at the equinoxes
course of the sun at winter solstice

HEMICYCLIVM AESTIVVM

PROS ORTHAS = "AXON"

LAXOTOMVS

Horizon = local horizon at this latitude

¼₆ OF CIRCLE = 24°

circulis menstrui

gnomon

ray at winter solstice

HEMICYCLIVM HIBERNVM

ray at summer solstice

equinoctial   shadow of gnomon

ray at equinox

Circle of the
Months, i.e., rate
at which angle of sun climbs
through the Belt of Signs (Zodiac)

latitude

latitude

horizon

sun at summer solstice

sun at equinox

sun at winter solstice

Figure 114. The Analemma (9.7.1–7).

THE ANALEMMA (9.7.1-7)

Partial demonstration of the derivation of a "pelecinum" sundial
for the latitude of Rome from the analemma. This drawing shows the
projection of the lines of the signs (months) on to the equinoctial line,
with the rest of the sundial added. All of the features of the sundial
are derived from the analemma.

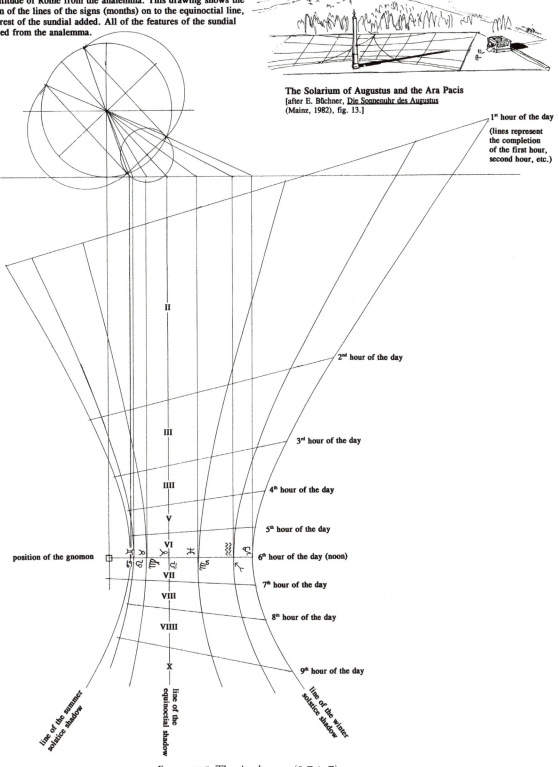

The Solarium of Augustus and the Ara Pacis
[after E. Büchner, <u>Die Sonnenuhr des Augustus</u>
(Mainz, 1982), fig. 13.]

1ˢᵗ hour of the day

(lines represent
the completion
of the first hour,
second hour, etc.)

II

2ⁿᵈ hour of the day

III

3ʳᵈ hour of the day

IIII

4ᵗʰ hour of the day

V

5ᵗʰ hour of the day

VI

6ᵗʰ hour of the day (noon)

position of the gnomon

VII

7ᵗʰ hour of the day

VIII

8ᵗʰ hour of the day

VIIII

9ᵗʰ hour of the day

X

line of the summer
solstice shadow

line of the
equinoctial shadow

line of the winter
solstice shadow

Figure 115. The Analemma (9.7.1–7).

WATER CLOCKS (9.8.4-7)

Waterclocks with mechanisms driven by a float (<u>phellus</u>)

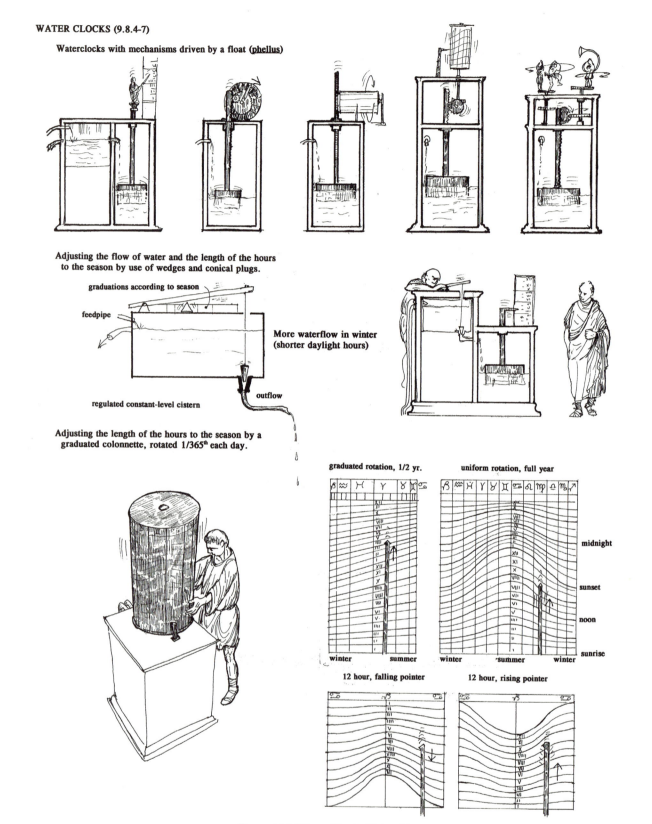

Adjusting the flow of water and the length of the hours to the season by use of wedges and conical plugs.

graduations according to season

feedpipe

More waterflow in winter (shorter daylight hours)

regulated constant-level cistern

outflow

Adjusting the length of the hours to the season by a graduated colonnette, rotated 1/365th each day.

graduated rotation, 1/2 yr.

uniform rotation, full year

midnight

sunset

noon

sunrise

winter   summer   winter   summer   winter

12 hour, falling pointer

12 hour, rising pointer

Figure 116. Water Clocks (9.8.4–7).

WATER CLOCKS (9.8.8)

Winter Clocks ("Anaphoric")(9.8.8-10)

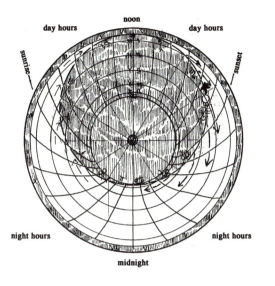

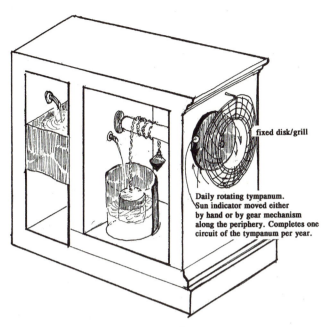

Daily rotating tympanum.
Sun indicator moved either
by hand or by gear mechanism
along the periphery. Completes one
circuit of the tympanum per year.

Adjustment to Season by Regulation of Waterflow (9.8.11-15)

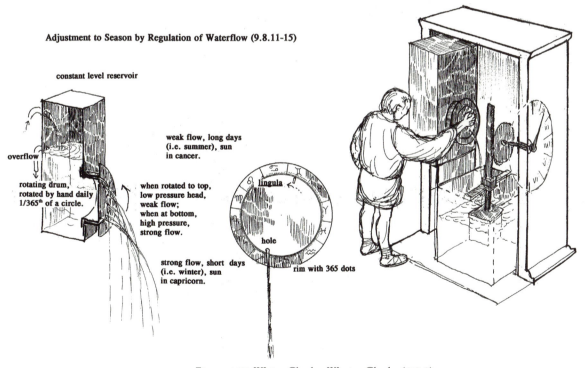

Figure 117. Water Clocks: Winter Clocks (9.8.8).

BOOK 10

people who can assemble
four hundred thousand sesterces (10.praef.2)

Four hundred thousand sesterces were the minimum property qualification for senatorial rank in Vitruvius's day, 100,000 for equestrian rank. The daily wage of a workman would be about one to three denarii. Large sums were usually tallied in 1000s of sestertii, or talents. The property qualification of a senator was 400,000 sestertii in the first century B.C. One of the largest fortunes was that of M. Licinius Crassus, which rose from 300 to 7,000 talents (42 million denarii).[1] L. Licinius Lucullus threw dinner parties costing as much as 50,000 denarii.[2] Top prices for luxurious *domus* (townhouses/mansions) in prime locations in Rome would be a couple of million sestertii; in 62 B.C. Cicero paid 3.5 million sestertii for his house in the Velia (in the upper Forum), and he complained about the high cost and heavy debts caused by this political necessity.[3] The highest known price paid for a house in Rome in the Republic was 14.8 million sestertii.[4]

endowments made by magistrates
for the festival games: the gladiators
the Forum . . . the awnings (10.praef.3)

Temporary, and apparently quite elaborate, wooden theaters were erected every year, usually under the supervision of the aediles, for certain festivals, and gladiatorial combats continued in the Forum until the end of the Republic. The theaters were usually built in the Campus Martius or on the site of the Augustan Theater of Marcellus. In 52 B.C. C. Curio built two rotating wooden theaters, M. Aemilius Scaurus, aedile in 58, built a theater with 360 marble columns for the scaenae frons, and later removed several of them to his house. In 46 Caesar built a "hunting" theater, stadium, and artificial lake for sea fights (naumachiae).[5] M. Claudius Marcellus, aedile in 25, built an awning over the entire Forum for gladiatorial combats.[6] At the time Vitruvius wrote the only stone theater in Rome was that of Pompey (60–55 B.C.); that of Marcellus may have been visible (begun c. 45 or 23, dedicated 17 B.C.); that of L. Cornelius Balbus (19–13 B.C.) was probably not yet begun. The first stone amphitheater in the City (of T. Statilius Taurus) was dedicated in 29 B.C.

grounding in mechanics (10.praef.3)

Perhaps one further reason that architects were supposed to know mechanics is that, in some circumstances, they (or the contractor) were responsible for furnishing the equipment of a building as well as its construction. This is implied in an example of a contract for building a villa given by Cato the Elder that specifies benches, stools, mortars, and so on, as well as window fittings, doors, cabinetry.[7]

praetors and aediles (10.praef.4)

Normally throughout the Republic aediles administered the festival entertainments, but in 22 Augustus transferred responsibilities to the much more senior officials of the praetors.

circular motion (10.1.1) (Figure 118)

This appears to be an original piece of analysis, but it is based on scientific attempts to see circular motion behind all mechanical action, such as Hero's (unsuccessful) attempt to demonstrate the relation of circular motion and the mechanical advantage of the inclined plane. See figure.

type used for mounting (10.1.1) (Figure 118)

This ambiguous definition probably relates to any kind of scaffolding or ladder; cf. 7.2.2 where "the machines" seems to be scaffolding for plasterers.

baruoison (10.1.1)

Reading *barouison* for MSS *baruison*, to mean "weight-bearing."

mechanically . . . instrumentally (10.1.3) (Figure 118)

This analytical device seems to derive from Greek writers on mechanics, but the sense is changed by Vitruvius to a functional point of view.

scorpion or anisocycles (10.1.3) (Figure 118)

The scorpion is the term for a small arrow-shooting catapult. The interesting implication here is that it is handled by one person. If the reading "anisocycles" means "unequal circles," then this may refer to *baruoulkon*, a reduction gear lifting device, described by Hero.[8] See figure.

This type of machine (10.2.3)

Ratio is a term of classification for machines, presumably translating the infinitely flexible Greek word *logos*. We see this peculiar Hellenizing use of *ratio* throughout Book 10. There are three *genera* (mounting, pneumatic, and tractor), and then each example within the *genus* seems to be a *ratio*. Within each *ratio* there can be further *genera*.

supporting ropes . . . shoulders (10.2.3) (Figure 120)

Supporting ropes = stays. Shoulders (*scapulae*) are presumably some upper part of the crane, perhaps where the two beams join.

1 Plutarch, Crassus, 2.1. seq.
2 Plutarch, Lucullus, 41.7.
3 Cicero, *Epistulae ad familiares* 5.6.2. Velleius, 2.14.2.
4 This was the notoriously luxurious house of M. Aemilius Scaurus, praetor in 67, who had to sell his house quickly when he went into exile in 54 B.C. The atrium featured four 38-foot columns of lucullean marble. It was located in the same area as Cicero's. Pliny the Elder, *Natural History* 36 113–114. F. Coarelli, "La casa dell'aristocrazia romana secondo Vitruvio," in *Munus non Ingratum*, 178–187.
5 Suetonius, *Caesar* 37.
6 Dio Cassius, 53.3.1. See D. Favro, *The Urban Image of Augustan Rome* (Cambridge, 1996), 39–40, 62.
7 *De Agri cultura*, 14.1–5.
8 *Mechanica* 1.1; 2.21; *Dioptra* 37, postdating Vitruvius (c. A.D. 65).

FIRST PRINCIPLES OF MACHINES (10.1.1-3)

CIRCULAR MOTION as the basis of all machines:

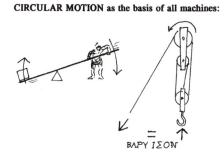

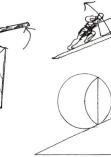

BAPY IΣON

Heron's attempt to analyze
the inclined plane as circular
motion (after Heron, Mech. 1.23)

TYPES:

Mounting Machines (scansoria)   **Pneumatic**   **Tractors**

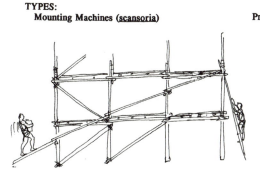

TYPES OF USE:

mechanicos
many (unskilled?) workers

organicos
one skilled operator

"anisocycle" = βαραλκός
(Heron, Mech. 1.1)

(βάλλ' ἐς κόρακας
βαρύς ἐστιν)

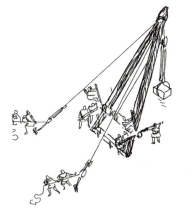

5 TALENTS
APPLY 4 TAL.
TO HANDLE
(+1 FOR RESISTANCE)

TT = 2×RS
= 8 TALENTS

RS=8×FQ
= 40 TAL.

SO=5×MNK
= 200 TAL.

HT=5×HZ
= 1000 TAL.

1000 TAL.

Figure 118. First Principles of Machines (10.1.1–3).

CRANES: <u>TRISPASTOS/PENTASPASTOS</u> (10.2.1-4)

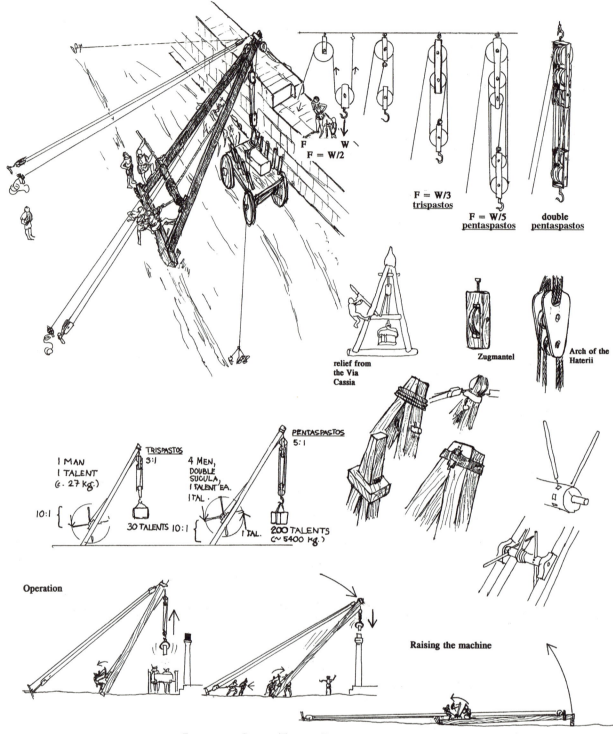

Figure 119. Cranes: *Trispastos/Pentaspastos* (10.2.1–4).

CRANES FOR HEAVIER LOADS (10.2.5-7)

WITH REDUCTION GEAR (amphiesis, perithêkion)

TREADMILL-DRUM PLACED TO THE SIDE

relief from Capua

capstan, [after
Nicolai Zabaglia,
Contignationes ad pontes,
(Romae, 1743).]

reconstruction based
on the Arch of the
Haterii

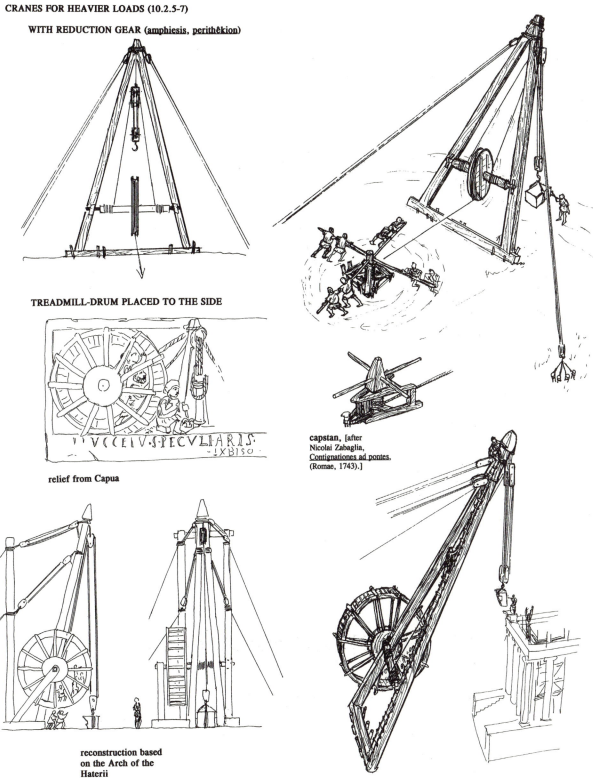

Figure 120. Cranes for Heavier Loads (10.2.5–7).

maneuvered by control ropes (10.2.8) (Figure 121)

Maneuvered (*distendo*) = "made to reach." This type of motion is indeed very difficult to coordinate between four rigging gangs.

the colossal statue of Apollo (10.2.13)

From the context this must be an Apollo at Ephesus, but the exact identification is debatable; possibly it is to be identified with a work of Myron, stolen by Marc Antony and returned by Augustus.[9]

Paconius (10.2.13) (Figure 122)

Unknown by any other source, Paconius may be a Roman working in Asia Minor, or if read as Paeonius, he may be identified with Paeonius of Ephesus mentioned in 7.praef.16. The latter, however, is a fourth-century B.C. architect, and this Paconius is a contemporary of Vitruvius.

Paros, Proconnesus, Heraclea, Thasos (10.2.15)

Parian is the basic statuary marble of Greek antiquity; Proconnesian, a blue-white marble from quarries on the isle of Proconnesus in the Sea of Marmara; and Thasian a bright white coarse-grained marble from Thasos in the northern Aegean. The latter two were exported in large quantities throughout the Empire. Heraclea may be Heraclea ad Latmos.

linear motion . . . circular motion (10.3.1–8)

This analytical section is partly original, and partly derives from the tradition continued (later) by Heron of Alexandria in trying to see circular motion underlying all levers, inclined planes, and so on.[10] The notion that sailboats go faster when their sails are raised higher up the mast because the sail has a longer lever arm is, of course, wrong; speed is proportional to sail area, torque (heeling) is proportional to height of mast (and weight of ballast). See figure.

the pilot of the largest cargo ship (10.3.5) (Figure 123)

Lucian gives a vivid picture of a precarious passage from Alexandria to Rome on a 180-foot ship in which "all depended for its safety on one little old man who turns those great steering oars with a tiller that's no more than a stick!"[11]

double iron chain (10.4.4) (Figure 125)

Presumably attached at each side of each bucket. *Congius* = 6 *sextarii* = c. 3.275 liters.

Water mills (10.5.2) (Figure 126)

Water mills were apparently a fairly recent invention, probably appearing only in the late first century B.C. Vitruvius does not mention the overshot wheel or the horizontal wheel, but both were certainly used by later antiquity. Vitruvius's mill is geared down, that is, with the grindstone rotating more slowly than the waterwheel; later, larger European overshot wheels were geared up.[12]

water screw (10.6.1) (Figure 127)

Literally, "water snail."

Ctesibius . . . many others (10.7.4) (Figure 128)

This is another reference to the ingenious automata used mainly as scientific playthings and theater entertainments. There were even plays, like the *Nauplius*, which were performed solely by automata.[13]

water organs (10.8.1–6) (Figure 129)

Water organs were very loud instruments, and they commonly appeared as part of the entertainment for large crowds, such as in circuses.[14] The bronze dolphins are presumably counterweights for the air intake valves. See figure.

a device that is not idle (10.9.1) (Figure 130)

Vitruvius's wording implies strongly that this odd gadget was an actual part of the repertoire of land surveyors. A similar device is also described by Heron, *Dioptra* 34.

four feet . . . twelve and one-half feet (10.9.1)

Vitruvius gives no actual value for pi. MSS read 4 1/6 feet for the diameter of the wheel, 12 1/2 for its presumed circumference, giving a value of pi of 3.00. Reading MSS as 4 feet gives a value of 3.125. Archimedes demonstrates a range of approximations from 3 1/8 (= 3.125) to 3 1/7 (= 3.1429).[15] The number 22/7 is a fairly common approximation in antiquity.

scorpions and ballistae (10.10.1) (Figures 118, 131, 132)

Vitruvius seems to use *scorpio* to distinguish an arrow- or bolt-launching catapult from a *ballist(r)a* or stone-launching catapult, but in 10.1.3 *scorpio* also seems to imply a smaller, one-man weapon. The catapult was invented c. 399 B.C. in Syracuse as a bow-shooter[16] and in the course of the fourth century B.C. developed into the sophisticated twin-arm, twin-spring

---

9 Pliny the Elder, *Natural History* 34.58.
10 Heron, *Mechanica* 1.9, 2.7, 2.9.
11 Lucian, *Navigium* 5; cited in L. Casson, *Travel in the Ancient World* (Toronto, 1974),158–159.

12 One of the first references is from an epigram from the *Palatine Anthology* (9.418), which celebrates the release from drudgery brought to women servants who previously had to grind by hand. The verse presumably dates from the late first century B.C. Also Lucretius, *De rerum natura* 5.509–33. An overshot wheel is represented in a mosaic from the Palace of the Emperors in Constantinople; *Antiquity* 13 (1939), 354–356, pl. vii. See J. G. Landels, *Engineering in the Ancient World* (Berkeley, 1978), 16–26.
13 The principal source for such information are Heron's *Pneumatica* and *Automata*. See R. S. Brumbaugh, *Ancient Greek Gadgets and Machines* (New York, 1966), 113–129.
14 Pliny the Elder, *Natural History* 7.125; Suetonius, *Nero* 41.4; Tertullian *Animadversiones* 14.
15 J. Pottage, "The Vitruvian Value of pi," *Isis* 59 (1968), 190–197.
16 A large group of expert craftsmen was lured to Syracuse by Dionysius I with the hope of developing weaponry that would give him the advantage over Carthaginian forces. Diodorus Siculus 14.41.4, 42.1. E. W. Marsden, *Greek and Roman Artillery: Historical Development* (Oxford, 1969), 48–49.

machine described in Vitruvius. In more general terms, the Latin *catapulta* meant the arrow- or bolt-shooter, *ballista* the stone-shooter, and a *scorpio* was a smaller *catapulta*. Between c. A.D. 100 and 300 the nomenclature changed, and *catapulta* became the one-armed stone-throwing machine (onager), and *ballista* became the bolt-shooter.[17]

Hellenistic town fortifications were heavily influenced by the development of sophisticated siegecraft and artillery in the fourth century B.C. Because of artillery, crenellations were abandoned on the curtain and replaced with a continuous screen with firing apertures. Towers appeared in order to hold artillery, and to raise it higher, to provide greater range over besieging artillery, and to offer flanking fire to clear the walls; they were roofed and most fighting moved inside, with large ports in the upper stories for artillery (catapults) and smaller loopholes in the lower stories for archers. Small artillery was sometimes placed on the curtain as well. Greek walls continued to be of drystone masonry, but became higher and thicker, commonly developing into header and stretcher or "compartment" walls with mud and rubble infill, to resist stone-throwing catapults. Stone-throwing catapults (*petroboloi*) could often shatter crenellations or cave in chambers of towers, but never an earth-backed wall. From the later fourth century, fortifications developed ditches and outworks (*proteichismata*) whose purpose was to keep siege machinery at a distance from the walls[18] (Figures 15–19).

proposed length of the arrow (10.10.2)

Usually measured in "spans," 1 span = 3 palms.

five-digit (10.11.3)

The principal texts on catapults are Ctesibius of Alexandria (mid-third century), Biton (third century), Philo of Byzantium (c. 200 B.C.), Vitruvius, and Hero of Alexandria (first century A.D.). Vitruvius follows Philo on the dimensions of the *ballista* in all but a few details.[19] Marsden emends Vitruvius's dimensions in digits to unciae, on the grounds that otherwise his machines have springs three-quarters the diameter of Philo's.[20]

their tension is tempered by ropes (10.11.9; 10.12.1–2) (Figure 133)

A similar device is also described in Hero's *Belopoeica*, 107–113.[21] The material of springs was either sinew or nerve, presumably woven to a rope, although women's hair also could be used.[22]

First of all, the ram . . .
is said to have been invented . . . (10.13.1)

Chapters 13, 14, and 15 of Book 10 are almost identical to chapters on siegecraft from Athenaeus Mechanicus's *Peri Mechanêmatôn*,[23] so much that either could be a translation of the other. The common source is probably the late second-century B.C. engineer Agesistratus, whom Vitruvius credits in 7.praef.14; Athenaeus was likely a contemporary of Vitruvius.[24]

Gades (10.13.1)

Cadiz, possibly c. 500 B.C. Most siegecraft up to c. 400 B.C. was developed by Carthaginians; to conquer Selinus in 409, Carthaginian attackers used six siege towers, six rams, archers, and slingers. At Himera, (407) they used mines and pit props, at Akragas (406), siege mounds.[25]

Philip . . . siege to Byzantium (10.13.3)

The first sieges at which Philip II made extensive use of artillery were Perinthos and Byzantium, both in 340 B.C., and afterward technical leadership in siegecraft passed to the Macedonians. The torsion catapult (as opposed to the bow-shooter) was probably a Macedonian development.[26]

Hegetor of Byzantium (10.15.2) (Figure 137)

Possibly a siege engineer of Demetrius Poliorcetes.

Diognetus . . . Callias . . . Demetrius (10.16.3–4) (Figure 138)

These events are part of the siege of Rhodes in 304 by Demetrius, son of Antigonus of Macedon. It was one of the most spectacular and famous sieges in antiquity and caught the attention of the world on account of the sophistication of the siege machinery.

on Chios . . . sambucae (10.16.9) (Figure 138)

It is not known which siege this refers to, but presumably some event in the third or second century B.C. The *sambuca* is a type of ship-borne scaling ladder suspended from a mast, and it is given this name because it resembles the type of stringed harp of the same name.

in Apollonia (10.16.9–10) (Figure 138)

Again uncertain, but possibly the siege of Apollonia in Illyria by Philip V of Macedon in 214. Octavian was in Apollonia in 44 when he learned of Julius Caesar's death.

17 Ibid., 1.
18 F. E. Winter, op. cit., 311–333. Other general studies of importance: J. P. Adam, *L'Architecture militaire grecque* (Paris, 1982); F. Krischen, *Die Stadtmauer von Pompeii und die griechische Festungsbaukunst in Unteritalien und Sizilien* (Die Hellenistische Kunst in Pompeii 7) (Berlin, 1941).
19 E. W. Marsden, *Greek and Roman Artillery: Technical Treatises* (Oxford, 1971), 1–14.
20 Ibid., 198–199.
21 Ibid., 37–41.

22 Heron, *Belopoeica* 110–113.
23 ed. Wescher, 9–26.
24 See Marsden, *Greek and Roman Artillery: Technical Treatises*, 4–5, with earlier references.
25 Diodorus Siculus 13.54.7, 13.59.8, 13.86.1–3.
26 Marsden, *Greek and Roman Artillery: Technical Treatises*, 58.

OTHER CRANES (10.2.8-10)

POLYSPASTOS

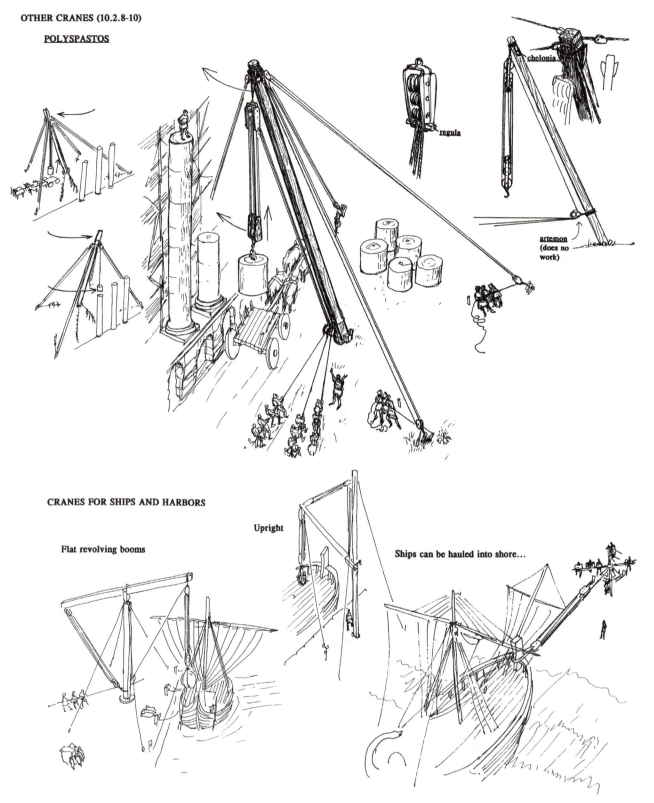

CRANES FOR SHIPS AND HARBORS

Upright

Flat revolving booms

Ships can be hauled into shore...

Figure 121. Other Cranes (10.2.8–10).

SPECIAL METHODS OF HAULING LARGE BLOCKS (10.2.11-15)

Metagenes' Machine

Chersiphron's Machine

Paconius' Disaster

Cylindri for levelling ambulationes of palaestrae

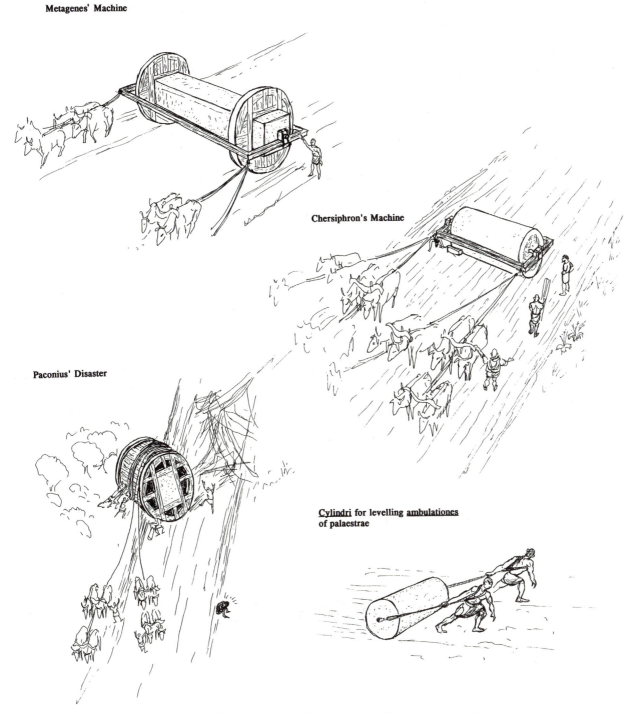

Figure 122. Special Methods of Hauling Large Blocks (10.2.11–15).

ALL MACHINES USE TWO TYPES OF MOTION (10.3.1-8)

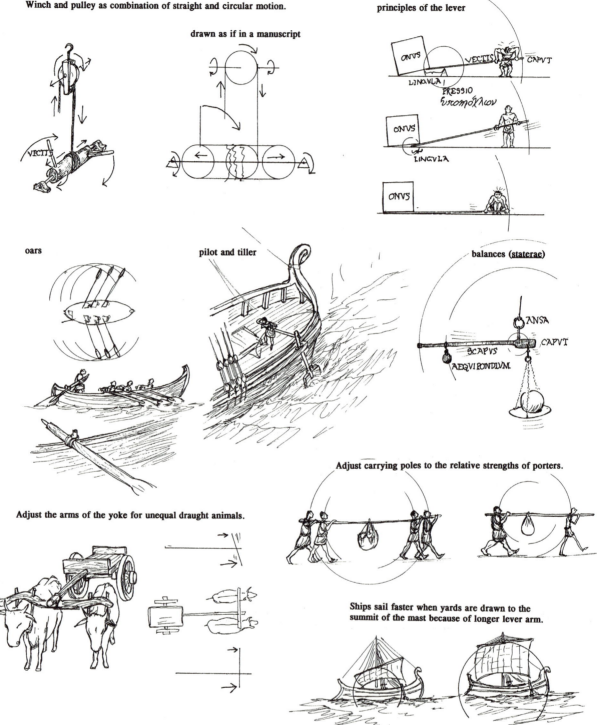

Figure 123. All Machines Use Two Types of Motion (10.3.1–8).

WATER RAISING MACHINES (10.4.1-4)

THE DRUM (TYMPANUM)

WHEEL WITH "SQUARE BUCKETS" (modioli quadrati)

modius

modiolus quadratus?

rise

rise

Rio Tinto Mines, Spain; eight pairs of wheels with total rise of 97 ft.
[after J.F. Healy, Mining
and Metallurgy in the Greek
and Roman World (London, 1978).]

**bucket wheel in Louisiana
rice paddies, 19/20C.**

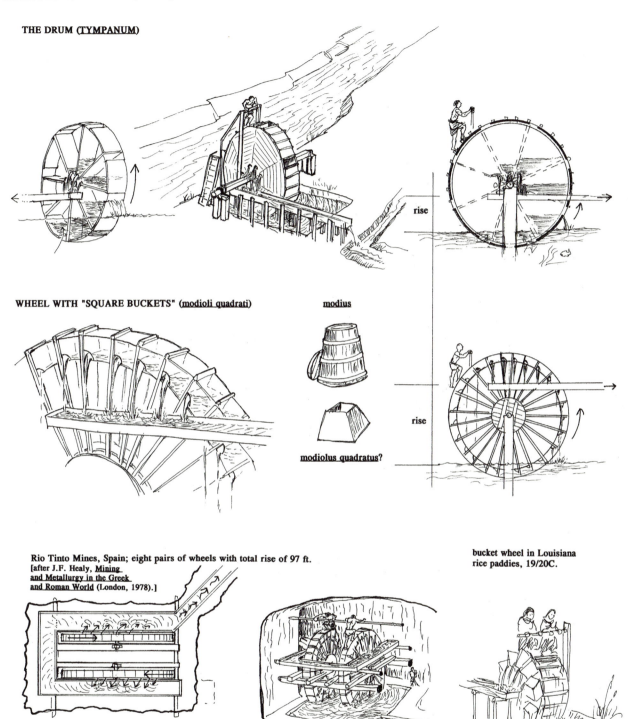

Figure 124. Water Raising Machines (1.4.1–4).

BUCKET CHAINS (10.4.4)

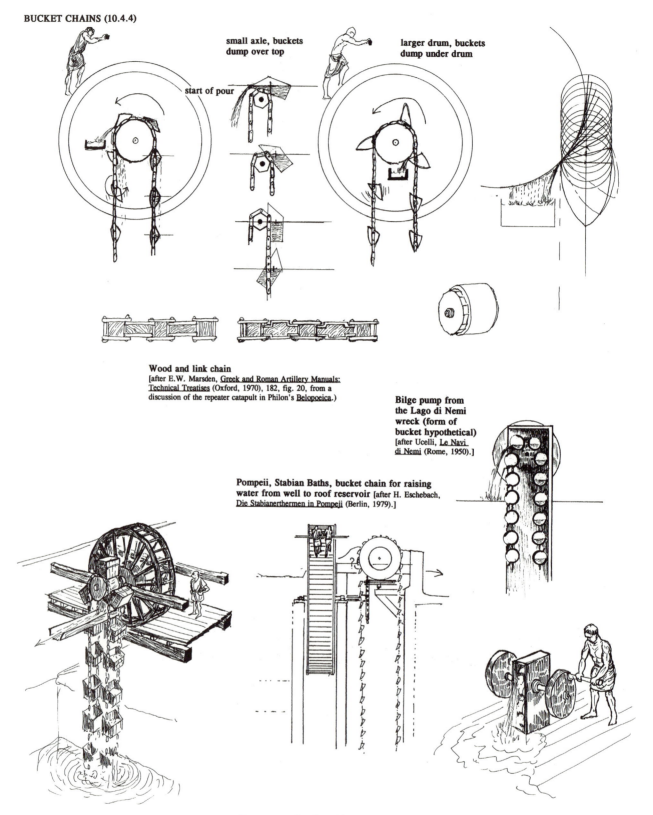

small axle, buckets
dump over top

larger drum, buckets
dump under drum

start of pour

Wood and link chain
[after E.W. Marsden, Greek and Roman Artillery Manuals:
Technical Treatises (Oxford, 1970), 182, fig. 20, from a
discussion of the repeater catapult in Philon's Belopoeica.)

**Bilge pump from
the Lago di Nemi
wreck (form of
bucket hypothetical)**
[after Ucelli, Le Navi
di Nemi (Rome, 1950).]

**Pompeii, Stabian Baths, bucket chain for raising
water from well to roof reservoir** [after H. Eschebach,
Die Stabianerthermen in Pompeji (Berlin, 1979).]

Figure 125. Bucket Chains (10.4.4).

WATERWHEELS (10.5.1-2)

"...wheels are made in rivers by the same principles as those above..."

Water mills:
Vitruvian

more common practice

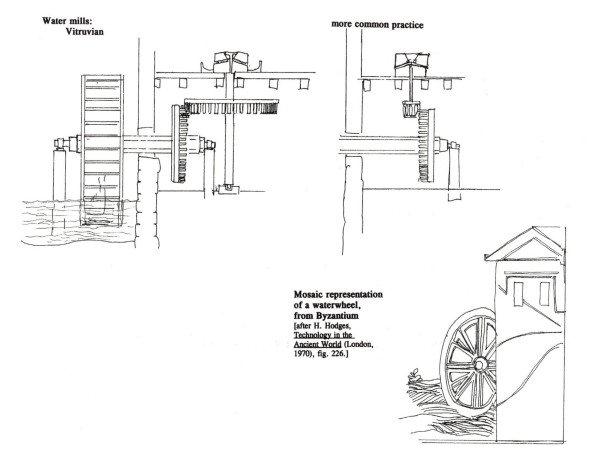

Mosaic representation
of a waterwheel,
from Byzantium
[after H. Hodges,
Technology in the
Ancient World (London,
1970), fig. 226.]

Figure 126. Waterwheels (10.5.1–2).

THE WATER SCREW ("Water Snail," Coclea)(10.6.1-4)

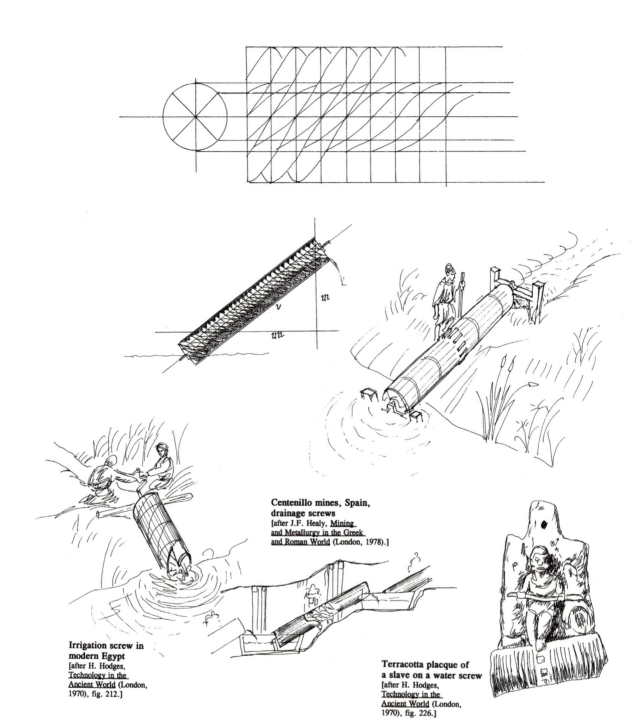

Centenillo mines, Spain,
drainage screws
[after J.F. Healy, Mining
and Metallurgy in the Greek
and Roman World (London, 1978).]

Irrigation screw in
modern Egypt
[after H. Hodges,
Technology in the
Ancient World (London,
1970), fig. 212.]

Terracotta placque of
a slave on a water screw
[after H. Hodges,
Technology in the
Ancient World (London,
1970), fig. 226.]

Figure 127. The Water Screw ("Water Snail," *Coclea*) (10.6.1–4).

CTESIBIUS'S WATER PUMP (10.7.1-3)

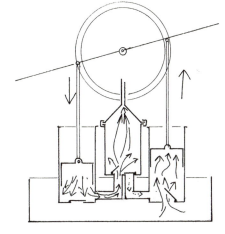

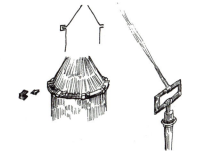

"penny valves"
(asses), reconstructions

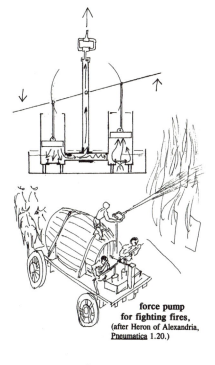

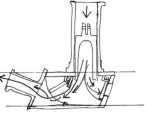

force pump
for fighting fires,
(after Heron of Alexandria,
Pneumatica 1.20.)

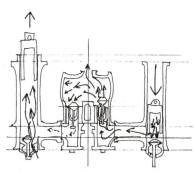

force pump from Bolsena
[from British Museum, in Guide to
the Exhibition Illustrating Greek and
Roman Life (London, 1920²), figs.127, 128.]

force pump from
Sotiel, Coronado Mines,
Valverde, Spain
[after J.G. Landels, Engineering
in the Ancient World (Berkeley and
Los Angeles, 1978), fig.24.]

force pump from a merchant ship wreck
[after Landels, [after J.G. Landels, Engineering
in the Ancient World (Berkeley and
Los Angeles, 1978), fig.25.]

Figure 128. Ctesibius's Water Pump (10.7.1–3).

WATER ORGANS (10.8.1-6)

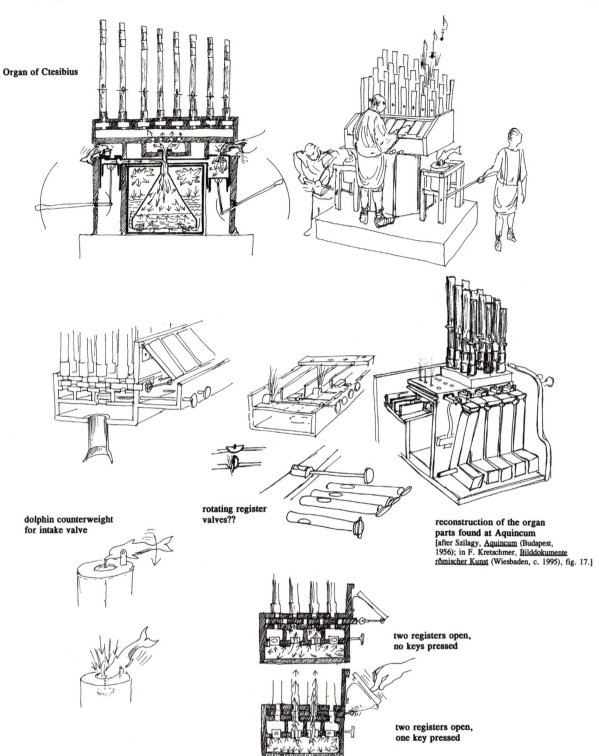

Organ of Ctesibius

dolphin counterweight
for intake valve

rotating register
valves??

reconstruction of the organ
parts found at Aquincum
[after Szilagy, Aquincum (Budapest,
1956); in F. Kretschmer, Bilddokumente
römischer Kunst (Wiesbaden, c. 1995), fig. 17.]

two registers open,
no keys pressed

two registers open,
one key pressed

Figure 129. Water Organs (10.8.1–6).

THE HODOMETER (10.9.1-7)

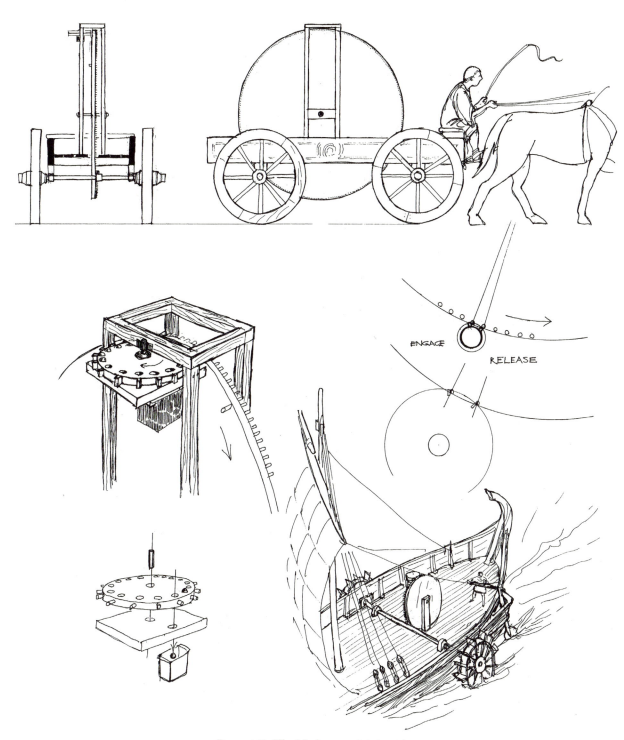

Figure 130. The Hodometer (10.9.1–7).

ARTILLERY: THE <u>SCORPIO</u> (10.10.1-6)

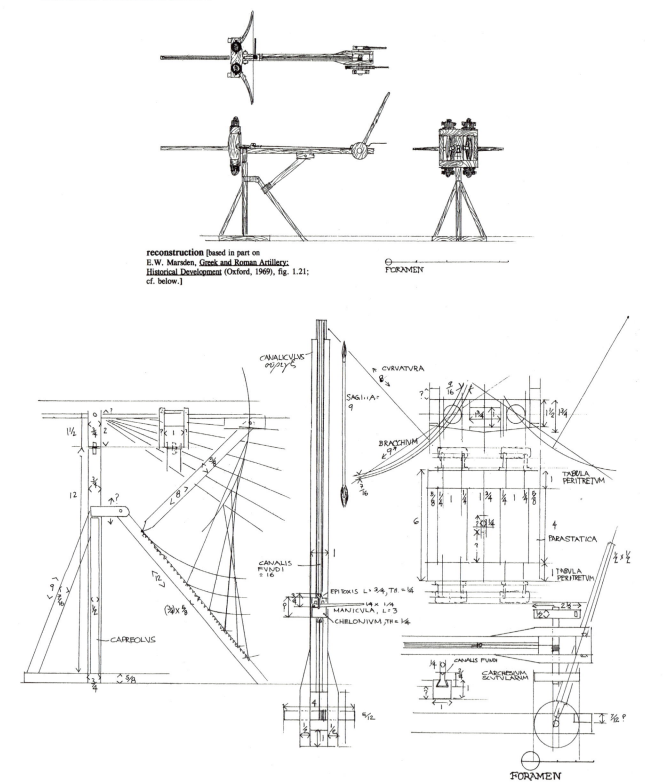

reconstruction [based in part on
E.W. Marsden, <u>Greek and Roman Artillery:
Historical Development</u> (Oxford, 1969), fig. 1.21;
cf. below.]

Figure 131. Artillery: The *Scorpio* (10.10.1–6).

ARTILLERY: THE BALLISTA (10.11.1-9)

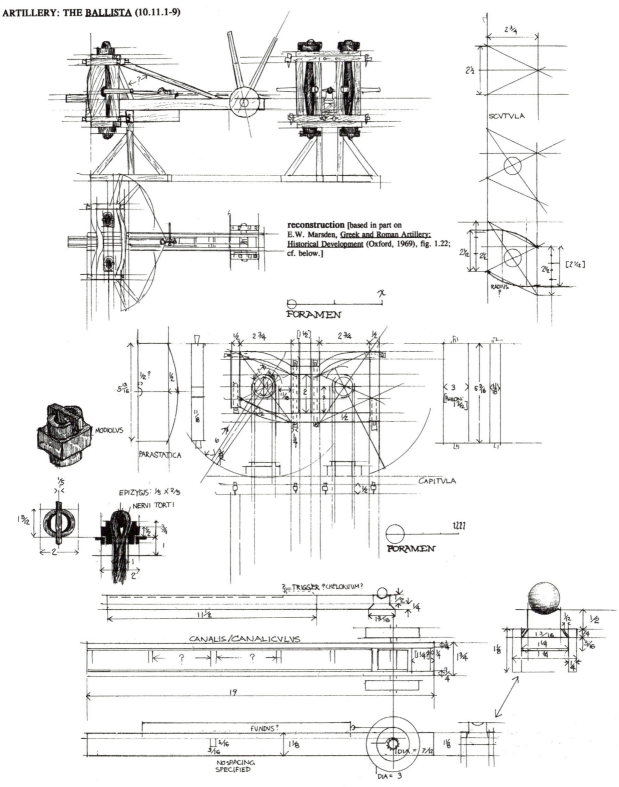

Figure 132. Artillery: The *Ballista* (10.11.1–9).

THE TENSIONING OF WAR MACHINES (10.12.1-2)

stretching frame for a catapult spring
[after Heron, Bel. 107-110, and figure
in E.W. Marsden, Greek and Roman Artillery:
Technical Treatises (Oxford, 1971), 59, fig. 23.]

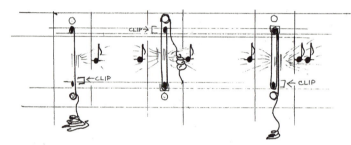

**hypothetical reconstruction of stretcher
for entire headpiece (two springs)**

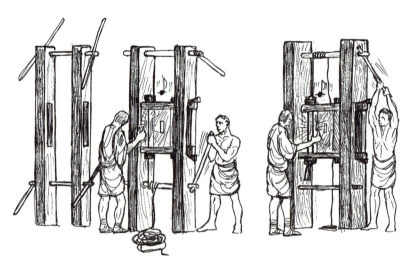

Figure 133. The Tensioning of War Machines (10.12.1–2).

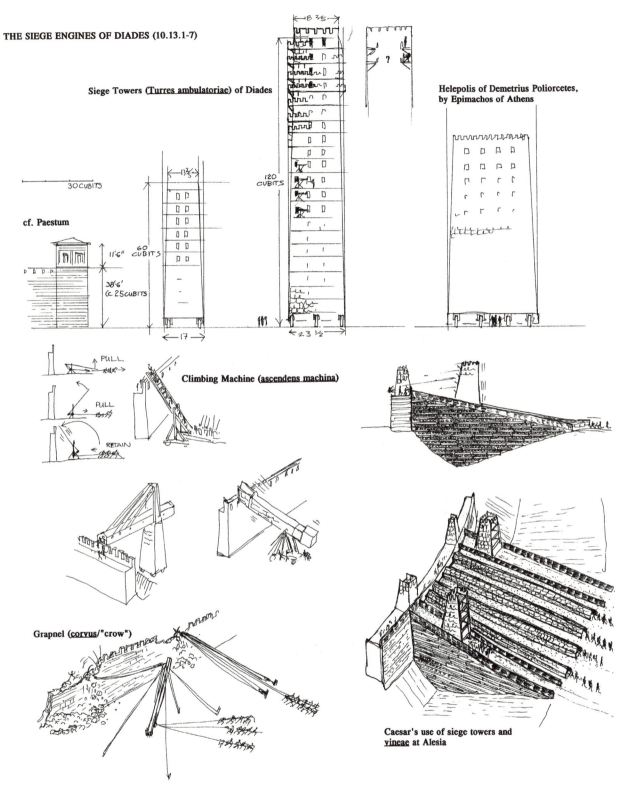

Figure 134. The Siege Engines of Diades (10.13.1–7).

SIEGE ENGINES OF DIADES (10.13.6-7)

"TORTOISE FOR A RAM" (testudo arietaria)

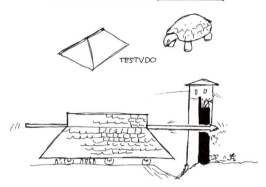

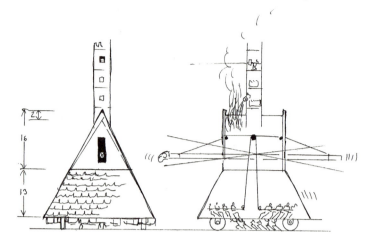

Purpose of the terebra as to punch through the wall at one spot, by hitting repeatedly and precisely.

Purpose of a ram was to knock of the top courses of the walls, course by course.

Alternatives (in part after P. Fleury, La méchanique de Vitruve (Caen, 1993), fig. 72).

tornus

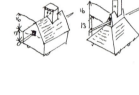

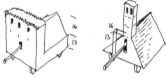

BORER (gouge, penetrator, punch)(terebra)

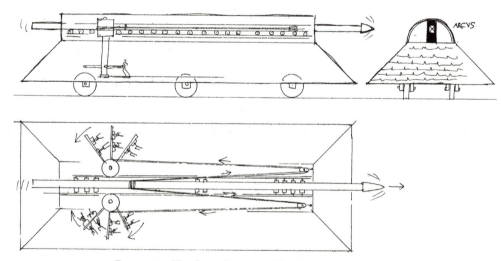

Figure 135. The Siege Engines of Diades (10.13.6–7).

THE TORTOISE FOR FILLING MOATS
(<u>testudo ad congestionem fossarum</u>) (10.14.1-3)

OTHER TYPES...(10.15.1)

DIGGERS (<u>oryges</u>)(10.15.1)

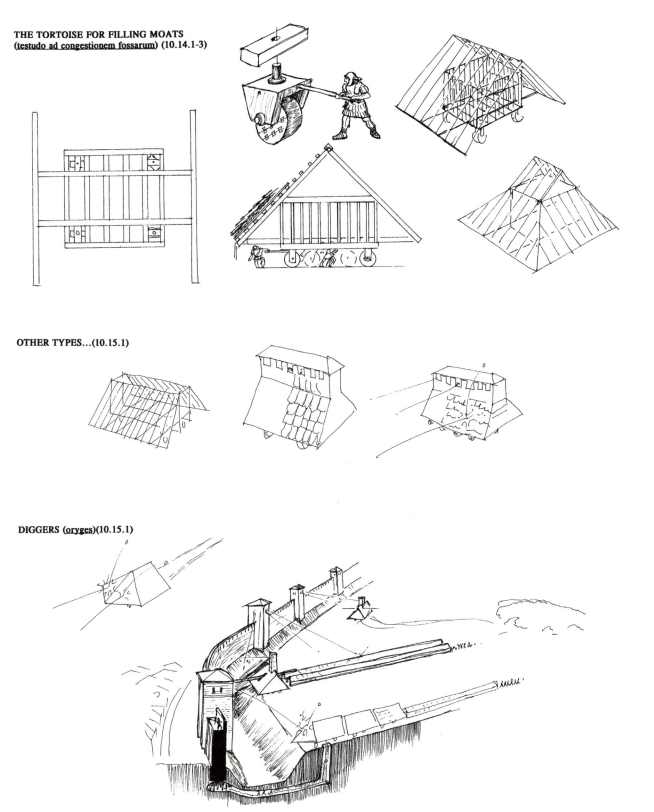

Figure 136. The Tortoise for Filling Moats (10.14.1–3).

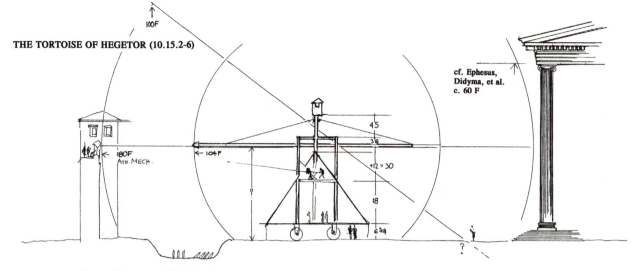

use of <u>arectaria</u> for suspension halyards

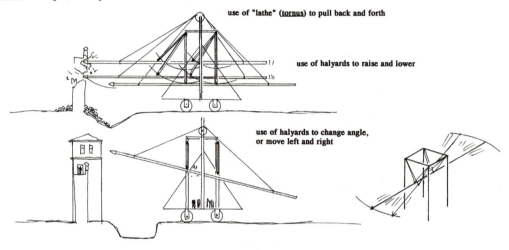

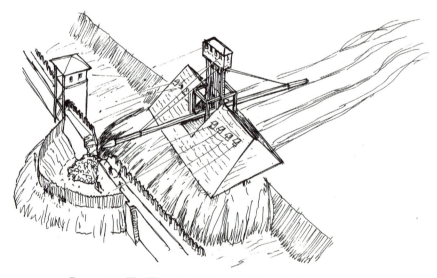

Figure 137. The Tortoise of Hegetor (10.15.2–6).

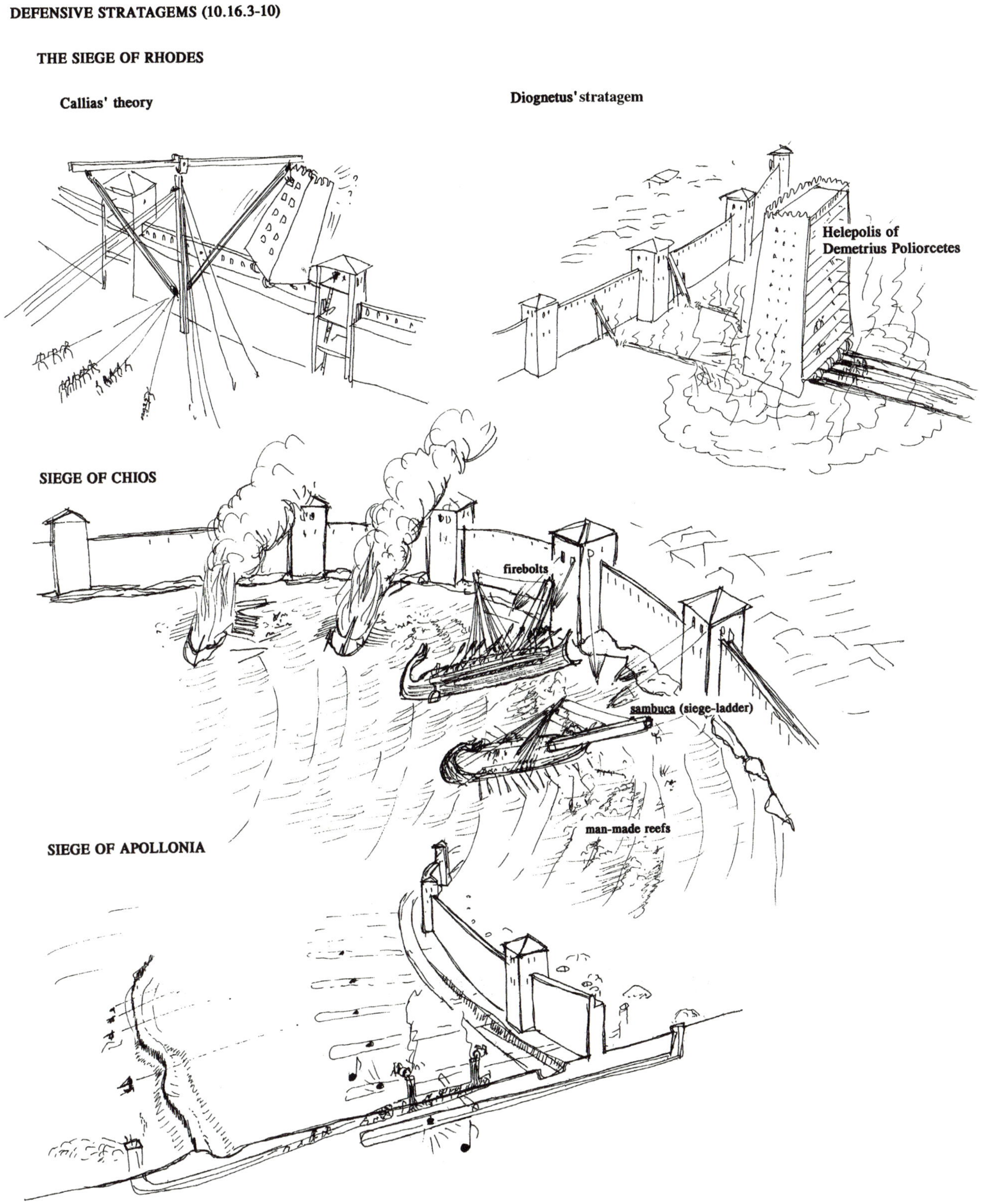

DEFENSIVE STRATAGEMS (10.16.3-10)

THE SIEGE OF RHODES

Callias' theory

Diognetus' stratagem

Helepolis of
Demetrius Poliorcetes

SIEGE OF CHIOS

firebolts

sambuca (siege-ladder)

man-made reefs

SIEGE OF APOLLONIA

Figure 138. Defensive Stratagems (10.16.3–10).

DEFENSIVE STRATAGEMS: THE SIEGE OF MASSILIA (10.16.11-12)

Lowering the moat to below
the level of the sapping
tunnel

tank to flood the
sapping tunnel

ramp burnt by
firebolts

wooden shoring
for ramp

filled-in siege ditch

crane with noose siezes
the battering ram

Figure 139. Defensive Stratagems: The Siege of Massilia (10.16.11–12).

Massilia (10.16.11–12) (Figure 139)

This is presumably the siege of Massilia in 49 B.C. The city had been induced by Pompey to make an isolated stand, and the siege, conducted largely by D. Brutus and C. Trebonius in Caesar's absence, was intended to secure Caesar's rear before going on to face Pompey at Pharsalus. Massilia was one of the leading cities in siegecraft and one of those which possessed staffs of trained engineer/architects; others included Alexandria, Byzantium, Rhodes, Syracuse, and Athens. Vitruvius terminates the *Ten Books* with this historical anecdote in order to drive home the point that the ingenuity and "cleverness of architects" (*architectorum sollertia*) triumph over mechanical methods. Oddly, his closing anecdote features a siege in which the Caesarians, and Vitruvius, if he was present, were (temporarily) among the losers. Caesar's account of the siege focuses mainly on the sea battles, although later[27] he does describe the failure of the siege machines and of various stratagems, but makes no mention of problems with the mines and the moat. Caesar was present to accept the capitulation of Massilia before moving on to cross the Rubicon.[28]

27 *Bellum Civile* 2.2.
28 Caesar, *Bellum Civile* 1.34–36; 1.56–58; 2.1–16; 2.22.

INDEX

Page numbers in *italics* refer to illustrations.

Abdera 92, 115
Academy, of Plato 136
Accius, Lucius 109, 281
Achaea 38, 54
Achinapolus 115
Acid 101–102
Acoustics 229n., 283n.
Acroteria 53
Actium 1, 3
Actors 8, 63, 69, 71, 119, 245
    scenic 70, 245
    thymelic 70, 245
Actus 167, 277
Adjustments 69, 76, 80, 128
    optical 16, 50, 52–53, 59, 78, 221, 228
Adriatic 2, 6, 38, 44, 45
Aedile 4, 6n., 10, 13n., 119, 142, 281, 292
Aedis sacra 152n.
Aemilia, Via 172, 173
Aeolipiles 17, 29, 163n., *164*
Aeolus 29
Aequicoli 102
Aeschylus 86, 173n., 266
Aesthetics xiii, 14, 143, 149
Aether 177
Aetiology 135
Aetna, Mount 38
Africa 6, 44, 99, 102, 275
Agatharchus 86, 266
Agennius Urbicus 172
Agesistratus 7n., 86, 267, 297
Agger and *fossa 162*
Agger, river 98
Agnus castus 43, 97, 125
Agora 166
    Agricultural land 151
    Agricultural villa 152
Agrigento *157*, 297
Agrimensores xvi n., 151, 152, 156n., 163,
    167, 172, 173, 277, 281, 296
Agrippa, Marcus Vipsanius 3, 6, 8, 10,
    136, 275, 277
Akragas *157*, 297
Akrobatikon 119

Alabanda 48, 49, 92, 192, 268
Alae 79, 256, *258*
Alba 38
Alban hills 39
Albarium 249
Alberti, Leone Battista xiii
Albula, river 99, 275
Alcibiades 266
Alder 43, 97, 178
Alexander of Aphrodisias 143n.
Alexander the Great 12, 33, 85, 101,
    130, 173, 174, 213, 266, 267
Alexandria 3, 15n., 17, 33, 85, 86, 94,
    109, 115, 116, 139, 142, 143,
    163n., 167, 169, 173, *174*, 188n.,
    256, 266, 268, 277, 281, 296, 317
    Library 85, 142, 143, 266, 267, 281
Alexis 75, 249
Allocation 25–26, 31–32, 151, 153
Alps 6, 44, 101, 102
Altars 59, 152n.
    Ara Maxima Herculis 156n.
    of Consus 156n.
    of the Lares 156n.
Altinum 27
Alum 99, 105
Amaltheum 14n.
Amateurs 76
Ambitio 75, 80, 249
Amiternae 38
Amphithalamos 82
Amphitheater 2, 10, 292
    of Statilius Taurus 12n., 292
Amusium 167, *168*, *170*
Analêmma 109, 114, 115–116, 117, 165,
    284, 288, 289
Analogia 47
Analogists 15n.
Analysis 25, 149, 151
Anaxagoras of Clazomenae 85, 86, 96,
    115, 266, 275, 286
Anaximenes 266
Ancestors; see also *Maiores* 14, 17n., 63,
    76, 79, 85, 89, 107, 119, 127

Ancients 91
Ancona 44
Andrias 116
Androcydes of Cyzicus 46
Andron of Ephesus 46
Androns 83, 126n.
Andronicus Cyrrestes 29, 166, 218n.
Andronitis 82, 256, *263*
Anecdotes xiii
Anemoscope 165
Anician quarries 39
Anisocycles 120, 292, *293*
Anterides 17, 83–84, *265*
Anthropology xv, 173
Antigonus Gonatas, king of Macedon 286
Antimachides 87
Antiochus, King 87, 267
Antipater 101, 115
Antiperistasis 163n., *165*, 235
Antiquarians 221n.
Antistates 87
Antony, Marc 1, 3, 8, 93, 135, 296
Aosta *157*, 225
Apartment houses 30, 41; see also *Insulae*
Apaturius of Alabanda 92, 268
Apelles of Colophon or Cos 23, 142
Apennines 38, 44
Apollo 46, 54, 108, 122
Apollodorus of Damascus 5
Apollonia 100, 134, 297, *315*
Apollonius of Perge 24, 116, 143
Apparitores 14
Appian Way 156
Approval 92, 151
Apse 16
Apulia 28
Aqua Marcia 99, 275
Aqueducts xiii, 5, 6n., 10, 13, 22, 275,
    277, 280, 281
Aquileia 27
Aquitania 4, 5, 34
Ara Maxima Herculis 156n.
Arabia 100, 101
Araeostyle 49, 50, 51, *196*, *197*

Aratus of Soli 115, 140, 286
Arausio (Orange) 151, 163, *171*
Arcadia 101, 102, 136
Arcesius 57, 86, 221, 267
Arches
  keystone 12, 83, 266
  relieving 83
  triumphal 12
Archimedes of Syracuse 16, 17, 23, 24,
    86, 104, 108, 138, 143, 144, 267,
    277, 281, 296
Architects 5, 13, 66, 68, 69, 75, 76, 84,
    87, 119, 134, 142, 151, 249, 267
  city 14, 68
  cleverness of 134, 317
  education 5, 13, 21–24, 75, 76
  Greek 5
  Roman 87
Architectura 13
Architecture 7, 13, 18, 75, 87, 109, 134,
    138, 151, 229, 267
  Augustan 18
  body of 35, 134
  Campanian 11
  elements of, *145, 146*
  Hellenistic 5, 10
  invention of 34
  Ionian 5, 6
  Republican 11
Archytas of Tarentum 24, 86, 108, 143,
    267, 281
Ardea 99
Arevanias 41
Argos 41, 54, 102
Ariobarzanes, King 71
Aristarchus of Samos, astronomer 23,
    24, 112, 116, 143, 283
Aristarchus of Samothrace, grammarian
    and librarian 23, 142
Aristides, author 103, 275, 277
Aristippus of Cyrene 75, 249
Aristomenes of Thasos 46
Aristophanes of Athens, comic poet 75,
    249
Aristophanes of Byzantium, librarian of
    Alexandria 85–86, 266
Aristotle 7, 85, 107, 136, 140, 142, 163,
    165, 167, 173, 177, 178, 189, 229,
    244n., 249, 266, 275
Aristoxenus of Taras 15n., 23, 66, 68,
    142, 144, 235, 244n.
Arithmetic xvi n., 7, 8, 22
Armenia 94
Army 5, 6
Arretium 40

Arsenic 93, 101
Arsinoë 54
Art 10, 46, 120, 283
Artemisia 41, 184
Artemision; see Temples, Diana at Ephesus
Artes liberales; see Arts, liberal
Artifices 245
Artillery 6, 156, 159, 297, 308, *309*; see
    also Catapults
Artisans xvi, 84
Artists 70, 86, 188
Arts 18, 34, 35, 75, 91, 151n., 173, 175
Arts, liberal xv, 7, 13, 14, 18, 75, 142, 267
As 189, 192
Asclepiades of Bithynia 142
Ash (timber) 43
Ashlar masonry 11, 39, 180, *180*, 184
Asia 36, 38, 49, 54, 98, 111
asphalt marsh 100
Assessment, property 40
Astansoba, river 98
Astoboa, river 98
Astrologers 69, 115
Astrology 114–115, 256, 283, 286
Astronomical tables 115, 286
Astronomy xv, 7, 22, 23, 24, 114–115,
    143, 177, 283, 286
Astynomoi 142
Aswan; see Syene
Atellan farce 245
Athenaeus Mechanicus 7n., 267, 297
Athenians 54, 55, 75, 93, 213
Athens 5, 7, 29, 35, 40, 49, 61, 71, 86,
    87, 93, 100, 109, 115, 136, 163,
    166, 175, 266, 267, 317
  Acropolis 61, 86, 100
  Agora 166, *239*
  Areopagus 35, 175
  Erechtheion 61, 136
  Lysicrates Monument 213n., 215
  Odeum of Themistocles 71, *250*
  Portico of Eumenes 71, *250*
  silver mines 92
  Temple of Olympian Jupiter 49, 87
  Theater of Dionysus 71, *250*
  Tower of the Winds 29–30, 163, *166*,
    218
Athletes 85, 107, 109, 281
Athos, Mount 33, 173, *174*
Atlantes 83, 135
Atlantids 83
Atlas 83
Atlas, Mount 98, 99
Atomism 16, 135, 138, 142, 177, 221, 266
Atoms 17, 35, 90

Atria 79, 80, 81, 82, 91, 256, *258*, 260
Atrium Libertatis 2, 151
Attalids, kings of Pergamum 40, 85, 266
Attalus 54
Attica 61
Atticus, Titus Pomponius 1, 14n., 268
Attractiveness 26, 49, 79, 120; see also
    Venustas
Augur 4, 31, 152, 156n.
Auguraculum 152n.
Augury 18n., 152, *154*, 275, 286
Augusta Praetoria (Aosta) *157*, 225
Augustus 1, 2, 3, 4, 5, 6, 10, 12, 21, 24,
    46, 54, 63, 75, 86, 109, 119, 135,
    142, 157, 188, 235, 268, 281, 286,
    296
Auspices 152
Authority 24, 46, 49, 50, 63, 65, 66, 87,
    91, 109, 151, 245
Authors 85, 86, 103, 107
  Greek xiii, 103
Automata 116, 126–127, 286, 296
Aventine 3, 93, 152n.
Awnings (*velaria*) 119, 292
Axis 109, 156n.
Axon 116

Babylon 12n., 100, 283
Babylonians 29, 283
Baiae 37
Balances 123, *300*
Balbus, Lucius Cornelius 4
Balearic Islands 93, 103
Ballistae 23, 25, 120, 124, 128, 129–130,
    131, 132, 133, 134, 138, *148*, 296,
    297, *309*
  tuning 130, 138, *310*
Banquets 82, 83
Barbarians 77
Barns 81, 82
Baruoison 120
Bases, column
  Attic 51, 203
  Ionic xvi n., 51–52, 203
  Tuscan 61
Basilica xvi, 10, 12, 16, 64, 80, 81, *240*,
    256
  Aemilia 221, 225
  Aquiliana 64
  Fano 4, 5, 11, 13, 16, 17, 64–65, 235,
    241, 242
  Julia 3, 64
Bassae 213, 215
Baths 11, 12, 16, 17, 25, 72, 80, 81, 104,
    108, 249, *251, 252*, 256, 260

Battering ram 13, 28, 130, 131, 132, 134, 297, *312*

Beauty 18, 83, 84, 87; see also Attractiveness; *Venustas*

Bedrooms 25, 82, 256

"Belly" (inverted siphon) 105, 277, 280

Belt of Signs; see Zodiac

Benchmark 30, 163, 167

Bernini, Gianlorenzo 150

Berosus the Chaldaean 111–112, 115, 116, 283, 286

Biton 297

Bitumen 29, 99, 100, 105

Black 94

"Blackbirds" 125

Blocks, city 167, 173

Blue 94

Boarding bridges (*sambucae*) 131, 134, 297, *315*

Body 23, 25, 42, 47, 48, 55, 71, 76, 77, 78, 101–102, 103, 105, 107, 109, 150, 188, 189, 213n.
    of architecture 134
    of text 63, 86

Boedas of Byzantium 46, 188

Boeotia 101, 136

Boethius 7n.

Books 1, 80, 85, 86, 103; see also Scroll
    copying 1
    trade 1

Borysthenes, river 98

Boundaries 142, 163, 167, 170

Bow 156
    portable 156

Brick 12n., 41–42
    fired 11, 12
    inlaid 40
    mud; see Mud brick

Britannia 6n.

Brown, Frank xv

Bruma 113

Brutus, Decimus 317

Bryaxis 86, 267

Bucket chains *302*

"Bucket-climbers" (*angobatai*) 125

Bug, river (Hypanis) 98, 100

Building types xvi, 16

Businessmen 16n., 63, 64, 235, 256

Buttresses 84, *265*

Byzantium 130, 167, 297, 317

Caelian Hill 152n.

Caementicium; see Opus caementicium

Caesar, Gaius Julius 1, 2, 3, 4, 5, 6, 7, 10, 11, 15n., 21, 44, 86n., 93, 103,

135, 156, 163, 188, 249, 275, 292, 297, 311, 317
    assassination 3, 135
    De Bello Gallico 156n., 163
    Bellum Civile 6
    Epistulae 4

Calculation xvi n., 129

Calendar 283

Calibration 118

Caligula 12

Callaeschros 87

Callebat, Louis 125n., 132n.

Callet 36

Callias of Arados 133, 314

Callimachus, sculptor 55, 213

Callippus of Cyzicus 115, 177, 286

Calpurnius Piso, Lucius 136

Calvinus, Gaius Domitius 3

Camenae 99, 275

Campania 2, 5, 6, 11, 12n., 14, 37, 38, 45, 101, 173, 213, 267, 275

Campus Cornetus 101

Campus Martius 3, 8, 10, 136, 213n., 292

Canon of Polycleitus 142, *148*, 188, 189, *190*, 213n.

Canopus 114, 286

Cantilevering 10

Capitals, column 16, 52, 54, 56, *217*, *218*, 235
    composite 218
    Corinthian 54, 55, 213, *215*, *216*, *217*
    Doric 57, *218*
    Ionic 52, 202, *205*, *206*
    Mycenaean 218
    new types 15, 56, *217*, 235
    Tuscan 61

Capitolium (Capitoline) 10, 11n., 35, 175, 193

Cappadocia 100

Cardo 109n., 152, 156

Caria 40, 41, 54, 184

Carians 41, 55, 184

Carpion 86, 266

Carrying poles 123–124, *300*

Carthage 100, 130, 173, 297

Carving 56

Caryae 22, 136

Caryatids 22, 136, *137*

Casius 100

Castellum aquae 17, 104, 105, 277, *279*, 280, 281

Castra Praetoria 12

Catapults xvi n., 5, 14, 15, 21, 23, 28, 128–129, 130, 131, 132, 133, 138, 296, 297, *310*

tuning 130, 138, 297, *310*

Cathetoe 52, *205*

Cato, Marcus Porcius the Elder 17–18, 138, 152, 292

Catoptrics 229

Caucasus 98

Cavaedia 78–80, *257*, 260
    Corinthian 78, *257*
    covered 78, 79, *257*
    displuviate 78–79, *257*
    testudinate 78, 79, *257*
    tetrastyle 78, *257*
    Tuscan 78, *257*

Cavea 13n., *247*, *248*

Cea 102

Cedar 44

Ceilings 36, 72, 89–90, *271*
    suspended 11, 13, 72, *271*

Cella, temple 13, 48, 49, 50, 58, 59, 60, 61, 92, *194*, *195*, 227, 235, *236*

Cellars 13n.

Celsus 142

Celts 98

Cement, hydraulic; see also Opus signinum 106, 281

Centuriae *154*, 170

Centuriation 163, 167, *170*, *171*, *172*, 173, 277

Cephisos, river 101

Chalcidian porches 64, *240*

Chaldaeans 111, 115, 143n., 286

Chalk 93

Charias 86, 130, 267

Cheirokmêton 109

Chemistry xv, 138, 163, 173, 176, 177, 178, 180, 235, 256, 275, 283

Chersiphron of Cnossus 16, 86, 87, 122, 267, 299

Chion of Corinth 46, 188

Chionides 75, 249

Chios 54, 86, 297, *315*

Chorobate (*Chorobates*) 17, 103–104, 277, *278*

Chrobs 101

Chronometer 167

Chrysippus 188

Cicero xiii, 1, 7, 8, 13n., 14, 15n., 136, 151, 152n., 268, 281, 286, 292
    De Natura Deorum 14
    De Officiis 13n., 136, 143, 151n.
    De Oratore 15n., 143n.
    Epistulae ad Atticum 14n.

Cilbian fields 93

Cilicia 100

Cinnabar 91, 92, 93–94, 268

Circus 31
Circus Flaminius 10, 61, 237
Circus Maximus 49, 156n.
Cistern 106
Citadel (Arx) 35
Citizens, Roman 151, 249
Citizenship, Roman 5, 275
City, the 2, 11, 38, 235, 292
Civitates 38n.
Classicism 11, 14, 15, 17
Claudius Marcellus, Marcus 292
Clazomenae 54, 101
Cleopatra 1, 3
Cleverness 126, 127, 134, 317
Clients 2, 135, 249, 256
Climates 23, 76–78, 138, *139, 140, 141,*
    177n., 249
Clitor, spring 102
Clocks 106, 116–118, 143, 283
    calibration 118
    water 116–118
    winter 117–118
Cnossus 27
Codes, building 10
Coffers 82
Colchis 34, 98, 175
Collaxaria 105, *280, 281*
Colocci, Angelo x, 15n., 19, 150n.
Colonnade, temple 13, 192, 218
Colonists 163
Colony 5, 11, 12n., 54, 151, 156, 163,
    173, 213, 235
Colophon 54
Color 90, 92–95
Colosseum 12n.
Columella 138, 142, 281
Columns 14, 25, 192
    contraction 50, 61, 193, *198, 199,* 221
    corner 50, 52, 229n.
    Corinthian xv, 10, 16, 54–56, 211,
        212, 213, 215, 218
    Doric 213, *214,* 218
    engaged 11, 12, 14
    Ionic 208, *212, 214,* 218
    inclination 53, *204*
    interior 16n., 58–59
    spacing 49, *197*
    superposed 16
    wooden 12n., 218
Column types xiii, 11, 56, 211, 218
Comedies 63, 75
Comedy 245, 249
Comic poets 63, 75, 249
Comitium 40, 152n.

Commensurability 150, 186
Compasses 22, 24, 30, 52, 58, 109, 116,
    125
Compluvia 79
Concameratio 13, 266
Concrete 2, 11, 12, 13n., 36–40,
    179–180, 184
    brick-faced 11, 14, 17, 184
Conduct 109
"Cone of vision" 229
Conic sections 143
Conjectures, textual xiii, 82, 235, 281
Conjunction 77
Consuetudo 15n., 151
Constellations 109, 110, 113–114, 117,
    287
Consuls 10
Contractors 14, 92, 104, 108
Contracts 18n., 142
Convention 25, 57
Cooking 72, 105
Copernicus 285
Copper 94, 102
Copying 1
Cori 225
Corinth 68, 213, 215, 245
Corinthian bronze 213, 277
Corinthian column type xv, 10, 16,
    54–56, 211, *212,* 213, 215, 218
    invention of 55, 211, 213, 215
Cornices 12, *215,* 219
    Modillion *215, 219*
Cornificius, Lucius 3
Correctness 24, 25, 78, 80–81, 84,
    91–92, 150–151, 153; see also
    Decor
Corridors 82, 83
Cos 115
Cosa 11, 156, *157,* 173
Cosmology 143, 177, 283, 286
Cosmos 77, 83, 109–111, 103, 112, 120,
    138, 143, 177, 256, 283, 286
Cossutii, family of contractors 14, 267
Cossutius, Roman architect 87, 267
Cottius 101
Courses of the stars 109, 110, 111, 112
Courtyards; see Peristyle
Craftsmanship 84, 120
Craftsmen 76, 84
Cranes and hoists 120–122, *294, 295,*
    298
Crassus, Marcus Licinius 292
Crates of Mallos 15n., 140
Crathis, river 101

Crete 27, 44
Creusa 54
Criticism, art 149, 189
Crocodiles 99
Croesus, king of Lydia 40, 85, 266
"Crow" (demolition grapnel) 130, 131,
    311
Ctesibius of Alexandria 23, 86, 116–117,
    138, 267, 297
Cube 63
    doubling 143, *282*
Cubicula 80, 82, 256, 260
Cult, Imperial 4
Cult statues 58, 59, 213, *230*
Culture xv
Cumae 37, 73
Cuniculi 275
Cura aquarum 6, 17
Curia 3; see also Senate House
Curiae Veteres 156n.
Curio, Gaius 292
Cursus honorum 6n., 18n.
Curvature 51, 52, 193
    column *199,* 221
    stylobate 16n., 51, 52, 193, *201, 202,*
        204, 221, 229n.
Custom 83, 107, 151
Cutiliae 99
Cydnos, river 100
Cymatium xvi n., *202,* 221
Cypress 43, 44, 89
Cyrene 101, 249

Danube 5
Daphnis of Miletus 87, 267
Daring 120
Darius 173
Darkness 110, 111, 120
Days 112, 113, 115, 116, 141, 283
Decempeda 167, *170*
Decimals xvi
Declamation 8
Decor 14, 150–151
Decumanus 152, 156, 173
Decussis 152, *170*
Defense 26, 28–29, 133–134, 151, 153,
    156, 173
Deferents xv
Delivery (*pronuntiatio*) 8
Delos 108
Delphi 46, 54
    Tholos 86, 266
Demetrius, architect and temple slave at
    Ephesus 87, 267

Demetrius of Phaleron 87, 266, 267
Demetrius Poliorcetes 133–134, 297,
    311, 315
Democles 86, 267
Democritus of Abdera 17, 35, 85, 86,
    107, 109, 114, 115, 173, 177, 221,
    266, 281, 286
Demophilos 86, 267
Denarius 189, 192
Dentils 56, 57
Design xv, xvi, 6n., 14, 16, 24, 62, 84,
    143, 149, 150, 244
Dewar, Michael xiv, 1n., 76n.
Diades 86, 130–131, 267, 311, 312
Diagram 31, 50, 66, 68, 107, 108, 143
Dialectic 7
Diathyra 83
Dicaearchus of Messana 139, 165
Dice 63
Didyma 136, 193, 199
Dies brumales 113
Diesis 67
Dimensions xiii, xvi, 72, 76, 78, 150
Dining rooms 80, 91, 256, 272; see also
    Oecus; Triclinia
Dinocrates 33, 173, 174
Diodorus Siculus 173
Diognetus of Rhodes 14n., 133–134,
    315
Diomedes 28
Dionysodorus 116
Diopter 103, 277
Diphilos 86, 267
Disciplina Etrusca 152, 154
Disciplinae 7, 142
Disciplines 35, 46, 87, 142
Discoveries 107–109
Discus Thrower 142
Dispositio 14, 24, 143, *145*, 149, 150, 235
Distributio 14, 151
Divination 152
Dnieper, river 98
Doctors 5, 138, 142
Dominus 256
Domus 11, 249, 256, 292
    of Marcus Aemilius Scaurus 11n., 292n.
Don, river 98
Doors, 59–60, 79, 80, 83, 233
Doorways 59–60, 79, 82, 83, *231*, *232*,
    258
Dorians 55
Doric column type 16, 54, 55, 57–58,
    225, *226*
    angle conflict 221, *222*

Augustan *225*
Egyptian origin 218, 220
flutes *224*
invention 54–55
Republican *225*
symmetries *223*, *226*
wooden origin 218, *219*, 220
Dorus 54
Doubling the cube 143, *282*
Doubling the square 107, *282*
Draftsmanship 7, 8, 22, 23
Drainage 71
Drama 70, 245
Drawings xvi, 149, 193
Dura Europos *157*
Durability; see Firmitas; Soundness
Dyrrachium 100

Earth 109, 114, 156n.
    circumference 16, 30, 31, 167, 169,
        283
    creation of 14
    curvature of 104
Echea 13n., 17, 23, 67–68, 138, 245, *246*
Eclecticism 18
Ecliptic 138, 256
Ecole des Beaux-Arts 149
Editions, printed xiii, xiv, 19
    1511 xiii, xiv, 19, 150n.
    1522 xiv, 19
Education 7–8, 13, 21–24, 75, 76, 119,
    135, 249
Egypt 3, 33, 59, 76, 93, 100, 114, 167n.,
    173, 230, 268
Egyptians 96, 167
Ekklêsiasterion 268
Ekphorá 51, 52
Elements xv, 27, 33, 35, 37, 39, 43, 96,
    105, 138, 163, 173, 176, 177, 178,
    256
Elephantis 98
Eleusis
    Telesterion 87, 266, 268
Elevation 24, 25, 149
Elm 43
Elpias the Rhodian 28
Embatêr 57, 150, 221
Emendation 235; see also Conjectures
Empedocles xv, 96, 138, 173, 275, 283
Emplekton 12, 40, *161*
Encaustic 268
Encyclios disciplina; see Arts, liberal
Engineer 14, 15
Enkyklios paideia 7

Ennius 2, 109, 156n.
Entasis 16n., 50, 53, 58, 193, *199*, 211,
    221, 229n.
Entertainment 82
Environment xv, 178, 179
Ephesus 44, 54, 92, 93, 94, 119, 122,
    136, *157*, 213
    statue of Diana 44
    temple of Diana 44, 86, 87, 122, 173
Epicharmos 96, 275
Epicurean philosophy 135, 136
Epicurus 35, 75, 85, 177, 266
Epicycles xv
Epidaurus 213
    Tholos 213, 215
Epidemics 29
Epigrams 102
Epimachus of Athens 14n., 133, 311
Epistyles, Ionic xvi n., 207, 208
Eptabolos, Lake 98
Equestrian class 5
Equilibrium 27
Equinoxes 23, 109, 112, 114, 115, 283
    precession of 283
Eratosthenes of Cyrene 16, 24, 30, 31,
    108, 139, 143, 166, 167, 169, 266,
    281, 282, 283
Erechtheion 61, 136, *137*
Erismae 266
Erythrae 54, 101
Ether 111
Ethiopia 100
Ethiopians 98
Etruria 38, 44, 45, 100
Etruscan 167n., 229
Etruscans 12, 151, 152
Euclemon 115, 286
Euclid 143, 189, 229
Eucrates 75, 249
Eudoxus of Cnidus 115, 116, 140, 177,
    286
Eumenes, king of Pergamum 71, 266
    Eumenes II 266
Euphranor 86
Euphrates, river 98
Eureka! 108
Euripides, tragedian 96, 101, 111, 266,
    275
    Phaethon 111
Eurythmia 14, 25, 143, *147*, 149, 150,
    189, 213n., 244
Exedrae 73, 79, 82, 91, 93, *259*
Expense 22, 65, 84, 119, 151
Extravagance 92

Faberius 93
Failure 16
Faliscan 101
Fame 75
Fano 4, 5, 6, 11, 13, 16, 17, 44, 64, 235
    forum 64
    Temple of Jupiter 64
Faventinus, Marcus Cetius 2, 7
Favonius 188
Favor 46, 75, 76
Fensterbusch, Kurt xiv
Ferentum 39
Festus 65n., 156n.
Finitores 151
Fir 43
Fire 11, 38, 42, 74
    discovery 34
Fire brigades 6n., 10, 18n.
Firmament 83, 109, 110, 111, 112, 114
    inclination 77, 78, 101, 103
    rotation 111, 114
Firmitas 14
Fleury, Philippe 125n., 132n.
Floors 87–88, *269*
    suspended 72
Flutes, column 16n., 53, 58, 209, 211,
    221, 224, 228
Foot 213n. , 214
    Greek 167n.
    Roman 167n., 189, *190*, 192
Formia 2
Fornix 12, 13
Fortification 17, 27, 29, 156, *158*, *159*,
    160, *161*, *162*, 297
    Hellenistic xvi, 156, *158*, 297
    Roman xvi
Forum 63–64, 119, *153*, 235, *239*, 256
    Augustum 136, *137*
    Boarium 156n.
    of Caesar 3, 49
    Greek 64, *239*
    Holitorium 4
    Italic 64, *239*
    Romanum 3, 4, 8, 10, 11, 119, 152n.,
        193, 215, 292
Foundation of cities 151
Foundations 13n., 50–51, 65, 74, 83,
    156, *161*, 193, 200, *264*, 266
    Etruscan 193
    Greek 193
    Imperial 193
    Republican 193
Fountains 104, 125, *279*
Fractions, unitary xvi
France xiv

Fresco 82, 89–90, 91–92, 95, 249, 268
Frieze xvi n.
    Doric 56, 57, 58, *212*, 220, 221, 223,
        224, *225*
    Ionic 52–53, 56–57, 202, 207
Frontinus, Sextus Julius 6, 7, 10, 17n.,
    179, 229, 277, 281
Fufius 86, 267
Fulvius Nobilior, Marcus 10
Function 25, 79, 84, 151; see also
    Thematismos
Fundi 2, 101

Gades 130, 297
Gaeta 2
Galen 143, 167, 178, 188
Galleries, picture 25, 79, 80, 81, 82, 256,
    259
Gallia 4, 5
    Belgica 4, 5
    Celtica 4, 5
    Cisalpina 6, 27, 98
    Lugdunensis 5
    Narbonensis 5; also see Gaul
Games 4, 64, 107, 119, 235, 249, 281,
    292
Ganôsis 94, 268
Gardens 10, 11, 71, 80, 81, 124
Gates xv, 17, 156, *158*, *160*
Gaul 4, 5, 6, 34, 86n., 95, 98
Genres xiii
Genus xiii , 11, 15, 16, 138, 214, 235,
    244, 245, 257, 292
Geography xv, 138, 167, 275, 277
Geology 177
Geometry xvi n., 7, 8, 22, 24, 129, 143,
    229
Geras of Carthage 130
Gerasimus 7n.
Giocondo, Fra Giovanni x, xiii, xiv, 19,
    38n., 51n., 63n., 64n., 66n., 76n.,
    90n., 97n., 99n., 109n., 126n.,
    131n., 132n., 150n., 235
Gladiators 64, 119, 235, 239, 249, 292
Globe 109
Gnomon 30, 109, 114, 115, 167n., *168*,
    170, 286
Gnomonics 26, 109
Goiter 102
Golden Mean 249n.
Gortyna 27
Gracchi 1, 192n.
Grammar 7, 8
Grammaticus 8, 135, 142, 143
Granaries 26, 80, 81

Granger, Frank xiv, 19, 64n., 74n., 76n.,
    81n., 100n.
Gravitas xiii
Greece 6, 7, 12, 22, 54, 68, 77, 142, 283
Greek xiii, 17, 20, 66, 75, 82, 83, 86,
    86n., 94, 100n., 102, 103, 108,
    109, 167n., 266, 283, 292
Greeks 12, 17, 47, 50, 63, 64, 69, 73, 75,
    77, 80, 82, 83, 91, 109, 138, 183,
    256, 281
Green, malachite 92, 94
Grid 14, 167, 170, 173
Groma 152, 167, *170*
Gymnasium 249, *253*
Gynaeconitis 82, 256, *263*

Half-timbering (*opus craticium*) 10, 11,
    12, 42, 90, *186*, *271*
Halicarnassus 6, 40–41, 184, *185*, 266
Handbook 1
Hannibal 192
Harbors 73
Harmony 15n., 24, 66, 67, 69, 77, 84,
    143, 151, 188, 244, *255*
Harp xv, *255*
Haruspices 155
Haterii, family of contractors 14, 295
Hauling 16, *299*
Heads of Households; see *Paterfamilias*
Health 25, 29, 42, 71, 101, 102, 103,
    105, 143, 151, 152, 153, 167, 178,
    188, 281
Heat, attractive power xv, 179, 283
Hegesias, of Magnesia or Maroneia 103,
    277
Hegetor of Byzantium 132, 297, 314
Hegias of Athens 46, 188
Height, of buildings 142
Heliocentrism 283
Helios 111
Hellen 54
Hellenistic culture xv, 7
Heraclea 122
Heracleides of Pontus 284
Heraclitus "The Obscure" of Ephesus 35,
    96, 179, 275
Herculaneum 1, 253
Heredium 167, 170
Hermodorus of Salamis 5, 14, 17, 48,
    192, 267, 268
Hermogenes 5, 6n., 13, 14, 17, 48, 49,
    57, 86, 146, 149, 192, 195, 221, 267
Herodotus of Halicarnassus 103, 275, 277
Hero (Heron) of Alexandria 163n., 166,
    277, 292, 296, 297

Herringbone tilework 88; see also Opus
    spicatum
Hierapolis 100
Hieron of Syracuse 108, 281
"High Style" xiii, 15
Himera 297
Himeras, river 100
Hipparchus of Nicaea xvi n., 115, 141,
    277, 283n., 286
Hippocrates of Chios 282
Hippocrates of Cos 23, 136, 142, 165,
    167, 173, 178n.
Hippopotami 99
Hispania 34, 36, 76, 93, 94
Historia 135, 173, 175
History 8, 17n., 22, 63, 135, 175, 275,
    277, 283
    early Roman 17n.
Hodometer 127–128, 307
Homer 2, 86, 266
Horace 4, 5, 6n., 7, 188, 275
Horizon 77, 115, 116, 152, 163
Hornbeam 43
Horoscopes 115, 283
Horti; see also Gardens 11
Hortulorum, Collis 10
Hospitalia 69, 263
Hostilius, Marcus 28
Hours 109, 112, 113, 116, 117, 283
Houses xvi, 12, 25, 26, 35, 75–84, 256,
    262, 292
    of Augustus 2, 3
    Country xvi, 16, 26, 81–82
    Greek xvi, 82–83, 256, 263
    Pompeiian 256
    Pseudourban 81
    Roman xvi, 75–82
    of Romulus 35, 175
Humors 167
Huts 4, 34–35, 175
Hybrid temples 61–62
Hydraulic devices 23, 117–118
Hydraulics 16
Hygiene 151
Hyginus, astronomer 283
Hyginus Gromaticus 154, 163, 167, 170,
    172, 229
Hymettus, Mount 40
Hypanis, river (Bug) 93, 98, 100

Ichneumons 99
Ichnography 24–25, 145, 149, 150n.
Ictinus 86, 87, 213, 266
Illustrations xiii, xv, 15, 22, 31, 50, 66,
    68, 70, 125, 245, 281

Illyricum 3
Imagery 3
Imagines 79
Imitation 56, 57, 64, 91, 109, 114, 120
Imperator 10, 21, 33, 44, 46, 54, 119, 135
Imperium 151
Inclination
    of columns 204
    of the cosmos 77, 78, 101, 103, 114,
        138, 177n., 256, 275, 286
Inclined plane 292, 294
India 94, 98, 100
Indigo 94, 275
Indus, river 98
Inertia 163
Influence 21, 46
Inlay 91
    fresco 90
    stone; see also Opus sectile 88
Innovation xv, 5, 16, 18
Inscriptions 267
Instruments 120
Insulae 10, 14, 30, 41–42, 186, 188
Integers 47
Intelligence, divine 21, 77, 109, 114, 115
Interest, readers' xii, 63
Interiors 25, 78–79
    domestic 78–79, 257
    temple 58–59
Interpolation 16
Intervals, musical 15n., 24, 66, 67, 138,
    143, 144, 189, 244, 245, 255
Invention (*inventio*) 15n., 16, 17, 25, 77,
    107–109, 116, 117, 119, 126–127,
    143, 149, 175
Iollas 101
Ion 54, 55
Ionia 55
Ionian League 54
Ionic column type 16, 51–53, 54, 55
    invention of 55
    wooden origins 219
Ismuc 102
Isocrates 266
Italy xiv
Iugerum 167, 170

Jail 65
Jetties 74
Joppa 100
Juba of Numidia 6, 102, 275
Julius, Gaius, son of Masinissa 6n., 103,
    275
Juniper 44
Jupiter (planet) 77, 110, 111

Justice 107

K 156n.
Kermes 95, 275
Kitchen 81
Knowledge xv, 143
    scientific xv
    technical xv
    unity of xv
Krohn, Friedrich xiv
Kydna 158

Laconicum ("Spartan sauna") 72, 94, 249,
    251, 253
Lacus Iuturnae 156n.
Lakes 100
Landscape 91
Language xiii, 15n., 34, 83, 275
Laodicaea 101
Larch 17, 44
Larignum 6, 44, 188
Latin xiii, xiv, 13n., 15, 83, 109, 126n.,
    156n., 266
    plebeian 286
Latium 2
Latitude 138, 140, 141, 167, 177, 255,
    283
Laurentum 11
Lavinium 11
Law 7, 22, 23, 41, 85, 107, 119, 142
Law courts xiii, 16n., 85
Lawyers 80
Lead 94, 102, 104, 105, 275
    poisoning 105, 281
    white 94, 102, 105
Leleges 41, 55
Lemnos 93
Leochares 40, 86, 267
Leonidas 86
Lepidus, Marcus Aemilius 3, 10
Lesbos 29, 101
Leuctra 136
Level 103–104, 277, 278
Liberal education xv, 5, 7, 75, 249
Libraries 5, 25, 80, 81, 82, 235, 256,
    260, 266
    of Alexandria 85, 142, 266
    in Atrium Libertatis 151
    of Pergamum 85, 266
    in Porticus Octavia 135
    private 1, 2, 5, 256
    public 2, 151
Licymnius 92, 268
Lighting 25, 82, 262
Lime 37, 39, 88, 89, 90, 179–180, 270

Liming 106
Limitatio 163, *170*, *172*
Limites 170; see also Boundaries
Limestone 37
Linden 43
Liparis, river 100
Literature 22
Lituus *154*
Liver divination 18, 27, 152, *155*
Livia 10
Livy 152n., 186
Logic 7
Logos 292
Longitude 167
"Low Style" xiii
Loxotomus 116
Lucania 101
Lucian 296
Lucifer 110
Lucretius (Titus Lucretius Carus) 16, 17,
    50n., 109, 135, 138, 173, 177, 235,
    281
Lucullus, Lucius Licinius 11, 292
Ludi Actiaci 281
Ludi Saeculares 4
Lusitania 34
Lyceum 249, 275
Lydia 101
Lyncestus 101
Lysimachus of Thrace 213
Lysippus 46, 186, 189, 213n.

Macedon 10, 33, 86, 94, 101, 297
Machines 73, 89, 108, 116, 118,
    119–134, 138
    classification 119–120
    hydraulic 116
    mounting 119, 120
    pneumatic 119, 120, 138
    tractor 119, 120
Madder 95
Magi 96
Magister ludi 8
Magistrates 14, 63, 64, 81, 119, 256
Magnesia 48, 86, 92, 102
Magnificence 120
Maintenance
    of temples 10
    of water pipes 277
Maiores 17n., 18
Maison Carrée *238*
Malachite 94
Mamurra 2
Management 25–26
Manilius 235, 283, 286

Mantinea *157*
Mantua 151, 163, 172
Manuscripts xiii, xiv, 4, 19, 20, 38n.,
    39n., 51n., 55n., 60n., 63n., 64n.,
    66n., 73n., 74n., 76n., 86n., 90n.,
    95n., 97n., 99n., 100n., 105n.,
    106n., 113n., 114n., 118n., 126n.,
    131n., 134n., 150n., 235, 245, 267,
    268, 277, 281, 286, 292, 296
    G (Gudianus 69) 19, 66n., 81n., 83n.,
        86n., 90n., 104n., 108n., 109n.
    H (Harleianus 2767) 19, 66n., 76n.,
        81n., 83n., 86n., 90n., 100n., 104n.,
        108n., 109n., 113n.
Maps 138, *139*, 151–152, 167, 275, *276*
Marble 2, 10, 40, 55, 87, 92, 122, 296
Marcellus, Marcus Claudius 2
Mariana 48
Marius, Gaius 1, 13n., 48, 87, 268
Marketplaces 73
Mars (planet) 77, 110, 111
Martial 1, 14
Martianus Capella 152
Masinissa 6n., 193, 275
Masonry 11n., 12, 13n., 17n., 36–40,
    41–42, 72, 84, 100, 104, *161*, 179,
    182, *183*, 184
    brick 40–41
    emplêkton 40, *161*, *182*, 184
    Greek 39–40, *182*, 184
    isodomic 40, *182*, 184
    pseudoisodomic 40, *182*, 184
    styles 39–40, *181*, *182*
Massilia (Marseilles) 6, 8, 34, 134, *316*,
    317
Materials, building 2, 10, 29, 33–45, 84,
    142
Mathematics 7, 24, 66, 67, 108, 112,
    115, 116, 143, 150, 189, 229,
    244n., 282, 283
Matter 26, 179
Mauretania 98, 99, 275
Mausoleum
    of Augustus 3, 10, *265*
    of Halicarnassus 5, 40, 86, 142, 184,
        185, 188, 266, 267
Mausolus 40, 184
Mazaca 100
Maeonia 101
Measure, units of *148*, 150, 167, 189,
    190, 192
Measurement 22, 25, 47, 48, 167, 189
Mechanics 119, 292
Medicine 7, 8n., 16, 22, 23, 136, 138,
    142, 177, 178, 179, 267

rational 16, 138, 142, 152
Mediterranean 163, *164*, 276
Medulli 102
Melampus, author 86
Melampus, hero 102
Melas, colonist 41
Melas, river 101
Melinum 93
Melite 54
Melos 93
Memory 22, 23, 24, 63, 85, 87, 95, 109,
    135, 143, 235
Menaeus 116
Menesthenes 49, 192
Mercury (element) 93
Mercury (planet) 110
Meroë 98, 167
Mesauloe 83
Mesolabe 108, 281, *282*
Metagenes, son of Chersiphron 16, 86,
    87, 122, 267, 299
Metapontum 163
Metellus Macedonicus, Quintus Caecil-
    ius 5, 10
Meton 115, 283, 286
Metope 53, 56–57, *58*, 221
    split 221
Metrodorus of Skepsis 103, 275
"Middle Style" xiii
Mile 167n.
Miletus 54, 173, 213, *239*, 267
Milo of Croton 107, 281
Mime 245
Mining 28, 132, 134, 297
Mint 193
Minucius Rufus, Marcus 10
Mithridatic War 71
"Mixed Orders" 211, 213
Mixture of elements; see Temperament
Moats 131, 134
Models 133
Modes, musical 67
Modillion cornice *215*, 218, *219*
Modular design 14, 87, 149, 150
Modulation, musical 66–67
    chromatic 66–67, 68, 244, 245
    diatonic 66–67, 68, 244, 245
    enharmonic 66–67, 68, 244, 245
Module 49, 57, 129, 149, 150, *187*, 189,
    221
Moldings xvi n.
Moles 73–74, *254*
Monades 47
Moneychangers 64
Moneylenders 26, 80

Monopteroe 61
Monsters 91
Month, lunar 110, 112
Moon 83, 110, 111–112, 115, 120, 138
Morgan, Morris Hicky xiv
Mortar 12, 39, 40
Mos maiorum 18n.
Mosaic 88
Motion 163n., 177, 235
    celestial *284*, 286
    circular 119, 122–124, 292, *293*, 296,
        300
    instrumental (organic) 120, 292
    linear 122–124, 296, *300*
    mechanical 120, 292
    planetary *284*, 286
Mucius, Quintus, Roman architect for
        Gaius Marius 48, 87, 192, 268
Mucius Scaevola, Gaius 13n., 268
Mucius Scaevola, Quintus 13n.
Mud brick 10, 11, 12, 29, 36, 40, 100,
        180, *181*, *187*
Müller-Strübing, Hermann xiv
Mummius, Lucius 68, 245
Munatius Plancus 3
Mundus 109, 177
Murus gallicus 17, 156, *161*
Muses 108
Music xiii, 7, 8, 15n., 22, 23, 24, 66–67,
        69, 130, 143, 244, 245
    of the spheres 143, *255*
    theory 7, 66–67, 143, 235, 244
Myagrus 188
Mycale, Mount 213
Myron of Athens 23, 46, 142, 188, 296
Mylasa 40, 184
Myrrh 101
Mysia 38
Myth 17
Mytilene 29
Myus 54

Naples 2, *168*
    Bay of 11
Narrative xiii
Nature 25, 39, 47, 57, 66, 67, 76, 77, 78,
        85, 109, 114, 115, 120, 151, 283
    as architect 109
Naulochoi 3
Near East 12
Neologisms 13n., 15n.
Nero 12, 188
Nexaris 86, 267
Nicomachus 189
Nigidius Figulus 286

Nile 33, 59, 98–99, 173, 230, 275
Nîmes 277
Nitrous springs 99–100
Nonacris 101
North, true 167, 168
Notes, musical 66, 67, 77, 244–245, 255
Numbers xiii, 107, 281
    irrational xvi n., 107, 150, 281
    perfect 16, 47–48, 189
Numerals, Hindu-Arabic xvi
Numidia 6n., 100, 275
Nymphodorus 86
Nymphs 102

Oak 43, 87
Ocean 99
Ochre 91, 92–93, 94
    burnt 38, 94
Octavia 2, 6, 21, 135
Octavian (Gaius Julius Caesar Octa-
        vianus; see also Augustus) 2, 3, 4,
        6, 8, 135, 275, 297
Octavius, Gaius 3
Octavius, Gnaeus 10
Oecus 79–80, 82, 83, 256, *259*
    Corinthian 79–80, *259*
    Cyzicene 80, 82, *259*
    Egyptian 11, 79–80, *259*
    tetrastyle 79–80, *259*
Oil room 81
Olbia 167
Olive press 81
Olympia 253
Olympic Games 281
Olynthus 12n.
Opimius, Lucius 10
Oppida 38n.
Optics 16, 22, 24, 52–53, 78, 202, 221,
        229
Opus africanum *186*
Opus caementicium 11, 12, *182*, *186*
Opus craticium 10, 11, 12, 13n., 42, 90,
        186, *271*
Opus incertum 12, 39, 180, *182*
Opus reticulatum 11, 39, 180n., *182*,
        184
Opus sectile 88
Opus signinum 37, 73, 106, 184, 266,
        281
Opus spicatum tiburtinum 88, 268
Opus testaceum 11n., 17, 268
Opus vittatum 12n., *182*
Oracles 46, 54, 108
Orators 73, 81, 143
Oratory 8

Orbits 110, 111, 112, 113, 177n., *255*,
        284
Orchestra 69, 70
Order 18, 45, 54, 56, 57, *145*, 149n.
    of the *Ten Books* 35, 45, 54, 63, 87,
        127, 143
Ordering 24
"Orders" xiii, 12n., 14, 15, 16, 150; see
        also Types
Ordinatio 14, 15, 24, *145*, *146*, 149, 150
Organ, water 23
Oribasius 167
Orientation xvi, 29–31, 59, 76, 80,
        152n., 163, 165, 166, 167, 168,
        229, 230, 251, 260, 261
Ornament 22, 54, 55, 56–57, 70, 87,
        143, 211, 218
    origin 218
Orpiment 93
Orthography 24, 25, 149
Ostia 12, 156, 275
Oven 82
Ovid 4, 245

Paconius 16, 122, 296, *299*
Padus, river 98; see also Po
Paeonius of Ephesus 87, 267, 296
Paestum *157*, 173, 213
Painters 80, 83, 267
Painting 7, 23, 83, 89–90, 95, 213n.
    correctness in 91–92
Paints 89–90; see also Pigments
Palaestra xvi, 16, 73, 122, 249, *253*, 299
Palatine 10, 11, 152n., 156n., 175, 217,
        265
Palla 38, 39
Palladio, Andrea xvi, 15
Palladius 7n.
Panaetius 136
Pantheon *147*, 150, 237
    of Agrippa 136, *237*
Pantry 82
Paphlagonia 102
Papyrus 1n., 44, 266
Paraetonium 93, 100
Parchment 266
Parma 172
Parmenides 140
Parmenion 116
Paros 122
Parthenon 86, 221n.
Parti *146*, 149
Party walls 40, 41, 82
Pastas 82, *263*
Paterfamilias 8, 13n., 76, 80, 83, 84, 138

Patrae 40
Patrician 13
Patrocles 116
Patrons 92
Pausanias, Spartan general 22, 136
Pausanias, travel writer 136
Pavement 88
Pax Augusta 1, 3, 235
Pedagogue 8
Pella 256
Peloponnese 54
Pentaspastos 121
Pentele, Mount 40
Peoples 76–77, 78
Pephrasmenos of Tyre 130
Pepper 101
Pergamum 85, 142, 218, 256, 266, 277
    library 85, 266
Periaktoi 69, 245
Peripteroe 61
Peristyle (*peristylion*) 73, 79, 80, 81, 82,
    83, 91, 93, 256, 259, 260
    Rhodian 82, 263
Perrault, Claude 73n.
Persia 22, 102
Persian Wars 22, 71, 136
Perspective 149, 229, 266
Pesaro (Pisaurum) 44, 165
Petrarch xiii
Pharsalus 317
Phidias 46, 188
Philadelphus, Ptolemy 86
Philander (edition of 1540) 81n., 97n.,
    108n., 113n.
Philip II of Macedon, son of Amyntas
    130, 267, 297
Philip V of Macedon 297
Philippi 151
Philippus 115
Philo of Athens 86, 87, 266
Philo of Byzantium (Philo Mechanicus)
    17n., 86, 156, 163n., 267, 297
Philodemus of Gadara 136
Philolaos of Tarentum 24, 143, 189
Philosophers 73, 85, 96, 143, 268, 277
Philosophy 7, 8, 22–23, 75, 135, 136,
    142, 143, 177, 188, 249, 255, 277
    moral 136, 266
    natural or physical xv, 22–23, 24, 35,
        85, 96, 135, 136, 138, 142, 173,
        177, 178, 249, 266, 275
Phocaea 54
Phrygia 100, 175
Phrygians 34

Phthia 54
Physicists 78, 85
Physics 163
Physiology 22, 138, 167
Pi 296
Piacenza liver 152, 155
Picenum 38
Piers 13n., 41, 74, 83
Pigments 7, 92–95
    substitute 95
Pile drivers 193n., 254
Pilings 43, 51, 74, 193, 254
Pinacothecae; see Galleries
Pincio 10
Pine 43–44
Pinna Vestina 99
Pipes, water 6n., 10, 17, 79, 104–105,
    280, 281
    ceramic 105, 279
    lead 104–105, 277, 279, 281
Piraeus 86, 100
    Arsenal of Philo 86, 266
Pisistratus 87, 267
Piso, Lucius Calpurnius 1
Pit sand 13n., 25, 36–37
Pitane 36
Pixodarus 122
Placentia 109, 283
Plagiarism 85
Plan 22, 24, 149, 235, 268
Planning 173
    Greek 173
    Hellenistic 173
    Roman 173
Planets; see Stars
Plaster 36, 37, 40, 42, 88–91, 93, 249,
    268, 271
    in damp locations 90–91, 272
    Greek 90
Plataea 22, 136
Plato 47, 85, 107, 189, 221, 229, 266,
    281, 282, 286
Plautus 14
    Miles Gloriosus 14
Pleiades 83
Pliny the Elder 6, 7, 55n., 138, 167,
    184n., 188, 266, 267
Plumbers 6, 17n.
Pluteus 235
Pneuma 178
Pneumatics 116–117, 120, 138
Pneumatikon 119, 120
Po, river 44, 98, 156, 163, 173
Podium 51, 69, 193, 200

Poetry 63, 109, 135, 235
Poets 75, 281
Points, cardinal 163
Pole Star 114, 286
Poles (*poloi*) 109, 140
Police 6, 10
Polishing 88, 89, 268
Pollarding 43
Pollio, Gaius Asinius 2
Pollis 86
Polycleitus of Argos 23, 46, 142, 188,
    189, 190, 213, 267
Polycles of Cyzicus 46, 188
Polyidos 267
Polyspastos 121
Pompeii 2, 12, 38, 215, 217, 225, 239,
    250, 251, 253, 256, 273, 274, 279
Pompey (Gnaeus Pompeius Magnus) 3,
    5, 8, 10, 11, 136, 317
Pompey, Sextus 3
Pomptine Marshes 28, 156
Pontedera (Polenus edition of 1825–30)
    60n.
Pontus 34, 76, 93, 98, 100
Pools, public 104
Poplar 43
Population 64
Pores 65
Porinos 87
Porta Collina 48
Porticoes 64, 6, 71–72, 73, 82, 83,
    213n., 249, 250
    of Eumenes 71
    of Pompey 71, 249, 250
Porticus Aemilia 12
    Liviae 10, 11
    Metelli 2, 4, 5, 10, 48, 213n., 268
    Minucia 10
    Octavia 2, 10, 135, 213n.
    Octavii 213n.
    Vipsania 275
Ports 73–74, 156, 254
Posidonius of Apamaea 103, 136, 140,
    275, 277
Posotês 24, 145, 146
Potassium nitrate 94
Pound 189
Pozzolana 12n., 37–38, 73–74, 180
Practice 13, 21, 135
Praeneste 12
Praetor 4, 119, 281, 292
Praxiteles of Athens 86, 136n., 188, 267
Precepts 1
Preface 3, 4, 5

Prescriptions xvi
Presses 124
Pressure 119, 120
    water 22, 105, 277
Prestige 26
Priene 5, 23, 86, 142, *157*, 173, *239*,
    253, 262
Priests 96, 152
Principles xvi, 25, 26, 27, 33, 47, 68, 71,
    80, 81, 95, 105, 116
    of correctness 80–81, 91–92
    first 35, 96, 173, 177, 293
    of mechanics 119, 293
    of symmetry 35, 54, 55
Privacy 83
Proconnesus 122
Proetus 102
Professionalism 7n., 8, 13, 14, 76, 142
Program xvi
Progress 16, 17
Projection 91
Promenades; see Walkways
Pronuntiatio 143; see also Delivery
Proportion xvi, 14, 17, 21, 25, 26, 27, 31,
    33, 45, 47, 49, 51, 53, 55, 57, 64, 69,
    71, 78, 79, 80, 87, 128, 142, 150,
    188, 189, 192, 213, 214, 229n., 258
Pros orthas 115, 116
Prostas 82, *263*
Protagoras 177
Prothyra 83
Provinces 21, 68
Ptolemy, astronomer 141, 144, 277, 283,
    285
Ptolemy, king of Egypt 85, 86, 266
    Ptolemy I Sôtêr 266
    Ptolemy V Epiphanes 266
Public spaces 31–32, *260*
Public works 120
Publication 1, 4, 21, 85
Pumice 36, 38
Purple 92, 95
Puteoli 12n., 94, 180n., 268
Pyrrhus of Epirus 267
Pythagoras of Rhegium, artist 188
Pythagoras of Samos, philosopher 63,
    107–108, 115, 143, *189*, *209*, 235,
    255, 266, 275, 281, 286
Pythagorean Theorem 108, 281, *282*
Pythagoreans 35, 63, 143, 173, 189
Pytheas of Massilia 169
Pytheos 5, 23, *23*, 57, 86, 142, 146, 195,
    221, 266, 267
Pythian priestess 46

Quadrivium 7n.
Quantity 24
Quarries 38, 39, 100, 122
Quartering 18n., 152, *154*
Quicksilver 93
Quintilian 8n., 15n., 17n., 142
Quirinal hill 268

Raeder, J. 256
Ramparts, 157
Raphael 15
Ratio 16, 138, 292
Ravenna 27, 43, 44
Rays 235, 283
    equinoctial 116
    solar 109, 110, 115, 284, 285
    visual 14n., 16, 78, 86, *228*, 229
Reading 63, 76, 235
Reasoning 21, 24, 61, 78, 135
Reconstructions xvi
Records 163
Refinements, architectural 221n., 229
Reggio Emilia 172
Regia 3, 215
Regions 76
    of heaven 22, 27, 76, 80, 81, 103,
    152, 155, 165, 230, 275
Religion xv, 18, 26, 151
    Etruscan 18n., 152
Remus 152n.
Renaissance xiv
Republic, Roman 1, 3, 8, 14, 18, 26, 292
Reputation 22, 75
Reservoir; see *Castellum aquae*
Resources 25–26
Retrograde motion xv, 110, 111, 114,
    283, *285*, 286
Revolution, of the stars 83, 110, 114
Rhenus, river 98
Rhetor 8
Rhetoric xiii, 1, 3, 7, 8, 15, 17n., 46,
    109, 135, 143
Rhetorica ad Herennium 8n.
Rhine, river 98
Rhineland *limes* 156
Rhodanus, river 98
Rhodes 8, 14n., 41, 75, 94, 95, 115,
    133–134, 156, 165, 167, 184, 297,
    315, 317
Rhoecus, architect 266
Rhone, river 98
Rhythm 143
Rhythmos 149
Ritual 151, 152

    sacrificial 62, 152
Rivers 98
Roads 59, *156*, 230
Rode, A. von 95n.
Rollers 122
Roma Quadrata 154, 156n.
Roman People 21, 28, 77, 104, 119
Rome 109, 115
    reconstruction *9*
    regions *11*
Romulus 35, 152n., 156n.
Roof
    double-ridged 16, 64, *242*
Roof tiles 209
Rooms
    private *260*
    public *260*
Rose, Valentin xiv, 19, 50n., 60n., 106n.,
    118n., 150n.
Rostra xiii
Rotation
    of the firmament 120, 256, 275
    of the stars 110, 112, 120, 275
Rubble 38, 39
Rubblework 11, 39, 41, 180
Rubicon, river 317
Rubrics 21n.
Rules 11
Rutilius Rufus, Publius 1

Sacrifice 62, 102, 108, 152
Saepta Julia 249
Sages 107, 109, 115
    Seven 96
Salmacis, fountain of 40–41
Salpia 6n., 28, 156
Salutatio 249, 256
Sambucae (storming bridges) 131, 134,
    297, *315*
Sambykê 77, *255*, 256, 297
Samos 86
Sand 25, 36–37, 38, 39, 179
    excavated (=pit sand) 13n., 25, 36–37
Sangallo, Giuliano da 225
Sapping 156; see also Mining
Sardis 40
Sarnacus 86
Saturn (planet) 77, 110, 111
Satyrus 86, 266
Saxa Rubra 38, 39
Scaenae frons 69
Scaenographia *145*, 149
Scale 24, 25, 65, 150
Scales, musical *243*, 244

Scamilli impares 51, 71, 193, *201*, 202
Scansorium 119
Scenography (scene painting) 24, 25, 86, *145*, 149, 245
Scholasticus 8
Scholars xiv
School, grammar 8
Schott 100n.
Schramm 129n.
Science 18, 42, 109, 115, 135, 138, 229, 286
   Ancient 15, 17, 18, 34, 177
   Hellenistic 18n.
   Modern 15, 138
Scipio Aemilianus, Publius Cornelius 136
Scipionic circle 7
Scopas 86, 267
Scopinas of Syracuse 24, 116, 143
Scorpiones 23, 120, 124, 128, 138, 292, 296, 297, *308*
Scriba, Faberius 6n.
Scribes xiv, 1
Scriptorium 1
Scroll 1n., 44
Sculptors 86, 213n., 267
Sculpture 7, 23, 229
Sea 109
Seasons 115, 177n., 179, 283, 284
Seats 69, 70, 73, 119, 235
Segesta 202
Selinus 297
Semiramis 100
Senate 1, 3, 21, 28, 249
Senate and People of Rome (S.P.Q.R.) 28, 92
Senate House xiii, 65; see also Curia
Senator 11, 69
Senatorial rank 292
Seneca, Lucius Annaeus 14
Sensory experience 16
Septimius, Publius 87, 267
Sequences, proportional 32, 47, 62
Servants' quarters 82
Servian Wall 179
Service 26, 82, 109, 120
Service, military 8
Servius 7
Set square 107–108, 115, 266
Sets, theatrical 70, 78, 91, 92, 245
Seven Sages 96
Seven Wonders of the World 40, 86
Sextus Empiricus 135
Shadows 109, 114, 115

Shapeliness 24, 25, 78, *147*, 149; see also *Eurythmia*
Ship sheds 73, 74
Ships 25, 73, 74, 78, 122, 123, 127–128, 131, 134, 296, *298*, *300*
Shops 11n.
Sicily 3, 12n., 100, 101, 277
Sidonius Apollinaris 7
Siege engines 130–133, *311*, *312*, *313*
   of Diades 130–131, *311*, *312*
   of Vitruvius and his teachers 131–132
Siegecraft 5, 267, 297, *315*, *316*, *317*; see also War machines
Signbearing circle; see Zodiac
"Signified" and "Signifier" 22, 135
Sight 78
Silanion 86
Silenus, author 86, 266
Silex 37, 38, 97, 102, 180
Silphium 101
Simas 209, *211*
Sinope 93
Siphons, inverted 277, 280; see also "Belly"
Siting 26, 31–32, 65, 70, 71, 72, 81, 151, *153*, *157*, 167
Six, as perfect number 47–48, 189
Sixteen, as perfect number 48, 189
Skill 120
Skiothêrês 30
Slaves 14
Slope, of aqueducts 277
Smyrna 54, 71, 86, 93
Social wars 156
Socrates 46, 85, 249, 266, 281
Socratics 75
Soli 100
Solstice 23, 109, 112, 116, 118, *141*, 163
Solunto 12n.
Sophists 7
Sophocles 173n.
Soracte 38
Sosius, Gaius 3
Soubiran, Jean 109n.
Sounding vessels; see *Echea*
Soundness 26, 83, 87, 90, 95; see also *Firmitas*
Space 177
Spacing, of columns *197*
Spain; see also Hispania 86n.
Sparta 40, 136
   Stoa of the Persians 136
Spartan sauna 72, 94, 249, *251*, *253*
Spartans 22
Species 192

Spectators 65, 66, 71
Spelling 267, 275
Spheres, celestial 143, 177, 256, 286
Spices 101
Spouts, lion-head 53, *210*, 211
Springs 25, 38, 40–41, 96, 97, 98, 99–103, 105, 186, 235, 275
   acid 101–102
   alum-saturated 99
   bitter 100–101
   bituminous 99, 100
   deadly 101
   hot 99
   metallic 100
   mineral 100–101
   nitrous 99
   oily 100
   pitch 100
   salt 100
   sulphurous 99
Square, doubling 108
Staberius Eros 15n.
Stables 81, 82
Stade (*stadion*)
   Egyptian 167
   Greek 167n.
Stairs 16, 69, 82, 108, *200*
Stalls 81
Stars 23, 24, 69, 83, 109, 110, 111, 112, 115, 120, 143, 177, 283, *285*, 286
   evening 110
   morning 110
Staterae 123
Statilius Taurus, Titus 292
Statonia 39
Statues 83
Steps 16, 51, 69, 108, 193, *200*
Stipulatio 18
Stoicheia 27
Stoics 15n., 135, 136, 142, 178, 188
Stone 7, 38–40, 180
Stones
   gall 102
   kidney 101–102
Storehouses 71–72
Storerooms 80
Strabo 10, 139, 140
Strategy 133–134
Strato of Lampsacus 177n.
Stratoniceum 71
Streets 29, 31, 167, 173
   orientation of 166
Structura 180
   testacea 184

Stucco 17n., 18, 82, 92, 218, 249, 268
Study 120
Style, literary xiii, 1, 3, 15, 63, 143
Stylobates 51, 71
    curvature 16n., 51, 71
"Styx Water" 101
Sublunary realm 177, 178
Subpavement 87–88
Substructures 83–84
Sudatio 13n., 72, 249, *251*, *253*
Suetonius (Gaius Suetonius Tranquillus)
    8n.
Sulla, Lucius Cornelius 1, 11, 12
Sulphur 99, 105
Sulpicius, Johannes of Veroli 100n.
Summi viri 18n., 26
Sun 25, 26, 36, 45, 65, 71, 76, 77, 78,
    83, 97, 99, 101, 109, 110, 111,
    112–113, 114, 115, 117, 120, 256,
    275, 283, 285
    triangular rays of 111, 283
Sundials 23, 30, 106, 107, 108, 109,
    115–116, 143, *166*, *168*, 286, *289*
Sunium 61
Supercilia 13
Supplies 33, 35, 69, 71–72
Surveying 17, 142, 151, 152, 154, 156n.,
    163, 167, *170*, 171, 172, 173, 193,
    277, 296
Susa 102
Swamp, The 98
Swamps 26, 27, 28, 65, 71, 98
Sweating chambers 37–38, 72, 245, *253*;
    see also *Sudationes*
Syene 98, 167, 286
Symmetria 14, 16, 24, 143, *147*, 188,
    189, 244
Symmetries xvi, 16, 22, 33, 45, 49, 54,
    55, 56, 62, 64, 65, 71, 74, 76, 78,
    79, 82, 84, 86, 87, 149, 211, 215,
    217, 221, 223, 235, 266, 267, 268
    Corinthian 54, 55–56
    discovery of 55, 211
    Doric 54, 55
    Ionic 54, 55
Symmetry 24, 26, 35, 47, 51, 69, *148*,
    150, 213n.
Syracuse 108, 281, 296, 317
Syria 44, 100, 101, 157

Tablinum 79, 80, 256, *258*
Tabularium 12, 152
"Tabulation" 19
Tacitus 156n.

Talent 18, 22, 46
Tapping, of water pipes 277
Tarentum 115
Tarsus 100, 102
Taste 213
Tax revenue 104
Taxis 24, *145*, 149
Teachers 2, 5, 7, 57, 143, 249
Teanum 101
Technical vocabulary xiii, 143
Technology 11
Tectorium 249
Tegea 213n., 215, 267
Telamones 83, 135
Temperament 27, 35, 173, 178, 179, 256
Temples 25, 33, 45, 46–62, 63, 86, 120,
    153, *197*, 229, 230, 264
    on the Acropolis at Athens
        (Erechtheion) 61, *237*
    Aesculapius at Epidaurus 267
    Aesculapius at Tralles 86
    amphiprostyle 48
    in antis 48
    Apollo at Alabanda 48, 192
    Apollo and Diana 49
    Apollo at Didyma 136, 193, 199, 267
    Apollo at Miletus 87
    Apollo Epikourios at Bassae 213
    Apollo Palatinus 2, 3, 4
    Apollo Sosianus 3, 4, 227
    Araeostyle 49, 50, 51, *196*, *197*
    Athena Alea at Tegea 213n., 215, 267
    Augustus at Fano 4, 64
    Capitoline 49
    Castor in the Circus of Flaminius 61,
        237
    Castor in the Forum 218, *238*
    Ceres on the Aventine 4, 49
    Ceres and Proserpina at Eleusis
        (Telesterion) 87, 268
    Concord 10, 218
    correctness in 25
    at Cosa 11n.
    Deified Julius; see Divus Julius
    Diana 10, 55
    Diana at Ephesus 44, 49, 86, 87, 193,
        267
    Diana (Artemis Leukophryne) at
        Magnesia 48, 86, *146*, 192, *195*,
        227, 267
    Diana Nemorensis 61, *237*
    Diana of the Plebs 3
    Diastyle 49, 50, 51, 58, *196*, *197*
    Dipteral 48

    Divus Julius 3, 4, 49, 215, 218
    doors 60
    doorways 59–60
    Equestrian Fortune (Virtue) 4, 49
    Etruscan 10, 49
    Eustyle 49, 50, 51, *196*
    Father Liber (Dionysus) at Athens 71
    Father Liber at Teos 49, 57, 86, 192,
        195, 267
    flora 268
    foundations 50–51
    Greek 152n.
    Hercules 49
    Hercules Musarum 10
    Honor and Battle-courage (Honos
        and Virtus) 13n., 48, 87, 192, 267
    hybrid 61, *237*, *238*
    Hypaethral 48
    interiors 58–59, 227
    Italic 10
    Juno (Hera) at Argos 54
    Juno Moneta 193
    Juno Regina 10
    Juno (Hera) at Samos 86, 266, 267
    Jupiter Ammon 100
    Jupiter at Fano 64
    Jupiter and Faunus 48
    Jupiter Stator 48, 192, 267
    Magna Mater 218
    maintenance of 10
    Mars 192
    Mars Ultor 3, 227
    Minerva on the Acropolis
        (Parthenon) 86, 266
    Minerva (Athena Polias) at Priene 23,
        86, 142, *146*, *195*, 264
    Minerva (Athena) at Sunium *236*
    Moon 68
    new types *237*, *238*
    Olympian Jupiter at Athens 49, 87,
        267
    orientation 59
    Pallas Minerva at Sunium 61
    Panionian Apollo 55, 213, 214
    peripteral 48
    prostyle 48
    pseudodipteral 13, 16, 48, 49–50, 86
    pseudoperipteral 11, 61–62, *238*
    pycnostyle 49, 50, 51, *196*, *197*, *198*
    Quirinus 49, 268
    rebuilding 10
    round 61, *236*
    Saturn 3, 4, 193, 218
    siting of 25, 31–32

Temples (continued)
  species 192, 196
  steps 16, 51
  systyle 49, 50, 51, 58, 196, 197
  Three Fortunae 48
  Tuscan 60–61, 229, 234
  types 192, 194
  Veiovis-between-two-Groves 61, 237
  Venus Genetrix 49
  Zeus at Magnesia 195, 225
Templum 152, 229, 275
Ten, as perfect number 48, 189
Tenements 10; see also insulae
Teos 49, 86
Terminology xiii, 14, 15, 20, 21, 24–26,
    33, 63, 66, 135, 143, 266
Terracina 101, 172
  centuriation of 172
  fountain of Neptune 101
Terracotta 10, 268
Tertullian 268
Testing water 103
Tetrachords 66, 67, 244, 255
Tetraktys 189
Tetrans 202
Thalamos 82
Thales of Miletus 35, 85, 96, 115, 209,
    266
Thasos 122
Theaters 2, 13, 17, 23, 65–70, 86, 119,
    246, 249, 264, 283, 292
  of Aemilius scaurus 292
  of Athens 71, 86
  of Balbus 292
  Greek 70, 245, 248
  of Marcellus 4, 11, 12n., 221, 225,
    235, 292
  of Pompey 4, 12n., 49, 249, 250, 292
  Roman 247
  siting of 31
  of Statilius Taurus 292
  stone 2, 4, 49, 68, 292
  temporary 245, 292
  of Tralles 71, 92
  wooden 68, 245, 292
Thebes 136
Thematismos 25, 151
Themistocles 71
Theo of Magnesia 46, 188
Theocydes 86
Theodorus of Phocaea 86, 266
Theodosius 116, 140
Theophrastus 14n., 103, 275
Theory 15, 18, 21, 24, 62, 66, 138, 143,
    188, 218, 235

Thessaly 101
Tholus, in Delphi 86
Thymelê 245
Thyrôreion 82
Thrace 10, 101
Tiber, river 98
Tiber Island 48
Tiberius 4, 12
Tibur 38
Tiles 12, 42
Tilework 11
Timaeus of Tauromenium 103, 275, 277
Timavus, river (Timavo) 98
Timber 7, 10, 13n., 25–26, 42–45, 72,
    187, 249
Timosthenes of Rhodes 165
Timotheos 40, 86, 267
Tivoli xv, 11, 265, 275
Tobin, Richard 189
Toga virilis 8
Tomb 10
Tones, musical 67, 244
"Tortoises" (testudines) 130–134, 312,
    313, 314
Tower of the Winds 163, 166
Towers xv, 17, 28–29, 73, 156, 158, 159,
    163, 297
Trabeation 15
Tractors 119, 120–122
Tradition xv, 16, 18, 25, 75, 83, 120, 151
Tragedy 245
Trajan 5, 275
Tralles 40, 71, 86, 92, 221
Transliteration 20
Transport 25, 44, 72, 104, 122
Travertine 38, 275
Treasury 65
Treatises xiii, 24, 75, 85, 86, 87, 103,
    115, 126, 138, 142, 143, 149, 179,
    188, 221, 249, 266, 267, 283, 286
Trebonius, Gaius 317
Trees 42–43, 64, 73
  evergreen 10
Trials 6n., 81, 256
Triangles 68, 69, 77, 110, 111, 189, 256,
    281, 283, 286
  equilateral 286
  isosceles 286
  Pythagorean 16, 107–108, 125,
    167n., 281
Tribunal 13, 16, 64, 69, 235
Triclinia 79, 80, 82, 256, 260
Trigarium 10
Trigon 110, 283, 284
Trigonometry xvi n., 141, 277, 283

Triglyphs 56, 57, 224
Trispastos 121
Triumph 3, 107, 275
Triumphatores 10
Triumvirate, Second 1, 3, 4
Trivium 7n.
Troezen 41, 100
Troy 28, 85, 91, 101
Trypho of Alexandria 134
Tufa 11, 17n., 37, 38, 39
Tuning, tempered 244n.
Tuscan temple xiii, 16, 60–61, 229, 234;
    see also Tuscanicae dispositiones
Tuscanicae dispositiones 229, 234
Tusculum 11
Tyana 100
Types xiii, 11, 15, 235
Tyrrhenian Sea 44

Ulysses 91
Umbria 38
Unciae 189
Underwater construction 38
Universe 177
Urbs 38n.; see also City
Usage xiii
Ustrinum
  of Augustus 10
Utica 36
Utilitas 14
Utility 26, 49; see also Utilitas

Vapors 27, 38, 65, 71, 98, 106
Varro, Marcus Terentius, writer 8n.,
    13n., 14, 15n., 87, 109, 143n., 152,
    256, 261, 267, 281, 286
Varro Murena, Aulus Terentius, aedile 40
Vatican Library 163
Vaulting 11, 12, 13, 14, 17, 72
Vedius Pollio 11
Vegoia 152n.
Veins 27, 42, 45, 100, 105, 106, 179,
    235
Veleia 12n.
Velinus 101
Velleius Paterculus 142
Veneer, marble 91
Venetia 38
Venus (planet) 110
Venustas 14, 15
Verdigris 94, 102
Vergiliae 83
Vergina 256
Verona 2, 157, 239
  Arch of the Gavii 2

Vesperugo 110
Vestibules 80, 81, 82, 83, 260
Vestorius 6n., 268
Vesuvius, Mount 38
Vettius Cyrus, Roman architect 14n.
Vicomagistri 142
Villa 10, 11, 81–82, 152, 256, *261*
   of Lucullus 10
"Vitruvian Man" 189, *191*
Vitruvius 96n.
   apprenticeship 5, 8
   career 5, 8
   education, liberal arts 5, 7, 8, 75, 135
   education, professional 5, 7, 8, 75
   erudition 5, 7, 14, 135
   family (gens) 2, 5
   as hydraulic engineer 15
   influence 6–7
   method of writing 16
   military campaigns 5, 6, 15
   name 2
   parents 5, 7, 75
   reading 143n.
   teachers 5, 7, 8, 57, 75, 129
   Ten Books on Architecture
      date 4
      as theorist 15
      travel 6, 8
Vittatum; see Opus vittatum
Vocabulary xiii
Voice xv, 23, 65, 66, 69, 70, 76 , 77,
   103, 235, 283n.
Void 177
Volsiniensis, Lacus 39
Vomitorium 13
Voussoirs 12, 13n., 83, 266

Wages 292
Walkways 10, 71–72, 73, 81, 83, 122

Wall painting, Roman 218, 245, 268,
   273, 274
Walls, city xv, 7, 26–29, 33, 81, 83,
   130–134, *161, 162*, 264, 297
War 71, 72, 128–134
War, Civil 1, 3, 5
War machines xiii, 21, 23, 28, 128–134,
   138, 297
   calibration and tuning 23, 130, 138, 297
Warehouses 73
Water 5, 23, 25, 95, 96–106, 275
   distribution *279*
   finding 96–98
   raising 124
   sources 17, 72, *276*
   supply 6 n., 10, 23, 25, 72, 104–106
   testing 103, 106
   underground 97
Water clock 166, 286, *290, 291*
Water jets 116, 125, 286
Water mills 124, 296
Water organ of Ctesibius 126–127, 296,
   306
Water pump of Ctesibius 125–126, *305*
Water screw 16, 74, 124–125, *304*
Water spouts, lion-headed 53, 209, *211*
Water wheels 124, *301, 303*
Waves 66
Wedges 286
Weight, units of 189
Weld 95, 275
Wells 97, 105–106
White chalk 93
White lead 93, 94, 102, 105
Willow 43, 125
Wind rose 31, 165, *166*, 168
Windows 13n., 22, 56, 80, 82, 264
Winds 16, 17, 29–31, 42, 80, 98–99,
   138, 163, 164, 165, 166, 167, 275

Wine 101, 275
Wine cellars 26
Wisdom 18, 75, 134
Woad 95, 275
Women
   Greek 82, 83, 256
Women's quarters 82
Words
   creation of new 13n., 15n.
Workshops 80
World 109, 177
Writing 63
   on architecture 63
   of history 63
   of poetry 63

Xanthus 101, 186
Xenia 83
Xenocrates 186, 189
Xenophanes of Colophon 85, 115, 266
Xenophon of Athens 167
Xerxes 173
Xuthus 54
Xysta 73, 83
Xystos 73, 83, 126n., *253*

Year 110
Yokes 123, 124

Zacynthus 100
Zama 102
Zeno of Elea 85, 266
Zodiac 69, 76, 109, 110, 111, 112–113,
   114, 115, 117, *144*, 249, 283, *287*,
   288; see also Belt of Signs,
   Signbearing circle
Zoilus of Amphipolis, scourge of Homer
   86, 266
Zoning 142